Harm Reduction in Substance Use and High-Risk Behaviour

International Policy and Practice

This book is dedicated to Dominic Pates, Helen Jamet and Suzanne Pates, and Gemma and Cleo Pates, all of whom have been my strength and support.
RP

Harm Reduction in Substance Use and High-Risk Behaviour

International Policy and Practice

Edited by

Richard Pates
D.Clin.Psy., C.Psychol., AFBPS

Diane Riley
Ph.D.

WILEY-BLACKWELL
A John Wiley & Sons, Ltd., Publication

Addiction **Press**

This edition first published 2012
© 2012 by Blackwell Publishing Ltd

Wiley-Blackwell is an imprint of John Wiley & Sons, formed by the merger of Wiley's global Scientific, Technical and Medical business with Blackwell Publishing.

Registered office: John Wiley & Sons, Ltd, The Atrium, Southern Gate, Chichester, West Sussex, PO19 8SQ, UK

Editorial offices: 9600 Garsington Road, Oxford, OX4 2DQ, UK
The Atrium, Southern Gate, Chichester, West Sussex, PO19 8SQ, UK
2121 State Avenue, Ames, Iowa 50014-8300, USA

For details of our global editorial offices, for customer services and for information about how to apply for permission to reuse the copyright material in this book please see our website at www.wiley.com/wiley-blackwell.

The right of the author to be identified as the author of this work has been asserted in accordance with the UK Copyright, Designs and Patents Act 1988.

Library of Congress Cataloging-in-Publication Data

Harm reduction in substance use and high-risk behaviour : international policy and practice / edited by
  Richard Pates, Diane Riley.
      p. ; cm.
  Includes bibliographical references and index.
  ISBN 978-1-4051-8297-3 (pbk. :alk. paper)
 I. Pates, Richard. II. Riley, Diane M. (Diane Mary), 1953–
[DNLM: 1. Harm Reduction. 2. Substance-Related Disorders–therapy. 3. Risk Reduction Behavior. 4. Risk-Taking.
WM 270]
  362.19686—dc23

                                                                                2012007474

A catalogue record for this book is available from the British Library.

Cover image: Gracey Stinson/Morguefile.com
Cover design by Steve Thompson

Wiley also publishes its books in a variety of electronic formats. Some content that appears in print may not be available in electronic books.

Set in 10/12.5 pt Sabon by Thomson Digital, Noida, India
Printed and bound in Malaysia by Vivar Printing Sdn Bhd

1 2012

CONTENTS

FOREWORD

The prevention of the spread of the human immunodeficiency virus among and from whole communities of people who inject drugs is no less than a public health triumph – one of the public health triumphs of the 20th century, as far as I am concerned. There is much history in this volume, about harm reduction, its antecedents, and other aspects of humankind's relationship with drugs and other fancies; and very welcome it is, because much of the extraordinary history of the current movement is in danger of disappearing. In this historical spirit, my own small involvement in this public health triumph came about relatively accidentally, in a way which introduced me to the predominant feature of the field: prejudice and discrimination, based on man's inhumanity to man.

Those who use drugs (of any kind, legal, illegal, anodyne or exciting) participate in one of the most useful tools for defining who's in and who's out, who's in power and who is not . . . I learnt this again when I ran a harm reduction workshop with WHO in the mid-1990s, in Guizhou in the south of China, for Public Security and Public Health officials from 10 Chinese Provinces. The Public Security officials traveled to the workshop straight from organizing the public executions which marked National Drug Control Day, executions of low level heroin user dealers and small time heroin traders. Each evening was marked with copious quantities of the local Maotai, 55-plus % alcohol, a slower but reliable form of execution. The extreme irony of celebrating the death of those using a pharmacologically pretty harmless drug by drinking large amounts of a severely harmful one brought home to me the utility of labeling people by the drugs they use, and selectively dealing with them on that basis. Using the drugs as an excuse, a cover, a blind to draw away attention, to effectively silence and subjugate the people.

The more I look at drugs, the more I see people. The more I look at people, the more I see a propensity to dehumanize so as to control. The more I look at the harm reduction movement of the last three decades, the more I see hope. Harm reduction drives towards re-humanizing the dehumanized, de-demonizing the demonized, normalizing and welcoming back to the human fold the outcast person, and the outcast behaviour . . . and reclaiming them as part of our humanity, so we can confront and deal with them in properly human ways.

The accident that happened to me, that I referred to above, was when I worked in the AIDS Branch at the Centers for Disease Control in the late 1980s. I was very supernumerary, and reputations were being made; territory was strongly claimed and fiercely guarded. But there was a bit of turf no-one wanted, and it was the scrap thrown to me – HIV among injecting drug users. I remember at the time, around 1988, noting that in an epicentre of the epidemic in the US, in the northeast states of New York and New Jersey, the number of people diagnosed with AIDS with histories of injecting drug use outnumbered those diagnosed who had histories of male to male sex – and yet there was no-one in the AIDS Branch at CDC, the home of the discovery of AIDS, the world leading public health institution, specifically studying this massive and devastating part of the epidemic. A first exposure to the depth to which prejudice permeates our institutions . . . and a surprise to a youngish public health practitioner, whose aspiration was to get the science right, and had trouble seeing, let alone understanding, the basis on which some people with AIDS were worth more than others.

It has always seemed to me that there is a parallel between our drug policies and the practice of execution of deserters in war (who have always seemed to me far more heroic in their humanness than the adrenalin charged killer who wins the medal; perhaps only because I can completely identify with the former and do not for a moment understand the latter). The more dangerous we can make the use of a particular drug, by removing any possibility of quality control or regulation of access or informed use, the more likely are users likely to suffer harm from its use, so bolstering our initial proposal that its use is dangerous . . . if we do our job well enough, we might be fortunate in that a few will die, providing us with exactly what we need *pour encourager les autres*.

'Harm reduction' as a name may have started with HIV, but as we read in these pages as a concept it is co-contingent with humanity – it is in essence part of the definition of being human. Harm reduction is a normal human response to intractable, usually behaviourally-based, problems that allow no immediate solution – what could be more sensible than to ensure that the harm they cause is lessened to the extent possible? Is this not, indeed, simply good public health practice under a different guise? And again as we read within these pages, is not the best public health synonymous with human rights?

HIV is just the starting point, the entry into the world of systematic discrimination and dehumanization. Harm reduction takes us through the door that HIV opens, a door to ourselves; and we betray it and our selves if we do not follow up, and confront the beast within.

This current book is as good a guide to this journey as it is possible to produce – a guide through personal experiences, from activists to users to educators and policy makers and police; a global guide, spanning the world as do the phenomena, the problems, the philosophy and the response; and a guide that takes us into the many paths that harm reduction, branching out from its beginnings with injecting drug use and HIV, is beginning to explore. It will serve us for many years, as textbook and inspiration.

Professor Nick Crofts
Senior Research Fellow
UN Interregional Crime and Justice Research Institute
Turin, Italy

LIST OF FIGURES AND TABLES

Figures

Tables

LIST OF CONTRIBUTORS

Editors

Richard Pates
Consultant Clinical Psychologist/Independent Consultant, UK

Diane Riley
Canadian Foundation for Drug Policy; School of Public Health, University of Toronto; Founder, International Harm Reduction Association, Canada

Contributors

Eliot Ross Albert
International Network of People Who Use Drugs, Deputy Director/Programme Coordinator, UK

Tina Alwyn
Reader in Health Psychology, Cardiff Metropolitan University, UK

Monica J. Barratt
Research Fellow, National Drug Research Institute at Curtin University, Perth, Australia

Ingrid van Beek
Director, Kirketon Road Centre, Sydney, Australia

Calum Bennachie
Coordinator, Wellington, New Zealand

Alex Blaszczynski
School of Psychology, University of Sydney, Australia

Steven Branstetter
Assistant Professor, Department of Biobehavioral Health, Pennsylvania State University, USA

Stefan Brugger
Medical Student and Researcher, Neuropsychopharmacology Unit, Imperial College, London, UK

Dave Burrows
Director, AIDS Projects Management Group, Sydney, Australia

Adrian Carter
NHMRC Postdoctoral Research Fellow, UQ Centre for Clinical Research, University of Queensland, Australia

Walter Cavalierri
Canadian Harm Reduction Network, Canada

Allan Clear
Harm Reduction Coalition, New York, USA

Julian Cohen
Independent Consultant and Trainer, UK

Jan Copeland
National Drug and Alcohol Research Centre, University of New South Wales, Australia

Jon Derricott
Co-founder/Writer/Filmmaker, Exchange Supplies, UK

Paul Dillon
Manager, National Drug and Alcohol Research Centre, University of New South Wales, Australia

Kate Dolan
National Drug and Alcohol Research Centre, University of New South Wales, Sydney, Australia

Jimmy Dorabjee
Chairperson, Asian Network of People Who Use Drugs, Harm Reduction Advisor, Australia

Richard Elliott
Executive Director, Canadian HIV/AIDS Legal Network, Canada

Michael Farrell
Professor and Director, National Drug and Alcohol Research Centre, University of New South Wales, Australia

Amanda Fielding
Countess of Wemyss, Founder and Director, Beckley Foundation, Beckley, Oxford, UK

Jonathan Foulds
Professor of Public Health Sciences & Psychiatry, Pennsylvania State University, College of Medicine, USA

Sally Gainsbury
Centre for Gambling Studies, Southern Cross University, Australia

Patrick Griffiths
Communications and Research Officer, Anex, Victoria, Australia

Jean Paul Grund
Centrum voor Verslavingsonderzoek/Addiction Research Centre, Utrecht, The Netherlands; Centre for Addictology, First Faculty of Medicine, Charles University, Prague, Czech Republic; CVO – Research & Consultancy, The Netherlands

Wayne Hall
Professor and NHMRC Australia Fellow, Deputy Director (Policy), UQ Centre for Clinical Research, University of Queensland, Australia

Catherine Healy
National Coordinator, New Zealand

Robert Heimer
Professor of Epidemiology and Public Health, Yale School of Public Health, USA

Neil Hunt
Researcher and Trainer; Honorary Senior Research Associate at the School of Social Policy, Sociology and Social Research, University of Kent; Honorary Research Fellow with the Centre for Research on Drugs and Health Behaviour, London School of Hygiene and Tropical Medicine, UK

Bev John
Reader and Head of Research in Psychology, School of Psychology, University of Glamorgan, UK

Ralf Jürgens
Consultant, HIVAIDS, Health Policy and Human Rights, Canada

Danny Kushlik
Head of External Affairs, Transform Drug Policy Foundation, UK

Simon Lenton
Deputy Director National Drug Research Institute, Curtin University, Perth, Australia

Alisher Latypov
Eurasian Harm Reduction Network, Vilnius, Lithuania; Columbia University Global Health Research Center of Central Asia, New York, USA

Mags Maher
Freelance Specialist Trainer and Consultant, Hertfordshire, UK

Raewyn Marshall
Community Liaison Worker, Wellington, New Zealand

Peter G. Miller
Senior Research Fellow, School of Psychology, Faculty of Health, Deakin University, Australia

Geoffrey Monaghan
HIV/AIDS Prevention and Care Expert, UNODC, Russia

Lisa Moore
Department of Community Health Education at San Francisco State University, USA

Neo K. Morojele
Deputy Director, Alcohol and Drug Abuse Research Unit, Medical Research Council, Pretoria, South Africa

Danny Morris
Freelance Trainer and Consultant, Hereford, UK

Geoffrey Noller
Research Fellow, Department of Psychological Medicine, University of Otago, Dunedin, New Zealand

David J. Nutt
Professor of Neuropsychopharmacology, Neuropsychopharmacology Unit, Imperial College London, UK

Patrick O'Hare
Independent Consultant; Former CEO of the International Harm Reduction Association, HIT, UK

David Otiashvili
Addiction Research Centre, Union Alternative Georgia, Tbilisi, Georgia Centre for Addictology, First Faculty of Medicine, Charles University, Prague, Czech Republic

Charles D.H. Parry
Director, Alcohol & Drug Abuse Research Unit, Medical Research Council, Pretoria, South Africa

Richard Pates
Consultant Clinical Psychologist/Independent Consultant, UK

Laurence J. Reed
Clinical Senior Lecturer, Neuropsychopharmacology Unit, Imperial College, London, UK

Diane Riley
Canadian Foundation for Drug Policy; School of Public Health, University of Toronto; Founder, International Harm Reduction Association, Canada

Ana Rodas
Research Officer, National Cannabis Prevention and Information Centre, Randwick, New South Wales, Australia

Diana Rossi
Professor and Researcher of the Faculty of Social Sciences at the University of Buenos Aires; Social Worker and Specialist in youngsters' social problems, Intercambios Asociacón Civil, Buenos Aires, Argentina

John Ryan
Chief Executive Officer, Anex, Victoria, Australia

Otilia Scutelniciuc
United Nations Joint Programme on AIDS (UNAIDS), Almaty, Kazakhstan

Edmund Silins
Senior Research Assistant, National Drug and Alcohol Research Centre, University of New South Wales, Australia

Pavlo Smyrnov
International HIV/AIDS Alliance in Ukraine, Kyiv, Ukraine

James Stone
Clinical Senior Lecturer, Neuropsychopharmacology Unit, Imperial College, London, UK

Raminta Stuikyte
European AIDS Treatment Group, Brussels, Belgium; Eurasian Harm Reduction Network, Vilnius, Lithuania

Jallal Toufiq
The National Centre for Drug Abuse Prevention, Treatment and Research, Morocco

Bruce Trathen
Consultant Addiction Psychiatrist; Sub-Saharan Harm Reduction Network Executive Committee, UK

Ivan Varentsov
Eurasian Harm Reduction Network, Vilnius, Lithuania; Andrey Rylkov Foundation for Health and Social Justice, Moscow, Russia

Alex Wodak
Director, Alcohol & Drug Service, St Vincent's Hospital, Darlinghurst, Australia

Tomas Zabransky
Centre for Addictology, First Faculty of Medicine, Charles University in Prague ResAd, LLC, Prague, Czech Republic

Section I
Background

Chapter 1

INTRODUCTION

Diane Riley and Richard Pates

Harm reduction for psychoactive substance has been practised for centuries (see chapter 2) but harm reduction as we now know it was first developed in the 1980s, mainly as a response to HIV and hepatitis transmission among people who use drugs. There is now an extensive literature on harm reduction in academic journals and books and there are numerous publications aimed at advising and informing on best practice in many areas. We have come a long way since the days when all attempt at limiting the harm from psychoactive substances and high-risk behaviours simply involved prohibition, bans, and telling people not to partake. We know that the use of alcohol and other psychoactive substances goes back many thousands of years, sex work is called 'the oldest profession', and gambling has a very long history too. All of these have attracted opprobrium from the establishment in almost all countries and at most times in history, and attempts to recognise their inevitability and render them safer have been scant.

That harm reduction around psychoactive substances has been controversial is of interest in itself. If we look at another major cause of death and injury throughout the world, that of the motor car, we see a very different situation. It has never been seriously suggested that cars should be banned because of the number of deaths caused through their use (far more than heroin overdoses), but we have put in numerous harm reduction measures in an attempt to ameliorate these accidents. In terms of cars themselves we have introduced safer cars that stop more efficiently, that have greater protection for the occupants through stronger construction and crumple zones, and so forth. We provide seat belts and airbags so that in the event of an accident the occupants have a lesser chance of being injured. We have laws to limit the amount of alcohol people may consume before driving; we impose speed limits and enact a considerable amount of legislation to make the roads safer. We also make the motoring environment safer by constructing crash barriers, traffic lights, roundabouts and other physical changes to the infrastructure. These are all harm reduction measures designed to reduce death and injury on the road, and apart from some people feeling it infringes their personal liberty to be made to wear a seat belt or crash helmet, nobody really objects. The situation regarding harm reduction for psychoactive substances and gambling has been very different indeed.

This book covers a number of areas pertaining to harm reduction. The first section is an introduction by way of a history of harm reduction (which deserves a book in itself and is thus brief) and a discussion about the role of education in primary prevention, an attempt to remove the harm before it occurs. The second section looks at policy, offers a critique of various policy matters, examines law and policing, and raises questions about ethics and legalisation. The third section is centred around harm reduction for individual substances and behaviours, offering expert views on current best practice and ideas. The chapter on opiate harm reduction has been written from the 'recovery' perspective. There is much discussion elsewhere in the book about opiate substitution therapy (OST), so this is not included in this chapter, but current thinking is that the use of substitute medication such as methadone is necessary in the treatment of opioid problems but not sufficient, it

Harm Reduction in Substance Use and High-Risk Behaviour: International Policy and Practice, First Edition.
Edited by Richard Pates and Diane Riley.
© 2012 Blackwell Publishing Ltd. Published 2012 by Blackwell Publishing Ltd.

stabilises those dependent on opioids but is not a cure. In the UK and a number of other countries we have created a system for helping people stop using opiates but we have not really helped them become free of dependence (on both the drugs and the services that provide them). In some countries such as Canada, methadone is being given to users of Oxcycontin, many of the young people, to help them discontinue use of the pain killer; the result has been an increase in methadone users who are also buying Oxycontin on the street. This is not an example of best practice in harm reduction.

The fourth section is a global geographical review highlighting what services have been available in all the continents and where the deficiencies lie. Whereas we are well informed about Western Europe, North America and Australia we are less well informed about parts of the world with large populations, increasing problems, and a marked deficiency of services. This comprehensive survey has highlighted how far harm reduction has come since the 1980s, from being a mainly northern European and Australian concern to being truly global and reaching some of the most disadvantaged people in the world.

We have assembled a distinguished group of experts to write this book, some well known and some less well known, but all experts in their fields. There may appear to be some gaps in the content and this is not accidental; there are some subjects that deserve more space than this long book allows and it is our intention to include them in another book. There is, for example, discussion of gender issues in a number of the chapters, but no specific chapter on girls and women. This is one example of a subject which needs more space than allowed here.

The chapter on Australasia is different in format to the other regional chapters. The author who was to write this was unable to do so due to unforeseen circumstances and we therefore gathered, at short notice, a distinguished panel of Australian and New Zealand authors to write a number of perspectives on these two countries.

Any book on a subject like this is only as good as its current content and we are aware that this is only a snapshot of harm reduction a decade into the twenty-first century. It is hoped that this will provide a useful resource for students, academics, policy-makers, law enforcement officers and all those interested in the reduction of harm. An attempt has been made to be comprehensive, but even in a book of this length there will be gaps. The subject of performance and image enhancing drugs was to have been included but again the authors were unable to deliver the chapter (for reasons beyond their control and not because of performance deficit) and it is hoped to devote another book to this increasingly relevant area.

Harm reduction has become part of accepted practice in many parts of the world. It is inevitable that new challenges will arise, new drugs that will cause moral panics and new political systems that will reject the libertarian ideas of harm reduction. What is important is that in both policy and practice the foundations have been laid to continue this work, to develop it, and to try to reduce the harm that is associated with the inevitable use of psychoactive substances and the other behaviours associated with human beings such as gambling and sex work.

Chapter 2

A BRIEF HISTORY OF HARM REDUCTION

Diane Riley, Richard Pates, Geoffrey Monaghan and Patrick O'Hare

The first few thousand years

Harm reduction has no doubt been part of the human behavioural repertoire since psychoactive substances were first used by our early ancestors. In most cultures which used such substances (and this appears to have been almost all), social rituals and religious codes often regulated consumption and associated behaviours. In many societies today these rites of passage, rituals and codes have all but eroded, leaving a void that risks and harms can fill. Until the industrial revolution, harms related to human-machine interaction (or collision) were, while still an occurrence (the arm caught in the grindstone, the leg in the plough), were not of such high risk to so many as to demand the regulations that we have today. In this chapter we give a brief overview of some of the historical underpinnings of harm reduction as we know it, including the role of police in reducing drug related harm.

Historical understandings of the risks of injecting

The practice of injecting substances into the body has been around for centuries. For example, Christopher Wren, in the seventeenth century, conducted experiments of injecting a dog with various substances including opium using a bladder and a quill as a form of syringe (Wren, 1665). He injected into the veins and reported that '*the opium, being soon circulated into the brain, did within a short time stupefy, though not kill the dog*', this probably being one of the first reports of the injecting of an opiate. He also reported '*that liquors thus injected into the veines without preparation and digestion, will make odde, commotions in the blood, disturb nature, and cause strange symptoms in the body*' (sic) indicating again an early example of the knowledge that injecting into a vein will produce sensations in the brain.

It was not until the invention of the hypodermic syringe in the 1850s that the practice of injecting became a popular and regular feature of medical treatment. The syringe as we now know it, with a barrel, plunger, hollow needle with a chamfered end was first produced by Charles Hunter (1858) who improved a design produced by Alexander Wood in 1853 (Wood, 1855) by adding a lateral opening in the needle. (For a full discussion of the history of injecting see Macht, 1916; Howard-Jones, 1947; Pates and Wichter, 2005.) In the latter part of the nineteenth century the use of injection to administer medication became increasingly popular especially for the injection of morphine. Kane (1880) in the preface to his classic text on the injection of morphia said that 'a physician of the present day without a hypodermic syringe in his pocket or close at hand would be looked upon as would have been a physician 50 years ago, did he not own and use a lancet'. But he went on to say 'There is no proceeding in medicine that has become so rapidly popular; no method of allaying pain so prompt in its action and permanent in its effect; no plan of medicine that has been *so*

Harm Reduction in Substance Use and High-Risk Behaviour: International Policy and Practice, First Edition.
Edited by Richard Pates and Diane Riley.
© 2012 Blackwell Publishing Ltd. Published 2012 by Blackwell Publishing Ltd.

carelessly used and thoroughly abused; and no therapeutic discovery that has been so great a blessing and *so great a curse* to mankind as the hypodermic injection of morphia.' So within 30 years of introduction and widespread use there were already concerns about the use of the syringe.

By 1870 Allbutt became concerned about indiscriminate use of the syringe and complained that 'patients are now injecting themselves daily or more than daily during long periods of time, for neuralgia, which are as far from cured as they were at the outset'. Levinstein (1878) also was concerned about the misuse of the hypodermic syringe and attributed the problems of morphine addiction to allowing patients to have access to the syringe allowing them to inject at will. A Professor Gaillard Thomas (quoted by Kane, 1880) stated that he would never teach a patient how to inject him/herself for fear of developing a morphine habit.

As early as 1862 there has been concerns about the accidental transmission of disease by injecting, a case of the possible transmission of syphilis as a result of a contaminated small pox vaccination was discussed in the *British Medical Journal* (Acton, 1862). Although no conclusion was reached the possibility was raised. One of Kane's (1880) recommendations was that needles should always be thoroughly cleansed after using on syphilitic or carcinomatous patients and patients ill with contagious or infectious diseases.

Kane (1880) reports a number of cases of patients dying from tetanus following injections. He quotes cases back as far as 1867 as reported in the Lancet where a case was reported as being 'due probably to the use of rusty needles'. He also quotes a case of a woman dying in 1871 where the syringes were in a very dirty condition apparently not having been wiped after use and that the steel needles were in a very rusty state. Three other cases of death from tetanus were reported in the *Lancet* following the injection of sulphate of quinine, again rusty needles being associated with the deaths.

Calvel (quoted by Kane, 1880) 'collected many cases of abscess, traumatic fever and other accidents produced by hypodermic injection of morphia', but believes they were all caused by 'the state of the needle, improperly prepared solutions and to the cachexia produced by the morphia habit'.

It is clear that there has been concern about injecting virtually since the invention of the syringe and as will be seen later in the book (see chapter 11 on injecting) the risks associated with injecting are one of the main areas of concern in the harm reduction arena.

The eighteenth-century gin craze

Concern about the dangers of alcohol use has also had long historical precedents. In eighteenth-century London there was what is known as 'The Gin Craze'. Daniel Defoe wrote in 1728 about the heavy drinking of gin especially among the poor, 'common people get so drunk on Sunday that they cannot work for a day or two following. Ney [sic], since the use of 'Geneva' [gin] has become so common they cannot work at all, but run from one irregularity to another 'til they become arrogant rogues' (Defoe 1728 quoted in Linnane, 2008).

The reasons for the excessive use of gin were partly due to the cheapness of gin and its availability. Duties on home produced spirits were very low compared to imported spirits and Britain was producing a huge amount of grain which was distilled into gin (Linnane, 2008). Duty was 2d per gallon and there was no need for retail licences to sell it and it was therefore sold in thousands of premises across the capital. Men, women and children all drank gin, using it as an anaesthetic to quieten starving children and as a food substitute for starving parents.

Over the next 22 years a number of Acts were passed in an attempt to control the gin craze (and the consequent harm). In 1729 a licence fee of £20 was imposed for retailing spirits and duty was raised from 2d to 5 shillings per gallon. By 1733 these were repealed as they were apparently unworkable and further drunkenness and disorder occurred. In 1736 another Gin Act was introduced requiring those retailing spirits to pay a £50 licence fee. Spies were paid to inform on people circumventing the Act and this led to rioting and the stoning to death of some of those informers. In 1751 the Gin Act suppressed some retail outlets and initiated further increase in taxes so that within a few years the annual consumption of gin fell from 11 million to 1 million gallons. This was clearly an attempt to reduce the harm being done to London's poor and eventually worked through legislation, taxation and through the use of paid informers.

The history of policing and harm reduction

The historical literature on police services in Britain contains a number of examples of laws, programmes and practices which fall neatly under the rubric of harm reduction. Of course, British police services prior to the late 1980s did not use the term to describe these programmes and practices but few would now disagree that they were formulated and underpinned by similar considerations as their modern-day examples; namely the reduction of harms caused by infectious diseases, alcohol and drug misuse and sex work and a desire to divert some offenders, particularly young people, alcohol and drug misusers and sex workers away from the criminal courts. Indeed, some of the so-called modern or new approaches have their historical links to policies and programmes which stretch back decades; at least one practice dates back some four hundred years.

Alternatives to prosecution for offences involving alcohol and other drugs

For decades, the most widely used alternative to prosecution in Britain has involved the use of the *formal caution*. Following the introduction of Home Office Circular 30/2005, the *formal caution* is now referred to as a *simple caution by* Home Office officials and police services in order to distinguish it from *conditional cautioning*.

The practice of using the simple caution has its origins in the discretion given to police whether or not to initiate a prosecution when an offence is disclosed; a point reinforced by Lord Denning in delivering his judgment in the case of *R. v. Metropolitan Police Commissioner ex parte* Blackburn:

> Although the chief officers of police are answerable to the law, there are many fields in which they have discretion with which the law will not interfere. For instance, it for the Commissioner of Police or the chief constable, as the case may be, to decide in any particular case whether enquiries should be pursued, or whether an arrest should be made, or a prosecution brought . . . He can also make policy decisions and give effect to them, as for instance was often done when prosecutions were not brought for attempted suicide.

MPS records show that something akin to simple cautioning was being used in 1833 (Steer, 1970) causing the Commissioner to issue the following instruction during that year:

> In some returns of charges refused, when the charge has been preferred by a police constable for disorderly conduct, the reason alleged by the Inspector for not taking the charge is 'Dismissed upon promising not to be guilty of such conduct for the future'. The Commissioner altogether condemns such practice.

Regarding the specific practice of using the simple caution for adult drug offenders, there is a widely held belief that this practice has its origins in the Home Office Circular of 26/1983 which laid down the Attorney General's Guidelines on the criteria to be applied by all persons or agencies who had to decide whether these should be a prosecution in a particular case. Some believe that it was a practice first introduced by the Merseyside Police, England, in the late 1980s as part of the 'Mersey model of harm reduction'. Neither supposition is correct. As in the case for other offences, the practice has a long history. Although no precise date can be assigned, the practice dates back to at least the sixteenth century. A book entitled *Quacks of old London*, published in 1928 (Thompson), recounts how one John Halle 'a worthy doctor of Maidstone' described the quacks – known as 'counterfeit javels' – who thronged to that town in 1565. Among them was John Bewley, a notorious quack from London, who having been arrested in Maidstone was brought before the local justices: 'He was let off with a caution, and advised "to leave such false and naughty deceits and begone".'

The following examples, drawn from MPS prosecution and policy files, and police service Annual Reports to the Home Office, clearly show that simple cautions were administered for a variety of drug offences, including those which are now defined as 'drug trafficking offences', over one hundred years before the Home Office Circular 26/1983:

- In October 1877, the Registrar of the Pharmaceutical Society issued 'caution letters' to some twenty offenders for offences under the Pharmacy Act 1868.
- In 1903, a chemist received a simple caution by the MPS for offences relating to the unauthorised sale of opium tincture under the Pharmacy Act 1868.
- In 1926, a man appeared at the Greenwich Police Court, London, for offences under section 5 of the Poisons and Pharmacy Act 1908. The summonses were dismissed but a caution was nevertheless administered by the magistrate.
- Two chemists and one other person received simple cautions by Manchester City Police in 1926, for offences contrary to the Dangerous Drugs Acts 1920–3.
- On 30 July 1931, a MPS police inspector administered a simple caution to a woman by for attempting to obtain 36 grains of morphine by means of a forged prescription.
- In September 1932, the daughter of the Dean of Exeter, received a simple caution by the MPS (following advice from the Director of Public Prosecutions) for two offences of supplying drugs.
- On 19 October 1932, Mrs Leonie Fester was cautioned by the MPS (following advice from the DPP) for unlawfully obtaining prescriptions, and in turn unauthorised supplies of morphine, from two doctors.
- Of the 118 persons arrested by the MPS Dangerous Drug Squad in 1965, 45 (38%) were cautioned at the request of the DPP.

It is also worth noting that in some cases the drug involved would now be described as Class A drugs – i.e. the opium tincture and morphine. Since administering simple cautions to drug offenders is thought to avoid the stigmatisation and the damaging effects a conviction can have for an offender, numerous commentators view the practice as an important component of police services' harm reduction policies (O'Hare, 1992; Kaal, 2001; Task Force to Review Services for Drug Misusers, 1996). And, over the years, this is how the British police services have come to see the practice.

Drug treatment in police stations

In Britain, the practice of providing controlled drugs such as dihydrocodeine and methadone to detainees held in police stations so as not to disrupt their treatment regimens or to help them stave off withdrawal is longstanding. According to MPS archives, morphine was occasionally prescribed to detainees held in London police stations as long ago as the 1930s. Certainly, dihydrocodeine (in the form of DF 118 tablets) was often prescribed to heroin addicts held in London police stations in the 1980s and the early 1990s. Arrestees who were able to prove that they were entitled to receive methadone on prescription would also be prescribed the drug if their time in police detention was expected to be lengthy or s/he exhibited signs of withdrawal distress. In accordance with medical guidelines and rules governing the treatment of persons in police detention, methadone could only be administered to a detainee under the direct supervision of a 'police doctor/surgeon' (or Forensic Medical Examiner as they were late called).

Drug referral schemes

Long before Drug Referral Schemes were established and evolved into the well-defined pro-grammes of the late 1990s, British police services had been experimenting with the idea of refer-ring drug misusers to appropriate drug treatment programmes. In general terms, the idea of intervening at the point of arrest in order to divert offenders thought to have problems relating to their use of alcohol or other drugs can be traced to the latter part of the nineteenth century following the passing of the Inebriates Act and the Habitual Drunkards Act in 1879, and the twentieth century saw sporadic initiatives aimed at introducing 'detoxification centres', safer alternatives to police cells for people under the influence and schemes aimed at providing infor-mation about services. Specifically, the origins of DRS can be traced back to a letter dated 11 September 1934 from a Home Office civil servant to the Assistant Commissioner, Crime, at New Scotland Yard, suggesting that 'drug addicts . . . in many cases' could be coerced into treatment as an alternative to prosecution.

The history of two different systems

In the first 3 decades of the twentieth century there were very different responses to the problems of opiate addiction in the UK and the USA. In the late nineteenth century opiate addiction in America was legal although stigmatised (Courtwright, 2001). A series of laws beginning with the Smoking Opium Exclusion Act (1909) and culminating in the Harrison Act in 1914 made access to legal opiates very difficult. Although opiates were not prohibited the Harrison Act made physicians and pharmacists and others who dealt with narcotics register with the US Department of the Treasury, pay a tax and maintain records of the narcotics they dispensed. The Act also demanded that physi-cians who prescribed narcotics followed certain provisions. However, there arose the question as to whether they could prescribe opiates to 'maintain' an opiate addict's habit and the Treasury and courts refused this provision. Physicians who did continue to prescribe were harassed and prose-cuted and this led to the majority of the clinics established to treat and supply addicts were closed (Courtwright, 2001).

In contrast in the UK questions were being raised about prescription and control of narcotic drugs for addicts (Spear, 2002). In 1923 an Assistant Under Secretary of State, Sir Malcolm Delevingne, wrote a letter to the Minister of Health asking 'for an authoritative statement on the prescribing of morphine to an addict'. This eventually led to the establishing of a commission under the Chairman-ship of Sir Humphrey Rolleston, then President of the Royal College of Physicians to examine the question. The main conclusions of the Rolleston report (Ministry of Health, 1926) which estab-lished what came to be known as the British System were as follows:

> There are two groups of persons suffering from addiction to whom the administration of morphine and heroin may be regarded as legitimate medical treatment, namely:

    a. Those who are undergoing treatment for the cure of addiction by the gradual withdrawal method.;

    b. Persons for whom, after every effort has been made for the cure of addiction, the drug cannot be completely withdrawn, either because:

        i. Complete withdrawal produces serious symptoms which cannot be satisfactorily treated under the ordinary conditions of private practice; or where

        ii. A patient, who while capable of leading a useful and fairly normal life so long as he takes a certain non-progressive quantity, usually small, of the drug of addiction, ceases to be able to do so when the regular allowance is withdrawn.

So while in the USA maintenance of addicts became difficult and virtually disappeared until the mid-1960s, when the early methadone clinics researched by Dole and Nyswander in New York started, in the UK maintenance, a firm plank of harm reduction, has been continued for more than a century.

The twentieth century

Harm reduction as we know it is a social policy with respect to drugs which has gained popularity since the 1980s, primarily as a response to the spread of Acquired Immune Deficiency Syndrome (AIDS) among injection drug users. Although harm reduction can be used as a framework for all drugs, including alcohol, it has primarily been applied to injection drug use because of the pressing nature of the harm associated with this activity (Riley, 1993; Riley and O'Hare, 2000).

Harm reduction has as its first priority a decrease in the negative consequences of drug use. This approach can be contrasted with abstentionism, the dominant policy in North America, which emphasises a decrease in the prevalence of drug use. According to a harm reduction approach, a strategy which is aimed exclusively at decreasing the prevalence of drug use may only increase various drug related harms, and so the two approaches have different emphases. Harm reduction tries to reduce problems associated with drug use and recognises that abstinence may be neither a realistic nor a desirable goal for some, especially in the short term. This is not to say that harm reduction and abstinence are mutually exclusive but only that abstinence is not the only acceptable or important goal. Harm reduction involves setting up a hierarchy of goals, with the more immediate and realistic ones to be achieved in steps on the way to risk-free use or, if appropriate, abstinence; it is consequently an approach which is characterised by pragmatism.

The main characteristics or principles of harm reduction are (Riley, 1993; Riley et al., 1999):

- *Pragmatism*: Harm reduction accepts that some of use of mind-altering substances is inevitable and that some level of drug use is normal in a society.
- *Humanistic values*: The drug user's decision to use drugs is accepted as fact, as his or her choice; no 'moralistic' judgment is made either to condemn or to support use of drugs, regardless of level of use or mode of intake. The dignity and rights of the drug user are respected.
- *Focus on harms*: The extent of a person's drug use is of secondary importance to the harms resulting from use.
- *Hierarchy of goals*: Most harm reduction programmes have a hierarchy of goals, with the immediate focus on addressing the most pressing needs.

The roots of harm reduction as we now know it are in the United Kingdom, the Netherlands and North America.

Liverpool, United Kingdom

In the mid-1980s, there was an influx of cheap brown heroin on Merseyside. It was estimated that there were about 20,000 drug users in the Region in a population of about two and a quarter million people (O'Hare, 2007). Liverpool, Wirral and Bootle had high levels of heroin use. Parker, Newcombe and Bakx estimated that there were about 5000 heroin users in the Wirral out of a total population of about 300,000 (1988). In 1985, John Ashton of the University of Liverpool Department of Public Health and later Mersey Regional Director of Public Health and Howard Seymour, Head of the Health Promotion of the Mersey Regional Health Authority (MRHA) had been developing the ideas of the New Model for Public Health, bringing together the old ideas of environmental change, prevention and therapeutic interventions but adding the importance of 'those social aspects of health problems which are caused by life-styles. In this way it seeks to avoid the trap of victim blaming' (Ashton and Seymour, 1988: 21). They were interested in applying it to the emerging public health problem, drugs and AIDS, using a strategy, which involved political organisation, market research of groups at risk, creative use of mass media, activism, the involvement of the risk groups in programmes and community support.

This resulted in the implementation of a harm reduction approach to drug use in the region, especially the threat of HIV through the sharing of infected injecting equipment, based on public health principles that influenced the later historic recommendations of the UK's Advisory Council on the Misuse of Drugs (ACMD) 1988 report. Services were created from 1985 involving the consumer, which gave drug users the information and the means to protect themselves, especially those drug injectors most at risk.

A crucial part of the strategy was the opening of the Mersey Drug Training and Information Centre (MDTIC), which later became HIT, which was a drop-in centre whose brief was to give honest information to anyone who requested it and training to the public and professionals. It was next door to the Liverpool Drug Dependency Unit (LDDU), which prescribed methadone and, in a few cases, heroin. It was part of the New Public Health approach, oriented to prevention rather than treatment and based 'on the premise that this can best be achieved through involving the population at risk in the solution to problems of public health (being consumer-led); that they be informed of the risk and be able to make healthy choices' (Eaton et al., 1998: 309).

The realisation that HIV could be contracted through sharing contaminated injection equipment was met with an immediate pragmatic response based on public health principles. If the danger was infected equipment, clean equipment had to be made available. A syringe exchange service was started in 1986 in a converted toilet at MDTIC. Methadone was used to attract people to come to services to find out how to reduce risk and to get clean equipment. If there were still people who had not come in to services, the services had to go out to where they were. User friendliness was a key concept. It had to be easy to access (low threshold), open at the right times with a committed non-judgmental staff.

The target group was identified. Making and maintaining contact with that target group and delivering specific interventions to that population at risk, the 'population' rather than an 'individual' approach, was the method used. Cooperation was sought from the target group, the public, professionals (which was indeed the hardest group to convince with many doctors using their clinical freedom to provide what they thought was best for their patients) and the police. The objectives were very simple: to reduce sharing of injection equipment; to reduce injecting drug use; to reduce street drug use; to reduce drug use; and if possible you increase abstinence. This was presented as a hierarchy of objectives. The emphasis was very much on the more achievable aims of reducing risk behaviour rather than reducing drug use. Needle exchange, prescribing mainly of methadone, outreach and the provision of information were the instruments used. Service uptake was rapid with 733 people making 3,117 visits to the Syringe Exchange Service in the first 10 months. In the first 2 years, 1090 people attended the Drug Dependency Unit. Hitherto, 200 people per year coming to a traditional agency would have been the norm. Soon the Maryland Centre was opened to provide basic health care as well as HIV prevention services. This all became known as the Mersey Harm Reduction Model.

The police were becoming disillusioned with arresting the same people time after time. They recognised the new approach's potential to reduce this and made the decision not to target drug users coming to services, to stay away from the vicinity of services and to refer drug users they arrested to those services. They didn't use possession of injection equipment as evidence of drug use and referred people to needle exchanges and saw public health as part of their role alongside public order. 'Consequently, as a Force, we support the needle exchange schemes and have a non-prosecution policy with regard to possession of used needles that are to be exchanged' (O'Connell, 1990).

It is interesting to contrast the approach of the police with the approach of Liverpool City Council, which was controlled by the Labour Party and which was vehemently against the policy. They saw methadone as the 1980s version of the 'opium of the people' and were a constant thorn in the side of everyone involved with the project in Liverpool. The local Labour Party position also contrasted with the attitude of the right wing central government led by Margaret Thatcher, which made a substantial amount of funding available to roll out the approach across the country.

The approach resulted in behaviour change; there was a reduction in sharing of needles and syringes and use of street drugs. Many more people were attracted into services who had never been before. Some people who had been injecting heroin for 25 years made their first appearance at a drug service. A range of physical problems relating to injecting drug use were found and dealt with. The drug using population of Merseyside became healthier and more knowledgeable. In the late 1980s, Liverpool was responsible for about one third of the methadone prescribed in England. Contact was made with over 50% of the high-risk population. An HIV epidemic did not happen among injecting drug users in Mersey. By 1996 there had been 20 people who had contracted the virus through injecting drug use and some of these seem to have contracted the virus before moving to Liverpool.

In 1988, the British Advisory Council on the Misuse of Drugs stated: 'We have no hesitation in concluding that the spread of HIV is a greater danger to individual and public health than drug misuse. Accordingly, services which aim to minimise HIV risk behaviour by all available means should take precedence in developmental plans.'

In 1990, the harm reduction approach was applied to the new phenomenon of the use of MDMA (Ecstasy) with the publication by MDTIC of the milestone leaflet, *Chill Out*. Key features of this leaflet were that it was culturally attuned, attractive, non-judgmental and user friendly. This leaflet created a controversy with the Director of MDTIC being attacked on the front pages of the *Daily Star* and the *Sun*. MRHA decided that the leaflet was in line with their strategy and decided it should be defended against accusations of encouraging drug use and so the director also appeared on national television programmes. However, its publication was a turning point in the public's understanding of harm reduction in that a debate about the issue took place on Merseyside and nationally, with a favourable outcome in terms of public opinion (McDermott et al., 1993).

The first conference on the reduction of drug related harm was organised by Pat O'Hare and colleagues in Liverpool, UK, in 1990. The conference has taken place every year since then in cities around the world with attendance by representatives from more than 80 countries.

The Netherlands

The Netherlands was one of the first countries to implement harm reduction programmes, recognising that reducing harm means providing medical and social care in order to avoid some of the more harmful consequences of injection drug use. The Dutch approach was pragmatic and non-moralistic, encompassing needle exchange, information and education, a law enforcement focus on traffickers rather than users, methadone prescribing and a tolerance area policy. Needle exchange began in 1984 and has been widely adopted. Police stations in Amsterdam provided clean needles on an exchange basis – this was possible because of police support for harm reduction. Agencies began methadone prescribing programmes in the 1970s, expanding and liberalising them in the 1980s to deal with hepatitis, HIV, drug related crime and other harms. This 'low threshold programme' approach aimed to contact heroin users and to regulate or stabilise heroin use (Hartgers et al., 1992). One innovative approach was the methadone bus project in Amsterdam, where mobile methadone clinics cruised the city, stopping at different locations daily. Oral methadone was consumed on the spot, and clean needles and condoms were also available (Buning et al., 1990). The Amsterdam Municipal Health Service had a small number of registered users on injectable methadone or morphine (Derks, 1990). The number of people entering drug-free treatment and resocialisation programmes in Amsterdam more than doubled following the introduction of the methadone bus project and needle exchange schemes; one of the main reasons for success is that they do not require users to provide urine samples or to have contact with counsellors. Police in the Netherlands focused attention and resources on drug traffickers, not users.

North America

Methadone maintenance programmes for opiate users began in Canada in the late 1950s and in the United States in the early 1960s. The spread of AIDS in opiate users led to expansion and liberalising of methadone programmes in a number of countries with good results, but many other countries, including Canada and the United States, were slow to expand and improve methadone services and even today these are often beset by problems of lack of accessibility and respect for the rights of users.

From these roots, harm reduction emerged and spread around the world. One of the countries that best exemplifies harm reduction as a national strategy as well as a local response is Australia.

Australia

Australia rapidly revised its drug policies in response to the threat of HIV/AIDS. National and state advisory committees on AIDS and drug use were set up early, and priority was given to containing HIV and other drug related harms. A harm reduction approach was adopted in 1985, which included needle exchange, drug information and education programmes, and an expansion of methadone programmes. These programmes developed more flexible criteria for admission, including clients who were not motivated to change their drug-using behaviour. The effectiveness of the Australian response was greatly enhanced by a comprehensive national strategy on HIV/AIDS, first implemented in 1986. The strategy was based on wide consultation with those infected and affected as well as those working in the area. It targets those at high risk of infection because of behaviour and/or social circumstances: men who have sex with men, injecting drug users, sex workers and people from diverse cultural and linguistic backgrounds. Five priority areas are identified: education and prevention, treatment and care, research, international assistance and cooperation, and legal and ethical matters.

Australia's national strategy stresses the importance of a supportive legal environment to the success of initiatives. A 1991 report by a select committee on HIV, Illegal Drugs and Prostitution concluded that, on the basis of international experience, prohibition policies are not effective in reducing drug supply or use and work actively against health policies seeking to prevent HIV transmission (National Centre for Epidemiology and Population Health, 1991). This report, together with the work of the Australian Drug Law Reform Foundation (made up of parliamentarians, professionals and members of the community concerned about the damage done by drugs and drug policies) (Wodak, 1990), provided an important impetus for consideration of alternatives to prohibition and abstinence policies.

One alternative considered was heroin prescribing, and a trial was designed to provide evidence about the potential benefits of controlled availability of opiates (reduced crime, reduced corruption, prevention of HIV spread, improved health and lifestyle of users) and the potential limitations (leakage of supplies onto the street, failure to address the relationship with crime, since many users are involved in crime before they are involved in heroin, and failure to address other problems of drug users). The committee concluded that the risks can be minimised and are outweighed by potential benefits, and the project was approved in 1997. This coincided with a new government, however, and as a result of external and internal political pressure (Symonds, 1997) the federal cabinet decided not to go ahead with the trial. Currently, the premiers of several states are pressing for the commencement of heroin trials. As a result of the harm reduction measures adopted, Australia has an HIV prevalence among IDUs of less than 5%. Efforts to curb the increase in drug related crime and overdose deaths have been less successful, indicating that the approach to harm reduction may have focused too narrowly on HIV and not on other harms. This has been reinforced by public and political pressure, leading to the opening of a safe injecting room in Sydney on a trial basis in 2002.

IHRA, International Harm Reduction Association

The International Harm Reduction Association (IHRA) was formed in 1996 as a result of the rapidly increasing popularity of the International Conference on the Reduction of Drug Related Harm and the demand for services and support with respect to harm reduction policies and programmes extending beyond the brief period of the annual meeting. Several friends and colleagues involved with the harm reduction conference (Pat O'Hare, Ernie Drucker, Diane Riley, Alex Wodak, Ernst Buning, Fabio Mesquita, Bill Stronach, Patrick Aeberhard, Dave Burrows, Marsha Rosenbaum) from several different countries formed IHRA to continue the work of the conference throughout the year and around the world. IHRA was an international, professional association for individuals and organisations concerned with the development and adoption of more appropriate and effective drug policies which seek to reduce the harmful consequences of drug use. IHRA sought to intervene in the process of formulating drug policy, such that harm reduction principles are widely adopted: it informs the wider population of the issues; to those providing interventions it offers information, training and educational materials; and for policy shapers, makers and implementers, it engages in specific, targeted programmes.

Pat O'Hare and Diane Riley respectively were Executive Director and Deputy Director of this new organisation, based in Liverpool, UK, which operated for many years on a shoe-string budget, a hope and a prayer and in the face of often open hostility to the concept of harm reduction and those that practiced, or even spoke, of it. Despite the opposition, the harm reduction movement grew rapidly. In 1998 in Sao Paolo, Brazil, Diane Riley and Fabio Mesquita together with representatives of the harm reduction networks founded Global Voice (now the Network of Networks), the consortium of the regional and interest-focused networks (this includes the networks for each region of the world, the drug users network, the youth network and the womens' network). The networks have been the key to the success and endurance of harm reduction. For example, starting in 1996 the Asian Harm Reduction Network has played a crucial role in the establishment of harm reduction programmes and the development of more supportive policies throughout the region. It runs a website, publishes a newsletter, carries out training, prepares training materials and is actively involved in advocacy.

The conference together with the work of IHRA and the *International Journal of Drug Policy* (IHRA's journal) were a vehicle for documenting and broadcasting the effectiveness and humanity of harm reduction, gaining more support and winning converts. Amongst these converts were politicians, police officers, commissioners of prisons and even the UN system. Harm reduction is now the official position of many national and international and multilateral bodies, including the UN.

The history of harm reduction in particular countries and regions of the world is reviewed in individual chapters of this book.

References

Acton, W. (1862) Can syphilis be communicated by vaccination, letter to *British Medical Journal*, 22 February, 214–15.

Allbutt, T.C. (1870) On the abuse of hypodermic injections of morphia, *Practitioner*, 5, 327–31.

Ashton, J. and Seymour, H. (1988) *The New Public Health*, Milton Keynes: Open University Press.

Buning, E.C., van Brussel, G.H.A. and van Santen, G. (1990) The 'Methadone by Bus' project in Amsterdam, *British Journal of Addiction*, 85 (10), 1247–50.

Courtwright, D. (2001) *Dark Paradise: A History of Opiate Addiction in America*, Cambridge, MA: Harvard University Press.

Derks, J. (1990) The efficacy of the Amsterdam Morphine-Dispensing Program. In H.A. Ghodse, C.D. Caplanand R.D. Mann (eds), *Drug Misuse and Dependence*, Park Ridge: Parthenon, 75–98.

Eaton, G., Seymour, H. and Mahmood, R. (1998) The development of services for drug misusers on Mersey, *Drugs: Education, Prevention and Policy*, 5 (3), 315–18.

Hartgers, C., van den Hoek, A., Krijnen, P. and Coutinho, R. (1992) HIV prevalence and risk behaviour among injecting drug users who participate in 'low threshold' methadone programs in Amsterdam, *American Journal of Public Health*, 82 (4), 547–51.

Howard-Jones, N. (1947) A critical study of the origins and early development of hypodermic medication, *Journal of the History of Medicine and Allied Sciences*, 2 (2), 201–49.

Hunter, C. (1858) On narcotic injections in neuralgia, *Medical Times and Gazette*, 2, 408–9.

Kaal, H.L. (2001) Police cautioning of drug offenders: policies, practices and attitudes. Unpublished dissertation submitted to the University of Bristol in accordance with the requirements of the degree of the Doctor of Philosophy in the Faculty of Law.

Kane, H.H. (1880) *The Hypodermic Injection of Morphia: Its History, Advantages and Dangers*, New York: Chas. Bermingham and Co.

Levinstein, E. (1878) *The Morbid Craving for Morphia*, London: Smith, Elder and Co.

Linnane, F. (2008) *Drinking for England*, London: JR Books.

Macht, D.I. (1916) The history of intravenous and subcutaneous administration of drugs, *Journal of the American Medical Association*, 56 (12), 856–60.

McDermott, P., Matthews, A., O'Hare, P. and Bennett, A. (1993) Ecstasy in the United Kingdom: recreational drug use and subcultural change. In N. Heather, A. Wodak, E. Nadelmannand P. O'Hare (eds), *Psychoactive Drugs and Harm Reduction: From Faith to Science*, London: Whurr, 230–44.

Ministry of Health (1926) *Departmental Committee on Morphine and Heroin Addiction (The Rolleston Report)*, London: HMSO.

National Centre for Epidemiology and Population Health and the Australian Institute of Criminology (1991) *Feasibility Research into the Controlled Availability of Opioids, Vol. 1: Report and Recommendations*, Canberra: Australian National University.

O'Connell, D. (1990) The role of the police in Merseyside. First International Conference on the Reduction of Drug Related Harm, Liverpool, 9–12 April.

O'Hare, P.A. (1992) A note on the concept of harm reduction. In P.A. O'Hare, R. Newcombe, A. Matthews, E. C. Buningand E. Drucker (eds), *The Reduction of Drug-Related Harm*, London and New York: Routledge.

O'Hare, P.A. (2007) Merseyside, the first harm reduction conferences, and the early history of harm reduction, *International Journal of Drug Policy*, 18 (2), 141–4.

Parker, H., Newcombe, R. and Bakx, K. (1988) *Living with Heroin: The Impact of a Drugs 'Epidemic' on an English Community*. Milton Keynes: Open University Press.

Pates, R. and Wichter, J. (2005) History of injecting. In R. Pates, A. McBride, and K. Arnold (eds), *Injecting Illicit Drugs*, Oxford: Blackwell Publishing, 1–10.

Riley, D.M. (1993), *The Policy and Practice of Harm Reduction*, Ottawa: Canadian Centre on Substance.

Riley, D.M. and O'Hare, P.A. (2000) Harm reduction: history, definition and practice. In J. Inciardiand L. Harrison (eds), *Harm Reduction and Drug Control*, Newbury Park: Sage, 1–26.

Riley, D., Sawka, E., Conley, P., Hewitt, D., Mitic, W., Poulin, C. Room. R., Single, E, and Topp, J. (1999) Harm reduction: concepts and practices, *Substance Use and Misuse*, 34 (1), 9–24.

Spear, H.B. (2002) *Heroin Addiction Care and Control: The British System 1916–1984*, London: Drugscope.

Steer, D. (1970) *Police Cautions: A Study in the Exercise of Police Discretion*, Oxford: Oxford University Penal Research Unit, Basil Blackwell.

Symonds, A. (1997) The Australian heroin trial. Paper presented at the Drug Policy Foundation Conference, New Orleans, October 1997.

Task Force to Review Services for Drug Misusers (1996) *Report of an Independent Review of Drug Treatment Services in England*, London: Department of Health.

Thompson, C.J.S. (1928) *Quacks of Old London*, London: Brentano's.

Wodak, A. (1990) Chair, Sydney: Australian Drug Law Reform Foundation, personal communication.

Wood, A. (1855) A new method of treating neuralgia by the direct application of opiates to the painful points, *Edinburgh, Med. Surg. Journal*, 82, 265–81.

Wood, E., Kerr, T., Small, W., Li, K., Marsh, D.C., Montaner, J.S., and Tyndall, M.W. (2004) Changes in public order after the opening of a medically supervised safer injecting facility for illicit injection drug users, *Journal of the Canadian Medical Association*, 171, 731–4.

Wren, C. (1665) An Account of the rise and Attempts, of a Way to Conveigh Liquors Immediately into the Mass of Blood, *Philosophical Transactions of the Royal Society*, 1, 128–30.

Chapter 3

DRUG EDUCATION OR DRUG PROPAGANDA?

Julian Cohen

I have worked in the drug education field all over the UK as a trainer, lecturer, teacher, youth worker, counsellor, researcher and as an author of many published drug education resources for use with children and young people, professionals who work with them and parents. I have also lectured, run training courses or carried out research in America, Australia, Canada, France, Ireland, the Netherlands, Romania and Spain and witnessed some of the drug education in these countries. I have closely followed debates about good practice in drug education and kept abreast of the research studies that have evaluated the impact of drug education and information initiatives in schools, youth and community settings and through the mass media. Some decades on I am struck by how little actual drug education there has been for young people. Unfortunately, much of what has been called drug education has not really been educational at all. It has had much more in common with propaganda. What is the difference between education and propaganda? In a broad sense education is an act, or experience, that has a formative effect on the mind, character and abilities of a person. An educational approach teaches you *how* to think and act for yourself and encourages you to develop your own informed opinions and to make your own decisions. In contrast, propaganda tells you *what* to think and how to behave in specific ways that have been decided by someone else for you. Education is open, expansive, explorative and divergent. Propaganda is closed, narrow, predictable and convergent.

When it comes to drug education an educational approach teaches *about* drugs, whilst propaganda tries to teach *against* drugs. Anti-drug campaigns, usually conducted through the mass media, are clearly propaganda but in this article I focus on the drug education delivered to groups of young people in schools and youth and community projects and suggest that much of it is also propaganda. A disproportionate amount of this drug education has addressed illegal drugs but a lot of what I argue also applies to education about alcohol, solvents and tobacco. What I say is relevant as well to media initiatives and one-to-one work with young people, in fact to any form of drug education or drug information provided for young people.

I define drugs as all mind-altering substances. We all have a lifetime drug career of using a range of mind-altering substances, be they currently 'legal' drugs (such as alcohol, tobacco, caffeine, solvents and poppers), currently 'illegal' drugs or medicines. Drug careers often begin before birth because many drugs cross the placenta during pregnancy. We nearly all self-medicate for most of our lives and search out drugs, and ways of using them, that are useful and acceptable to us, even if we may have some mishaps on the way. In this sense we are all drug users, even though many people do not like to think of themselves as such. In this chapter I explore how the differences between

Harm Reduction in Substance Use and High-Risk Behaviour: International Policy and Practice, First Edition.
Edited by Richard Pates and Diane Riley.
© 2012 Blackwell Publishing Ltd. Published 2012 by Blackwell Publishing Ltd.

education and propaganda are played out in the drug education targeted at young people, with regard to its three, interrelated components:

- provision of information about drugs;
- exploration of attitudes towards drug use;
- development of skills relevant to decision-making about drug use.

I go on to look at the differences between educational and propagandist approaches to drug education with regard to the teaching methods used and who should lead sessions with groups of young people. I then discuss how educational and propagandist approaches relate to the aims and effectiveness of drug education and their associations, respectively, with *primary prevention* and *harm reduction*. This leads me to emphasise the need to reclaim the education in drug education as a way of moving forward. I conclude by suggesting ways that a more educational approach to drug education can be developed in the future, even though the possibility of this happening seems very remote at the present time. Rather than writing an academic piece I have used examples from my own experience as a drug educator.

Provision of information about drugs

A lot of drug education pays little, if any, attention to exploration of attitudes and development of skills and is based almost solely on the provision of drug information. While this might be expected in the media – TV and radio advertisements, posters, leaflets, pamphlets and so forth – it is also often true of much of the drug education delivered to groups of young people in schools and youth and community groups. Given little time in the curriculum to work with young people around drugs issues many teachers, and youth and social care workers, focus mainly on information provision. Concentrating on information provision also means there is likely to be less debate, questioning and controversy and the drug educator can feel more in control of what is going to be explored and said. We will all agree that information about drugs and drug use is an important aspect of drug education. However, we may not agree about what information is provided, whether it is accurate or true, and what information is omitted. The drug information given to young people is rarely balanced and often inaccurate. Commonly, risks and dangers are exaggerated in an attempt to present drugs in a bad light and to deter young people from using. The possibility that taking a drug might kill you, or lead to serious impairment, is often emphasised, despite the fact that the probability of these things happening is often highly unlikely, and statistically a lot less likely than the dangers arising from many normal, everyday activities and situations (British Medical Association, 1990; Gardner, 2008). Discussion of the relative dangers of different drugs, and ways of using them, and comparison with the dangers of many accepted and promoted activities for young people, such as outdoor pursuits and action sports, is often taboo, despite the fact that many such activities are often more dangerous than drug use. This was recently witnessed in the UK when Professor David Nutt was sacked as chairperson of the Government's Advisory Council on the Misuse of Drugs after publicly comparing the risks of ecstasy use with horse riding, and criticising the way the dangers of use of legal drugs are often downplayed, and of illegal drugs exaggerated.

Emotive films about young people dying after taking drugs have been a feature of drug education. The tragic deaths of Leah Betts and Rachel Whitear in the UK are two examples. Both films were shown in many schools and youth clubs throughout the country. The problem was that neither girl died simply from the drugs that were implicated in the films – respectively ecstasy and heroin – as coroners' reports into their deaths later showed. Similarly, recent deaths in the UK, that were thought to be associated with mephedrone, led to media hysteria and the government rushing to make mephedrone illegal, only for the subsequent coroner's report to show that the boys, who were highlighted as the victims of mephedrone, had not even taken the drug.

Drug education often presents extreme cases as norms, such that there have been many attempts to shock and scare young people from taking drugs, what is called fear arousal. Slogans like 'one pill kills', talks by the ex-drug addicts about how low they became on drugs, emotive films and theatre productions about young people dying using drugs and garish poster campaigns have been predominant in the history of drug education in the UK and used widely in schools and youth and community projects. The fact that the information given is often inaccurate, and that dangers are exaggerated, is largely ignored. A lot of young people, and especially those who are more involved with drugs, and at greatest risk, see through such propaganda, feel they are not being told the truth and start mistrusting the information about drugs that they are given. Young people are often fed 'prophylactic lies' (Trebach, 1987), resulting in what sociologists have termed 'deviancy amplification' (Young, 1971; Cohen, 1972).

I was showing a Band of Hope 'anti-drug' pamphlet to a group of young people. On one page were two drawings of a young man. In one drawing he looked bright and happy. In the other he looked dishevelled and depressed. According to the Band of Hope drug use had led to his downfall. One young man in the group looked at the drawings and said to me 'No. They've got it all the wrong way round. Look at him. What a miserable slob. Took some ecstasy and look how happy he is now.'

The propagandist aspect of a lot of drug education is also to the fore in the omission of information that is deemed unsuitable for young people to know because it might put drug use in a more favourable light. The benefits and pleasures of using drugs are often ignored or, if they are addressed at all, portrayed as being short lived as users inevitably begin to have problems and become hooked. The fact that many people use drugs in relatively moderate and controlled ways over long periods of their lives, with few if any problems, is seen as something that either cannot happen or, if it does occur, should not be acknowledged with young people. With the exception of alcohol use, many drug educators see no benefits to drug use, which leaves the unanswered question as to why we use mind altering substances in the ways that we do. Nearly all drug use is portrayed as very dangerous, which means that strategies for using drugs, and especially illegal drugs, in safer and less damaging ways are rarely discussed with young people. Many drug educators become caught in the circle of 'if you don't condemn drug use, you condone it', despite the fact that we nearly all, including drug educators themselves, have a lifetime career of using mind altering substances, be they currently legal or illegal drugs.

Drug educators often ask young people to brainstorm the reasons that people use drugs. The answers given, and discussed, rarely make much sense because the distinction between different forms of drug use – experimental, recreational, binge and dependent use – and the different motivations for each form, is rarely fully explored. In particular recreational use, with few problems, is usually ignored.

And there are also omissions of many other uncomfortable facts. These commonly include not giving a full picture of current drug laws within the UK (and even sometimes giving a deliberately dishonest one, such as examples I have witnessed of making out to children and young people that it is illegal for them to smoke cigarettes, drink alcohol or use solvents or poppers), little or no information about young people's legal rights and ignoring, or playing down, statistics concerning the extent of drug use. A lot of drug education also fails to make comparisons with other countries that deal with drugs in different ways to the UK, airbrushes the often contradictory history of drug use and controls, and ignores religious uses of drugs and cross cultural differences in drug use and production. The propagandist approach to drug education censors uncomfortable facts.

A few years ago I was commissioned by the UK Government Department for Education to help write a drug education guidance document for schools. One thing they asked me to do was to give examples of ways teachers could integrate the issue of drugs into the various subjects taught in schools. For the teaching of history I suggested a number of possibilities, including the Opium Wars, medicinal cannabis use in Victorian times and the history of drug laws and controls in the UK. These examples were later censored from the document. When I asked the senior history adviser why this had been done he said 'We don't want young people getting the wrong idea about drugs. We need to give them a consistent message'.

Propagandist approaches see young people as ignorant about drugs or having the wrong ideas about drugs. The fact that even young children already have information, feelings, views and experiences concerning drugs, is often ignored. Instead they are to be given, what is deemed, the correct information. In this sense a lot of drug education is something that is done to, rather than with, young people and they are not encouraged to question the information they receive about drugs from various sources. By teenage years many young people have tired of being talked at. They begin to feel patronised and that they have heard it all before, are only being told part of the picture and know more about drugs than the people who are teaching them.

I was asked to chair a large public meeting of over 200 parents and young people about the rise in young people's drug use in Leeds. The organisers had arranged for four speakers on the expert panel. The prison governor assured the audience that there was no drug use in his prison. The police officer's talk about the law presented inaccurate information about the legal status of cannabis, magic mushrooms and poppers. The judge gave a lurid account of drug dealers and how the courts dealt with them, kept confusing ecstasy and LSD, and seemed a bit worse for wear from drinking alcohol. The solicitor was supposed to talk about legal rights but spent most of his time talking about how smoking a few joints of cannabis could, in itself, cause young people to have severe mental health problems. I later found out that he was having a lot of difficulties with his son's use of cannabis. It was a very difficult meeting to chair. I struggled to correct so much inaccurate information without appearing to put the speakers down.

In contrast, an educational approach tries to ensure that information about drugs is accurate and balanced. It acknowledges the benefits people may derive from use of drugs and examines the dangers of drug use in a realistic way, without exaggeration. It also encourages young people to learn that the dangers of drug use have as much to do with the ways that drugs are used, the set (the people using, what is happening in their lives, how they feel about themselves etc.) and the setting of use (where they are, what they are doing, who they are with etc.) as the actual drugs themselves (Zinberg, 1984). Methods of using drugs in safer and less safe ways, in other words harm reduction, is seen as an essential element. Broader social, political, historical and cross-cultural information and issues are included, rather than omitted. Young people are encouraged to question the drug information they are given and to critically evaluate different sources of information.

Exploration of attitudes towards drug use

Drug education sessions with groups of young people often involve little debate. The ways that drugs are dealt with by the government and presented in the media are rarely questioned. The pretence is often that we all agree about drugs – they're bad and nasty, only weak people use them, only wicked people supply them and the current laws and Government policy are right. The many differences in how people view drugs, and how they believe we should deal with drugs as a society, are rarely addressed. By default, young people are told what they should think. If their views or experiences differ from those presented they soon realise that they are not to be expressed in front of anyone in authority.

I was at a school in a very poor area of Washington, USA watching a drug education lesson led by two uniformed police officers. The 13- and 14-year-olds were performing the anti-drug songs they had penned with great gusto and at the end of the lesson signed a pledge not to use drugs. Later I was walking around the neighbourhood when I spotted a group of the same students sitting on a wall smoking joints. I went up and asked them how come they were smoking joints when a few hours before they were singing anti-drug songs and had signed a pledge not to use drugs. One of the students looked at me, shrugged his shoulders, and said 'Well it keeps them happy and this – waving the joint – keeps me happy.'

Rather than challenging stereotypes a lot of drug education perpetuates them. Users are often portrayed as weak and naive people who are bullied or tricked into using drugs. Dealers are seen as evil, dangerous people who are not to be trusted and try to force dangerous drugs on innocent young people to get them hooked. The term drug 'pusher' is often used, even though it is at variance with the way most young people acquire drugs from friends and acquaintances, and regard it as a favour when they do (Coggans and McKellar, 1994). In many cases drugs are pulled, rather than pushed, in that a lot of young people want to use drugs and seek them out. Perpetuating these stereotypes fails to prepare young people for the reality of drug use and does nothing to create understanding of, or empathy with, other people who may be different from themselves and may be experiencing difficulties in their lives. Instead, it creates stigmatisation, particularly of problem drug users (Lloyd, 2010).

By a young age most children already have very stereotypical and negative perceptions of drug users and dealers. When I have asked groups of young children to make up a play about 'drugs' the atmosphere becomes dark and dangerous with seedy characters and very soon someone drops dead. When I ask the same groups to make up a play about drinking beer and wine they stumble about drunk like, laugh a lot, sometimes shout and argue and square up for a fight, and if there are boys and girls they often show physical affection and flirt with each other. No one ever dies in the alcohol play. Even into adolescence when young people are asked to draw drug users and dealers, or brainstorm words for them, the same negative stereotypes tend to occur time and time again, even amongst young people who are using various drugs themselves.

Many drug education policy-makers and practitioners talk about the need to give young people the 'right', 'correct' or 'consistent' 'messages' about drugs. They also sometimes speak of their concerns about 'putting the wrong ideas in young people's heads'. These concepts are more in the realms of propaganda, than an educational approach.

In one county in the UK, the police arranged for a 'reformed', convicted drug dealer, who was serving a long prison sentence, to go into schools to talk to young people about the evil world of drug dealing and how they should have nothing to do with drugs. The prisoner was an articulate, good looking young man. The talks were very well received in the schools but were stopped after evaluations showed that many young people, and especially girls, found the prisoner, and his lifestyle, very attractive.

In contrast, an educational approach to drug education enables young people to explore a range of views about drugs and the meanings drug use might have for different people and encourages them to challenge stereotypes. Debate, questioning and difference are welcomed and facilitated. Young people are helped to think for themselves, to recognise that there are many different views about drugs and to reach their own opinions and conclusions. An educational approach also makes the point that we are all drug users.

I was talking to a small group of 17- and 18-year-olds in the UK who were into music and art big style, including making their own works. They told me about their use of ecstasy, ketamine, cannabis and a range of legal highs. They did not drink much alcohol and looked down on young people who were always getting drunk. One young woman in the group made it clear that they could not stand 'dirty druggies', by which she meant heroin users. I asked them how they could square their own drug use with not liking 'druggies'. One of the young men explained that 'When it comes to it, drugs is something other people do.' I've found this one of the most useful definitions of drugs I have ever heard and one that can generate a lot of discussion and debate.

Development of skills relevant to decision-making about drug use

In recent years many drug education policy-makers and practitioners have talked about the importance of developing decision-making skills amongst young people. They often emphasise the need to teach young people how to make 'healthy', 'informed' or 'rational' choices about drugs. However, this usually boils down to telling young people not to take drugs at all. In other words young people are told what decisions they should make, rather than encouraged to make decisions for themselves. The circumstances in which people use drugs, and the various ways they might use, including safer and less safe ways, are rarely explored. There have been some exceptions, such as in alcohol education programmes and harm reduction initiatives concerning heroin injecting and HIV, and ecstasy use and over-heating, but most drug education with groups of young people in schools and youth and social care projects still focuses on saying no to drugs, especially illegal drugs.

When decision-making skills are addressed in drug education the focus is usually on drug offer situations and the development of refusal skills. Case studies, role play, film, drama, expert speakers and posters have been used to try to teach young people how they can say no to an offer of drugs. The assumption is that young people are under a lot of overt peer pressure from friends, acquaintances and evil drug 'pushers' to start using drugs and that they lack the confidence and skills to refuse these offers of drugs. However, this is not how young people are usually initiated into using drugs and it does not correlate with young people's likely experiences in the real world. As stated earlier, drugs are more commonly pulled, rather than pushed, and young users have an interest in using and seek out people who can supply them; a case of peer preference, rather than peer pressure (Coggans and McKellar, 1994).

The classic 'say no to drugs' role play usually involves young people working in pairs, one trying to persuade or trick the other into taking a drug and the other coming up with strategies to say no. The young people are often put on the spot, by having to play themselves, rather than a fictitious character. With a teacher, youth or social care worker and/or police officer and their peers, watching, they have little choice but to say no.

The focus on peer pressure and saying 'no', means that key skills – such as assessment of risks in a variety of drug-related situations, harm reduction strategies, ways of getting help and advice if needed, communicating about drugs and managing conflict with peers, parents and the police are often off the agenda. Again, those young people who are most at risk from drug use learn little of practical help. A lot of this drug education is individualistic, rather than based on collectivism and peer, family and community support. The focus on the individual's use of drugs, means that skills to help and advise friends and family members, who may be having difficulties with drug use, and important skills, like drug related first aid, are also rarely addressed.

Over the years I must have seen more than twenty different theatre productions dealing with drug issues, staged in schools and youth clubs. With one or two notable exceptions they have all had an explicit anti-drug 'message' and a format of stereotypical goodies and baddies, much like a classic 1950s American western movie. Common elements have included someone dying, young people forced or tricked into drug use, evil drug 'pushers' who eventually get their come uppence and goodies who have a close shave but, in the end, learn their lesson not to use any drugs. The plays are often followed by workshops that try to re-enforce the 'anti-drug' message and use role play to try to teach young people to say no to drugs.

An educational approach to skills recognises that young people may be faced with many different situations and dilemmas regarding their own, and other people's, use of drugs and helps them to develop a broad range of decision-making and practical skills, by exploring various options, rather than blandly telling them what to do. 'Third person' techniques can be adopted so that young people can consider, and sometimes role play, fictitious characters, rather than themselves, and can explore situations and possible outcomes, without being personally put on the spot.

The methods used

Propagandist approaches to drug education see young people as empty vessels who are deficient in knowledge of drugs and the skills that they need to resist peer pressure, and may have the wrong attitudes to drug use. The assumption is that the person leading drug education needs to be an expert about drug use so they can use their knowledge to correct these assumed deficiencies in young people. Young people tend to be talked at and the teaching methods used are relatively passive, with little active involvement. Where more active methods are employed, such as role play, they are used in a closed manner, where there is little questioning and the outcomes have already been decided by the educator. The educator closely controls and directs what is said and what happens.

Peer education, where one group of young people, usually an older group, educate another group of young people, has become fashionable in recent years. Whilst some peer education projects have been used in an educational way many have not. As one advocate of peer education, who was concerned that young people would not listen to her message of 'Say no to drugs', put it to me 'They don't seem to listen to me, but perhaps they will listen to other young people telling them not to use drugs.'

In contrast, an educational approach to drug education is based on the assumption that young people, even young children, already have valuable information, ideas, thoughts, feelings, skills and experiences and these should form an important basis, and starting point, for drug education. Active, participatory teaching methods are used to do this and discussion and debate is valued. Young people are encouraged to say what they think and feel and to question. The educator and the young people work together and what is said is less predictable and more open ended.

Tapping into, and using, what young people bring means we have a better idea of 'where they are at' and can tailor what we do to meet the needs of specific groups. Young people are not faced with a set programme, and are involved in directing their own learning so they are less likely to feel that they have heard it all before. Using participative methods means that young people are more likely to be engaged and motivated and to develop confidence and skills in listening, speaking, debating, empathising with and helping others, conflict resolution and working cooperatively in groups.

There are many different active methods that can be used. They include use of:

artwork, board games, body maps, brainstorming, card games, carousels, case studies, collage making, dance/movement, debates, demonstrations, displays, drama, drawing and painting, (questioning) expert speakers, guided fantasies, ice breakers, interactive media, leaflet reviews and making, line continuums, matching activities, mime work, music projects, use of objects and paraphernalia, pairs work, analysing photographs, problem pages, poster making, use of puppets, questionnaires, question boxes, quizzes, ranking activities, research (including via the internet), role play, rounds, sequencing, simulations, small group discussion and presentations, sorting activities, story making and reading, time and life lines and visits to places and to meet people.

An educational approach also often benefits from the group facilitator playing 'devil's advocate', by introducing new concepts and ways of thinking and encouraging young people to consider a wide range of perspectives. Expert speakers may be used as part of a programme, but not in a passive way. Young people are encouraged to closely question them. It also helps if the educator negotiates ground rules with young people at the start of drug education sessions so everyone is clear which behaviours are, and are not, acceptable and what people can say about their own drug use and experiences without getting themselves, or other people, into trouble.

Who should lead drug education for groups of young people?

Most drug education with groups of young people takes place in schools and youth and community projects and is led by teachers and youth and social care workers. Many of them feel that they need to be very knowledgeable about drug use to teach drug education. The fact that drug education is regarded as a controversial and sensitive subject, and the expectation often put upon them to take a propagandist approach and to 'sort young people out', also means many teachers, and youth and social care workers, are anxious about leading sessions. If they can, many are keen to hand the job over to outside 'experts'.

However, drug educators do not need to be 'walking encyclopaedias' of drug information to effectively teach drug education. They do not need to be the source of all drug information for young people. They can use, and work with, young people's knowledge and views, have access to drug information sources and teaching packs that provide background information and can always explain to young people that they do not know certain things but can later find out. It is a valuable educational experience for drug educators and young people to work together to research drug information by talking to other people, reading books, using the internet and so forth.

There has been a long procession of ex-drug addicts doing the rounds of schools and youth clubs. They've been there, worn the tattered tee-shirt, feel they know all about drug use and are seen by many, and often by themselves, as ideal drug educators. Many are on an evangelical mission to tell young people about the evils of drugs. However, they have had very problematic drug careers and what they really know about is how *not* to use drugs. An analogous situation would be allowing people who have had lots of convictions for dangerous driving to become driving instructors. Yet, having speakers who have had relatively successful drug careers, and have used drugs without experiencing many problems, is seen as taboo and as promoting drug use.

Teachers, and youth and social care workers, should be helped to appreciate that the skills they use in other areas of work with young people are transferable to drug education work. If they are leading drug education they can use teaching methods and approaches that they use to address other subject areas and in their pastoral work supporting young people. It is also important for them to realise that effective drug educators need to have the skills and confidence to actually teach and facilitate groups, and to listen to and engage with young people, rather than just knowing a lot about drugs. In this sense teachers, and youth and social care workers, should be encouraged to take an educational, rather than propagandist approach, and to teach drug education on a similar basis to how they teach other, possibly less contentious, subject areas.

Some parents, who have had the great misfortune to have children who have died using drugs, are immediately put forward as expert drug educators who young people should listen to. These parents may be able to be good drug educators but I know that if my daughter died from a drug overdose I would be so traumatised that I would probably not be a good person to take drug advice from. Acting out of anger and grief may lead parents to be evangelical about stopping other young people from using drugs. The information they give may be selective and exaggerated and their approach very emotive and propagandist.

It helps when drug education is led by people who young people already know, and have a relationship with, rather than staff from specialist external agencies. This avoids sensationalising the drugs issue and encourages drugs to be a normal, everyday thing that can be talked about. I have known many specialist drug education workers who go into schools and youth projects to give talks and run sessions about drugs. A lot of them take an educational approach and do a good job. However, some of them work in ways that undermine the confidence of teachers, and youth and social care workers, to lead drug education. They sometimes agree to taking over the teaching of the whole programme and may tell, or imply to, young people that their teachers, and youth and social care workers, know little about drugs and are not worth talking to about drugs. It would be good if these workers could empower, rather than undermine, teachers and youth and social care workers.

Over-use of specialist external agencies may inadvertently undermine open discussion of drugs between teachers, youth and social care workers and young people. It may give young people the impression that discussion of drugs with school, and youth and social care, staff is taboo and something that these staff cannot, or will not, do. Once teachers, and youth and social care workers, become confident in delivering drug education they can ensure that programmes are in place for years to come, rather than becoming dependent on the availability of external agencies. They can also design programmes to meet the needs of particular groups of young people and adapt them as circumstances change.

Specialists from external agencies, such as drug and community projects and the police, can enhance drug education if they add something important and useful that teachers, or youth and social care workers, cannot do. They need to be used in a limited and appropriate manner and their credibility and what they are going to do, and say, need to be checked out before they are invited to speak, something that is not always done. It is also good to encourage young people to question speakers, and not just relate to them passively. Rather than schools and youth and community projects becoming dependent on their input for their drug education, external agencies should help teachers, and youth and social care workers, to become more confident in the delivery of drug education.

The aims and effectiveness of drug education

The overall aim of most of the drug education targeted at young people has been to deter them from using drugs – what is called *primary prevention*. Primary prevention is synonymous with the propagandist approach to drug education that I have described in this article. Over the years there have been many evaluations of the outcomes of such programmes, particularly in America but also in the UK and other countries. These research studies have consistently found that primary prevention is ineffective in preventing, or reducing, young people's drug use (ACMD, 2006; Jones et al., 2006; McGrath et al., 2006). Despite the recent fashion in the UK for governments, and national drug, health and law enforcement agencies, to talk about the need for 'evidenced-based approaches', these research findings have been virtually ignored and primary prevention remains by far the most common form of drug education in the UK and also in other countries.

Evaluations of drug education programmes based on proper social science methods and conventions (large samples, properly matched control groups, sufficient time delay after the drug education intervention etc.) have nearly all focused on measuring primary prevention outcomes. Very few have considered any possible harm reduction outcomes, such as young people's actual experiences of drug use and safer, and less dangerous, drug using patterns. On a couple of occasions I have worked with colleagues to try to persuade UK government health and law enforcement agencies, who were funding large-scale research evaluation studies, to include consideration of harm reduction outcomes from drug education. In both cases our pleas quickly fell on deaf ears. The discussions with the agencies led me to believe that it would be unacceptable to them if evaluations did find that some drug education programmes actually reduced harm. For them it had to be primary prevention . . . or nothing.

In response to the ineffectiveness of primary prevention, and the way it skews drug education away from meeting the needs of young people, a number of practitioners, including myself, have attempted to develop *harm reduction* drug education as an alternative (Cohen, 1993). Since the 1980s we have held conferences, written articles, debated with, and run training courses and workshops for, drug educators and policy-makers. We have also produced, what were often regarded as radical, drug education resources to use with children, young people, parents and professionals in schools, youth and community settings and also through drug and health agencies, local media and in pubs and clubs. We have had some positive influences on the way drug education has been delivered to young people but not a lot, especially in the majority of schools and through the mass media, where propagandist approaches still predominate. It is clear that many practitioners are still nervous about harm reduction and are concerned that if they do not condemn drug use outright, they must be condoning it. In particular, many practitioners are scared about what parents, politicians and the media might think if they moved away from primary prevention and propaganda.

Reclaiming the education in drug education

I suggest that we should now move away from posing harm reduction as the alternative to primary prevention, and instead reframe the debate by advocating for the need for drug education, rather than propaganda. Advocating for education means we can move away from a focus on behavioural outcomes, and instead prioritise educational aims for most of the drug education work that we do with young people. In other words, we can aim to make young people more knowledgable about drugs and drug use, more aware of different views about drugs and help them to develop skills and confidence to deal with a wide range of potential situations involving their own, and other people's, use of drugs. We also know, from research evaluations, and from the evaluations of individual practitioners, that meeting educational aims is actually achievable, unlike primary prevention behavioural outcomes (ACMD, 2006; Jones et al., 2006; McGrath et al., 2006).

We should aim to help young people to become drug literate, rather than to think and behave in narrow, specific ways. This may lead to a reduction in drug-related harm and help young people to have safer drug careers as individuals, and collectively in the ways they can help and support each other. It may also help them to make a better job of drug policy in the future, compared to the mess that we have created.

In my experience advocating for education, rather than propaganda, makes much more sense to many drug educators and policy-makers, compared to trying to persuade them of the virtues of harm reduction. In particular, I have found that many teachers, and youth and social care workers, begin to see that drug education should, and can, be taught on a similar educational basis to the way they address other subjects. Indeed, many people would be horrified and object if other subjects were taught in such a propagandist manner. We need to reclaim the education in drug education.

There will need to be some exceptions to this focus on educational aims in situations where identified groups of young people are using certain drugs in particularly dangerous ways. In such cases, drug education based on specific behavioural, harm reduction outcomes will be needed.

What can be done?

Table 3.1 summarises the main differences between educational and propagandist approaches to drug education.

To help move away from a propagandist approach to drug education with young people, and towards an educational one, I can make many practical suggestions.

Table 3.1 Approaches to drug education

	Education	Propaganda
Overall	• About drugs • Drug use as normal • Open, expansive • Collectivist • Engage with young people's ideas and views • Harm reduction	• Against drugs • Drug use as deviant • Closed, prescriptive • Individualist • Young people treated as empty vessels • Primary prevention
Information	• Accurate • Balanced	• Selective • Exaggerate dangers • Extremes as norms • Shock/scare
	• Benefits and dangers • Include all aspects – social, political and historical • Honest • Question information	• Ignore benefits • Omission of uncomfortable facts • 'Prophylactic lies' • Accept what you are told
Attitudes	• Explore and debate a range of views • Challenge stereotypes	• No or little debate • Perpetuate stereotypes of users, dealers etc.
	• Think for yourself	• Think as we tell you to
Skills	• Develop a range of relevant skills	• Focus on refusal skills • 'Just say no'
	• Make your own, informed decisions	• Do what we say
Methods used	• Active • Done with young people	• Passive • Done to young people

These include:

1. Introduce drug educators to the differences between educational and propagandist approaches to drug education and challenge them to base their approach on education, rather than propaganda.
2. Discuss the differences between education and propaganda with parents, politicians, funders and policy and decision-makers and challenge them to support educational approaches, rather than propaganda.
3. Focus on educational, rather than behavioural outcomes, unless addressing specific and dangerous drug using practices.
4. Whenever possible, balance information provision, attitude exploration and skill development, rather than just focus on drug information.
5. Value and use what young people already know, think and feel. Create an environment, and employ active teaching methods, that enables young people to feel comfortable to speak out, question and debate, consider a range of views and to actively participate.
6. Support drug educators, and especially teachers and youth and social care workers, by the provision of quality training and educational teaching resources.
7. Develop new drug education teaching resources based on an educational model.
8. Develop new media initiatives (I am loathe to use the word 'campaigns' because of the propaganda connotations) based on an educational approach.
9. Encourage specialist agencies to work in ways that develop the confidence and skills of teachers, and youth and social care workers, to deliver drug education, rather than creating dependency and undermining them.
10. Fund research that evaluates the educational and harm reduction outcomes from drug education programmes.

I am interested in what people think of this chapter. Let's converse and debate. I can be contacted at julian.cohen@virgin.net

References

ACMD (2006) *Pathways to Problems: Hazardous Use of Tobacco, Alcohol and Other Drugs by Young People in the UK and Its Implications for Policy*, London: Advisory Council on the Misuse of Drugs.

British Medical Association (1990) *The BMA Guide to Living with Risk*, London: Penguin Books.

Coggans, N. and McKellar, S. (1994). Drug use among peers: peer pressure or peer preference?, *Drugs: Education, Prevention and Policy*, 1 (1), 15–26.

Cohen, J. (1993) Achieving a reduction in drug-related harm through education. In N. Heather, A. Wodak, E. Nadelmann and P. O'Hare (eds), *Psychoactive Drugs and Harm Reduction, From Faith to Science*. London: Whurr, 65–76.

Cohen, S. (1972) *Folk Devils and Moral Panics: The Creation of Mods and Rockers*, London: MacGibbon and Kee.

Gardner, D. (2008) *Risk: The Science and Politics of Fear*, London: Virgin Books.

Jones, L., Sumnall, H., Burrell, K., McVeigh, J. and Bellis, M. (2006) *Universal Drug Prevention*, Liverpool: National Collaborating Centre for Drug Prevention.

Lloyd, C. (2010) *Sinning and Sinned Against: The Stigmatisation of Problem Drug Users*, London: UK Drug Policy Commission.

McGrath, Y., Sumnall, H., Edmonds, K., McVeigh, J. and Bellis, M. (2006) *Review of the Grey Literature on Drug Prevention among Young People*, London: National Institute for Health and Clinical Excellence (NICE).
Trebach, A. (1987) *The Great Drug War*, New York: Macmillan.
Young, J. (1971) *The Drug Takers: The Social Meaning of Drug Use*, London: MacGibbon and Kee.
Zinberg, N. (1984) *Drug, Set and Setting: The Basis for Controlled Intoxicant Use*, New Haven: Yale University Press.

Recent drug education teaching resources written by Julian Cohen are:

Drug Education & Training Photo Pack: Exciting & innovative learning activities to use with young people & adults, 2005, Liverpool: HIT.
Drugs and Me: A structured programme for working one-to-one with young drug users and with small groups, 2010, Liverpool: HIT.
Spiral Drug Education 1: a developmental drug education programme for 11 to 14 year olds in schools, youth clubs and other settings, 2010, HIT.
Spiral Drug Education 2: a developmental drug education programme for 14 to 18 year olds in schools, youth clubs and other settings, 2010, HIT.

For further information about these resources contact www.hit.org.uk.

Section II
Policy

Chapter 4

HARM REDUCTION AND INTERNATIONAL LAW: DRUG CONTROL VS. HUMAN RIGHTS

Richard Elliott

Introduction

There is ample evidence that drug control laws have exacerbated the harms sometimes associated with drug use, including undermining efforts to prevent HIV and reduce harms in other ways (Wolfe and Malinowska-Sempruch, 2004; OSI, 2009; Count the Costs, 2011). It is increasingly evident that implementing harm reduction approaches at least requires countries to defend and take advantage of the flexibility that exists within the current international legal regime of drug control. Where that regime, in interpretation or application, cannot accommodate evidence-informed measures aimed at preventing illness and saving lives, it is deficient on both public health and human rights grounds.

This chapter outlines the basic elements of the international architecture of drug control, consisting of three treaties and three related bodies. It then examines the extent to which those treaties and mechanisms have been or could be open to harm reduction measures. A brief discussion of the most directly relevant aspects of international human right law not only bolsters, but also compels, the case that the drug control treaties must allow for harm reduction programmes. The chapter concludes with some observations about the growing challenges to prohibition, as some countries increasingly seek to temper harsh criminal policy and adopt more public health-oriented approaches to drugs.

International drug control regime: treaties and bodies

The international legal system of drug control consists of three core treaties. The 1961 *Single Convention on Narcotic Drugs* not only codified but also added to various international drug control conventions dating back to 1912, creating the basic structure of the current international legal regime for controlling substances such as opium, coca and marijuana and their derivatives. The 1971 *Convention on Psychotropic Substances* expanded the scope of international control to include synthetic psychotropic substances (e.g., amphetamines, barbiturates, benzodiazepines and psychedelics) and their precursor chemicals. The focus of the 1988 *Convention against Illegal Traffic in Narcotic Drugs and Psychotropic Substances* is prohibiting and punishing the illicit traffic of substances controlled under the previous two conventions. Almost all of the world's countries are parties to all three conventions. Under these treaties, States Parties must adopt measures to criminalise drug-related activities such as cultivation, production, manufacture, export, import, distribution, trading, and the possession of controlled substances except for 'medical and scientific

Harm Reduction in Substance Use and High-Risk Behaviour: International Policy and Practice, First Edition.
Edited by Richard Pates and Diane Riley.
© 2012 Blackwell Publishing Ltd. Published 2012 by Blackwell Publishing Ltd.

purposes' (1961 Convention, Articles 4, 33, 35 and 36; 1971 Convention, Articles 21 and 22; 1988 Convention, Article 3).

Three core bodies supplement the treaties in the architecture of the international drug control system and play key roles in interpreting the treaties, the global policy atmosphere and the treaties' actual implementation at country level. Each of these bodies, and their stance on harm reduction measures in their approach to the treaties' parameters, is described below.

UN Commission on Narcotic Drugs

The UN Commission on Narcotic Drugs (CND) is a 'functional commission' of the UN's Economic and Social Council (ECOSOC), consisting of 53 member states elected for four-year terms from among ECOSOC members. The CND meets annually and is the central body in the UN system responsible for shaping global drug control policy. This includes bringing forward amendments to existing treaties or proposing new treaties and amending the 'schedules' of drugs that determine the degree of control required by the treaties with respect to a scheduled substance.[1] Despite its own rules of procedure and ECOSOC rules governing its functional commissions providing for making decisions by voting, historically the CND has operated by consensus, meaning that any single country among the 53 member states can block a resolution or other initiative. This has proven a major obstacle to pursuing resolutions supportive of harm reduction – to date, not a single CND resolution uses the phrase. Similarly, it has frustrated any significant reform of international drug control policy, including efforts to address in any meaningful way the human rights consequences of said policy (Crocket, 2010).

This consensus approach has increasingly begun to show signs of strain since the new millennium (Jelsma and Metaal, 2004; Bewley-Taylor, 2009; Jelsma, 2010). In recent years, the CND increasingly has faced the challenge of reconciling the prohibitionist provisions and emphasis of the UN drug control treaties with the demands for harm reduction and recognition of human rights, including during its review of global drug control policy ten years after the UN General Assembly (IDPC, 2009). This has included offers from UN special rapporteurs on human rights to provide 'guidance' to the CND (Nowak and Grover, 2008).

International Narcotics Control Board

The International Narcotics Control Board (INCB) is the other treaty-based body in the global drug control sphere. As 'the independent and quasi-judicial control organ for the implementation of the United Nations drug conventions', the Board seeks in various ways to ensure governments comply with (its interpretation of) those treaties.[2] ECOSOC member states elect the Board's 13 individual members (3 of them from a list proposed by the WHO), who sit in their personal capacities for 5-year terms. Although INCB interpretations of the conventions are not legally binding, they help determine the political climate in which decision-makers determine national drug policies. The INCB comments on states' compliance with their obligations under the drug control conventions and recommends changes to national drug control regimes, including through its annual reports. (The Board's correspondence with governments, its country visits and reports, and the minutes of

[1] The World Health Organization also plays an important advisory role in Commission deliberations regarding the scheduling of substances (pursuant to 1961 Convention, Article 3). However, the INCB has regularly weighed in on the issue of scheduling, even though this is the purview of the WHO under the drug control conventions: e.g., see INCB (2010) and INCB (2011a).
[2] The INCB was established in 1968 in accord with the provisions of the 1961 Convention, with a mandate subsequently expanded to cover the two later conventions.

its meetings are rarely public.) The INCB can also propose 'consultations' with a government, request explanations for the government's actions, and bring matters of concern to the attention of the CND, ECOSOC and, ultimately, the UN General Assembly (pursuant to 1961 Convention, Article 14).

Historically, the INCB has manifested a general hostility toward both harm reduction and human rights, although that position may be softening in recent years in the face of sustained criticism (Csete and Wolfe, 2007a; 2007b; 2008; Barrett, 2008; IDPC, 2008; Bewley-Taylor and Trace, 2006). The INCB has lamented that harm reduction has 'diverted the attention (and in some cases, funds) of Governments from important demand reduction activities such as primary prevention or abstinence-oriented treatment' (INCB, 2001). Notwithstanding legal advice to the contrary from its own secretariat (UNDCP, 2002), the INCB has repeatedly declared that harm reduction initiatives such as supervised drug consumption sites – which it regularly mischaracterises as 'shooting galleries' or 'opium dens' – amount to governments 'promoting the abuse of drugs' (e.g., Emafo, 2007) and denounces them virtually annually in breach of the international drug control conventions (INCB, 2001; 2002; 2004; 2005; 2007; 2008; 2009; 2010; 2011). The INCB has also called on governments to end other harm reduction programmes such as the distribution of safer crack-use kits and other 'drug paraphernalia', declaring that these programmes also contravene the 1988 Convention (INCB, 2008).[3]

Also noteworthy is the INCB's failure, until very recently, to devote much attention to the other part of its mandate explicitly set out in the 1961 Convention – ensuring access to opioids for medical purposes. One such purpose is opioid substitution therapy (OST) using medications such as methadone and buprenorphine, both of which the WHO recognises as 'essential medicines' (WHO, 2011). OST is a critical harm reduction intervention, recognised by the UN system for its benefits in reducing HIV risk among people who inject opioids and in supporting effective antiretroviral treatment for those living with HIV (UN, 2001; WHO, UNODC and UNAIDS, 2004a; 2004b; UN ECOSOC, 2004; WHO, 2005; 2009). Yet the INCB has done little to engage countries in ensuring access to OST.

This reticence to speak out about countries' policies that deny access to proven health services such as OST is symptomatic of a broader unwillingness to articulate concerns about countries' abuses of human rights in the context of enforcing drug control laws. The INCB's response to such criticisms has been disappointing. For example, in 2007, in response to a widely publicised report highlighting the ways in which the INCB had become an obstacle to programmes aimed at preventing HIV and in other ways reducing drug-related harms (Csete & Wolfe, 2007a), the President of the Board declared that it is mandated only 'to discuss with governments', a claim demonstrably false upon review of the conventions (Barrett, 2008). Meanwhile, the Board's Secretary declared that it would 'not discuss human rights' (Kouame, 2007). The INCB has also continued to question the widely accepted definition of harm reduction, usually referring to it in scare quotes as 'harm reduction', thereby suggesting that the concept is suspect, and insisting that only abstinence-oriented programmes are legitimate (e.g., INCB, 2009). Even as the foreword to the Board's most recent Annual Report (for 2010) explicitly mentions that both drug supply and demand reduction efforts must respect human rights, the Board continues to remain silent on well-documented human

---

[3] Note that the 'drug paraphernalia' must presumably include needle exchanges, even though the Board has previously accepted such programmes as legal under the drug control conventions, consistent with the advice of the UNDCP Legal Affairs Section (UNDCP, 2002). Distribution of sterile materials to reduce the risks of harm from the unsafe smoking of crack is qualitatively equivalent to distributing sterile materials to reduce the risks of harm from unsafe injection, so it is hard to understand the Board's inconsistency here.

rights abuses – such as mandatory minimum sentences for drug offences (including the death penalty in some cases), torture and other abuse of people who use drugs (even in some cases in the name of 'treatment'), and extrajudicial executions (HRI, 2011).

United Nations Office on Drugs and Crime

The third key entity within the global drug control architecture, and the one that has demonstrated the greatest evolution in its institutional thinking in recent years, is the UN Office on Drugs and Crime. UNODC is the technical agency mandated to assist Member States in their struggle against illicit drugs, crime and terrorism, which it does through technical cooperation projects in the field, research and analysis to inform policy and operational decisions, and normative work to assist states in the ratification and implementation of the relevant international treaties, the development of domestic legislation on drugs, crime and terrorism. It also acts as the secretariat to treaty-based bodies such as the CND and the INCB.

Commentators have previously observed that the UNODC has been grappling with the contradictions between the predominantly prohibitionist orientation of the drug control treaties and 'core values' of the UN such as human rights and public health (Bewley-Taylor, 2005). That tension has certainly intensified with the agency's role as a co-sponsor agency of the Joint UN Programme on HIV/AIDS (UNAIDS), with lead responsibility for the UN system's response to HIV among people who inject drugs and people in prison or other places of detention. In addition, there has been growing pressure from the evidence and from civil society groups to revisit key elements and assumptions of global drug control policy, particularly in the face of the global HIV pandemic.

As a result, notwithstanding certain pressures,[4] UNODC has increasingly supported harm reduction measures, at least insofar as it relates to preventing HIV among people who use drugs, and the greater consideration of human rights in the development, interpretation and implementation of drug control, including in regions particularly hard-hit by injection-driven HIV epidemics (e.g., WHO, UNODC and UNAIDS, 2009; UNODC and Canadian HIV/AIDS Legal Network, 2011). In January 2008, the then Executive Director of UNODC, Antonio Maria Costa, issued a report that went further than any such previous reports in expressing, albeit with some qualifications, support for harm reduction:

> 'Harm reduction' is often made an unnecessarily controversial issue as if there was a contradiction between prevention and treatment on one hand and reducing the adverse health and social consequences of drug use on the other. This is a false dichotomy. They are complementary.
>
> (UNODC, 2008)

The report went on to recommend specific interventions such as easy access to OST and needle/syringe exchange programmes. Shortly thereafter, in his report to the 2008 CND session, Costa acknowledged numerous unintended consequences of international drug control efforts under the current system (see chapter 8 for details).

Whether, and to what extent, the incorporation of harm reduction and human rights concerns in UNODC's work will continue remains to be seen. Much concern greeted the appointment in mid-2010 of Yury Fedotov, a Russian diplomat, as the new Executive Director, given Russia's long history of staunch prohibition – including to the point of banning methadone in the face of

---

[4] In one troubling episode, in 2005, UNODC acceded to US demands that it avoid any reference to harm reduction and needle/syringe exchange in agency publications. It subsequently backtracked in the face of widespread condemnation (Open Letter, 2005; TNI, 2005a; TNI, 2005b).

extensive evidence and widespread international criticism. In the early months of his tenure, Fedotov affirmed to UN Member states 'the centrality of public health and human rights to our work' (Fedotov, 2010a). He has further stated that '[a] well-coordinated network of services for drug-dependence treatment, HIV prevention measures, AIDS treatment interventions and social protection will succeed in stopping HIV' (Fedotov, 2010b) and that 'instead of punishment, what they [the drug users] need is treatment, care and social integration. Like all people, they deserve to be treated humanely' (Fedotov, 2010c). However, on the occasion of his first report to the CND, while he declared the need to 'seriously rethink our strategy on drug control', as the International Drug Policy Consortium pointed out, 'the scope of the proposed rethink is somewhat limited' and his proposed programme amounted to 'another ritual incantation of support for the creaking drug control conventions' (IDPC, 2011a).

While UNODC may continue, at the programmatic level, to support more harm reduction-friendly interpretation and implementation of the drug control conventions, the reality is that any more fundamental shift in global drug control policy ultimately requires political will on the part of a critical number of states. In the meantime, the flexibility that is afforded to states under the existing treaties can and should be exploited to the fullest by countries seeking to replace strict prohibition and punishment with more pragmatic, evidence-based, health-friendly and human rights-respecting responses.

Flexibility in the international drug control regime

While prohibitionist states in the CND and bodies such as the INCB have focused on the provisions in the drug control treaties requiring the criminal prohibition and punishment of drug-related activities, there remains 'room for manoeuvre' (Dorn and Jamieson, 2000; Krajewski, 1999). Responding to a request from the INCB, the UNODC's legal advisory branch has explicitly advised that the UN drug control conventions can be interpreted to permit such harm reduction measures as OST, needle and syringe programmes and supervised drug consumption sites (UNDCP, 2002). Noting the emergence of new threats such as HIV transmission through injection drug use, the memorandum observed that: 'It could even be argued that the drug control treaties, as they stand, have been rendered out of synch with reality, since at the time they came into force they could not have possibly foreseen these new threats.'

In assessing the flexibility found in the current drug control treaties, a number of observations are in order.[5] First, both the 1961 Single Convention and the 1971 Convention allow for the production, distribution or possession of controlled substances for 'medical and scientific purposes'. States determine how they will interpret and implement these provisions in their domestic law.

Second, the drug control conventions also note the importance of measures aimed at protecting and promoting the health of those who use drugs. The 1961 Single Convention requires the government to 'to give special attention to and take all practicable measures to provide treatment, education, aftercare, rehabilitation and social reintegration of drug users' (Article 38). In addition, even though there is a requirement to criminalise possession other than as may be allowed for medical and scientific purposes, the convention states that measures for treatment, care and support of people who use drugs may be provided 'either as an alternative to conviction or punishment or in addition to conviction or punishment' (Article 36(2)). The 1971 Convention contains the same

---

[5] The observations that follow are adapted with permission from text prepared for Canadian HIV/AIDS Legal Network (2006).

obligation to 'take all practicable measures' for the care, treatment and social reintegration of people who use drugs (Article 20), and the same provision allowing for measures of treatment, care, rehabilitation and social reintegration 'as an alternative to conviction or punishment' (Article 22).

Harm reduction measures – such as prescription of opioids or opioid substitutes, programmes ensuring access to sterile drug use equipment, and drug consumption facilities that provide less harmful methods of using drugs and access to other health services including drug dependence treatment – also fall under the rubric of providing treatment, education, care and rehabilitation to people who use drugs and of facilitating their social reintegration. As such, they are permissible under the 1961 and 1971 UN conventions on drug control. This is consistent with States Parties' own subsequent agreements – to which regard must be had in interpreting the treaties, according to basic international law principles of treaty interpretation. At the 1998 UN General Assembly Special Session on Drugs, the General Assembly adopted a Declaration on the Guiding Principles of Drug Demand Reduction, in which it declared that demand reduction policies should aim not only at 'preventing the use of drugs' but also at 'reducing the adverse consequences of drug abuse' (i.e., harm reduction) (UNGA, 1998b). Certainly, it is the common understanding of UN administrative organs that the response to harms related to drug use must be multi-faceted and include these health-based approaches: the UN system as a whole has adopted a position paper (UN, 2002) in which it recognised that 'drug abuse problems cannot be solved simply by criminal justice initiatives. A punitive approach may drive people most in need of prevention and care services underground'.

Third, the 1988 Convention Against Illicit Traffic, the primary focus of which is criminalising trafficking (not the individual drug user), has often been incorrectly interpreted as requiring the full criminalisation of any possession of a prohibited drug. Article 3(2) says that each state party to the Convention must make it a criminal offence under its domestic law to intentionally 'possess, purchase or cultivate narcotic drugs or psychotropic substances for personal consumption contrary to the provisions of the 1961 Convention, the 1961 Convention as amended or the 1971 Convention'. Note that the obligation to impose criminal liability goes no further than the equivalent obligations in the 1961 and 1971 Conventions. The 1988 Convention only requires signatory states to criminalise possession for personal consumption that is 'contrary to the provisions' of the 1961 and 1971 Conventions. The correct interpretation of this qualifier remains somewhat uncertain, with states having adopted different interpretations. The Official Commentary on the 1988 Convention (UN, 1988) leaves this question of interpretation unresolved. The preferable interpretation is that the flexibility found in the two earlier conventions is preserved. As noted above, those Conventions include a number of provisions that make it legally permissible to remove, at least to some degree, the criminalisation of people who use or possess drugs – if, for example, decriminalisation is in pursuit of 'medical or scientific purposes' or forms part of practicable measures to provide care, treatment or support to people who use drugs. It is therefore arguably incorrect to interpret the 1988 Convention as requiring the complete criminalisation, without exception, of possession of a controlled substance for the purposes of personal consumption.

What is certainly clear is that the 1988 Convention does not require either conviction or punishment for the possession, purchase or cultivation of a controlled substance for personal consumption. Article 3(4)(d) says that, in the case of the offence of possession, purchase or cultivation for personal consumption, a state may provide for 'measures for the treatment, education, aftercare, rehabilitation, or social reintegration' of the offender, 'either as an alternative to conviction or punishment, or in addition to conviction or punishment'. (Such leniency is also available in 'appropriate cases of a minor nature' where a person is charged with manufacturing, offering, distributing, selling or transporting a controlled substance for something other than personal consumption: Article 3(4)(c).) Just as with the 1961 and 1971 Conventions, in addressing personal consumption States can adopt laws and policies that focus more on treating drug use and dependence as health issues, rather than imposing harsh criminal penalties.

Finally, remember that the 1961 and 1971 Conventions, although they require states to impose restrictions on the manufacture, export, import, distribution, use and possession of the controlled substances, also say that a state's obligations under the conventions are 'subject to its constitutional limitations' (1961 Convention, Article 36; 1971 Convention, Article 22). In the case of the 1988 Convention, the treaty explicitly provides that the state's obligation to criminalise personal possession, purchase or cultivation contrary to the 1961 and 1971 Conventions is 'subject to its constitutional principles' (Article 3(2)). Such constitutional principles usually include respect for and protection of human rights; some countries' constitutions explicitly incorporate international legal obligations (such as human rights) into domestic law. Therefore, uniform measures and responses are not required; states have discretion to determine the policies they wish to adopt, in line with the constitutional principles reflected in their own domestic legislation, including respecting and protecting the human rights of people who use drugs.

International human rights law: the further case for harm reduction and for flexibility in international drug control law

While setting out the substantive provisions of the international regime of drug control, the treaties outlined above form but one part of international law. The other key domain for purposes of sharing drug policy, domestic and international, is the international law of human rights. It is lamentable that the only explicit reference to human rights in any of the three drug control treaties is the recognition in the 1988 Convention (Article 14(2)) that measures taken to eradicate illicit crops must 'respect fundamental human rights'. Yet there can be little doubt that the drug control conventions, and states' implementation thereof, must be in accord with human rights norms. This flows from the higher-order position of such norms in international law; it has also been recognised explicitly and repeatedly by states themselves – even if their actual conduct falls far short of this stated obligation.

The UN Charter, the foundational legal document of the international legal system, specifically states (in Article 55) that the UN 'shall promote . . . solutions of international economic, social, health, and related problems; and universal respect for, and observance of, human rights and fundamental freedoms for all without distinction as to race, sex, language or religion'. Furthermore, by virtue of Article 56, all UN member states are legally bound 'to take joint and separate action in cooperation with' the UN to achieve these purposes. The content of those human rights obligations, and states' duties to respect, protect and fulfil them, is set out further in a range of instruments negotiated and adopted by states. The *Universal Declaration of Human Rights* (UDHR) 'gives expression to' the Charter's human rights requirements (UN Secretary General, 2005) by setting out basic civil, political, economic, social and cultural rights to be enjoyed by all; its norms have achieved the status of customary (i.e., non-treaty) international law that bind all states. A wide range of human rights treaties, including the nine core human rights treaties of the UN (e.g., ICCPR, 1966; ICESCR, 1966), fleshes those norms out further. Under its Article 103, States' obligations under the UN Charter, including with respect to human rights, enjoy primacy over any other treaty obligations: 'In the event of a conflict between the obligations of the Members of the United Nations under the present Charter and their obligations under any other international agreement, their obligations under the present Charter shall prevail'. Consequently, as a matter of international law, compliance with the drug control conventions can never excuse the violation of human rights.[6]

---

[6] The Commentary on the 1988 Convention also explicitly notes that a state is free to adopt stricter drug control measures than required under the convention, 'subject always to the requirement that such initiatives are consistent with applicable norms of public international law, in particular norms protecting human rights' (UN, 1988).

Indeed, UN Member States have repeatedly affirmed the primacy of states' human rights obligations in international law: 'Human rights and fundamental freedoms are the birthright of all human beings; their protection and promotions is the first responsibility of Governments' (Vienna Declaration, 1993; see also Proclamation of Teheran, 1968). Specifically in the context of drug control, CND member states have explicitly reaffirmed their 'unwavering commitment to ensuring that all aspects of demand reduction, supply reduction and international cooperation are addressed in full conformity with the purposes and principles of the Charter of the United Nations, international law and the Universal Declaration of Human Rights, and, in particular, with full respect for . . . all human rights and fundamental freedoms' (UNCND, 2008; UNCND, 2009; UNCND, 2010a; UNCND, 2010b).[7] The UN General Assembly has also repeatedly reaffirmed the same proposition in the same language – including in the *Political Declaration* adopted by the 1998 UN General Assembly Special Session on Drugs (UNGA, 1998a),[8] as well as a decade later following the global review of the implementation of that declaration (UNGA, 2011a).[9]

Such repeated solemn affirmations are largely rhetorical – and have not prevented states from simultaneously balking at specific commitments on harm reduction. The 1998 General Assembly declaration on drugs is, of course, a prime example of this doublethink, which persists to this day. Consider, for example, the UN General Assembly's own high-level meeting on HIV/AIDS in June 2011. Even as member states reaffirmed in their *Political Declaration* that human rights are essential to effective HIV responses and proposed to reduce injection-related HIV transmission (UNGA, 2011b), they backtracked on previous commitments to ensure expanded access to harm reduction, now saying merely that states should 'give consideration' to expanding harm reduction programmes recommended by the UN's specialised technical agencies, 'in accordance with national legislation,' while also reiterating the war-on-drugs mantra 'that much more needs to be done to effectively combat the world drug problem' (Barrett, 2011).

Why is human rights law important to harm reduction?

There are several reasons to consider human rights in any discussion of international (or domestic) drug control law. First, harm reduction is fundamentally a human rights project, in that it seeks to realise the human right to enjoy the highest attainable standard of physical and mental health (discussed further below).

Second, a fundamental principle running throughout human rights law is that of non-discrimination and its corollary, a concern for ensuring the realisation of human rights for the most vulnerable and marginalised. People who use drugs are often among those most dehumanised and subjected to

[7] States have also specifically recognised the need to 'ensure that drug demand reduction measures respect human rights and the inherent dignity of all individuals and facilitate access for all drug users to prevention services and health-care and social services, with a view to social reintegration' (UNCND, 2009). The CND has reiterated this more recently, with states again recognising 'the need to base programmes for the treatment and rehabilitation of drug use disorders on scientific evidence while respecting human rights and human dignity' (UNCND, 2011).

[8] For more on the original UN special session that articulated the goal of a 'drug-free world' through the implementation of the drug control treaties, see Jelsma (2003).

[9] See also: UNGA (2006); UNGA (2007); UNGA (2008); UNGA (2009). Note that the General Assembly resolutions in 2010 and 2011 also both include explicit reference to the *Vienna Declaration and Programme of Action* on human rights cited above.

widespread, daily, systematic violation of human rights, by both state and non-state actors – from the casual discrimination experienced when seeking services to harsh sentences of imprisonment, from egregious forms of physical and mental abuse (sometimes in the name of 'treatment' for drug dependence) to extrajudicial execution. Criminalisation is state-sanctioned stigmatisation of people who use drugs, which contributes to such abuses. A human rights response therefore demands that we interrogate whether and in what circumstances the application of criminal sanction is justifiable, and hence that we question the contours of prohibition.

> Third, securing human rights is necessary for the success of harm reduction, because it encourages and enables access to health services.
>
> (Wodak, 1998)

And in a more general sense, the political viability of harm reduction practice itself may be human rights-dependent in some contexts:

> Protection of human rights makes harm reduction – and thus life itself – possible . . . [Some harm reduction methods] will not be started or survive unless they are protected by a public culture of rights and liberties.
>
> (Fridli, 2003)

Finally, human rights principles point toward harm reduction, rather than criminal prohibition, in our policy responses to drug use. As discussed further below, States' human rights obligations under international law carry at least two implications of relevance to any discussion of harm reduction. First, states have a legal duty to implement harm reduction measures that are known to protect and promote health, or that can reasonably be expected to have such benefits. Second, to the extent that international or domestic law on drug control impedes harm reduction measures, or otherwise causes or contributes to the harms suffered by people who use drugs, states have an obligation to reform said law to remove such obstacles

Harm reduction and the human right to health

Numerous human rights are compromised by the enactment and enforcement of drug control laws. For purposes of this discussion, however, consider the application of one specific human right's relevance to harm reduction.[10] States that are parties to the *International Covenant on Economic, Social and Cultural Rights* (ICESCR) have recognised (in Article 12) the right of every person to enjoy 'the highest attainable standard of physical and mental health'. The states also have a binding legal obligation under this same Article to take steps to realise fully this right, including those steps 'necessary for . . . prevention, treatment and control of epidemic, endemic . . . and other diseases' and 'the creation of conditions which would assure to all medical services and medical attention in the event of sickness'. The UN Committee on Economic, Social and Cultural Rights, the expert body charged with assessing states' compliance with their obligations under the ICESCR, has explained that 'the right to health must be understood as a right to the enjoyment of a variety of facilities, goods, services and conditions necessary for the realization of the highest attainable

---

[10] The synopsis that follows in this section is adapted with permission from Canadian HIV/AIDS Legal Network (2006).

standard of health' (UNCESCR, 2000). The Committee has also specified that states have the legal duty to *respect*, to *protect* and to *fulfil* the right:

> [t]he obligation to respect requires States to refrain from interfering directly or indirectly with the enjoyment of the right to health. The obligation to protect requires States to take measures that prevent third parties from interfering with article 12 [i.e. the right to health] guarantees. Finally, the obligation to fulfil requires States to adopt appropriate legislative, administrative, budgetary, judicial, promotional and other measures towards the full realisation of the right to health.
>
> (UNCESCR, 2000)

The spreading HIV epidemic, and the other harms encountered by people who use drugs in unsafe ways or conditions, highlight that governments have good public health reasons to ensure that their domestic legislation and policies on drug control do not contribute to these harms and do not impede health promotion efforts among people who use drugs. However, governments also have legal obligations to act. The implementation of various harm reduction measures, and making legislative and policy reforms if necessary for this purpose, is not only permissible under the international drug control treaties but is also consistent with – and required by – states' obligations under the international law of human rights. The UN's position paper on preventing HIV transmission among people who inject drugs explicitly notes that the *Universal Declaration of Human Rights* and human rights principles are part of the foundation for HIV prevention efforts in this field (UN, 2002). The Office of the UN High Commissioner on Human Rights and UNAIDS have also produced guidelines for states on how to respond to HIV/AIDS through legislation, policies and practice that protect human rights and achieve public health goals. These include the basic recommendation that 'criminal law should not be an impediment to measures taken by States to reduce the risk of HIV transmission among injecting drug users and to provide HIV-related care and treatment for injecting drug users' (OHCHR and UNAIDS, 2006).

Conclusion

Almost all countries have ratified the three UN drug control treaties, meaning their impact on global and domestic responses to drugs is therefore a concern for all those witnessing the human and economic devastation wreaked by the 'war on drugs'. Harm reduction measures are an important component of the larger struggle to realise fully the human right to health of all people who use illicit drugs. Pursuing more health-friendly interpretation and implementation of the existing drug control treaties, and pursuing complementary strategies for reforming them, are an important aspect of scaling up harm reduction approaches to drugs across the globe. As outlined above, States Parties to the drug control treaties do have some significant leeway in how they interpret and implement their treaty obligations; mustering domestic political will has led to the implementation of harm reduction initiatives. However, there is no doubt that there has been a 'chilling' effect of the international drug control regime and of the actions of influential countries that have been heavily committed to a prohibitionist agenda (Jelsma, 2003; Levine, 2003; Wolfe and Malinowska-Sempruch, 2004). As Room puts it: 'The impact of the system comes instead from the implementation of the treaties, and with the international politics that surrounds that, which can be characterised as an international environment where states have been reluctant to break openly with a governing orthodoxy describing drug control in terms of a war on drugs' (Room, 2003). Meanwhile some other states have been willing and eager to invoke the drug control treaties and claim that their hands are bound as a means of resisting domestic pressures for reform and for harm reduction services. But aside from these questions of global politics, there are also limits in international law on the 'policy space' available to countries, another prompt to question the overall regime.

Consequently, 'cracks in the consensus' are emerging (Jelsma and Metaal, 2004). A number of countries are shifting away from, or at least tempering, criminalisation as their dominant approach to illicit drugs and a growing chorus is calling for a fundamental reconsideration of prohibition as the globe's predominant response to HIV – be it decriminalising possession of drugs for personal consumption as in Portugal (Hughes and Stevens, 2007; 2010), tolerating use of drugs such as cannabis under certain circumstances as in the Netherlands (Jelsma, 2010), or implementing harm reduction services such as prescription heroin programmes as in Switzerland (Csete, 2010) or supervised consumption sites in numerous countries (e.g., Canada and Australia joining various European countries despite criticism from entities such as the INCB or pressure from certain heavily prohibitionist countries: Malkin et al., 2003).

Most recently, a number of developments have accelerated the push for reform. In 2009, the Latin American Commission on Drugs and Democracy, including numerous former heads of state, released its report calling for a 'paradigm shift' in global drug policy away from prohibition toward a more public health approach (Latin American Commission on Drugs and Democracy, 2009a; Latin American Commission on Drugs and Democracy, 2009b). Two years later, the Global Commission on Drug Policy echoed the call, declaring that 'the global war on drugs has failed' and 'fundamental reforms in national and global drug control policies are urgently needed' (Global Commission on Drug Policy, 2011). The UN Special Rapporteur on the right to health has called for 'a human rights-based approach to drug control', stating that the current 'excessively punitive regime has not achieved its stated public health goals, and has resulted in countless human rights violations' (Grover, 2010). He has recommended that countries 'decriminalize or depenalize possession and use of drugs' and 'repeal or substantially reform laws and policies inhibiting the delivery of essential health services to drug users, and review law enforcement initiatives around drug control to ensure compliance with human rights obligations'. A Global Commission on HIV and the Law, supported by the UN Development Programme, was also actively studying, through a series of extensive regional dialogues around the globe, the impact of punitive drug laws on HIV prevention and treatment among people who use drugs, among other issues. The evidence and analyses gathered to date confirm the need for a policy shift in order to support effective HIV responses, particularly given the extensive role of unsafe drug injecting in fuelling the global epidemic.

Meanwhile, the treaty regime itself has also recently seen an important denunciation by a State Party. After years of objections to the legal treatment under the conventions of the longstanding indigenous uses of coca and years of unsuccessful efforts to have this issue resolved within the CND, Bolivia formally withdrew from the 1961 Single Convention, indicating its intention to re-accede to the Convention with a reservation regarding coca leaf chewing (IDPC, 2011b). True to form, the move provoked condemnation from the INCB, which warned Bolivia 'to consider very seriously all the implications of its actions in this regard' (INCB, 2011c). According to the INCB, 'The international community should not accept any approach whereby Governments use the mechanism of denunciation and re-accession with reservation, in order to free themselves from the obligation to implement certain treaty provisions. Such approach would undermine the integrity of the global drug control system' (INCB, 2011c). The INCB's claim is bizarre in that this is precisely the purpose of the mechanisms of denunciation and of acceding to treaties with reservations, as expressly contemplated in the 1961 Convention itself (Articles 46, 49 and 50).

There can remain little doubt that the interpretation and application of the drug control treaties is increasingly contested. Harm reduction has been one particular flashpoint, but the challenges to prohibition itself are mounting: a growing body of analysis exists that explores alternatives to prohibition that would seek to regulate drugs in ways that minimise their harmful use and protect public health while avoiding the myriad harms caused by criminalisation (TDPF, 2004; 2007; 2009). Even as resolution after resolution in the CND and in the General Assembly reaffirms states' commitment to the three drug control conventions and to the basic edifice of drug prohibition, the facade is slipping. As Jelsma (2010) has speculated, we may soon reach a tipping point:

> Over the last decade rapidly widening cracks have begun to split global drug control consensus. The zero-tolerance ideology is increasingly challenged by calls for decriminalisation, harm reduction and embedding human rights principles in drug control . . . What the world needs is a group of countries willing to declare that the current treaty framework is no longer fit for purpose. A small group of countries initiated the development of an international drug control system a century ago. In 2012 another small group of countries could initiate its needed reform and design the outlines of a new legal framework for the next century, based on the many lessons learned over the past hundred years.

References

Barrett, D. (2008) *Unique in International Relations?: A Comparison of the International Narcotics Control Board and the UN Human Rights Treaty Bodies*, London: International Harm Reduction Association.

Barrett, D. (2011) HIV/AIDS at the UN: Battleground of the war on drugs, openDemocracy, www.opendemocracy.net/damon-barrett/hivaids-at-un-battleground-of-war-on-drugs, accessed 18 February 2012.

Barrett, D., Lines, R., Schleifer, R., Elliott, R. and Bewley-Taylor, D. (2008) *Recalibrating the Regime: The Need for a Human Rights-Based Approach to International Drug Policy*, London: Beckley Foundation Drug Policy Programme.

Bewley-Taylor, D.R. (2005) Emerging policy contradictions between the UNODC 'universe' and the core values and mission of the UN, *International Journal of Drug Policy*, 16 (6), 423–32.

Bewley-Taylor, D. (2009) The 2009 Commission on Narcotic Drugs and its high level segment: more cracks in the Vienna consensus, *Drugs and Alcohol Today*, 9 (2), 7–12.

Bewley-Taylor, D.R. and Fazey, C. (2003) The mechanics and dynamics of the UN system for international drug control, www.aidslex.org/site_documents/J027E.pdf, accessed 18 February 2012.

Bewley-Taylor, M. and Trace, M. (2006) *The International Narcotics Control Board: Watchdog or Guardian of the UN Drug Control Conventions?*, London: Beckley Foundation for Drug Policy.

Canadian HIV/AIDS Legal Network (2006) *Legislating for Health and Human Rights: Model Law on Drug Use and HIV/AIDS -- Module 1: Criminal Law Issues*, Toronto: Canadian HIV/AIDS Legal Network.

Clement, T.(Minister of Health of Canada) (2008) Letter to P. Emafo (INCB President), 6 March, on file.

Costa, A. (2008) *Making Drug Control 'Fit for Purpose': Building on the UNGASS Decade*. Report of the UNODC Executive Director, Commission on Narcotic Drugs, 51st Session, E/CN. 7/2008/CRP. 17, Vienna: UNODC.

Costa, A. (2010) *Drug Control, Crime Prevention and Criminal Justice: A Human Rights Perspective*. Note by the UNODC Executive Director, Commission on Narcotic Drugs, 53rd Session, Vienna, 8-12 March, E/CN.7/2010/CRP.6, Vienna: UNODC.

Count the Costs (2011) *Count the Costs: 50 Years of the War on Drugs*, www.countthecosts.org.

Crocket, A. (2010) The function and relevance of the Commission in Narcotic Drugs in the pursuit of humane drug policy (or the ramblings of a bewildered diplomat), *International Journal on Human Rights and Drug Policy*, 1, www.humanrightsanddrugs.org/2011/04/function-and-relevance-of-the-cnd, accessed 18 February 2012.

Csete, J. (2010) *From the Mountaintops: The Evolution of Drug Policy Change in Switzerland and its Lessons for the World*, New York: Open Society Foundations.

Csete, J. and Wolfe, D. (2007a) *Closed to Reason: The International Narcotics Control Board and HIV/AIDS*, Toronto: Canadian HIV/AIDS Legal Network & Open Society Institute.

Csete, J. and Wolfe, D. (2007b) The International Narcotics Control Board and HIV/AIDS, *GMHC Treatment Issues*, 3 (3), 3–5 at 4.

Csete, J. and Wolfe, D. (2008) Progress or backsliding on HIV and illicit drugs in 2008?, *Lancet*, 371, 1820–1.

Dorn, N. and Jamieson, A. (2000) *Room for Manoeuvre: Overview of Comparative Legal Research into National Drug Laws of France, Germany, Italy, Spain, the Netherlands and Sweden and Their Relation to Three International Drugs Conventions*, London: DrugScope.

Emafo, P. (2007) Remarks at press conference, New York, 7 March, www.un.org/webcast/pc2007.htm (summary note at www.globalsecurity.org/security/library/news/2007/03/sec-070307-unconf01.htm), accessed 18 February 2012.

Emafo, P.(INCB President) (2008) Letter to T. Clement (Minister of Health of Canada), 9 April, on file.

Fedotov, Y. (2010a) Vienna: a mainstay of the United Nations development and security agenda. Address by the UNODC Executive Director to the Plenary Meeting of Member States, Vienna, 29 September, Vienna: UNODC.

Fedotov, Y. (2010b) Access to HIV and drug dependence treatment services is a right. Remarks by the UNODC Executive Director on World AIDS Day, Vienna, 1 December, Vienna: UNODC.

Fedotov, Y. (2010c) Remarks by the UNODC Executive at the reconvened 53rd Session of the Commission on Narcotic Drugs, Vienna, 2 December, Vienna: UNODC.

Fridli, J. (2003) Harm reduction is human rights, *Harm Reduction News*, 4 (1), 3.

Global Commission on Drug Policy (2011) *War on Drugs: Report of the Global Commission on Drug Policy*, www.globalcommissionondrugs.org, accessed 18 February 2012.

Grover, A. (2010) *Report to the UN General Assembly of the UN Special Rapporteur on the Right of Everyone to the Highest Attainable Standard of Physical and Mental Health*, UN Doc. A/65/255, 6 August 6.

Harm Reduction International (2011) *Annual Report of the International Narcotics Control Board: Corruption, human rights and OST*, Blogpost, 3 March 3, www.ihra.net/contents/896, accessed 18 February 2012.

Hughes, C. and Stevens, A. (2007) *The Effects of Decriminalization of Drug Use in Portugal*, Briefing Paper 14, London: Beckley Foundation Drug Policy Programme.

Hughes, C. and Stevens, A. (2010) What can we learn from the Portuguese decriminalization of illicit drugs?, *British Journal of Criminology*, 50 (6), 999–1022.

International Drug Policy Consortium (2008) *The International Narcotics Control Board: Current Tensions and Options for Reform*, IDPC Briefing Paper 7, London: IDPC.

International Drug Policy Consortium (2009) *Why Is the Outcome of the United Nations Drug Policy Review So Weak and Inconclusive?*, IDPC Briefing Paper, London: IDPC.

International Drug Policy Consortium (2011a) *The 2011 Commission on Narcotic Drugs: Report of Proceedings*, London: IDPC.

International Drug Policy Consortium (2011b) *IDPC Advocacy Note: Bolivia's Reconciliation with the UN Single Convention on Narcotic Drugs*, London: IDPC.

International Narcotics Control Board (2001) *Report of the International Narcotics Control Board for 2000*, E/INCB/2000/1, Vienna: INCB.

International Narcotics Control Board (2002) *Report of the International Narcotics Control Board for 2001*, E/INCB/2001/1, Vienna: INCB.

International Narcotics Control Board (2004) *Report of the International Narcotics Control Board for 2003*, E/INCB/2002/1, Vienna: INCB.

International Narcotics Control Board (2005) *Report of the International Narcotics Control Board for 2004*, E/INCB/2004/1, Vienna: INCB.

International Narcotics Control Board (2007) *Report of the International Narcotics Control Board for 2006*, E/INCB/2006/1, Vienna: INCB.

International Narcotics Control Board (2008) *Report of the International Narcotics Control Board for 2007*, E/INCB/2007/1, Vienna: INCB.

International Narcotics Control Board (2009) *Report of the International Narcotics Control Board for 2008*, E/INCB/2008/1, Vienna: INCB.

International Narcotics Control Board (2010) *Report of the International Narcotics Control Board for 2009*, E/INCB/2009/1, Vienna: INCB.

International Narcotics Control Board (2011a) *Report of the International Narcotics Control Board for 2010*, E/INCB/2010/1, Vienna: INCB.

International Narcotics Control Board, (2011b) *Report of the International Narcotics Control Board on the Availability of Internationally Controlled Drugs: Ensuring Adequate Access for Medical and Scientific Purposes,* UN Doc. E/INCB/2010/1/Supp.1, New York: United Nations.

International Narcotics Control Board (2011c) International Narcotics Control Board regrets Bolivia's denunciation of the Single Convention on Narcotic Drugs, press release, July 5, 2011, UNIS/NAR/1114.

Jelsma, M. (2003) Drugs in the UN system: the unwritten history of the 1988 United Nations General Assembly special session on drugs, *International Journal of Drug Policy*, 14, 188–95.

Jelsma, M. (2010) *The Development of International Drug Control: Lessons Learned and Strategic Challenges for the Future*, Amsterdam, Transnational Institute.

Jelsma, M. (2011) Treaty guardians in distress: the inquisitorial nature of the INCB response to Bolivia, TNI Blogpost, 11 July, www.undrugcontrol.info/en/weblog/item/2626-treaty-guardians-in-distress, accessed 18 February 2012.

Jelsma, M. and Metaal, P. (2004) *Cracks in the Vienna Consensus: The UN Drug Control Debate*. Drug War Monitor, A WOLA Briefing Series, Washington, DC.

Kouame, K. (2007) Remarks at press conference, New York, 7 March, www.un.org/webcast/pc2007.htm (summary note at www.globalsecurity.org/security/library/news/2007/03/sec-070307-unconf01.htm), accessed 18 February 2012.

Krajewski, K. (1999) How flexible are the United Nations drug conventions?, *International Journal of Drug Policy*, 10, 329–38.

Latin American Commission on Drugs and Democracy (2009a) Drugs and democracy: toward a paradigm shift – statement by the Latin American Commission on Drugs and Democracy, www.drogasedemocracia.org/Arquivos/declaracao_ingles_site.pdf, accessed 18 February 2012.

Latin American Commission on Drugs and Democracy (2009b) Drogas y Democracia: Hacia un Cambio de Paradigma, www.drogasedemocracia.org/Arquivos/livro_espanhol_04.pdf, accessed 18 February 2012.

Levine, H.G. (2003) Global drug prohibition: its uses and crises, *International Journal of Drug Policy*, 14, 145–53.

Malkin, I., Elliott, R. and McRae, R. (2003) Supervised injection facilities and international law, *Journal of Drug Issues*, 33, 539–78.

Mathers, B., Degenhardt, L., Phillips, B., Wiessing, L., Hickman, M., Strathdee, S.A., Wodak, A., Panda, S., Tyndall, M., Toufik, A., and Mattick, R.P.for the 2007 Reference Group to the UN on HIV and Injecting Drug Use (2008) Global epidemiology of injecting drug use and HIV among people who inject drugs: a systematic review, *Lancet*, 372, 1733–45.

Mathers, B., Degenhardt, L., Ali, H., Wiessing, L., Hickman, M., Mattick, R.P., Myers, B., Ambekar, A., and Strathdee, S.A.for the 2009 Reference Group to the UN on HIV and Injecting Drug Use (2010) HIV prevention, treatment, and care services for people who inject drugs: a systematic review of global, regional, and national coverage, *Lancet*, 375, 1014–28.

Nowak, M. and Grover, A. (2008) Letter to H.E. S. Ashipala-Musavyi, Chairperson, 52nd Session of the Commission on Narcotic Drugs, 10 December, www.hrw.org/de/news/2008/12/10/un-human-rights-experts-call-upon-cnd-support-harm-reduction, accessed 18 February 2012.

Office of the UN High Commissioner for Human Rights and Joint United Nations Programme on HIV/AIDS (2006) *International Guidelines on HIV/AIDS and Human Rights (2006 Consolidated Version)*, Geneva: OHCHR & UNAIDS.

Open Letter to the delegates of the Forty-eighth session of the Commission on Narcotic Drugs (2005) 1 March 1, www.hrw.org/en/news/2005/03/01/open-letter-delegates-48th-session-commission-narcotic-drugs-cnd, accessed 18 February 2012.

OSI (2009) *At What Cost? HIV and Human Rights Consequences of the Global 'War on Drugs'*, New York: OSI Public Health Program, March.

Room, R. (2003) Impact and implications of the international drug control treaties on IDU and HIV/AIDS prevention and policy. Paper prepared for 2nd International Policy Dialogue on HIV/AIDS, Warsaw, Poland, 12-14 November 12-14.

Sinha, J. (2001) *The History and Development of the Leading International Drug Control Conventions.* Research report prepared for the Senate Special Committee on Illegal Drugs, Ottawa: Library of the Parliament of Canada.

Small, D. and Drucker, E. (2008) Return to Galileo? The inquisition of the International Narcotic Control Board, *Harm Reduction Journal*, 5, 16, doi:10.1186/1477-7517-5-16.

Transform Drug Policy Foundation (2004) *After the War on Drugs: Options for Control*, London: TDPF.

Transform Drug Policy Foundation (2007) *After the War on Drugs: Tools for the Debate*, London: TDPF.

Transform Drug Policy Foundation (2009) *After the War on Drugs: Blueprint for Regulation*, London: TDPF.

Transnational Institute (2005a) *The United Nations and Harm Reduction*, Drug Policy Briefing no. 12, Amsterdam: TNI.

Transnational Institute (2005b) *The United Nations and Harm Reduction: Revisited*, Drug Policy Briefing No. 13, Amsterdam: TNI.

United Nations (1988) *Commentary on the United Nations Convention against Illicit Traffic in Narcotic Drugs and Psychotropic Substances*, 1988, UN Doc. E/CN.7/590, New York: UN.

United Nations (2002) *Preventing the Transmission of HIV Among Drug Abusers: A Position Paper of the United Nations System*, approved on behalf of the Administrative Committee on Coordination by the High-Level Committee of Programmes, 1st regular session of 2001, Vienna, 26-27 February 2001, UN Doc. E/CN.7/2002/CRP.5 (12 March 2002).

UN Commission on Narcotic Drugs (2008) *CND Resolution 51/12 (2008)*, UN Doc. E/CN.7/2008/15.

UN Commission on Narcotic Drugs (2009) *Political Declaration and Plan of Action on International Cooperation towards an Integrated and Balanced Strategy to Counter the World Drug Problem*, in Commission on Narcotic Drugs, Report of the 52nd Session, ECOSOC Official Reports, 2009, Supp. No. 8, UN Doc. E/2009/28, E/CN.7/2009/12 (pp. 37ff).

UN Commission on Narcotic Drugs (2010a) CND Resolution 53/2, UN Doc. E/CN.7/2010/18 (pp. 8–10).

UN Commission on Narcotic Drugs (2010b) CND Resolution 53/8, UN Doc. E/CN.7/2010/18 (pp. 24–6).

UN Commission on Narcotic Drugs (2011) CND Resolution 54/5, in Commission on Narcotic Drugs, Report on the 54th session, ECOSOC OR 2011, Supp. No. 8, UN Doc. E/CN.7/2011/15 (p. 12).

United Nations Committee on Economic, Social and Cultural Rights (2000) *The Right to the Highest Attainable Standard of Health*, General Comment 14, UN Doc. E/C/12/2000/4.

United Nations Drug Control Programme (Legal Affairs Section) (2002) *Flexibility of Treaty Provisions as Regards Harm Reduction Approaches*, E/INCB/2002/W.13/SS.5, www.aidslex.org/site_documents/Z121E.pdf, accessed 18 February 2012.

United Nations Economic and Social Council (ECOSOC) (2004) *Guidelines for Psychosocially Assisted Pharmacological Treatment of Persons Dependent on Opioids*, Resolution 2004/40, UN Doc. E/2004/INF/2/Add.2.

United Nations General Assembly (1998a) *Political Declaration*, Resolution S-20/2, UN Doc. A/RES/S-20/2.

United Nations General Assembly (1998b) *Declaration on the Guiding Principles of Drug Demand Reduction*, Resolution S-20/4, UN Doc. A/RES/S-20/4.

United Nations General Assembly (2006) Resolution 60/178, UN Doc. A/RES/60/178.

United Nations General Assembly (2007) Resolution 61/183, UN Doc. A/RES/61/183.

United Nations General Assembly (2008) Resolution 62/176, UN Doc. A/RES/62/176.

United Nations General Assembly (2009) Resolution 63/197, UN Doc. A/RES/63/197.

United Nations General Assembly (2010) Resolution 64/182, UN Doc. A/RES/64/182.

United Nations Assembly (2011a) Resolution 65/233, UN Doc. A/RES/65/233.

United Nations General Assembly (2011b) *Political Declaration on HIV/AIDS: Intensifying our Efforts to Eliminate HIV/AIDS*, Resolution 65/277, UN Doc. A/RES/65/277.

United Nations Human Rights Committee (1982) *The Right to Life (Art. 6): General Comment 6*, UN Doc. HRI/GEN/1/Rev.1, 6.

United Nations Office on Drugs and Crime and Canadian HIV/AIDS Legal Network (2011) *Accessibility of HIV Prevention, Treatment and Care Services for People who Use Drugs and Incarcerated People in Azerbaijan, Kazakhstan, Kyrgyzstan, Tajikistan, Turkmenistan and Uzbekistan: Legislative and Policy Analysis and Recommendations for Reform*, Almaty: UNODC & Canadian HIV/AIDS Legal Network.

United Nations Office on Drugs and Crime (2008) *Reducing the Adverse Health and Social Effects of Drug Use: A Comprehensive Approach*, Vienna: UNODC.

United Nation Secretary General (2005) *Explanatory Note by the Secretary-General on the Human Rights Council*, UN Doc. A/59/2005/Add.1.

Wodak, A. (1998) Health, HIV infection, human rights, and injecting drug use, *Health & Human Rights: An International Journal*, 2 (4), 24–41, 38-9.

Wolfe, D. and Malinowska-Sempruch, K. (2004) *Illicit Drug Policies and the Global HIV Epidemic: Effects of UN and National Government Approaches*, New York: Open Society Institute.

World Health Organization (2004) *Effectiveness of Sterile Needle and Syringe Programming in Reducing HIV/AIDS among Injecting Drug Users*, WHO Evidence for Action Technical Papers, Geneva: WHO.

World Health Organization (2005) *Effectiveness of Drug Dependence Treatment in Preventing HIV among Injecting Drug Users*, WHO Evidence for Action Technical Papers, Geneva: WHO.

World Health Organization (2011) *WHO Model List of Essential Medicines, 17th list*, www.who.int/medicines/publications/essentialmedicines/en/index.html.

World Health Organization, UN Office on Drugs and Crime and UN Joint Programme on HIV/AIDS (2004a) *Position Paper: Substitution Maintenance Therapy in the Management of Opioid Dependence and HIV/AIDS Prevention*, Geneva/Vienna: WHO, UNODC, UNAIDS.

World Health Organization, UN Office on Drugs and Crime and UN Joint Programme on HIV/AIDS (2004b) *Policy Brief: Reduction of HIV Transmission through Drug-Dependence Treatment*, Evidence for Action on HIV/AIDS and Injecting Drug Use Series, UN Doc. WHO/HIV/2004.04. Geneva: WHO.

World Health Organization, UN Office on Drugs and Crime and UN Joint Programme on HIV/AIDS (2009) *Technical Guide for Countries to Set Targets for Universal Access to HIV Prevention, Treatment and Care for Injecting Drug Users*, Geneva: WHO, UNODC & UNAIDS.

Treaties and Declarations

Charter of the United Nations (1945), T.S. 993.

Convention on Psychotropic Substances, 1971, 1019 U.N.T.S. 14956.

Convention against Illegal Traffic in Narcotic Drugs and Psychotropic Substances, 1988. UN Doc. E/CONF. 82/15 (1988), reprinted in 28 I.L.M. 493 (1989).

International Covenant on Civil and Political Rights (1966), 999 U.N.T.S. 171, entered into force 23 March 1976.

International Covenant on Economic, Social and Cultural Rights (1966), 993 U.N.T.S. 3, entered into force 3 January 1976.

Proclamation of Teheran, UN Doc. A/CONF.32/41, subsequently endorsed by UNGA Res. 2442 (XXIII) (19 December 1968), GAOR 23rd Session, p. 49.

Single Convention on Narcotic Drugs, 1961 (as amended by the 1972 *Protocol amending the Single Convention on Narcotic Drugs*), 976 U.NT.S. 14152.

Universal Declaration of Human Rights, UNGA Res. 217A (III), UN Doc. A/810 (1948).

Vienna Declaration and Programme of Action, UN Doc. A/CONF/157/23 (1993), subsequently endorsed by the UN General Assembly, UNGA Res. 48/121, UN GAOR, 48th Session, 85th Mtg., UN Doc. A/RES/48/121 (1993).

Chapter 5

A BRIEF, PERSONAL HISTORY OF HARM REDUCTION ADVOCACY

Dave Burrows

Michel Sidibe, Executive Director of UNAIDS, addressed the February Board Meeting in 2010 of the Global Fund to Fight AIDS, TB and Malaria (GF). His staff wanted a theme for his speech that would be as successful as the previous year's speech on scaling up prevention of mother-to-child transmission of HIV. The chosen topic was 'Scaling up harm reduction' and I was asked to write a briefing paper for Dr Sidibe on this topic.

The briefing paper gave several reasons for scaling up harm reduction. Injecting drug users (IDUs), it said, are among those most at risk for HIV infection. Of the 11–21 million IDUs globally, only 8% have access to opioid substitution treatment (target: 40%) and only 4% of those who are HIV-positive (up to 2 million) have access to antiretroviral therapy (ART). In the absence of scaled-up harm reduction services, 850,000 new cases of HIV among IDUs can be expected between 2010 and 2015: already in 2010, IDUs are estimated to constitute 10% of new HIV infections each year. A frequent argument against harm reduction is that it has never been taken to scale anywhere in the developing/transitional world, despite the fact that GF and now PEPFAR funds can be (and are being) used for harm reduction.

Yet we have excellent evidence for harm reduction interventions:

- *Effective:* 2 decades for needle-syringe programmes (NSP), 3 decades for Medication-Assisted Treatment (MAT)[1]: consistent findings that HIV transmission is reduced.
- *Safe:* NSPs lead to no greater numbers of injectors, new injectors or problems with discarded syringes; MAT medications are controlled like all other opioid medicines.
- *Feasible:* NSPs now in 82 countries; MAT in 70 countries; both in 66 countries.
- *Cost-effective:* NSP provides $5 in benefits for every dollar invested (Australian Dept of Health and Ageing, 2009); MAT $4 (Harwood et al., 1988).

The paper also noted that political support was now almost unanimous for harm reduction. Until 2009, there was strong opposition to harm reduction methods from a few key countries (especially the USA, Japan and the Russian Federation). Political changes and ongoing increases in evidence and advocacy mean the number of those countries has now dwindled to approach zero (with Russian Federation now the only country to consistently disapprove of the term 'harm reduction' and to argue loudly against MAT).

---

[1] This is the US term for opioid substitution therapy (OST) with medications such as methadone and buprenorphine. MAT is used in preference to OST as the word 'substitution' often leads to confusion among policymakers who think that this treatment simply substitutes one drug for another.

Harm Reduction in Substance Use and High-Risk Behaviour: International Policy and Practice, First Edition.
Edited by Richard Pates and Diane Riley.
© 2012 Blackwell Publishing Ltd. Published 2012 by Blackwell Publishing Ltd.

The paper argued that UNAIDS together with its partners had worked for more than a decade to ensure that a comprehensive intervention for IDUs is designed and (now) accepted by all relevant global agencies, including the US government (in July 2010) (PEPFAR, 2010). Similarly, UNAIDS with its partners had developed targets for coverage of harm reduction interventions (WHO/UNAIDS/UNODC, 2009). It also noted that a series of costing studies had been carried out, concentrated mostly on scale-up of specific interventions rather than all elements of the comprehensive intervention. While the long-term goal must be the implementation of the comprehensive intervention such that there is universal access for all injecting drug users globally to all elements of the intervention, an appropriate short-term goal would be to assist countries to meet key targets. The cost of the Comprehensive Intervention at scale globally could be US$1.46 billion to US$8.6 billion per year. Scaling up the key interventions of NSP and MAT to reach high coverage globally could cost around US$2 billion per year.

As part of writing this paper, I was given early access to the report to be released by the International Harm Reduction Association in April 2010: '3 cents a day is not enough: Resourcing HIV-related harm reduction on a global basis' (IHRA, 2010). This paper found that harm reduction is relatively invisible in national and international budgets, but that it was possible to calculate a plausible estimate of HIV-related harm reduction expenditure in low and middle income countries between 2007 and 2009. The results:

> demonstrate the degree to which the international community is failing to address the issue of HIV among injecting drug using populations. Despite the difficulties in identifying harm reduction expenditure, and of obtaining accurate estimates, there is no doubt that the overall volume of spending on HIV-related harm reduction is small. A cautious estimate for 2007 is that approximately US$160 million was invested in HIV-related harm reduction in low and middle income countries, of which US$136 million (90%) came from international donors. *This spending equates to US$12.80 for each injector each year in low and middle income countries, or just three US cents per injector per day.* This figure is almost certainly an overestimate of actual spending on harm reduction services, which would have received only one-third to one-half of this total harm reduction investment.
>
> (Original emphasis)

The Executive Summary of the document finishes: 'More money is needed for harm reduction, and it is needed now.'

Two decades of advocacy

Harm reduction advocacy has come a long way since we were arguing for this 'new' and 'radical' approach to drugs and HIV in the 1980s. My first article on this topic was in January 1987 (Burrows, 1987). At that time, the New South Wales (NSW) government had decided to provide clean needles in exchange for used needles in a three-part programme – through government and non-government services and through pharmacies – in an attempt to stem the HIV epidemic which had already reached (in one study, Kaldor, 1987) 9% of injecting drug users in Sydney.

By acting early on providing widespread access to injecting equipment through needle-syringe programmes (NSP), through peer education by injecting drug users (including an IDU group funded by the NSW government, starting in 1989), and through expansion of the methadone maintenance programme, Sydney and, ultimately, Australia reduced its HIV epidemic among IDUs so that HIV prevalence never again rose to more than 1% among IDUs to this day (National Centre in HIV Epidemiology and Clinical Research, 2010).

After writing about HIV and drug use and developing videos, audio and print materials on HIV and drug use, I moved to the IDU group, NSW Users and AIDS Association, ending up as coordinator (1993–5); then became National IDU Policy Officer (1995–6) at the Australian Federation of AIDS Organisations, the peak body of all Australian non-government organisations working on HIV. In these roles, the advocacy work was about survival more than anything else. Fledgling NSPs were harassed by the media, neighbours, politicians, ex drug users, even some doctors and other health workers.

Even close friends found harm reduction hard to understand. 'Isn't giving a needle to a heroin addict the same as giving a criminal a gun?' This sentiment and the uglier version – 'They're just junkie scum, does it matter if they die?' – underlay many of the outraged media reports, angry neighbourhood meetings, speeches in parliament by shocked politicians, and so on. It took me some years to realise that harm reduction is counter-intuitive: an example of that most difficult issue where 'common sense' is invalidated by research. Surely, giving needles to drug users would create a whole new generation of drug injectors; allowing drug users to tell their own stories in print – as we did in *NUAA News* – would encourage curiosity among non-users to try injecting; giving methadone was just substituting one addiction with another.

But the research found that these were not true. Literally hundreds of papers published on the effects of NSP, outreach, MAT and other harm reduction interventions found, that within certain boundaries of quality and targeting, these interventions had an enormous impact on drug users' lives with very little impact on the rest of society. Slowly, gradually, the data from this research was shared among researchers, then among practitioners, added to each year with more studies from more countries – invariably western countries before the mid-1990s – to assemble a knowledge base from which to argue that harm reduction works.

The primary discussion and dissemination point for this research was the International Harm Reduction Association's Annual Conference (originally called the International Conference on the Reduction of Drug Related Harm, to avoid having the term 'harm reduction' in the title), held each year since 1990. At these conferences, those of us who worked as harm reduction practitioners, researchers, policymakers or – as in my case – consultants/advisers, met and discussed the latest evidence which could guide both the practice of carrying out harm reduction activities and our work in advocating for more countries to adopt these approaches.

Advocacy in developing and transitional countries

Because we had the experience from our own country, Australians were among the first group of harm reduction advocates that worked in developing and transitional countries, trying to persuade governments, politicians, doctors, health workers, sometimes trying to convince drug users themselves that harm reduction was the most effective way to protect the health of injecting drug users, especially in the burgeoning HIV epidemics around the globe.

Joining that group, I worked first in Malaysia, India and Nepal then, in quick succession, most of the countries in Eastern Europe, Central Asia and South East Asia. In the process, I found the same issues arising over and over again. The counter-intuitive nature of harm reduction meant that people found it very difficult to believe that these ideas would work in their country. By 2002, I had heard these arguments so often, I wrote a book for IHRA, (WHO/UNAIDS/UNODC, 2004) published two years later by WHO to assist others advocating for harm reduction.

This *Advocacy Guide* notes that the major, relevant UN agencies working on HIV and injecting drug use already agreed that a set of activities could be labelled 'effective HIV prevention for injecting drug users'. It detailed these (virtually the same as the set now promoted by all parties including the US government), but stated that, 'despite the support from international agencies and signatures on international agreements, effective programmes related to HIV/AIDS and injecting drug use comprising at least some of the key interventions mentioned above, had been implemented in only about 55 countries worldwide, fewer than half of all countries where HIV has been found among injecting drug users. Even in countries that have implemented one or more effective programmes, such activities are often provided at very small scale or on a pilot basis, and not as part of a national policy.

Vigorous opposition to the introduction and maintenance of such effective programmes has occurred in many countries. This opposition has taken many forms, including:

- Concern, for instance among the police, unsupported by any evidence, that some HIV/AIDS prevention activities, especially needle-syringe programmes, increase illicit drug use;
- Concern that methadone maintenance and other programmes are not appropriate forms of drug treatment because cessation of illicit drug use is not their immediate goal;
- Criticism that some measures are too liberal and should be replaced by punishment of drug users;
- Media descriptions contrasting 'generous' programmes for allegedly incorrigible drug users while 'innocent' patients who are not drug users are unable to obtain proper medical care;
- Opposition from city administration and neighbourhood groups to the establishment of sites for programmes on the grounds that these services attract injecting drug users, diminishing the amenity of the neighbourhood;
- Perception by some health staff that medical treatment for injecting drug users wastes scarce resources on 'worthless' drug users or replaces one addiction with another;
- Concern that emphasis on HIV/AIDS prevention programmes for injecting drug users compromises primary prevention of drug and abstinence-oriented drug treatment programmes;
- Concern that HIV/AIDS prevention for injecting drug users could divert resources otherwise available for the prevention of sexual transmission of HIV among the general population;
- Criticism often based on limited or no knowledge of prevention programmes, that such programmes go against the culture of a country or the tenets of a prevailing religion.

Possible reasons for this opposition vary according to the culture of each country, but some common themes have been observed including:

- Lack of or late recognition by officials and politicians that injecting drug use exists in a country or is of serious concern, often coupled with a lack of experience in dealing with drug issues and related problems such as substance dependence (especially in transitional and some developing countries, where such problems may have been rare previously);
- Lack of knowledge among decision-makers regarding how quickly HIV infection can spread among and from injecting drug users, and of the evidence for the effectiveness and cost-effectiveness of the approaches outlined above;
- Traditional reliance in many countries on law enforcement mechanisms and an abstinence-only approach to 'solve' drug issues (including HIV infection related to drug use);
- Lack of experience or training in drug and HIV/AIDS prevention approaches among health professionals and non-governmental organisation staff;
- Lack of community awareness of the effectiveness of these approaches and the benefits of controlling and reducing HIV epidemics among injecting drug users;

- Lack of experience or training in advocacy and lobbying among health professionals, staff of non-governmental organisations, policymakers, and others to start, manage, or promote HIV/AIDS prevention for injecting drug users.

The *Advocacy Guide* provided various methods to overcome these and other obstacles. Although the *Guide* is quite detailed, provides planning and analysis tools and assists readers to discover entry points for working with politicians, law enforcement, doctors etc., my favourite section of the book is labelled 'Beliefs and attitudes opposing interventions', in which I tried to assemble the most common arguments against harm reduction together with some draft responses that I had found effective in at least some circumstances. Some extracts from this section:

There is no problem

This is a common argument in countries with few recorded cases of HIV infection among injecting drug users. **Reply:** Few recorded cases do not mean a small number of cases. Every country where injecting drug use has been found is at risk of an epidemic of HIV/AIDS among injecting drug users. Prevention which starts early is much cheaper and much more effective in saving lives than prevention efforts after an epidemic is established. Rapid assessment should be done immediately to determine the extent of injecting drug use and related risk behaviours. If these behaviours exist, then action should be taken immediately at a scale large enough to prevent a HIV/AIDS epidemic among injecting drug users or bring an existing epidemic under control.

Drug users do not matter

Some people believe that drug users are 'bad' or 'evil' and therefore should not be provided with health services. **Reply:** Use of drugs is an activity, which may change across a person's lifetime. Many drug users are young people experimenting with drugs. In any case, no one deserves to die of AIDS. Drug users are members of the society and the signatories to the Health for All policy have stated that the health of all people in a society is important and must be protected.

There are bigger health problems

This is a very common argument, especially in developing and transitional countries. It is also often true, at least in the short-term. **Reply:** The truth about HIV/AIDS epidemics is that they overwhelm health systems with AIDS five to ten years after the initial epidemic has occurred. Unless HIV/AIDS is brought under control, a massive wave of AIDS cases can occur which will dwarf all of the country's other health problems. The only way to prevent this from happening is to prevent HIV transmission now, although malaria, tuberculosis, or other diseases may look like a much greater problem at present.

Needle syringe programmes and substitution treatment encourage drug use and drug injecting

This is especially common among those who only look at some of the proposed activities and do not read background papers about evidence. **Reply:** This is untrue. Harm reduction activities have been studied extensively to determine specifically whether they lead to any negative consequences such as increased drug use or increased injecting. In no research has this been shown to occur. In fact, the effect is often the opposite with drug users attracted to outreach or needle and syringe programmes voluntarily seeking help to stop using drugs. This comes about as a result of the trust established by such programmes with injecting drug users.

The AIDS epidemic will fix the drugs problem

This is quite a common response, usually said with a laugh but meant at least partly seriously. **Reply:** This is not the case. In no country where HIV has spread among injecting drug users has there been a massive reduction in drug use. HIV/AIDS affects men, women and children- not just drug users and their families, but many other people in society as well.

Police must enforce the law and therefore apprehend drug users

This is a very common argument. It is also true. **Reply:** That is true. However, there are many areas in which the law is enforced with some discretion. Police are able to determine whether to enforce laws more or less vigorously, in which areas to place their resources and on what crimes they will concentrate. Evidence shows that fear of arrest by the police is often stronger than fear of acquiring HIV/AIDS, so that drug users are likely to take greater risks in injecting drugs when they fear arrest. They will also not come forward for education in an atmosphere of trust unless they are sure they will not be arrested. Health workers need to be able to provide this education and build up this trust so that education is successful.

Needle syringe programmes and substitution treatment send the wrong message

This is extremely common, especially from politicians, in almost every country. It means that the government is committed to a 'fight against drugs' and that the politician or policymaker believes that the advocated activities are in opposition to this policy. **Reply:** This is not true. Implementing the advocated activities does not imply 'weakness' or being 'soft on drugs'. All countries, which have implemented these activities also continue to have strong policies on reducing the supply of and the demand for drugs. A balanced approach is needed which allows a government to maintain control over drug use by its citizens and prevent a HIV/AIDS epidemic among drug users.

Ideas from western (or developed) countries are unsuitable in this country

This is a common argument even from health professionals, lawyers and especially police and politicians in some countries. **Reply:** It is possible that these approaches will not be effective in this country. For this reason, pilot programmes may be needed to begin with. If the programmes are shown to be effective in this country and they will reduce or stop an HIV/AIDS epidemic, then they are suitable for this country.

During and immediately after development of the *Advocacy Guide*, the evidence for harm reduction approaches to HIV and injecting drug use became so overwhelming that a number of agencies published the evidence in various ways to try to sway decision-makers. The leading agency in this area was WHO with its 'Evidence for Action' series which included both papers summarising the evidence for various elements of the comprehensive package as well as policy briefs which attempted to summarise the summaries in a form that might interest politicians and other policymakers. WHO was also the lead agency in ensuring there were practical guides to starting and managing needle-syringe programmes, outreach programmes, methadone maintenance and other elements of the comprehensive package.

Other agencies joined in this process until, today, a remarkable range of international bodies promote harm reduction. The list now includes the UK Government – whose Department for International Development was one of the first bilateral aid agencies to have its own harm reduction strategy -, the aid arms of the Australian, Dutch, German and Swiss governments; virtually all the relevant UN organisations including UNAIDS, UNODC, UNDP, UNFPA, UNICEF, as well as the World Bank, Asian Development Bank and other similar donors; and, in 2010, the US government through its USAID, PEPFAR and Centers for Disease Control (CDC) operations.

Country by country, city by city

It would be a wonderful thing to report one success after another, that this harm reduction advocacy has wrought in every region. Unfortunately, in 2010, as the Sidibe speech and the IHRA report emphasise, there is still much to be done. The 82 countries with NSP, 70 countries with MAT, and 66 countries with both sounds impressive, until an analysis is undertaken of the regular reach or coverage of these programmes. In western countries, coverage approaches very high percentages of injecting drug users, but in most developing and transitional countries, small numbers are reached each year with each element and very few are reached with the full comprehensive package of services.

Until recently, it was assumed that we had neither strong enough evidence to overcome opposition to harm reduction, nor sufficient funds to scale up harm reduction programmes. Those two conditions have, at least for the present, been cancelled by the overwhelming level of evidence and agreement on the effectiveness of harm reduction and the funding available through all HIV funds worldwide (with the possible exception of JICA – the Japanese international aid agency). The challenge now is to use the funds available in the most effective and efficient way to provide universal access for IDUs to HIV prevention, treatment and care. This will only happen if we transmute the global technical knowledge and political support now available into specific advocacy activities at every local, state/provincial and national level where opposition remains.

One of the largest current challenges is to transfer control from (hopefully) benign foreign funders to the governments and people of the developing and transitional countries where harm reduction needs to be scaled up. By far the largest such programme is currently under way in China. Although the Government of China (GoC) was able, with little outside assistance, to scale up its methadone programmes towards its target of 200,000 clients, there has been little activity yet in scaling up needle-syringe programmes. In 2010, I worked with a group of American agencies, led by USAID, to try to persuade the governments of Yunnan and Guangxi Provinces, and ultimately the Government of China, that USAID-funded interventions to address HIV among IDUs, combined with scaled-up NSP for active IDUs and the ongoing expansion of methadone clinics would bring about a rapid reduction in HIV incidence among and from drug users.

An extensive process was used to show this point to the Government of China (GoC). Research was carried out in two tracks. Track 1 objectives include:

- describing the IDU model (of USAID-funded services in Yunnan and Guangxi) in substantial detail, including the development of a collective view of the model, its inputs, activities, outputs, and outcomes;
- describing the achievements, strengths, shortcomings and weaknesses of the IDU activities implemented in the framework of the CPS in Guangxi and Yunnan; and
- developing – collectively with collaborating agencies, IDUs, and other stakeholders (including GoC) – strategic recommendations to improve key IDU activities implemented as part of the IDU Model.

The track 1 report (RTI International, 2010), made seven major recommendations for the key attributes of a suggested model for replication that would enhance the quality of services targeted at IDUs in Yunnan and Guangxi:

- enhanced drop-in centres;
- strengthened referral networks;
- increased emphasis on a peer-based approach;
- improved outreach to and NSPs for active IDUs;
- developed minimum package of gender-sensitive services;
- standardised monitoring and evaluation of service delivery; and
- enhanced partnerships with GoC authorities.

The objectives of the surveys undertaken as part of track 2 (RTI International, 2011) included:

- evaluating the CPS IDU services that have been implemented among IDUs; and
- comparing levels and types of risk behaviour and other outcomes among IDUs in sites where CPS services are available with those of IDUs in matched sites where no such services are available.

The track 2 study examined differences in behaviour – specifically, levels and types of risk behaviour and other outcomes – between IDUs in four sites where USAID-funded projects are operating (survey: $N = 421$ in project sites) and two matched sites where no such projects exist ($N = 200$ in control sites). In addition, qualitative data were collected from 40 respondents in project sites and 20 in control sites. This study found that the USAID-funded IDU projects had made a substantial difference in the lives of the drug users they reached. IDUs in China are difficult to find and reach because of the policies and laws governing the behaviour of all who come into contact with drug users. Within this difficult environment, the USAID-funded projects managed to achieve a real engagement with drug users on a number of levels related to knowledge and service utilisation. The IDU services, provided together, appeared to lead to increased knowledge and access to services.

The results of the two tracks (over 500 pages of research results) were distilled down to a 4-page report for presentation to the Government of China (RTI International, 2011). This advocacy document stated that the USAID-funded IDU Model, now called the Comprehensive Package of Services, with some additions and changes, is appropriate for HIV prevention, treatment, care, and support of HIV among IDUs in China. It listed key recommendations from the evaluation for the Government of China and other agencies:

1. The Comprehensive Package of Services for IDUs should be expanded to new districts and provinces in China. The package includes the best practices detailed in the track 1 report, working framework, standard operating procedures, and quality control methods.
2. Central to reducing HIV risk related to IDUs is the provision of sterile needles and syringes to drug users through NSPs run by staff whom IDU clients perceive as friendly. Given the legal and regulatory barriers to accessing NSPs, it is recommended that these services should be linked to outreach where possible and also be provided through non-outreach modes such as pharmacy distribution. Enhanced drop-in centres (DICs) should utilise innovative outreach approaches capable of reaching active IDUs, including by mobile phones and the internet.
3. Policy work on legal, regulatory and policing issues is needed to achieve access to active IDUs, and the stigma reduction under way for former IDUs needs to be extended to active IDUs. The policy environment needs to be addressed at national, provincial and local levels and needs to involve both the Ministry of Health and the Public Security Bureau to determine a way to allow access to active IDUs that is acceptable to both.
4. DICs are critical to the improved regularity, frequency and duration of high-quality service-client contact required for sustained behaviour change among IDUs. Current and new DICs should be enhanced to provide a safe space, IEC materials, access to a broad range of services (either directly or via strengthened referral networks), and as wide a range of activities as possible to attract and support clients. Specific, centrally located enhanced DICs should be considered as training centres and supported to provide training for key intervention personnel as well as for community and Government of China stakeholders. The role of Comprehensive Package of Services DICs in working with families of IDUs should be emphasised during scale-up.

5. Although the level of referrals in project sites was much higher than in control sites, only 45% of respondents from project sites had accepted referrals of any type during the previous 12 months. Enhanced DICs should act as hubs for referrals to other general and specialist health and social services for former IDUs, MMT patients and stopping IDUs, including those who are also HIV positive. Referral networks should help service clients to access a continuum of care. Referrals should ideally be accompanied, then followed up or case managed, to ensure that referrals are utilised, that referred services meet quality standards, and that further client needs identified by referred services are met.

6. Peer education was shown to be an essential factor in the success of the Comprehensive Package of Services. Accordingly, the enhanced DICs should act as a base for peer-based approaches, which are increasingly integrated not only into obvious areas – such as outreach and support to MMT patients at clinics, homes, and hospitals; the development of appealing and useful IEC materials; and the training of peer educators – but into all aspects of service planning, implementation, monitoring, and evaluation. Peer education should be extended to active IDUs to ensure improvements in safer behaviour.

7. A gender-sensitive Comprehensive Package of Services should be used across all services. This package should focus on building independence, involving women in designing services and formulating policies, making programmes available for mothers, incorporating sexual and reproductive health into services, providing gender-sensitive drug treatment and integrated HIV prevention and care programmes for drug-using sex workers, providing information and referrals to the Women's Federation, supporting women to access national hotlines and services for domestic violence and rape prevention, and educating mainstream providers.

Human rights: the way forward?

As this chapter has shown, my own work on harm reduction advocacy has tended towards the concrete, the specific, the arguments that I felt would sway an opponent, a police officer, a government. Increasingly this is not the language of the International Harm Reduction Association, the International Harm Reduction Conference, many of the regional harm reduction networks and many of the new groups working on harm reduction. These groups concentrate increasingly on the human rights of drug users and abuse or protection of these rights.

Reports seem to emerge each month detailing the human rights abuse of drug users in general, drug users in treatment, drug users in prison, drug users in Russia, drug users in Thailand etc. Indeed IHRA had a huge success a couple of years ago in showing that UNODC was breaching its own undertakings on human rights by commending governments who applied the death penalty to drug traffickers. Not unexpectedly, drug user groups who are once more striving for a global voice through the unfortunately acronymed INPUD – International Network of People Who Use Drugs – and national networks in many European countries, Australia, Thailand and North America, have welcomed this approach. Finally, I am told at every conference, the stories of the mistreatment of drug users are being told.

This is a good thing of course. But I can't help remembering the constant tales of the village girl who was raped, impregnated and left HIV-positive. The girl may be Indian, Chinese, South African, Rwandan, Tajik, Argentinean or from Papua New Guinea. But it seems to me I hear her story at every conference when the topic comes up of stigma and discrimination. Never or extremely rarely do presenters give evaluated methods of reducing stigma and discrimination. Instead, using a human rights 'witnessing' approach, speaker after speaker tells the story of the village girl (or a thousand variants). And I wonder, if the world can't protect the human rights of 50% of its population – i.e., women and girls – what hope is there really for protecting the human rights of drug users?

References

Burrows, D. (1987) *Clean Needles: New Weapons in the War on AIDS*, Sydney: Connexions Centre for Information and Education on Drugs and Alcohol.

Commonwealth Department of Health and Ageing (2009) *Return on Investment 2: Evaluating the Cost-Effectiveness of Needle and Syringe Programs in Australia*, Canberra: Commonwealth of Australia.

Harwood, H.J., Hubbard, R.L., Collins, C.J. and Valley, R.V. (1988) *The Costs of Crime and the Benefits of Drug Abuse Treatment*, NIDA Monograph Series 86, Rockville: NIDA.

IHRA (2010) *Global State of Harm Reduction 2010: Key Issues for Broadening the Reponse.* Report from the International Harm Reduction Association, London: IHRA.

Kaldor, J. (1987) Personal communication.

National Centre in HIV Epidemiology and Clinical Research (2010) *Australian NSP Survey National Data Report 2005–2009*, Sydney: University of New South Wales.

PEPFAR (2010) *Comprehensive HIV Prevention for People Who Inject Drugs: Revised Guidance*, US President's Emergency Plan for AIDS Relief (PEPFAR), Washington, DC: US Bureau of Public Affairs.

RTI International (2010) *Report on the Comprehensive Package of Services Model for Injecting Drug Users: Yunnan and Guangxi*, Raleigh-Durham: RTI International.

RTI International (2011a) *Strengthening HIV Prevention, Care, Support, and Treatment Services for Injecting Drug Users in Yunnan & Guangxi Provinces, China: A Model for Moving Forward*, Raleigh-Durham: RTI International.

RTI International (2011b) *Study of Outcomes of the Comprehensive Package of Services Model for Injecting Drug Users: Yunnan and Guangxi*, Raleigh-Durham: RTI International.

WHO/UNAIDS/UNODC (2004) *Advocacy Guide: HIV/AIDS Prevention for Injecting Drug Users*, Geneva/Vienna: WHO/UNAIDS/UNODC.

WHO/UNAIDS/UNODC (2009) *Technical Guide for Countries to Set Targets for Universal Access to HIV Prevention, Treatment and Care for Injecting Drug Users*, Geneva/Vienna: WHO/UNAIDS/UNODC.

Chapter 6

HARM REDUCTION AND THE ROLE OF POLICE SERVICES

Geoffrey Monaghan

By the late 1980s some western academics began exploring the possibility of expanding harm reduction principles to criminal justice systems. Consequently, a number of police services, primarily those operating in Australia, North America and Western Europe began to revise their drug enforcement policies and practices to take account of the threats posed by HIV, hepatitis and alarming increases in levels of injecting drug use. In a number of countries, senior police chiefs and their advisers were quick to factor into their thinking the emerging evidence demonstrating the effectiveness of key harm reduction interventions such as needle and syringe schemes, methadone maintenance therapy, and condom distribution programmes. This chapter is intended to provide the reader with an overview of the ensuing harm reduction policies and practices developed by selected police services. The chapter also analyses some of the persistent tensions arising from police services' legal and professional obligations when enforcing drug and sex work laws, protecting their staff, community expectations, and modern-day public health imperatives. In addition, historical examples of police-initiated harm reduction policies and practices are also highlighted. Although framed largely within the British context, I also draw on examples from other countries.

> when overdose is identified, witnesses may be reluctant to call an ambulance for fear that the police will also become involved, and prosecution under some heading ensue. Our view is that a call to a person who has overdosed should be regarded by the ambulance and police services as a *medical emergency* in the first instance, rather than as a call to the scene of a crime.' *Reducing Drug Related Deaths*.
>
> (ACMD, 2000)

> THINK MURDER until the investigation proves otherwise. Initial attendance [at the scene of a suspicious death] encompasses basic crime scene and evidence preservation as a precursor to launching the investigation.
>
> (ACPO and the Forensic Science Service, 1989: 19)

The above excerpts indicate the inherent difficulties police services face in their efforts to adopt and implement 'harm reduction' policies and practices. On the one hand, it is likely that a good many practitioners working in the HIV and drug misuse prevention, treatment and care fields would unhesitatingly agree with the view expressed by Advisory Council on the Misuse of Drugs (ACMD). On the other hand, it is likely that a majority of the public and police officers would think it a good idea that any drug overdose incident is investigated so as to determine whether or not a crime has been committed by a third party. For example, the overdose might have occurred after a drug addict had injected a friend, also a drug addict, with a controlled drug. In such a case at least two serious offences may have been committed under English law, namely the unlawful supply of a

Harm Reduction in Substance Use and High-Risk Behaviour: International Policy and Practice, First Edition.
Edited by Richard Pates and Diane Riley.
© 2012 Blackwell Publishing Ltd. Published 2012 by Blackwell Publishing Ltd.

controlled drug, or the unlawful administration of a poison or noxious substance. Or perhaps the overdose had occurred in circumstances where the suspect had administered a drug to his/her victim in order to facilitate an offence of theft or indecent assault whilst the victim was sedated. In fatal overdose cases, it is essential that the circumstances are thoroughly investigated to determine whether or not a murder, manslaughter, or other serious offence has been committed – hence the advice contained in the Association of Chief Police Officers (ACPO) and the Forensic Science Service (FSS) *Murder Investigation Manual*. In these and similar circumstances, whether any person is prosecuted or even arrested will be largely determined by a thorough police investigation. In many cases, the course of the investigation will be guided by the evidence the police were able to retrieve from the scene of the overdose.

In the absence of police to safeguard the scene, the risk of its contamination by family members, friends, onlookers or even paramedics is increased. The ACMD recommended that 'a call to a person who has overdosed should be viewed as a medical emergency [and] confidentiality should be maintained . . . and the police should not routinely attend' (ACMD, 2000). Preliminary research showed that police officers in London did not *routinely* attend emergency calls relating to drug overdoses, but a study of drug related deaths in Scotland, found that the police were in attendance at 90% of the scenes of the overdose following a call from either the ambulance service or a friend or acquaintance. At the scene the police undertook no activity in 87% of cases, in 5% of cases they were called to obtain access to overdosed persons (e.g. force entry through a locked door, and some cases police performed cardiopulmonary resuscitation (CPR).

The ACMD recommendation begs a central question: was there a risk that a marked reduction in police attendance at drug overdose incidents would actually *increase* the number of overdose fatalities? Taking into account the heavy traffic congestion in London, it is likely that in some cases police officers, if asked to respond, would reach the scene of an overdose before the London Ambulance Service (LAS). Given that all police officers in London are required to be proficient in first aid including emergency resuscitation techniques, on arrival at the scene, they could be in a position to perform CPR, and therefore prevent loss of life. This is supported by the Scottish study where police officers performed CPR on ten occasions, which suggests they arrived at the scene before the ambulance. In this light, a recommendation which could mean a *reduction* of the number of people trained to administer CPR attending overdose incidents suddenly seems less attractive.

Having carefully considered the ACMD recommendation and related proposal, the Commander in charge of the Drugs Directorate issued a more general statement reiterating the fact that the police in London do not routinely attend suspected drug overdose incidents and that if called, the primary reason for police attendance would be to render first aid, assist the LAS, or maintain public order. We don't know if the limited media coverage had any impact on the number of emergency calls made in the ensuing months. However, some three years later, in September 2007, the London Drug Policy Forum with the support of the MPS, LAS and the NHS launched a new campaign aimed at preventing overdose deaths. The campaign, Staying Alive, encourages the friends and family of problem drug users to call an ambulance if someone collapses or overdoses. Helping to launch the campaign, Detective Superintendent Neil Wilson of the MPS said:

> We know people often hesitate to call an ambulance if there has been a suspected overdose. However, the fact is that we are not routinely called to attend suspected overdose incidents and our overwhelming prime concern is the saving of lives. By phoning an ambulance you can help save a life.

The role of police services in supporting harm reduction

Whilst an increasing number of police officers accept that they have a role to play in supporting harm reduction policies and practices, relatively few appear to have much idea as to what that role entails. Many police officers struggle to get beyond bald statements such as: 'Well, we support needle syringe/methadone programmes' when asked to elaborate. Even though any number of senior police officers have introduced policies and pioneered practices which are underpinned by the basic principles of harm reduction, they fail to recognise them as such. Having trawled the historical literature on police services in Britain for many years, I have found a number of examples of laws, programmes and practices which fall neatly under the rubric of harm reduction. British police officers prior to the late 1980s did not use the term to describe these programmes and practices but few would now disagree that they were formulated and underpinned by similar considerations as those which exercise the minds of their present-day counterparts; namely the reduction of harms caused by infectious diseases, alcohol and drug misuse, and prostitution, and a desire to divert some offenders, particularly young people, alcohol and drug misusers and prostitutes away from the criminal courts. Indeed, some of the so-called new approaches have their historical links to policies and programmes which stretch back decades. As detailed in the history chapter, at least one practice dates back some four hundred years. The following list is intended to provide the reader with some sense of the what some police services have been doing since the 1980s, picking up from the historical references in chapter 2.

Police services and harm reduction: some examples

As noted by Riley et al. (1999), 'harm reduction' is neither a 'new' nor an 'alternative' approach so much as it an extension and focusing of existing and accepted approaches. In the context of public health policies and practices, Riley's observation hold just as true for police services as it does for the medical profession, drug service workers, public officials, and other professionals. And although there is still a tendency for many police officers to distance themselves from initiatives or interventions which are informed by public health considerations, the literature on their participation in public health programmes is extensive in both time spanned and quantity.

Alternatives to prosecution for offences involving alcohol, drugs and prostitution

For decades, the most widely used alternative to prosecution in Britain has been the *formal caution*. Following the introduction of Home Office Circular 30/2005, the *formal caution* is now referred to as a *simple caution* by Home Office officials and police services in order to distinguish it from *conditional cautioning*. (Unless the context dictates otherwise, I use the term *simple caution* to include the practice of cautioning offenders prior to 2005.) A simple caution is a non-statutory disposal for adult offenders and is commonly used in cases where there is evidence of a criminal offence but the public interest does not require a prosecution. Simple cautions are administered by police and other law enforcement agencies in England and Wales. The aims of a simple caution are to deal quickly and simply with offences, divert offenders where appropriate from appearing in the criminal courts, and reduce the likelihood of offending.

Table 6.1 Sub-sample of the 797 MPS simple caution cases recorded in 1984: adult simple cautions involving class A drugs

Attempting to possess cocaine	1
Attempting to possess diamorphine	3
Possession of cocaine	4
Possession of diamorphine	8
Possession of diamorphine and cannabis	1
Concerned in the supply of diamorphine	1
Importation of diamorphine	1
Total	*19*

Source: Monaghan, G. (1992) Memorandum to the Metropolitan Police Service Drug Strategy Group, unpublished.

Since 1983, Home Office Circulars have been issued for the purposes of providing guidance to police services and prosecutors on the use of simple cautions and to remind practitioners that simple cautions should generally be used for low-level offending; encouraging greater consistency in the use of the simple caution on a national basis; providing a clear outline of the practical process of administering a simple caution; emphasising the importance of accurate recording of simple cautions because of the possible impact on the individual offender; to help maintain public confidence and for data collection purposes; and providing a standard simple pro forma for operational use. Following the issuance of the Home Office Circulars 26/1983, 14/1985, 59/1990, and 18/1994, the rate of cautioning drug offenders increased dramatically across Britain. By 1998, no fewer than 55% of drug offenders in England and Wales were dealt with by means of the simple caution (Kaal, 2001). Nowhere was the increase more dramatic – or more liberal – than in London. In 1981, the percentage of persons cautioned for drug offences by the MPS was less than 0.5%; by 1984, this had increased to 9% (797 persons). Although the bulk of these cautions involved the possession of cannabis or cannabis resin (class B drugs) as is apparent in table 6.1, an increasing number involved class A drugs (i.e. diamorphine and cocaine) and two of these were for drug trafficking offences.

From 1984 to 1994 the number of simple cautions for drug offences in Britain increased from 2,000 to 44,000, compared with an increase in convictions over the same period from 18,700 to 34,600. In other words, the national simple cautioning rate for 1994 was 61.5% (although the rate varied between police services; from 16% to 77%) (Department of Health, 1996). By 1995, the percentage of those cautioned for drug offences by the MPS had increased to 68% (16,414 persons). The percentage of those cautioned for drug trafficking offences (everything from importing, exporting, supplying, possession with intent to supply etc.) also increased.

Further increases in the number of cases where simple cautions had been administered for drug trafficking offences involving class A, B and C drugs, followed the issuance of *A Guide to Case Disposal Options for Drug Offenders* by the Association of Chief Police Officers Drug Sub-Committee, London in 1999 (Monaghan and White, 1999). For example, in 2004 the MPS and City of London Police (CoL) administered 14 simple cautions to persons for class A drug trafficking offences under section 4(3) MDA 1971 (supply, offering to supply, and being concerned in the supply), and 30 simple cautions for class A drug trafficking offences under section 5(3) MDA 1971 (possession with intent to supply). Simple cautions were also administered by the MPS and CoL for drug trafficking offences involving class B and C drugs; see table 6.2.

Table 6.2 Number of adult offenders administered simple cautions for drug trafficking offences involving class A, B or C drugs in 2004: Metropolitan Police Service and City of London Police

Section 4(3) Misuse of Drugs Act 1971 (class A)	14
Section 4(3) Misuse of Drugs Act 1971 (class B)	17
Section 4(3) Misuse of Drugs Act 1971 (class C – mainly cannabis)*	18
Section 5(3) Misuse of Drugs Act 1971 (class A)	30
Section 5(3) Misuse of Drugs Act 1971 (class B)	57
Section 5(3) Misuse of Drugs Act 1971 (class C – mainly cannabis)*	108
Total	*244*

Note:* In January 2004 cannabis was reclassified from a class B to class C controlled drug. In January 2009 it was reclassified as a class B controlled drug.
Source: RDS Office for Criminal Justice Reform, UK.

In the same year, most of the police services in England and Wales administered simple cautions for drug trafficking offences involving class A, B or C drugs with West Yorkshire Police apparently operating a more liberal policy than other police services outside London; see table 6.3.

In terms of simple cautions for possession offences (section 5(2) MDA) involving class A, B and C, the published data for 2004 show that the practice was widespread and in the case of cannabis, routine. Table 6.4 is intended to convey these points by highlighting the police service areas with the highest numbers of offenders:

In her 2001 dissertation entitled 'Police cautioning of drug offenders: policies, practices and attitudes', Kaal makes the point that in the relatively brief history of the criminalisation of the possession of drugs such as cannabis, cocaine, diamorphine (heroin), morphine and opium in Britain, the simple caution, has become an important method of disposal for drug offenders. Whilst the increase in simple cautioning rates is to be welcomed, I know of many cases where the use of simple cautions for drug offences has been wholly inappropriate. To be fair, plenty of British police officers have also been less than dispassionate when deciding to recommend the administration of a simple caution. In the 1980s and 1990s, administering a simple caution required a lot less paperwork than preparing a prosecution file. On occasions, simple cautions were issued bcause the officers concerned had misunderstood the guidance.

Simple cautions are still widely used to dispose of thousands of drug offences alongside other alternatives to prosecution, including reprimands and final warnings for young offenders, 'cannabis possession warnings' for adults, Penalty Notices for Disorder (for cannabis possession), and

Table 6.3 Number of adult offenders administered simple cautions for drug trafficking offences involving class A, B, or C drugs in 2004: West Yorkshire Police

Section 4(3) Misuse of Drugs Act 1971 (class A)	11
Section 4(3) Misuse of Drugs Act 1971 (class B)	2
Section 4(3) Misuse of Drugs Act 1971 (class C – mainly cannabis)*	4
Section 5(3) Misuse of Drugs Act 1971 (class A)	30
Section 5(3) Misuse of Drugs Act 1971 (class B)	16
Section 5(3) Misuse of Drugs Act 1971 (class C – mainly cannabis)*	37
Total	*100*

Note:* In January 2004 cannabis was reclassified from a class B to class C controlled drug. In January 2009 it was reclassified as a class B controlled drug.
Source: RDS Office for Criminal Justice Reform, UK.

Table 6.4 Number of adult offenders administered simple cautions for possession offences involving class A, B, or C drugs in 2004 in four police service areas

Metropolitan Police Service and City of London Police	
Section 5(2) Misuse of Drugs Act 1971 (class A)	769
Section 5(2) Misuse of Drugs Act 1971 (class B)	2,674
Section 5(2) Misuse of Drugs Act 1971 (class C – mainly cannabis)*	3,373
Total	*6,816*
West Midlands Police	
Section 5(2) Misuse of Drugs Act 1971 (class A)	229
Section 5(2) Misuse of Drugs Act 1971 (class B)	310
Section 5(2) Misuse of Drugs Act 1971 (class C – mainly cannabis)*	1,246
Total	*1,785*
West Yorkshire Police	
Section 5(2) Misuse of Drugs Act 1971 (class A)	242
Section 5(2) Misuse of Drugs Act 1971 (class B)	389
Section 5(2) Misuse of Drugs Act 1971 (class C – mainly cannabis)*	660
Total	*1,291*
South Wales Police	
Section 5(2) Misuse of Drugs Act 1971 (class A)	204
Section 5(2) Misuse of Drugs Act 1971 (class B)	139
Section 5(2) Misuse of Drugs Act 1971 (class C – mainly cannabis)*	399
Total	*742*
Grand total	*10,634*

Note:* In January 2004 cannabis was reclassified from a class B to class C controlled drug. In January 2009, it was reclassified as a class B controlled drug.
Source: RDS Office for Criminal Justice Reform, Ministry of Justice, UK.

conditional cautions (theoretically for any controlled drug). Other countries also have cautioning policies in place for drug offenders. The Victoria Police, Australia, for example, has been operating such a system for years (Victoria Police, 2007).

Drug treatment in police stations

In Britain, the practice of providing controlled drugs such as dihydrocodeine and methadone to detainees held in police stations so as not to disrupt their treatment regimens or to help them stave off withdrawal is longstanding, as it is in the Netherlands (see chapter 2 for more details).

Buprenorphine and methadone are also provided to arrestees in police stations in Australia. Although arrestees cannot begin a buprenorphine or methadone programme while in police custody, it is a requirement that they be provided this service if they are already registered with a programme (Victoria Police, 2007). According to Alice Ryan, a nurse with the Victoria Police Custodial Health & Alcohol Programme:

> We don't want to interfere with the positive influence of substitution therapy whilst a person is in custody. Nor do we want the behavioural problems sometimes associated with persons beginning to withdrawal [sic] in custody . . . As part of the pre-custody assessment, the offender notifies police that they are a registered patient on a methadone programme. Police then contact the offender's doctor, who is asked to complete a Prescription form confirming the therapy, dose and dose intervals.

The cost of dispensing the named drug is covered by the Victoria Police for the period the person is in police custody. In an effort to avoid disputes between the police and detainees arising from any delay, and reduce detainees' anxiety, Nurse Ryan and her colleagues urge drug counsellors and health workers to inform their clients of the possibility of delays in getting their drugs (Victoria Police, 2007).

Referral from police stations to drug treatment services

Drug Referral Schemes (DRS) are partnerships between the police and local drug services that use the point of arrest within police stations as an opportunity for independent drug workers to offer arrestees help and refer them to appropriate treatment services as a means for reducing their drug related offending (see chapter 2 for a brief history of DRS).

Although modest, the successes of the pilot DRS across England and Wales in the early 1990s led the Conservative government to recommend that police services include DRS in their drug strategies (Department of Health, 1995). The government believed that it was through the introduction of such schemes that the police might make the greatest impact in the areas of harm reduction, drug use and community safety. By 1998, a survey conducted by Newburn and Elliot showed that DRS were running in 37 of the 43 police service areas in England and Wales. In some areas, however, they were still at the pilot stages, a few police services had no plans to introduce DRS, and some schemes had already disappeared. Although there were a range of responses by police officers to such schemes, including indifference and active opposition, there was increasing evidence that this approach to accessing drug treatment was gathering momentum. As anticipated by the ARPP Monitoring Group, the DRS research also showed that the majority of those who are most likely to benefit from such schemes will not have been arrested for drug offences. For example, the South London Drugs Referral Project (1995–9) showed that two-thirds of those who engaged with the scheme at the point of arrest had been arrested for theft and kindred offences. This underscores the important point that drug misuse problems, associated HIV and hepatitis risks, and the need for help, may not always be apparent at the time of arrest.

Misunderstandings as a result of conversations between a police officer and detainee triggered by the offer of referral could undermine the idea of DRs and any breach of the Code could amount to a disciplinary offence, which in turn could jeopardise an investigation. Having identified the problem in 1997 (Monaghan, 1999, Monaghan, 2001, DPAS, 1999) and set out the issues in detail in a briefing paper to the MPS Drugs Directorate, I contacted Michael Zander, Professor Emeritus of Law at the London School of Economics and Political Science and the country's leading expert on Police and Criminal Evidence Act 1984 (PACE) and sought his advice. Professor Zander and officials from the Home Office Drug Prevention Advisory Service (DPAS) wrote a Guidance Manual which made the following recommendations:

- It should be the Custody Officer (police sergeant) who brings the DRS to the attention of the suspect as part of the booking in procedure.
- Since paragraph 3.4 of Code C prohibits the Custody Officer from engaging in conversation with the suspect about anything to do with his or her involvement with the offence, the Custody Officer should restrict what he or she says about DRS to a statement of factual information without being drawn into conversation.
- The following form of words should be used: 'A drug referral scheme operates at this police station. If you are interested, I can arrange for you to see an independent worker. Are you interested?'

- Wherever possible the words of the Custody officer should be accompanied by a leaflet which explains more about DRS and the local arrangements in place (DPAS, 1999).

Police services' role in multi-agency approaches to drugs and drug related crime

As described in chapter 2, there is a long history of British police services working with local authorities, health services and CSOs to tackle drug related harm. In 1995, the British government published its White Paper and recommended the setting up of Drug Action Teams (DATs), multi-agency partnerships, in each health authority area in England. In essence, the DAT's role was strategic; to assess the nature and scale of local drug problems, ensure that local agencies' response was coordinated and to implement the White Paper's recommendations. DAT membership included senior representatives from health, probation, police, social services and other local authority departments such as education and housing, as well as the prison service and, in some cases, Customs and Excise. In their 1998 survey of police service drugs strategies, Newburn and Elliot noted that police services: 'appear to have responded with some vigour to the White Paper's approach to multi-agency partnership approaches to drugs and drug related crime' (Newburn and Elliot, 1998). Duke and MacGregor in 1997 found that DAT chairs and members identified the health service and the police as the 'key players' in their local partnership arrangements. Almost four-fifths of DAT chairs identified the police as a key player on the DAT (compared, for example, with just over half who said the same of either education or social services representatives). Newburn and Elliot also found that senior officers (superintendents and above) were active members of DATs.

Needle syringe programmes

Soon after they were first introduced, some police services set about promoting and supporting NSPs and in some cases their support extended far beyond lip-service. According to a paper written in 1991 by Leo Zaal, the former Chief Narcotics Officer, Municipal Police, Amsterdam, the police in the capital city were actively supporting NSPs and PWIDs were able to obtain sterile syringes in exchange for used ones, from police stations (Zaal, 1992). In 1988 in New South Wales (NSW), Australia, an instruction from the Commissioner of Police stated that 'Without restricting their day to day duties and obligations, police should be mindful not to carry out unwarranted patrols in the vicinity of NSPs that might discourage injecting drug users from attending' (Hansen, 2011). Similar instructions have been issued by other Australian police services.

Police support for NSPs operating in Sverdlovsk Oblast, Russia, is set out in Order No. 1564, 2 December 1999, published by Department of the Interior. The Order, signed by Major-General A. Krasnikov, Head of the Main Department, is really a testament to the courage, hard work and foresight of the General's Staff Officer, Colonel Alexander ('Sasha') Nikolaevich Yelin (Yelin, 2001). Sadly, since the creation of the Federal Drug Control Service (FDCS) in 2003 there has been a crack-down on NSPs (and all other forms of harm reduction) and Russian police support for NSPs is, save in a handful of cities, virtually non-existent. Senior Russian police officers in Chelyabinsk, Irkutzk and Voronezh, however, still lend their tacit support not only to fixed-site NSPs but also to mobile schemes operating in and around these cities.

A 2003 report by Human Rights Watch notes that whilst NSPs were technically illegal in Los Angeles they were ostensibly tolerated by the police (Human Rights Watch, 2003). Since then, things have moved on and the Los Angeles Police Department (LAPD) participated in the production of a video documentary entitled *Risks of the Job* in which the role of NSPs are described and advice provided as to how officers can reduce the risk of needle stick injuries. In recent years, many other police chiefs across the USA have made public their support for NSPs. For example, Chief of Police, City of Portland, Oregon, Rosanne Sizer has stated that: 'In Portland, syringe exchange has helped protect law enforcement and first responders from injuries caused by syringes during body searches or rescue operations' (Foundation for AIDS Research, 2010).

The Royal Malaysian Police Force (RMPF) policy support for NSPs is evident in the related Guidelines for Police prepared by the Ministry of Health in cooperation with the RMPF in 2006. In 2004, whilst acting as an unpaid consultant to Futures Group Europe, and working with Susan Beckerleg (Project Leader, the Omari Project Kenya) and Maggie Telfer (Director of the Bristol Drug Project, UK) I managed to enlist the support of a number of senior police officers in Kenya to set up pilot NSPs in the country's coastal region (Monaghan, 2004). The pilots never materialised but in September 2011, following years of advocacy, the United Nations Office on Drugs and Crime (UNODC) in Kenya announced that pilot NSPs, with the support of the Kenyan police service, would start soon.

In the late 1980s, when most NSPs in the UK were strictly operating a 'one-for-one' policy, the MPS police stations in the three boroughs agreed to provide stamped receipts to drug injectors (who, following arrest had had their used syringes confiscated) which they could give to NSPs to explain where the used syringes had gone. Further support for NSPs operating in London came from the MPS in June 1989, which issued a Police Order stating that it was service policy that drug users in possession of a *sterile* hypodermic syringe and needle in a public place should not be arrested (although possession was unlawful under section 139 of the Criminal Justice Act 1988). The Home Office issued a letter to all Chief Officers of Police in November 1988 informing them that drug misusers were being advised to obtain supplies of clean needles for individual use from needle exchange schemes and that this advice would be questionable if they thought they could not have (empty) needles and syringes with them in public places.

So far as I'm aware, no drug injector in possession of sterile needles in a public place was prosecuted or even cautioned in Britain under section 139 before the Home Office letter was sent to police services, but drug injectors were concerned that section 139 would be used. Their anxiety was shared by drug workers. Release, the UK drugs charity that provides free legal advice to young people in trouble with the police, was concerned for some time after the Home Office letter was issued that the law and police practices would thwart the work of NSPs, but the published arrest, simple cautioning and prosecution data suggests these fears were largely unfounded (Release, 1992; Monaghan, 1998). The Home Office advice was welcomed by Chief Officers and incorporated into their service policies. In June 1990, the MPS advised its officers not to submit hypodermic syringes containing residual amounts of controlled drugs to the MPS Forensic Science Laboratory for examination to support investigations relating to unlawful possession offences. This advice was issued because of the perceived risks to police officers and laboratory staff of contracting HIV and hepatitis B through needle-stick injuries. (During 1983–6, a total of 105 needle-stick injuries involving MPS officers were recorded by the Department of Virology, St Thomas's Hospital in London: Welch et al., 1988.)

In recent years, many British police services have enabled their officers to supply sterile injecting equipment to PWIDs on their release from police stations. Avon and Somerset Constabulary, the MPS, and Staffordshire Police ran pilot NSPs in the early 2000s (Police Review, 2001b). More recently, a policy developed by Kent Police (England) and the KCA Harm Reduction Team (a CSO), states that in cases where detainees (age 17 and over) have used or unused needles and syringes in their possession, the police will seize these and dispose of them. Detainees are then informed that they will be provided with a 'needle replacement pack' on their release from the police station, a fact recorded on their custody records. In 2006, a review of NSPs in Scotland identified six schemes operating from police stations (Griesbach et al., 2006).

This is not the place to document in any detail police resistance to NSPs, which since the 1980s has been considerable and continues to be so in some countries, but examples are useful. Stöver and Schuller (1992) note that the opening of the NSP on in September 1986 in Bremen, north Germany, was observed by police and after the press covering the event had left, the police moved in and seized the syringes. Police later resorted to seizing the NSP waste bins containing used syringes, seemingly with the intention of mounting some form of proceedings against the staff on the basis that the barrels of the used syringes contained residual amounts of controlled drugs.

As noted above, in Russia the FDCS has been resistant to NSPs despite the fact since December 2003 the provision of injecting 'tools and equipment' for 'the purposes of preventing HIV infection' was legally recognised following the insertion of a Note to Article 230 of the 1996 Criminal Code of the Russian Federation. This Article creates the offence of 'inclining to consumption of narcotic drugs or psychotropic substances' and is still cited by senior FDCS officers as grounds for closing NSPs or objecting to their opening. In the summer of 2008 a CSO in the Kaliningrad Region notified the local FDCS department that it intended to start a NSP in September of that year. The notification was made in line with the requirements indicated in the Note to Article 230. In its reply the FDCS department threatened to initiate a prosecution under Article 230 if it started the NSP and the CSO dropped the idea. To date, there are no NSPs in Kaliningrad, but the number of new HIV and hepatitis C infections continue to rise.

In 2006, Richard Brunstrom, the former Chief Constable for North Wales Police, Britain. backed a proposal to buy a vending machine designed to dispense sterile syringes to PWIDs in exchange for a token inserted into the machine. Such vending machines had been in use for many years (Druglink, 1991), but Brunstrom wanted to attach this machine to the wall of the police station in the resort of Colwyn Bay where there was only limited access to NSPs at that time. The idea encountered some strong resistance from local community leaders and groups, partly on the grounds that Brunstrom, had made some radical statements regarding drug policy. Whilst in office he had called for the legalisation of all drugs including cocaine and heroin and urged the British government to declare an end to the 'failed war on drugs'. The bid for the vending machine failed and after legal wrangling and public debate, Brunstrom was publicly accused of wasting £50,000 of taxpayers' money (£40,000 in legal fees on the back of a public inquiry and £10,000 for the cost of the vending machine). The Brunstrom case is a salutary lesson to chief officers, not so much because they need to think carefully before promoting access to sterile injecting equipment or other harm reduction measures but more from the standpoint that they need to think very carefully as to how they go about doing it. When promoting harm reduction measures, chief officers need to be able to navigate with credibility between the opposing camps and factions to avoid unexpected or undesirable outcomes. See also chapter 22 of this book where Derricott discusses drug injecting paraphernalia.

In Britain, the MPS was instrumental in bringing about legislative changes regarding the supply of drug injecting articles (paraphernalia) in 2003. Although the supply of a hypodermic syringe or any part of one has been specifically exempted from the scope of section 9A of the MDA 1971 (described above) since its introduction, the supply of other injecting paraphernalia, such as medi-swabs, filters or ampoules of water for injection, wasn't. Accordingly, doctors, pharmacists or a person working for drug treatment services, risked prosecution under section 9A of the MDA. The situation was clearly unsatisfactory and presented particular difficulties for staff working in NSPs. Acutely aware that the legislation was an obstacle to the prevention of HIV and hepatitis, the MPS had lobbied the Home Office for years for the necessary amendments to be made to section 9A of the MDA (Monaghan, 1997). In some parts of London, police superintendents had given assurances, sometimes in writing, to local drug services that their staff would not be the subject of an investigation if they decided to distribute ampoules of sterile water and medi-swabs to their clients. The Drug and Alcohol Service in Barnet, North London had brokered such an arrangement with local police in 1990.

The MPS Drugs Directorate prepared a detailed briefing paper on drug paraphernalia law in Britain in the summer of 2000 and sent it to the United Kingdom Anti-Drugs Coordinating Unit for consideration (Monaghan, 2000). The paper also contained draft legislation for the provision of injecting paraphernalia some of which found its way into the legislation which finally came into force in August 2003. The Misuse of Drugs (Amendment) (No. 2) Regulations 2003, a statutory instrument (SI) amended the Misuse of Drugs Regulations 2001 by inserting Regulation 6A which gives doctors, pharmacists and persons employed or engaged in the lawful provision of drug treatment services to the authority to supply specified items of drug injecting articles, namely swabs, utensils for the preparation of a controlled drug, citric acid, filters and ampoules of water for injection, 'only when supplied or offered for supply in accordance with the Medicines Act 1968 and of any instrument which is in force thereunder'.

Although ascorbic acid was included in the articles listed in the MPS briefing paper, the 2003 Regulations did not include it. Based on subsequent evidence provided to the ACMD which indicated that addicts who inject crack or freebase cocaine tend to use ascorbic acid rather than citric acid, Regulation 6A was amended to include ascorbic acid in the list of articles which could be supplied by the listed persons. The amendment, which came into force on 14 November 2005, aims to reduce the level of harm that addicts face when choosing an acidifier to use for injecting crack or 'freebase' cocaine. Again, the MPS Drugs Directorate was instrumental in helping bring about this amendment and as an interim measure, advised senior officers to refrain from initiating investigations in cases where local drug services were supplying ascorbic acid to their clients.

At the time of writing, the supply of foil for the purposes of smoking controlled drugs, generally heroin, is illegal in Britain and drug services providing foil to drug misusers, to encourage smoking as a safer alternative to the practice of injecting, could be prosecuted under section 9A of the MDA. However, evidence presented to the ACMD (2010) during its consideration of the use of foil as a harm reduction measure, showed that the some police services are supportive of the provision of foil as a harm reduction measure, and have upon request, provided so-called 'letters of comfort' which in effect, is an undertaking by the police not to submit a report to the CPS recommending prosecution. Avon and Somerset Constabulary provided such a letter to the national drugs charity, Turning Point, when its NSPs in south west England started to provide foil to clients (Pizzey and Hunt, 2008). In November 2010, in a letter to the Home Secretary and Secretary of State for Health, the ACMD stated that it had found evidence of the benefits of foil provision, but wasn't able to find any evidence of harms, and it recommended that foil be exempted under section 9A of the MDA.

Drug referral schemes

Besides Britain, DRS are operating in a number of countries, including Australia, the Republic of Ireland (Health Research Board, Ireland, 2005) and parts of the Russian Federation, and have been shown to be effective in identifying arrestees at high-risk of HIV and hepatitis, getting them into drug treatment, and reducing their levels of drug related offending. In the Russian Federation, they have also helped arrestees to contact HIV/AIDS prevention, treatment and care services. (The pilot DRS in Voronezh found that the majority of those referred did not know their HIV status and were not in contact with prevention, treatment or care services at the time of their arrest.) The Voronezh DRS, set up in December 2006, is one of a number now operating in nine Russian cities. Whilst the Russian police should be congratulated on their support for DRS and their willingness to expand them, the schemes are able to offer little in the way of referral to effective drug treatment due to the ongoing ban on the prescribing of buprenorphine, dihyrocodeine, methadone or slow-release oral morphine, so the schemes will only produce modest results in terms of bringing about significant reductions in acquisitive crime. Referral to HIV prevention, treatment and care services is also limited in the cities operating DRS. The schemes operating in Russia are modeled on the Southwark ARPP and draw heavily on lessons from the published research. They were all set up by the United Nations Office on Drugs and Crime (UNODC), Moscow, local police services and CSOs using funding provided by the Dutch Ministry of Health, Welfare and Sports as part of its US$ 25 million programme to scale-up HIV prevention, treatment and care services in the Baltic States, Romania and Russia.

At the time of writing, the UNODC Country Office in Vietnam is working with the Ministry of Public Security's Anti-narcotics Department (C47) to set up a pilot DRS in Hanoi. As part of this initiative, the head of C47, Major-General Nguyen Anh Tuan and colleagues from his department and Hanoi city police travelled to London in December 2010 to see first-hand how the referral process operates from Charing Cross police station. Unlike Russia, Vietnam has methadone programmes and many senior police officers are avid supporters so UNODC anticipates that it will be possible for the police to refer arrestees to community-based methadone maintenance treatment (MMT) programmes as an alternative to the compulsory drug treatment centres. In Vietnam, the police also have responsibility for running prisons and it is pleasing to report that a number of senior police officers have recently called for the introduction of pilot MMT programmes in prisons. Vietnamese police officers working in prisons are also keen to promote harm reduction approaches and prison guards, medical staff and inmates, have all recently benefited from UNODC organised training sessions which are underpinned by harm reduction principles.

Since their inception in the late 1980s, DRS in Britain have developed into the well-resourced Drug Interventions Programme (DIP) which engage and direct arrestees who test positive for opiates or cocaine to drug treatment services. Research on DIP supports the notion of using arrest as one route for getting opiate and cocaine users into treatment. It also shows that rates of entry into treatment for DIP referrals were higher than for previous DRS, that the levels of retention in treatment for DIP entrants equalled those of non-criminal justice route entrants to treatment (Skodbo et al., 2007), and that coercive approaches can improve engagement in drug treatment services. The overall volume of offending by a cohort of 7,727 individuals was 26% lower following DIP identification. Based on these research findings, drug referral workers are now routinely based in police stations in London and other British cities.

Preventing drug overdose deaths

In recent years, a handful of police services have developed and implemented policies and training programmes which enable their officers to administer naloxone in the case of overdose. Naloxone, a prescription drug, carries no potential for abuse and is inexpensive. The drug is used as the standard treatment for opiate overdose, and is administered in hospital emergency rooms and by first responders. As police are often the first to arrive at the scene of an overdose, some police services have introduced policies that allow their officers to administer naloxone to overdose victims. The State of New Mexico, USA, for example allows its police and highway patrol officers to carry and administer intranasal naloxone. The two-day training programme was first introduced in August 2004. Policies and training programmes are developed in partnership with national health agencies and emergency services and seek to protect officers against legal liability should the treatment prove ineffective.

To help reduce drug overdose deaths, particularly those which occur in police stations, a number of police services have developed guidance which emphasises the need to treat suspected drug swallowing as a medical emergency that requires urgent hospitalisation. When confronted by police officers, suspects sometimes attempt to destroy evidence by orally ingesting drugs in their possession. Given the inherent dangers of drug swallowing and the myriad of legal questions arising from the use of force by officers in an effort to prevent the imminent destruction of evidence, chief police officers should ensure that their own services introduce similar guidance to that introduced by the MPS, London, in August 1988: 'The Chief Medical Officer has advised that where [arrestees] are suspected of having swallowed drugs they are to be treated as having taken a potential overdose and an ambulance is to be called immediately to take them to hospital. This is necessary as it is impossible to estimate the concentration of a drug from a visual inspection.'

Drawing on technological advances, some police services have installed cell occupant and occupancy monitoring systems (COMS) or similar, in police cells and other places of temporary detention. Monitoring systems of this kind utilise sensor equipment capable of detecting breathing trouble such as experienced by a detainee choking on their vomit or by a sleep apnoea. Such systems are already in place in a number of police stations in Britain. COMS is intended to supplement rather than replace the statutory or administrative cell visiting/monitoring requirements police officers make as part of their duty of care to arrestees/detainees.

Police support for drug consumption rooms

For the purposes of this chapter, the term, 'drug consumption rooms' is used to describe any room specifically set up for the hygienic consumption of pre-obtained, controlled drugs under professional supervision (Joseph Rowntree Foundation, 2006; Roberts et al., 2004). This definition distinguishes DCRs from 'crack houses', 'shooting galleries', and other premises given over to the illicit and unhygienic consumption of drugs bought at the same location. The definition also distinguishes DCRs from the supervised injectable maintenance clinic, where the attendee is a known patient, receiving treatment from their doctor, and self-administering the prescribed injectable drug, usually diamorphine or methadone, under the direct supervision of a nurse or other worker within the clinic (Strang and Forston, 2004).

Some DCRs in Europe, such as that in the city of Frankfurt, allow for the smoking or inhalation as well as the injection of drugs. DCRs have been running in a number of countries since the 1980s. As noted by the Independent Working Group (IWG) on Drug Consumption Rooms (DCRs), the idea of providing drug misusers with a place to go to use their illegally obtained drugs is highly contentious and one which has triggered passionate (and on occasions acrimonious) debate.

The International Narcotics Control Board (INCB, 2004) rejects DRCs, largely on the grounds that such facilities are contrary to the fundamental provisions of the international drug control treaties, which oblige state parties to ensure that controlled drugs are used only for medical and scientific purposes. This view deserves detailed analysis elsewhere; suffice to say, some prominent lawyers take a different view (Forston, 2006). There is even disagreement between legal experts in the UN and INCB on this issue. Writing in 2004, Roberts, Klein and Trace note that the United Nations on Drugs and Crime (UNODC) had no official position on DCRs. At the time of writing (September 2011) the UNODC has still to adopt an official position on this topic; although research findings of DCRs indicate a number of health benefits (including a statistically significant relationship in four German cities between the establishment of DCRs and a reduction in drug related deaths), the impact on crime and public nuisance is more equivocal (Andresen and Boyd, 2010). According to the IWG, DCRs do not appear to act a 'magnet' for drug misusers outside the local area.

According to Cook (2010), there are over 90 DCRs operating in countries around the world, including Australia, Canada, Germany, the Netherlands and Spain. There are none operating in Britain although former and serving senior police officers have called for their introduction. Police support or at the very least, tolerance, is needed to ensure that clients will not be harassed or arrested when entering or exiting, or just being in the immediate vicinity, of a DCR. In some cities, the police are supportive of DCRs. For example in Vancouver, nearly 17% of DCR clients reported being referred to the facility by police (DeBeck et al., 2008). Many Australian, Dutch, German, Spanish and Swiss police also support DCRs.

Conclusion

We can safely conclude from the above examples that the notion of harm reduction, at least in the context of preventing HIV, hepatitis and injecting drug use, is gradually becoming more acceptable to police services in a number of countries. It's also evident that many are working hard to balance the pressures of national drug control strategies with public health agendas. Increasing numbers of officers (particularly those working in prisons) now accept that they have an important role to play in helping to prevent HIV, hepatitis, drug overdose deaths and much other harm associated with drug misuse. Some of the examples provided also show that it is possible for police services to overcome the legal and administrative barriers to harm reduction, and a number of programmes and initiatives have been implemented which have reduced harms arising from drug misuse or sex work. Many police officers are ready to accept that the principles of harm reduction may also be applied to the community safety aspects of policing such as retail drug markets.

The role of police services in helping governments to realise the ambitions of Millennium Development Goal (MDG) 6 (combating HIV/AIDS, malaria and other diseases) and MDG Target 6A (halt by 2015 and begin to reverse the spread of HIV/AIDS) and the UNAIDS 2011–2015 strategy, Getting to Zero, is likely to become one of the most central issues for the next few years (LEHRN, 2010). In many countries, the targets will only be achieved if police services wholeheartedly embrace harm reduction approaches and do their utmost to support the key nine interventions which make up the comprehensive package, namely:

1. needle and syringe programmes (fixed and mobile);
2. opioid substitution treatment (using drugs such as buprenorphine, methadone, and slow-release oral morphine) and other kinds of evidence-based drug dependence treatment;
3. HIV testing and counseling;
4. antiretroviral therapy;
5. prevention and treatment of sexually transmitted infections;

6. condom programmes for injecting drug users and their sexual partners;
7. targeted information, education and communication for injecting drug users and their partners;
8. vaccination, diagnosis and treatment of viral hepatitis;
9. prevention, diagnosis and treatment of tuberculosis.

These interventions should be provided in the context of a continuum of services that includes outreach, other evidence-based drug dependence treatment, overdose prevention and management, free-of-charge social and legal services, and other services depending on specific needs (UNODC, 2009).

How should police services go about supporting the MDG 6 Goal and the UNAIDS strategy Getting to Zero? Building on Pearson's work from the late 1980s/early 1990s (Pearson, 1992) and the work of Spooner, McPherson and Hall (2002) in early 2000s, and drawing on the published research, the role of police services vis-à-vis harm reduction, can be organised under the following areas:

1. Encouraging entry of most-at-risk-populations into drug treatment programmes via drug referral and similar schemes. (In order to ensure sufficient numbers of arrestees take up the offer of referral, police services should allow drug referral workers (or specially trained outreach workers) to access arrestees whilst they are in police stations.)
2. Preventing the spread of HIV and hepatitis caused by injecting by supporting community-based and prison-based NSPs, and providing arrestees with sterile injecting equipment on their release from police stations.
3. Preventing drug overdose fatalities by allowing specially trained officers to carry and administer naloxone, treating all cases of drug swallowing as a medical emergency requiring immediate hospitalisation and ensuring that all drug using arrestees are examined by a doctor to determine their fitness to be detained at the police station.
4. Reducing drug related crime, illicit drug consumption, HIV, hepatitis and drug overdose deaths in communities and prisons by promoting opioid substitution treatment programmes.
5. Helping to reduce incarceration rates by adopting or scaling-up warning, cautioning, and cautioning-plus programmes as alternatives to prosecuting offenders for minor drug use/possession/trafficking crimes and minor offences relating to adult prostitution.
6. Preventing sexually transmitted infections in prisons and other closed settings by making condoms and dental dams readily available and setting up mechanisms which allow for the voluntary referral of sex workers to local prevention, treatment and care services.
7. Tackling in-service stigma and discrimination by adopting and implementing liberal recruitment and retention policies for homosexuals and PLWH and ensuring they have the same career opportunities in terms of promotion and specialisation as their colleagues.
8. The reduction of collateral harms (e.g. large-scale public disorder, allegations of evidence fabrication and 'cracked trials'), by focused intelligence-led tactics (e.g. test purchase and undercover buy operations and controlled deliveries), in conjunction with other prevention strategies and, where possible, in consultation with community leaders and community groups.
9. Making sure they focus on those drug and sex markets which are causing or are likely to cause, most harm to individuals and communities. The misuse of some drugs such as alcohol, cocaine, heroin and methamphetamine create far more harms than say, cannabis or ecstasy.
10. Ensuring that the principles of harm reduction are embedded in police service training curricula. In this respect, UNODC together with its consultants, is taking a global lead in developing training manuals and other materials.

11. Forging durable partnerships with health authorities, drug and HIV prevention, treatment and care services and PLWH support groups.
12. Regularly reviewing their policies, strategies, tactics and performance indicators/targets to ensure they support the broader agenda of public health imperatives and are underpinned by rights-based international treaties.

If the majority of police services frame their drug and sex work enforcement strategies and tactics in the context of the above areas, then I for one have no doubts that we really will move towards a situation where public health goals such as getting to 'zero new infections' is just as important to police services as it is to public health officials and practitioners; where methadone maintenance programmes are seen as more effective than 'stop and searches' or street-level 'crackdowns' in terms of bringing about significant reductions in rates of acquisitive crime and illicit opiate use; where police officers are able to rattle off the definition of harm reduction in much the same way as they do the legal definitions of theft and burglary or the words of the caution or the 'Miranda warning'; where police services regard the number of cocaine, heroin and methamphetamine users they have referred to local drug and HIV prevention, treatment and care services as important as the number of arrests and seizures and where in-service stigma and discrimination is minimised to the extent that drug misusers, sex workers, homosexuals and people living with HIV/AIDS (PLWHA) are represented in the police/community consultative groups and police service authorities and boards.

A few police services are already there, others are well on the way. However, many – too many – still cling to outdated policies and practices which serve only to impede HIV, hepatitis and injecting drug use prevention efforts. In a handful of countries, police services have gone out of their way to thwart HIV prevention efforts; boasting that they have engineered the closure of NSPs or threatening to arrest distinguished psychiatrists and clinicians for the 'crime' of promoting essential medicines such as methadone and buprenorphine. In some parts of the world, drug misusers, sex workers, homosexuals and men who have sex with men (MSM) are frequently harassed, tormented, persecuted and unlawfully detained by police officers. Such behaviour is nothing short of disgraceful and violates a number of fundamental human rights: freedom of expression, the right to enjoy the benefits of scientific progress and its applications, freedom from torture, inhuman or degrading treatment or punishment and freedom from arbitrary arrest or detention.

When it comes to harm reduction and the role of police services, it's high time some chief police officers started examining the evidence.

Note

The views and opinions expressed in this chapter are those of the author and do not necessarily reflect official policies or positions of the United Nations Office on Drugs and Crime or indeed any other United Nations organisation.

References

ACMD (2000) *Reducing Drug Related Deaths*, London: Advisory Council on the Misuse of Drugs, Home Office.
ACMD (2010) *Consideration of the Use of Foil, as an Intervention, to Reduce the Harms of Injecting Heroin*, London: Advisory Council on the Misuse of Drugs, Home Office.

Andresen, C. and Boyd, N. (2010) A cost-benefit analysis of Vancouver's supervised injection facility, *International Journal of Drug Policy*, 21 (1), 70–6.

Association of Chief Police Officers (ACPO) and the Forensic Science Service (1989) *Murder Investigation Manual*, London: ACPO and the Forensic Science Service.

Cook, J. (2010) *Global State of Harm Reduction 2010: Key Issues for Broadening the Response*, London: International Harm Reduction Association.

DeBeck, K., Wood, E., Zhang, R., Tyndall, M., Montaner, J. and Kerr, T. (2008) Police and public health partnerships: evidence from the evaluation of Vancouver's supervised injection facility, *Substance Abuse Treatment, Prevention and Policy*, 3 (11), 1–5.

Department of Health (1995) *Tackling Drugs Together: A Strategy for England 1995–1998*, London: HMSO.

Department of Health (1996) *The Task Force to Review Services for Drug Misusers*, Report of an Independent Review of Drug Services in England, London: Department of Health.

DPAS (1999) *Drug Interventions in the Criminal Justice System: Guidance Manual*, London: Drugs Prevention Advisory Service, Home Office.

Druglink (1991) Britain's first syringe vending machine now available, *Druglink*, January/February, 5, ISDD, London.

Duke, K. and MacGregor, S. (1997) *Tackling Drugs Locally: The Implementation of Drug Action Teams in England*, London: HMSO.

Forston, R. (2006) Harm reduction and the law of the United Kingdom. Paper submitted to the independent Working Group on Drug Consumption Rooms, York: Joseph Rowntree Foundation.

Foundation for AIDS Research (2010) *Fact Sheet: Public Safety, Law Enforcement and Syringe Exchange*, New York: Foundation for AIDS Research.

Griesbach, D., Abdulrahim, D., Gordon, D. and Dowell, K. (2006) *Needle Exchange Provision in Scotland: A Report of the National Needle Exchange Survey*, Edinburgh: Scottish Executive.

Hansen, F. (2011) *Are Police Interfering with Harm Reduction? The Role of Police in Harm Reduction*, www.cdc.gov.tw/public/Attachment/81321254371.pdf, accessed 20 July.

Health Research Board, Ireland (2005) Arrest referral in the north inner city, *Drugnet*, 14 (summer), 13–14.

Human Rights Watch (2003) Injecting reason: human rights and HIV prevention for injecting drug users, California, a case tudy, *Human Rights Watch*, 15 (2) (G) 22.

INCB (2004) *International Narcotics Control Board, Report of the INCB for 2003*, Vienna: INCB.

Joseph Rowntree Foundation (2006) *The Report of the Independent Working Group on Drug Consumption Rooms*, York: Joseph Rowntree Foundation.

Kaal, H.L. (2001) Police cautioning of drug offenders: policies, practices and attitudes, unpublished doctoral dissertation submitted to the University of Bristol, Faculty of Law.

LEHRN (2010) Law enforcement and harm reduction at the Nossal Institute partnership, *HIV Matters*, 2 (1), 14–16.

Monaghan, G. (1997) *Drugs and the Pharmacist in Drugs and the Community*, ACPO National Drugs Conference, Final Report, London: ACPO.

Monaghan, G. (1998) *Aspects of Policing: Harm Production or Harm Reduction*. In G.V. Stimson, C. Fitch and A. Judd (eds), *Drug Use in London*, London: Centre for Research on Drugs and Health Behaviour, 89.

Monaghan, G. (1999) Legal problems for Arrest referral, *Druglink*, 14 (3), 9.

Monaghan, G. (2000) Kits, bits, balloons and spoons: drug paraphernalia law in Britain. Unpublished briefing paper on section 9a of the Misuse of drugs Act 1971 for the United Kingdom Anti-Drugs Coordinating unit, Metropolitan Police Service, Drugs Directorate, London.

Monaghan, G. (2001) Daily challenges to policing in a democracy: notes from the front line. In S. Einsteinand A. Menachem (eds), *Policing, Security and Democracy: Special Aspects of Democratic Policing*, Texas: Office of International Criminal Justice, 127–76.

Monaghan, G. (2004) *Overcoming the Legal Barriers to Needle Exchange Programmes in Kenya*, Final Report to Futures Group, Europe, Kenya Office.

Monaghan, G. and White, A. (1999) *A Guide to Case Disposal Options for Drug Offenders*, London: Association of Chief Police Officers, Drug Subcommittee.

Newburn, T. and Elliot, J. (1998) *Police Anti-Drugs Strategies, Tackling Drugs Together Three Years On*, Crime Detection and Prevention Series, Paper 9, London: Home Office.

Pearson, G. (1992) Drugs and criminal justice: a harm reduction perspective. In P.A. O'Hare, R. Newcombe, A. Matthews, E.C. Buning and E. Druker (eds), *The Reduction of Drug-Related Harm*, London and New York: Routledge, 17.

Pizzey, R. and Hunt, N. (2008) Distributing foil from needle and syringe programmes (NSPs) to promote transitions from heroin injecting to chasing: an evaluation, *Harm Reduction Journal*, 5 (24), www.harmreductionjournal.com/content/5/1/24, accessed 10/10/2011.

Police Review (2001a) An eye for an eye, *Police Review*, 20 July.

Police Review (2001b) Needle scheme approved for use, *Police Review*, 16 November.

Release (1992) *A Release White Paper on Reform of the Drug Laws*, London: Release.

Riley, D., Sawka, E., Conley, P., Hewitt, D., Mitic, W., Poulin, C., Room, R., Single, E. and Topp, J. (1999) Harm reduction: concepts and practice – a policy discussion paper, *Substance Use and Misuse*, 34 (1), 9–22.

RMPF (2006) *The National Needle and Syringe Exchange Programme, Guidelines for Police*, Kuala Lumpur: Royal Malaysian Police Force.

Roberts, M., Klein, A. and Trace, M. (2004) *Drug Consumption Rooms*, Drug Scope Briefing Paper, Oxford: Drug Scope and the Beckley Foundation.

Skodbo, S., Brown, G., Deacon, S., Cooper, A., Hall, A. and Millar, T. (2007) *The Drug Interventions Programmes (DIP): Addressing Drug Use and Offending through 'Tough Choices'* Research Report 2, Key Implications, London: Home Office.

Spooner, C., McPherson, M., and Hall, W. (2002) The role of police in illicit drug **harm** minimization: an overview. Presentation for 2nd Australasian Conference on Drug Strategy, Perth, 9 May.

Stöver, H. and Schuller K. (1992) AIDS prevention with injecting drug users in the ormer West Germany: a user-friendly approach on a municipal level. In P. O'Hare, R. Newcombe, A. Matthews, E.C. Buning and E. Drucker (eds), *The Reduction of Drug Related Harm*, London: Routledge, 189–90.

Strang, J. and Forston, R (2004) Supervised fixing rooms, supervised injectable maintenance clinics – understanding the difference, *British Medical Journal*, 328 (7431), 102–3.

UNODC (2009) *Responding to the Prevalence of HIV/AIDS and Other Blood-Borne Diseases: Report of the Executive Director*, 21 December 2009 E/CN.7/2010/11.

Victoria Police (2007) *Victoria Police and Harm Minimisation*, Community Information Bulletin, Melbourne: Victoria Police.

Welch, J., Tilzey, A.J., Bertrand, J., Bott, E.C.A. and Banatvala, J.E. (1988) Risk to Metropolitan police officers from exposure to hepatitis B, *British Medical Journal*, 297, 835–6.

Yelin, A.N. (2001) *Drug Use and Harm Reduction: Participation of the Department of the Interior in its Implementation*, Ekaterinburg: Russian Federation.

Zaal, L. (1992) Police policy in Amsterdam. In P. O'Hare, R. Newcombe, A. Matthews, E.C. Buning and E. Drucker (eds), *The Reduction of Drug Related Harm*, London: Routledge, 93.

Chapter 7

HARM REDUCTION IN PRISONS AND OTHER PLACES OF DETENTION

Ralf Jurgens

We don't need to take things away. We need to add things to the system. We need needle exchange programmes. We need the safer tattooing programme. We need to start taking seriously what's going on inside prisons. But before we can do that we have to give prisoners some value. They have it. Let's give it to them, and let's try and convince communities to give it to them. Let's turn this thing around because until we include everybody, we lose.

(James Motherall, 2006)

In an article I wrote in 1997 with Diane Riley, co-editor of this book, we concluded as follows: 'For those of us who have started to feel that we have begun to make headway in introducing harm reduction as an acceptable policy in our countries, the situation in prisons should make us realise how much has still to be done. Reducing drug-related harm in society means reducing such harm in prisons too, and in that regard we have so far had only limited success' (Jürgens and Riley, 1997). Years later, little has changed – prisons[1] continue 'to fail the AIDS test' (Jürgens, 1997). This is despite clear recommendations made by international bodies as early as 1987 (WHO, 1987), stressing the importance of providing adequate care and treatment to prisoners living with HIV and preventing further transmission of HIV in prisons. These recommendations have been repeated and further developed in a large number of documents and declarations since, and have consistently urged countries to introduce harm reduction measures in prisons and to take other necessary measures, including improving prison conditions and providing alternatives to incarceration, particularly for people dependent on drugs (see, e.g., Council of Europe, 1988, paras 14A(i)–14A(viii); United Nations, 1990; WHO, 1993; 2007; Correctional Service Canada, 1994; UNAIDS, 1997; UNODC, WHO and UNAIDS, 2006; 2008; WHO, UNODC and UNAIDS, 2007).

---

[1] Different jurisdictions use different terms to denote places of detention, which hold people who are awaiting trial, who have been convicted or who are subject to other conditions of security, and different terms for the people in these. In this chapter, the term 'prison' has been used for all places of detention and the term 'prisoner' has been used to describe all who are held in such places, including males and females detained in criminal justice and prison facilities during the investigation of a crime; while awaiting trial; after conviction and before sentencing; and after sentencing. The considerations in this chapter also apply to those detained for reasons relating to immigration or refugee status, those detained without charge, and those sentenced to compulsory 'treatment' and 'rehabilitation' centres as they exist in some countries.

Harm Reduction in Substance Use and High-Risk Behaviour: International Policy and Practice, First Edition.
Edited by Richard Pates and Diane Riley.
© 2012 Blackwell Publishing Ltd. Published 2012 by Blackwell Publishing Ltd.

This chapter will briefly review what is known about HIV and drug use in prisons. It will then discuss what is being done to prevent HIV infection and to reduce the harms from drug use in prisons and, importantly, what is not being done. Some priorities for action will be suggested. While its focus will be on HIV and drug use, it will also address other risk behaviours and other related infections, in particular viral hepatitis and tuberculosis.

Two epidemics: HIV and incarceration

HIV hit correctional facilities early and hit them hard. The rates of HIV infection among prisoners in many countries are significantly higher than those in the general population. Coincident with the HIV epidemic, many countries have been experiencing a significant increase in the incarcerated population. Each of the two 'epidemics' – HIV and incarceration – has affected the other.

The HIV epidemic in prisons

Reviews of HIV prevalence in prison have shown that HIV infection is a serious problem, and one that requires immediate action (WHO, UNODC and UNAIDS, 2007). In most countries, HIV prevalence rates in prison are several times higher than in the community outside prisons and this is closely related to the rate of HIV infection among people who inject drugs[2] in the community and the proportion of prisoners convicted for drug-related offences (Macalino et al., 2004). In other countries, particularly in sub-Saharan Africa, elevated HIV prevalence rates in prisons reflect the high HIV prevalence rates in the general population (Jürgens et al., 2009). Everywhere, the prison population consists of individuals with greater risk factors for contracting HIV (and hepatitis C virus and tuberculosis) compared to the general population outside of prisons. Such characteristics include injecting drug use, poverty, alcohol abuse and living in medically underserved and minority communities (Reindollar, 1999).

Studies have shown HIV prevalence ranging from zero in a young male offenders institution in Scotland (Bird et al., 1993) and among prisoners in Iowa, United States, in 1986 (Glass et al., 1988), to 33.6% in an adult prison in Catalonia, Spain (Martin et al., 1990), to over 50% in a female correctional facility in New York City (Vlahov et al., 1991). In Eastern Europe and Central Asia, HIV prevalence is particularly high in prisons in Russia and Ukraine, and in Lithuania, Latvia and Estonia. In Russia, by late 2002 the registered number of people living with HIV/AIDS in the penal system exceeded 36,000, representing approximately 20% of known HIV cases. In Latin America, prevalence among prisoners in Brazil and Argentina was reported to be particularly high, with studies showing rates between 3 and over 20% in Brazil and 4 to 10% in Argentina. Rates

---

[2] Participants in the consultations for a report on greater involvement of people who use (or have used) illegal drugs in the response to HIV and hepatitis C (Canadian HIV/AIDS Legal Network, International HIV/AIDS Alliance, Open Society Institute. *Nothing about Us without US: Greater, Meaningful Involvement of People Who Use Illegal Drugs – A Public Health, Ethical, and Human Rights Imperative*, Toronto, 2008) rejected the terms 'drug user', 'injection drug user' or 'IDU' as stigmatising. They urged the use of a term that, instead of reducing people to the fact that they use or inject drugs, identifies them as people first and foremost, clarifying that drug use or injection drug use is just one aspect of their lives. After a review of documents by organisations of people who use drugs and further consultation, the term 'people who use drugs' was chosen as preferable. Since then, UN organisations and many authors have adopted this term. Other terms, such as 'drug user', 'injection drug user' or 'IDU' are used in the article only when citing from other documents using these terms.

reported from studies in other countries, including Mexico, Honduras, Nicaragua, and Panama are also high (Dolan et al., 2007). In India, one study found that the rates were highest among female prisoners, at 9.5% (Nagaraj et al., 2000). In Africa, a study undertaken in Zambia found a rate of 27% (Simooya et al., 2001). The highest HIV prevalence reported among a national prison population was in South Africa, where estimates put the figure as high as 41.4% (Dolan et al., 2007). Conversely, some countries report zero prevalence; most of these are in North Africa or the Middle East (Dolan et al., 2007).

The HIV epidemic in prisons is not occurring alone: Prevalence of HCV ranges from between 4.8% in an Indian jail (Singh et al., 1999) to 92% in two prisons in northern Spain (Pallas et al., 1999). Tuberculosis (TB) is also common: in some countries, it is 100 times more common in prisons than in the community (Veen, 2007). Sub-standard prison living conditions, including overcrowding, poor ventilation, poor lighting and inadequate nutrition, make the attempts to control the spread of TB in prisons more difficult. TB incidence rates are therefore very high in many prisons. Moreover, prisons in geographically disparate places (from Thailand to New York State to Russia) have reported high levels of drug-resistant TB. TB poses a substantial danger to the health of all prisoners, staff, and the community outside prisons. Prisoners living with HIV are at particular risk. HIV infection is the most important risk factor for the development of TB and TB is the main cause of death among people living with HIV. TB mortality in prisons is elevated (Tuberculosis Coalition for Technical Assistance and International Committee of the Red Cross, 2009).

Within prison populations, certain groups have higher levels of infection. In particular, the prevalence of HIV and HCV infection among women tends to be higher than among men (WHO, UNODC and UNAIDS, 2007).

The epidemic of incarceration

Coincident with the emergence of HIV and later HCV, many countries have been experiencing a significant increase in the size of their incarcerated population. As of 1998, over 8 million people were held in penal institutions throughout the world, either as pretrial detainees or having been convicted and sentenced. As of December 2008, more than 9.8 million people were incarcerated (Walmsley, 2009). If prisoners in 'administrative detention' in China are included the total was over 10.6 million. Between 2005 and 2008, prison populations rose in 71% of countries (Walmsley, 2009). Each year some 30 million people enter and leave prison establishments.

The USA has the highest prison population rate in the world (748 per 100,000 of the national population), followed by Russia (595), Rwanda (593) and a number of countries in Eastern Europe and in the Caribbean. On average, the prison population rate is 145 per 100,000. Certain regions, such as the Caribbean, Eastern Europe, Central Asia and Southern Africa have much higher rates, while others, such as Northern and Western Europe, Western Africa and Oceania (with few exceptions) have much lower average rates (Walmsley, 2009).

In many parts of the world, the growth in prison populations (and often the resulting increase in overcrowding) has been the result of an intensification of the enforcement of drug laws in an effort to limit the supply and use of illegal drugs. As a result of the large number of prisoners convicted for drug-related offences, the demographic and epidemiological characteristics of the incarcerated population are significantly different today in many countries from what they were in the 1990s. Consistent with the nature of the crimes for which they are convicted, incarcerated individuals have a high prevalence of drug dependence, mental illness and infectious diseases (Boutwell and Rich, 2004).

By choosing mass imprisonment as the main response to the use of drugs, countries have created a de facto policy of incarcerating more and more individuals with HIV infection (US National Commission on AIDS, 1991). Many prisoners serve short sentences and recidivism to prison is common. Consequently, HIV-positive people (and at-risk individuals) move frequently between prisons and their home communities. For example, in the Russian Federation, each year 300,000 prisoners, many of whom living with HIV, viral hepatitis, and/or TB, are released from prisons (*Prison Healthcare News*, 2003). Most prisoners will return to their home communities within a few years. The high degree of mobility between prison and community means that communicable diseases and related illnesses transmitted or exacerbated in prison do not remain there. When people living with HIV and HCV (and/or TB) are released from incarceration, prison health issues necessarily become community health issues.

An important – and often neglected – component of the epidemic of incarceration is the excessive use and arbitrary application of pretrial detention, which has wide ranging negative consequences for detainees, detainees' families and the larger community and, in particular, for the health of pretrial detainees (Csete, 2010; Jürgens and Tomasini-Joshi, 2010). Approximately every third incarcerated person in the world today is a pretrial detainee (Schönteich, 2008). However, in many countries around the world, a majority of people incarcerated are awaiting trial or the finalisation of their trial, often for many years. Many of these people will be acquitted at the end of their trials, and some will never be tried as prosecutors and judges realise that the evidence against them is too weak to justify a trial. A significant number of those who are convicted are given a non-custodial sentence such as a fine or probation.

Throughout their detention, most pretrial detainees never see a lawyer, paralegal or legal adviser and often lack information on their basic rights. When they eventually reach a courtroom – without representation and likely despondent due to months of mistreatment – the odds are stacked against them. The longer an accused is detained before trial, the more likely he or she will be found guilty (Tomasini-Joshi and Schönteich, 2010).

Risk behaviours in prisons

Injecting drug use

In many countries, a substantial proportion of prisoners are drug dependent. Estimates of drug use or dependence in male prisoners (eight studies, n = 4,293) range from 10.0% to 48%; in female prisoners (six studies, n = 3,270), from 30.3% to 60.4% (Fazel, Bains and Doll, 2006). For people who inject drugs, imprisonment is a common event, with studies from a large number of countries reporting that between 56% and 90% of people who inject drugs had been imprisoned at some stage (Ball et al., 1995; Normand et al., 1995; Beyrer et al., 2003). Multiple prison sentences are more common for prisoners who inject drugs than for other prisoners (Gore et al., 1995).

Some people who use drugs prior to imprisonment discontinue their drug use while in prison while many carry on using on the inside, often with reduced frequency and amounts (Shewan et al., 1994), but sometimes maintaining the same level of use (Plourde and Brochu, 2002; Swann and James, 1998). Prison is also a place where drug use is initiated, often as a means to release tension and to cope with being in an overcrowded and often violent environment (Taylor et al., 1995; Hughes and Huby, 2000).

Injecting drug use in prison is of particular concern given the potential for transmission of HIV and HCV. Those who inject drugs in prisons often share needles and syringes and other injecting equipment, which is a very efficient way of transmitting both viruses. A large number of studies from countries around the world report high levels of injecting drug use, including among female prisoners (DiCenso et al., 2003; Elwood Martin et al., 2005). Although more research has been carried out on injecting drug use in prisons in high-income countries, studies from low and middle income countries have found similar results. In Iran, for example, about 10% of prisoners are believed to inject drugs while incarcerated, and more than 95% of them are reported to share needles (Rowhani-Rahbar et al., 2004). Injecting drug use has also been documented in prisons in countries in Eastern Europe and Central Asia (Russia: Frost and Tchertkov, 2002; Drobniewski et al., 2005; Ukraine: Zhivago, 2005; Armenia: Weilandt et al., 2005; Tajikistan: Godinho, 2005), and in Latin America (Cravioto et al., 2003) and sub-Saharan Africa (Adjei et al., 2006).

Consensual and non-consensual sexual activity

It is difficult to obtain reliable data on the prevalence of sexual activities in prisons because of the many methodological, logistical and ethical challenges of undertaking such a study. Sex – with the exception of authorised conjugal visits – violates prison regulations. Many prisoners decline to participate in studies because they claim not to have engaged in any high-risk behaviour (Pearson, 1995). Prisoners who do participate may be too embarrassed to admit to engaging in same-sex sexual activity and they may fear punitive measures.

Despite these challenges, studies undertaken in a large number of countries show that consensual and non-consensual sex does occur in prisons. Estimates of the proportion of prisoners who engage in consensual same-sex sexual activity in prison vary widely, with some studies reporting relatively low rates of 1 to 2% (Rotily et al., 2001; Strang et al., 1998), while other studies report rates between 4 and 10% (Frost and Tchertkov, 2002; Simooya and Sanjobo, 2002; Marins et al., 2000; Correctional Service Canada, 1996) or higher (Albov and Issaev, 1994), particularly among female prisoners (DiCenso et al., 2003; Butler and Milner, 2001). Some same-sex sexual activity occurs as a consequence of sexual orientation but most men who have sex in prisons do not identify themselves as homosexuals and may not have experienced same-sex sex prior to their incarceration (Zachariah et al., 2002).

Distinguishing coerced sex from consensual sex in prison can be difficult: Prisoner sexual violence is a complex continuum that includes a whole host of sexually coercive behaviours, including sexual harassment, sexual extortion and sexual assault. It can involve prisoners and/or staff as perpetrators (WHO, UNODC and UNAIDS, 2007). Sexual violence occurs in prisons around the world (Human Rights Watch, 2001; Observatoire international des prisons, 1996). Overtly violent rapes are only the most visible and dramatic form of sexual abuse behind bars. Many victims of sexual violence in prison may have never been explicitly threatened, but they have nonetheless engaged in sexual acts against their will, believing they had no choice (Human Rights Watch, 2001).

In prisons, with the exception of countries in which injecting drug use is rare, sexual activity is considered to be a less significant risk factor for HIV transmission than sharing of injecting equipment. Nevertheless, sexual activities can place prisoners at risk of contracting HIV and other STIs. Violent forms of unprotected anal or vaginal intercourse, including rape, carry the highest risk of HIV transmission (Schoub, 1995).

Other risk factors

Additional risk factors for blood-borne infections include the sharing or reuse of tattooing and body piercing equipments, sharing of razors for shaving, blood sharing/'brotherhood' rituals and the improper sterilisation or reuse of medical or dental instruments.

Factors related to the prison infrastructure and prison management contribute indirectly to vulnerability to HIV and other infections. They include overcrowding, violence, gang activities, lack of protection for vulnerable or young prisoners, prison staff that lack training or may be corrupt, and poor medical and social services.

HIV transmission resulting from risk behaviours in prisons

The prevalence of risk behaviours, coupled with the lack of access to prevention measures in many prisons, can result in frighteningly quick spread of HIV. There were early indications that extensive HIV transmission could occur in prisons. In Thailand, the first epidemic outbreak of HIV in the country likely began among people who inject drugs in the Bangkok prison system in 1988 (Dolan et al., 2003). Since then, a large number of studies from countries in many regions of the world have reported HIV and/or HCV seroconversion within prisons or shown that a history of imprisonment is associated with prevalent and incident HIV and/or HCV and/or hepatitis B virus (HBV) infection among people who inject drugs (WHO, UNODC and UNAIDS, 2007).

HIV infection has been significantly associated with a history of imprisonment in countries in western and southern Europe (including among female prisoners: Richardson et al., 1993; Koulierakis et al., 2000; Davies et al., 1995; Granados et al., 1990; Martin et al., 1998; Estebanez et al., 2000), but also in Russia (Heimer et al., 2005), Canada (Calzavara et al., 2005), Brazil (Hacker et al., 2005), Iran (Zamani et al., 2005) and Thailand (Choopanya et al., 1991). Using non-sterile injecting equipment in prison was found to be the most important independent determinant of HIV infection in a number of studies (WHO, UNODC and UNAIDS, 2007).

The strongest evidence of extensive HIV transmission through injecting drug use in prison has emerged from documented outbreaks in Scotland (Taylor and Goldberg, 1996), Australia (Dolan et al., 1994), Russia (Bobrik et al., 2005) and Lithuania (MacDonald, 2005). Outbreaks of HIV have also been reported from other countries (Dolan et al., 2004).

Well-documented evidence exists for STI intra-prison transmission through sexual contacts among prisoners (Bobrik et al., 2005; Zachariah et al., 2002). Evidence also exists of HIV intra-prison transmission through sexual contacts among prisoners. In one United States study of HIV transmission in prison, sex between men accounted for the largest proportion of prisoners who contracted HIV inside prison (Krebs and Simmons, 2002). HCV infection by sharing of injecting equipment in prison has been reported in Australia and Germany (Haber et al., 1999; O'Sullivan et al., 2003; Keppler and Stöver, 1999).

International human rights and the responsibility of prison systems

By its very nature, imprisonment involves the loss of the right to liberty, but prisoners retain their other rights and privileges except those necessarily removed or restricted by the fact of their incarceration. In particular, prisoners, as every other person, have a right to the highest attainable level of physical and mental health: the state's duty with respect to health does not end at the gates of prisons (Jürgens and Betteridge, 2005).

The failure to provide prisoners with access to essential HIV prevention measures and to treatment equivalent to that available outside is a violation of prisoners' right to health in international law. Moreover, it is inconsistent with international instruments that deal with rights of prisoners, prison health services and HIV/AIDS in prisons, including the United Nations' *Basic Principles for the Treatment of Prisoners* (1990), the World Health Organization's *WHO Guidelines on HIV Infection and AIDS in Prisons* (WHO, 1993), and the International Guidelines on HIV/AIDS and Human Rights (1997).

According to the *WHO Guidelines*, '[a]ll prisoners have the right to receive healthcare, including preventive measures, equivalent to that available in the community without discrimination, in particular with respect to their legal status or nationality' (WHO, 1993). The *International Guidelines on HIV/AIDS and Human Rights* identify the following specific action in relation to prisons:

> Prison authorities should take all necessary measures, including adequate staffing, effective surveillance and appropriate disciplinary measures, to protect prisoners from rape, sexual violence and coercion. Prison authorities should also provide prisoners (and prison staff, as appropriate), with access to HIV-related prevention information, education, voluntary testing and counselling, means of prevention (condoms, bleach and clean injection equipment), treatment and care and voluntary participation in HIV-related clinical trials, as well as ensure confidentiality, and should prohibit mandatory testing, segregation and denial of access to prison facilities, privileges and release programmes for HIV-positive prisoners. Compassionate early release of prisoners living with AIDS should be considered.
>
> (International Guidelines on HIV/AIDS and Human Rights, 1997)

Responding to HIV and other infections in prisons: a human rights and public health imperative

Four elements are key to responding to HIV and other infections such as hepatitis B and C and TB in prisons:

- introducing comprehensive harm reduction and other prevention measures;
- providing health services in prisons that are equivalent to those available in the community, including provision of antiretroviral treatment for HIV, and ensuring continuity of care between prisons and the community;
- improving prison conditions; and
- reducing prison populations.

Providing comprehensive harm reduction and other prevention measures

Needle and syringe programmes (NSPs)

The first prison NSP was established in Switzerland in 1992. Since then, NSPs have been introduced in over 60 prisons in 11 countries in Europe and Central Asia (Jürgens et al., 2010). In some countries, only a few prisons have NSPs. However, in Kyrgyzstan and Spain, NSPs have been rapidly scaled up and operate in a large number of prisons.

Germany remains the only country in which prison NSPs have been closed. At the end of 2000, NSPs had been successfully introduced in seven prisons, and other prisons were considering implementing them. However, since that time six of the programmes were closed as a result of political decisions by the newly elected conservative state governments, without consultation with prison staff. Since the programmes closed, prisoners have gone back to sharing injecting equipment and to hiding it, increasing the likelihood of transmission of HIV and HCV (Lines et al., 2004). Staff have been among the most vocal critics of the governments' decision to close down the programmes, and have lobbied the governments to reinstate the programmes (2004).

In most countries with prison NSP, implementation has not required changes to laws or regulations in order to allow it. Across the 11 countries, various models for the distribution of sterile injecting equipment have been used, including anonymous syringe dispensing machines, hand-to-hand distribution by prison health staff and/or NGO workers and distribution by prisoners trained as peer outreach workers (Lines et al., 2006).

Systematic evaluations of the effects of NSPs on HIV-related risk behaviours and of their overall effectiveness in prisons have been undertaken in 10 projects. These evaluations and other reports demonstrate that NSPs are feasible in a wide range of prison settings, including in men's and women's prisons, prisons of all security levels and small and large prisons. Providing sterile needles and syringes is readily accepted by people who inject in prisons and contributes to a significant reduction of syringe sharing over time. It also appears to be effective in reducing resulting HIV infections (Jürgens et al., 2009). At the same time, there is no evidence to suggest that prison-based NSPs have serious, unintended negative consequences. In particular, they do not lead to increased drug use or injecting, nor are they used as weapons (2009). Evaluations have found that NSPs in prisons actually facilitate referral of people who use drugs to drug dependence treatment programmes (Menoyo et al., 2000; Stöver, 2000).

Studies have shown that important factors in the success of prison NSPs include easy and confidential access to the service, providing the right type of syringes and building trust with the prisoners accessing the programme (WHO, UNODC and UNAIDS, 2007). For example, in Moldova, only a small number of prisoners accessed the NSP when it was located within the healthcare section of the prison. It was only when prisoners could obtain sterile injecting equipment from fellow prisoners, trained to provide harm reduction services, that the amount of equipment distributed increased significantly (Hoover and Jürgens, 2009).

Ultimately, since most prisoners leave prison at some point to return to their community, implementing NSPs in prisons will benefit not only prisoners and prison staff, but also society in general. Therefore, experts and UN agencies recommend that NSPs be introduced in prisons and other places of detention. Following an exhaustive review of the international evidence, WHO, UNODC and UNAIDS in 2007 recommended that prison authorities in countries experiencing or threatened by an epidemic of HIV infections among IDUs should introduce and scale up NSPs *urgently* [emphasis added]'(WHO, UNODC and UNAIDS, 2007).

Bleach programmes

Already in 1991, 16 of 52 prison systems surveyed made them available, including in Africa and Central America (Harding and Schaller, 1992). Today, bleach or other disinfectants are available in many more prison systems, including in Australia, Canada, Indonesia, Iran and some systems in Eastern Europe and Central Asia (WHO, UNODC and UNAIDS, 2007).

Evaluations of bleach programmes in prisons have shown that distribution of bleach or other disinfectants is feasible and does not compromise security. However, WHO has concluded that the 'evidence supporting the effectiveness of bleach in decontamination of injecting equipment and other forms of disinfection is weak' (WHO, 2004). While the efficacy of bleach as a disinfectant for inactivating HIV has been shown in laboratory studies, field studies have cast considerable doubt on the likelihood that these measures could ever be effective in operational conditions (2004). Moreover, studies assessing the effect of bleach on HCV prevalence did not find a significant effect of bleach on HCV seroconversion (Kapadia et al., 2002; Hagan et al., 2001). For these reasons, bleach programmes are regarded as a second-line strategy to NSPs. WHO, UNODC and UNAIDS (2007) have recommended that bleach programmes be made available in prisons where 'authorities continue to oppose the introduction of NSPs despite evidence of their effectiveness, and to complement NSPs'.

Opioid substitution therapy and other drug dependence treatment

The first experimental OST programme in prison, offering methadone pre-release to prisoners in New York City, was initiated in 1968 (Dole et al., 1969). The early literature noted that, in addition to Rikers Island in New York (Joseph et al., 1989), over the next twenty years such programmes either existed or had existed at some point at a prison in California (Contra Costa Country), in Rotterdam in the Netherlands, at Wolds Remand Prison in the United Kingdom (Daines et al., 1992) and in Denmark and Sweden (Gorta, 1992).

In New South Wales, Australia, a pilot pre-release methadone programme started in 1986. It was later expanded so that the pre-release programme became just one component of a larger prison methadone maintenance therapy (MMT) programme (Hall et al., 1993). Initially, the programme focused on breaking the cycle of criminal activity associated with drug use. However, as early as 1987, it became the first prison MMT programme to move towards a HIV prevention strategy and to include the reduction of injecting heroin use and HIV and hepatitis B transmission among its objectives (1993).

Since the early 1990s, and mostly in response to raising HIV rates among people who inject drugs in the community and in prison, there has been a marked increase in the number of prison systems providing OST to prisoners. Today, prison systems in nearly 40 countries offer OST to prisoners (Jürgens et al., 2010). In Spain, according to 2009 data, 12% of all prisoners received MMT (correspondence, 2010). However, in many other prison systems, OST programmes remain small and benefit only a small number of prisoners in need (WHO, UNODC and UNAIDS, 2007). Reflecting the situation in the community, most prison systems make OST available in the form of MMT. Buprenorphine maintenance treatment is available only in a small number of systems (Black et al., 2004; Stöver et al., 2004; 2006).

Generally, drug-free treatment approaches continue to dominate interventions in prisons in most countries (Zurhold et al., 2004). OST remains controversial in many prison systems, even in countries where it is accepted as an effective intervention for opioid dependence in the community outside of prisons. Prison administrators have often not been receptive to providing OST, due to philosophical opposition to this type of treatment and concerns about whether the provision of such therapy will lead to diversion of medication, violence and/or security breaches (Magura et al., 1993).

A recent comprehensive review showed that OST, in particular with MMT, is feasible in a wide range of prison settings (WHO, UNODC and UNAIDS, 2007b). As is the case with OST programmes outside prisons, those inside prisons are effective in reducing the frequency of injecting drug use and associated sharing of injecting equipment, if a sufficient dosage is provided (more than 60 mg per day) and treatment is provided for longer periods of time (more than six months), or even for the duration of incarceration (Dolan et al., 2005).

A four-year follow-up study to a randomised controlled trial of MMT versus waiting list control in prison examined the longer-term impact of MMT on mortality, re-incarceration and HCV and HIV seroconversion. Retention in treatment was associated with reduced HCV infection, while short MMT episodes (less than 5 months) were significantly associated with greater risk of HCV (2005).

In addition, evaluations of prison-based MMT found other benefits, both for the health of prisoners participating in the programmes, and for prison systems and the community. For example, re-incarceration is less likely among prisoners who receive adequate OST, and OST has been shown to have a positive effect on institutional behaviour by reducing drug-seeking behaviour and thus improving prison safety (Magura et al., 1993; Johnson et al., 2001; Wale and Gorta, 1987; Hume and Gorta, 1988; Herzog et al., 1993). While prison administrations have often initially raised concerns about security, violent behaviour, and diversion of methadone, these problems have not emerged or have been addressed successfully where OST programmes have been implemented (WHO, UNODC and UNAIDS, 2007b).

WHO, UNODC and UNAIDS have recommended that 'prison authorities in countries in which OST is available in the community should introduce OST programmes urgently and expand implementation to scale as soon as possible' (ibid).

In contrast to OST, which has become increasingly available in many prison systems at least in part because of its potential to reduce injecting drug use and the resulting risk of spread of infection, other forms of drug dependence treatment have not usually been introduced in prison with HIV prevention as one of their objectives. Therefore, there is little data on their effectiveness as an HIV prevention strategy (Jürgens et al., 2009).

Nevertheless, good quality, appropriate and accessible treatment has the potential of improving prison security, as well as the health and social functioning of prisoners, and might reduce reoffending. Studies have demonstrated the importance of providing ongoing treatment and support and of meeting the individual needs of prisoners (WHO, UNODC and UNAIDS, 2007b). Therefore, WHO, UNODC and UNAIDS have recommended that, in addition to providing OST, prison authorities also provide a range of other drug dependence treatment options for prisoners with problematic drug use, in particular for other substances such as amphetamine type stimulants. Because data on the effectiveness of these other forms of treatment as an HIV prevention strategy are lacking, they recommended that evaluations of their effectiveness in terms of reducing drug injecting and needle sharing should be undertaken (WHO, UNODC and UNAIDS, 2007b).

In some countries, including Cambodia, China, Indonesia, Laos, Malaysia, Myanmar, Thailand and Vietnam, people who use drugs can face coerced 'treatment' and 'rehabilitation' in compulsory drug detention centres, which results in many human rights abuses (Jürgens et al., 2010). In many of these centres the services provided are of poor quality and do not accord with either human rights or scientific principles. Treatment in these facilities takes the form of sanctions rather than therapy, and relapse rates are very high (2010). These centres should be closed and replaced with drug treatment that works.

Efforts to reduce drug supply in prisons

A broad range of search and seizure techniques and procedures are being used by prison systems in an attempt to reduce the availability of drugs in prisons. These supply reduction measures include random cell searches, staff and visitor entry/exit screening and searches, drug detection dogs and other drug detection technologies, perimeter security measures, and urinalysis programmes, often referred to as 'mandatory drug testing programmes' or 'MDT' (Weekes et al., 2004; Hughes, 2003).

Many prison systems, particularly in high income countries, have placed considerable and growing emphasis on these measures to reduce the supply of drugs. In particular, urinalysis has been adopted as policy in several prison systems. In these systems, and others, the goal is to reduce the use of and demand for drugs in prison. Urinalysis, combined with self-report surveys of prisoners, is also used to obtain an estimate of the extent of drug use (Her Majesty's Government, 1995) as well as to target programmes and treatment services (MacPherson, 2004).

Many prison systems make substantial investments in drug supply reduction measures, but there is no evidence that these measures may lead to reduced HIV risk. Indeed, mandatory drug testing programmes may increase, rather than decrease, prisoners' risk of HIV infection. There is evidence that implementing such programmes may contribute to reducing the demand for, and use of, cannabis in prisons. However, such programmes seem to have little effect on the use of opiates. In fact, there is some evidence that a small number of people switch to injectable drugs to avoid detection of cannabis use through drug testing. Given that smoking cannabis presents no risk of HIV transmission while injecting opiates presents a significant risk of HIV and other health risks, the evidence that some prisoners switch from cannabis use to use of more harmful drugs by injecting is worrisome.

Therefore, WHO, UNODC and UNAIDS have recommended that 'improving the documentation and evaluation of supply reduction measures should be a priority for prison systems making substantial investments in such measures'. They further recommended that 'prison systems with MDT programmes should reconsider whether to include urinalysis testing for cannabis. At a minimum, they should make clear distinctions in punitive terms between those testing positive to cannabis and opiates' (WHO, UNODC and UNAIDS, 2007b).

Other prevention measures

The harm reduction measures described above should be implemented in conjunction with the following other elements of a comprehensive prison HIV prevention programme: HIV education; voluntary and confidential HIV testing and counselling; condom provision; and prevention of rape, sexual violence and coercion (WHO, UNODC and UNAIDS, 2007). These are described in more detail in table 7.1.

Providing Equivalent Health Services in Prisons to Those in the Community, Including Provision of Antiretroviral Treatment for HIV

In addition to providing harm reduction measures and the other elements of comprehensive HIV prevention programmes, prison systems have a responsibility to provide prisoners with treatment, care and support equivalent to that available to other members of the community.

Effective HIV treatment in prison settings

The right to medical care in prisons includes the provision of antiretroviral therapy (ART) in the context of comprehensive HIV care (WHO, UNODC and UNAIDS, 2007d). The advent of combination ART has significantly decreased mortality due to HIV infection and AIDS in countries around the world where ART has become accessible. There has been a parallel decrease in the mortality rate among incarcerated individuals in prison systems in those countries.

Providing access to ART for those in need in prisons is a challenge, but it is necessary, feasible and even more important now that there is evidence that ART not only benefits individuals but also plays a key role in decreasing HIV transmission (Donnell et al., 2010; Editorial, 2011).

Studies have documented that, when provided with care and access to medications, prisoners respond well to antiretroviral treatment (Bellin et al., 1999). As ART is increasingly becoming available in developing countries and countries in transition, and as countries are moving towards the goal of universal access to HIV prevention, treatment, care and support, it is critical to ensure that treatment is also available to all prisoners who need it. Ensuring continuity of care from the community to the prison and back to the community, as well as continuity of care within the prison system, is a fundamental component of successful treatment scale-up efforts. Treatment discontinuation for short or long periods of time may happen upon arrest and detention in police cells, within the prison system when prisoners are transferred to other facilities or have to appear in court, and upon release. Each of these situations should be addressed and mechanisms established to ensure

Table 7.1 Elements of a comprehensive programme to prevent HIV transmission in prisons

According to UN guidance, governments should urgently adopt or expand comprehensive, evidence-based programmes for preventing HIV transmission in prisons. In addition to the interventions to reduce the risk of HIV transmission through injecting drug use described in more detail above, the following programmes have been recommended (see, e.g., WHO, UNODC and UNAIDS, 2007)

HIV education
• Well-designed information and education programmes can improve prisoners' knowledge about HIV (Vaz et al., 1996; Braithwaite et al., 1996; Dolan et al., 2004; Lurigio et al., 1992; Connolly, 1989; Dolan and Rouen, 2003).
• A few evaluations have indicated self-reported behavioural change (particularly upon release) as a result of prison-based educational initiatives (Grinstead et al., 1999; Grinstead et al., 2001). Education programmes are more likely to be effective if developed and delivered by peers (Grinstead et al., 1999; Van Meter, 1996).
• The effectiveness of educational efforts in influencing prisoners' behaviour and in reducing HIV transmission among prisoners remains largely unknown (Braithwaite et al., 1996; Lurigio et al., 1992; Connolly, 1989).
• Education and counseling are not of much use to prisoners if, while they are in prison, they do not have the means (such as condoms or sterile injecting equipment) to act on the information provided (Dolan et al., 2004; Simooya and Sanjobo, 2001).

HIV testing and counselling
• HIV testing and counselling programmes in prison reach a clientele at high risk of HIV infection that often has not accessed such services on the outside (Beauchemin and Labadie, 1997; Sabin et al., 2001), offering important prevention and care opportunities (Dean-Gator and Fleming, 1999).
• Voluntary HIV counselling and testing programmes can achieve high rates of acceptance among prisoners, but documented rates vary considerably, ranging from 39% to 83% (Hoxie et al., 1990; Cotton-Oldenburg et al., 1999; Behrendt et al., 1994).
• Where testing and counselling is not offered (and recommended) to all prisoners, 'the need for prisoners to actively request the test when dealing with the myriad issues involved in prison life' may lead to lower acceptance rates (Basu et al., 2005). Testing acceptance rates are particularly low where testing is done in the view of other prisoners, with inadequate counselling services and confidentiality measures, and with inadequate follow-up care, treatment and support for those testing HIV-positive (2005).
• Prison systems that have implemented routine 'opt-out' testing have reported high HIV testing rates of more than 90% (Ramratnam et al., 1997; Grinstead et al., 2003).
• When health-care providers state that they will proceed with testing unless prisoners say no, prisoners sometimes feel they cannot refuse (or 'opt-out' of) testing. Prisoners often consider this virtually synonymous with mandatory or compulsory testing (Basu et al., 2005; Grinstead et al., 2003; UNODC and WHO, 2009; Walker et al., 2004).
• To minimise the risk of misperception, staff in prison settings that routinely offer HIV testing upon entry should assure incarcerated people that testing is voluntary and provide adequate, safe opportunities for individuals to refuse testing (UNODC and WHO, 2009).
• Mandatory HIV testing is unethical (UNODC and WHO, 2009; Jürgens and Betteridge, 2005; Canadian HIV/AIDS Legal Network, 2006) and there is evidence suggesting that mandatory testing and segregation of HIV-positive prisoners is costly, inefficient (Centers for Disease Control and Prevention, 2006), and can have negative health consequences for segregated prisoners (Basu et al., 2005; Centers for Disease Control and Prevention, 1999; Centers for Disease Control and Prevention, 2000; Spaulding et al., 2002; Patterson et al., 2000).

Condom provision
• Provision of condoms is feasible in a wide range of prison settings (Lowe, 1998; Correctional Service Canada, 1999; Dolan et al., 2004; May and Williams, 2002; Yap et al., 2007).

- No prison system allowing condoms has reversed its policy, and none has reported security problems or any other major negative consequences (WHO, UNODC and UNAIDS, 2007).
- Condom access is unobtrusive to the prison routine (May and Williams, 2002), represents no threat to security or operations (Dolan et al., 2004; Yap et al., 2007), does not lead to an increase in sexual activity or drug use (May and Williams, 2002; Yap et al., 2007), and is accepted by most prisoners and prison staff once it is introduced (Correctional Service Canada, 1999; Dolan et al., 2004; May and Williams, 2002).
- Condoms need to be easily accessible in various locations in the prison, so that prisoners do not have to ask for them and can pick them up without being seen by staff or fellow prisoners (Correctional Service Canada, 1999; Calzavara et al., 1996; Jürgens, 1996).
- Studies have not determined whether infections have been prevented thanks to provision of condoms in prisons, but there is evidence that prisoners use condoms to prevent infection during sexual activity when condoms are accessible in prison. It can therefore be considered likely that infections have been prevented (Dolan et al., 2004; May and Williams, 2002).
- Prevention of rape, sexual violence and coercion
- Rape and other forms of sexual violence occur in prisons around the world (WHO, UNODC and UNAIDS, 2007c), posing a serious threat to the health of prisoners, including the risk of HIV and other sexually transmitted infections (2007c).
- Some prison systems continue to deny the existence of the problem (O'Donnell, 2004), but others have shown that it is possible to fundamentally change the way in which sexual violence is addressed in prison, within a relatively short timeframe (Stop Prisoner Rape, 2005; Dumond, 2006). These systems typically adopt methods to document incidents of prisoner sexual violence, undertake preventive measure, provide staff training, undertake investigation and response efforts, and provide services to victims, including access to post-exposure prophylaxis (Zweig et al., 2006).
- To date little if any research has been undertaken to assess which strategies are most effective. In addition to evaluating the various components of policies and programmes to address sexual violence, it has been recommended that prison systems allow external, independent researchers to carry out, at regular intervals, a review of the incidence of rape and other forms of sexual violence in prisons (WHO, UNODC and UNAIDS, 2007c).

uninterrupted ART (Springer et al., 2004; Pontali, 2005). Policies and guidelines should be developed specifying that people with HIV or AIDS are allowed to keep their HIV medication upon them, or are to be provided with their medication, upon arrest and incarceration and at any time they are transferred within the system or to court hearings. Police and prison staff need to be educated about the importance of continuity of treatment. Particular attention should be devoted to discharge planning and linkage to community aftercare.

Prison healthcare: the need for increased funding and a new model

Health services in prison settings often work in complete isolation from the general healthcare system, hampering the quality of healthcare and making continuity of care a challenge. HIV/AIDS, HCV and TB have exacerbated existing problems in healthcare provision in prisons. Prison healthcare budgets must reflect the growing needs of the prison population. Prison healthcare should be recognised as an integral part of the public health sector, and evolve from its present reactive 'sick call' model into a proactive system that emphasises early disease detection and treatment, health promotion, and disease prevention. There is a need for a public health infrastructure to fulfil the core functions of public health services within prisons, i.e., to assess the health status of prisoners; have an effective surveillance system for infectious and chronic diseases; undertake health promotion efforts; have coordinated actions to prevent diseases and injuries; protect the health of prisoners; and evaluate the effectiveness, accessibility, and quality of health services (Correctional Service Canada, 2004). Addressing prisoners' health needs will contribute to the prisoner's rehabilitation and successful reintegration into the community (UNODC, WHO and UNAIDS, 2008).

Transferring control of prison health and ensuring prisoners are included in HIV programming

In the longer term, transferring control of prison health to public health authorities could have a positive impact on HIV care in prison (2008). In the vast majority of prison systems in the world, healthcare is provided by the same ministry or department responsible for prison administration, not by the ministry or department responsible for healthcare. Prisons were not designed and are generally not equipped to deal with prisoners infected with chronic, potentially fatal diseases such as AIDS, HCV and TB. They do not have adequate staffing levels, adequate staff training or adequate equipment to meet the health needs of prisoners suffering from these diseases. The authority and influence of prison authorities may compromise healthcare professionals' ethical obligations. Trust and confidence are crucial to an effective, ethical relationship between patient and healthcare provider. When health services for prisoners are 'captured' within, or subservient to, the prison administration it is unlikely that prisoners will trust or have confidence in the healthcare providers. This lack of trust contributes to sub-standard healthcare for prisoners (2008).

Experience in a range of prison systems has shown that healthcare in prisons can be delivered more effectively by public health authorities than by prison management. This has the advantage of strengthening the link between health in the community and health in prisons (Pontali, 2005; Editorial, 1991; UNAIDS, 1997). Some countries. like Norway, have already introduced such a change in prison health administration. In France, where prison health was transferred to the Ministry of Health in 1994, a positive impact was soon evident (UNAIDS, 1997).

At a minimum prison systems need to become an integral part of national (and international) efforts to provide access to comprehensive HIV prevention, treatment, care and support. Currently, sustainable HIV prison programmes, integrated into countries' general HIV programmes (and in their requests for funding from international sources) or at least linked to them, remain rare (table 7.2).

Special attention should be given to women prisoners

As women prisoners are fewer than males, the health services provided for women are sometimes minimal or second-rate. With the advent of HIV/AIDS, a new problem has arisen for women prisoners. Women prisoners need the same preventive measures and the same level of care, treatment and support as male prisoners. Pregnant prisoners need access to the full range of prevention of mother-to-child transmission interventions. In addition, there is a need for initiatives that acknowledge that the problems encountered by women in the correctional environment often reflect, and are augmented by, their vulnerability and the abuse many of them have suffered outside prison. The task of protecting women prisoners from HIV transmission and of providing those living with HIV with care, treatment and support, therefore presents different – and sometimes greater – challenges than that of dealing with HIV infection in male prisoners (UNODC and UNAIDS, 2008).

Table 7.2 Ensuring that prisoners are included in national scale-up efforts

At the *international level*, initiatives to support scale-up efforts should include a prison- and pre-trial detention-specific component and ensure that:
• Prison systems (and pre-trial detention facilities) are included in technical assistance missions.
• Data about access to HIV prevention, treatment, care and support, and coverage in prisons is collected and published.
• Best practice models are developed and disseminated.
• The public health and human rights implications of inadequate efforts in prisons are brought to the attention of policy-makers.

At the *country level*:
• Prison departments (and departments responsible for pre-trial detention facilities) should have a place within the national HIV coordinating committees and the country coordinating mechanisms that develop and submit grant proposals to the Global Fund to Fight AIDS, tuberculosis and malaria.
• Prison issues should be part of the agreed HIV/AIDS action framework and monitoring and evaluation system.
• Prison departments and departments responsible for pre-trial detention facilities should be involved in all aspects of scale-up of prevention and treatment, care and support, from funding applications (to ensure that funds are specifically earmarked for prisons), to development, implementation, and monitoring and evaluation of roll-out plans.
• The ministry responsible for health and the ministry (or ministries) responsible for the prison system and pre-trial detention facilities should collaborate closely, recognising that prison health is public health; alternatively, governments could assign responsibility for health care in prisons and pre-trial detention facilities to the same ministries, departments and agencies that provide health care to people in the community.

At the *regional and local level*, prisons and pre-trial detention facilities should
• form partnerships with health clinics, hospitals, universities and NGOs, including people living with HIV organisations, to provide services for prisoners; and
• develop integrated rather than parallel care and treatment programmes.

Undertaking broader prison reform

Addressing HIV and HCV in prisons effectively cannot be separated from wider questions of human rights and prison reform.

Overcrowding, violence, inadequate natural lighting and ventilation, and lack of protection from extreme climatic conditions are common in many prisons in many regions of the world. When these conditions are combined with inadequate means for personal hygiene, inadequate nutrition, poor access to clean drinking water, and inadequate health services, the vulnerability of prisoners to HIV infection and other infectious diseases is increased, as is related morbidity and mortality. Sub-standard conditions can also complicate or undermine the implementation of effective responses to health issues by prison staff. Therefore, action to prevent the spread of infections in prisons and to provide health services to prisoners living with HIV and HCV is integral to – and enhanced by – broader efforts to improve prison conditions. This is why efforts to stop the transmission of HIV in prisons must start with making HIV prevention measures available, but should include reforms aimed at addressing these underlying conditions.

In particular, action to reduce the size of prison populations and prison overcrowding should accompany – and be seen as an integral component of – a comprehensive strategy to prevent HIV and HCV transmission in prisons, to improve prison healthcare, and to improve prison conditions. According to UN agencies, this should include legislative and policy reforms aimed at reducing the criminalisation of non-violent drug offences and significantly reducing the use of incarceration for non-violent users of illicit drugs and developing alternatives to prison and non-custodial diversions for people convicted of offences related to drug use, so as to significantly reduce the number of people who use drugs sent to prison, the overall prison population and levels of prison overcrowding (WHO, 1987; WHO, UNODC and UNAIDS, 2007; UNODC, WHO and UNAIDS, 2008).

Action to reduce the excessive use of pretrial detention – the arrest and incarceration of people who have not yet been convicted of any crime – is also essential. Pretrial detainees account for over a third of all the people in jails and prisons around the world, and are frequently held in overcrowded, substandard conditions without medical treatment, or any measures for infection control. Incarceration exposes detainees to a range of health risks, including interruption of critically important medications to treat HIV, TB, or drug dependence and exposure to new infections. As in prisons, drug use and sex occur in pretrial detention centers, while tools to promote protection such as condoms, drug dependence treatment and sterile syringes are largely unavailable – even in jurisdictions where these measures are available in prisons. The health risks associated with pretrial detention affect not only those detained but also societies at large, as people cycle in-and-out of pretrial detention and back into the community (Schönteich, 2008; Csete, 2010; Jürgens and Tomasini-Joshi, 2010).

International standards clearly state that pretrial detention should be an 'exceptional' measure used sparingly. For health, human rights, and prison reform advocates, it is imperative to advocate for programmes that provide safe alternatives to pretrial detention for persons accused of low-level crimes, for effective disease prevention and treatment for those who must remain in pretrial detention, and for better conditions while in pretrial detention.

Conclusion

We know what works – and what does not work – when it comes to preventing the further spread of HIV (and HCV and TB) in prisons and providing prisoners living with HIV with the treatment, care and support they need. In particular, harm reduction interventions have been introduced successfully in prisons, have been well accepted by prisoners, prison staff and administrations, and found to be effective in reducing injecting drug use and sharing of injecting equipment. Provision of ART to every prisoner in need is also essential, not only for the individual living with HIV, but also because HIV treatment is prevention.

Nevertheless, most prison systems continue to fail to take effective action, pretending that drug use (and sexual activity) do not occur in their prisons – despite evidence from studies around the world that risk behaviours are prevalent and put prisoners and their families at high risk of infections. At the same time, the number of prisoners, including a growing number of prisoners with HIV, HCV and/or drug dependence, continues to increase in most countries, further straining limited prison budgets and leading to even more unsanitary and overcrowded prison conditions. In many countries, people spend years in pretrial detention, under even worse conditions. Prisoners themselves are rarely involved in any policy-making on HIV and drug use in prisons, their voices hardly ever listened to – and most people and policy-makers simply do not seem to care, as James Motherall so eloquently put it (Motherall, 2006). Much will have to change to make harm reduction in prisons a reality. Those involved in harm reduction in the community can make an important contribution by expanding their interest and advocacy to prison and pretrial detention issues.

Note

The author would like to acknowledge the contribution of Annette Verster, Andrew Ball, Rick Lines, Catherine Cook, Manfred Nowak and Marcus Day to other reports and articles on HIV in prisons recently published by the author; thank all those who are working to improve the health and human rights of prisoners and pretrial detainees; and dedicate this article to James Motherall, for speaking out loudly and clearly on behalf of prisoners at risk.

References

Adjei, A.A., Armah, H.B., Gbagbo, F., Ampofo, W.K., Quaye, I.K.E. and Hesse, I.F.A. (2006). Prevalence of human immunodeficiency virus, hepatitis B virus, hepatitis C virus and syphilis among prison inmates and officers at Nsawam and Accra, Ghana, *Journal of Medical Microbiology*, 55, 593–7.

Albov, A.P. and Issaev, D.D. (1994) Homosexual contacts among male prison inmates in Russia, *Int Conf AIDS*, 10 (2), 53. Ministry of Internal Affairs, Dept of Reformatory Affairs, St. Petersburg, Russia, 7–12 August.

Ball, A. et al. (1995) *Multi-Centre Study on Drug Injecting and Risk of HIV Infection: A Report Prepared on Behalf of the International Collaborative Group for World Health Organization Programme on Substance Abuse*, Geneva: WHO.

Basic Principles for the Treatment of Prisoners (1990) UN GA Res. 45/111, annex, 45 UN GAOR Supp (No 49A) at 200, UN Doc A/45/49 (1990).

Basu, S., Smith-Rohrberg, D., Hanck, S. and Altice F.L. (2005) HIV testing in correctional institutions: evaluating existing strategies, setting new standards, *AIDS & Public Policy Journal*, 20 (1/2) 1–20.

Beauchemin, J. and Labadie, J.F. (1997) *Évaluation de l'utilité et de l'accessibilité des services de counselling et de dépistage du VIH en milieu carcéral – Services offerts par le CLSC Ahuntsic à la Maison Tanguay et à l'Établissement de détention de Montréal. Rapport final: août 1997*, Montréal: Direction de la santé publique de Montréal-Centre et CLSC Ahuntsic.

Behrendt, C., Kendig, N., Dambita, C., Horman, J., Lowler, J. and Vlahov, D. (1994) Voluntary testing for human immunodeficiency testing (HIV) in prison population with a high prevalence of HIV, *Am J Epidemiol*, 139 (9), 918–26.

Bellin E., Wesson J., and Tomasino V. (1999) High dose methadone reduces criminal recidivism in opiate addicts, *Addiction Research*, 7, 19–29.

Beyrer, C., Jittiwutikarn, J., Teokul, W. and Razak, M.H. (2003) Drug use, increasing incarceration rates, and prison-associated HIV risks in Thailand, *AIDS and Behavior*, 7 (2), 153–61.

Bird, A.G., Gore, S.M., Burns, S.M. and Duggie, J.G. (1993) Study of infection with HIV and related risk factors in young offenders' institution, *British Medical Journal*, 307, 228–31.

Black, E., Dolan, K. and Wodak, A. (2004) *Supply, Demand and Harm Reduction Strategies in Australian Prisons: Implementation, Cost and Evaluation. A Report Prepared for the Australian National Council on Drugs*, Sydney: Australian National Council on Drugs.

Bobrik, A., Danishevski, K., Eroshina, K., and McKee, M. (2005) Prison health in Russia: the larger picture, *Journal of Public Health Policy*, 26, 30–59.

Boutwell, A. and Rich, J. (2004) HIV infection behind bars, *Clinical Infectious Diseases*, 38, 1761–3.

Braithwaite, R.L., Hammett, T.M. and Mayberry, R.M. (1996) An analysis of current educational and prevention efforts. In Braithwaite, Hammettand Mayberry (eds), *Prisons and AIDS: A Public Health Challenge*, San Francisco: Jossey-Bass, 31–50.

Butler, T. and Milner, L. (2001) *The 2001 Inmate Health Survey*, Sydney: NSW Corrections Health Service, www.justicehealth.nsw.gov.au/pubs/Inmate_Health_Survey_2001.pdf.

Calzavara, L. et al. (1996) Inmates' view on harm reduction tools in Canadian prisons. 11th International Conference on AIDS, Vancouver, 7–11 July. Abstract MoD, 1845.

Calzavara, L. et al. (2005) *Prevalence and Predictors of HIV and Hepatitis C in Ontario Jails and Detention Centres: Final Report,* Toronto: HIV Social, Behavioural, and Epidemiological Studies Unit, Faculty of Medicine, University of Toronto.

Canadian HIV/AIDS Legal Network (2006) *Legislation to Authorize Forced Testing of Federal Prisoners for HIV: An Unjustified Violation of Human Rights*, Toronto: The Network.

Centers for Disease Control and Prevention (1999) Tuberculosis outbreaks in prison housing units for HIV-infected inmates: California, 1995–1996, *Morbidity and Mortality Weekly Report*, 48 (4), 79–82.

Centers for Disease Control and Prevention (2000) Drug-susceptible tuberculosis outbreak in a state correctional facility housing HIV-infected inmates: South Carolina, 1999–2000, *Morbidity and Mortality Weekly Report*, 49 (46), 1041–4.

Centers for Disease Control and Prevention (2006) HIV transmission among male inmates in a state prison system: Georgia, 1992–2005, *Morbidity and Mortality Weekly Report*, 55 (15), 421–6.

Choopanya, K., Vanichseni, S., Des Jarlais, D.C. et al. (1991) Risk factors and HIV seropositivity among injecting drug users in Bangkok, *AIDS*, 5, 1509–13.

Connolly, L. (1989) *Evaluation of the AIDS Education Programme for Prisoners in the NSW Department of Corrective Services: March, 1987 to March 1989*, Research publication no. 20, Sydney: NSW Department of Corrective Services.

Correctional Service Canada (1994) *HIV/AIDS in Prisons: Final Report of the Expert Committee on AIDS and Prisons,* Ottawa: Minister of Supply and Services Canada.

Correctional Service Canada (1996) *1995 National Inmate Survey: Final Report,* Ottawa: CSC (Correctional Research and Development) no. SR-02.

Correctional Service Canada (1999) *Evaluation of HIV/AIDS Harm Reduction Measures in the Correctional Service of Canada,* Ottawa: CSC.

Correctional Service Canada (2004) A health care needs assessment of federal inmates in Canada, *Canadian Journal of Public Health*, 95 (supple. 1), S1–S63.

Correspondence received from Enrique Acin (2010) *Jefe de Area de Salud Pública,* Coordinación de Sanidad Penitenciaria, dated 1 March, on file with authors.

Cotton-Oldenburg, N.U., Jordan, B.K., Martin, S.L. and Sadowski, L.S. (1999) Voluntary HIV testing in prison: do women inmates at high risk for HIV accept HIV testing?, *AIDS Education and Prevention*, 11 (1), 28–37.

Council of Europe (1988) Recommendation 1080 on a Co-ordinated European Health Policy to Prevent the Spread of AIDS in Prisons of 30 June 1988.

Cravioto, P., Medina-Mora, M.F., de la Rosa, B., Galván, F., and Tapia-Conyer, R. (2003) Patterns of heroin consumption in a jail on the northern Mexican border: barriers to treatment access, *Salud Publica de Mexico*, 45, 181–90.

Csete, J. (2010) Consequences of injustice: pre-trial detention and health, *International Journal of Prisoner Health*, 6 (2), 47–58.

Daines, N. et al. (1992) Results of the study tour undertaken in May–June 1992 to the United States, Canada, The Netherlands and England to research correctional facilities in connection with the Metropolitan Remand Centre Project, Sydney: NSW Department of Corrective Services, unpublished report.

Davies, T., Dominy, N., Peters, A. and Bath, G. (1995) HIV and injecting drug users in Edinburgh: prevalence and correlates, *Journal of Acquired Immune Deficiency Syndrome Human-Retroviral*, 8, 399–405.

Dean-Gator, H.D. and Fleming, P.L. (1999) Epidemiology of AIDS in incarcerated persons in the United States, 1994–1996, *AIDS*, 13, 2429–35.

DiCenso, A., Dias, G. and Gahagan, J. (2003) *Unlocking Our Futures: A National Study on Women, Prisons, HIV, and Hepatitis C,* Toronto: PASAN.

Dolan, K., Rutter, S. and Wodak, A.D. (2003) Prison-based syringe exchange programs: a review of international research and development, *Addiction*, 98, 153–8.

Dolan, K. and Rouen, D. (2003) Evaluation of an educational comic on harm reduction for prison inmates in New South Wales, *International Journal of Forensic Psychology*, 1 (1), 138–41.

Dolan, K., Bijl, M. and White, B. (2004) HIV education in a Siberian prison colony for drug dependent males, *International Journal of Equity in Health*, 3, 7.

Dolan, K., Lowe, D. and Shearer, J. (2004) Evaluation of the condom distribution program in New South Wales prisons, Australia, *Journal of Law, Medicine & Ethics*, 32, 124–8.

Dolan, K., Hall, W., Wodak, A. and Gaughwin, M. (1994) Evidence of HIV transmission in an Australian prison, *Medical Journal of Australia*, 160 (11), 734.

Dolan, K., Kite, B., Black, E., and Aceijas, C. (2004) Review of injection drug users and HIV infection in prisons in developing and transitional countries, New York: UN Reference Group on HIV/AIDS Prevention and Care among IDUs in Developing and Transitional Countries.

Dolan, K., Kite, B., Aceijas, C. and Stimson, G.V. (2007) HIV in prison in low-income and middle-income countries, *Lancet Infectious Diseases*, 7, 32–43.

Dolan, K., Shearer, J., White, B., Zhou, J., Kaldor, J. and Wodak, A. (2005) Four-year follow-up of imprisoned male heroin users and methadone treatment: mortality, re-incarceration and hepatitis C infection, *Addictions*, 100 (6), 820–8.

Dole, V.P., Robinson, J.W., Orraca, J., Towns, E., Searcy, P. and Caine, E. (1969) Methadone treatment of randomly selected criminal addicts, *N Engl J Med*, 280 (25), 1372–5.

Donnell, D., Baeten, J.M., Kiarie, J., Thomas, K.K., Stevens, W., Cohen, C.R. and McIntyre, J (2010) Heterosexual HIV-1 transmission after initiation of antiretroviral therapy: a prospective cohort analysis, *Lancet*, 375 (9731), 2092–8.

Drobniewski, F.A., Balabanova, Y.M., Ruddy, M.C., Graham, C., Kuznetzov, S.I., Gusarova, G.I., Zakharova, S.M., Melentyev, A.S. and Fedorin, I.M. (2005) Tuberculosis, HIV seroprevalence and intravenous drug abuse in prisoners, *Eur RespirJ*, 26 (2), 298–304.

Dumond, R.W. (2006) The impact of prisoner sexual violence: challenges of implementing public law 108–79: The Prison Rape Elimination Act of 2003, *Journal of Legislation*, 32, 142.

Editorial (1991) Health care for prisoners: implications of 'Kalk's refusal', *Lancet*, 337, 647–8.

Editorial (2011) HIV treatment as prevention: it works, *Lancet*, 377, 1719.

Elwood Martin, R. et al. (2005) Drug use and risk of bloodborne infections: a survey of female prisoners in British Columbia, *Canadian Journal of Public Health*, 96 (2), 97–101.

Estebanez, P.E., Russell, N.K., Aguilar, M.D., Béland, F. and Zunzunegui, M.V. (2000) Women, drugs and HIV/AIDS: results of a multicentre European study, *International Journal of Epidemiology*, 29, 734–43.

Fazel, S., Bains, P. and Doll, H. (2006) Systematic review of substance abuse and dependence in prisoners, *Addiction*, 101, 81–91.

Frost, L. and Tchertkov, V. (2002) Prisoner risk taking in the Russian Federation, *AIDS Education and Prevention*, 14 (supple. B) 7–23.

Glass, G.E., Hausler, W.J., Loeffelholz, P.L. and Yesalis, C.E. (1988) Seroprevalence of HIV antibody among individuals entering the Iowa prison system, *American Journal of Public Health*, 78 (4), 447–9.

Godinho, J. (2005) *Reversing the Tide: Priorities for HIV/AIDS Prevention in Central Asia*, Washington: World Bank.

Gore, S.M., Bird, A.G., Burns, S.M., Goldberg, D.J., Ross, A.J. and Macgregor, J. (1995) Drug injection and HIV prevalence in inmates of Glenochil Prison, *British Medical Journal*, 310, 293–6.

Gorta, A. (1992) *Monitoring the NSW Prison Methadone Program: A Review of Research 1986–1991*, Sydney: Research and Statistics Division, NSW Department of Corrective Services, publication no. 25, with reference to Lynes, D. (1989) Methadone maintenance in prison: a realistic programme, *Journal of Prisoners on Prisons*, 1, 9–15.

Granados, A., Miranda, M.J. and Martin, L. (1990) HIV seropositivity in Spanish prisons. Presented at the 6th International AIDS Conference, San Francisco, Abstract no. Th.D.116.

Grinstead, O. et al. (1999) Reducing post-release HIV risk among male prison inmates: a peer-led intervention, *Criminal Justice and Behavior*, 26, 453–65.

Grinstead, O., Zack, B. and Faigeles, B. (2001) Reducing postrelease risk behavior among HIV seropositive prison inmates: the Health Promotion Program, *AIDS Education and Prevention*, 13, 109–19.

Grinstead, O. et al. (2003) HIV and STD testing in prisons: perspectives of in-prison service providers, *AIDS Education and Prevention*, 15 (6), 547–60.

Haber, P., Parsons, S., Harper, S., White, P., Rawlinson, W. and Lloyd, A. (1999) Transmission of hepatitis C within Australian prisons, *Medical Journal of Australia*, 171, 31–3.

Hacker, M.A., Friedman, S.R. and Telles, P.R. (2005) The role of 'long-term' and 'new' injectors in a declining HIV/AIDS epidemic in Rio de Janeiro, Brazil, *Subst Use Misuse*, 40 (1), 99–123.

Hagan, H. Thiede, N.S., Weiss, S.G. and Hopkins, J.S. (2001) Sharing of the drug preparation equipment as a risk factor for hepatitis C infection among young adult injection drug users?, *Epidemiology*, 13 (6), 738–41.

Hall, W., Ward, J. and Mattick, R. (1993) Methadone maintenance treatment in prisons: the New South Wales experience, *Drug and Alcohol Review*, 12, 193–203.

Harding, T.W. and Schaller, G. (1992) *HIV/AIDS and Prisons: Updating and Policy Review: A Survey Covering 55 Prison Systems in 31 Countries*, Geneva: WHO Global Programme on AIDS.

Herzog, C., Fasnacht, M., Stohler, R. and Ladewig, D. (1993) Methadone substitution as an AIDS-preventive measures in the prison environment. Presented at the European Symposium Drug Addiction & AIDS, Siena, Italy, 4–6 October.

Heimer, R. et al. (2005) Imprisonment as risk for HIV in the Russian Federation: evidence for change. 16th International Conference on the Reduction of Drug Related Harm.

Her Majesty's Government (1995) *Tackling Drug Use Together: A Strategy for England 1995–1998*, London: HMSO.

Hoover, J. and Jürgens, R. (2009) *Harm Reduction in Prison: The Moldova Model*, New York: Open Society Institute.

Hoxie, N.J., Vergeront, J.M. and Frisby, H.R. (1990) HIV seroprevalence and the acceptance of voluntary HIV testing among newly incarcerated male prison inmates in Wisconsin, *American Journal of Public Health*, 80 (9), 1129–31.

Hughes, R.A. (2003) Illicit drug and injecting equipment markets inside English prisons: a qualitative study, *Journal of Offender Rehabilitation*, 37 (3/4) 47–64.

Hughes, R.A. and Huby, M. (2000) Life in prison: perspectives of drug injectors, *Deviant Behavior*, 21 (5), 451–79.

Human Rights Watch (2001) *No Escape: Male Rape in U.S. Prisons*, New York: Human Rights Watch.

Hume, S. and Gorta, A. (1988) Views of key personnel involved with the administration of the NSW prison methadone program: process evaluation of the NSW Department of Corrective Services Prison Methadone Program, Study no. 5, unpublished report, Sydney: Research and Statistics Division, New South Wales Department of Corrective Services.

International Guidelines on HIV/AIDS and Human Rights (1997) UNCHR Res. 1997/33, UN Doc. E/CN.4/ 1997/150 (1997), para. 29(e).

Johnson, S.L., van de Ven, J.T.C. and Gant, B.A. (2001) *Research Report: Institutional Methadone Maintenance Treatment: Impact on Release Outcome and Institutional Behaviour*, Ottawa: Correctional Service Canada, no. R–119.

Joseph, H. et al. (1989) Heroin addicts in jail: New York tries methadone treatment program, *Corrections Today*, 5, 124–31.

Jürgens, R. (1996) *HIV/AIDS in Prisons: Final Report*, Montréal: Canadian HIV/AIDS Legal Network and Canadian AIDS Society.

Jürgens, R. (1997) Will prisons fail the AIDS test? In P. G. Erickson, D. M. Riley, Y.W. Cheung and P.A. O'Hare (eds), *Harm Reduction: A New Direction for Drug Policies and Programs*, Toronto, Buffalo, London: University of Toronto Press, 151–73.

Jürgens, R. and Riley, D.M. (1997) Responding to AIDS and drug use in prisons in Canada, *International Journal of Drug Policy*, 8 (1), 29–37.

Jürgens, R. and Betteridge, B. (2005) Prisoners who inject drugs: public health and human rights imperatives, *Health & Human Rights*, 8 (2), 47–74.

Jürgens, R. and Tomasini-Joshi, T. (2010) Editorial, *International Journal of Prisoner Health*, 6 (2), 45–6.

Jürgens, R., Ball, A. and Verster, A. (2009) Interventions to reduce HIV transmission related to injecting drug use in prison, *Lancet Infect Dis*, 9, 57–66.

Jürgens, R., Cook, C. and Lines R. (2010) Out of sight, out of mind? Harm reduction in prisons and other places of detention. In C. Cook (ed.), *The Global State of Harm Reduction 2010* London: International Harm Reduction Association.

Jürgens, R., Csete, J., Amon, J.A., Baral, S. and Beyrer, C. (2010) People who use drugs, HIV, and human rights, *Lancet*, 376 (9739), 475–85.

Kapadia, F., Vlahov, D., Des Jarlais, D.C., Strathdee, S.A., Ouellet, L., Kerndt, P., Morse, E.E.V., Williams, I., and Garfein, R.S. (2002) Does bleach disinfection of syringes protect against hepatitis C infection among young adult injection drug users?, *Epidemiology*, 13 (6), 738–41.

Keppler, K. and Stöver, H. (1999) Transmission of infectious diseases during imprisonment – results of a study and introduction of a model project for infection prevention in Lower Saxony, *Gesundheitswesen*, 61 (4), 207–13. Summarised in English in *Canadian HIV/AIDS Policy & Law Newsletter*, 1996, 2 (2), 18–19.

Koulierakis, G., Gnardellis, C., Agrafiotis, D., and Power, K.G. (2000) HIV risk behaviour correlates among injecting drug users in Greek prisons, *Addiction*, 95 (8), 1207–16.

Krebs, C.P. and Simmons, M. (2002) Intraprison HIV transmission: an assessment of whether it occurs, how it occurs, and who is at risk, *AIDS Education and Prevention*, 14 (Supple. B) 53–64.

Lines, R., Jürgens, R., Betteridge, G., Stöver, H., Laticevschi, D. and Nelles, J. (2004) *Prison Needle Exchange: A Review of International Evidence and Experience*, Montreal: Canadian HIV/AIDS Legal Network.

Lines, R., Jürgens, R., Betteridge, G, Stöver, H., Latishevschi, D. and Nelles, J. (2006) *Prison Needle Exchange: A Review of International Evidence and Experience*, Montreal: Canadian HIV/AIDS Legal Network, 2nd edn.

Lowe, D. (1998) *Evaluation of the Condom Trial in Three Correctional Centres in New South Wales*. Final Report for the Department of Corrective Services.

Lurigio, A.J., Petraitis, J. and Johnson, B.R. (1992) Joining the front line against HIV: an education program for adult probationers, *AIDS Education and Prevention*, 4, 205–18.

Macalino, G.E., Hou, J.C., Kumar, M.S., Taylor, L.E., Sumantera, I.G. and Rich, J.D. (2004) Hepatitis C infection and incarcerated populations, *International Journal of Drug Policy*, 15, 103–14.

MacDonald, M. (2005) *A Study of Health Care Provision, Existing Drug Services and Strategies Operating in Prisons in Ten Countries from Central and Eastern Europe*, Finland: Heuni.

MacPherson, P. (2004) *Use of Random Urinalysis to Deter Drug Use in Prison: A Review of the Issues*, Ottawa: Addictions Research Branch, Correctional Service of Canada, no. R-149.

Magura, S., Rosenblum, A. Lewis, C. and Joseph, H. (1993) The effectiveness of in-jail methadone maintenance, *Journal of Drug Issues*, 23 (1), 75–99.

Marins, J.R., Page-Shafer, K., Berti de Azevedo Barros, M. Hudes, E.S., Chen, S. and Hearst, N. (2000) Seroprevalence and risk factors for HIV infection among incarcerated men in Sorocaba, Brazil, *AIDS and Behavior*, 4 (1), 121–8.

Martin, R.E., Gold, F., Murphy, W., Remple, V., Berkowitz, J. and Money, D. (1998) Predictive factors of HIV-infection in injecting drug users upon incarceration, *European Journal of Epidemiology*, 14 (4), 327–31.

Martin, V. et al. (1990) Seroepidemiology of HIV-1 infection in a Catalonian penitentiary, *AIDS*, 4, 1023–6.

May, J.P. and Williams, E.L. (2002) Acceptability of condom availability in a US jail, *AIDS Education and Prevention*, 14 (5 supple: HIV/AIDS in Correctional Settings), 85–91.

Menoyo, C., Zulaica, D. and Parras, F. (2000) Needle exchange in prisons in Spain, *Canadian HIV/AIDS Policy & Law Review*, 5 (4), 20–1.

Motherall, J. (2006) Giving a voice to (former) prisoners in the debate on prisoners' health. *International Journal of Prisoner Health*, 2 (3), 253–5.

Nagaraj, S.G., Sarvade, M., Muthanna, L., Raju, R., Aju, S. and Sarvade, N.M. (2000) HIV seroprevalence and prevalent attitudes amongst the prisoners: a case study in Mysore, Karnataka state India. Paper presented at 13th International AIDS Conference, Durban.

Normand, J., Vlahov, D.and Moses, L.E. (eds), (1995) *Preventing HIV transmission: The Role of Sterile Needles and Bleach*, Washington, DC: National Academy Press.

Observatoire international des prisons (1996) *Le guide du prisonnier*, Paris: Les Editions Ouvrières.

O'Donnell, I. (2004) Prison rape in context, *British Journal of Criminology*, 44 (2), 241–55.

O'Sullivan, B.G., Levy, M.H., Dolan, K.A., Post, J.J., Barton, S.G., Dwyer, D.E., Kaldor, J.M. and Grulich, A. E. (2003) Hepatitis C transmission and HIV post-exposure prophylaxis after needle-and syringe-sharing in Australian prisons, *Medical Journal of Australia*, 178 (11), 546–9.

Pallas, J., Farinas-Alvarez, C., Prieto, D., Llorca, J., Delgado-Rodriguez, M. (1999) Risk factors for monoinfections and coinfections with HIV, hepatitis B and hepatitis C viruses in northern Spanish prisoners, *Epidemiol Infect*, 123, 95–102.

Pearson, M, (1995) Voluntary screening for hepatitis C in a Canadian federal penitentiary for men, *Canadian Communicable Disease Report*, 21 (14), F4–F5.

Patterson, S. et al. (2000) Drug-susceptible TB outbreak in a state correctional facility housing HIV-infected inmates: South Carolina, 1999–2000, *Morbidity and Mortality Weekly Review*, 49 (46), 1041-4.

Plourde, C. and Brochu, S. (2002) Drugs in prison: a break in the pathway, *Substance Use Misuse*, 37, 47–63.

Pontali, E. (2005) Antiretroviral treatment in correctional facilities, *HIV Clinical Trials*, 6 (1), 25–37.

Prison Healthcare News (2003) Disease control in north west Russia, 4 (spring).

Ramratnam, B., Rich, J.D., Parikh, A., Tsoulfas, G., Vigilante, K.C. and Flanigan, T.P. (1997) Former prisoners' views on mandatory HIV testing during incarceration, *Journal of Correctional Health Care*, 4, 155–64.

Reindollar, R.W. (1999) Hepatitis C and the correctional population, *American Journal of Medicine*, 107 (6B), 100S–103S.

Richardson, C., Ancelle-Park, R. and Papaevangelou, G. (1993) Factors associated with HIV seropositivity in European injecting drug users, *AIDS*, 7, 1485–91.

Rotily, M., Weilandt, C., Bird, S., Kall, K., van Haastrecht, H.J.A., Landolo, E. and Rousseau, S. (2001) Surveillance of HIV infection and related risk behaviour in European prisons: a multicentre pilot study, *Eur J Public Health*, 11 (3), 243–50.

Rowhani-Rahbar, A., Tabatabee-Yazdi, A. and Panahi, M. (2004) Prevalence of common blood-borne infections among imprisoned injection drug users in Mashhad, north-east Iran, *Archives of Iranian Medicine*, 7 (3), 190–4.

Sabin, K.M., Frey, R.L., Jr, Horsley, R. and Greby, S.M. (2001) Characteristics and trends of newly identified HIV infections among incarcerated populations: CDC HIV voluntary counseling, testing, and referral system, 1992–1998, *Journal of Urban Health*, 78, 241–55.

Schönteich, M. (2008) The scale and consequences of pretrial detention around the world, *Justice Initiatives*, spring, 11–43.

Schoub, B.D. (1995) *AIDS and HIV in Perspective: A Guide to Understanding the Virus and Its Consequences*, New York: Cambridge University Press.

Shewan, D., Gemmell, M. and Davies, J.B. (1994) Behavioural change amongst drug injectors in Scottish prisons, *Soc Sci Med*, 39 (11), 1585–6.

Simooya, O., Sanjobo, N. (2001) 'In but free': an HIV/AIDS intervention in an African prison, *Culture, Health & Sexuality*, 3 (2), 241–51.

Simooya, O. and Sanjobo, N. (2002) Study in Zambia showed that robust response is needed in prisons, *British Medical Journal*, 324, 850.

Simooya, O., Sanjobo, N., Kaetano, L., Sijumbila, G., Munkonze, F., Tailoka F. et al. (2001) 'Behind walls': a study of HIV risk behaviours and seroprevalence in prisons in Zambia, *AIDS*, 15, 1741–4.

Singh, S., Prasad, R. and Mohanty, A. (1999) High prevalence of sexually transmitted and blood-borne infections amongst the inmates of a district jail in Northern India, *International Journal of STD & AIDS*, 10 (7), 475–8.

Spaulding, A., Stephenson, B., Macalino, G. and Ruby, W. (2002) Human immunodeficiency virus in correctional facilities: a review, *Clinical Infectious Diseases*, 35, 305–12.

Springer, S.A., Pesanti, E., Hodges, J., Macura, T., Doros, G. and Altice, F. (2004) Effectiveness of antiretroviral therapy among HIV-infected prisoners: reincarceration and the lack of sustained benefit after release to the community, *Clinical Infectious Diseases*, 38, 1754–60.

Stop Prisoner Rape (2005) *PREA Update: Stop Prisoner Rape's Report on the Prison Rape Elimination Act*, Los Angeles: Stop Prisoner Rape.

Stöver, H. (2000) Evaluation of needle exchange pilot project shows positive results, *Canadian HIV/AIDS Policy & Law Newsletter*, 5 (2/3) 60–4.

Stöver, H., Hennebel, .LC. and Casselmann, J. (2004) Substitution Treatment in European prisons: A Study of Policies and Practices of Substitution in Prisons in 18 European Countries, London: European Network of Drug Services in Prison (ENDSP).

Stöver, H., Casselmann, J. and Hennebel, L. (2006) Substitution treatment in European prisons: a study of policies and practices in 18 European countries, *International Journal of Prisoner Health*, 2 (1), 3–12.

Strang, J. et al. (1998) *HIV/AIDS Risk Behaviour among Adult Male Prisoners*, Research Findings no. 82, London: Home Office Research, Development and Statistics Directorate.

Swann, R. and James, P. (1998) The effect of the prison environment upon inmate drug taking behaviour, *Howard Journal of Criminal Justice*, 37, 252–65.

Taylor, A. and Goldberg, D. (1996) Outbreak of HIV infection in a Scottish prison: why did it happen?, *Canadian HIV/AIDS Policy & Law Newsletter*, 2 (3), 13–14.

Taylor, A., Goldberg, D., Emslie, J., Wrench, J., Gruer, L., Cameron, S., Black, J., Davis, B., McGregor, J., Follet, E., Harvey, J., Basson, J. and McGavigan, J. (1995) Outbreak of HIV infection in a Scottish prison, *British Medical Journal*, 310 (6975), 289–92.

Tomasini-Joshi, T. and Schönteich M. (2010) Promoting community and prison health through pretrial release for people with transmissible diseases, *International Journal of Prisoner Health*, 6 (2), 59–71.

Tuberculosis Coalition for Technical Assistance and International Committee of the Red Cross (2009) *Guidelines for Control of Tuberculosis in Prisons*.

United Nations (1990) *Infection with Human Immunodeficiency Virus (HIV) and Acquired Immunodeficiency Syndrome (AIDS) in Prisons*. Resolution 18 of the Eighth United Nations Congress on the Prevention of Crime and the Treatment of Offenders, U.N. Doc. A/CONF.144/28 of 5 October 1990, New York: United Nations.

UNAIDS (1997) *Prisons and AIDS: UNAIDS Point of View*, Geneva: UNAIDS.

UNODC and UNAIDS, (2008) *Women and HIV in Prison Settings*, Vienna: UNODC.

UNODC and WHO (2009) *Policy Brief: HIV Testing and Counselling in Prisons and Other Closed Settings*, Vienna and Geneva: UNODC and WHO.

UNODC, WHO and UNAIDS (2006) *HIV/AIDS Prevention, Care, Treatment and Support in Prison Settings: A Framework for an Effective National Response*, New York: UNODC, WHO, UNAIDS.

UNODC, WHO and UNAIDS (2008) *HIV and AIDS in Places of Detention: A Toolkit for Policymakers, Programme Managers, Prison Officers and Health Care Providers in Prison Settings*, New York: United Nations.

US National Commission on AIDS (1991) *Report: HIV Disease in Correctional Facilities*. Washington, DC: US National Commission on AIDS.

Van Meter, (1996) *Adolescents in Youth Empowerment Positions: Special Projects of National Significance*, Washington, DC: US Department of Health and Human Services.

Vaz, R.G., Gloyd, S. and Trindade, R. (1996) The effects of peer education on STD and AIDS knowledge among prisoners in Mozambique, *International Journal of STD and AIDS*, 7, 51–4.

Veen, J. (2007) Tuberculosis control in prisons. In: World Health Organization, Regional Office for Europe, *Health in Prisons: A WHO Guide to the Essentials in Prison Health*, Copenhagen: WHO.

Vlahov, D., Brewer, F., Castro, K.G., Narkunas, J.P., Salive, M.E., Ullrich, J. et al. (1991) Prevalence of antibody to HIV-1 among entrants to US correctional facilities, *Journal of the American Medical Association*, 265, 1129–32.

Wale, S. and Gorta, A. (1987) *Views of Inmates Participating in the Pilot Pre-Release Methadone Program*, Study No. 2, Sydney: Research and Statistics Division, NSW Department of Corrective Services.

Walker, J., Sanchez, R., Davids, J., Stevens, M., Whitehorn, L., Greenspan, J. and Mealey, R. (2004) Is routine testing mandatory or voluntary?, *Clinical Infectious Diseases*, 40, 319.

Walmsley, R. (2009) *World Prison Population List*, 8th edn, King's College/International Centre for Prison Studies, www.kcl.ac.uk/depsta/law/research/icps/downloads/wppl-8th_41.pdf.

Weekes, J., Thomas, G. and Graves, G. (2004) *Substance Abuse in Corrections: FAQs*, Ottawa: Canadian Centre on Substance Abuse.

Weilandt, C., Eckert, J. and Stöver, H. (2005) *Anonymous Survey on Infectious Diseases and Related Risk Behaviour among Armenian Prisoners and on Knowledge, Attitudes and Behaviour of Armenian Prison Staff towards Infectious Diseases and Drugs*, Bonn: WIAD, ENDIPP, ICRC.

World Health Organization (1987) *Statement from the Consultation on Prevention and Control of AIDS in Prisons*, Global Programme on AIDS, Geneva: WHO.

World Health Organization (1993) *WHO Guidelines on HIV Infection and AIDS in Prisons*, Geneva: WHO (WHO/GPA/DIR/93.3).

World Health Organization (2004) *Evidence for Action Technical Papers: Effectiveness of Sterile Needle and Syringe Programming in Reducing HIV/AIDS among Injecting Drug Users*, Geneva: WHO.

World Health Organization (2007) *Promoting Health in Prisons: The Essentials, a WHO Guide*, Copenhagen: WHO Regional Office for Europe.

WHO, UNODC and UNAIDS (2007) *Interventions to Address HIV in Prisons: Comprehensive Review*, Evidence for Action Technical Paper, Geneva: World Health Organization.

WHO, UNODC and UNAIDS (2007b) *Interventions to address HIV in Prisons: Drug Dependence Treatments*, Evidence for Action Technical Paper, Geneva: WHO.

WHO, UNODC and UNAIDS (2007c) *Interventions to Address HIV in Prisons: Measures to Decrease Sexual Transmission*, Evidence for Action Technical Paper, Geneva: WHO.

WHO, UNODC and UNAIDS (2007d) *Interventions to Address HIV in Prisons: HIV Care, Treatment and Support*, Evidence for Action Technical Paper, Geneva: WHO.

Yap, L. et al (2007) Do condoms cause rape and mayhem? The long-term effects of condoms in New South Wales' prisons, *Sexually Transmitted Infections* (online edn).

Zachariah, R., Harries, A.D., Chantulo, A.S., Yadidi, A.E., Nkhoma, W. and Maganga, O. (2002) Sexually transmitted infections among prison inmates in a rural district of Malawi, *Trans R Soc Trop Med Hyg*, 96 (6), 617–19.

Zamani, S., Kihara, M., Gouya, M.M., Vazirian, M., Ono-Kihara, M., Razzaghi, E.M. and Ichikawa, S. (2005) Prevalence of factors associated with HIV-1 infection among drug users visiting treatment centres in Tehran, Iran, *AIDS*, 19 (7), 709–16.

Zhivago, S. (2005) HIV/AIDS epidemic situation in penitentiary system of Ukraine. Presentation at 'HIV/AIDS in Prisons in Ukraine – From Evidence to Action: Prevention and Care, Treatment, and Support', Kiev, 1–2 November.

Zurhold, H., Stöver, H. and Haasen, C. (2004) *Female Drug Users in European Prisons: Best Practice for Relapse Prevention and Reintegration*, Hamburg: Centre for Interdisciplinary Addiction Research, University of Hamburg.

Zweig, J.M., Naser, R.L., Blackmore, J. and Schaffer, M. (2006) *Addressing Sexual Violence in Prisons: A National Snapshot of Approaches and Highlights of Innovative Strategies. Final Report*, Washington, DC: Urban Institute.

Chapter 8

INTERNATIONAL SECURITY AND THE GLOBAL WAR ON DRUGS: THE TRAGIC IRONY OF DRUG SECURITISATION

Danny Kushlick

It can be argued that the apparently successful global securitisation of drugs constitutes one of the greatest threats to international and human security.

(Danny Kushlik)

First, one would be hard-pressed to think of another subject where we, as a nation, have engaged in more self-deception than about the effectiveness, or even efficacy, of our 'war on drugs' and the likely impact of even tougher and more expensive, but likely equally futile, counternarcotics programmes'. So long as there is an insistent market in a country like the United States for illegal narcotics and a sufficient profit to be made, they will probably be produced. And so long as they are illegal, their production and distribution will be through organised crime.

(Ambassador David Passage, former Director of Andean Affairs at the US State Department, SSI, 2000)

Introduction

Global drug policy is in crisis on many fronts. Deaths in turf wars are undermining Mexican society, Colombian and Afghan coca and opium production appear singularly intractable and Guinea Bissau turned from being a fragile state to a narco state almost overnight. The balance has shifted as the unintended consequences of the war on drugs are now threatening the security of numerous states. We have created the ultimate irony whereby the securitisation of drugs has itself become one of the greatest threats to international security. The level of crisis is demonstrated in the recent calls by Presidents Calderon and Santos for a debate on alternatives to prohibition – including legalisation and regulation. There is a concurrent loss of popular support for the war and increasing scrutiny of drug war expenditure in the context of a global economic crisis.

The fact that the war on drugs has not achieved its stated objectives of reducing drug supply and use, as well as its severe unintended consequences, makes it highly vulnerable to criticism. The most cursory analysis exposes its overwhelming shortcomings, and many are bewildered by prohibition's longevity. The resilience of the war on drugs since the mid-twentieth century is usefully explained by the international relations theory – securitisation – this forms the foundation of the geopolitical steel that protects the soft centre within. It expressly excludes other policy positions, protects the prohibition from criticism and from evidence-based scrutiny.

Harm Reduction in Substance Use and High-Risk Behaviour: International Policy and Practice, First Edition.
Edited by Richard Pates and Diane Riley.
© 2012 Blackwell Publishing Ltd. Published 2012 by Blackwell Publishing Ltd.

Drugs and security

There can be little doubt that drugs are an international security issue. Fragile and vulnerable states that are involved in the production, supply and use of drugs proscribed under international prohibition, are politically and economically destabilised. Producer and transit countries Colombia, Mexico, Afghanistan and West Africa are prime examples. The UN Associations estimate the value of the global drugs market at $320 billion a year – rivalling the worldwide markets in oil, wheat and arms. The proportions of this anarchic trade dwarf the GDP of many smaller states.

Industrialised countries with low levels of well-being, and that have high levels of drug misuse, are also doubly afflicted. The UNICEF league table of the level of child wellbeing in industrialised countries, invariably puts the United States and United Kingdom at or near the bottom. Both counties have higher than average populations of problematic drug users, operate overwhelmingly prohibitionist drug policies and have disproportionately high prison numbers. The incendiary combination of low societal well-being and high demand for prohibited drugs is a major cause of crime and ill health, and wastes money, resources and political attention.

Securitisation is a theory developed in the mid-1990s by the Copenhagen School (Buzan, Waever and de Wilde (1997). The authors outline a process whereby: a securitising actor identifies an existential threat to a referent object and makes it a security issue – in a speech act to a specific audience. The actor then applies an 'extraordinary measure' to nullify the perceived threat (see table 8.1)

According to the Copenhagen School, in *Security: A New Framework for Analysis*: '"Security" is the move that takes politics beyond the established rules of the game and frames the issue either as a special kind of politics or as above politics.'

The significance of this statement should not be underestimated. It is well understood that much of the political discourse around drug policy appears to be divorced from other policy issues. However, if, as this chapter argues, drugs have undergone two securitisations, drug policy isn't just isolated from other policy discourses, it exists in a securitised world all of its own. Its continuation is not subject to democratic input. Rather its continuance is based on achieving support from world leaders in non-democratic forums. In the framework of the Copenhagen School, the Audience for the Speech Act is not voters, but other heads of UN member states. This total isolation from normal policy-making structures explains why our failing drug policy is so persistent. International policy exists in the rarified world of security, 'beyond the established rules of the game', 'above politics'. Before exploring this further, it is useful to present a counterfactual example.

Table 8.1 How this applies to drug policy

Speech act	Referent object	Existential threat	Extraordinary measure
1961 UN Convention	'Mankind'	'Evil' of addiction to drugs	Global prohibition
1988 UN Convention	'States'	Organised crime and trafficking	Escalation/militarisation of war on drugs

Source: Emily Crick, University of Swansea. See also Crick, E. (2012), *International Journal of Drug Policy*.

A comparison with the legal opiates market

But Repeal changed that, replacing the almost-anything-goes ethos with a series of state-by state codes, regulations and enforcement procedures. Now there were closing hours and age limits and Sunday blue laws, as well as a collection of geographic proscriptions that kept bars or package stores distant from schools, churches or hospitals. State licensing requirements forced legal sellers to live by the code, and in many instances statutes created penalties for buyers as well. Just as Prohibition did not prohibit, making drink legal did not make drink entirely available.

(Okrent, 2010)

It is a little known fact that, in parallel with the enormous illegal opium and heroin market, there exists a regulated legal market to match it. When the UN Drugs Convention of 1961 was drawn up, as well as calling on member states to support a global ban on non-medical use of opiates, it made provision for governments to grow, trade, supply and oversee the use of opiates for medical use. Indeed, more than half of global opium production is for the legal opiates market – pharmacy preparations, co-codamol, vicodin, codeine, and prescribed opiates – morphine, diamorphine, and the like.

Opium poppies are legally grown in the fields of the United Kingdom, Australia, Turkey, Hungary and India. Their production and supply operates within global frameworks that govern pharmaceutical drugs. These are detailed in Transform's report 'Blueprint for Regulation', that also shows how a post-prohibition regulatory framework for currently prohibited drugs might work (Transform Drug Policy Foundation, 2009). It is instructive to compare this legal market with the poppy fields in Helmand province and the supply chain that leads to the illicit heroin on the streets of most industrialised nations. Why is it that the legally grown, produced and supplied opiates do not constitute an international security issue, and yet those whose production, supply and use is prohibited, do? Security cannot be undermined by the plant or the drug it contains. The difference must be the result of the respective policy contexts they inhabit (see table 8.2).

How and when did the global securitisation of drugs happen? The UN Single Convention on drugs, ratified in 1961, to consolidate previous drug control treaties, mentioned 'health' 24 times and 'criminal' 6. In the guise of protecting children and other vulnerable people, 'drugs' (not tobacco or alcohol) were designated 'threat' status; identified as a threat to individuals,

Table 8.2 Securitising the drugs threat

Russia
In March 2010, during an expanded session of the Russia-NATO Council in Brussels, Viktor Ivanov, the head of Russia's Federal Drug Control Service (FSKN), presented Moscow's seven-point plan on fighting drug production in Afghanistan and suggested creating a joint group with NATO to tackle Afghan poppy production. Among other ideas, the plan included *'an upgrade of the status of the Afghan drug production problem in the UN Security Council to the level of a threat to world peace and security'*.

Equador
At the Commission on Narcotic Drugs of 2009, Ecuador's statement to the High Level Meeting described its approach as a *'De-securitisation of drug policy which allows us to address the problem from the perspective of health and human rights'*.

Source: Emily Crick, University of Swansea.

communities and nation states. The preamble to the 1961 UN Single Convention places it within a health and welfare framework:

> Concerned with the health and welfare of mankind . . . But quickly asserts the threat:
> 'Recognizing that addiction to narcotic drugs constitutes a *serious evil* for the individual and is fraught with social and economic danger to mankind . . . Conscious of their duty to prevent and *combat this evil*.'

The Convention goes on to say in article 2, section 5:

> A Party shall, if in its opinion the prevailing conditions in its country render it the most appropriate means of protecting the public health and welfare, prohibit the production, manufacture, export and import of, trade in, possession or use of any such drug except for amounts which may be necessary for medical and scientific research only.

It is obvious that individual member states could not seriously have contemplated an alternative to prohibition, even had it been in their 'opinion' a more appropriate means of protecting public health and welfare. Having identified in the preamble that 'drugs' are 'evil' and a 'danger to mankind' (with US backing), it would be a foolhardy representative who suggested during the negotiation process that this evil be legally regulated, rather than prohibited. In this environment it is unsurprising that support for this Convention and the two that followed became almost total.

In 1961 levels of drug use, production and supply were relatively low, compared with the rates we have now, although some must have foreseen the potentially negative consequences of '*protecting the public health and welfare*', by imposing a prohibitionist regime; indeed, parts of the Convention were written in the 1940s whilst Al Capone was still in prison. The lessons from alcohol prohibition could have informed the development and implementation of global illicit drug control. They did not. The clear and present danger was that a significant increase in levels of demand, combined with the gifting of a gargantuan and highly lucrative market to organised criminals, would conspire to create a nightmare scenario.

The early 1960s saw the birth of a burgeoning drug subculture. It was the worst case scenario – drug use took off, and collided with the immovable object of prohibition. This helped create the setting in 1971 for President Richard Nixon to officially declare a 'War on drugs', identifying 'drug abuse' as 'public enemy No. 1'. Whatever the underlying motive, war was the rhetoric. And very soon, war became the modus operandi.

With this global regime in place the scene was set for an overwhelmingly ideological commitment to fight the 'evil' in our midst. By this point a number of moves had been made that would set the stage for the monolith of prohibition to assume the proportions of the empire that we now see:

- The declaration of 'war' against 'evil', and the construction of drugs as a threat, had moved illicit drugs into a category all of their own, beyond the normal public health policy setting inhabited by licit drugs. Indeed all other policy discourses now played a seriously poor second fiddle to police and military.
- By virtue of placing the responsibility for the global prohibition in the UN, the structures that oversaw the foundation for domestic, nation state prohibition, were now moved 'beyond' national policy-making processes and beyond democratic norms. (Indeed to this day, the Home Office claims that its hands are tied with regard to discussing UK prohibition, because the UK is a signatory to the UN Conventions.)

- The securitisation is very heavily resourced, politically and financially – creating a substantial power base for the securitised status quo -- for example UN Office on Drugs and Crime, UK Serious Organised Crime Agency, US Office of National Drug Control Policy, private prison industry, customs and police, security and intelligence agencies.
- The creation of a symbiotic relationship between drug warriors and organised criminal networks. By virtue of having created the opportunity for organised crime through the enormous criminal drugs market, enforcement agencies must then counter them, and so the vicious circle is closed.
- The corollary also involves the demonisation of users and indeed, the marginalisation of those who challenge the prohibitionist orthodoxy.

Unintended consequences of the war on drugs

The construction of the threat approach to drugs, perversely led to prohibition causing significant negative consequences. In a world in which demand was increasing exponentially, prohibition was creating profit margins in the cocaine and heroin markets that were unheard of in any other commodity trade.

By 2008 even the Executive Director of the UN Office on Drugs and Crime, Antonio Maria Costa, was prepared to admit that the drug control system creates major negative consequences (Costa, 2008):

> The first unintended consequence is a huge criminal black market that thrives in order to get prohibited substances from producers to consumers, whether driven by a 'supply push' or a 'demand pull', the financial incentives to enter this market are enormous. There is no shortage of criminals competing to claw out a share of a market in which hundred fold increases in price from production to retail are not uncommon.
>
> The second unintended consequence is what one night call policy displacement. Public health, which is clearly the first principle of drug control . . . was displaced into the background.
>
> The third unintended consequence is geographical displacement. It is often called the balloon effect because squeezing (by tighter controls) one place produces a swelling (namely an increase) in another place.
>
> A system appears to have been created in which those who fall into the web of addiction find themselves excluded and marginalised from the social mainstream, tainted with a moral stigma, and often unable to find treatment even when they may be motivated to want it.

This is a remarkable admission from the head of the agency tasked with implementing global prohibition, and one that demonstrates above all else how the prohibition itself creates many of the problems at every level that prohibition is supposed to neutralise. And it must not be forgotten that the harms created by the regime intended to protect humankind fall overwhelmingly upon the most disenfranchised, marginalised, disadvantaged and poor the world over.

It can now be argued that the apparently successful global securitisation of drugs ironically constitutes one of the greatest threats to international and human security:

> Over the past decades we have witnessed: A growth in unacceptable levels of drug-related violence affecting the whole of society and, in particular, the poor and the young; The criminalization of politics and the politicization of crime, as well as the proliferation of the linkages between them, as reflected in the infiltration of democratic institutions by organized crime; The corruption of public servants, the judicial system, governments, the political system and, especially the police forces in charge of enforcing law and order.
>
> (Latin American Commission on Drugs and Democracy, 2009)

Outside of the bribes and official political corruption, it can also be argued that there is a corruption of the political structures that support prohibition. Many in positions of senior political leadership know that the securitisation is overwhelmingly counterproductive, and yet remain silent publicly or even claim success for the war on drugs. President Barack Obama described the war on drugs as an 'utter failure' in 2004 but laughed off calls to legalise marijuana when he came into office. Prime Minister David Cameron called on the UK government to initiate a debate at the UN on the legalisation and regulation of drugs in 2002, but has positioned himself and his party as supporters of prohibition since assuming leadership of the conservatives.

Securitising organised crime

After some three decades of global prohibition, many had accepted the 'evil' nature of drugs and those who supplied them, and perceived the need to ramp up the war on drugs. Those in charge of 'doing something about drugs' (already on a permanent war footing) embarked upon a second securitisation, this time addressing the threat of trafficking and organised crime.

In 1988 the third Convention was ratified:

> Deeply concerned by the magnitude of and rising trend in the illicit production of, demand for and traffic in narcotic drugs and psychotropic substances, which pose a serious *threat to the health and welfare of human beings and adversely affect the economic, cultural and political foundations of society,*
> Recognizing the links between illicit traffic and other related organized criminal activities which undermine the legitimate economies *and threaten the stability, security and sovereignty of States.*

In the 1988 protocol (principally a piece of transnational criminal law), 'Crime' or 'criminality' receives twenty-five mentions, 'health' four. Note how the focus of concern has now shifted from 'evil' drugs in 1961, to the 'threat' to state security arising from illicit production and trafficking. And now we have come full circle; over the course of twenty-seven years, 'evil' drugs have now become truly harmful through the enforcement of the global prohibition:

> Aware that illicit traffic generates large financial profits and wealth enabling transnational criminal organizations to penetrate, contaminate and corrupt the structures of government, legitimate commercial and financial business, and society at all its levels.

Many years on from this second securitisation, and even further from the first, many are confused about what precisely it is that they are fighting, partly because the two securitisations are conflated. We now have a self-referential feedback loop: drugs are identified as a 'threat', the war is fought to eradicate the threat and global prohibition is put in place to hermetically seal the world against the threat. Key international agencies in the drugs field are set up to do only one thing – fight - and securitisation can be the only response to the emergence of organised crime. This second securitisation obscures the first one and over time the two are conflated in such a way as to make it appear that we are now fighting 'drugs and crime' (as reflected in the creation of the UN Office on Drugs and Crime).

Maintaining the status quo

After decades of securitisation, the war on drugs is fundamentally integrated into much of the world's geopolitical frameworks. Substantial international relations frameworks are premised upon the war, its infrastructure, and finance.

Now we have a triple seal protecting the soft centre of prohibition: the initial securitisation of drugs and 'abuse', the second securitisation of trafficking and organised crime, and now the commitment to a geopolitical status quo, whose raison d'être is lost in the mists of time, but whose maintenance is perceived as absolutely essential to the preservation of a long standing world order.

This commitment to the status quo overrides any suggestion that the modus operandi is hopelessly outdated and totally unfit for purpose. Any challenge is now perceived as a threat to the world order, and cannot be countenanced. Evidence is anathema and must be sidelined at all costs. In 1995 the WHO failed to publish a study that outlined, amongst other things, the evidence on the harms of using coca and cocaine (WHO and UNICRI, 1995). At the 48th World Health Assembly, the US representative to the WHO threatened to withdraw US funding for WHO research projects:

> The United States Government considered that, *if WHO activities relating to drugs failed to reinforce proven drug control approaches, funds for the relevant programmes should be curtailed.* In view of the gravity of the matter, he asked the Director-General for an assurance that WHO would dissociate itself from the conclusions of the study and that, in substance abuse activities, an approach *would not* be adopted that could be used to justify the continued production of coca.
>
> (WHO, 1995)

This is from a debate in the UK House of Commons (9 September 2010):

Tom Brake MP: 'I seek reassurance that when sound, factual evidence is produced to show what is effective in tackling drug crime and addressing health issues, the hon. Gentleman will sign up to that.'

Alan Campbell MP: 'I cannot give the hon. Gentleman the assurance he seeks because he is sending me along a route he knows I cannot go down.'

The route, of course, was towards decriminalisation or legal regulation of currently illicit drugs.

In an atmosphere where politicians are calculating whether to change policy on the basis of balancing effectiveness against political expediency and expenditure of political capital in a hostile environment, it is no wonder that genuine debate is stifled. However, this self-referential balancing act is being challenged by the reality of the overwhelmingly negative consequences that the war on drugs is now producing.

Shifts in power dynamics

> *I also take note of the debate that has come up here regarding the regulation of drugs. It is an essential debate. Firstly I think it should be considered in a pluralistic democracy and it's great that we have that in this country and that the pros and cons should always be deeply analysed.*
>
> (President Felipe Calderon of Mexico, August 2010)
>
> *President Calderon is right to call for [legalisation] to be discussed, without meaning that one is in agreement or not with the position of legalization.*
>
> (President Juan Manuel Santos of Colombia, August 2010)
>
> *There is as much chance of repealing the Eighteenth Amendment as there is for a hummingbird to fly to Mars with the Washington Monument tied to its tail.*
>
> (Morris Sheppard, author of the Eighteenth Amendment, September 1930)

US Alcohol Prohibition was repealed on 7 April 1933. The 13-year experiment had ended in complete and utter disaster. The crisis this mistaken policy had engendered had corrupted state and federal institutions and helped create the US Mafia. Its ultimate demise had been brought about by the loss of popular support for Prohibition and, in the context of the Great Depression, Government's dire need to raise alcohol revenue.

The forces at play then are strikingly similar to those leading senior statesmen and women to call into question the contemporary prohibition – polls all over the world show that support for fundamental reform is growing and we are clearly in the midst of deep economic recession.

The 28,000 deaths in Mexican turf wars in the last few years, have brought the extensive collateral damage of the securitisation as close to the US (the political home of the war on drugs) as they have ever been. Cocaine production has enabled paramilitaries and parapoliticians to fully integrate themselves into Colombian society. Afghanistan produces most of the world's illicit poppy in its virtually ungovernable southern states. Guinea Bissau became a narco state virtually overnight when the balloon effect moved the cocaine trade into west Africa.

We have now reached the point where the tragic irony of securitisation is made truly manifest. The power dynamics have shifted such that significant power is moving from the state to criminals and paramilitaries. Far from preserving and promoting security, the extraordinary measures of the global securitisations have fundamentally compromised the security of a number of nation states. This is providing the wake up call that is stirring former and serving government leaders in Latin America to call for substantive debates on alternatives to global prohibition.

A three-pillar impact assessment

What is needed is to shift from a securitised approach to one that is founded upon the three pillars of the United Nations, namely human rights, development and security (Barnett, 2010). In an influential report on UN reform former Secretary General of the UN, Kofi Annan noted that 'we will not enjoy development without security, we will not enjoy security without development, and we will not enjoy either without respect for human rights. Unless all these causes are advanced, none will succeed' (Annan, 2005).

Exposing drug policy to evidence based scrutiny is one of the keys to building a bridge between the threat-based approach and a three pillar approach, as per UN norms. One way to do this is to call upon policy-makers to apply the established policy scrutiny tool of Impact Assessment (IA) (International Drug Policy Consortium, 2007) to expose the failure of the war on its own terms.

The following is taken from: 'Time for an Impact Assessment of Drug Policy', International Drug Policy Consortium, 2009 (International Drug Policy Commission, 2009):

> For too long, the debate around improving drug policy has been emotive, polarised and deadlocked. A useful way to determine the best mix of evidence-based drug policies is through an independent, neutral process that all stakeholders can support, because it does not commit anyone to a particular position in advance. One way to achieve this is through IAs of drug policy, at the national and international levels, that compare the economic, environmental and social costs and benefits of existing policies with a range of alternatives. To ensure all stakeholders can support the process, the alternatives assessed should range from more intensive/punitive enforcement approaches, through options for decriminalisation of personal use, to models for legal regulation of drug production and supply.

The historic nature of the drug policy debate has meant that policy development has often lacked objective scrutiny. By rationally and methodically focusing on the evidence, in terms of costs and benefits of different options, and using established methodologies already embedded in most governments' processes, IA brings drug policy back into the arena of science, avoiding the polarising clashes that have long defined the debate. A call for IA is essentially a call for better evidence, and a structured approach to assessing policy options to inform debate and determine the best way forward. As such it is politically neutral, and a very reasonable request to policy-makers.

IA serves a number of very useful functions, because it:

- challenges policy-makers to apply evidence to policy;
- drives drug policy into the realm of the normal in policy-making terms;
- helps bring drug policy out of the securitised and into the normal policy arena;
- helps develop the evidence base for the current regime;
- encourages policy-makers to explore alternatives to prohibition;
- enables public scrutiny of a comparison between regimes.

Policy-makers need to show that prohibition is really delivering on development, security and rights.

Conclusion: the global drug control system is in crisis: the time has come to explore alternatives

> We recommend that the Government initiates a discussion within the Commission on Narcotic Drugs of alternative ways – including the possibility of legalisation and regulation – to tackle the global drugs dilemma.
>
> (UK Parliamentary Home Affairs Select Committee, 2002)

One of the members of the Committee who voted for the above recommendation was an up and coming backbencher, David Cameron. He has failed to repeat this call since becoming Prime Minister.

There is no doubt that prohibition is in crisis – from producer and transit countries, to predominantly consumer nations. However, the geopolitical obstacles to reform are significant and substantial moves, at a global level, away from the status quo are, more than likely, years away. In the meantime it is the responsibility of all those involved in the policy-making process to assert the need for an evidence based approach that includes exploration of alternative policy options. In the security field this could take the form of a series of security impact assessments.

The need for a normalised approach to drug policy (based upon promoting development and security within the context of a human rights approach), is needed now more than ever – to create a policy environment conducive to ending the war on drugs, and replacing it with one that is effective, just and humane.

Transform drug policy foundation

Mission

To end the War on Drugs and establish effective and humane systems of drug regulation

Our activities

- Carry out research, policy analysis and innovative policy development.
- Challenge government to demonstrate rational, fact-based evidence to support its policies and expenditure.
- Promote alternative, evidence-based policies to parliamentarians, government and government agencies.
- Advise non-governmental organisations whose work is affected by drugs in developing drug policies appropriate to their own mission and objectives.
- Provide an informed, rational and clear voice in the public and media debate on UK and international drug policy.

Acknowledgement

I am indebted to my colleague Emily Crick, for bringing me the securitisation framework and the numerous conversations we had about it. This paper would not have come about were it not for her input. My heartfelt thanks are also due to Damon Barrett of IHRA for his help in clarifying my views on wellbeing and three pillars.

References

Annan, K. (2005) *In Larger Freedom: Towards Development, Security and Human Rights for All*, UN Doc No. A/59/2005, 21 March, New York: United Nations.

Barrett, D. (2010) Security, development and human rights: Normative, legal and policy challenges for the international drug control system, *International Journal of Drug Policy*, 21, 140–4.

Buzan, B., Waever, O. and de Wilde, J. (1997) *Security: A New Framework for Analysis*, Boulder: Lynne Reinner.

Costa, A. (2008) *Making Drug Control 'Fit for Purpose': Building on the UNGASS Decade*, Vienna: United Nations, Commission on Narcotic Drugs.

International Drug Policy Consortium (2007) *Towards Better Regulation?*, ed. Colin Kirkpatrick, Cheltenham: Edward Elgar.

International Drug Policy Consortium (2009) *Time for an Impact Assessment of Drug Policy*, London, International Drug Policy Consortium.

Okrent, Daniel (2010) *Last Call: The Rise and Fall of Prohibition*, New York: Scribner's.

Strategic Studies Institute (2000) *The United States and Colombia: Untying the GordianKnot*, Carlisle Barracks: Strategic Studies Institute.

Latin American Commission on Drugs and Democracy (2009) www.drogasedemocracia.org/Arquivos/declaracao_ingles_situ_pdf, accessed 10 February, 2011.

Transform Drug Policy, Foundation (2009) *After the War on Drugs: Blueprint for Regulation*, Bristol: Transform.

UK, Parliamentary Home Affairs Select Committee (2002) *The Government's Drugs Policy: Is It Working?*, Command Paper 5573, London: The Stationery Office.

WHO (1995) www.dpf.org.uk/WorldHealthAssembly1995pdf, accessed 9 February 2011.

WHO/UNICRI (1995) www.tdpf.org.uk/WHO-UNICRIcocainestudypdf, accessed 9 February 2011.

Chapter 9

THE ETHICS OF HARM REDUCTION

Adrian Carter, Peter G Miller and Wayne Hall

Introduction

Harm reduction is an approach to drug policy that emerged in the 1980s largely in response to the HIV (human immunodeficiency virus) epidemic among injecting drug users, although there were earlier anticipations (Ball, 2007).

There are many definitions of harm reduction, some more contested than others (Kleinig, 2008). In illicit drug policy, it is often used as a shorthand term for interventions for which there is good evidence of public health benefit and a strong humanitarian warrant for their provision such as: providing clean injecting equipment to injecting drug users (IDUs); methadone maintenance treatment (MMT) for opioid dependence; educating IDUs about ways of reducing blood-borne virus (BBV) transmission and drug overdoses; HIV testing and counselling; access to antiretroviral therapy (ART) for HIV; and access to effective treatments for chronic hepatitis C virus (HCV) infection (Hall, 2007). Harm reduction now also includes policies towards alcohol, tobacco, other regulated drugs and gambling, such as: promoting less hazardous forms of tobacco use; encouraging the use of low alcohol beers; responsible service of alcohol; and setting maximum bet and loss limits for gamblers.

Harm reduction is regarded by its advocates in developed countries as an evidence-based and humane way of reducing drug-related harm. This view is not universally accepted. Some critics see 'harm reduction' as a morally objectionable approach that facilitates, or is at least complicit in, what they regard as a moral evil: using illicit drugs. Similarly, many tobacco control researchers have opposed proposals to introduce new less harmful tobacco products onto the market. There has also been very strong resistance from alcohol treatment circles to controlled drinking as a treatment goal for problem drinkers.

Some critics oppose harm reduction on grounds that are more open to empirical test. One common claim is that in failing to condemn the use of illicit drugs, harm reduction sends a message that illicit drug use is acceptable, thereby increasing the number of illicit drug users and drug-related harm (e.g. G.W. Bush cited in Kleinig, 2008: 1).

Other critics argue that harm reduction approaches fail to get people 'off drugs'. There is considerable evidence that these claims are false. Evaluations of both NSP and supervised injecting facilities, for example, have found that users who may not have otherwise sought treatment do so as a result of participating in these programmes (Hagan et al., 2000; Wood et al., 2006).

The other chapters of this book describe many examples of harm reduction practices that are effective in meeting their goals. These approaches seem self-evidently 'good' to supporters of harm reduction, but they remain controversial primarily because they do not interpret drug use through the same moral lens as those who insist upon abstinence from drug use as the only acceptable drug policy goal. How is harm reduction understood in response to such moral claims? We build upon

Harm Reduction in Substance Use and High-Risk Behaviour: International Policy and Practice, First Edition.
Edited by Richard Pates and Diane Riley.
© 2012 Blackwell Publishing Ltd. Published 2012 by Blackwell Publishing Ltd.

the work of thoughtful authors before us, in considering harm reduction from an ethical and moral viewpoint (e.g. Keane, 2003; Christie et al., 2008; Hathaway and Tousaw, 2008; Kleinig, 2008; Fry and Irwin, 2009). We also use two examples to illustrate some of the ethical issues raised by harm reduction policies in the alcohol and other drug fields.

What is harm reduction?

Reducing drug-related harm could be said to be the goal of every intervention and policy related to drugs, whether they focus on preventing, stopping, or reducing drug use, or alleviating its adverse consequences. What is it that distinguishes 'harm reduction' policies from other policies towards drug use?

The term 'harm reduction' is most often used by its advocates to describe policies that aim to reduce the harmful consequences of drug use without requiring drug users to stop or reduce their drug use (Lenton and Single, 1998). According to the International Harm Reduction Association (IHRA):

> 'Harm Reduction' refers to policies, programmes and practices that aim primarily to reduce the adverse health, social and economic consequences of the use of legal and illegal psychoactive drugs without necessarily reducing drug consumption.
>
> (International Harm Reduction Association, 2010).

Underlying this concept of harm reduction is the recognition that many people will engage in illegal drug use, despite the strongest efforts of government and civil society to prevent or discourage such use.

Harm reduction involves the following key principles.

1. Some people who use drugs and experience problems are either unable or unwilling to stop using.
2. It is important to encourage these people to seek treatment and, failing that, to provide advice on how to reduce the harms that their drug use causes.
3. Harm reduction is a targeted approach that focuses on specific risks and harms and targets the causes of risks and harms using approaches that are practical, feasible, effective, safe and cost-effective.
4. Keeping people who use drugs alive and preventing irreparable damage is a higher priority than achieving abstinence in the short term.

Is harm reduction a value-neutral approach to drug use?

Many harm reductionists claim that they adopt a value neutral attitude towards drug use and drug users. Some commentators see this as a major advantage of harm reduction (Strang, 1993; Erickson et al., 1997; Rumbold and Hamilton, 1998; Keane, 2003), and a 'powerful rhetorical intervention' in an area that is highly moralised (Keane, 2003; Tammi and Hurme, 2007). Kleinig (2008) argues that the claim that harm reduction is morally neutral is implausible for a number of reasons.

First, harm reduction unavoidably makes ethical assumptions in identifying harms and in its core principle that reducing harms experienced by drug users and others is a worthy social goal.

Second, there is a major ethical issue in deciding which harms matter most in setting drug policies. What importance do we place upon the harms experienced by: drug users; non-users directly affected by others' drug use (e.g. family members, neighbours); and the broader society (which is affected by lost productivity, criminal acts, the costs of policing drug use, neglected family members and the treatment of health problems arising from drug use)?

Third, questions of how to prioritise and make trade-offs between qualitatively different drug-related harms require ethical judgments that in liberal pluralistic societies are resolved by social and political deliberation (Kleinig, 2008; Weatherburn, 2009). It is difficult to accurately or objectively measure and balance all drug-related harms. Street-level law enforcement can lead some drug users to engage in risky injecting practices, such as injecting rapidly and carelessly or needle sharing to avoid apprehension (Weatherburn, 2009). It can also encourage other drug users to stop or seek help to do so. We do not have the means of quantifying the aggregate effects of these competing harms.

Even if we were able to accurately measure them, many of these harms are qualitatively different. How do we balance the wide variety of harms associated with different drug policies? For example, can one easily balance the harms arising from increased street surveillance (such as stopping and searching youth suspected of drug offences, increased needle-related harm and the loss of civil liberties for non-drug users) against the reduction in public drug dealing without some ethical judgment about their comparative moral worth?

The failure to acknowledge the ethical basis of harm reduction policies can also have undesirable consequences. First, value-neutral approaches do not provide ethical guidance when valuing and balancing the effects of different policies on a range of invested individuals and society. Second, programmes lacking an ethical basis close off dialogue with critics of harm reduction policies. By assuming that the need for harm reduction is self-evident, advocates of harm reduction miss the opportunity to convince those that do not share their view (Kleinig, 2008). Third, while a value-neutral harm reduction approach may have attracted broad support in countries such as Australia and western Europe, such an approach has received much less public and political support in countries such as the USA and Russia (Keane, 2003; Kleinig, 2008).

Fourth, harm reduction policies may win support from the broader community for tax-funded programmes that improve the health of 'drug users' by focusing on their social and economic benefits. They can, however, also unwittingly reinforce prevailing social prejudices (Kleinig, 2006). A programme without a sound ethical basis for their provision can result in punitive approaches that make the programmes less effective, provide inadequate healthcare, and increase harm to society. While an aggregative approach may convince governments to provide MMT, the absence of an ethical warrant for the programme (e.g. providing effective medical healthcare) can lead to low doses of methadone being given that are insufficient to prevent craving and drug use. Punitive responses to positive urines in MMT can lead to patients being kicked off the programme. Both of these responses undermine the effectiveness of MMT and lead to greater social harm. A clear distinction needs to be made between the ethical justification for a health policy, and the sorts of arguments that may be used to garner support for these policies.

Liberalism and ethical presumptions of harm reduction

A key ethical issue for harm reduction is how to reconcile the conflict between an individual's 'right' to use potentially harmful drugs and the use of State power to prohibit or regulate how drugs are used (Hathaway, 2001). This reflects wider debates about whether society can legitimately draw legal boundaries around the right to engage in some forms of risky behaviour (e.g. drug use) while allowing others (e.g. bungee jumping, mountain climbing) (Keane, 2003) or glamorising successful risk takers as 'heroes' who define the boundaries of human endeavour (e.g. adolescents who sail solo around-the-world) (Miller, 2001).

Much harm reduction discourse assumes that drug use is an individual's choice. This is reflected in the priority given within liberal democracies to individual autonomy and in the harm principle of John Stuart Mill (1892): if an individual wants to do something – even if it may harm them – then that is their business unless it harms someone else. Some follow Mill in arguing that individuals have the 'right' to use drugs so long as they do not harm others (Husak, 1992; Hathaway, 2001; Cohen and Csete, 2006).

Other ethicists have argued that the illegality of using some drugs adversely affects the dignity of an already marginalised group of people. Ethical responses to drug-related problems, these commentators argue, must include measures that maintain or enhance the dignity of drug users (Ashcroft, 2005). This position has some force when one considers that cultural factors, such as social disadvantage (e.g. lack of education and social resources, discrimination) and mental illness increase the risk of developing drug problems (Hathaway and Erickson, 2003).

Critics of the liberal principle of respect for autonomy argue that some drug users lack the ability to make autonomous decisions. In their case, they argue, society may intervene to make decisions on their behalf that will restore their autonomy (Charland, 2002; Cohen et al., 2002; Caplan, 2008). On this view, harm reduction policies that mitigate the harm caused by drug use without attempting to restore addicted individual's autonomy are unethical. A full discussion of this issue is beyond the scope of this paper but we have argued elsewhere that the view that addiction overrides an individual's autonomy is not supported by scientific evidence (Carter and Hall, 2008).

Ethical theories and frameworks for assessing harm reduction approaches

Ethical debate in controversial areas of public policy is often represented as a competition between two different approaches to moral reasoning: *consequentialism* and *deontology* (Rachels, 1999). In consequentialism the rightfulness or wrongfulness of competing courses of action (or moral rules) are determined solely by weighing up the costs and benefits to determine which action (or moral rule) produces the greatest good for the greatest number (Singer, 1993). The most well known form of consequentialism is the *utilitarianism* of Jeremy Bentham and John Stuart Mill.

A harm reduction approach, as it is often constructed by its proponents, is a form of utilitarianism that seeks to minimise suffering rather than to maximise happiness. As a result, harm reduction is open to many of the criticisms often levelled at utilitarianism. As Stephen Mugford (1993) has pointed out, highly punitive anti-drug policies can be justified on the utilitarian grounds that the individual rights of the drug-addicted minority are outweighed by the greater public good that results when the suffering of the addicted few deters the majority from using these drugs. Such a policy rationale, which arguably implicitly underlies some commonly used justifications for prohibition, would be unacceptable to many libertarian harm reductionists.

Deontology is an approach to ethics that appeals to natural or universal rules or principles (e.g. the categorical imperative, 'natural law' or the principle that persons should always be treated as ends rather than means (Kant, 1996)). A common criticism of deontological approaches is that the absolute adherence to universal principles (e.g. that one should always tell the truth regardless of the consequences) can cause harm that might otherwise have been avoided (e.g. by lying to the Gestapo about the location of Jewish people in occupied Europe in the 1940s). Christie et al. (2008) argue that a Kantian approach to ethics requires that all individuals should refrain from using drugs that impair individual autonomy. On this view, any harm reduction policies that implicitly or explicitly condone such drug use would be morally unacceptable, irrespective of how much harm they avoided. The counter to this argument would be that an individual expresses their autonomy while not intoxicated by choosing to use drugs and accepting the consequences of their actions.

Principlism

Principlism emerged in the USA in the 1970s as an approach to bioethics that identified four common moral principles shared by different ethical theorists that could be used to guide practical ethical decision-making (Beauchamp and Childress, 2001). Its language still forms the backbone of many codes of research ethics (see National Health and Medical Research Council, 1999).

The four major ethical principles are: respect for *autonomy* (interpreted as respecting the actions of rational persons and requiring informed voluntary consent, confidentiality and privacy); *non-maleficence* (minimising risks and harms to individuals); *beneficence* (ensuring that the benefits of interventions outweigh risks); and *distributive justice* (ensuring an equitable distribution of risks and benefits of research participation) (National Health and Medical Research Council, 1999; Beauchamp and Childress, 2001).

Principlism is a pluralistic approach that attempts to find a balance between a respect for persons within a utilitarian cost–benefit analysis (beneficence and non-maleficence) that seeks to achieve the best outcome using scientific evidence and principles of societal fairness. Autonomy is often regarded as the pre-eminent value within this framework, reflecting its liberal origins in the USA (Callahan, 2003). It also features prominently in ethical discussions of addiction where drug users' autonomy is called into question (Cohen, 2002).

A major challenge for principlism is how to resolve the conflicts that often arise between these four ethical principles. In the treatment of addiction, for example, respecting the autonomy of the addicted person to engage in drug use may conflict with the principles of beneficence and non-maleficence that require us to intervene to prevent harm and do good.

Principlism has two key virtues: (1) it reflects the ethical values of the western liberal society from which it emerged, and; (2) its simplicity in conceptualisation and application makes it an attractive way to structure ethical debates and guide clinical decision-making. Few other ethical frameworks have shown the same utility and popularity as principlism in the clinical setting.

Dignity and human rights

A human rights approach to ethics gives the highest priority to the dignity of the individual and the rights that this is seen as entailing. It recognises that drug addicted individuals are persons first and foremost and, like all persons, are deserving of human dignity, and the protection of basic human rights (Gostin, 2001; Carter and Hall, 2010). As the IHRA states: 'People who use drugs do not forfeit their human rights, including the right to the highest attainable standard of health, to social services, to work, to benefit from scientific progress, to freedom from arbitrary detention and freedom from cruel inhuman and degrading treatment.' Unfortunately, this laudable position is not reflected in the treatment of drug users in many countries around the globe.

A human rights approach is less likely to be influenced by powerful competing interests: 'Human rights inhere to the *person* and are not contingent on consensus or majority view' (Cohen and Csete, 2006: 103). A human rights approach also potentially allows for a better balance between public health and law enforcement approaches to drug use (Cohen and Csete, 2006). Threats of incarceration of drug users can adversely affect public health initiatives. It can deter addicted individuals from accessing harm reduction programmes (e.g. NSPs, supervised injecting centres) and other treatment services. Under a human rights framework, law enforcement agencies and officials, like drug users, are accountable to the law. This can limit the type of interventions that law enforcement officials can use and reduce law enforcement activities that adversely affect public health initiatives.

Critics argue that human rights does not resolve debates about the moral basis of harm reduction or specify how to reconcile the conflicting rights of different parties affected by drug use, such as the rights of parents to use drugs and the rights of their children to be growing up in an environment free from drug abuse and addiction

Virtue ethics

Virtue ethics approaches specify the qualities that an ethical decision-maker needs to possess such as: honesty, loyalty, courage, compassion, kindness and fairness (Christie et al., 2008). While virtue ethics promotes respect, tolerance and compassion, it is not clear how such an approach would assist policy-makers and clinicians in running harm reduction programmes. Given that addiction and those that suffer from it are often discriminated against, stigmatised and vulnerable, a compassionate approach is one that might require respect for the dignity of those suffering from addiction. However, a virtue ethics approach still needs to strike a balance between too much and not enough compassion that does not depend upon appeal to moral intuitions, a criticism also made of principlist approaches

Communitarian ethics

Communitarianism, like virtue ethics, 'is meant to characterise a way of thinking about ethical problems, not to provide any formulas or rigid criteria for dealing with them' (Callahan, 2003: 288). It has been proposed as a solution to some of the problems with principlism because it gives more weight to the common good and public interests than to individual autonomy.

In the case of drug use, it is not always clear what the 'common good' or who the 'community' is. Communitarian ethics has been criticised for reifying 'the community' and for assuming that societal agreement is possible in the case of contested issues and that the views of all members of the community contribute equally to 'the community view'. Experience suggests this is unlikely to be the case (Keane, 2005).

The behaviour of the uninformed and often uninterested majority towards a disenfranchised minority may not always be 'ethical'. Indeed, it might support policies that violate the rights of a vulnerable minority of 'drug users' who are seen as the source of social harm. A consensus approach might privilege the 'majority' preference for 'drug free' streets and justify intrusions into the personal liberty of a vulnerable drug addicted population whose interests are not taken into account. If it is the process of seeking consensus that is most important, then communitarian ethics potentially adds a valuable element to ethical deliberation about harm reduction.

The communitarian ethics model also has a number of positives in dealing with drug policy. Firstly, it can add other ethical principles, such as, honesty and fidelity in deliberations about ethical dilemmas. Secondly, communitarian ethics accepts that there is often conflict between principles and attempts to resolve them by appealing to shared ideas of 'community benefit'. Some addiction and drug policy issues may, however, still require tailored responses that do not fit notions of community benefit. For example, reducing hepatitis C among IDUs might mean accepting more discarded needles in public spaces.

A pluralist approach to ethical decision-making based on dignity

The variety of ethical frameworks reflects the reality that there is no consensus on a single universal theory of ethics (Miller et al., 2010). None of the ethical approaches described above provides a complete framework that encompasses all the ways in which individuals, groups, and institutions make ethical decisions. Each approach captures a small part of the multiple ways in which ethical decisions are made: some approaches are more applicable to different types of ethical decision-making or ways of thinking about ethical decision-making (e.g. the types of character traits that one should cultivate to make good ethical judgments), mindfulness of the wider community and community processes (e.g. considering vulnerable groups and garnering consensus) in ethical decision-making; human dignity and the individual rights that this confers.

In the absence of agreement, we argue for a pluralist approach that considers actions from a variety of different ethical frameworks. Programmes that can withstand interrogation from a range of ethical frameworks are arguably more ethically robust and more likely to attract public support. In a pluralistic democracy, when conflicting ethical judgments are encountered, a policy outcome is sought that achieves the broadest support. Ideally, respect for the dignity of all individuals, as embodied in both principlist and human rights approaches, should be at the centre of this approach but in reality the outcome is often an untidy compromise that fully satisfies no one approach.

Case studies of harm reduction ethics

The self-evident good of reducing drug-related harm can often mask questions about the ethical basis of harm reduction policies. It is often only when we consider boundary cases of harm reduction policies, those that are at the periphery of generally accepted forms of harm reduction, that debates about the ethical basis of harm reduction policies becomes apparent.

For example, the proposal to use harm reduction approaches (e.g. minor genital cuts) to minimise the harm caused by full female circumcision (Shell-Duncan, 2008), has not been greeted with the same enthusiasm as harm reduction approaches in drug policy. The arguments used to denounce the use of minor genital cuts are similar to those employed by opponents of harm reduction in drug policy: that this approach is complicit in genital mutilation which should be opposed absolutely. Giving tacit approval to this practice, it is argued, will lead to an increase in or at least a persistence of a morally abhorrent behaviour.

In this section, we consider two such boundary case studies of harm reduction drug policy in order to illustrate some of the ethical questions discussed in the previous section. First, we examine the controversial question of whether we should provide IDUs with information on groin injecting. While harm reduction has traditionally been reserved for drug policies that are aimed at illicit drug users, we will also consider the ethics of harm reduction in tobacco policy.

Providing information on 'safer' groin injecting

Groin injecting (GI), or injecting into the femoral vein in the groin region, is an often dangerous practice reported by up to 50% of injecting drug users (IDUs) in the UK (Maliphant and Scott, 2005). It has also been seen at different periods in Australian injecting populations (Darke et al., 2001). It is almost impossible to guarantee that groin injection will be safe (although a small minority of GIs never develop complications). There is a small margin for error with this type of injecting because the femoral vein, artery and nerve run alongside each other, deep under the skin. The risk is exacerbated when injectors are hurrying to avoid withdrawal or are intoxicated. Deep venous thrombosis (DVT), accidental arterial injection, venous ulceration and local infections are possible complications that can have serious health consequences for the injector (Rhodes et al., 2006).

Recent UK research in London and Bristol suggests that an increasing proportion of novice and new injectors engage in groin injecting, after using as little as one or two other injection sites (Maliphant and Scott, 2005: 4). The apparent 'normalisation' of groin injecting among UK IDU is a major problem for which effective solutions are currently lacking (Rhodes et al., 2006).

Given the risks of groin injecting, there has been serious debate about how best to respond to individuals who engage in it (e.g. Rhodes et al., 2007; Rhodes and Kimber, 2007; Miller et al., 2008; Zador et al., 2008; Miller et al., 2009). The most common response has been the distribution of 'how to' booklets and posters in NSPs. According to the value-neutral approach to drug use, these policies should be promoted to allow individuals who engage in GI to reduce the harms. Some are concerned, however, that the distribution of booklets and posters might increase groin injection, and in doing so, produce more harm in aggregate while marginally reducing harm for individuals (Miller et al., 2008). Is it ethical to provide information that might encourage novice or early career injectors to see groin injecting as a viable option, or will the provision of such information ameliorate harm experienced by people who are already groin injecting or are certain to do so in the future?

Analysis of the ethical issues: a principlist perspective

In a previous attempt to understand the ethical issues associated with groin injection, Miller et al. (2008) used a principlist framework to investigate a range of possible responses from agencies dealing with potential and current groin injectors. They included: (1) provision of harm reduction information about how to groin inject; (2) training IDUs to find other injecting sites and to use good injecting techniques; (3) permitting groin injectors to access treatment (such as drug consumption rooms (DCRs) and injecting clinics (ICs)), but banning them from groin injecting within these services; and (4) excluding groin injectors from accessing services. We consider the first of these here.

Supplying information can be seen as supporting an individual's *autonomy* by allowing them to make their own decisions. However, it may also be that IDUs choose to groin inject because of the social pressures when injecting (Rhodes et al., 2006) or a lack of skill or knowledge about how to inject elsewhere. Similarly, the influence of 'addiction' on their ability to make a rational choice also needs to be considered (Cohen, 2002).

Given that it is impossible to guarantee the safety of groin injection, supplying such information to all IDUs may well have unintended consequences. Therefore, simply handing out advice without any assessment of whether the information is suitable for the person's injecting career may breach the tenants of *non-maleficence* and *beneficence*. On the other hand, not supplying harm reduction information to an individual who is determined to start groin injection could allow them to seriously harm themselves.

A more appropriate response might distinguish between 'last resort' and 'convenience' groin injectors. Harm reduction information would be provided at a lower threshold for last resort injectors, whereas convenience groin injectors would be strongly encouraged to use other injection sites. In this case, a principlist framework suggests a tailored dissemination of information to address ethical concerns.

A human rights perspective

Using a human rights perspective, it could be argued that respect for the autonomy of drug users would require the provision of information on the risks and 'best practice' groin injecting. This would allow IDUs to make an informed choice about whether to do so and assist them to reduce their risks if they decided to do so. On the other hand, critics may argue that such a 'rights-based' approach relies too much on the assumptions that individuals who are addicted are able to make informed judgments under the exigencies of intoxication and withdrawal and social pressures to inject, all of which might compromise their ability to make a free choice.

Smokeless tobacco and harm reduction

Sweden has a similar prevalence of tobacco use to its neighbours but one of the world's lowest tobacco-attributable mortality rates. Some observers have suggested that this is because of the high rates of use of a smokeless tobacco product, called snus, by former male Swedish smokers (Ramström, 2000; Ramström and Foulds, 2006), although this interpretation is disputed (Tomar et al., 2003). Snus is pasteurised and refrigerated to greatly reduce the formation of nitrosamines, the main carcinogens in tobacco. This, and the absence of the combustion products associated with smoking (e.g. tars and carbon monoxide), are believed to reduce the risks of cardiovascular disease, chronic obstructive pulmonary disease and cancer, when compared to smoking (Foulds et al., 2003; Critchley and Unal, 2004; Luo et al., 2007). Snus use appears to carry some residual risks of pancreatic cancer (Boffetta et al., 2005; Luo et al., 2007), cardiovascular disease (Bolinder et al., 1994) and possibly diabetes (Persson et al., 2000; Eliasson et al., 2004), but the risks are much lower (perhaps 90%) than smoking.

Some researchers have argued that smokers who are unable to quit should be provided with low nitrosamine smokeless tobacco products, such as snus, to reduce tobacco-related harm. There has been strong resistance to such proposals by tobacco control advocates. They argue that tobacco use of any kind is addictive and harmful we should be trying to eliminate all tobacco use, not opening more avenues to nicotine dependence. These arguments are similar to those used by zero tolerance advocates in illicit drugs.

Analysis of the ethical issues

A liberalist *respect for autonomy* holds that individuals should be able to use any form of tobacco, given that it is a licit and broadly available substance. However, this freedom may be overridden if their tobacco use caused harm to others (e.g. smoking bans in public places to prevent the harm of passive smoking). However, snus is a product that has no direct adverse health impacts upon others.

There are also *beneficent* and *non-maleficent* warrants for allowing smokers to access snus-like products. While quitting all tobacco use is the only health advice that doesn't carry *any* risk, many smokers fail to follow this advice. Advocates of tobacco harm reduction argue that 'quit or die', should not be the only health options available to smokers (Fagerström, 2002).

If snus is an effective way of improving the health of 'nicotine dependent' persons, then a human rights approach arguably provides a strong warrant for allowing smokers to use snus. It would be a denial of smokers human rights to prevent access to a product that substantially lowers the risk of harm when cigarettes, the most harmful tobacco product, are readily available (Kozlowski, 2002).

Critics allow that while snus may reduce the individual user's risks, its widespread use could increase population level harm. First, if snus proved more popular among non-smokers than smokers, then overall harm could increase. Second, the promotion of snus could keep current smokers smoking (instead of quitting) or lead some non-smokers to commence smoking.

If these critics were correct, policies to prevent the widespread use of snus might be justified on the utilitarian grounds that the gains to the greater public good (health) would override any benefits to individual snus users. There is considerable evidence against this argument. The large difference in health risk between smoking and snus use (approx. 90%) means that even if all non-smokers used snus its adverse health effects would be less than the health gains achieved from all smokers switching to snus (Tobacco Advisory Group of the Royal College of Physicians, 2002; Gartner et al., 2007a). In Sweden, moreover, most snus users are former smokers, few non-smokers use snus, and very rarely do snus users become smokers (Ramström and Foulds, 2006). See Gartner et al. (2007b) for a detailed discussion of these issues.

Conclusions

Harm reduction is not a morally neutral approach to drug policy. Ethical judgments and reasoning are central to harm reduction approaches to drug policy; they are also important in guiding how harm reduction programme operators can best administer them.

An important consideration in examining the ethics of a harm reduction programme is determining whether the reductions in harms to the individual who use these programmes outweighs any possible increases in broader social harm that may rise from allowing individuals to engage in harmful behaviours. As our case studies show, these questions cannot always be answered simply by an empirically driven cost-benefit analysis. An ethical analysis enables harm reduction programmes to be delivered in ways that maximises benefits while minimising any additional social harm. An ethical analysis can also assist in identifying empirical evidence that is critical in evaluating what the impact of different policies might be on drug-related harm.

References

Ashcroft, R. (2005) Making sense of dignity, *Journal of Medical Ethics*, 31 (11), 679–82.

Ball, A.L. (2007) HIV, injecting drug use and harm reduction: a public health response, *Addiction*, 102 (5), 684–90.

Beauchamp, T. L. and Childress, J. F. (2001) *Principles of Biomedical Ethics*, New York: Oxford University Press.

Boffetta, P., Aagnes, B., Weiderpass, E. and Andersen, A. (2005) Smokeless tobacco use and risk of cancer of the pancreas and other organs, *International Journal of Cancer*, 114 (6), 992–5.

Bolinder, G., Alfredsson, L., Englund, A. and de Faire, U. (1994) Smokeless tobacco use and increased cardiovascular mortality among Swedish construction workers, *American Journal of Public Health*, 84 (3), 399–404.

Callahan, D. (2003) Principlism and communitarianism, *Journal of Medical Ethics*, 29 (5), 287–91.

Caplan, A. (2008) Denying autonomy in order to create it: the paradox of forcing treatment upon addicts, *Addiction*, 103 (12), 1919–21.

Carter, A. and Hall, W. (2008) The issue of consent in research that administers drugs of addiction to addicted persons, *Accountability in Research*, 15 (4), 209–25.

Carter, A. and Hall, W. (2010) The rights of individuals treated for addiction. In D. Dudley, D. Siloveand F. Gale (eds), *Mental Health and Human Rights*, London: Oxford University Press, 519–29.

Charland, L.C. (2002) Cynthia's dilemma: consenting to heroin prescription, *American Journal of Bioethics*, 2 (2), 37–47.

Christie, T., Groarke, L. and Sweet, W. (2008) Virtue ethics as an alternative to deontological and consequential reasoning in the harm reduction debate, *International Journal of Drug Policy*, 19 (1), 52–8.

Cohen, J. and Csete, J. (2006) As strong as the weakest pillar: harm reduction, law enforcement and human rights, *International Journal of Drug Policy*, 17 (2), 101–3.

Cohen, M.J.M., Jasser, S., Herron, P.D. and Margolis, C.G. (2002) Ethical perspectives: opioid treatment of chronic pain in the context of addiction, *Clinical Journal of Pain*, 18 (4, supple.) S99–S107.

Cohen, P.J. (2002) Untreated addiction imposes an ethical bar to recruiting addicts for non-therapeutic studies of addictive drugs, *Journal of Law Medicine & Ethics*, 30 (1), 73–81.

Critchley, J.A. and Unal, B. (2004) Is smokeless tobacco a risk factor for coronary heart disease? A systematic review of epidemiological studies, *European Journal of Cardiovascular Prevention and Rehabilitation*, 11 (2), 101–12.

Darke, S., Ross, J. and Kaye, S. (2001) Physical injecting sites among injecting drug users in Sydney, Australia, *Drug and Alcohol Dependence*, 62 (1), 77–82.

Eliasson, M., Asplund, K., Nasic, S. and Rodu, B. (2004) Influence of smoking and snus on the prevalence and incidence of type 2 diabetes amongst men: the northern Sweden MONICA study, *Journal of Internal Medicine*, 256 (2), 101–10.

Erickson, P., Riley, D., Cheung, Y. and O'Hare, P. (1997) *Harm Reduction: A New Direction for Drug Policies and Programs*, Toronto: University of Toronto Press.

Fagerström, K. (2002) Quit or die: nothing in between?, *Respiration*, 69 (5), 387–8.

Foulds, J., Ramström, L., Burke, M. and Fagerström, K. (2003) Effect of smokeless tobacco (snus) on smoking and public health in Sweden, *Tobacco Control*, 12 (4), 349–59.

Fry, C.L. and Irwin, K. (2009) Engaging the values-based ethical dilemmas in harm minimization: a response to Weatherburn, *Addiction*, 104 (5), 862–3; author reply 863–4.

Gartner, C.E., Hall, W.D., Vos, T., Bertram, M.Y., Wallace, A.L. and Lim, S.S. (2007a) Assessment of Swedish snus for tobacco harm reduction: an epidemiological modelling study, *Lancet*, 369 (9578), 2010–14.

Gartner, C. E., Hall, W.D., Chapman, S. and Freeman B. (2007b) Should the health community promote smokeless tobacco (snus) as a harm reduction measure? *PLoS Medicine*, 4 (10), 1703–4.

Gostin, L.O. (2001) Beyond moral claims: a human rights approach in mental health, *Cambridge Quarterly of Healthcare Ethics*, 10 (3), 264–74.

Hagan, H., McGough, J.P., Thiede, H., Hopkins, S., Duchin, J. and Alexander, E.R. (2000) Reduced injection frequency and increased entry and retention in drug treatment associated with needle-exchange participation in Seattle drug injectors, *Journal of Substance Abuse Treatment*, 19 (3), 247–52.

Hall, W. (2007) What's in a name?, *Addiction*, 102 (5), 692.

Hathaway, A.D. (2001) Shortcomings of harm reduction: toward a morally invested drug reform strategy, *International Journal of Drug Policy*, 12 (2), 125–37.

Hathaway, A.D. and Erickson, P.G. (2003) Drug reform principles and policy debates: Harm reduction prospects for cannabis in Canada, *Journal of Drug Issues*, 33 (2), 465–95.

Hathaway, A.D. and Tousaw, K.I. (2008) Harm reduction headway and continuing resistance: Insights from safe injection in the city of Vancouver, *International Journal of Drug Policy*, 19 (1), 11–16.

Husak, D.N. (1992) *Drugs and Rights*, Cambridge: Cambridge University Press.

International Harm Reduction Association (2010) *What Is Harm Reduction?*, London: IHRA.

Kant, I. (1996) *The Metaphysics of Morals*, New York: Cambridge University Press.

Keane, H. (2003) Critiques of harm reduction, morality and the promise of human rights, *International Journal of Drug Policy*, 14 (3), 227–32.

Keane, H. (2005) Moral frameworks, ethical engagement and harm reduction: commentary on 'Ethical challenges and responses in harm reduction research: promoting applied communitarian ethics' by C. L. Fry, C. Treloar and L. Maher, *Drug and Alcohol Review*, 24 (6), 551–2.

Kleinig, J. (2006) Thinking ethically about needle and syringe programs, *Substance Use and Misuse*, 41 (6–7), 815–25.

Kleinig, J. (2008) The ethics of harm reduction, *Substance Use and Misuse*, 43 (1), 1–16.

Kozlowski, L. T. (2002) Harm reduction, public health, and human rights: smokers have a right to be informed of significant harm reduction options, *Nicotine & Tobacco Research*, 4 (4, supple. 2) S55–S60.

Lenton, S. and Single, E. (1998) The definition of harm reduction, *Drug Alcohol Rev*, 17 (2), 213–19.

Luo, J., Ye, W., Zendehdel, K., Adami, J., Adami, H.-O., Boffetta, P. and Nyrén, O. (2007) Oral use of Swedish moist snuff (snus) and risk for cancer of the mouth, lung, and pancreas in male construction workers: a retrospective cohort study, *Lancet*, 369 (9578), 2015–20.

Maliphant, J. and Scott, J. (2005) Use of the femoral vein ('groin injecting') by a sample of needle exchange clients in Bristol, UK, *Harm Reduction Journal*, 2 (1), 6.

Mill, J.S. (1892) *On Liberty*, London: Longmans, Green.

Miller, P., Carter, A. and Hall, W. (2010) Ethics in drugs research. In P.G. Miller, J. Strangand P.M. Miller (eds), *Addiction Research Methods*, Oxford: Wiley-Blackwell, 79–96.

Miller, P.G. (2001) A critical review of the harm minimization ideology in Australia, *Critical Public Health*, 11 (2), 167–78.

Miller, P.G., Forzisi, L., Zador, D., Lintzeris, N., Metrebian, N., Waal, R.V.D., Mayet, S. and Strang, J. (2009) Groin injecting in injectable opioid treatment service users in South London, *Addiction Research & Theory*, 17 (4), 381–9.

Miller, P. G., Lintzeris, N. and Forzisi, L. (2008) Is groin injecting an ethical boundary for harm reduction?, *International Journal of Drug Policy*, 19 (6), 486–91.

Mugford, S. (1993) Harm reduction: does it lead where its proponents imagine? In N. Heather, A. Wodak, E. Nadelmanand P. O'Hare (eds), *Psychoactive Drugs and Harm Reduction: From Faith to Science*, London: Whurr, 21–33.

National Health and Medical Research Council (1999) *National Statement on Ethical Conduct in Research Involving Humans*, Canberra: National Health and Medical Research Council, Commonwealth of Australia.

Persson, P.-G., Carlsson, S., Svanstrom, L., Ostenson, C.-G., Efendic, S. and Grill, V. (2000) Cigarette smoking, oral moist snuff use and glucose intolerance, *Journal of Internal Medicine*, 248 (2), 103–10.

Rachels, J. (1999) *The Elements of Moral Philosophy*, Boston: McGraw-Hill.

Ramström, L.M. (2000) Snuff: an alternative nicotine delivery system. In R. Ferrence, J. Slade, R. Roomand M. Pope (eds), *Nicotine and Public Health*, Washington, DC: American Public Health Association.

Ramström, L.M. and Foulds, J. (2006) Role of snus in initiation and cessation of tobacco smoking in Sweden, *Tobacco Control*, 15 (3), 210–14.

Rhodes, T. and Kimber, J. (2007) Safer groin injecting interventions are needed and justifiable as part of a harm reduction approach, *Addiction*, 102 (12), 1987–8.

Rhodes, T., Briggs, D., Kimber, J., Jones, S. and Holloway, G. (2007) Crack-heroin speedball injection and its implications for vein care: qualitative study, *Addiction*, 102 (11) 1782–90.

Rhodes, T., Stoneman, A., Hope, V., Hunt, N., Martin, A. and Judd, A. (2006) Groin injecting in the context of crack cocaine and homelessness: from 'risk boundary' to 'acceptable risk'?, *International Journal of Drug Policy*, 17 (3), 164–70.

Rumbold, G. and Hamilton, M. (1998) Addressing drug problems: the case for harm minimisation. In Hamilton et al. (eds), *Drug Use in Australia: A Harm Minimisation Approach*, Melbourne: Oxford University Press, 130–45.

Shell-Duncan, B. (2008) From health to human rights: female genital cutting and the politics of intervention, *American Anthropologist*, 110 (2), 225–36.

Singer, P. (1993) *A Companion to Ethics*, Oxford: Blackwell Reference.

Strang, J. (1993) Drug use harm reduction: responding to the challenge. In N. Heather, A. Wodak, E. Nadelmannand P. Ohare (eds), *Psychoactive Drugs and Harm Reduction: From Faith to Science*, London: Whurr.

Tammi, T. and Hurme, T. (2007) How the harm reduction movement contrasts itself against punitive prohibition, *International Journal of Drug Policy*, 18 (2), 84–7.

Tobacco Advisory Group of the Royal College of Physicians (2002) *Protecting Smokers, Saving Lives: The Case for a Tobacco and Nicotine Regulatory Authority*, London: Royal College of Physicians of London.

Tomar, S.L., Connolly, G.N., Wilkenfeld, J. and Henningfield, J.E. (2003) Declining smoking in Sweden: is Swedish Match getting the credit for Swedish tobacco control's efforts?, *Tobacco Control*, 12 (4), 368–71.

Weatherburn, D. (2009) Dilemmas in harm minimization, *Addiction*, 104 (3), 335–9.

Wood, E., Tyndall, M., Montaner, J. and Kerr, T. (2006) Summary of findings from the evaluation of a pilot medically supervised safer injecting facility, *Canadian Medical Association Journal*, 175 (11), 1399.

Zador, D., Lintzeris, N., Van der Waal, R., Miller, P., Metrebian, N. and Strang, J. (2008) The fine line between harm reduction and harm production: development of a clinic groin injecting policy, *European Addiction Research*, 14 (3), 213–18.

Chapter 10

HARM REDUCTION: CONTRIBUTION TO A CRITICAL APPRAISAL FROM THE PERSPECTIVE OF PEOPLE WHO USE DRUGS

Eliot Ross Albert

This chapter introduces a critical perspective on harm reduction theory and practice from the perspective of people who use drugs. It will be contested that the dominant way in which harm reduction interventions are delivered is predicated upon the assumption that the presenting client is an atomised individual suffering from harms that need remedying at the individual level, rather than recognising that 'an individual's health status is determined not solely by that person's attributes but also by the social and economic indicator's of his or her community's well-being, such as the unemployment, crime and infant mortality rates' (Molina and Aguirre-Molina (1994). A secondary assumption derives from the pathologising discourse that dominates most discussion of the 'drugs problem' in which the consumption of illicit drugs (or of prescribed drugs in an unauthorised way) is that they are inherently harmful. This chapter, guided by a critique of the addiction-as-illness paradigm, proposes instead to view such consumption as a multiply determined, socially located assemblage of practices, technologies and decisions about risk and pleasure, and looks to 'a critical reinterpretation of Social Justice' to produce 'insights that can illuminate structural inequities that contribute to the harms associated with the context of drug use' (Pauly, 2008). In this regard, most of the harms that arise from illicit drug use are reconceptualised not primarily as symptoms produced by the properties of the substances themselves, but rather as ramifications of the punitive prohibitionist architecture within which people who use drugs live and operate. As a result of the contention that those living at the sharp end of criminalising prohibition experience the greatest harms, and human rights abuses, the focus will be on consumers of illicit drugs.

Put more strongly, I will contend that the 'harms' that are being 'reduced' are ones that are largely produced, manufactured and sustained by prohibition, social policy and the attendant discrimination and stigma directed towards people who use illicit drugs. This is a concatenation of forces that produces the person who uses drugs as both victim (of drugs) and culprit (of crime, not merely limited to that of using drugs in the first place). I here follow Jamrozik in his assessment that most literature focuses 'on the victims of social and economic policies rather than on the process of 'victim creation' through such social and economic policies' (Jamrozik, 2001). The result of the dominant construction of the drug user as an addict or abuser (the former being synonomous with the latter in 'official' discourse) is that, as John Booth Davies put it in his seminal *The Myth of Addiction*, 'the more we treat drug problems as if they were the domain of inadequate, sick or helpless people, the more people will present themselves within that framework, and the more we will produce and encounter drug users who fit that description' (Davies, 1997).

That people who use drugs and their organisations have been broadly supportive of, and in some respects key drivers of the harm reduction agenda is not in doubt. Indeed, one of the pioneering

Harm Reduction in Substance Use and High-Risk Behaviour: International Policy and Practice, First Edition.
Edited by Richard Pates and Diane Riley.
© 2012 Blackwell Publishing Ltd. Published 2012 by Blackwell Publishing Ltd.

harm reduction interventions and a key event in the early history of the movement was the opening up of a needle exchange, the world's first, in Rotterdam in 1985 by activists of the MDHG *Belangenvereniging Druggebruikers* (Interest Association for Drug Users) in response to a hepatitis-B outbreak amongst the injecting community of that city. Similarly, numerous other examples of peer led harm reduction initiatives can be found the world over. By the same token, the development of the international movement of people who use drugs has been inextricably entwined with the history of the harm reduction movement (Albert and Byrne, 2010).

Up until now, I have, for convenience's sake been operating with the working assumption that harm reduction is one thing with a fixed essence. This assumption needs some considerable unpacking and analytic examination.

The *International Harm Reduction Association*, the world's leading promoter of harm reduction policies, services, interventions, and research offers the following definition for harm reduction:

> 'Harm Reduction' refers to policies, programmes and practices that aim primarily to reduce the adverse health, social and economic consequences of the use of legal and illegal psychoactive drugs without necessarily reducing drug consumption. Harm reduction benefits people who use drugs, their families and the community.

> (IHRA, 2011)

Over the last few years, the harm reduction movement has moved beyond its public health emphasis and taken a turn towards augmenting it with a strong advocacy for human rights, as the IHRA statement puts it, the harm reduction approach 'is based on a strong commitment to public health and human rights'. This commitment was formalised in 2007 with the establishment of IHRA's 'Harm Reduction and Human Rights Monitoring and Policy Analysis Programme', which from an analysis of the international architecture of drugs control policy, concludes that the latter, focused as it is on punitive prohibition, acts as the predominant driver of drug related harms. I will argue that, whilst not explicitly stated, this human rights turn has been substantially driven by the demands, and development of, a coherent international movement of people who use drugs, a movement that is both explicitly anti-prohibitionist and firmly grounded on the defense of, and advocacy for, the human rights of people who use drugs. *The Death Penalty for Drug Offences*, the first publication of the Harm Reduction and Human Rights Monitoring and Policy Analysis Programme, states that 'a key principle of IHRA's approach is to support the engagement of people and communities affected by drugs and alcohol around the world in policy-making processes, including the voices and perspectives of people who use illicit drugs' (Lines, 2007). To what extent these perspectives are heard, let alone coherently acted upon in the development of harm reduction initiatives will be a prevailing concern of this inquiry, as will a questioning of the unspoken assumption that such initiatives are always conducted in the best interests of those at whom they are aimed, that is, people who use drugs. will press this issue further by examining the extent to which the harm reduction movement does or does not confront the growing consensus that prohibition is the primary producer of drug related harm, and will insist that a harm reduction that is really in the interests of people who use drugs is one that strongly supports the right to use drugs as a fundamental human right. It is evident that not all bodies and individuals who claim to operate within the remit of harm reduction see the abolition of prohibition as being the logical extension of the harm reduction agenda.

Neil Hunt has argued that one way of looking at differing strands in the harm reduction movement is to identify 'two philosophies of harm reduction: a "weak rights" version, in which people are entitled to good treatment and a "strong rights" version that additionally recognises a basic right to use drugs. Prioritising human rights or public health can lead to different concepts of harm reduction and different forms of "right action"' (Hunt, 2004). Activists involved in the movement of people who use drugs, have a clear, and unrelenting commitment to the 'strong rights' version and take it to its logical conclusion by calling for an alternative, legal regulatory framework to prohibition. I would argue further that a harm reduction that doesn't do so is not worthy of the name, but is instead a part of the harm producing assemblage. Indeed, the 'weak rights' version is so broad that it could be taken to include the entire panoply of services that are offered to active people who use drugs, including methadone maintenance and syringe and needle exchange, the latter two often being seen as synonymous with harm reduction. However, as has been argued by a number of critical scholars as well as activists, much of what passes for harm reduction can instead be understood as an 'approach that simultaneously pathologizes and vilifies' (White, 2001) and as a form of social control, or as a regime for normalising the perceived deviance of the illicit drug user. Some of theses arguments are well summarised in Helen Keane's 'Foucault on Methadone: Beyond Biopower' (Keane, 2009). One of the key essays that she discusses contends, accurately in my opinion, that the 'phenomenon of the methadone clinic is an unhappy compromise between competing discourses: A criminalizing morality versus a medicalizing model of addiction-as-a-brain-disease' (Bourgois, 2000). I would go further though and generalise the point beyond the methadone clinic, by arguing that illicit drug use per se is constructed by these two competing discourses, both of which are unequivocally rejected by the politics of the burgeoning movement for the human rights of people who use drugs.

The critical force of this critique of the operation of methadone clinic is predicated upon Michel Foucault's critique of the normalising power of much health based discourse:

> I am merely emphasizing that the fact of 'health' is a cultural fact in the broadest sense of the word, a fact that is political, economic and social as well, a fact that is tied to a certain state of individual and collective consciousness. Every era outlines a 'normal' profile of health.
>
> (Foucault, 2002)

It will be my contention that most interventions directed at illicit drug users are aimed at imposing this 'normal' profile through the imposition of what Scott Vrecko has called 'civilising technologies' (Vrecko, 2010), manifested in, amongst other things the 'byzantine rules' and often invasive surveillance practices of the methadone clinic. Bourgois describes the American federal methadone dispensing system as 'the state's attempt to inculcate moral discipline into the hearts, minds, and bodies of deviants who reject sobriety and economic productivity' (Bourgois, 2000). This description of methadone prescribing and dispensing practices will be familiar to almost every opiate user who has come into contact with them, and whilst there is of course an enormous variety in the amount and nature of control embedded in each different setting, what is common to all of them is that in addition to the intention to minimise harm through the provision of a legal, pharmaceutically known, quality controlled opiate, there is an additional layer of behaviour modification. The latter very often takes the form of imprecations to accede to a state of abstinence from the drug of choice, and confessions on the part of the self-declared patient or client as to the extent of their transgressing behaviour. These demands are part of what Foucault would describe as the normalising tendencies of biopower.

Briefly put, biopower refers to the panoply of techniques, powers, and legislations that the state puts in place to control its subjects' bodies, and bodily conduct. In the context of harm reduction and the services that are provided for drug users this includes a multitude of legal and medical definitions and structures, distinctions, practices, demands and controls, all of which are aimed at disciplining the unruly pleasures of the person who uses drugs. A key instrument of the biopolitical state is a new form of power that Foucault defines as a medico-legal one whose function is neither 'judicial nor medical, it is a power of a new type, one that I shall, provisionally at least, call, "the power of normalization" the meeting of the medical and the legal realms, transforms both judicial power and psychiatric knowledge into the control of the abnormal or deviant'. The peculiarity of this power is that it controls 'neither crime, nor sickness, but the abnormal, the deviant individual' (Foucault, 2003). In direct opposition to this power stand organisations of people who are identified within this rubric as abnormal, in our context this means organisations of people who use drugs. Such organisations have been helpfully described as ones whose 'struggles are against forms of exclusion, stigma and discrimination; their fight might be against uneven distribution of social power, uneven access to health services; medical authority or the dominant biomedical paradigm' (Valenzuela and Mayrhofer, 2011).

Nothing better instantiates Foucault's *medico-legal*, 'power of normalisation' (Foucault, 2003), than the treatment currently offered to 'drug misusers', to quote the term that those working within the field in the UK are specifically compelled to use. That one of the explicit – perhaps the primary – objectives of the medico-legal power embodied in the drug treatment system is to force its subjects to conform to morally, and indeed economically, determined standards of 'normality' (as opposed to treating a medical condition), is attested to in the 1926 Rolleston Report, the landmark document that formalised what came to be known as the 'British system'. According to Rolleston, one of the questions that must be factored in to a physician's decision to give a patient a regular supply of heroin is if it would allow the patient to lead 'a useful and normal life'. I could have quoted such a sentiment from countless different sources, for it is practically endemic to the literature. That I have quoted it from the Rolleston Report, which was, and to a considerable degree, still is, an extremely enlightened document, only attests to the fact that this drive towards 'normalisation' is a fundamental principle of drug treatment under prohibition.

The Rolleston Report is also a key reference point in discussions of harm reduction practice as it embodies the spirit underlying much of the spirit of contemporary harm reduction interventions, in that they are pragmatic attempts to enable drug users to continue using their drug of choice, but in the safest way possible. For drug user activists, harm reduction needs to take several further steps. We have already alluded to the first, in that harm reduction professionals must recognise that the services they provide, necessary as they are, must question the source of the harm that they are addressing, namely the criminalisation of drug users in the name of the chimerical war on drugs. Furthermore, harm reduction services need to fully acknowledge that those who use their services are not necessarily either willing or capable of stopping their drug use, and as such imprecations to abstinence are inappropriate.

An issue that we have not yet touched on is the professionalisation of harm reduction, and its increasingly institutional character. It is widely recognised in the literature that the most effective interventions, whether that be the delivery of services or information, are those that are given by peers, that is to say members of the same community with equivalent lived experience and the experiential knowledge that comes from it. The position of the 'peer' has been institutionalised in many front-line services including needle exchange. Whilst activists largely recognise this as a progressive step, it does have its limitations and it to these that I now turn.

We have seen harm reduction taxonomised along the lines of respective positions taken towards rights, however, I wish to introduce a further distinction. Namely that between what we can crudely call 'bottom up' or drug user led and 'top down' or professional approaches to harm reduction. The latter model currently accounts for most harm reduction services and is a model in which services are provided by non-drug using professionals to 'service users'. As the latter term indicates, this is a consumerist model, and one that rests upon the securing of large-scale service provision contracts from government agencies to similarly large NGOs or charities. There still remains, even within the harm reduction industry, a strong reluctance to employ people who actively use drugs in positions of responsibility or authority, at the very most they are used as voluntary peers, usually directed by a worker who has either never been a person who uses drugs, or is a former user. This is not meant to denigrate the sincerity of the actions and intentions of most of those who work in the sector, even though there is strong evidence that many working in the field do in fact have highly negative and stigmatising attitudes to those that they are supposed to be helping (Kelly and Westerhoff, 2010).[1] Drug user activists militate for harm reduction services that are run, delivered and conceived by people who use drugs. A significant element in the development of such services and of challenging the hegemony of top-down professional harm reduction lies in the development of autonomous organisations of people who use drugs.

Whilst more progressive elements within the harm reduction movement clearly welcome the development of such organisations, and openly encourage their involvement, expertise and contributions, the response from the harm reduction industry is more unclear, ambiguous, and discouraging. The latter, in its statutory (that is to say state provided) and voluntary sector (charity run) manifestations has become increasingly professionalised, profoundly distanced from, and distancing of, its target population. In the UK at least, since the 2001 Health and Social Care Act there has been a statutory obligation for health and social services to involve service users in the course, design and delivery of treatment (Frischer et al., 2007; Patterson et al., 2008; Patterson et al., 2009), from the perspective of the drugs field this has included not just prescribing, but also harm reduction services. However the 'service user activism' that has resulted has been strictly delimited by a medical model of drug use, and the operational requirements of the host organisations. This has led to a canalising of many drug users into a de facto championing of a weak rights model of harm reduction and the acceptance of a sick identity, of the drug user as in need of cure, or treatment for the medical condition of being a user of illicit drugs.

Autonomous organisations of people who use drugs, operate, as has been indicated, with a very different set of founding assumptions. Notably one that 'in contrast to views that see IV drug use as simply a matter of individual pathology describe IV drug users as constituting a subculture as this term has been used within sociological and anthropological research' Friedman et al., 1986). In this crucial respect groups that define themselves as being of people who use drugs constitute a decisive attempt to forge positive community out of a long marginalised, heavily stigmatised section of society that faces systematic assaults on its dignity, human rights, and access to social justice. This is an explicitly political movement, one that takes its inspiration from other struggles for social justice, most notably the gay rights movement. The two groups are of course united by the disproportionate degree to which both were and are struck by the impact of HIV/AIDS, and by the social stigma to which they are subject, a stigma that played and in some areas still plays a significant role in the delaying, and sometimes total lack of, public health efforts to mitigate its effects. Both movements are still dealing with the increased vulnerability to blood borne diseases that stigmatisation and marginalisation can create. Equally both groups have been the object of changing frames of reference, 'for instance, in the gay movement the medical definition of homosexuality was a very important tool against the oppression of homosexuality in the last part of the nineteenth century and in

---

[1] This paper concludes 'the commonly used "substance abuser" term may perpetuate stigmatizing attitudes'. The authors note that 'ways of describing individuals with such problems may perpetuate or diminish stigmatizing attitudes yet little research exists to inform this debate'. Whilst the term 'abuser' is primarily an American one, the point is of near universal relevance.

the early twentieth century' (Foucault, 1997), however whilst a medicalising gaze can be seen as a means of resistance to moralising condemnation it can also act as a means of oppression. This is a point that I will now go on to explore and unpack.

A call to conceive the drug 'problem' as a medical rather than a criminal, still less a moral one is often raised by mainstream harm reductionists, and whilst this might on the surface seem like a progressive move to make it must be handled carefully as it also entails its own problems, principal amongst them being, as we have already seen, the inherent pathologisation that it brings with it. Organisations of people who use drugs such as the *International Network of People who Use Drugs* (INPUD, 2011) and its major constituent organisations, which include but are by no means limited to the French *Auto-Support pour Usagers de Drogues* (ASUD), the Danish *BrugerForeningen*, the Swedish *BrukarForeningen*, the *Australian Injecting and Illicit Drug Users' League* (AIVL) are active in resisting the medical model of addressing drug related issues, and attempt to forge and celebrate positive drug using identities. INPUD defines its mission as being to 'expose and challenge stigma, discrimination and the criminalisation of people who use drugs and its impact on our community's health and rights' (INPUD, 2011). All of these groups explicitly renounce the status of being organisations of patients, insisting instead on being militant organisations of people who use illicit drugs and all of whom are dedicated to the abolition of global prohibition as a long term goal, and in the interim, the decriminalisation of drug use. All of these groups work closely, but critically with the harm reduction movement, and with local harm reduction delivery services to ensure that all services that are aimed at our community take our perspectives on board, act on them, and seriously engage with us in their design, implementation, and monitoring.

Accepting that under prohibition, we have to engage with health services for assistance when we do run into difficulties with our drug use is a strategic necessity, indeed acceptance of a patient role is the only one that is functional within the medical paradigm within which most harm reduction services function. The supposedly objective criteria of harm that institutionalised harm reduction services work with is one that is questioned by the movement of people who use drugs, who, resisting the moralising implicit in the construction of addiction, insist that harm is only present when the drug user herself deems that her habit is becoming problematic. Construction of a positive drug using identity thus becomes a crucial role played by the kinds of militant organisations that I have referred to above. The construction of such identities and of communities acts as a necessary corrective to the internalised stigma carried by so many illicit drug users who, given the moral condemnation attached to drug use often reproduce the commonly held view of them, namely that they are helpless, weak minded people who need to be cured. As J.B. Davies stresses, this is not to say that drug users are being dishonest when they present as sick in this way, but rather that such a positioning is the only one that is functional within the medical discourse of official harm reduction services.

To offer some provisional conclusions then, whilst drug user activists were at the foundation of the modern harm reduction movement, a bifurcation has set in, one in which the provision of harm reduction interventions has increasingly become the domain of non-drug using professionals whose jobs are dependent on the exclusion of active drug users from positions of responsibility. This situation is one that can occasion trenchant criticisms of the manner in which harm reduction is often delivered from drug user activists. All too often the only means by which drug users are invited to contribute to the running, design and implementation of harm reduction services has been via 'service user groups' which are both led and organised by professional workers in the services themselves. These groups are by definition circumscribed in the kinds of questions that they can ask and the agenda is set more by the productivity targets of the organisation itself than by the desires of those whom the service notionally serves. Participation in these groups is by grace and favour of the organisation whose functioning and performance they are supposed to be criticising, and any critical input that might be found to be useful is all too often instrumentalised by the organisations, and turned into a professional product. To offset this, independent groups of active drug users have formed with their own agendas, which refuse to accept the supine nature of patient or service user, and attempt to push the services that are offered beyond mere harm reduction and onto the field of human rights, including the right to use drugs, and pleasure maximising techniques.

References

Albert, E. and Byrne, J. (2010) Coexisting or conjoined: the growth of the International drug users' movement through participation with IHRA Conferences, *International Journal of Drug Policy*, 21 (2), 110–11.

Bourgois, P. (2000) Disciplining addictions: the bio-politics of methadone and heroin in the United States, *Culture, Medicine and Psychiatry*, 24, 165–95, 165.

Davies, J.B. (1997) *The Myth of Addiction*, London: Routledge, 23.

Foucault, M. (1997) Sex, power, and the politics of identity. In Paul Rabinow (ed.), *Ethics: Subjectivity and Truth: Essential Works of Foucault*, vol. 1, New Press: New York, 163–73, 168.

Foucault, M. (2002) The risks of security. In J.D. Faubion (ed.), trans. R. Hurley et al., *Power: Essential Works of Foucault 1954–1984* vol. 3, London: Penguin, 365–81.

Foucault, M. (2003) [1999] *Les anormaux: Cours au college de France, 1974–5*, Paris: Gallimard: 1999; trans. Graham Burchell as *Abnormal*, London: Verso, 39. Unless otherwise stated I have used my own translations and refer to the book as *The Abnormals*.

Friedman, S., des Jarlais, D. and Sotheran, J. (1986) AIDS health education for intravenous drug users, *Health Education Quarterly*, 13, 383–93, 385.

Frischer, J., Jenkins, N., Bloor, M., Neale, J. and Berney, L. (2007) *Drug User Involvement in Treatment Decisions*, York: Joseph Rowntree Foundation.

Hunt, N. (2004) Public health or human rights: which comes first?, *International Journal of Drug Policy*, 15, 231–7, 231.

IHRA (2011) www.ihra.net/what-is-harm-reduction, accessed March.

INPUD (2011) www.inpud.net/mission-statement, accessed March.

Jamrozik, A (2001) *Social Policy in the Post-Welfare State: Australians on the Threshold of the 21st Century*, Frenchs Forest, NSW: Pearson Education, 279. I owe this citation to Lea Campbell, Chemical intent: imagining the drug using client and the human service worker in harm minimisation policy (2007), Australian Catholic University, PhD thesis, accessed at http://dlibrary.acu.edu.au/digitaltheses/public/adt-acuvp172.09092008/index.html, accessed March 2011.

Keane, H. (2009) Foucault on methadone: beyond biopower, *International Journal of Drug Policy*, 20, 450–2.

Kelly, J.F. and Westerhoff, C.M. (2010) Does it matter how we refer to individuals with substance-related conditions? A randomized study of two commonly used terms, *International Journal of Drug Policy*, 21 (3), 202–7.

Lines, R. (2007) *The Death Penalty for Drug Offences: A Violation of International Human Rights Law*, 1, London: International Harm Reduction Association.

Molina, C. and Aguirre-Molina, M. (1994) *Latino Health in the US: A Growing Challenge*, Washington, DC: American Public Health Association. Cited in Merill Singer (2006) What is the 'drug user community'?: implications for public health, *Human Organisation*, 65 (1), 71–9.

Patterson, S., Weaver, T., Agath, K., Rutter, D., Rhodes, T., Albert, E. and Crawford, M. (2008) User involvement in efforts to improve the quality of drug misuse services in England: a national survey, *Drugs: Education, Prevention & Policy*, 16 (4), 364–77.

Patterson, S., Weaver, T., Agath, K., Rutter, D., Rhodes, T., Albert, E. and Crawford, M. (2009) 'They can't do it without us': a qualitative study of user involvement in drug treatment, *Health & Social Care in the Community*, 17 (1), 54–62.

Pauly, B. (2008) Harm reduction through a social justice lens, *International Journal of Drug Policy*, 19, 4–10.

Valenzuela, H.C. and Mayrhofer, M.T. (2011) A new configuration of power/knowledge in the realm of bio-power: the cases of two patient-user organizations, www.congresafsp2009.fr/sectionsthematiques/st43/st43cuevas.pdf, accessed March 2011.

Vrecko, S. (2010) 'Civilizing technologies' and the control of deviance, *Biosocieties*, 5 (1), 36–51.

White, C. (2001) Beyond professional harm reduction: the empowerment of multiply-marginalized illicit drug users to engage in a politics of solidarity towards ending the war on illicit drug users, *Drug and Alcohol Review*, 20, 449–58.

Section III
Specific Interventions

Chapter 11

INJECTING

Richard Pates, Robert Heimer and Danny Morris

Introduction

Injecting, whether it is intravenous, intra muscular or subcutaneous, carries risks which must be minimised for the sake of the health of the injector. When the syringe was invented in its modern form, in the mid-nineteenth century, it was a tool used by doctors and not immediately used by drug users themselves. Even in doctors' hands it could sometimes be subject to misuse and the method of disease transmission partly through a lack of understanding of the hygiene imperatives associated with injecting.

Injecting carries the risk of the transmission of blood-borne viruses, (e.g. hepatitis B and C, HIV), blood-borne bacterial infections, (e.g. syphilis, cellulitis, bacterial endocarditis, tetanus) blood-borne parasites (e.g. malaria) and blood-borne prions. Infections may also be contracted through infected drugs (e.g. anthrax in heroin), through infections at the sites of the injections through poor hygiene (abscesses etc) and fungal infections (e.g. candida albicans). There are also risks of thrombosis, both of air and blood clots, damage to veins, arteries and nerves, contaminants mixed in with drugs to be injected, and of course the risks of overdose.

This chapter will look at the practice of injecting and the health risks involved, particularly the role of injecting and contaminated syringes in the transmission of HIV and hepatitis. It will conclude with a section on safer injecting.

Diseases spread by injection equipment

Viral infections, especially those that are blood borne, can be efficiently transmitted through unsafe injections, and under appropriate conditions this can lead to epidemic conditions. In some cases, the epidemic has been iatrogenic while in others it is a result of non-medical injections, usually in populations of people who inject drugs illicitly.

Epidemics of HIV, HCV and hepatitis B virus (HBV) among people who inject drugs are now evident throughout the world (Aceijas and Rhodes 2007; Aceijas et al., 2004; Alter, 2006). Most frequently, increases in the prevalence of the hepatitis viruses occur more rapidly than the prevalence of HIV. However, when conditions favour high rates of unsafe injection and syringe scarcity, HIV prevalences can rapidly increase (figure 11.1). Sometimes the scarcity is the result of poverty and sometimes it results from active legal or policy measures to limit access. The latter has been shown to contribute to HIV epidemics among people who inject drugs in many parts of the world (Friedman et al., 2006; Brettle, 1990; Sarang and Platt, 2008; Kitsenko and Kitsenko 2007). It is, however, possible to keep HIV prevalence among IDUs low and even reverse high prevalence through expansion of harm reduction and HIV treatment efforts (Des Jarlais et al., 1995; Des Jarlais

Harm Reduction in Substance Use and High-Risk Behaviour: International Policy and Practice, First Edition.
Edited by Richard Pates and Diane Riley.
© 2012 Blackwell Publishing Ltd. Published 2012 by Blackwell Publishing Ltd.

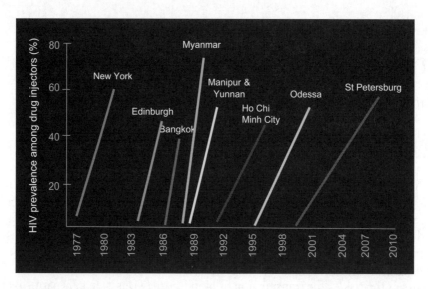

Figure 11.1 Rapid expansion of HIV prevalence among people who inject drugs in a sample of cities worldwide.

et al., 2005, Burns et al., 1996, Kerr et al., 2010). It has been found more difficult to accomplish the same for HCV, which has proven approximately tenfold more easily transmitted than HIV. However, there is some evidence from studies in New York and Australia (Short and Bell, 1993) that harm reductions can slow the HCV epidemic among people who inject drugs (Des Jarlais et al., 2005).

It remains uncertain why HCV is an order of magnitude more infectious through unsafe syringe use, but possibilities are related to virus and/or to the host. Virus-related factors include higher titres per equal volume of blood or longer survival of HCV. In efforts to elucidate which, if any, virus-related factors contribute to the differences in transmissibility, one of us (Heimer) has led a set of studies exploring the viability of HIV-1 and HCV in syringes and other paraphernalia used for the injection of illicit drugs and investigation procedures to reduce viral transmissibility. This work integrated the careful observational studies of how injection users prepare drugs for injection, make injections and share injection equipment made by medical anthropologists and ethnographers into replications of these activities under laboratory conditions that allow the viruses to be recovered and quantified.

In the first of these experiments it was determined that HIV-1 remained infectious within the barrel of a contaminated syringe for far longer than if the virus was simply found in a fomes containing dried, virus-contaminated blood (or, for that matter, dried in a cooker or filter used as part of illicit drug preparation). In the latter case, the viability of HIV-1 stored at room temperature was reduced by approximately 98% within several days (Tjøtta et al., 1991). When stored in syringes at room temperature, we found that virus recovery was linked to type of syringe and the resultant amount of blood retained in the barrel of the syringe. For instance, using 1 ml insulin syringes with fixed needles that retained approximately 2 µl of fluid when the plunder was fully depressed, we could recover virus from 15% of syringes after one week and from more than 5% of syringes after three weeks. When syringes with detachable needles were tested, the volumes retained were tenfold higher and viable HIV-1 was recovered from 75% of syringes after two weeks and from 10% of syringes after 6 weeks (Abdala et al., 1999). We subsequently compared the duration of viability at five different temperatures (4 °C, 20 °C, 27 °C, 32 °C and 37 °C) to replicate conditions that might be experienced in different locations and found that increasing temperatures was associated with decreasing viability. For instance, we could recover potentially infectious virus even from insulin type syringes after six weeks if stored at 4 °C whereas viability disappeared from all syringes within 3 days at 37 °C and one week at 27 °C and 32 °C (Abdala et al., 2000).

The next set of experiments with HIV-1 demonstrated that disinfection of contaminated syringes was possible, that a single instantaneous rinse with undiluted bleach solutions (5.25% w/v sodium hypochlorite) reduced viability by more than 99% when 40 µl or less of blood remained inside syringes, and that three rinses with water reduced recovery, through decreases in viral titer, by more than 95% (Abdala et al., 2001). Almost no other standard disinfection solution we tested was more effective than water alone in reducing HIV-1 recovery when the exposure time of the virus to the solution was limited to that required to draw the solution into the syringe and immediately expel it (Abdala et al., 2004). Only ethanol at concentrations of 70% v/v or higher and isopropyl alcohol at volumes of greater than 0.3 ml in a 1 ml syringe were any more effective than water. In contrast, strong acids (pH less than or equal to 1.7) eliminated recovery and weaker acids equivalent to that found in lemon juice or vinegar (pH 2.4–2.7) were only partially effective at reducing HIV-1 viability (Heimer et al., 2007).

Most recently, building on the newly developed assay system to propagate hepatitis C virus (HCV) in culture, we have begun to reproduce the set of study conducted to ascertain HIV-1 viability. To date, we have been able to demonstrate that HCV can be recovered from syringes with detachable needles for up to nine weeks after storage regardless of storage temperature (Paintsil et al., 2010). Recovery was greater at lower temperatures; more than 50% of syringes yielded viable virus up to 56, 42 and 7 days, respectively, at 4 °C, 22 °C or 37 °C. However, in experiments using the insulin syringes with fixed needles, HCV viability closely paralleled that for HIV-1.

Our work suggests that the host factors must play a role in the relative ease of HCV transmission since survival times for and the probability of recovering HIV-1 and HCV from within the barrels of syringes are roughly equivalent over a range of volumes and storage temperatures (Abdala et al., 1999; 2000; Paintsil et al., 2010). What these factors are remains a mystery and needs to be investigated. Potentially any blood-borne disease could be spread by the use of contaminated injecting equipment. The selection of diseases discussed is not exhaustive and there are probably many not yet identified.

Malaria

The spread of malaria by contaminated injecting equipment can be traced back at least to the 1920s. Biggam (1929) reported malaria as being thus transmitted in Egypt among a group of intravenous drug users who shared injecting equipment. Helpern (1934) reported cases of malaria in New York City among injecting drug users. Because of the locality and climate of New York City the presence of malaria transmitting mosquitoes the diagnosis was not taken seriously by the users themselves. The role of needle sharing in disease transmission was not then recognised. However, Helpern stated that the disease was directly transmitted from addict to addict as a result of sharing unsterilised hypodermic syringes. In 1986 Gonzalez Garcia et al. reported an outbreak of malaria among drug injectors in Madrid who shared injecting equipment, one of whom regularly visited Equatorial Guinea.

Infective endocarditis

Endocarditis is a disease which is a bacterial or fungal infection affecting the muscles of the heart, particularly the heart valves. Cherubin (1971) reported on endocarditis treated in New York in an 8-year period, 29 of whom were hospitalised and 7 non-hospitalised. He found that most frequently the aortic and mitral valves were affected and less frequently the tricuspid valve or a bilateral infection involving the tricuspid valve. The most common causative organism was staphylococci (48%), streptococci (14%) and candida fungal infection (10%). It was noted that major embolic episodes were common in this group of patients 7 of whom died suddenly outside the hospital from cerebral or myocardial emboli. In another study in a different hospital half of the patients had Streptococcus viridans as the infecting organism. In a third study of 12 addicts with endocarditis, 6 were infected with Staphylococcus aureus, 2 with Candida, 1 with Streptococcus viridans, 1 with Klebsiella and 1 with no identified organism. The author comments that the frequency of these infections is probably related to multiple, daily unsterile injections and to superficial infections.

Clostridium infections

The clostridium group of spore forming bacteria are responsible for a number of different infections most of which are soft tissue infections often resulting from subcutaneous or intramuscular injection.

Tetanus (Clostridium tetani)

In 1971 Cherubin commented that tetanus and narcotic addiction 'form the most unusual and dramatic association of drug abuse with any disease' and when this was published that association was already 90 years old. In the 1950s the majority of patients treated in 2 hospitals in Chicago and New York for tetanus were drug addicts. In 1942 there was an epidemic of tetanus stemming from a commonly used adulterated source of the drug. From 1950 to 1961 tetanus contributed to 8.3% of deaths of addicts seen by the Office of the Chief Medical examiner. From 1955 to 1971 the majority of cases in New York were in the addict population mainly in black Americans in their twenties and thirties who were 'skin popping' (injecting subcutaneously). Cherubin commented that the increased mortality rate among addicts with the disease seemed to be related to the nature of the initial tissue (ie the puncture of the skin in injecting) and possibly to the inclusion of quinine in the injected material. MMWR (1998) pointed out that drug injection provides several potential sources for infection with Clostridium tetani, including the drug, its adulterants, injection equipment and unwashed skin. The mortality rate in drug users is much higher than in the general population.

Cherubin and Sapira (1993) reviewed the medical complications of intravenous drug use and commented that diseases that complicated drug abuse 25 years previously, are now more widely disseminated and diseases such as tetanus and malaria are now rare but other diseases which were previously unknown, such as HIV, now occur frequently.

Wound botulism (Clostridium botulinum)

In California among users of black tar heroin an increase of cases of wound botulism due to Clostridium botulinum and an increase in tetanus (Clostridium tetani) (Kimura et al., 2004). In a study of wound botulism Werner et al (2000) reviewed clinical, epidemiological and laboratory features of the infection. They commented that California had reported most of the world's cases and 75% of the cases in the United States. They found that the first case was reported in 1951 and up until 1998 a total of 127 cases were reported but that the infection had drastically increased 93 cases having been identified in the last 5 years of the period. It appeared that the increase in cases was due to an epidemic of wound botulism in injectors of black tar heroin. All but one of the last 102 cases had been in people skin popping. The authors commented that the infection occurred disproportionately in people of Hispanic origin and in women and that misdiagnosis occurred as did diagnostic delays.

Passaro and colleagues (1998) undertook a case-control study to investigate the factors associated with wound botulism. Using 26 patients who had the infection and 110 controls who were recruited from methadone detoxification programmes they found that patients were more likely to inject subcutaneously or intramuscularly and to use these routes more times per month with a greater cumulative monthly dose of black tar heroin. In a final regression model the subcutaneous or intramuscular injection of black tar heroin was the behaviour associated with wound botulism in injecting drug users. Crucially, they found that cleaning the skin, cleaning injecting equipment and sharing needles did not affect the risk of developing wound botulism.

Clostridium sordellii

Necrotising soft tissue wound infections due to a variety of clostridia was reported by Kimura and colleagues (2004). Nine injecting drug users developed necrotising fasciitis of whom four died. This appeared to be caused by Clostridium sordellii which was cultured from some of the wounds. One aspect of this was that some of the patients appeared to have a toxic shock syndrome which is characteristic of infections caused by Clostridium sordellii. The suspected source of the outbreak was the drug that was infected and this was often injected intramuscularly or subcutaneously. The authors commented that this outbreak of Clostridium sordellii infection was an example of how black tar heroin can serve as an agent for the transmission of deadly infections and the need for educating injecting drug users about the dangers of skin popping.

Clostridium novyi

Christie (2000) reported an outbreak which killed 22 drug users in Scotland and Ireland and at the time the cause was unknown but suspected to be anthrax although this was later discounted. All were injecting into the muscle and severe inflammation developed around the injection site followed by shock, collapse and then death. The suspicion around anthrax arose because of the case of a Norwegian drug injector had contracted the disease and two of the Scottish sample had a positive reaction to testing. The source was eventually believed to be heroin contaminated with Clostridium novyi (Ramsey et al., 2010). Brett et al. (2005) reviewed the incidence of soft tissue infections caused by spore forming bacteria in the UK in injecting drug users. They identified an increase between 2000 and 2004 of these infections and identified 63 cases of severe illnesses caused by Clostridium novyi in 2000 and a further 7 cases from 2001. They also identified infections caused by Clostridium botulinum (6 cases in 2000 and a further 51 cases up to 2004), Clostridium hystolyticum (9 cases), Clostridium sordellii and bacillus cereus in one case each. In discussing the reasons for the increase in infections the authors found this to be unclear but found the major risk factor to be skin popping and intramuscular injection.

Taylor et al. (2005), investigating the consequences of the outbreak of severe illness thought to be caused by Clostridium novyi in injecting drug users in Scotland in 2000 looked at associated environmental factors. Using a case control study they used the 19 definite and 32 probable cases in Glasgow. For the 19 deceased cases 3 proxy cases per deceased individual were interviewed and three controls per case were identified. They found that injecting into the muscle or skin and injecting most of the time with a filter already used by another drug injector were the variables most strongly associated with illness. For the muscle injecting cases and controls the cases were significantly likely to have injected larger amounts of heroin per average injection than the controls.

Anthrax

Reports of heroin injectors contracting anthrax appear from time to time. The sporadic nature of this would suggest that it is the drug that is contaminated or adulterants which have been added to the drug. However, in 2010 an outbreak of anthrax was confirmed in Scotland (Ramsey et al., 2010). By 14 January, 14 cases had been confirmed, half of whom had died, all of whom had a history of injecting heroin. Cases usually presented with inflammation around the injection site and in some cases localised lesions developed into necrotising fasciitis. In some cases cellulitis with very marked oedema was noted in limbs with the infection site. In a few cases patients presented with advanced stages of systemic sepsis some of whom died within hours and two presented with symptoms suggestive of sub-arachnoid haemorrhage or haemorrhagic meningitis. Others presented with relatively localised lesions which did not progress. The only common feature of these cases across Scotland appeared to be the heroin itself, there was no common factor for the possible anthrax exposure other than the acquisition and taking of heroin by one or more methods. As Ramsey and colleagues commented there was difficulty in providing harm reduction advice because even in the absence of injection there was a potential risk from inhaling the anthrax spores from smoking or snorting the heroin. Christie (2010) reported further deaths in this outbreak, at the time of writing 11 drug users had died. Christie reported that the heroin may have been contaminated at its original source in Afghanistan through contact with infected soil or animal skins. At the same time as this outbreak a death was reported in Germany of an injecting drug user from anthrax. This individual had no history of travel to Scotland so the assumption was that it might have been the same source of heroin (Radun et al., 2010).

Other infections

Many other infections have been reported including a report of four drug users who shared 'venepuncture equipment' and who all contracted tick borne relapsing fever. Lopez-Cortez et al. (1989) suggested that this could have been transmitted through the shared equipment in a similar way to the transmission of malaria by this route. The authors recommend examining peripheral blood films for intravenous drug abusers in cases of acute febrile illness during spring to autumn months in endemic areas.

Efstratiou and colleagues (2003) reported an increase in streptococcal infections amongst drug injectors in England and Wales. They argue that the increase is not just due to greater surveillance but may be due to an increased vulnerability in injecting drug users to skin sepsis through a change in risk behaviour suggesting an increase in sharing behaviour since the late 1990s.

Fungal infections

As discussed above, endocarditis may be caused by Candida albicans and as Derricott discusses in chapter 22 of this book there is the risk of infection from the use of lemon juice and vinegar which can lead to fungal infections (particularly Candida albicans, commonly known as 'thrush') being introduced into the circulatory system, causing eyesight problems through retinal damage.

Leen and Brettle (1991) suggested that fungal infections may account for 5–50% of serious infections in intravenous drug users and that the fungi most commonly encountered are Candida and Aspergillus, that Candidosia may be disseminated with lesions in superficial structures, the eye, or the skeletal system or may be limited to one system such as the eye, the heart or the central nervous system. Aspergillosis usually presents as an infection of the eye (the intraocular cavities) or the central nervous system. The authors conclude that systemic fungal infections in intravenous drug users are uncommon and some resolve spontaneously while others strike rapidly and may lead to death. Mortality from established fungal infections is high and may increase (quoted in 1991) as a co-factor in HIV in drug injectors.

In a study among injecting drug users in Barcelona between 1983 and 1990 Bisbe and colleagues (1992) found that disseminated candidiasis was diagnosed in 83 heroin users in one hospital. All had consumed brown heroin diluted with fresh lemon juice. Some 75% had skin lesions, 49% had ocular lesions and 42% had costochondral (articulations between the ribs and the costal cartilage) tumours. Twenty-nine of the patients developed varying degrees of loss of vision and one patient died having developed endocarditis involving the aortic valve. Candida albicans was grown in culture or histo-pathologically identified in 41% of cases. The authors comment that ocular lesions are the most harmful manifestation of the infection with loss of vision being the most serious consequence.

As has been seen there are many potential infections which may be transmitted as part of the process of injecting drugs, some via contaminated blood in shared injecting equipment, some as a result of contaminated drugs and some as a result of poor hygiene. Clearly, education and the provision of safe injecting equipment can reduce risks and improved hygiene may help. Vlahov and colleagues (1992) conducted a study of 1,057 injectors in Baltimore. Of the sample, 12 reported endocarditis and 113 reported subcutaneous abscesses in the 6 months before being interviewed. Among the questions asked at the interview was about skin cleaning prior to injection (556 cases reported doing so) or skin cleaning all the time (173 cases reported). The frequency of subcutaneous abscesses and the frequency of endocarditis was lower in those who cleaned their skin all the time. The authors conclude that encouraging injectors to clean their skin prior to injection will not eliminate but may reduce these infections.

Injecting other substances and the resulting consequences

When drugs are sold they are inevitably cut with some other substance to bulk up the product. This might be something relatively benign such as glucose powder or might be a substance less soluble which in itself may cause problems. The accumulation of non-soluble products can cause blockages to veins and capillaries and lead to thromboses. The practice of injecting temazepam gel capsules in the UK in the late 1980s and 1990s led to thrombophlebitis, abscesses and deep vein thrombosis (Ruben and Morrison, 1992) despite the fact that temazepam were reformulated in an attempt to make it more difficult to inject them. Partanen and colleagues (2009) reported on a study of the consequences of injecting crushed tablets among patients at a hospital in Helsinki. Of 24 patients treated, 16 had acute limb ischaemia, 8 had infections and 8 cases led to proximal or distal amputation.

Lalhmingliana (2003) in an unpublished study described how in the closed north-eastern Indian state of Mizoram propoxyphene became the drug of choice and frequently used by injection. Propoxyphene is an opioid, comes in a powdered form and is easily available and cheap. However, when injected the drug can cause major problems. Between 1990 and 2002 there were 738 drug related deaths in Mizoram, 26 related to heroin use, 4 related to other drugs and 704 related to propoxyphene. These deaths are either direct (as a result of overdose) or indirect (illnesses caused by the use of the drug or injecting; examples of these illnesses include septicaemia, pulmonary embolism, tetanus and congestive heart failure). There were also many cases of gangrene and necrotising fasciitis leading to amputations and many abscesses.

Iatrogenic spread of infection by injection

In a review of injections in healthcare settings worldwide, Hutin et al. (2003) estimated that in the year 2000 in South America and Eastern and Central Europe, 39.3% of medical injections were given with reused medical equipment. They defined reuse as 'the administration of an injection to a recipient with a syringe or a needle that has been previously used on another person and that was reused in the absence of sterilisation'. They also suggested that injection practices in sub-Saharan Africa were safer than in the Middle East and South Asia and that the proportion of the population aware of the potential risk of the transmission of HIV infection through unsafe injections was 24% in Pakistan, 19% in India but 52% in Burkina Faso. There are other suggestions about the rate of iatrogenic infection of HIV in sub-Saharan Africa. Gisselquist et al. (2002) commented that many studies report HIV in African adults with no sexual exposure to HIV, and unexplained high rates of HIV infection in the postpartum and antenatal periods in African women. They also comment that many studies show that 20% to 40% of adult HIV infections are associated with injections, although direction of causation is unknown. The authors call for more research to clarify a health-care route for HIV transmission, as their findings challenge the conventional hypothesis suggesting that unsafe medical care may be an important factor in Africa's HIV epidemic.

In a 2004 article Schmid and colleagues reviewed the epidemiological evidence on the role of unsafe sex in the transmission of HIV-1 and concluded that there was little evidence that unsafe injections were a predominant mode of transmission of HIV-1 in sub-Saharan Africa. They commented that although there is a need to eliminate unsafe injection practices, sexual transmission is still the most important route for the transmission of HIV-1.

An attempt to estimate the transmission efficiency of HIV through medical injections and other invasive procedures was made by Gisselquist and colleagues (2006). They concluded that evidence from iatrogenic outbreaks and percutaneous exposures among health care workers provide a basis to estimate HIV transmission where grossly insufficient or no effort is made to clean or discard used medical equipment. In these circumstances they estimate for procedures with lower risks (e.g. intramuscular injections) the range to be 0.5% to 3% and for higher risks (maintaining intravenous lines or phlebotomy procedures) 10% to 20%. They also conclude that estimates of the efficiency of HIV transmission from iatrogenic causes are based on limited information about numbers types and circumstances of healthcare procedures delivered to HIV infected individuals. They also comment that there are many unexplained HIV infections that have yet to be investigated in Africa and Asia.

A specific example of iatrogenic causes of disease is the spread of hepatitis C in Egypt via the treatment of schistosomiasis. Egypt has the highest prevalence of hepatitis in the world, population prevalence has reached 15% and most infections are genotype 4, which is uncommon outside of the Middle East and Central Africa (Kamal and Nassar, 2008). The first reports of the epidemic, from the 1990s, described an association between receiving treatment for schistosomiasis and HCV infections (reviewed in Hibbs et al., 1993). Treatment of schistosomiasis at that time required intravenous delivery of anti-parasite medication and re-use of needles spread the virus efficiently. The evidence suggests that unsterilised needles used during a campaign to eradicate schistosomiasis were responsible for the spread of the infection (Rao et al., 2002). Schistosomiasis is a parasitic infection passed from snails that harbour the disease. Between the 1960s and 1980s mass campaigns were conducted to treat schistosomiasis during which all individuals over the age of 5 were treated with tartar emetic injections. Rao and colleagues demonstrated that there was a clustering in households of HCV infection and that these households were more likely to have participated in the anti-schistosomiasis programme. Rao and colleagues are firm in their conclusion that the spread of hepatitis C in the Nile Delta was associated with the schistosomiasis treatment campaign. Iatrogenic transmission was demonstrated by molecular virology, which showed the HCV to be largely clonal, and by spatial analysis, which found that the highest prevalence of HCV was in the towns and villages of the Nile floodplain that were the targets of the anti-schistosomiasis campaigns (Frank et al., 2000). Although the campaign against schistosomiasis was largely successful, the resultant epidemic spread a genotype that is often resistant to currently available therapeutic approaches (Kamal and Nassar, 2008)

Flashblood

The sharing of injecting equipment results usually from ignorance, poor hygiene or being prepared to take risks because of the need for the drug. However, a new phenomenon was reported among female sex workers who inject heroin in Tanzania (McCurdy et al., 2005). Known as flashblood it involves the deliberate sharing of injecting equipment and blood, where blood is drawn into the barrel of the syringe, which is then passed to other injectors. The practice has developed because the women believe that 4 cc of blood contains enough heroin to avoid opiate withdrawals. The potential for disease transmission is very high.

Evidence for efficacy for NES

Needle and syringe exchange (NES) has been an important part of harm reduction since the early 1980s. Although syringes had been offered to injectors previously in an attempt to stop the spread of hepatitis it only became a major issue with the arrival of HIV. Initially it was controversial in many countries where it was perceived to be acquiescing to illicit drug use. It has since become mainstream public health practice in many countries of the world.

In the mid-1980s there was a major epidemic of HIV among injectors in the Scottish city of Edinburgh where at one point prevalence was estimated at 85% (Robertson et al., 1986). In the neighbouring city of Glasgow, only 40 miles distant, the prevalence was assessed at 4%. The major difference between the two cities was the availability of clean needles and syringes and a more understanding police response of not confiscating injecting equipment. Stimson (1996) reviewed the evidence of the efficacy of harm reduction including NES in the UK and concluded that Britain had averted a major epidemic because of those measures.

Blumenthal et al. (2000) reviewed the effects of needle exchanges on the behaviour of drug users in the Oakland area in California. They found an overall decline in syringe sharing (60% of the sample reported ceasing sharing of syringes) and that injector who used the NES were significantly more likely to stop sharing syringes than those who did not use the NES. They also found that NES use contributed to reductions in HIV risk behaviour among high-risk injectors. In a review of HIV incidence among injectors at a New York NES, Des Jarlais and colleagues (1996) found that HIV incidence among NES attendees was much lower than non-attendees and that there was an individual-level protective effect against HIV infection associated with participation in the needle exchange. Wodak and Cooney (2006) in an international review of the effectiveness of NES to reduce HIV incidence found compelling evidence of effectiveness, safety and cost-effectiveness.

In a comprehensive review of the effectiveness and cost-effectiveness of needle and syringe programmes for injecting drug users, Jones et al. (2008) examined a number of different aspects of needle and syringe exchange. Using systematic reviews, meta analyses and primary study they concluded that participation in needle exchange programmes reduced injection risk behaviours particularly self-reported needle and syringe sharing. There was evidence that it reduced the risk of acquiring HIV although the evidence for the impact on hepatitis C was less compelling and that access to needles and syringes via pharmacies provides specific benefits in addition to those available from specialist needle and syringe programmes (NSPs). They also found that reducing HIV incidence and prevalence among IDUs was cost-effective but this was not the case for HCV. There was evidence that the setting of the NSP did not impact on injection risk behaviours but that mobile NSPs and vending machines may attract younger IDUs or IDUs with higher-risk profiles. On the role of prison based NSPs there is evidence to show that these can work in small prisons but less evidence of the effectiveness of these on a larger scale. There is also evidence to suggest that the provision of vending machines does not have adverse effects on HIV and HCV seroconversion and reduces sharing and other injection risk behaviours. They found that where there were NSP based health care services attendance at emergency departments was reduced. Finally, there was evidence to suggest that low threshold methadone maintenance programmes at NSPs can reduce injection risk behaviours among IDUs and that the combination of methadone maintenance programmes and full participation in NSPs can reduce the incidence of HIV and HCV among drug users.

While examining the effectiveness of harm reduction approaches, Ryder et al. (2001) reviewed the evidence and found that the cost-effectiveness of needle exchange in relation to HIV was overwhelming. The cost of needle exchange was $AU350 per person (1991 figures) compared to $AU90,000 for medical treatment of HIV/AIDS (1992/3 figures) and that where NES was implemented early in the AIDS epidemic the incidence of the infection was much lower.

The UK experience of combined heroin and crack cocaine injection

Among people who inject drugs, the term 'speedball' has been used variably to describe the use of assorted depressants (including heroin, morphine, methadone and barbiturates) in conjunction with different stimulants (including cocaine, amphetamine and methamphetamine), but it mainly refers to the combined use of heroin and cocaine. Using heroin and crack cocaine together may involve any route of administration, such as smoking or chasing heroin with crack, or, sniffing heroin with powder cocaine. Speedballing widely refers to the injection of both drugs simultaneously and it can also encompass serial or sequenced injecting where one drug is injected after the other. Alternatively, heroin might be injected and crack cocaine then smoked, or vice versa.

In the context of UK use the term speedballing is primarily employed to refer to the combined injection of heroin and cocaine/crack. Treatment and research experience in the UK suggests that this particular combination is becoming more common and is a cause for special concern due to evidence of injecting related harms.

Speedball injectors often report a superior effect from this combination of drugs. However, neuro-pharmacological studies suggest that the simultaneous administration of cocaine and heroin does not induce a novel set of subjective effects. Studies also suggest that this simultaneous administration is no more reinforcing than either drug alone, especially when the doses of heroin and cocaine are high.

Speedballing is associated with: high rates of sharing of injecting equipment, an increased risk of HIV and Hepatitis C infection and increased risk of bacterial infection and soft tissue injuries. Some evidence points to a heightened risk of overdose. Reports of serious mental health problems among speedballers are common. Speedballing has also been linked to increased sexual health risks including those associated with commercial sex work.

Pharmacology and neurobiology

The pharmacology and neurobiology of combined heroin and cocaine use and the exact mechanisms that cause tolerance, dependence and overdose risks are not fully understood (Leri et al., 2003). However it is known that although opioids and cocaine have different mechanisms of action within the brain, both drugs share important characteristics and serve as powerful motivators of appetitive behaviour by stimulating the pleasure or reward systems. There is considerable evidence that common reinforcing and incentive effects of these drugs are mediated by increasing dopamine levels (Cornish et al., 2005).

Opiates modify the action of dopamine deep within the parts of the brain that form the brain's reward pathway. Dopamine is a neurotransmitter, which is associated with feelings of pleasure, and heroin indirectly boosts dopamine, leading to euphoria and the 'high' associated with heroin use. Cocaine also modifies the action of dopamine in similar parts of the brain but through different mechanisms. When cocaine/crack is present in the brain it inhibits re-absorption of dopamine that results in a substantial dopamine build-up, producing feelings of euphoria and the 'high' associated with cocaine use. Research indicates that when heroin and cocaine are combined they may cause a net and dramatic increase in dopamine levels. Animal studies suggest that injecting heroin and cocaine together has a synergistic effect, where one drug enhances the effects of the other (Hemby et al., 1999; Gerasimov and Dewey, 1999). These processes may account for the effects described by some speedballers, which sometimes suggest a qualitatively enhanced and more pleasurable experience than when either drug is taken in isolation. However, fully translating these insights into the experiences of speedballers is not straightforward because they are also influenced by factors such as repeated use, increased or fluctuating tolerance, duration of drug use, dependency, and withdrawal (Leri et al., 2003).

'Street pharmacology' and speedballing culture

Injecting drug users sometimes explain their speedballing use as a consequence of the availability of crack and heroin in the same markets. When both drugs are sold together, they are more likely to be used in combination. There are indications that buying of 'brown & white' together in metropolitan drug markets such as London, is becoming more common and normalised amongst injectors and may reinforce this pattern of use.

Although drug markets appear to have an important role, a key reason suggested by people as to why they inject heroin and crack together is the elevated pleasure they perceive. One possible explanation for this discrepancy from Leri's findings (Leri et al., 2003) may be that street users' doses are not high, relative to their tolerance. One study has also suggested that people move from crack smoking to speedball injection as injection of crack was smoother and less 'edgy' than smoking (Boreham, 2005).

Prevalence and geographic variation

In general, drug use prevalence data within the UK is derived from the British Crime Survey (BCS); in common with almost all epidemiological research in Britain, this does not ask explicitly about speedballing and is also known to underestimate heroin and crack cocaine use (Hay et al., 2007). This contrasts with the USA, where speedballing appears to be more established and questions about its prevalence are asked more routinely. A national estimate for England suggested around 117,000 injectors of heroin or crack-cocaine in 2006 (0.34% of those aged 15 to 64), down from 137,000 in 2004 (HPA, 2007).

Risks associated with speedballing

There are no risks that are entirely unique to speedballing but there is a growing body of literature suggesting that speedballing is associated with increased drug specific and technique specific risks and a more rapid onset of injecting related damage.

In general, speedball use is associated with increased frequency of injection. People who report speedballing as their main drug are twice as likely to inject five or more times a day than those injecting heroin (Turning Point 2007). Some speedballers inject as many as eight to 16 times a day (Newcombe, 2007). Increased injecting frequency, when coupled with the local anaesthetic and vasocontrictive properties of cocaine/crack, typically results in accelerated vascular and soft tissue damage. Further, these risks may be compounded by other factors. Speedballing seems to be associated with situational and environmental risk factors, notably homelessness, which are in turn associated with poorer health and well-being (Newcombe, 2007; Rhodes et al., 2006). Furthermore, speedballing sometimes intersects with commercial sex work, which can increase risk exposure in assorted ways (Newcombe, 2007).

Blood-borne infections

The most extensive literature concerning speedballing and risk relates to blood-borne infections – especially HIV/AIDS. Several studies have found that speedball injectors report increased injecting risk (Johnson et al., 2002, Koester, Booth and Zhang, 1996,) and, consistent with this finding, a range of studies report higher rates of HIV/AIDS infection among speedballers (Doherty et al., 2000; Craib et al., 2003; Kral et al., 1998). A smaller number of studies have also found associations between hepatitis C infection and speedballing (Garfein et al., 1998; Miller et al., 2002).

More recently, among the current IDUs participating in the UAPMP survey throughout England, Wales and Northern Ireland, the prevalence of antibodies to hepatitis C has increased since the beginning of the decade, from 34% in 2000 (791 of 2,364) to 40% (758 of 1,891) in 2008 and that here was a higher prevalence of hepatitis C infection among several sub-groups of current IDUs, notably those injecting crack-cocaine. In 2008, 54% (343 of 640) of those who reported injecting crack cocaine during the past four weeks had hepatitis C, compared to 33% (415 of 1,251) of those who had not, and 48% (96 of 199) of those who reported injecting cocaine had hepatitis C, compared with 39% (662 of 1,692) of those who had not.

Direct sharing in the last four weeks was more common among those current IDUs who reported injecting crack cocaine (23%, 139 of 616, compared with 17%, 204 of 1,182, of those who had not), injecting cocaine (31%, 58 of 189, compared with 18%, 285 of 1,609, of those who had not), injecting an amphetamine (27%, 86 of 321, compared with 17%, 257 of 1,477, of those who had not), and having been homeless in the last year (22%, 154 of 705 compared with 17%, 171 of 997, those who had not) (HPA Shooting UP update 2010).

Bacterial infection and venous damage

Recent British research has drawn attention to an apparent rise in speedballing and corresponding concern about an increase in femoral injecting and accompanying problems (Rhodes et al., 2006; Rhodes et al., 2007; Newcombe, 2007). Complications include local bacterial infections/ abscesses, septicaemia, deep vein thrombosis (DVT), pulmonary embolism (PE), cerebrovascular accidents and transient ischemic attacks (CVA/TIA). Other complications, such as needle breakage, can occur (Thorne and Collins, 1998). The risk of vein damage appears to be higher for speedballers and suggested explanations include: 'missed hits' due to the local anaesthetic and vasoconstrictive actions of cocaine; 'flushing' when having a hit (Rhodes et al., 2007). American research has previously identified speedball injecting as a cause of increased risk for skin and soft tissue infections – risks which appear to be greater for women – which can be reduced if the skin is cleaned with alcohol before injecting (Johnson et al., 2002; Murphy et al., 2001). The Health Protection Agency (HPA, 2007) reported that about a third of all IDUs within their surveillance have had an abscess, sore or opened wound at an injecting site in the last year and also discuss a recent increase in injecting into the groin and crack injecting – suggesting that speedballing is an important factor in this trend.

Overdose

Investigations of fatal overdose are often hindered by absent or poor-quality witness evidence, which means that details concerning the sequence and route of drug administration are unclear. Although toxicological evidence frequently shows that cocaine and opioids are each present, their interactions and the particular role of cocaine is harder to ascertain. There is considerable opinion among the drug using community and services that speedballing is associated with higher rates of overdose. Some possible mechanisms by which speedballing might increase risk are:

- The shorter-acting stimulant effect of the crack means that higher doses of heroin are tolerated initially but that risk of respiratory depression increases as the cocaine's initial effect wears off.
- The stimulant effect of cocaine increases the body's oxygen requirement, which is not adequately met due to respiratory depression.
- Risk is increased because speedballing is more common among people who have other risk factors for overdose such as homelessness, older age, recent imprisonment, malnutrition or various forms of systemic illness.

Sexual risk

There is extensive literature about cocaine use in general and the various ways this impacts on sexual risk. This almost certainly has some bearing on speedball use but it is beyond the scope of this chapter to summarise this here. Speedball use has been specifically associated with commercial sex work (Newcombe, 2007), having multiple sexual partners (for men) (Bogart et al., 2005), acquiring syphilis (López-Zetina et al., 2000), and also linked to HIV infection among sexually vulnerable females (Miller et al., 2002). Just as with other drug users attending treatment, and possibly more so, it will be important to assess and respond to sexual risk among speedball injectors.

Cardiovascular risk

The relationship between speedballing and cardiovascular risk seems to have received little specific research attention. Cocaine use is a known risk factor for cardiovascular disease and its use increases levels of circulating catecholamines and leads to prolongation of the heart's QT interval (Weaver et al., 2003; Karch, 2002). As speedballing involves regular crack cocaine use, it is regarded as a cause of increased risk compared to heroin use. These risks will be further increased if alcohol is simultaneously used, as the resulting coca-ethylene is thought to have greater cardiotoxicity than cocaine alone.

Overdose and the provision of naloxone

One of the risks of the use of CNS depressants, especially opioids, is the potential for overdose. In 1994 Gossop et al. (1996) surveyed 438 drug injectors, of whom 23% reported at least one overdose; the mean number of overdoses was 3.6. and the mean age of first overdose was 23.9 years. At least one overdose was reported by 41% in the previous year and 16% reported more than one overdose. Almost all overdoses were reported by injectors, with only 2% of non-injectors reporting an overdose.. Users who reported overdose were more severely dependent on heroin, older and more likely to have been in treatment but overdose was not related to gender or frequency of heroin use. Reasons for overdosing included taking a larger dose than usual, the heroin being more pure, using alcohol at the same time and resuming heroin after a period of abstinence (when tolerance has dropped).

When injecting street drugs purity is unknown and accidental overdose a constant risk even among experienced users. As Darke (1996) points out, however, fatalities are rarely from heroin alone but often a consequence of other CNS depressants, typically alcohol and benzodiazepines and those who die often have morphine levels no higher than those who survive. Deaths are more likely to occur in older heroin-dependent males who are not currently in treatment.

In a study of overdose among injectors in the Russian Federation, Sergeev et al. (2003) examined the characteristics of opiate overdose in 16 cities. In a group of 763 injectors studied, 59% reported experiencing an overdose, 81% reported seeing others experiencing an overdose and 15% reported seeing a fatal overdose. Heroin was the most common drug to cause an opiate overdose (73%) but in smaller towns home-produced opiates were the most common cause of opiate overdose. Mixing alcohol and tranquillisers increased the risk of overdose as did a longer history of opiate use. Injecting drug users were reluctant to seek medical assistance because of a perceived ineffectiveness of ambulance staff and fear of police prosecution. There was an acknowledged lack of appropriate skills to treat overdose by 57% of respondents.

Overdose is universal among opiate injectors but strategies may be put in place to reduce the risk of fatalities. Sporer (2003) suggest a number of measures that may be taken, involving education of drug users (including CPR training), formation of family support groups and supervised injecting facilities. Recently, a number of projects have tested the viability of the distribution of naloxone. Naloxone is an opiate antagonist with no euphoric properties, which reverses the effects of opiate overdose including the respiratory depression and sedation. Strang et al. (1999) in a pre-launch study of a take home naloxone scheme found that some users were opposed to these measures because they thought it may lead them to increase their drug use. Sporer (2003) points out that as naloxone has a shorter half-life than heroin there is concern that sedation and respiratory depression may recur. Ashworth and Kidd (2001) in a letter to the *British Medical Journal* raised the question of deliberate recreational 'flatlining' (near fatal overdose) for the experience it offered.

Naloxone

Dettmer, Saunders and Strang (2001) describe two pilot schemes of take home naloxone doses. In Berlin opiate users were offered training in emergency resuscitation after overdose, provided with naloxone, needles, syringes, information on naloxone and an emergency handbook. Of 124 injectors who received the training and naloxone, 40 reported back with 22 having given emergency naloxone. All those given naloxone recovered and no risky consumption was reported as a result of naloxone availability. In Jersey naloxone was provided to 101 drug users in contact with local services with instructions on intramuscular administration of the drug and principles of resuscitation from overdose and recovery. Five instances of resuscitation were reported; all fully recovered with no adverse consequences other than withdrawal symptoms being recorded.

Galea et al. (2006) describe a pilot overdose prevention and reversal programme implemented at a New York City needle exchange. Of 25 participants recruited, 22 were successfully followed up in the first 3 months of the project and of these 11 had witnessed a total of 2 overdoses. Naloxone was administered 10 times in 17 of the overdoses and all those who were administered naloxone survived. Galea et al concluded that in New York City naloxone administered by injecting drug users was a feasible overdose prevention measure.

Supervised injecting facilities (SIFs)

Safer injecting rooms (SIRs) or facilities are places where injectors may go where they will be supervised in their injecting, advised on injecting technique and observed following injection. Haemmig and van Beek (2005) give a good description of the history and function of injection rooms. The first was opened in Berne in Switzerland in 1986 and they are now operating in a number of countries. Haemmig and van Beek state that SIRs are a balanced approach to addressing both public health and pubic order issues arising from street based injecting drug use. They suggest that these facilities have a place in reducing immediate and sometimes fatal consequences of public drug use but that the philosophical debate about the merits of these facilities is likely to continue.

Conclusions

This chapter has discussed the many dangers and harms associated with injecting drug use. Although there are many possible interventions and safe practices which may reduce the risk of infections and overdose it is almost impossible to remove the risk entirely. Drug use is a personal choice and the risks that are associated with injecting may be minimised but remain part of that choice.

References

Abdala, N., Stephens, P.C., Griffith, B.R. and Heimer, R. (1999) Survival of human immunodeficiency virus type 1 in syringes, *Journal of Acquired Immune Deficiency Syndrome*, 20, 73–80.

Abdala, N., Reyes, R., Carney, J.M. and Heimer, R. (2000) Survival of HIV-1 in syringes: effects of temperature during storage, *Substance Use and Misuse*, 35, 1369–83.

Abdala, N., Gleghorn, A.A., Carney, J.M. and Heimer, R. (2001) Use of bleach to disinfect HIV-1 contaminated syringes, *American Clinical Laboratory*, 20 (6), 26–7.

Abdala, N., Tolstov, Y., Crowe, M. and Heimer R. (2004) Survival of human immunodeficiency virus type 1 after rinsing injection syringes with different cleaning solutions, *Substance Use and Misuse*, 39, 581–600.

Aceijas, C. and Rhodes, T. (2007) Global estimates of prevalence of HCV infection among injecting drug users, *International Journal of Drug Policy*, 18 (5), 352–8.

Aceijas, C., Stimson, G.V., Hickman, M. and Rhodes, T. (2004) United Nations Reference Group on HIV/AIDS Prevention and Care among IDU in Developing and Transitional Countries: global overview of injecting drug use and HIV infection among injecting drug users, *AIDS*, 18, 2295–303.

Allbutt, T.C. (1870) On the abuse of hypodermic injections of morphia, *Practitioner*, 5, 327–31.

Alter, M.J. (2006) Epidemiology of viral hepatitis and HIV co-infection, *Journal of Hepatology*, 44 (1, supple.) S6–9.

Ashworth, A.J, and Kidd, A. (2001) Apparent advantages may be balanced by hidden harm, letter to *British Medical Journal*, 323 (7318), 935.

Biggam, A.G. (1929) Malignant malaria associated with the administration of heroin intravenously, *Transactions of the Society of Tropical Medicine and Hygiene*, 23, 147–53.

Bisbe, J., Miro, J.M., Latorre, X., Moreno, A., Mallolas, J., Gatel, J.M., de la Bellacasa, J.P. and Soriano, E. (1992) Disseminated candidiasis in addicts who use brown heroin: report of 83 cases and review, *Clinical Infectious Diseases*, 15, 910–23.

Blumenthal, R.N., Kral, A.H., Gee, L., Erringer, E.A. and Edlin, G. (2000) The effect of syringe exchange use on high-risk injection drug users: a cohort study, *AIDS*, 14, 605–11.

Bogart, L.M., Kral, A.H., Scott, A., Anderson, R., Flynn, N., Gilbert, M.L. and Bluthenthal, R.N. (2005) Sexual risk among injection drug users recruited from syringe exchange programs in California, *Sexually Transmitted Diseases*, 32 (1), 27–34.

Boreham, M. (2005) *Exploring Factors Initiating and Sustaining a Culture of snowballing (Simultaneous I.V. Heroin and Crack Co-Use) amongst Drug Users Known to Treatment Agencies in the West End of London: Which Drug Treatment Agencies Does This Subpopulation Access and Why? A Qualitative Study*, London: University of London.

Brett, M.M., Hood, J., Brazier, J.S., Duerden, B.I. and Hahne, S.J. (2005) Soft tissue infections caused by spore forming bacteria in injecting drug users in the United Kingdom, *Epidemiology and Infection*, 133 (4), 575–82.

Brettle, R.P. (1990) Implications of the Edinburgh AIDS epidemic for the United Kingdom, *Journal of Infection*, 20, 215–17.

Burns, S.M., Brettle, R.P., Gore, S.M., Peutherer, J.F., Robertson, J.R. (1996) The epidemiology of HIV infection in Edinburgh related to the injecting of drugs, *Journal of Infection*, 32, 53–62.

Cherubin, C. (1971) Infectious disease problems of narcotic addicts, *Archives of Internal Medicine*, 128, 309–13.

Cherubin, C. and Sapira, J.D. (1993) The medical consequences of drug addiction and the medical assessment of intravenous drug user: 25 years later, *Annals of Internal Medicine*, 119, 1017–28.

Christie, B. (2000) UK heroin deaths prompt international alert, *British Medical Journal*, 320, 1559.

Christie, B. (2010) Heroin contaminated with anthrax has killed 11 people, *British Medical Journal*, 340, 937.

Cornish, J.L., Lontos, J.M., Clemens, K.J. and McGregor, I.S. (2005) Cocaine and heroin ('speedball') self-administration: theinvolvement of nucleus accumbens dopamine and μ-opiate, but not δ-opiate receptors, *Psychopharmacology*, 180 (1), 21–32.

Craib, K.J., Spittal, P.M., Wood, E., Laliberté, N., Hogg, R.S., LI, K., Heath, K., Tyndall, M.W., O'Shaugnessey, M.V. and Schecter, M.T. (2003) Risk factors for elevated HIV incidence among Aboriginal injection drug users in Vancouver, *Canadian Medical Association Journal*, 168 (1), 19–24.

Darke, S. and Zador, D. (1996) Fatal heroin 'overdose': a review, *Addiction*, 91 (12), 1765–72.

Des Jarlais, D.C., Hagan, H., Friedman, S.R., Friedmann, P., Goldberg, D., Frischer, M., Green, S., Tunving, K., Ljungberg, B., Wodak, A., Ross, M., Purchase, D., Millson, M.E. and Myers, T. (1995) Maintaining low HIV seroprevalence in populations of injecting drug users, *Journal of the American Medical Association*, 274, 1226–31.

Des Jarlais, D.C., Marmor, M., Paone, D., Titus, S., Shi, Q., Perlis, T., Jose, B. and Friedman, S. (1996) HIV incidence among injecting drug users in New York City syringe exchange programmes, *Lancet*, 348 (9033), 987–91.

Des Jarlais, D.C., Perlis, T., Arasteh, K., Torian, L.V., Beatrice, S., Milliken, J., Mildvan, D., Yancovitz, S. and Friedman, S.R. (2005) HIV incidence among injection drug users in New York City, 1990 to 2002: use of serological test algorithm to assess expansion of HIV prevention services, *American Journal of Public Health*, 95, 1439–44.

Des Jarlais, D.C., Perlis, T., Arasteh, K., Torian, L.V., Hagan, H., Beatrice, S., Smith, L., Wethers, J., Milliken, J., Mildvan, D., Yancovitz, S., Friedman, S.R. (2005) Reductions in hepatitis C virus and HIV infections among injecting drug users in New York City, 1990–2001, *AIDS*, 19 (supple. l3), S20–S25.

Dettmer, K., Saunders, B. and Strang, J. (2001) Take home naloxone and the prevention of deaths from opiate overdose: two pilot schemes, *British Medical Journal*, 322, 895–6.

Doherty, M.C., Garfein, R.S., Monterroso, E. and Brown, D. (2000) Correlates of HIV infection among young adult short term injection drug users, *AIDS*, 14 (6), 717–26.

Efstratiou, A., Emery, M., Lamagni, T.L., Tanna, A., Warner, M. and George, R.C. (2003) Increase incidence of group A streptococcal infections amongst injecting drug users in England and Wales, *Journal of Medical Microbiology*, 52, 525–6.

Frank, C., Mohamed, M.K., Strickland, G.T., Lavanchy, D., Arthur, R.R., Magder, L.S., El Khoby, T., Aly Ohn, El Said, Anwar, W. and Sallam, I. (2000) The role of parenteral antischistosomal therapy in the spread of hepatitis C virus in Egypt, *Lancet*, 355 (9207), 887–91.

Friedman, S.R., Cooper, H.L., Tempalski, B., Keem, M., Friedman, R., Flom, P.L. and Des Jarlais, D.C. (2006) Relationships of deterrence and law enforcement and drug related harms among drug injectors in US metropolitan areas, *AIDS*, 20 (1), 93–9.

Garfein, R.S., Doherty, M.C., Monterroso, E.R., Thomas, D.L. and Vlahov, D. (1998) Prevalence and incidence of hepatitis C virus infection among young adult injection drug users, *Journal of Acquired Immune Deficiency Syndrome Human Retrovirology*, 18 (supple. 1) S11–19.

Galea, S., Worthington, N., Piper, T.M., Nandi, V.V., Curtis, M. and Rosenthal, D.M. (2006) Provision of naloxone to injection drug users as an overdose prevention strategy: Early evidence from a pilot project, *Addictive Behaviours*, 31 (5), 907–12.

Gerasimov, M.R. and Dewey, S.L. (1999) Gamma-vinyl gamma-aminobutyric acid attenuates the synergistic elevations of nucleus accumbens dopamineproduced by a cocaine/heroin (speedball) challenge, *European Journal of Pharmacology*, 380 (1), 1–4.

Gisselquist, D., Upham, G. and Potterat, M.J. (2006) Efficiency of human immunodeficiency virus transmission through injections and other medical procedures: evidence, estimates and unfinished business, *Infection Control and Hospital Epidemiology*, 27 (9), 944–52.

Gisselquist, D., Rothenburg, R., Potterat, J. and Drucker, E. (2002) HIV infections in sub-Saharan Africa not explained by sexual or vertical transmission, *International Journal of STD and AIDS*, 13 (10), 657–66.

Gonzalez Garcia, J.J., Arnalich, F., Pena, J.M., Garcia-Alegria' J.J., Garcia Fernadez, F., Jiminez Herraez, C. and Vazquez, J.J. (1986) An outbreak of plasmodium vivax malaria among heroin users in Spain, *Transactions of the Royal Society of Tropical Medicine and Hygiene*, 80, 549–52.

Gossop, M., Griffiths, P., Powis, B., Williamson, S. and Strang, J. (1996) Frequency of non-fatal heroin overdose: survey of heroin users recruited in non-clinical settings, *British Medical Journal*, 313, 402.

Haemmig, R. and van Beek, I. (2005) Supervised injecting rooms. In Pates, R., McBride, A. and Arnold, K. (eds). *Injecting Illicit Drugs*, Oxford: Blackwell.

Hay, G., Gannon, M., MacDougall, J., Millar, T., Eastwood, C. and McKeganey, N. (2007) *National and Regional Estimates of the Prevalence of Opiate Use and/or Crack Cocaine Use 2005/06: A Summary of Key Findings*, Home Office, Online Report 21/07.

Health Protection Agency (HPA) (2007) *Shooting Up: Infections among Injecting Drug Users in the United Kingdom 2006*, London: Health Protection Agency.

Health Protection Agency (HPA) (2010) *Shooting Up: Infections among Injecting Drug Users in the UK 2009. An Update*: 2010, London: Health Protection Agency.

Heimer, R., Kinzly, M.L., He, H. and Abdala, N. (2007) The effect of acids on the survival of HIV during drug injection, *AIDS*, 45, 144–50.

Helpern, M. (1934) Epidemic of fatal estivo-autumnal malaria among drug addicts in New York City transmitted by common use of hypodermic syringe, *American Journal of Surgery*, 26, 111–23.

Hemby, S.E., Co, C., Dworkin, S.I. and Smith, J.E. (1999) Synergistic elevations in nucleus accumbens extracellular dopamine concentrations during self-administration of cocaine/heroin combinations (speedball) in rats, *Journal of Pharmacology and Experimental Therapeutics*, 288 (1), 274–80.

Hibbs, R.G., Corwin, A.L., Hassan, N.F., Kamel, M., Darwish, M., Edelman, R., Constantine, N, Rao, M.R., Khalifa, A.S., Mokhtar, S., Fam, N.S., Ekladious, E.M. and Bassily, S.B. (1993) The Epidemiology of Antibodies to Hepatitis C in Egypt. *Journal of Infectious Diseases*, 168, 789–90.

Hutin, Y.J.F., Hauri, A.M. and Armstrong, G.L. (2003) Use of injections in healthcare settings world wide, 2000: literature review and regional estimates, *British Medical Journal*, 327, 1075–8.

Johnson, R.A., Gerstein, D.R., Pach, A., Cerbonne, F.G. and Brown, J. (2002) HIV risk behaviors in African-American drug injector networks: implications of injection-partner mixing and partnership characteristics, *Addiction*, 97 (8), 1011–24.

Jones, L., Pickering, L., Sumnall, H., McVeigh, J. and Bellis, M. (2008) *A Review of the Effectiveness and Cost Effectiveness of Needle Exchange Programmes for Injecting Drug Users*, London: National Institute for Clinical Health and Excellence.

Kamal, S.M. and Nassar, I.A. (2008) Hepatitis C genotype 4: what we know and what we don't yet know, *Hepatology*, 47, 1371–83.

Karch, S.B. (2002) *Karch's Pathology of Drug Abuse*, 3rd edn, New York: CRC Press.

Kerr, T., Small, W., Buchner, C., Zhang, R., Li, K., Montaner, J. and Wood, E. (2010), *American Journal of Public Health*, 100 (8), 1449–53.

Kimura, A., Higa, J., Levin, R.M., Simpson, G., Vargas, Y. and Vugia, D.J. (2004) Outbreak of necrotizing fasciitis due to clostridium sordellii among black-tar heroin users, *Clinical Infectious Diseases*, 38, 87–91.

Kitsenko, N. and Kitsenko, G. (2007) A continuing epidemic of HIV among IDUs in Odessa, Ukraine: insights from a rapid policy assessment (abstract #1064). *18th International Harm Reduction Conference*. Warsaw, Poland.

Koester, S., Booth, R.E. and Zhang, Y. (1996) The prevalence of additional injection related HIV risk behaviors among injection drug users, *Journal of Acquired Immune Deficiency Syndromes*, 12 (2), 202–7.

Kral, A.H., Bluthenthal, R.V., Booth, R.E. and Watters, J.K. (1998) HIV seroprevalence among street-recruited injection drug and crack cocaine users in 16 US municipalities, *American Journal of Public Health*, 88 (1), 108–13.

Lalhmingliana, C. (2003) *The physical effects of propoxyphene*, unpublished dissertation, Presbyterian Hospital, Aizawl, Mizoram.

Leen, C.S. and Brettle, R.P. (1991) Fungal infection in drug users, *Journal of Antimicrobial Chemotherapy*, 28 (supple. A), 83–96.

Leri, F., Bruneau, J. and Stewart, J. (2003) Understanding polydrug use: review of heroin and cocaine co-use, *Addiction*, 98 (1), 7–22.

Lopez-Cortez, I., Lozano de Leon, F., Gomez-Mateos, J.M., Sanchez- Porto, A. and Obrador, C. (1989) Tick-borne relapsing fever in intravenous drug abusers, *Journal of Infectious Diseases*, 159, 804.

López-Zetina, J., Ford, W., Weber, M., Barna, S., Woerhle, T., Kerndt, P. and Monterroso E. (2000) Predictors of syphilis seroreactivity and prevalence of HIV among street recruited injection drug users in Los Angeles County, 1994–6, *Sexually Transmitted Infections*, 76 (6), 462–9.

McCurdy, S.A., Williams, M.I., Ross, M.W., Kilonzo, G.P. and Leshabari, M.T. (2005) New injecting practice increases HIV risk among drug users in Tanzania, letter to *British Medical Journal*, 331 (1 October), 778.

Miller, C.L., Spittal, P.M., Laliberté, N., Li, K., Tyndall, M.W., O'Shaughnessey, M.V. and Schecter, M.T. (2002) Females experiencing sexual and drug vulnerabilities are at elevated risk for HIV infection among youth who use injection drugs, *Journal of Acquired Immune Deficiency Syndrome*, 30 (3), 335–41.

Miller, C.L., Johnson, C., Spittal, P.M., Li, K., Laliberté, N., Montaner, J.S.G. and Schecter, M.T. (2002) Opportunities for prevention: hepatitis C prevalence and incidence in a cohort of young injection drug users, *Hepatology*, 36 (3), 737–42.

MMWR (1998) Tetanus among injecting drug users-California 1997, *Morbidity and Mortality Weekly Report*, 47 (8), 149–51. Cited in McBride, A.J. and Wichter, J. (2005) Odd commotions: some other health consequences of injecting. In R. Pates, A. McBride and and K. Arnold (eds), *Injecting Illicit Drugs*, Oxford: Blackwell.

Murphy, E.L., DeVita, D., Liu, H., Vittinghof, E., Leung, P., Ciccarone, D.H. and Edlin, B.R. (2001) Risk factors for skin and soft-tissue abscesses among injection drug users: a case-control study, *Clinical Infectious Diseases*, 331 (1), 35–40.

Newcombe, R. (2007) *Multi-Drug Injecting in Manchester: A Survey of 100 Injecting Drug Users Attending Lifeline Needle Exchange Scheme in 2006*, Manchester: Lifeline Publications.

Paintsil, E., He, H., Peters, C., Lindenbach, B. and Heimer, D. (2010) Survival of hepatitis C virus in syringes: implication for transmission among injection drug users, *Journal of Infectious Diseases*, 202, 984–90.

Partanen, T.A., Vikatmaa, P., Tukiainen, E., Lepäntalo, M. and Vuola, J. (2009) Outcome after injections of crushed tablets in intravenous abusers in the Helsinki University Central Hospital, *European Journal of Endovascular Surgery*, 37 (6), 704–11.

Passaro, D.J., Werer, S.B., McGee, J., Mackenzie, W.R. and Vugia, D.J. (1998) Wound botulism associated with black tar heroin among injecting drug users, *Journal of the American Medical Association*, 279 (11), 859–63.

Radun, D., Bernard, H., Altmann, M., Schöeneberg, I., Bochat, V., van Treek, U., Rippe, R.M., Grunow, R., Elschner, M., Biederbick, W. and Krause, G. (2010) Preliminary case report of fatal anthrax in an injecting drug user in North-Rhine-Westphalia, Germany, *Eurosurveillance*, 15 (2), 5.

Ramsey, C.N., Stirling, A., Smith, J., Hawkins, G., Brooks, T., Penrice, G., Browning, L.M., and Ahmed, S. (on behalf of the NHS GGC and the Scottish National Outbreak Control Teams) (2010) An outbreak of infection with bacillus anthracis in injecting drug users in Scotland, *Eurosurveillance*, 15 (2), 2–4.

Rao, M.R., Naficy, A.B., Darwish, M.A., Darwish, N.M., Schisterman, E., Clemens, J. and Edelamn, R. (2002) Further evidence for association of hepatitis C infection with parenteral schistosomiasis treatment in Egypt, *BioMed Central Infectious Diseases*, 2 (29), PMCID: PMC 139974.

Rhodes, T., Stoneman, A., Hope, V., Hunt, N., Martin, A. and Judd, A. (2006) Groin injecting in the context of crack cocaine and homelessness: From 'risk boundary' to 'acceptable risk'? *International Journal of Drug Policy*, 17, 164–70.

Rhodes, T., Briggs, D., KImber, J., Jones, S. and Holloway, G. (2007) Crack–heroin speedball injection and its implications for vein care: qualitative study, *Addiction*, 102 (11), 1782–90.

Robertson J.R., Bucknall, A.B.V., Welsby. P.D., Roberts, J.J.K., Inglis, J.M., Peutherer, J.F. and Brettle, R.P. (1986) Epidemic of Aids related virus (HTLV-III/LAV) infection among intravenous drug abusers in a Scottish general practice, *British Medical Journal (Clinical Research Edition)*, 292 (6519), 527–30.

Rubin, S. and Morrison, C.L. (1992) Temazepam misuse in a group of injecting drug users, *British Journal of Addiction*, 87 (10), 1387–92.

Ryder, D., Salmon, A. and Walker, N. (2001) *Drug Use and Drug Related Harm: A Delicate Balance*, Melbourne: IP Communications.

Sarang, A.T.R. and Platt, L. (2008) Access to syringes in three Russian cities: implications for syringe distribution and coverage, *International Journal of Drug Policy*, 19 (supple. 1), 25–36.

Schmid, G.P., Buvé, A., Mugvenyi, P., Garnett, G.P., Hayes, R.J., Williams, B.G., Calleja, J.G., De Cock, K.M., Whitworth, J.A., Kapiga, S.H., Ghys, P.D., Hankins, C., Zaba, B., Heimer, R. and Boerma, J.T. (2004) Transmission of HIV-1 infection in sub-Saharan Africa and the effect of elimination of unsafe injections, *Lancet*, 363, 482–8.

Sergeev, B., Karpets, A., Sarang, A. and Tikhonov, M. (2003) Prevalence and circumstance of opiate overdose among injection drug users in the Russian Federation, *Journal of Urban Health*, 80 (2), 212–19.

Short, L.J. and Bell, D.M. (1993) Risk of occupational infection with blood-borne pathogens in operating and delivery room settings, *American Journal of Infection Control*, 21, 343–50.

Sporer, K.A. (2003) Strategies for preventing heroin overdose, *British Medical Journal*, 326 (7386), 443.

Stimson, G. (1996) Has the United Kingdom averted a major epidemic of HIV-1 infection among drug injectors?, *Addiction*, 91 (8), 1085–8.

Strang, J., Powis, B., Best, D., Vingoe, L., Griffiths, P., Taylor, C., Welch, S. and Gossop, M. (1999) Preventing overdose fatalities with take-home naloxone: pre-launch study of possible impact and acceptability, *Addiction*, 94 (2), 199–204.

Taylor, A., Hutchinson, S., Lingappa, J., Wadd, S., Ahmed, S., Gruer, L., Taylor, T.H., Jr, Roy, K., Gilchrist, G., McGuigan, C., Penrice, G. and Goldberg, D. (2005) Severe illness and death among injecting drug users in Scotland: a case controlled study, *Epidemiology and Infection*, 133 (2), 193–204.

Thorne, L.B. and K.A. Collins, (1998) Speedballing with needle embolization: case study and review of the literature, *Journal of Forensic Science*, 43 (5), 1074–6.

Tjøtta, E., Hungnes, O. and Grinde, B. (1991) Survival of HIV-1 activity after disinfection, temperature and pH changes, or drying, *Journal of Medical Virology*, 35, 223–7.

Turning Point (2007) *At the Sharp End*, London: Turning Point.

Vlahov, D., Sullivan, M., Astemborski, J. and Nelson, K.E. (1992) Bacterial infections and skin cleaning prior to injection among intravenous drug users, *Public Health Reports*, 107 (5), 595–8.

Weaver, T., Madden, P., Charles, M.A., Stimson, G. and Renton, A. (2003) Comorbidity of substance misuse and mental illness in community mental health and substance misuse services, *British Journal of Psychiatry*, 183, 304–13.

Werner, S.B., Passaro, D., McGee, J., Schechter, R. and Vugia, D.J. (2000) Wound botulism in California, 1951–1998: recent epidemic in heroin injectors, *Clinical Infectious Diseases*, 3 (4), 1018–24.

Wodak, A. and Cooney, A. (2006) Do needle syringe programs reduce HIV infection among injecting drug users: a comprehensive review of the international evidence, *Substance Use and Misuse*, 41 (6–7), 777–813.

Chapter 12

RECOVERY AND HARM REDUCTION: TIME FOR A SHARED, DEVELOPMENT-ORIENTED, PROGRAMMATIC APPROACH?

Neil Hunt

Introduction

In recent years, the UK has seen a marked shift in its discourse on drug policy, in which a developing critique of its long-standing harm reduction based strategy has led to one that puts recovery at its core (Ashton, 2008; Scottish Government, 2008; Home Office, 2010). Official versions of recovery have been conflated with an expected goal of becoming abstinent, which is explicit in the coalition government's drug strategy 'Reducing Demand, Restricting Supply, Building Recovery: Supporting People to Live a Drug Free Life' (2010). This has generated a degree of debate about real or perceived tensions between these two approaches, in which one is frequently characterised as being in opposition to the other.

Proponents of the shift to recovery have been critical of the UK's harm reduction-based treatment system for its failure to produce people who are drug free. This has been attributed to an over-reliance on methadone within services that are driven by government targets and portrayed as doing little to develop people's hope, optimism and ambitions for a life beyond treatment. Treatment services have been criticised for failing to meet people's wider needs for psycho-social interventions within programmes that properly enable (re)integration. Simultaneously, they are portrayed as protective of professional power and reluctant to recognise the contribution that the wider recovery community does or could make (McKeganey, 2006, 2007; Best et al., 2008, 2009a; Best, 2010).

From a harm reduction perspective, a prominent concern has been that evidence-based interventions, which reliably achieve important public health impacts, health gains and benefits for community safety (chiefly needle and syringe programmes [NSPs] and opioid substitution treatment [OST]) may be undermined if spending is shifted towards programmes where the evidence is perceived to be weaker and a treatment goal is imposed rather than negotiated.

Alongside a process that continues to have undeniable strands of conflict, there has also been a discernible move towards consensus. Dialogue has generally increased between people who are primarily associated with a harm reduction perspective and those with a greater recovery-orientation. This has been evident at a number of levels including: the diverse UK discussion lists and online forums; numerous meetings and conferences with recovery-related themes; and, various print and online publications, for example see Bamber (2010). Polemical voices can still be heard, but any observer of this process would find it difficult to miss the more widespread and quietly developing respect among people whose views reflect different traditions, needs and experiences, and the corresponding exploration of ways they can best work together.

Harm Reduction in Substance Use and High-Risk Behaviour: International Policy and Practice, First Edition.
Edited by Richard Pates and Diane Riley.
© 2012 Blackwell Publishing Ltd. Published 2012 by Blackwell Publishing Ltd.

This chapter evaluates the considerable common ground that exists between harm reduction and the particular 'new recovery' that is developing in the UK. In doing so, areas that remain potentially divisive are examined as are opportunities for greater collaboration around shared values and goals.

Within a chapter that addresses readers from both harm reduction and recovery perspectives, it is necessary to clarify some of the terminology that will be used. Although many people readily describe themselves using terms such as 'alcoholic' or 'addict' and value the concept of 'addiction' as a way of making sense of their experiences, this language can also be experienced as offensive, subjugating and alienating by some of the people to whom it is applied. In particular, it can imply a disease model that is both contested and a focus for political struggle regarding drug-using identities (Davies, 1997; Albert, 2010). Within this chapter, it is nevertheless taken as uncontroversial that for some people who use alcohol or other drugs, loss of control over the frequency and pattern of use is sometimes experienced as a profound problem. The term preferred throughout this chapter is 'person experiencing an alcohol or other drug problem', because it places use within a continuum of life experience, rather than turning the person into the thing.[1]

Working across these two perspectives often requires looking past words that can seem toxic and working hard to keep people's underlying intentions and understanding clearly in view. It requires openness to the possibility that our worldview and the cherished concepts we use to describe it may need to become subtler, more fine-grained, amended or even discarded; and, that approaches which don't work for one person can, equally, be life-saving for others, when all the time our own beliefs, experiences, perhaps even our entire biography, shouts out that this can't be so.

'Harm reduction' and 'recovery' are concepts that are both contested and evolving. The comparative approach used in the chapter draws primarily on formal accounts that describe the principles on which each is based. The following two sections provide a brief historical context and the justification for selecting the versions that are compared.

Harm reduction

Harm reduction is commonly traced back to 1926 when the Rolleston report urged a medical approach of prescribing people's drug of dependence rather than the punitive, criminal justice approach that then (and still) prevailed in the USA; however, the term was first used by Russell Newcombe in 1987. It then entered widespread use as a term applied to the pragmatic responses to HIV/AIDS among people who inject drugs and has since been broadened to signify a philosophy that can potentially be applied to any harm that arises from the use of alcohol and other drugs.

Harm reduction's definition builds on Newcombe's early framework based upon a matrix of types and levels of harms (Newcombe, 1992). It is typically seen as operating across a hierarchy of types and levels of harm, focusing on those immediate threats to safety and well-being that are most amenable to change, yet recognising the importance of abstinence, where this can be achieved: Advisory Council on the Misuse of Drugs (ACMD, 1988).

The detailed practice and policies of harm reduction tend to vary in a way that is context dependent and according to factors including: a country's specific drug problems/harms; its economic situation; the stage of development of its services; and, broad socio-cultural factors (IHRA, 2010). See Rhodes and Hedrich (2010) and elsewhere in this volume for some illustrations of these variations

Since the inception of harm reduction, a variety of definitions have been proposed (Newcombe, 1992; Lenton and Single, 1998; Riley et al., 1999). In recent years, there has been a noticeable

---

[1] A convention for which I am grateful to William White.

development in the way that human rights have featured within harm reduction advocacy; a process that has received strong support from Harm Reduction International (HRI), the global body through which the different regional and national harm reduction networks are affiliated (formerly the International Harm Reduction Association). It seems likely that the meaning of harm reduction will continue to evolve; however, the IHRA position statement 'What is harm reduction?' (2010) is, in effect, an official definition and has therefore been used substantially as the basis for comparison within this chapter.

Recovery

The origins of the recovery and temperance movements are intertwined, with both emerging in the USA and UK during the first half of the nineteenth century amidst concern with the drinking patterns of an increasingly urbanised migrant labour force (Yates and Malloch, 2010). Alcoholics Anonymous (AA), the archetypal recovery fellowship, was founded in 1935, followed later by Narcotics Anonymous (NA), and a wide array of other peer-based groups that includes diverse religious, spiritual and secular addiction recovery mutual aid societies (White, 1998).

Until recently, the UK recovery movement has seemed largely synonymous with the 12-step fellowships: notably Alcoholics Anonymous (AA), Narcotics Anonymous (NA) and, increasingly, Cocaine Anonymous (CA). Consequently, in terms of people's general understanding of recovery within the UK, the 12-step approach has sometimes seemed like the only available model. For many harm reductionists, this has almost certainly engendered a degree of resistance to recovery due to a perceived clash between some of the central tenets of the 12-step movement and harm reductionists' values and worldview. For example, harm reduction's principle of promoting any positive change and focusing on immediate, urgent, achievable goals is in tension with the near-exclusive emphasis on abstinence as a control strategy that is embedded within the 12-step approach. Likewise, acknowledging being 'powerless' is inconsistent with a view which routinely incorporates behavioural change and self-control strategies to achieve moderation and risk reduction across populations that include experimental and occasional consumers and for whom a notion of powerlessness contradicts the daily reality of people's lives. Furthermore, the concept of a 'higher power' and the quasi-religious tenor of the 12-step approach evokes caution among some harm reductionists; many of whom tend to hold a rationalist, secular outlook. Reliance on an external higher power may also be seen to conflict with a view that harm is reduced when people are supported to achieve greater autonomy and self-empowerment, i.e. mobilising resources from within themselves. These are, of course, generalisations with all the caveats that generalisations require. Many 12-step advocates would immediately and rightly respond that their beliefs are considerably more nuanced than this somewhat superficial and stereotyped interpretation of the 12-step perspective. Nevertheless, this reading of recovery seems common among harm reductionists and worth noting as a potential source of some of the differences and misunderstandings within the unfolding debates about the interplay and respective roles of harm reduction and recovery within UK drug policy.

Despite the continued importance of the 12-step fellowships, in recent years there has also been a growth in the number of mutual aid groups operating outside of the 12-step tradition, which reflect a wider range of preferences and needs. Almost certainly, this expansion has been stimulated by the shift to a recovery focus within the UK's various drug strategies. It is difficult to fully catalogue this new diversity but, within it, a great variety of local groups have developed out of programmes linked to treatment services. Additionally, more formalised systems such as SMART Recovery® UK, which offer a secular approach and draw explicitly on psychological theory have become far more visible. These developments are one reason for any harm reductionist who simply equates recovery with the 12-step fellowships to reappraise their understanding of the broader concept and principles that recovery now comprises. These changes are evident within several attempts by prominent interest groups to formalise a modern vision of recovery for the UK.

A key contribution to the attempt to define this distinctive UK recovery is provided by a 'recovery consensus panel' convened by the UK Drug Policy Commission (UKDPC). This included both people in recovery (i.e. experts through experience) and other professional experts (UKDPC, 2008). The group took the work of the Betty Ford Institute Consensus Panel (2007) in the USA as a starting point and eventually developed a 'vision statement' as follows: 'The process of recovery from problematic substance use is characterised by voluntarily sustained control over substance use which maximises health and wellbeing and participation in the rights, roles and responsibilities of society.'

It is instructive to read the full report on this process, which explains some of the reasons for the ways in which this version differs from that of the Betty Ford Institute Consensus Panel (BFICP). For example, the BFICP (2007) uses the terms 'sobriety' and 'citizenship', whereas the UK statement talks of 'voluntarily sustained control' and 'participation in the rights, roles and responsibilities of society'; changes that reflect concerns about a simple equation between recovery and abstinence and caution about 'citizenship' as a term that might be interpreted to require active engagement in employment, which then becomes an absolute requirement for recovery (2008).

Another influential point of reference for any contemporary UK understanding of recovery is the set of 12 principles produced by the USA's Center for Substance Abuse Treatment (CSAT), within the Substance Abuse and Mental Health Services Administration (SAMHSA). Although American, this work is often referred to by UK recovery advocates; possibly because it has been developed through a careful consensus-building process and is therefore well-suited to bringing together different perspectives in a way that people feel to be needed here. Clearly, its recency and provenance as a government-promoted initiative in the country that is a global centre for the recovery movement also means that it carries considerable authority (Sheedy and Whitter, 2009). The CSAT group agreed the following 'working definition' – a term that suggests a degree of tentativeness:

> Recovery from alcohol and drug problems is a process of change through which an individual achieves abstinence and improved health, wellness, and quality of life.

It is, however, their 12 'guiding principles' that are most widely referred to in Britain. These provide a more elaborated understanding of recovery that is inclusive of diverse approaches and unhindered by some of the problems that some harm reductionists have found inherent within the 12-step philosophy. The principles state that:

1. There are many pathways to recovery
2. Recovery is self-directed and empowering
3. Recovery involves a personal recognition of the need for change and transformation
4. Recovery is holistic
5. Recovery has cultural dimensions
6. Recovery exists on a continuum of improved health and wellbeing
7. Recovery emerges from hope and gratitude
8. Recovery involves a process of healing and self-redefinition
9. Recovery involves addressing discrimination and transcending shame and stigma
10. Recovery is supported by peers and allies
11. Recovery involves (re)joining and (re)building a life in the community
12. Recovery is a reality.

(Sheedy and Whitter, 2009)

It could be said – unfairly perhaps – that some of these are illustrative of the sort of woolly, meaningless statements that result from consensus building between parties with very different worldviews; nevertheless, it will later be argued that some of these have considerable relevance to any discussion about an accommodation between harm reduction and recovery. One further reason for focusing on these principles is that they have recently been adapted by the UK Recovery Federation (UKRF)[2] – also within a consensus-building process – albeit one that was not as well-resourced and extensive as that in the USA. Any claim to represent *the* true voice of recovery in the UK might be premature and would probably still be contested but, still, the views of any initiative that is attempting to build consensus across a federated alliance of interested parties is relevant to the discussion here. The amended principles published by the UKRF still reflect the core of the CSAT principles, but among other things they have more explicit reference to: the role of families; the structural factors that contribute to people's experience of drug and alcohol problems; the development of 'recovery capital', which is emerging as a key concept within the new recovery; and, the relationship between recovery, abstinence and harm reduction (UK Recovery Federation, 2011). For more on recovery capital see Best and Laudet (2010).

The concept of recovery is not, however, restricted to the realm of problems people experience with alcohol and other drugs. In the UK, a mental health recovery movement has developed strongly since a vision for it was articulated in the early 1990s. Anthony (1993) characterises recovery as 'a deeply personal, unique process of changing one's attitudes, values, feelings, goals, skills, and/or roles. It is a way of living a satisfying, hopeful, and contributing life even with limitations caused by illness. Recovery involves the development of new meaning and purpose in one's life as one grows beyond the catastrophic effects of mental illness.' Mental health recovery also incorporates a notion of a hierarchy of needs and the mental health charity Rethink (2008) has argued that recovery requires the fulfilment of three basic conditions:

- The person has a place to live that is safe and free from threat
- The person has to be free from acute physical and psychological distress
- The person has to have basic human rights that mean they are able to make choices

Recovery has been an explicit, government principle for mental health services since 2001 and well before it ever featured in the UK's drug strategies (Department of Health, 2001). Consequently, alongside definitions of recovery embedded in the drugs field, an understanding of recovery in the UK is also, to some extent, informed by a concept of mental health recovery that is not directly connected with alcohol or other drugs; not least because many people experience overlapping mental health and drug and alcohol problems.

Recovery and harm reduction compared

The two previous sections have identified key, contemporary, formal accounts of harm reduction and recovery that contain consensus statements about the core beliefs, values and principles of these

---

[2] In the interests of transparency, please note that I am an advisory board member of the UKRF representing the UK Harm Reduction Alliance (UKHRA). The UKRF's initiative of extending an invitation to UKHRA to provide representation was an early signal to me that an inclusive, broad-based recovery was developing and that there were opportunities for a collaborative approach between parties who do not have a strong history of dialogue, which might yield benefits that were not then fully appreciated.

two perspectives and provide a basis for comparison. To what extent do harm reduction and recovery have common ground? Where are there differences of emphasis? And in what ways do tensions arise? This section offers a commentary on these questions with reference to several of the more obvious and important themes.

Abstinence: more agreement than disagreement

Much of the debate about the compatibility of harm reduction and recovery seems to revolve around the question of abstinence; however, in terms of the identified texts there seems to be a large measure of overlap. In its position statement IHRA (2010) explicitly acknowledges that abstinence is a desirable option:

> The objective of harm reduction in a specific context can often be arranged in a hierarchy with the more feasible options at one end (e.g. measures to keep people healthy) and less feasible but desirable options at the other end. Abstinence can be considered a difficult to achieve but desirable option for harm reduction in such a hierarchy.

This is tempered with the recognition that attaining abstinence is often difficult and will not always be feasible; nevertheless, it reflects an underlying logic that, for any given substance, not consuming the substance at all is, ultimately, the most effective way of avoiding its harms. Most harm reductionists would be quick to add a caveat that if the pursuit of abstinence results in a succession of lapses, the net result can be an overall increase in risk and harm. The reduced tolerance and heightened risk of fatal overdose after elective detoxification or enforced withdrawal through imprisonment are widely recognised hazards that need to be weighed against the benefits of any interim period of abstinence. There is also a need to understand the consequences of abstinence from a drug or drugs in the round. A programme that achieves abstinence from illicit and prescribed opiates, yet sees this replaced by increased reliance on alcohol in a person with a liver compromised by hepatitis C infection may lead to a net increase in harm. It is also arguable that in cases where a person is using a drug to self-medicate an underlying trauma or disturbance, abstinence will result in net harm unless the more fundamental problems can also be effectively addressed. Each of these caveats has implications for the design and operation of abstinence-oriented programmes, the way they are integrated with other services and the calculus between the likely risks and benefits of attempting to achieve abstinence. They do not, however, detract from the principle that abstinence is a desirable option, which can confer a net reduction in harms and is achieved and sustained by some people.

Conversely, the emerging UK model of recovery cannot reasonably be characterised as synonymous with or requiring abstinence. This is not to deny that abstinence from one or more substances is a widespread goal of people who define themselves as recovering or in recovery – it is. Recovery has, nevertheless, been reformulated as a broader concept that is not so exclusively predicated on the question of whether someone's life is drug and/or alcohol free. This is evident in several ways.

The Recovery Consensus Group convened by the UK Drug Policy Commission (2008) characterised recovery as 'voluntarily sustained control over substance use'. This is distinct from the definition agreed by the Betty Ford Institute Consensus Panel (2007) of 'a voluntarily maintained lifestyle characterised by sobriety'. 'Control' is privileged over 'sobriety' with the latter's implication of abstinence and the UK group further qualify their definition by saying recovery 'may mean abstinence supported by prescribed medication or consistently moderate use of some substances (for example, the occasional alcoholic drink)'.

In the CSAT/SAMHSA 'Guiding principles and elements of recovery-oriented systems of care' (Sheedy and Whitter, 2009) the participants agreed a working definition of recovery as 'a process of change through which an individual achieves abstinence and improved health, wellness, and quality of life'. Abstinence here is construed as *an* ultimate goal but not *the* ultimate goal and is regarded as integral to attaining goals of health, well-being and quality of life. The corresponding 12 principles also suggest a pragmatism that values a range of interim steps and diverse ways of approaching recovery that resonate strongly with a harm reduction approach. Three in particular warrant mention. The principle, '*There are many pathways to recovery*' embodies a non-prescriptive ethos that appears to allow the incorporation of any programme or intervention that confers benefit and enables the harm reduction maxim of '*any positive change*'. It also seems consistent with Lenton and Single's characterisation of harm reduction as an approach that 'maximises the intervention options' (Lenton and Single, 1998). Secondly, the view of recovery as '*self-directed and empowering*' seems very much in sympathy with the user-centred ethos of harm reduction encapsulated in the statement that '*In particular, people who use drugs and other affected communities should be involved in decisions that affect them.*' (International Harm Reduction Association, 2010) or, the pithier '*Nothing about us, without us*' (Canadian HIV/AIDS Legal Network, 2008). *Empowerment* here may refer largely to the degree of agency a person has to negotiate their available 'recovery-orientated system of care' within a given structural context. Nevertheless, it seems worth noting that a more comprehensive interpretation of empowerment could accommodate the notion of a recovering person as someone who also engages with the broader, social, structural factors that may thwart their health, well-being and quality of life. Viewed this way, empowerment may be aligned with harm reduction and its engagement with the

> Many policies and practices (that) intentionally or unintentionally create and exacerbate risks and harms for drug users. These include: the criminalisation of drug use, discrimination, abusive and corrupt policing practices, restrictive and punitive laws and policies, the denial of life-saving medical care and harm reduction services, and social inequities.
>
> (IHRA, 2010)

The third principle to highlight is that '*Recovery exists on a continuum of improved health and wellbeing.*' This seems strongly reminiscent of the concept of a hierarchy of goals that is intrinsic to harm reduction for which

> The objective of harm reduction in a specific context can often be arranged in a hierarchy with the more feasible options at one end (e.g. measures to keep people healthy) and less feasible but desirable options at the other end.

Just as the CSAT/SAMHSA definition of recovery sees abstinence as something towards which people travel, the phrasing of IHRA's position statement seems to imply that although abstinence is not necessary and may well not be feasible, it is generally desirable, insofar as this is the condition under which drug-related harms are entirely eliminated.[3]

---

[3] There is an emerging critique of harm reduction theory arising from its focus on harms and an implied neglect of the enjoyment and other benefits that can arise from drug-taking. From this point of view, abstinence would not necessarily be a desirable general goal; however, at present this perspective has not been adopted within mainstream accounts of harm reduction. HOLT, M. & TRELOAR, C. 2008. Pleasure and drugs. *International Journal of Drug Policy*, 19, 349–352, MOORE, D. 2008. Erasing pleasure from public discourse on illicit drugs: On the creation and reproduction of an absence. *International Journal of Drug Policy*, 19, 353–358.

The UK Recovery Federation has elected not to define recovery, but has adopted the CSAT/SAMHSA principles with some variations. The three principles discussed above are retained, albeit with changes of emphasis for two:

> There are many pathways to recovery and no individual, community or organisation has the right to claim ownership of the 'right pathway'.
> Recovery lies within individuals, families and communities and is self directed and empowering.

Another principle is expanded specifically to refer to a structural dimension of recovery, change and 'recovery capital'. This suggests a model of recovery with a clearer emphasis on social change, which is interesting to note in relation to the discussion of empowerment above:

> Recovery involves the personal, cultural and structural recognition of the need for participative change, transformation and the building of recovery capital.

Finally, an entirely new principle includes an important statement that addresses the dual role of abstinence and harm reduction within recovery, validating both:

> Recovery transcends, whilst embracing, harm reduction and abstinence based approaches and does not seek to be prescriptive.

Together, these contemporary accounts seem to suggest far more agreement than disagreement between harm reduction and the developing understanding of recovery within the UK. Although the attainment of abstinence is recognised as a valuable goal that people may aim for and from which they may benefit, the emerging UK recovery model is not prescriptive but largely flexible, pragmatic, inclusive and personalised.

Formal accounts concerning recovery are not, however, the only influence on people's understanding of the concept and one factor has particular potential to generate misunderstanding and distrust between approaches that otherwise appear to be converging. Notwithstanding the more nuanced way that the recovery movement itself addresses abstinence, the government's adoption of recovery has been conflated with an imposed expectation that abstinence is *the* goal of treatment. In particular, the UK Drug Strategy (Home Office, 2008) stated that '*The goal of all treatment is for drug users to achieve abstinence from their drug – or drugs – of dependency. For some, this can be achieved immediately, but many others will need a period of drug-assisted treatment with prescribed medication first.*' This conflicts with a view that people should determine their own goals, which may or may not include abstinence. The shift that it also signifies regarding the role of opioid substitution treatment is addressed later.

As people attempt to make sense of the new recovery, this government narrative prioritising abstinence is a critical point of reference, even though it might reasonably be argued that this has a lesser claim to authenticity than accounts of recovery developed within and by the recovery community. Although recovery comprises more than the sum of those services receiving government funding, it seems naïve to ignore the influence these have, as places through which many people pass and where recovery is implicitly defined by the government targets that are selected to measure how well providers perform within a recovery-oriented treatment system. If these focus too narrowly on indicators such as 'completing treatment drug free' and under-attend to other measures of health, wellbeing, quality of life, or participation in society, they are likely to muddy people's understanding of recovery and quite possibly construct recovery as something to be resisted rather than embraced by harm reductionists and recovery advocates alike.

Methadone and other medication: optimising their role, not whether they have one

As has been noted, a critique of the expanded UK treatment system developed as part of the New Labour government's shift to a focus on crime reduction has included the claim that there has been an over-reliance on methadone maintenance treatment (MMT).

Ashton (2008) attributes aspects of this critique to the 'new abstentionists'. In turn, this has been a prominent part of the argument with which the emergence of the new recovery is associated. For harm reductionists, this produced two main perceived threats: the replacement of MMT with residential rehabilitation; and, the imposition of time limits and constraints on MMT in a way that contradicts its evidence-base.

In 2007, the 'Addictions' report of the Conservative think-tank, the Centre for Social Justice (Centre for Social Justice, 2007) concluded that 'maintenance methadone prescribing which perpetuates addiction and dependency has been promoted under current policy while rehabilitation treatment has been marginalised'. This programme of policy analysis was overseen by the former Conservative leader the Rt Hon. Ian Duncan Smith and was initially anticipated to be influential over the drug strategy of a future Conservative government, which polls at the time suggested was increasingly likely. The report raised the prospect of a policy that would see MMT abandoned in favour of a wholesale switch to residential rehabilitation programmes: an approach with a less compelling evidence-base, which would greatly disrupt the lives of the many people whose treatment was being managed in the community. In practice, this threat has not materialised. Debate about the accessibility and role of residential treatment is ongoing, but it seems clear that, currently, there is no realistic plan for a major shift of resources towards residential services as part of the UK recovery agenda.

Earlier, it was noted that the UK drug strategy (Home Office, 2008) seemed to signal a change in the expectations surrounding OST. A prevailing maintenance model began to look under threat from a view that prioritised abstinence – defined to include abstinence from prescribed medication – and an implication that medicines such as methadone should have only an intermediate, time-limited role. For some, the journey towards abstinence was portrayed as something that could be achieved immediately, whereas *'many others will need a period of drug-assisted treatment with prescribed medication first'*. Again, this change coincided with the emerging recovery agenda, meaning that a link with more restrictive prescribing policies could readily be perceived. With the duration of any 'period of drug-assisted treatment' unspecified, and services simultaneously under escalating cost pressures and with performance targets for treatment episodes that are 'completed drug-free', shorter treatment episodes have an evident appeal, even if this risks abbreviating care that is protective and conferring benefit. From a harm reduction standpoint, this means that, rightly or wrongly, recovery can be construed as a threat.

What then is the role of OST within the new recovery? Three sources particularly help develop an answer to this question. The UKDPC Recovery Consensus Group (2008) conclude that *'Recovery may be achieved in a variety of ways including through medically maintained abstinence.'* They clearly regard 'maintenance' as a valid form of recovery.

The second point of reference is a recent monograph on 'recovery-oriented methadone maintenance' which is by far the most comprehensive treatment of the issue to date (White and Mojer-Torres, 2010). Their conclusions deserve attention because they can lay some claim to being the most definitive statements available. Regarding the status of the person on methadone maintenance their conclusions, contradict the view that abstinence requires someone to be free of medication:

Denying 'abstinence' or 'drug free' status to stabilised MM patients (who do not use alcohol or illicit drugs and who take methadone and other prescribed drugs only as indicated by competent medical practitioners) based solely on their status as methadone patients inhibits rather than supports their long-term recoveries.

The authors also conclude that from a recovery perspective the question of how continuation or cessation of methadone should be regarded is entirely a matter of personal choice and does not signify a demarcation between addiction and recovery. This suggests that any external requirement that people move beyond methadone maintenance when this is not wholly their own goal cannot be justified in terms of any recovery imperative.

For stabilized MM patients, continued methadone maintenance or completed tapering and sustained recovery without medication support represent varieties/styles of recovery experience and matters of personal choice, not the boundary between and point of passage from the status of addiction to the status of recovery.

In some ways the most important of White and Mojer-Torres' contributions is their review of the way that OST programmes in the USA during the 1970s and 1980s drifted and deviated from the early good practice established by Vincent Dole and Marie Nyswander (White and Mojer-Torres, 2010). Resemblances to the UK's experience are considerable; however, in essence, they argue that the original, comprehensive methadone maintenance treatment model became undermined and diluted through a poorly led process of rapid expansion for which a correspondingly knowledgeable and skilled workforce did not exist. Pressure to provide it on the cheap, with inadequate dosing and over-zealous tapering off of methadone – all driven by a relegation of a primary person-centred, rehabilitative ethos to an emphasis on the reduction of social harms all contributed to a corrosion of its reputation. People may argue about how to reconcile some of the tensions this analysis presents, but it is difficult to conclude anything other than that the question is one of how best to provide methadone – among newer approaches to medication-assisted recovery such as buprenorphine and heroin-assisted treatment, rather than whether it should be provided at all.

The third point of reference is the most recent UK drug strategy (2010) which has some differences from the previous strategy that merit noting. In a section entitled 'Recovery is an individual, person-centred journey' there is an acknowledgement that the government's aspiration is for people to be drug-free:

Our ultimate goal is to enable individuals to become free from their dependence; something we know is the aim of the vast majority of people entering drug treatment. Supporting people to live a drug-free life is at the heart of our recovery ambition.

Prescribing approaches, nevertheless, seem to receive a clearer endorsement than previously. The term 'maintenance' is not used directly, but the language seems to recognise the value of long-term prescribing and there is nothing to suggest that medication has to be time-limited or constrained, if that is what is needed. Diamorphine prescribing receives a qualified endorsement, which is notable as this is a treatment that remains controversial in some countries and is sometimes perceived to be at a more radical end of harm reduction.

Substitute prescribing continues to have a role to play in the treatment of heroin dependence, both in stabilising drug use and supporting detoxification. Medically assisted recovery can, and does, happen.

There are many thousands of people in receipt of such prescriptions in our communities today who have jobs, positive family lives and are no longer taking illegal drugs or committing crime. We will continue to examine the potential role of diamorphine prescribing for the small number who may benefit, and in the light of this consider what further steps could be taken, particularly to help reduce their re-offending.

There is, nevertheless, a clear view that:

> for too many people currently on a substitute prescription, what should be the first step on the journey to recovery risks ending there. This must change. We will ensure that all those on a substitute prescription engage in recovery activities and build upon the 15,000 heroin and crack cocaine users who successfully leave treatment every year free of their drug(s) of dependence.

Whatever White and Mojer-Torres (2010) might conclude about the continuing or tapering off of methadone as a personal choice between two varieties of recovery with equivalent merit, it is clear that the UK government wants more of the latter. If this is accomplished as a result of increased support, which enables more people to attempt and ultimately succeed in leading a life without OST in line with their own preferences, there is not necessarily any conflict with good practice. Indeed, depending on the cost of any increased support, there might even be a secondary societal benefit through a reduction in costs to the public purse. However, at a time of widespread public sector spending cuts in which there is an active objective of reducing the number of people receiving incapacity benefit, an evident concern must be that a clamour to produce people who are drug-free – in keeping with the government's goal – may lead to poor practice within systems and services that lack the resources to provide the required 'recovery activities', which then detrimentally affects people who are prescribed or in need of OST.

Reducing stigma and discrimination: time for a shared, programmatic approach?

The next theme to be developed here concerns stigma and discrimination, which can operate both to intensify problems and to prevent or delay help-seeking (Lloyd, 2010). Recognition of the need to engage effectively with stigma and discrimination has come increasingly to the fore and has been endorsed by recovery and harm reduction advocates alike. As has been seen, the 12 principles of recovery developed by CSAT identify discrimination and stigma as problems to be addressed and transcended and the UKRF (2011) adopt this principle with the slightly stronger language of 'challenging' discrimination rather than 'addressing' it. In the CSAT report, the discussion of stigma and discrimination in relation to recovery highlights its detrimental effects on people prior to receiving treatment (i.e. people who are still among the active drug users with whom harm reduction works), as well as its impact on people later in the recovery process who may well be drug free, yet are still subject to prejudice in areas such as employment practises arising from their history of drug use. The authors also discuss stigma reduction initiatives in a way that makes it evident that an active approach to reducing stigma and discrimination is required within recovery-oriented systems of care (Sheedy and Whitter, 2009).

IHRA's (2010) position statement also refers explicitly to stigma, the language that perpetuates it and its effects:

> Harm reduction practitioners oppose the deliberate stigmatisation of people who use drugs. Describing people using language such as 'drug abusers', 'a scourge', 'bingers', 'junkies', 'misusers', or a 'social evil' perpetuates stereotypes, marginalises and creates barriers to helping people who use drugs.

Discrimination is similarly identified as one of a range of related ways that people who use drugs are oppressed:

> Many policies and practices intentionally or unintentionally create and exacerbate risks and harms for drug users. These include: the criminalisation of drug use, discrimination, abusive and corrupt policing practices, restrictive and punitive laws and policies, the denial of life-saving medical care and harm reduction services, and social inequities.

It is uncertain how completely these understandings of stigma and discrimination overlap and point towards a fully shared programme of action across the recovery and harm reduction movements. The recovery account focuses on access to treatment and employment, whereas the harm reduction version is situated more broadly alongside a range of concerns that receive less consideration within formal accounts of recovery. Regardless, what these highlight is that there is a powerful case for people who are committed to both perspectives to explore ways that they can pursue a collaborative approach which would maximise their impact on the pervasive effects of stigma and discrimination. Indeed, combating stigma and discrimination may be one of *the* critical issues that unite these two social movements programmatically and in a fundamental way.

A hierarchically based development-orientation

Finally, recovery and harm reduction have overlapping concerns but do not deal with the same thing. Recovery is generally concerned with people who are experiencing serious problems with their drug or alcohol use. Becoming drug-free – whether permanently or temporarily – is a common goal for people aiming to achieve recovery and often favours particular control strategies and supports. Harm reduction's focus is wider, in the sense that it addresses the needs of people irrespective of whether their use is currently experienced as problematic. Its main emphasis is on continuing or active users, but these may be experimental, occasional or recreational users. As such, many people within the scope of a harm reduction approach have nothing – in any sense whatsoever – from which they need to recover. Comparisons that assume they do commit what is sometimes called a 'category error'. In other words, they contain a logical flaw that invalidates the comparison. Any debate about recovery and harm reduction needs to recognise and acknowledge this difference in their general focus.

Harm reduction programmes work routinely with people whose use has become profoundly problematic and who may benefit from a recovery approach. For this reason, if harm reduction programmes fail to take all reasonable and available opportunities to connect the population with whom they work with recovery-oriented services from which those same people are likely to benefit, they are squandering opportunities to reduce harm. Conversely, recovery-oriented services with a focus on supporting people who are endeavouring to become drug-free jeopardise the health and well-being of people who lapse and leave, if they do not take all corresponding measures to ensure that they then have access to services that can protect against immediate harms, most obviously NSPs and Take-Home Naloxone programmes.

The preceding discussion illustrates a major difference of emphasis. Being substantially rooted in the public health challenge of HIV/AIDS prevention, harm reduction prioritises: 'Keeping people who use drugs alive and preventing irreparable damage' (IHRA, 2010).

As its name suggests, harm reduction:

> refers to policies, programmes and practices that aim to reduce the harms associated with the use of psychoactive drugs in people unable or unwilling to stop. The defining features are the focus on the

prevention of harm, rather than on the prevention of drug use itself, and the focus on people who continue to use drugs.

(IHRA, 2010)

As the CSAT/SAMHSA principles show, the focus of recovery is towards change and transformation within a process of healing and self redefinition (Sheedy and Whitter, 2009) which, in the UKDPC Consensus Group's terms 'maximises health and wellbeing and participation in the rights, roles and responsibilities of society' (2008).

There seems to be nothing within these positions that creates any intrinsic conflict between recovery and harm reduction. Their emphasis is different and often this means that programmes traditionally associated with one approach or the other tend to work with people who are at different points of a process. This idea of a process is, nevertheless, a unifying feature embraced by both harm reduction and recovery. Without for a moment saying people *must* move along it, harm reduction incorporates the notion of movement along a hierarchy of risks and harms that are progressively harder to achieve, but which are generally associated with a reduction in harm at each step (IHRA, 2010). Likewise, recovery is discussed as 'a process of change, along a 'continuum of health and well-being' (Sheedy and Whitter, 2009). As has already been noted, Rethink's (2008) account of mental health recovery also incorporates a notion of hierarchy in which the fulfilment of basic needs is a prerequisite for recovery. Viewed this way, there appears to be considerable consensus about an organising principle of *development*, which suggests that the task of recovery advocates and harm reductionists alike is to do all that is within their power to enable people to do exactly that – develop – as far as their goals, potential and circumstances allow.

The principle of *development* may well be one that deserves to be more central to the debate and has already becoming an organising principle for drug policy in some German speaking regions. For example, in the municipal treatment system that incorporates the world's first drug consumption room in Berne, which opened in 1986 (Hedrich, 2004), a debate about how to reform and integrate abstinence-oriented services and those based on what is known in German-speaking countries as an 'acceptance' model (i.e. working within a harm reduction framework that accepts people irrespective of their lifestyle choices) has also taken place. This also reflected a perception that acceptance-based services were insufficiently ambitious on behalf of the people using them and failed to exploit opportunities which would enable people to develop. After much debate, the outcome was the adoption of an organising principle of *entwicklungsorientiert* (development-orientation), which was placed at the centre of the entire system.[4] Everyone working within services has a common goal of enabling people to develop to the fullest extent possible. As a result, acceptance-based services now have a greater emphasis on supporting people to make progress. Conversely, development was elevated as a goal within abstinence-oriented services. One possible benefit of bringing the language and principal of *development-orientation* to the centre is that, whereas the term *recovery* seems likely always to have connotations of a disease model that is problematic for some people, the idea that services should strive to enable personal development seems uncontroversial. Doubtless, many readers will also have been struck by the resonance between within this discussion and Maslow's hierarchy of needs, with its ultimate goal of self-actualisation (Maslow, 1943).

[4] Personal communication: Jakob Huber, director.

Conclusions

This chapter has very briefly traced the histories of the harm reduction movement and the 'new recovery' – a particular version of recovery that is developing in the UK. These have then been compared with reference to texts that appear to best represent formal, current, consensus accounts of their aims and principles. On this basis, it is apparent that recovery and harm reduction have far fewer differences than has sometimes been supposed. Although accounts of recovery vary in a way that suggest some differences, these are not pronounced and they diminish further when particular attention is paid to UK interpretations of recovery.

Given the immense amount of discussion of the new recovery that has played out at conferences, within online forums and in papers, editorials and letters addressing drug and alcohol policy, it is inevitable that this chapter does not reflect every position that has been expressed. The focus here on consensus statements rather than some of the more polemical perspectives is intentional, as these marginal views often seem to generate more heat than light. In the UK, harm reduction and recovery can be characterised as having entered a phase of dialogue and rapprochement, an implication of which is that these more marginal perspectives, which are often also divisive and undermine dialogue should not be over-valued. This is not a prescription for censorship. On the contrary, debate is vital, but care is needed to ensure that this is undertaken in a way that helps build consensus, rather than undermining it.

Concerning abstinence, it is evident that harm reduction and recovery both value this without viewing it as an isolated, exclusive or overriding goal. Where harm reduction programmes can identify and support people who will derive a net benefit from abstinence, the implication is that they should do so. Conversely, although many recovery advocates have extremely good personal reasons to regard abstinence as an effective self-control strategy, a contemporary understanding of recovery implies that it is also necessary to recognise the other choices that people sometimes make. To adapt a common expression, striving for the 'perfection' of an unattainable abstinence should never be an enemy of the 'good', where this good is 'any positive change' and achievable.

The role of methadone has been emblematic within debates surrounding the new recovery. The analysis here has shown that although there are vocal critics of the use of methadone and other prescribed treatments, the more consensual accounts of recovery fully recognise that these have a legitimate and valuable contribution to make. It seems certain, however, that this will remain an area where best practice will remain disputed and that this will, in part, reflect differences in the emphasis attached to individual, rehabilitative goals as opposed to social goals such as crime prevention. Furthermore, this debate will be played out against a wider backdrop within the UK of cuts to public services driven by the economic crisis and an allied objective of reducing the number of people receiving incapacity benefit, with which changes occurring as part of a genuine commitment to recovery should not be conflated.

The concern to reduce stigma and discrimination that recovery and harm reduction share stands out as an area where both movements have common goals. There has been little attention to this within the discourse concerning the supposed polarisation between these two perspectives, yet this is an evident area where people's aims are closely aligned, which may well benefit from a closer, programmatic approach. Exploring how this might be done more effectively seems like a strategic priority for harm reduction and recovery advocates alike.

Finally, the underlying model for both harm reduction and recovery has much in common because of the way that it is grounded on ideas of progress along a series of hierarchical steps. The wider scope of harm reduction to encompass a concern with the whole population at risk of harm and not just those who are experiencing problems has to be borne in mind to avoid seeing disagreement where none exists. For harm reductionists, it is important to recognise that the term recovery does not necessarily connote a disease model and that care is needed to look past any visceral response to the term. Likewise, recovery advocates also need to be mindful that there are multiple understandings of recovery, some of which can undermine a constructive, collaborative approach between people from different perspectives. To this end, it may be that emphasising the German principle of *entwicklungsorientiert* (i.e. *development-orientation*) is a way that recovery and harm reduction can best work together to maximise the health and well-being of the populations they aim to serve.

Notes

I wish to express my appreciation to:

Peter Hawley, Michael Cronin, Anton Derkacz, Chris and his colleagues from NA in Kent, Andria Efthimiou-Mordaunt, Stephen Bamber, Annemarie Ward, Alistair Sinclair, Michaela Jones, David Clark, David Best (for his contribution to an initial draft), Bill White (for comments on an earlier version of this chapter), Danny Morris, Chris Ford, Matthew Southwell, Peter McDermott, Pat O'Hare, Lisa Mallen, Tim Bingham, Claire Robbins and Nigel Brunsdon; all of whom are among the many people who have shaped my thinking in this chapter in one way or another, irrespective of whether they agree with the final result.

Lastly, I'd particularly like to acknowledge Johnny Ruttledge who stands out among those people whose lives exemplify how harm reduction and recovery should be combined.

References

ACMD (1988) *AIDS and Drug Misuse,* part 1, London, HMSO.

Albert, E.R., (2010) The production of stigma by the disease model of addiction: why drug user activists must oppose it. Presentation at the Intercnational Conference for the Reduction of Drug Related Harm, Liverpool, 9–13 April.

Anthony, W.A., (1993) Recovery from mental illness: the guiding vision of the mental health service system in the 1990s, *Psychosocial Rehabilitation Journal,* 16, 11–23.

Ashton, M., (2008) The new abstentionists, *Druglink,* special insert, 1–16.

Bamber, S.J., (2010) The role of needle and syringe programmes in a recovery-orientated treatment system. In S.J., Bamber,(ed.), *Recovery Writing, Vol. 1: 2009–2010* Manchester: The Art of Life Itself.

Best, D. (2010) Recovery fights its corner, *Drink and Drugs News,* 16–17.

Best, D. and Laudet, A.B. (2010) *The Potential of Recovery Capital,*www.thersa.org/projects/our-projects/reports/the-potential-of-recovery-capital, accessed 13 June.

Best, D., Groshkova, T. and McTague, P. (2009a) The politics of numbers, *Druglink,* 16–17.

Best, D., Groshkova, T. and McTague, P. (2009b) The politics of recovery, *Druglink,* 14–19.

Best, D., Loaring, J., Ghufran, S. and Day, E. (2008) Different roads, *Drink and Drugs News,* 6–7.

Betty Ford Institute (2007) What is recovery? A working definition from the Betty Ford Institute, *Journal of Substance Abuse Treatment,* 33, 221–8.

Canadian HIV/AIDS Legal Network, IAA, Open Society Institute (2008) *'Nothing About Us Without Us' – Greater, Meaningful Involvement of People Who Use Illegal Drugs: A Public health, Ethical, and Human Rights Imperative: Eastern Europe and Central Asia Edition,* Toronto: Canadian HIV/AIDS Legal Network, International AIDS Alliance, Open Society Institute, www.aidslaw.ca/publications/interfaces/downloadFile.php?ref=1351, accessed 16 June 2009.

Centre for Social Justice (2007) *Breakthrough Britain, Vol. 4, Addictions: Towards Recovery*, London: Centre for Social justice.

Davies, J.B., (1997) *The Myth of Addiction*, Amsterdam: Harwood Academic Publishers.

Department of Health (2001) *The Journey to Recovery: The Government's Vision for Mental Health Care.* London: Department of Health.

Hedrich, D., (2004) *European Report on Drug Consumption Rooms*, Lisbon: European Monitoring Centre for Drugs and Drug Addiction.

Holt, M., and Treloar, C., (2008) Pleasure and drugs, *International Journal of Drug Policy*, 19, 349–52.

Home Office (2008) *Drugs: Protecting Families and Communities*, London: Home Office.

Home Office (2010) *Drug Strategy 2010, Reducing Demand, Restricting Supply, Building Recovery: Supporting People to Live a Drug Free Life*, London, Home Office.

IHRA, (2010) *What Is Harm Reduction?*, a position statement from the International Harm Reduction Association, www.ihra.net/files/2010/08/10/Briefing_What_is_HR_English.pdf, accessed 10 June 2011.

Lenton, S., and Single, E., (1998) The definition of harm reduction, *Drug & Alcohol Review*, 17, 213–220.

Lloyd, C., (2010) *Sinning and Sinned Against: The Stigmatisation of Problem Drug Users*, London: UK Drug Policy Commission.

Maslow, A.H., (1943) A theory of human motivation, *Psychological Review*, 50, 370–96.

McKeganey, N., (2006) The lure and the loss of harm reduction in UK drug policy and practice, *Addiction Research & Theory*, 14, 557–88.

McKeganey, N., (2007) Riding high, *Drink and Drugs News*, 6–7.

Moore, D., (2008) Erasing pleasure from public discourse on illicit drugs: on the creation and reproduction of an absence, *International Journal of Drug Policy*, 19, 353–8.

Newcombe, R., (1987) High time for harm reduction, *Druglink*, 2, 10–11.

Newcombe, R. (1992) The reduction of drug related harm: a conceptual framework for theory, practice and research. In P. O'Hare, R. Newcombe, A. Matthews, E. Buning and E. Drucker (eds), *The Reduction of Drug Related Harm*, London: Routledge.

RETHINK (2008) *A Brief Introduction to the Recovery Approach*, www.rethink.org/living_with_mental_illness/recovery_and_self_management/recovery, accessed 1 February.

Rhodes, T., and Hedrich, D., (2010) *Harm Reduction: Evidence, Impacts and Challenges*, Luxembourg: ECMDDA, European Union Press.

Riley, D., Sawka, E., Conley, P., Hewitt, D., Mitic, W., Poulin, C., Room, R., Single, E. and Topp, J. (1999) Harm reduction: concepts and practice: a policy discussion paper, *Substance Use and Misuse*, 34, 9–24.

Sheedy, C.K. and Whitter, M. (2009) *Guiding Principles and Elements of Recovery-Oriented Systems of Care: What Do We Know From the Research?*, Rockville, MD: NIDA.

Scottish Government (2008) *The Road to Recovery: A New Approach to Tackling Scotland's Drug Problem.* Edinburgh: Scottish Government.

UKDPC (2008a) *The UK Drug Policy Commission Recovery Consensus Group: A Vision of Recovery*, London: UKDPC.

UKDPC. (2008b) *A Vision of Recovery*, London: UK Drug Policy Commission.

UKRF (2011) *Revised and Finalised UK Recovery Federation Recovery Principles*, London: UKRF.

White, W.L. (1998) *Slaying the Dragon: The History of Addiction Treatment and Recovery in America*, Bloomington: Chestnut Health Systems.

White, W.L. and Mojer-Torres, L. (2010) *Recovery-Oriented Methadone Maintenance*, Chicago: Great Lakes Addiction Technology Transfer Center, Philadelphia Department of Behavioral Health and Mental Retardation Services, Northeast Addiction Technology Transfer Center.

Yates, R. and Malloch, M.S. (2010) The road less travelled? A short history of addiction recovery. In Y. Yates and M.S. Malloch (eds), *Tackling Addiction: Pathways to Recovery*, London: Jessica Kingsley Publishers.

Chapter 13

HARM REDUCTION FOR STIMULANTS

Diane Riley and Richard Pates

Introduction

Harm reduction for users of stimulants poses different questions because of the nature of the drugs but any of the risks from injecting (see chapter 11) are common with other drugs but may have some additional problems. The group of drugs known as stimulants include cocaine and amphetamine type substances (ATS) as well as drugs such as ecstasy (which is dealt with in chapter 14) and other more milder stimulants such as khat; this chapter will deal with cocaine and ATS as they are the drugs posing the greater risks.

Stimulant drugs such as cocaine and ATS give the user feelings of euphoria, well-being and mood elevation Becker (1999), and provide an increase in energy, wakefulness and stamina. For this reason they are used recreationally, for both mood elevation and to remain awake and alert for long periods of partying and so forth. ATS have been used for many years in a variety of professions to maintain alertness, as, for example by truck drivers on long drives in Australia (Williamson, 2007) and Brazil (Silva et al., 2003) by British, Japanese and German troops in World War II and by the American Air Force between 1960 and 1991 (Cornum et al., 1997) and by students to enable them to study for long periods of time (Hayward et al., 2008). ATS are still used in the treatment of a few medical problems such as narcolepsy and for attention deficit hyperactivity disorder (ADHD) in children and teens.

Cocaine, which has a shorter period of action but produces a greater sense of euphoria than amphetamine, has been used traditionally in the countries of the Andes, where it originates, to overcome altitude sickness and enable people to work for long periods of time, often with little food (Rudgely, 1998; hence one of the slang terms for it 'Bolivian marching powder'). It was praised by Sigmund Freud, an enthusiast for cocaine, who wrote a paper about it in 1884 'Über Coca'. In this he eulogised cocaine for its beneficial effects and saw it as a harmless panacea for many ills and even suggested its use as a cure for morphine addiction – but that in itself it was not addictive: 'it does not turn the morphine addict into a *coquero*; the use of coca is only temporary'. It was also used as an anaesthetic especially in dental and facial operations. Cocaine was a popular recreational drug in the 1920s and 1930s in many western countries. The increase in use of more pure forms of cocaine such as crack in the 1980s resulted in an increase in psychological, physical, social and financial problems related to the drug and the policies pertaining to it.

Risks and harms

Stimulant use can be associated both physical and psychological problems. While many people who use stimulants such as cocaine and ATS have no problems following use, minor use may affect some

Harm Reduction in Substance Use and High-Risk Behaviour: International Policy and Practice, First Edition.
Edited by Richard Pates and Diane Riley.
© 2012 Blackwell Publishing Ltd. Published 2012 by Blackwell Publishing Ltd.

susceptible people with both mental and physical problems because of the nature of the effects of the drug on the central nervous system. Heavy or long-term use can lead to serious consequences. Both cocaine and ATS increase blood pressure and heart rate which may lead to cardiovascular problems and there is some evidence to suggest that the use of these drugs may lead to neurotoxic effects. In terms of mental health, stimulant use may lead to paranoia and a full psychosis. While these do not necessarily appear to be dose related, for some people small doses can lead to stimulant related psychosis.

Physical health problems

Hildrey et al. (2010) list a number of physical effects associated with ATS use. These include effects on sleep, anorexia, cardiac effects and stroke, possible risk factor for the development of Parkinson's disease in later life, underweight birth weight in new-borns, oral damage including tooth loss, gingivitis, angular cheilitis (lesions at the corner of the mouth), and increased risks from blood-borne infections from injection, and an increase in risky sexual activity.

Sleep problems

As noted above, ATS are used to maintain wakefulness by various professional groups including soldiers, airmen, truck drivers and students. This is deliberate use to remain awake for long periods of time; they are also used in the treatment of narcolepsy (a disease causing sudden periods of sleep during waking hours: Szabadi, 2006). A side effect of recreational or illicit ATS use is remaining awake which may be related to the role that dopamine has in modulating wakefulness (Jankovic, 2002), caused probably by amphetamine blocking dopamine re-uptake or by stimulating uptake of dopamine (Erbert and Berger, 1998; Boutrel and Koob, 2004). When withdrawing from amphetamine, there is a rebound effect where total sleep time increases and the time getting to REM sleep decreases. Sometimes following long periods of ATS use, users experience a 'crash' where they may sleep for several days. Washton and Tatarsky (1983) in a study of the adverse effects of cocaine found that 58% reported sleeping difficulties. They found that there was no connection between route of administration (intranasally, intravenously of via smoking) and the reporting of problems

Anorexia

Until the 1960s when concern began about over-prescription, ATS were prescribed by general practitioners to aid slimming (Pates and Riley, 2010) until a voluntary ban was introduced and eventually led to a ban on the prescription of these drugs for anorectic purposes. This also may be why ATS drugs are popular among young women with eating disorders compared to those without eating disorders (Matsumoto et al., 2002). Studies have shown that there is a decrease in food intake with regular amphetamine use but this does return to normal as the individual becomes tolerant to the effects of ATS, with return to previous food intake more quickly in those on lower doses of the drug (Wolgin, 2004). In Washton and Tatarsky's study (1983) of the effects of cocaine on 55 chronic users, 38% reported significant weight loss.

Cardiac effects

Cardiomyopathy and myocardial infarction are a rare but well known side effect of stimulant use; death is rare, although recorded (Jacobs, 2006). Kaye and colleagues (2007), in a review of methamphetamine use and cardiovascular pathology, found that methamphetamine users are subject to a higher risk of cardiac pathology, that this was higher for chronic users and likely to continue after the cessation of use. Premature mortality was more likely among these users because the drug exacerbated other risks of cardiac pathology. The Centres for Disease Control and Prevention (1995) have found that cocaine is the most likely cause of a drug induced stroke, followed by amphetamine. This is true of both ischaemic strokes (blocking of the blood supply to the brain as by clot) and haemorrhagic strokes (the bursting of a blood vessel in the brain). Stimulants causes vasoconstriction and thus a decrease in blood flow. Stimulants also cause elevated blood pressure (hypertension) which is also a major cause of death in the general population through strokes.

Stimulant induced strokes tend to occur within a few minutes or hours of administration and a longitudinal study (Westover et al., 2007) found that the incidence of stroke among amphetamine users increased between 2000 and 2003, which correlated with the increased use of amphetamine in this period. The study showed a relationship between haemorrhagic stroke and amphetamine use but not with ischaemic stroke.

Oral problems

Users of amphetamine are at risk for damage to teeth by loss of teeth, blackening and staining of the teeth and general tooth decay because of the acidic nature of amphetamine and the damage to the enamel protective layer of the teeth (American Dental Association Division of Communication, 2005). Bruxism (the involuntary grinding of teeth) is known to be a side effect of amphetamine use. This can lead to erosion of the teeth, fine cracks in the posterior teeth, chips in the teeth and the flattening of the biting surface (See and Tan, 2003). Oral or nasal use of cocaine may lead to perforation of the nasal septum and palate, gingival lesions and erosion of the tooth surfaces. There is also a risk of hepatitis C and HIV transmission through the oral lesions caused by smoking crack cocaine using makeshift pipes that expose the user to hot smoke and metal (Ward et al., 2000; Tortu et al., 2004).

Sexual problems

Many stimulant users are more likely to have increased sexual activity and have more risky sexual activity such as unprotected sex. Amphetamine users are twice as likely to have had sex in exchange for drugs or have had sex with a sex worker (Molitor et al., 1998) and have a significantly higher number of casual or anonymous sexual partners. They have three times as much vaginal intercourse as non-amphetamine users, more anal sex and higher rates of sexually transmitted infections (Baskin-Sommers and Sommers, 2006).

Injection problems

The risks for the transmission of blood-borne viruses and other infections is similar to other drugs (see chapter 11) but because of the short acting nature of cocaine it may be injected far more frequently than cocaine or heroin. More frequent injection will lead to the greater risk of vein damage and the local anaesthetic effect may also increase the risk of vein damage. There are also increased risks from injecting cocaine and heroin combined in the same injection (snowballing) (see chapter 11 for a fuller description of this.)

Parkinson's disease

The long-term use of ATS has been shown to be neurotoxic towards the brains dopaminergic neurons (McCann and Ricaurte, 2004) by destroying dopamine neural pathways which lead to long-term dopamine depletion. There is a suggestion that long-term ATS use may leave users at risk of developing Parkinson's disease later in life. Parkinson's disease is a neurodegenerative disease caused by degeneration of dopaminergic neurons resulting in an insufficient supply of dopamine. This relationship has been suggested by the similarity of the dopaminergic neuron depletion and evidence from Garwood et al. (2006) which found that in a sample of sufferers of Parkinson's disease, 11% had prolonged use of prescribed or street amphetamines.

Prenatal effects

There has been concern expressed about the effects of psychostimulants on the unborn foetus. Although the evidence is equivocal it is clear that all unnecessary drugs should be avoided during pregnancy. Furara and colleagues (1999) found that 25% of amphetamine users have underweight babies and that 28% of the babies were delivered pre-term. Psychostimulants are thought to affect the unborn child by blocking the reuptake of catecholamines in the mother which results in cardiac stimulation and vasoconstriction leading to a decrease in uterine blood flow and consequent decrease in the delivery of oxygen and other nutrients to the foetus. There also may be restricted blood flow to the placenta and decrease in uterine contractility (Dean and McGuire, 2004). White et al. (2006) found that there was a foetal loss of 14.9% compared to the rate of 5% in the general population. One of the problems with these figures is that women who use amphetamines are likely to use tobacco and have poor nutritional habits and social status, all of which may have an effect on the foetus. Discontinuing amphetamine use during the pregnancy may improve the health of the baby. In a study comparing women who took amphetamine throughout pregnancy with those who took the drug only for the first two trimesters, lower birth weights and head circumference were found in those who took the drug throughout the pregnancy (Smith et al., 2003).

Mental health problems

Neurotoxic effects of psychostimulant use may include short- and long-term interference with neurotransmitters which may lead to hyperactivity, mental confusion, agitation, tachycardia and tremor; this is also known as serotonin syndrome, the effects of which may occasionally be fatal (Pates and Riley, 2010). Monoamine depletion may also lead to a depressed mood, anhedonia and lethargy post-use (i.e., during the come down).

Mental health problems have long been associated with stimulant use. Mental health problems seem to be reported and more often documented for amphetamine users than for cocaine or ecstasy users (Pates and Riley, 2010). Long-term psychostimulant use can lead to problems of paranoia, psychosis, mood disorders and anxiety (Lee, 2004). The psychosis which results from psychostimulant use is similar to non-drug induced psychosis but usually remits after drug use ceases and can be treated quickly with antipsychotic drugs. Symptoms can include hallucinations, paranoid delusions and uncontrolled violent behaviour. The association of amphetamine use and psychosis was first reported in 1938 when Young and Scoville reported that 2 out of 3 patients using Benzedrine as a treatment for narcolepsy developed a paranoid psychosis. Connell (1958) wrote an influential monograph on amphetamine psychosis based on observations of the increase of amphetamine use in London in the 1950s. This was an important milestone and led to the acceptance of the link between ATS use and psychosis.

Chen et al. (2003), in a study of 445 methamphetamine users recruited from a psychiatric hospital who had developed psychosis, found that the symptoms were closely related to the symptoms of paranoid schizophrenia. Auditory hallucinations were experienced by 84.5%, 71% experienced persecutory delusions, 62.8% experienced delusions of reference, 46.5% experienced visual hallucinations and 40.5% experienced delusions of influence. They found that earlier and larger use of methamphetamine was associated with increased risk of psychosis, that a premorbid schizoid or schizotypal personality will predispose an ATS user to develop psychosis, and that the greater the personality vulnerability the longer the psychosis will persist.

Curran et al. (2004) conducted a systematic review of studies of psychostimulant use and psychosis. One of the theories they were interested in was whether repeated low doses of psychostimulants led to changes in the central nervous system which may produce a 'kindling' effect, a psychotic illness similar to schizophrenia. They hypothesised that people who had developed psychosis resulting from psychostimulant use could have done so as a result of either a toxic reaction to the drug use or a chronic persisting response caused by long-term use. This distinction is important as it might explain why some people react quickly to small doses and some only after long-term use. They concluded that there was good evidence for the effect of psychostimulants on pre-existing psychotic illness but that there was less evidence for the kindling effect. They also found that one large dose of a psychostimulant can produce a brief psychotic reaction and for most people this is self-limiting.

Wetli and Fishbain (1985) reported fatal results in seven psychotic recreational cocaine users who presented with symptoms beginning with acute onset of intense paranoia. This was followed by bizarre and violent behaviour, necessitating forcible restraint, symptoms which were accompanied by unexpected strength and by hyperthermia. Fatal respiratory collapse occurred suddenly between a few minutes and an hour after the victim was restrained. Five of the 7 died while still in police custody and the average blood concentration of cocaine was 10 times less than a fatal dose.

Physical and mental health problems are not inevitable with the use of stimulants but clearly with longer and heavier use there are greater risks of harm occurring.

Harm reduction interventions

Riley (2010: 217) has described a number of categories of psychostimulant use based on categories found in the stimulant literature:

- *Experimental use*: described as part of normal youthful curiosity and risk taking; most do not experience extensive problems or continue psychostimulant use.
- *Occupational use*: use for the purpose of better/longer work performance such as truck drivers, students, restaurant staff and athletes. (This is mainly associated with ATS.)
- *Occasional use*: as exemplified by the rave or club scene use; use is restricted to weekend or event-specific use (which may be frequent or infrequent).
- *Heavy sessional use*: excessive use or prolonged use over a short period of time, usually a couple of days.
- *Chronic use*: heavy and prolonged use.
- *Problematic use*: this is usually related to heavy, sessional use or to chronic use but may also occur with other patterns of use; it is often characterised by chaotic and compulsive (dependent) use, often associated with injecting drug use and sometimes with smoking of amphetamines (especially methamphetamine) or crack cocaine; such use often results in psychological, social and legal problems.

These patterns may merge and people may move from one pattern to another. Consideration needs to be given to the method of harm reduction for different categories. This can range from information and education to peer interventions through to treatment and follow-up.

Many of the prevention activities that target illicit drug use in general have relevance for stimulant use (e.g., school drug education; school drug policy; building community and individual social capital). While there are a number of approaches that aim to specifically prevent and reduce problems related to stimulant use, there is little by way of scientific evaluation of many of these.

There are a number of challenges to applying prevention and harm reduction strategies to stimulant use and related problems. One of the most significant of these is the large number of stimulant users who do not identify themselves as drug users and are therefore unlikely to access services or resources. Another issue in designing strategies is the need to target a diverse range of stimulant users, using environments, and user practices. As a result, at present there is limited evidence to guide activities targeting stimulant use.

Role of health workers in psychostimulant harm reduction

Given the identification of GPs and community health services as services commonly accessed by stimulant consumers, GPs could take a critical role in communicating harm reduction messages and information. Many patients might attend their GP for problems that are potentially stimulant related (e.g., sleep disorders; depressed mood). Screening programmes for stimulant use could be established at a range of points of contact where high-risk individuals congregate or present for advice, such as sexual health clinics, GP services and other community health centres.

Health workers need to be aware of the warning signs of escalating use and increase the capacity for self-assessment among users (NSW Health, 2006). In addition, information is needed regarding drug pharmacology and interactions, and the immediate and long-term effects of stimulant use. Given the unpredictable nature of some stimulant presentations, training in effective interventions, dual-diagnosis, primary mental health assessment skills, de-escalation skills and risk-management skills are likely to enhance worker confidence and capacity to manage acutely intoxicated users (NSW Health, 2006). In order to ensure staff and client safety, such education and training needs to be supported by the development of policies and procedures for working with stimulant users, including the management of potentially violent clients.

Harm reduction education and young people

While some strategies targeting young people are school-based others may target a particular drug or context of use (such as nightclubs). However, it has been noted that both prevention and harm reduction strategies need to better target high-risk youth outside of these settings, such as homeless youth, those in juvenile justice environments and so on. In Australia, Streetwize Communications developed a psychostimulant specific comic, entitled *On the Edge*, targeted at these groups through distribution at venues such as youth centres and refuges. One key aspect to developing the resource was conducting focus groups to determine the information needs of young psychostimulant users to ensure the publication was relevant and appropriate. The information provided relates to issues of side-effects of use, harm reduction strategies, and treatment options, with preliminary evaluation showing recall of content four months after reading the material and sharing the resources with friends (www.streetwize.com.au/publications).

Peer education

Peer education refers to the use of people who are of the same group (age, or user, school friends etc.) to supply information to support and educate the user or potential user. This involves peers who are credible, influential and informed and who have been trained to deliver interventions to reduce the harm of stimulants to themselves and others.

Peer-based prevention approaches have been variously used to prevent the uptake of drugs and to reduce problems for those already using drugs. Such strategies have the advantage of being able to access groups who might not otherwise attend general health or drug specialist services. Access may instead be facilitated through outreach or centre based programmes delivered by peer educators and professionals. Peer education may be particularly helpful in targeting young people, during and after their formal education, and during transition periods (e.g., transition to post-secondary education or transition to work) when they may be at increased risk of being exposed to drugs and or make a transition to problematic drug use. Information and advice delivered in this manner may be more likely to be attended to. It has been observed that much of a young persons' knowledge about drug use, both accurate and inaccurate, is sourced from peers (National Drug Research Institute, 2007).

While the evidence in regard to the effectiveness of peer education is variable, it has been proposed that initiatives that are well designed and sufficiently supported can be effective in reducing drug use and related problems (MacDonald et al., 2003). These authors noted that, in general, peer education can have a positive influence on knowledge and, to a lesser extent, attitudes, skills and behaviour. There is also evidence to suggest that, for young people, peer education may be more effective than adult-led education. This could be because peer initiatives are more interactive and often occur outside formal settings (MacDonald et al., 2003).

Peer-based strategies also have a potential role in harm reduction, as well as being used to prevent psychostimulant uptake. Peer education and support have been shown to be effective in several countries as risk reduction strategies to prevent infection with HIV in injecting drug user communities. Further, it has been asserted that peer education can be effective in increasing knowledge about hepatitis C, preventing further transmission of hepatitis C and encouraging behaviour change.

Another example of peer education but from the perspective of secondary prevention has been described by the Australian Injecting and Illicit Drug Users League (AIVL) developed a framework for peer education for drug-user organisations (AIVL, 2006). How 'peer education' is defined will have obvious implications for how it is implemented. In relation to this point, AIVL (2006) states: 'Peer education exists independently and predates the existence of funded, externally supported structures or projects . . . Damon Grogan describes peer education as a 'naturally occurring, organic process that occurs within such groups independently of governments or organised structures, but which may be resourced and utilised to more effectively achieve positive outcomes' (p. 4). Guided by this perspective, AIVL (2006) propose the following principles for formal peer education by drug-user organisations: equality, self-determination and ownership, pragmatic learning, developing community, harm reduction, privacy and confidentiality.

It is widely accepted now that to be truly effective and relevant, harm reduction initiatives should involve drug users and former users the planning, delivery and evaluation. It has also been suggested that campaigns need to acknowledge the positive experiences expressed by ATS users if they are to be perceived as accurate and balanced in their approach, while others caution about glorifying drug use (see for example, the many useful comments in the consultation on the Australian drug strategy: National Drug Research Institute, 2007). While there is very limited information that specifically addresses the effects of peer education on stimulant use, there is no reason to think that these would be any different from with other illicit drugs.

New media

There have been suggestions that 'new' media such as the internet and social networking offer a means to communicate with many at-risk groups, particularly young people. The internet can also be a source of inaccurate information and misinformation. Some law enforcement agencies are concerned about the role of the Internet in producing and distributing precursor chemicals and ATS (National Drug Research Institute, 2007).

Crack kits

On their website the EMCDDA lists the current evidence on the effectiveness of the available harm reduction options for non-injecting routes of administration (EMCDDA, 2010). Under specific interventions entries for harm reduction interventions for smoking and inhaling drug use that have been proposed but not yet assessed are listed crack kits. Best practice guidelines for safer crack smoking recommend a single-use glass tube with a rubber or latex mouthpiece and a small-gauge brass mesh screen at the end of the tube on which the rock of crack is placed before heating. Crack kits contain the materials for safer inhalation, including glass stems, rubber mouthpieces, brass screens, chopsticks, lip balm and chewing gum. Such kits are provided by harm reduction pro-grammes in parts of a number of countries, including Canada and the UK, but they remain very controversial.

An evaluation of crack kit distribution by a needle exchange programme in Ottawa, Canada (Leonard et al., 2006, 2007) suggested that sharing of crack pipes decreased dramatically, while crack users reduced injecting and more often smoked cocaine. Leonard and her colleagues recommend that, since distributing safer crack-smoking materials by a NEP contributes to transition to safer methods of drug ingestion and significantly reduces disease-related risk practices, other NEPs should adopt this practice.

Workplace prevention

There is increasing evidence about the use of psychostimulants especially ATS in association with work, with associated risks of working under the influence of drugs and impact on absenteeism. The impact of ATS use in the workplace can result in:

- overwhelming tiredness at the onset of the working week;
- otherwise unaccountable irritability, agitation or mood swings;
- difficulty concentrating and reduced performance;
- mental health problems, such as paranoia, delusions, feeling despondent or depressed;
- lack of concern about otherwise serious matters; and
- health problems, such as palpitations, infected injection sites or lesions (National Centre for Education and Training on Addiction, 2006).

As noted earlier, the use of ATS is more common in some industries than others. In particular, use in the transport industry, especially among long-distance drivers, has been identified as one key area of concern in relation to the workplace. A project was conducted by the NSW Injury Risk Management Research Centre in collaboration with the University of NSW into stimulant use by long-distance truck drivers (Williamson et al., 2006). The first study aimed to identify factors that may predict drug use by reanalysing data from previous national surveys with long-distance truck drivers, while the second study aimed to update and expand this information by conducting an in-depth survey of drivers. The strongest predictors of stimulant use by long-distance truck drivers, according to self-reported reasons for use, were fatigue and productivity-based payment systems. The second study found that one in five truck drivers used stimulants at least sometimes and more than half had used these drugs at some point in their career. The most common stimulants used were illicit forms of amphetamine-type stimulants. As a result of concern about ATS use in this population, some state-based strategies have been introduced. In NSW, the Roads and Traffic Authority has developed edu-cational materials, including information booklets and posters, for drivers and operators highlight-ing the dangers of using drugs and the need for more appropriate fatigue management strategies.

At a number of consultations, concern was expressed regarding the use of psychostimulants in relation to work and it was suggested that the workplace should be a site for prevention and harm reduction strategies. Some participants suggested that there was a need to identify and disseminate models of managing psychostimulants use in the workplace, some identifying current programmes such as recently developed programmes in the Department of Defence and guidelines for responding to drug problems developed by organisations such as Work Cover.

Harm reduction in pregnancy

The best practice is not to use non prescribed drugs during pregnancy because of the potential damage to both mother and child. Psychostimulants may also be present in breast milk during lactation so good advice should be given to expectant mothers.

Dean and McGuire (2004) suggest that the following recommendations should be given:

- Even if a woman has been taking psychostimulants at the beginning of the pregnancy it is still worth stopping or cutting down as benefits can result and women should be encouraged to do this.
- Pregnant psychostimulant users should be advised not to binge during pregnancy.
- Pregnant psychostimulant using women should be advised to reduce or stop their use of other drugs during the pregnancy, especially alcohol and nicotine.
- If a woman is breast feeding and using psychostimulants, then exposure of the child to the drug can be minimised by breastfeeding just before using and not breastfeeding again for at least 2–3 hours.

Treatment

Although this is not a book about treatment it is important to discuss the treatment of psychostimulant use as a harm reduction measure. In terms of pharmacological intervention there has been seen to be successful work done with dexamphetamine substitution in the treatment of amphetamine dependency in the UK and Australia. This has been done on a substitution model similar to that which is common for the substitution of methadone or heroin. There are problems because the physical dependency on amphetamine has always been a question of debate. Although there were unsuccessful trials in the 1960s in the UK it became part of the tools used for treatment by many British drug services from the mid-1980s until 2009 (Fleming and Roberts, 1994; White, 2000; McBride et al., 1997; Pates et al., 1996) It brought users into the service and kept them engaged and there were reported reductions in injecting and the use of street drugs, and of course monitoring for mental health problems. A random controlled trial for amphetamine prescribing (Merrill *et al.*, 2005) found that both the prescribed group and the control group showed falls in self-reported amphetamine use which were maintained after the end of treatment, an improvement in physical health of the prescribed group and there was a tendency for better outcomes in the treatment group. There were no significant physical or mental health risks as a result of prescribing. Despite some promising evidence the Department of health decided that there was no evidence of benefits of this practice and have now reversed previous cautious but positive advice.

Australian experience has been shown to also have benefits for the prescribing of dexamphetamine (Shearer et al., 2002). Shearer (2010) discusses some promise in the prescription of modafinil in the treatment of both cocaine and amphetamine dependence although the precise pharmacological action of modafifnil is unknown. It is a non-amphetamine type stimulant used in the treatment of narcolepsy. There is little evidence of other pharmacological interventions for the treatment of cocaine although there have been reports of promising but statistically non-significant interventions of the use of disulfiram compared to placebo or naltrexone (Pani et al., 2011).

Shearer (2010) also reviewed the role of psychosocial treatments for psychostimulant use. He found that the efficacy of cognitive behavioural therapy (CBT) was show in multi-centred random controlled trials, both in terms of abstinence 6 months after treatment and also had an impact on post treatment depression. Other existing psychosocial interventions have not been subject to sufficient examination to test the comparative efficacy. Narrative therapy has shown promise in services in Sydney. In the United States both contingency management (a system of positive reinforcement for the desired behaviours) and the Matrix model have been shown to be successful in the treatment of methamphetamine and cocaine problems (Rawson, 2010). The matrix model is an intensive multifaceted approach which includes individual counselling, early recovery groups, relapse prevention groups, family education groups, 12-step meetings, urine and breath testing, relapse analysis and social support groups.

Conclusions

Stimulant drugs are very widely used in many countries; they are probably the second most commonly used drugs worldwide after cannabis. The risks associated with the use of the use drugs can be considerable, but generally most people avoid major problems. Harms can be greatly reduced if people are given legal access to safer means of ingestion, such as clean needles and crack kits, and if there are treatment options available that cater to stimulant users and provide appropriate responses to the effects of stimulants. Interventions, both from a prevention/harm reduction and a treatment perspective, are still being explored and developed, with promising results having been reported in both areas.

References

American Dental Association Division of Communication (2005) Methamphetamine use and oral health, *Journal of the American Dental Association*, 1 (36) 1491.

Australian Injecting and Illicit Drug Users' League (AIVL) (2006) *A Framework for Peer Education by Drug-User Organisations*, www.aivl.org.au/files/FrameworkforPeerEducation.pdf, accessed 1 September 2011.

Baskin-Sommers, A. and Sommers, I. (2006) The co-occurrence of substance use and high risk behaviours, *Journal of Adolescent Health*, 38, 609–11.

Becker, J.B. (1999) Gender differences in dopaminergic functions in striatum and nucleus accumbens, *Pharmacological Biochemistry and Behavioural Journal*, 73, 491–504.

Boutrel, B. and Koob, G.F. (2004) What keeps us awake: the neuropharmacology of stimulants and wakefulness promoting medication, *Sleep*, 27 (6), 1181–94.

Brand, H.S., Gonggrip, S. and Blanksma, C.J. (2008) Cocaine and oral health, *British Dental Journal*, 204, 365–9.

Centre for Disease Control and Prevention (1995) Increased morbidity and mortality associated with the abuse of methamphetamine: United States 1991–1994, *Morbidity and Mortality Weekly Review*, 44, 882–6.

Chen, C., Lin, S., Sham, P., Ball, D., Loh, E. and Hsiao, C. (2003) Pre-morbid characteristics and co-morbidity of methamphetamine users with or without psychosis, *Psychological Medicine*, 3 (8), 1407–14.

Connell, P. (1958) *Amphetamine Psychosis*, Oxford: Oxford University Press.

Cornum, R., Caldwell, J. and Cornum, K. (1997) Stimulant use in extended flight operations, *Airpower Journal*, 53–8.

Curran, C., Byrappa, N. and McBride, A. (2004) Stimulant psychosis:systematic review, *British Journal of Psychiatry*, 185, 196–204.

Dean, A. and McGuire, T. (2004) Psychostimulant use in pregnancy and lactation. In A. Baker, N. Lee and L. Jenner,(eds), *Models of Intervention and Care for Psychostimulant Users*, 2nd edn, Monograph Series no. 51, Canberra: Commonwealth of Australia, 35–50.

Erbert, D. and Berger, M. (1998) Neurobiological similarities in antidepressant sleep deprivation and psychostimulant use: a psychostimulant theory of antidepressant sleep deprivation, *Psychopharmacology*, 140, 183–92.

European Monitoring Centre for Drugs and Drug Addiction (2010) www.emcdda.europa.eu/best practice/ harm reduction/non-injecting routes of administration, accessed 17 August 2011.

Fleming, P. and Roberts, D. (1994) Is the prescription of amphetamine justified as a harm reduction measure?, *Journal of the Royal Society of Health*, 14 (3), 127–31.

Freud, S. (1884) Über Coca, Centralblatt für die ges. *Therapie*, 2, 289–314.

Furara, S.A., Carrick, P., Armstrong, D., Pairaudeau, P., Pullen, A.M. and Lindow, S.W. (1999) The outcome of pregnancy associated with amphetamine use, *Journal of Obstetrics and Gynaecology*, 19 (4), 377–80.

Garwood, E.R., Bekele, W., McCulloch, C.E. and Christine, C.W. (2006) Amphetamine exposure is elevated in Parkinson's disease, *Neurotoxicology*, 27 (2), 1003–6.

Hayward, A., Lawrence, S.M. and Johnson, B. (2008) *Stimulant Use among Professional Students*, www.StimulantUseAmongProfessionalStudents/StudentDoctorNetwork, accessed 17 August 2011.

Hildrey, Z., Thomas, S.E. and Smith, A. (2010) The physical effects of amphetamine use. In R. Pates and D. Riley (eds), *Interventions for Amphetamine Use*, Oxford: Wiley-Blackwell, Oxford.

Jacobs, W. (2006) Fatal amphetamine associated cardiotoxicity and its mediolegal implications, *American Journal of Forensic Medicine and Pathology*, 27 (2), 156–60.

Jankovic, J. (2002) Emerging views of dopamine in modulating sleep/wake state from an unlikely source: PD, *Neurology*, 58 (3), 341–6.

Kaye. S., McKetin, R., Duflou, J. and Darke, S. (2007) Methamphetamine and cardiovascular pathology:a review of the evidence, *Addiction*, 102, 1204–11.

Lee, N.K. (2004) Risks associated with psychostimulant use. In A. Baker, N.K. Lee and L. Jenner (eds), *Models of Intervention and Care for Psychostimulant Users*, Monograph series no. 51, Canberra: Commonwealth of Australia, 33–50.

Leonard, L., Meadows, E., Pelude, L., Seto, J. and Medd, E. (2006). Scaling up harm reduction for crack-smoking injection drug users indicated for needle exchange programmes, *Canadian Journal of Infectious Diseases*, 17 (A) 46A.

Leonard, L., DeRubeis, E., Pelude, L., Medd, L., Birkett, E. and Seto, J. (2007) 'I inject less as I have easier access to pipes': injecting, and sharing of crack-smoking materials, decline as safer crack-smoking resources are distributed, *International Journal of Drug Policy*, 19 (3), 1–10.

MacDonald, J., Roche, M.A., Durbridge, M. and Skinner, N. (2003) *Peer Education: From Evidence to Practice. An Alcohol and Other Drugs Primer*, Adelaide: National centre for education and Training on Addiction.

Matsumoto, T., Kamijo, A., Miyakawa, T., Endo, K., Yabana, T., Kishimoto, H., Okudaira, K., Iseki, E., Sakai, T. and Kosaka, K. (2002) Methamphetamine in Japan: the consequnces of methamphetamine abuse as a function of route of administration, *Addiction*, 97 (7), 809–17.

McBride, A.J., Sullivan, G., Blewett, A.E. and Morgan, S. (1997) Amphetamine prescribing as a harm reduction measure: a preliminary study, *Addiction Research*, 5, 95–112.

McCann, U.D. and Ricaurte, G.A. (2004) Amphetamine neurotoxicity: accomplishments and remaining challenges, *Neuroscience and Behavioural Reviews*, 27 (8), 821–6.

Molitor, F., Truax, S.R., Ruiz, J.D. and Sun, A.K. (1998) Association of methamphetamine use during sex with risky behaviours and HIV infection among non-injecting drug users, *Western Journal of Medicine*, 168 (2), 93–7.

National Centre for Education and Training on Addiction (2006) *Responding to Alcohol and Other Drug Issues in the Workplace: An Information and Resource Package*, Adelaide: National Centre for Education and Training on Addiction (NCETA), Flinders University.

National Drug Research Institute Australian Institute of Criminology (2007) *National Amphetamine-Type Stimulant Strategy Background Paper*. Report prepared for the Department of Health and Ageing, Canberra: Deparment of Health and Ageing.

NSW Health (2005) *Amphetamine, Ecstasy and Cocaine: A Prevention and Treatment Plan 2005–2009*, Sydney: NSW Health.

NSW Health (2006) *Psychostimulant Users: Clinical Guidelines for Assessment and Management*, North Sydney: NSW Dept of Health.

Pani, P.P., Trogu, E., Vacca, R., Amato, L., Vecchi, S. and Dvoli, M. (2011) Disulfiram as a medication for the treatment of cocaine dependence, *Cochrane Database of Systematic Reviews*, 8.

Pates, R. and Riley, D (2010a) *Interventions for Amphetamine Misuse*, Oxford: Wiley-Blackwell, introductory chapter.

Pates, R. and Riley, D. (2010b) The psychological and psychiatric effects of amphetamines. In R. Pates and D. Riley (eds), *Interventions for Amphetamine Misuse*, Oxford: Wiley-Blackwell.

Pates, R., Coombes, N. and Ford, N. (1996) A pilot programme in prescribing dexamphetamine for amphetamine users, *Journal of Substance Misuse*, 1, 80–4.

Rawson, R. (2010) Treatments for methamphetamine dependence: contingency management and the matrix model. In R. Pates and D. Riley (eds), *Interventions for Amphetamine Misuse*, Oxford: Wiley-Blackwell.

Riley D. (2010) Harm reduction and amphetamines. In R. Pates and D. Riley (eds), *Interventions for Amphetamine Use*, Oxford: Wiley-Blackwell, Oxford.

Rudgely, R. (1998) *The Encyclopaedia of Psychoactive Substances*, London: Little Brown.

See, S.-J. and Tan, E.-K. (2003) Severe amphetamine-induced bruxism: treatment with botulinum toxin, *Acta Neurologica Scandanavia*, 107, 161–3.

Shearer, J. (2010) Treatment response to problematic amphetamine use: the Australian experience. In R. Pates and D. Riley (eds), *Interventions for Amphetamine Misuse*, Oxford: Wiley-Blackwell.

Shearer, J., Sherman, J., Wodak, A. and van Beek (2002) Substitution therapy for amphetamine users, *Drug and Alcohol Review*, 21, 179–85.

Silva, O.A., Greve, J.M.D., Yonamine, M. and Leyton, V. (2003) Drug use by truck drivers in Brazil, *Drugs: Education, Prevention and Policy*, 10 (2), 135–9.

Smith, l., Yonekura, M.L., Wallace, T., Berman, N., Kuo, J. and Berkowitz, C. (2003) Effects of prenatal methamphetamine exposure on fetal growth and drug withdrawal symptoms in infants born at term, *Developmental and Behavioural Paediatrics*, 24 (1), 17–23.

Szbadi, E. (2006) Drugs for sleep disorders: mechanisms and therapeutic prospects, *British Journal of Pharmacology*, 61 (6), 761–6.

Tortu, S., McMahon, J.M., Pouget, E.R., and Hamid, R. (2004) Sharing of noninjection drug-use implements as a risk factor for hepatitis C, *Substance Use and Misuse*, 39, 211–24.

Ward, H., Pallecarros, A., Green, A. and Day, S. (2000) Health issues associated with increasing use of 'crack' cocaine among female sex workers in London, *Sexually Transmitted Infections*, 78, 292–3.

Washton, A. and Tatarsky, A. (1983) Adverse effects of cocaine use, *Problems of Drug Dependence 1983*, NIDA Research monograph 49, Rockville: NIDA.

Westover, A.N. McBride, S. and Hayley, R. W. (2007) Stroke in young adults who abuse amphemphetamines and cocaine: a population based study of hospitalized patients, *Archives of General Psychiatry*, 64, 495–501.

Wetli, C.V. and Fishbain, D.A. (1985) Cocaine-induced psychosis and suden death in recreational cocaine users, *Journal of Forensic Science*, 30 (3), 873–80.

White, R., Thompson, M., Windsor, D., Walsh, M., Coc, D. and Charnaud, B. (2006) Dexamphetamine substitute prescribing in pregnancy: a 10 year retrospective audit, *Journal of Substance Use*, 11 (3), 205–16.

Williamson, A. (2007) Predictors of psychostimulant use by long-distance truck drivers, *American Journal of Epidemiology*, 166 (11), 1320–6.

Williamson, A., Colley, M., Hayes, L. and O'Neill, L. (2006) *Final Report of Stimulant Use by Long Distance Road Transport Drivers Project*, Sydney: University of New South Wales, Injury Risk Management Research Centre.

Wolgin, D.L. (2004) Tolerance to amphetamine hypophagia: a real time depiction of learning to suppress stereotypes, *Behavioural Neuroscience*, 118 (3), 470–8.

Young, D. and Scoville, W.B. (1938) Paranoid psychosis in narcolepsy and the possible danger of Benzedrine treatment, *Medical Clinics of North America*, 22, 637–46.

Chapter 14

ECSTASY AND RELATED DRUGS (ERDS) AND HARM REDUCTION

Paul Dillon, Professor Jan Copeland and Edmund Silins

Introduction

Drugs can be classified in a number of ways, but the typical approach is by describing their effect on the body (i.e. stimulant, depressant or hallucinogen). Another option is to group them according to their context of use. Drugs most likely to be used in the 'dance' or 'nightlife' environment such as ecstasy, amphetamines, LSD, cocaine, Ketamine and GHB (gamma hydroxy-butrate) are an example of such a classification.

In Australia, the term 'party drugs' was once used to describe the wide range of different substances that were used in this context. During the 1990s, however, there was increasing pressure from policymakers, as well as sections of the general community, for the term to be phased out, as there was concern that it could potentially 'glamorise' the use of these substances.

Although this group of drugs are often referred to as 'dance drugs' or 'club drugs' in other parts of the world, Australian researchers believed that this terminology did not necessarily reflect the usage patterns of all of those who used these substances. Even though the majority of ecstasy users continue to take the drug in a nightlife environment, there was evidence that suggested that these drugs were increasingly being used in a variety of contexts. For example, in a 2010 Australian study more than two-fifths of the national sample of ecstasy users reported that they usually used in their own and/or friends' homes (Sindicich and Burns 2010).

In an effort to group such diverse drugs as entactogens (ecstasy), a stimulant (amphetamines), a dissociative anaesthetic (ketamine), and a depressant (GHB) under one classification, Australian authorities have adopted the term 'ecstasy and related drugs' (ERDs). This term will be used in this chapter to describe a wide range of substances that are used in a particular context (i.e., any environment where young people go to have fun or party), where ecstasy is the illicit drug most commonly used among this category of drugs.

The use of ERDs has increased across the world dramatically since the 1980s, with some of the drugs now being used only having been identified by authorities very recently (e.g., mephedrone). Although prevalence rates vary, ecstasy, in particular, continues to be popular in much of Europe (with the Czech Republic, Estonia and the UK reporting the highest prevalence rates in the EU) (EMCDDA, 2009), the USA (Substance Abuse and Mental Health Services Administration, 2008), Australia (AIHW, 2008) and parts of Asia (with recent increases being reported in Bangladesh, China and Vietnam), (UNODC, 2010). Some countries have reported significant increases in the use of a wider range of ERDs, for example in Hong Kong ketamine use has risen sharply (Loxton et al., 2008). Although there is some evidence to indicate that ecstasy and amphetamine use has

Harm Reduction in Substance Use and High-Risk Behaviour: International Policy and Practice, First Edition.
Edited by Richard Pates and Diane Riley.
© 2012 Blackwell Publishing Ltd. Published 2012 by Blackwell Publishing Ltd.

stabilised or decreased in some parts of the world (e.g., Europe and the USA), the EMCDDA (2009) suggests that ERDs users may simply be replacing these with other drugs, most particularly cocaine.

There has been little research investigating harm reduction initiatives that target ERDs users, with almost all of the work published in the area examining ecstasy in isolation. With polydrug user being the norm amongst the majority of ecstasy users, is it safe to assume that the harm reduction initiatives designed to target ecstasy users are appropriate for other contextually related drugs? It is of course imperative that harm reduction messages are drug specific, however, as it is often the context of use that contributes to a significant proportion of harm with this group of drugs, it can be argued that the strategies used to deliver them may not need to differ to any great extent. That said, considering the continuing popularity of ERDs, as well as the increasing number of young people involved in the dance culture, there has been a surprisingly limited number of studies published that have specifically investigated harm reduction practices by ERDs users and the environments in which these drugs are most frequently used.

Ecstasy and harm reduction

Reducing drug-related harm began to be discussed as a legitimate public health approach in the mid-1980s as a response to newly discovered HIV epidemics amongst injecting drug users. Needle exchanges had begun to be set up in the UK, Australia and many European cities, as well a supervised consumption room starting to operate in Berne, Switzerland in 1986 (Stimson and O'Hare, 2010).

Not surprisingly, harm reduction initiatives designed specifically for ecstasy users were pioneered in the Netherlands. In 1986, Adviesburo Drugs became the first Dutch agency to adopt an 'integral' approach to safety within the context of large-scale dance events (e.g., 'raves') which were beginning to grow in popularity across the country. Although originally frowned upon by authorities, the innovative approach was to eventually garner widespread acceptance amongst policy-makers, health agencies and, to a lesser extent, politicians (Uitermark and Cohen, 2005). In 1988, the 'Safe House Campaign' began to test ecstasy at raves (Niesink et al., 2010). According to Niesink and colleagues the pills were tested so 'we could get information on what people are using and reduce the harm involved in using ecstasy pills'. Over time the programme was expanded and eventually evolved into what is now known as the Drugs Information and Monitoring System (DIMS), a national monitoring system which will be discussed more fully later in this chapter.

In the late 1980s ecstasy began to increase in popularity across UK and other parts of Europe through the growing underground rave culture. In 1990, authorities responded to this phenomenon by introducing a new law which meant that party organisers could face imprisonment and confiscation of profits if they continued to run such events. The result was a dramatic growth in an already thriving nightclub industry as ravers were 'pushed' into dance clubs (Saunders, 1997).

Prior to the existence of the internet, brochures and pamphlets were the primary methods of disseminating specifically tailored harm reduction information to ERDs users. These resources were usually disseminated via outreach or made available at venues most likely to be frequented by those involved in the nightlife scene, such as music stores and cafes. These strategies continue to be popular with harm reduction agencies, although little, if any research has demonstrated their effectiveness.

In 1990, one of the first harm reduction brochures dealing with ecstasy and nightlife was published. *Chill Out* was produced by HIT, a Liverpool-based organisation formerly called the Mersey Drug Training and Information Centre. The nightlife scene was thriving in Liverpool at the time and this milestone leaflet was unique in that it was culturally attuned, attractive, non-judgemental and user friendly. Its publication was not without its controversies, but as O'Hare (2007) reported, *Chill Out* became a turning point in the public's understanding of harm reduction.

Unfortunately such public acceptance is not always the case. Harm reduction continues to be a public health concept that is misunderstood by many and is regarded by some critics as condoning or promoting drug use. Over the years this has led to some ERDs-related projects having their funding withdrawn and consequently being shut down. Dillon and colleagues (1996) documented one such example in Australia. After the ecstasy-related death of a 15-year-old schoolgirl in Sydney, a number of harm reduction initiatives were targeted by the media as promoting drug use and contributing to the increasing popularity of ecstasy. As a result, a drug education resource had to go undergo a public review and two harm reduction resources, one specifically for 'ravers', were withdrawn.

Guidelines for venue safety

In response to the increasing number of ecstasy-related deaths that appeared to be related to environmental factors, such as overheating and dehydration (White et al., 1997; Burke, 2001; Bellis et al., 2002), a strategy targeting the nightlife industry itself was introduced which complemented the existing harm reduction information available to ecstasy users.

Once again, Liverpool was a leader in this area. One of the most well-known and established brands in the nightclub industry is Cream. Opening in 1992, by the mid-1990s it faced possible closure as, like many clubs, they were experiencing great pressure from local police and other authorities over licensing issues, mainly due to illicit drug use and the resulting media coverage. Being pro-active, they reached out to a range of agencies to seek guidance on how to improve the health and safety of their patrons and to develop a range of preventive strategies for the club itself (Luke et al., 2010).

In many parts of the world, guidelines began to be developed by a range of stakeholders, usually led by government departments, in consultation with event organisers, club owners, user organisations and prevention agencies, with the aim of creating a safer physical environment for those involved in the nightlife scene.

In 2002, the London Drug Policy Forum produced one of the most comprehensive of these, *Safer Clubbing: Guidance for Licensing Authorities, Club Managers and Promoters*. The London Drug Policy Forum introduced the package by stating that it provides a range of strategies that would 'ensure the health and safety of anyone who attends dance events in England' (Webster, 2002). These guidelines acknowledged that the health hazards in these settings more often arose from how events were organised rather than directly from drug use. It was emphasised that the problems most commonly experienced in these environments included overcrowding, poor ventilation, lack of affordable drinking water, violence and accidents from broken glass. However, information on how to deal with drug dealing and the training of door supervisors to organise searches and supervise toilet areas was also provided, as well as training in first aid and early detection of drug-induced problems. The document recommended the distribution of drug prevention information and outreach teams within venues, as well as more controversial initiatives such as 'amnesty bins', where club attendees could drop objects (including illicit drugs) before being searched.

Practical information, such as that contained in the 2002 package, and then in the updated 'Safer nightlife' guidelines developed in 2008 (Webster, 2008), continue to provide valuable harm reduction tools for those involved in the nightlife industry.

In addition to the European experience, there have also been a number of attempts by some Australian state government departments, including Queensland (Queensland Government, 1997), NSW (New South Wales Government, 1998) and South Australia (Drug and Alcohol Services South Australia and South Australia Police, 2006), as well as New Zealand authorities (Ministry of Health, 1999) to develop similar guidelines.

On occasion there have been campaigns funded to support such guidelines. One example developed by Queensland Health (1997) involved a five-point public education campaign that comprised of a venue operators and event promoters kit; a peer helper/educator strategy; 'swap cards' and brochures containing health and safety tips; the placement of health and safety messages in selected nightclubs; and a venue training programme.

The latest innovation in this area is the development of 'safer nightlife charters or labels', which began in 2005 (Charlois, 2009). These charters are developed based on established guidelines and then 'signed off' by both a club owner and a local government representative (e.g. the Mayor). This process demonstrates the commitment of the club owners to safer practices and is seen as providing benefits to all parties – the club provides safer events, the local authorities are seen as being proactive on a controversial issue and the clubbers can be assured that the venue they are attending is providing a safer environment.

Unfortunately, as with harm reduction brochures and pamphlets, little information is collected on whether such guidelines or charters are in fact more widely utilised, and more importantly whether they are actually effective in reducing harm to their target audience.

Examining what little research has been conducted in this area, the results are not particularly positive. In 2008, 12 countries in the EU reported having developed guidelines for nightlife venues, however, only the Netherlands, Slovenia, Sweden and the UK reported that these were monitored and enforced (EMCDDA, 2009). In addition, the EMCDDA reported that there was limited availability of simple measures to prevent or reduce health risks and drug use in European nightlife settings. Outreach prevention work was reported to be available in some parts of the EU but was not available at all in six countries. Only five countries reported immediate availability of first aid in the majority of relevant nightclubs, and although free cold water was available in the majority of 11 countries and in a minority of them in 9 countries, it was not available at all in three others (EMCDDA, 2009).

Unfortunately, where guidelines have been introduced and resulting strategies implemented (such as outreach work and provision of free cold water), little is known about their effectiveness. It is the same story in other parts of the world, with no rigorous research being conducted on the Australian or New Zealand initiatives that have been developed.

Peer led interventions

Australian research indicates that the majority of ERDs users are unlikely to access or utilise treatment services in relation to their drug use (Mugavin et al., 2007; Johnston et al., 2007). One study investigating help-seeking behaviour found that despite the reported high levels of drug-related harms reported by the ERDs users in the sample, only one in ten of them reported having accessed professional help in relation to these problems (Proudfoot and Ward, 2005). With this in mind it is important to try to find other ways of providing them with information. Given that the majority of ERDs users will be involved in the nightlife scene at some point, drug agencies and organisations have increasingly sought to utilise these settings to disseminate harm reduction information (Bellis et al., 2002; Crew 2000, 2001). One of the challenges that agencies continue to face, however, is ensuring that the information will be regarded as credible by those that use ERDs.

Since the 1970s, peer-led interventions have become increasingly popular health promotion tools used to disseminate a wide range of information, including safer injecting practices and ways to reduce the risk of sexually transmitted infections (STIs), to specific target groups (Bament, 2001; Backett-Milburn and Wilson, 2000; Cuijpers, 2002).

Peer-led harm reduction interventions designed specifically for ERDs users have been developed in many countries, with the Netherlands (Unity), Scotland (Crew 2000) and Australia (RaveSafe) being amongst the first to adopt such strategies (Bleeker et al., 2009). Another initiative, the Ecstasy Harm Reduction Project (later to become known as DanceSafe) was developed originally in the Bay Area of San Francisco in the USA in 1997. In one of their earliest published articles, the founder of the project reported that their key objective was 'to reduce the harm to both the individual and society resulting from the use of ecstasy and other dance-related drugs' (Sferios 1999).

Terminology may be confusing, as many peer-led interventions for ERDs users have used the terms peer education and peer support interchangeably. Unity (Amsterdam) states it is a 'peer support project' for those in the dance scene, whereas Crew 2000 (Edinburgh) and another Australian initiative, KIS (Sydney) both identify with the term 'peer education'. The underlying methodology behind these three peer-led interventions, however, is the same in that 'credible and influential peers' are recruited from the nightlife scene and trained to provide information about drugs and their effects to people attending festivals, dance parties and nightclubs (Bleeker et al., 2009). The theoretical foundations that underpin these projects is that, through peer credibility; trained 'peers' can affect a change in knowledge, attitude and behaviour within a community of individuals who possess similar characteristics. Unity, Crew 2000 and KIS all utilise strategies to provide oral and written harm reduction information to ERDs users within their own nightlife setting (e.g., nightclub, dance festival, rave, etc.).

Evaluations of such initiatives have been positive, particularly in regard to the service's ability to access a traditionally 'hidden' population. In his 1998 process evaluation report of the Scottish-based 'Crew 2000', Parkin reported that they were seen as credible and accessible to young people, with many of those interviewed reporting that they never had approached a drugs agency prior to their contact with the service. An independent evaluation of Unity conducted by Geraci (2000), found that attendees of dance parties in Amsterdam preferred to receive information about drugs from someone who had experience with drugs and who also came from the 'house scene'. Most importantly, Geraci's research found that the majority of those surveyed (88%) regarded the information provided by Unity volunteers as credible.

Similar findings have been reported in Australia, with 91% of people reached by the KIS project reporting the peer educators to be 'extremely approachable' when seeking information and advice about drugs (Devlin et al., 2005). A recent study investigated the peer educator qualities which were perceived to be most important by ecstasy users in Australia and the Netherlands (Silins et al., 2010). Experience with illicit drug use, an affinity with the ecstasy-using subculture and age emerged as important peer educator characteristics. Generally, ecstasy users appear to differ little from other drug users in regard to the importance of peer educators sharing characteristics and experiences.

It would appear then that peer education programmes such as these are able to provide valuable and much needed contact with ERDs users who are currently not in contact with traditional and/or mainstream drugs services. The provision of harm reduction information, from a credible source (i.e., their peers), in these settings, would seem to be an appropriate strategy. However, there is little evidence in the literature of the effectiveness of such programmes, particularly those targeting ERDs users. Little is known about whether the messages delivered by peer educators are able to be recalled by the target group, and if they are, does behaviour change? The lack of such research has resulted in criticisms being raised about the efficacy of the peer education approach.

In response to these concerns an Australian study sought to discover if harm reduction messages could be effectively delivered to ERDs users utilising a peer-led intervention (Bleeker et al., 2009). The study utilised a rigorous quasi-experimental design in a 'real-life' peer education setting. The researchers developed two unique ecstasy-related messages not previously used in Australian harm reduction activities (the first relating to 'serotonin syndrome' and the second recommending 'preloading' with water prior to an event) and disseminated these to an experimental group via peer educators at dance events. A control group received routine ERDs peer education messages in the usual manner.

The findings were positive with the authors reporting that there was good recall of health messages disseminated to ERDs users using a peer-led methodology at three-month follow-up. The authors also reported that approximately half of the sample had changed their water consumption as a result of talking to the peer educator, thus demonstrating behaviour change. These results support the use of peer-led interventions in the dissemination of harm reduction messages to ERDs users. Findings also support previous research that such interventions are a valuable medium to use in conjunction with other methods of drug education for this difficult to access group.

Pill testing

In his introduction to the newly formed peer-led initiative now known as DanceSafe, Sferios (1999) noted that there was 'a tangible need for harm reduction within the community of ecstasy users in the Bay Area and nationwide, particularly in the form of peer education and direct health and safety services like drug identification'. Unlike the majority of today's ecstasy users, Sferios reported that the ecstasy users being accessed by their outreach workers were unaware pills sold as ecstasy often contained other substances. He went on to report that the primary concern of those who were aware, however, was to identify the contents of the pills they were using.

Although the term 'ecstasy' is used to refer to pills, capsules or powder that contain MDMA (3,4-Methylenedioxymethamphetamine), today there is widespread evidence that in fact they contain a range of substances of varying concentrations (Quinn et al., 2004; Winstock et al., 2001). There have been reports that since 2007, in particular, the ecstasy market has undergone significant transformations, particularly in Europe. Tablets sold as ecstasy increasingly contain greater proportions of a range of substitute psychoactive substances not under international control, such as various piperazines like BZP and mCPP (UNODC, 2010).

Many studies have supported Sferios in his belief that ecstasy users are concerned over the unknown content and purity of the drugs they take (Quinn et al., 2004; White et al., 2005). In addition, there is evidence that a proportion of the harms associated with ecstasy use can be attributed to substances other than MDMA (Kalasinsky et al., 2004; Parrott, 2004). In a small number of cases, these harms have included death (Ling et al., 2001; Caldicott et al., 2003; Johansen et al., 2003).

In response to this concern, the provision of 'pill testing' programmes, which aim to identify the contents of ecstasy pills and provide this information to users, has been put forward as an appropriate harm reduction initiative for those people who use, or are considering using the drug. A number of programmes have been set up across the world. They are primarily in Europe, however there is considerable variation in how they operate and the information they are able to provide to ERDs users.

One of the most sophisticated pill testing programmes in the world is based in the Netherlands. The Drugs Information and Monitoring System (DIMS) is a monitoring system for nightlife drugs. It analyses and keeps records on the chemical composition and the toxicity of a range of ERDs, including ecstasy, cocaine and amphetamines. ERDs users can have the chemical makeup of their drugs checked at one of the DIMS-affiliated agencies. This data is then used to inform a range of stakeholders of current changes in the ERDs market and of associated health risks. With the capacity to be an 'early warning system', DIMS also has the capacity to launch targeted local or national warning campaigns when the need arises (Keijsers et al., 2008; Niesink et al., 2010).

A number of European countries have, or have had, 'on-site' pill-testing interventions (i.e., the testing is conducted at the event, either at a nightclub or dance party/festival), these include Austria, Belgium, Switzerland, the Netherlands, France, Germany and Spain (EMCDDA, 2001). Although some of these projects receive government funding there has continued to be general uncertainty surrounding legislation, with, in some cases, changes in the law resulting in the closure of some of these projects (e.g., Techno+ in France in 2004) (DrugChecking Initiative Berlin Brandenburg, 2008).

One of the longest running pill testing services is the Austrian 'ChEck iT!' project. ChEck iT! has been offering testing opportunities for a range of drugs since 1997. Funded as a research project by the City of Vienna and by the Austrian Federal Ministry for Social Security and Generations, it forms an official part of Vienna's municipal drugs policy (Benschop et al., 2002). Pill testing is performed exclusively on-site at large dance events and is free of charge. While clients wait for their results, they can speak to trained staff or fill in a questionnaire. The test results are posted on a wall, but without the corresponding pill logo, so that only the person who submitted the pill for testing can connect the result to a particular type of pill. The EMCDDA reported that it is due to its status as 'scientific research' that has led to its continuing 'official support or tolerance' by authorities (EMCDDA, 2001).

Budgetary constraints usually dictate what analytical procedures are utilised by the different programmes. The more expensive and time consuming identification techniques such as gas chromatography/mass spectrometry (GCMS) (used by programmes such as DIMS and ChEck iT!) are unaffordable for many agencies and smaller projects. The simple reagent pill testing kits (i.e., Marquis and Mandelin Reagent tests) are often used on-site by volunteer harm reduction organisations and individuals conducting their own testing (Johnston et al., 2006).

Simple colour reagent test kits, are relatively inexpensive products and available for purchase online, or at 'headshops' in some countries. Designed to identify the presence of ecstasy-like substances (MDMA, MDA, MDE) (EMCDDA, 2001) the kit is comprised of a liquid containing a chemical substance called the Marquis Reagent, and a colour chart. This liquid is dropped onto a small sample of the pill being tested and a chemical reaction results in one of a variety of colours. This colour is then compared to the chart provided and the user is provided with some limited information regarding the contents of the pill. The Mandelin Reagent test enables the user to also identify the presence of ketamine and PMA, and as a result some harm reduction agencies recommend to use the two testing kits to increase the quality of the result (Johnston et al., 2006). Even though these tests have been criticised by some as being simplistic and giving as 'artificial "shine of safety"' (Winstock et al., 2001), they continue to be used across the world.

Although concerns have been raised about the limitations of pill testing, particularly the quality of the information provided by the reagent tests (EMCDDA, 2001), there is some evidence that there are a number of important benefits associated with the strategy.

Firstly, research shows that on-site pill testing allows users to avoid specific pills or otherwise modify their drug use based on test results (Benschop et al., 2002; van de Wijngaart, 1999). Benschop and colleagues (2002) also reported that due to the 'attractiveness' of pill testing to some 'harder to reach' ERDs users who may not otherwise access services, messages related to legal risks, safer sex practices and safer driving behaviour may also be effectively disseminated when they seek information on the quality of their pill. Finally, as with the DIMS project, on-site testing also has the capacity to disseminate warning information if there are particularly dangerous substances identified. This would not only assist potential users to make an informed choice but also provide valuable information to the organisers of the event and medical staff.

Increasingly the worldwide web is being used to disseminate a wide range of harm reduction information to ERDs users (Charlois, 2009), including pill content results. Launched in July 2001, EcstasyData.org is an independent laboratory pill testing programme based in the USA which is co-sponsored by Erowid and Dancesafe. Its purpose is to collect, manage, review, and present laboratory pill testing results. These are made publicly available to 'help harm reduction efforts', as well as to provide information to medical personnel and researchers (Ecstasydata.org, retrieved 2010). This strategy is in stark contrast to that of government agencies which routinely analyse seized illicit drugs but choose to restrict the data they collect and release it primarily to law enforcement personnel.

The EcstasyData.org site does have certain restrictions as set out by the US Drug Enforcement Agency (DEA) and as such is only permitted to provide quantitative data to the public (i.e., what known substances were found and in what ratios), reportedly for fear of providing 'quality control' to dealers and suppliers of black market products.

One unique element about this initiative, however, is that users are able to send in a sample for testing. It is a 'user pays' service, with the fee being paid to the laboratory for the costs of the testing. Once the testing is completed the samples are destroyed and will not be returned. The results are then posted on-line (Ecstasydata.org, retrieved 2010).

Instead of actual laboratory analysis of pills, Pillreports.com is a site that allows ecstasy users to post subjective user reports on the drugs they have recently taken. Where possible the site attempts to disseminate any scientific analysis that is available, but it does not offer the testing service of EcstasyData.org. Pillreports is one of the most popular ERDs websites amongst the user group (Bleeker et al., 2009), it is supported by Enlighten Harm Reduction, a lobbyist organisation based in Melbourne Australia. The site states that 'By identifying dangerous adulterants, Pillreports performs a vital harm reduction service that can prevent many of the problems associated with 'Ecstasy' use before they happen. Prevention is always better than cure, as you cannot cure death' (Pillreports.com, retrieved 2010).

There have been few studies on the effectiveness of pill testing, with few, if any, of the projects providing the service either conducting the necessary research or publishing the data they collect. The available evidence that does exist, however, suggests that ERDs users may change their drug use if test results indicate the presence of a substance which they do not want to use or which are of unknown content (van de Wijngaart et al., 1999; Benschop et al., 2002).

An Australian study supported this finding, with the authors giving the example of the vast majority of non-ketamine users in their sample reporting that they would not take a pill if they discovered it contained ketamine (Johnston et al., 2006). Not surprisingly, they recommended more detailed research be conducted to examine ways in which test results may influence drug using behaviour over and above simply not taking the pill (e.g., taking half, using in a different setting, etc.).

In a study conducted in three European cities that offered pill testing, Benschop and colleagues (2002) concluded that the strategy did not cause a direct and profound change in the careers of ecstasy users. They did discover, however, that the results of tests were used to disseminate harm reduction information. When the test indicated the presence of amphetamines, suspicious substances or a high dose of MDMA, testers warned their friends. They noted that this route of dissemination of information about possible harms linked to ecstasy use is a 'hidden strength' of pill testing.

Where to from here?

As has already been discussed, although a range of harm reduction initiatives have been used to target ERDs users, there is little research on the effectiveness of such strategies.

Peer-led harm reduction interventions are generally seen as credible and cost-effective ways to share information. Such strategies can provide information to those involved in the nightlife scene who may not access conventional drug health services. Methodologically robust evaluations of the effectiveness of peer-led harm reduction strategies in changing risky drug-using behaviours are scarce but findings are promising. Given the popularity of the peer education approach, there is a need for more empirical research into the effectiveness of peer-led harm reduction interventions. However, rigorous evaluations are generally costly and there are complexities in teasing out the effects of peer-led interventions on drug-using behaviours. Furthermore, relatively few studies of peer-led interventions have specifically focused on ERDs users. This group is likely to differ from other drug users, for example, street-based heroin injectors, in relation to age, education, employment and the context of drug use, and therefore require separate study in relation to responses to peer-led interventions.

It is clear that ERDs users are interested in obtaining harm reduction information about the drugs they choose to use, most particularly, the actual contents of their pill, powder or liquid, but we know little about how they use that information. Similarly, there is little evidence whether the provision of pill testing does encourage those users who would not otherwise seek out ERDS related information to engage with, and act on the information provided in these environments.

With dance culture continuing to grow in popularity across the world and the range of drugs used in the nightlife scene increasing, it is vital that more work is conducted in the development of innovative harm reduction strategies targeting ERDs users. In an environment where use is increasing in many countries, particularly among young people in countries with authoritarian regimes where drug use is marginalised and highly criminalised, a new approach to harm reduction may also need to be developed.

References

AIHW (2008) *2007 National Drug Strategy Household Survey: Detailed Findings*, Canberra: Australian Institute of Health and Welfare.

Allott, K. and Redman, J. (2006) Patterns of use and harm reduction practices of ecstasy users in Australia, *Drug and Alcohol Dependence*, 82 (2), 168–76.

Backett-Milburn, K. and Wilson, S. (2000) Understanding peer education: insights from a process evaluation, *Health Education Research*, 15, 85–96.

Bament, D. (2001) *Peer Education Literature Review*, Adelaide: South Australian Community Health Research Unit.

Bellis, M.A., Hughes, K. and Lowey, H. (2002) Healthy nightclubs and recreational substance use: from a harm minimisation to a healthy settings approach, *Addictive Behaviors*, 27, 1025–35.

Benschop, A., Rabes, M. and Korf, D. (2002) *Pill Testing, Ecstasy and Prevention: A Scientific Evaluation in Three European Cities*, Amsterdam: Rozenberg.

Bleeker, A., Silins, E., Dillon, P., Simpson, M., Copeland, J. and Hickey, K. (2009) *The Feasibility of Peer-Led Interventions to Deliver Health Information to Ecstasy and Related Drug (ERDs) Users*, NDARC Technical Report 299, Sydney: National Drug and Alcohol Research Centre.

Boot, B., McGregor, I. and Hall, W. (2000) MDMA (ecstasy) neurotoxicity: assessing and communicating the risks, *Lancet*, 55 (20 May), 1818–21.

Burke, J. (2001) Ecstasy's death toll 'set to go on rising', *Guardian*, Sunday.

Caldicott, D., Edwards, N.A., Kruys, A., Kirkbride, K.P., Sims, D.N., Byard, R.W., Prior, M. and Irvine, R.J. (2003) Dancing with 'death': P-methoxyamphetamine overdose and its acute management, *Journal of Toxicology Clinical Toxicology*, 41 (2), 143–54.

Camilleri, A.M. and Caldicott, D. (2005) Underground pill testing, *Forensic Science International*, 151 (1), 53–8.

Charlois, T. (2009) *Safer Nightlife in Europe*, EXASS Net, Pompidou Group, Council of Europe.

Crew (2001) *[2000] Development of Strategies for Secondary Prevention in Drug Use: Patterns of Drug Use amongst Young People at Clubs and Pre-Club Bars in Edinburgh*, Project Report, Edinburgh: Crew.

Cuijpers, P. (2002) Peer-led and adult-led school drug prevention: a meta-analytic comparison, *Journal of Drug Education*, 32, 107–19.

Devlin, K., Bleeker, A.M. and Gerber, S. (2005) *Evaluation report: Keep It Simple (KIS) peer education at clubs and events, unpublished paper*, Sydney: Manly Drug Education and Counselling Centre.

Dillon, P., Goldspink-Lord, L. and Parkhill, N. (1996) Sex, drugs and just say no: a media perspective, *International Journal of Drug Policy*, 7 (3), 183–6.

Drug and Alcohol Services South Australia and South Australia Police (2006) *Guidelines for Safer Dance Parties*, Adelaide: Drug and Alcohol Services South Australia.

DrugChecking Initiative Berlin Brandenburg (2010) *Pill-testing Dossier: Update 2008*, www.drugchecking.eu/pdf/pill%20testing%20projects%20in%20europe%20update%202008.pdf, accessed 8 July.

Ebreo, A., Feist-Price, S., Siewe, Y. and Zimmerman, R.S. (2002) Effects of peer education on the peer educators in a school-based HIV prevention programme: where should peer education research go from here?, *Health Education and Behavior*, 9, 411–23.

Ecstasydat.org (2010) *About Us*, www.ecstasydata.org/about.php, accessed 10 July.

EMCDDA (2001) *An Inventory of On-Site Pill-testing Interventions in the European Union*, Lisbon: European Monitoring Centre for Drugs and Drug Addiction.

EMCDDA (2009) *2009 Annual Report on the State of the Drugs Problem in Europe*, Lisbon: European Monitoring Centre for Drugs and Drug Addiction.

Falck, R.S., Carlson, R.G., Wang, J. and Siegal, H.A. (2004) Sources of information about MDMA (3, 4-methylenedioxymethamphetamine): perceived accuracy, importance and implications for prevention among young adult users, *Drug and Alcohol Dependence*, 74 (1), 45–54.

Geraci, D. (2000) *Evaluatie van het peerproject Unity drugsvoorlichtingsproject voor en door jongeren uit de house scene*, Utrecht: Rijksuniversiteit.

Hansen, D., Maycock, B. and Lower, T. (2001) Weddings, parties, anything . . . , a qualitative analysis of ecstasy use in Perth, Western Australia, *International Journal of Drug Policy*, 12, 181–99.

Jacinto, C., Duterte, M., Sales, P. and Murphy, S. (2008) Maximising the highs and minimising the lows: harm reduction guidance within ecstasy distribution networks, *International Journal of Drug Policy*, 19 (5), 393–400.

Johansen, S.S., Hansen, A.C., Müller, I.B., Lundemose, J.B. and Franzmann, M.B. (2003) Three fatal cases of PMA and PMMA poisoning in Denmark, *Journal of Analytical Toxicology*, 27 (4), 253–6.

Johnston, J., Quinn, B. and Jenkinson, R. (2007) *Victorian Trends in Ecstasy and Related Drug Markets 2006: Findings from the Ecstasy and Related Drug Reporting System (EDRS)*, NDARC Technical Report 282, Sydney: National Drug and Alcohol Research Centre.

Johnston, J., Barratt, M.J., Fry, C.L., Kinner, S., Stoové, M., Degenhardt, L., George, J., Jenkinson, R., Dunn, M., and Bruno, R. (2006) A survey of regular ecstasy users' knowledge and practices around determining pill content and purity: implications for policy and practice, *International Journal of Drug Policy*, 17 (6), 464–72.

Kalasinsky, K.S., Hugel, J. and Kish, S.J. (2004) Use of MDA (the 'love drug') and methamphetamine in Toronto by unsuspecting users of ecstasy (MDMA), *Journal of Forensic Science*, 49 (5), 1106–12.

Keijsers, L., Bossong, M.G. and Waarlo, A.J. (2008) Participatory evaluation of a Dutch warning campaign for substance-users, *Health, Risk and Society*, 10 (3), 283–95.

Ling, L.H., Marchant, C., Buckley, N.A., Prior, M. and Irvine, R.J. (2001) Poisoning with the recreational drug paramethoxyamphetamine ('death'), *Medical Journal of Australia*, 174 (9), 453–5.

Loxton, N.J., Wan, V., Ho, A., Cheung, B., Tam, N., Leung, F. and Stadli, A. (2008) Impulsivity in Hong Kong-Chinese club-drug users, *Drug and Alcohol Dependence*, 95 (1–2), 81–9.

Luke, C., Dewar, C., Bailey, M., McGreevy, D. and Morris, H. (2010) *A Little Nightclub Medicine: The Healthcare Implications of Clubbing*, www.drugtext.org/library/articles/luke.htm, accessed 10 July.

Marlatt, G.A. (2002) *Highlights of Harm Reduction: Harm Reduction: Pragmatic Strategies for Managing High-risk Behaviors*, New York: Guilford Press.

Ministry of Health (1999) *Guidelines for Safe Dance Parties*, Manatu Hauora, Wellington: Ministry of Health.

Mugavin, J., Swan, A. and Pennay, A. (2007) *Ecstasy, Ketamine and GHB: A Review of Users and Victorian Alcohol and Other Drug Treatment Interventions*, Melbourne: Turning Point Alcohol and Drug Centre Inc.

New South Wales Government (1998) *Guidelines for Dance Parties*, Sydney: New South Wales Government.

Niesink, R., Nikken, G., Jansen, F. and Spruit, I. (2010) *The Drug Monitoring Service (DIMS) in the Netherlands: A Unique Tool for Monitoring Party Drugs*, www.drugtext.org/library/articles/niesink.htm

O'Hare, P. (2007) Merseyside, the first harm reduction conferences, and the early history of harm reduction, *International Journal of Drug Policy*, 18 (2), 141–4.

Palamar, J.J. and Halkitis, P.N. (2006) A qualitative analysis of GHB use among gay men: Reasons for use despite potential adverse outcomes, *International Journal of Drug Policy*, 17 (1), 23–8.

Panagopoulos, I. and Ricciardelli, L. (2005) Harm reduction and decision making among recreational ecstasy users, *International Journal of Drug Policy*, 16 (1), 54–64.

Parkin, S.G. (1998) *A Process Evaluation of Crew 2000*, Glasgow: Centre for Drug Misuse, University of Glasgow.

Parrott, A.C. (2004) Is ecstasy MDMA? A review of the proportion of ecstasy tablets containing MDMA, their dosage levels and the changing perceptions of purity, *Psychopharmacology*, 173, 234–41.

Pillreports.com*PillReports Ecstasy Test Results Database*, www.pillreports.com/index.php.

Proudfoot, P. and Ward, J. (2005) *Drug Related Harm and Help-Seeking Behaviour among Regular Ecstasy Users in NSW and the ACT*, Sydney: Party Drug Trends Bulletin, National Drug and Alcohol Research Centre.

Queensland Health Alcohol, Tobacco and Other Drug Services (1997) *Dance Parties Info Kit*, health.qld.gov. au/atods/resources/dance.htm, accessed 10 July 2010.

Quinn, C., Breen, C. and White, B. (2004) Illicit tablet market in Victoria, *Party Drug Trends Bulletin*, Sydney: National Drug and Alcohol Research Centre.

Saunders, N. (1997) *Ecstasy Reconsidered*, London: Neals Yard.

Sferios, E. (1999) The Ecstasy Harm Reduction Program, *Bulletin of the Multidisciplinary Association for Psychedelic Studies MAPS*, 9 (1), 37–8.

Shewan, D., Dalgarno, P. and Reith, G. (2000) Perceived risk and risk reduction among ecstasy users: the role of drug, set, and setting, *International Journal of Drug Policy*, 10, 431–53.

Silins, E., Bleeker, A.M., Copeland, J., Dillon, P., Devlin, K., van Bakkum, F., Noijen, J. (2010) The importance of peer educator qualities: as perceived by ecstasy users, *SuchtMagazin*.

Sindicich, N. and Burns, L. (2010) *Findings from the Ecstasy and Related Drugs Reporting System (EDRS)*, Australian Drug Trends Series no. 46, Sydney, NDARC.

Stimson, G.V. and O'Hare, P. (2010) Harm reduction: moving through the third decade, *International Journal of Drug Policy*, 21 (2), 91–3.

Substance Abuse and Mental Health Services Administration (2009) *Results from the 2008 National Survey on Drug Use and Health: National Findings*, Office of Applied Studies, NSDUH Series H-36, HHS Publication no. SMA 09-4434, Rockville.

UNODC (2010) *World Drug Report 2010*, Vienna: United Nations Office on Drugs and Crime.

Uitermark, J. and Cohen, P. (2005) A clash of policy approaches: The rise (and fall?) of Dutch harm reduction policies towards ecstasy consumption, *International Journal of Drug Policy*, 16 (1), 65–72.

Webster, R. (2002) *Safer Clubbing: Guidance for Licensing Authorities, Club Managers and Promoters*, London: Home Office, London Drug Policy Forum.

Webster, R. (2008) *Safer Nightlife: Best Practice for Those Concerned about Drug Use and the Night-time Economy*, London: London Drug Policy Forum.

Winstock, A., Wolff, K. and Ramsey, J. (2001) Ecstasy pill testing: harm minimization gone too far?, *Addiction*, 96 (8), 1139–48.

White, B., Degenhardt, L., Breen, C., Bruno, R., Newman J. and Proudfoot, H. (2005) Risk and benefit perceptions of party drug use, *Addictive Behaviours*, 31, 137–42.

White, J.M., Bochner, F. and Irvine, R.J. (1997) The agony of 'ecstasy': how can we avoid more 'ecstasy'-related deaths?, *Medical Journal of Australia*, 166, 117–18.

van de Wijngaart, G., Braam, R., de Bruin, D., Fris, M., Maalsté, N. and Verbraeck, H. (1999) Ecstasy use at large-scale dance events in the Netherlands, *Journal of Drug Issues*, 29 (3), 679–702.

Winstock, A., Wolff, K. and Ramsey, J. (2001) Ecstasy pill testing: harm minimization gone too far?, *Addiction*, 96 (8), 1139–48.

Chapter 15

ALCOHOL: HARM REDUCTION

Tina Alwyn and Bev John

Stories about the effects of drinking alcohol appear in the UK press on a predictably regular basis, to a large extent relating to the binge drinking behaviour of young people and its related consequences. However, the majority of people who drink (and presumably also read these newspaper articles) have positive attitudes to their own use of alcohol (Plant and Plant, 2006) and do not view it as a pharmacological drug, in the same way they would, for example, view sedatives or opiates. In the UK, alcohol is often referred to as 'our favourite drug'; its legal status and wide availability pose particular problems when we consider ways of reducing associated harm.

Anecdotal evidence suggests that problematic drinking behaviour is increasing, yet, public health messages often seem conflicting. Public health messages regarding information about strengths and units are often confusing: For example, the UK government suggests that 14 units of alcohol for women and 21 units for men over a weekly period is a safe limit for consumption. Further, they advise that drinking more than 6 units for women and 8 units for men on any one occasion is regarded as binge drinking. The Royal College of Psychiatrists (2011) has suggested that for older adults the weekly limit should be 11 units. However, as the majority of people do not understand what units are and how they relate to sensible drinking advice this information becomes meaningless. The smoking ban, availability of cheap alcohol in supermarkets and other retail outlets have led to less drinking in pubs and increased the trend for drinking at home, where people are far less likely to drink alcohol in standard measures and may be drinking far more than they realise.

Alcohol related harm

The World Health Organization in their *Handbook for Action to Reduce Alcohol-related Harm* (2009) outlined the high costs of excessive alcohol consumption. For example, alcohol is the third-highest risk factor for serious health consequences and premature death, behind only tobacco and high blood pressure. The associated economic costs are substantial; estimated to be around 125 billion euros a year across the EU. The main focus of costs attributed to alcohol is on alcohol related problems such as: health care; crime; work-related absenteeism; unemployment; and premature mortality (WHO, 2009).

Since the 1990s the high levels of alcohol consumption in the UK has increasingly become a cause of concern, particularly in impact on the National Health System, where the consequences of hazardous and harmful drinking levels have been well documented. Alcohol is relatively quickly absorbed into the blood stream (via the stomach and intestines) and through this process alcohol affects the brain, liver, heart, kidneys and all other organs in the body. Over 60 conditions have been attributed to excessive alcohol consumption (European Alcohol Policy Alliance, 2011) including the risk of cancer through the carcinogenicity of alcohol beverages. Alcohol related admission to

Harm Reduction in Substance Use and High-Risk Behaviour: International Policy and Practice, First Edition.
Edited by Richard Pates and Diane Riley.
© 2012 Blackwell Publishing Ltd. Published 2012 by Blackwell Publishing Ltd.

A&E departments account for up to 70% of admissions at certain times in the day. Along with the detrimental effects on our health, there is also a substantial negative impact on the family and wider society.

In 2001 the Chief Medical Officer warned that during the latter third of the twentieth century, deaths from liver cirrhosis had increased steadily in all age groups. More recently Sheron et al. (2008) reported that nearly 75% of surveyed liver specialists had seen patients of 25 and under with alcohol related liver disease and 25% had treated a patient in their late teens.

Due to the way alcohol is metabolised, women are less tolerant to alcohol and thus are particularly at risk. Young women are increasingly consuming higher levels of alcohol and there appears to be a corresponding increasing trend in liver disease and mortality in this group. In a recent Lancet paper (2011) Professor Ian Gilmore and his colleagues warn of the increasing dangers of ignoring such statistics and warn that unless action is taking to reduce alcohol related harm mortality rates from liver disease will continue to rise.

Patterns and trends in consumption

In the recent British General Household survey (ONS 2010) 42% of men and 39% of women aged 16 to 24 years had exceeded safe recommended daily limits in the previous week, with over half of those drinking heavily or 'bingeing'. The United Kingdom has the heaviest drinking rates for young women in Europe, with nearly 40% having drunk six or more units in one session in the previous week.

Large-scale surveys and statistical data suggest that more and more people are binge drinking with detrimental effects; the age at which drinking is initiated is getting younger, with children as young as nine experimenting with alcohol (Alwyn and John, 2005); the lack of legal enforcement of drinking behaviour on the streets (a high percentage of arrests in city centres are alcohol related (ONS, 2010); licensing policy that encourages binge drinking with pricing and labelling policies that are loosely interpreted and applied. The idealised 'continental café culture' has quickly faded with the press reporting images of 'booze Britain'; an image facilitated through the increasing availability of cheap drinks. In response, there have been calls for minimum pricing and tougher law enforcement

Young people

The European Alcohol Policy Alliance reports that the Alcohol related harm in young people is 'disproportionately high' with 115,000 deaths in Europe per year as a result of alcohol consumption. The European School Survey Project on Alcohol and Other Drugs in 2007 survey found that UK students reported high consumption of alcohol and high levels of intoxication and drunkenness, with heavy episodic drinking (ESPAD study, Hibbel et al., 2007). Our own studies surveying young people and students support these findings with a large number reporting risk taking behaviour such as engaging in unprotected and regretted sex as a consequence of excessive alcohol consumption.

The countries of the UK are consistently near the top of league tables relating to alcohol consumption in the young; a recent study of health behaviour in school aged children found that the percentage of 13-year-olds in Wales reporting having been drunk at least twice was the highest in the 40 countries surveyed (WHO, 2008). Surveys in the UK have also demonstrated that initiating of drinking behaviour is occurring earlier. Alwyn and John (2005) found that children as young as nine reported drinking alcohol (whole drink rather than taste); and had a clear sense of the place of alcohol in our society, for both positive and negative reasons.

Definitions of alcohol related harm

There are a number of definitions used to categorise the impact alcohol has on an individual; they are summarised by NICE (2011) as:

> Hazardous drinking: consumption of alcohol to a level where an individual is at risk of harm and could include physical, mental and social consequences. For example, excess consumption might lead to an individual making unwise or risky decisions, such as mistaking an unlicensed taxi for a licensed taxi.
>
> Harmful drinking: A pattern of alcohol consumption that is causing mental or physical damage. For example, an increase in the number of missed days work.
>
> Dependence: The DSM-IV defines a person with alcohol dependence as someone who continues the use of alcohol despite significant alcohol-related problems.

Assessment for dependence can be difficult. Many individuals who may be dependent do not see themselves as conforming to the stereotypical view of a dependent drinker ('I am not an alcoholic') and many would regard themselves as heavy social drinkers. The cultural norms in relation to alcohol in the UK perpetuate this view.

Screening for alcohol related harm

A number of screening measures have been developed with the aim of identifying those individuals who may be drinking at hazardous or harmful levels and who may be at risk of developing physical and or, mental health problems as a result. The majority of screening measures are self completed and take just a few minutes to answer. Anyone identified as a hazardous or harmful drinker will not typically be in or need intensive treatment to reduce their alcohol consumption and the associated negative consequences. Rather, screening is seen as a pre-curser to the implementation of brief treatment, for example, brief motivational interventions. Since the new millennium there has been much debate over whether general population screening is beneficial. Beich et al. (2003) evaluated the effectiveness of screening in primary care (GP setting) as a pre-curser to a brief intervention. Their conclusions were that screening such large scale populations in order to treat relatively few individuals was not beneficial in terms of resources. However, this finding has been heavily criticised through commentaries and responses in the *British Medical Journal*. More recently, a number of projects have been implemented to evaluate the benefit of screening and implementation of brief interventions in a number of health care settings (SIPS, 2008).

The Audit was developed by Babor et al. (1989) specifically to identify those who may be drinking hazardously or harmfully. It has been shown to be a robust screening measure in non-medical, health care, social and research settings. It also faired favourably when compared to other screening measures such as the MAST and CAGE (Wittchen, 1994; Raistrick et al., 2007). The FAST (Fast Alcohol Screening Test), basically a shortened version of the Audit, was developed by Hodgson et al. (2002) for use in busy settings, such as Accident and Emergency departments and trauma clinics where time and resources are limited. It is a robust, reliable and valid measure (Hodgson et al., 2002) that is quick to complete and is scored in seconds. More recently, it has been used widely in general practice and other primary and secondary health care settings, dental surgeries and other non-medical settings.

The Paddington Alcohol Test (PAT) was developed by Touquet to be used in busy A&E departments. It is a clinical measure but is also used as a therapeutic tool for Early Identification and Brief Advice (EIBA) of hazardous, harmful and dependent drinking. The philosophy behind the measure is early identification can result in a 'teachable moment' (Williams et al., 2005). It has been shown that use of this measure and referral for a brief intervention results in a reduction in alcohol consumption (Crawford et al., 2004) and a reduction in the likelihood of re-attendance (Crawford et al., 2004).

The CAGE (cut-annoyed-guilty-eye) was developed to identify problems an individual may have with excessive alcohol consumption. The CAGE questionnaire has four questions and takes minutes to complete. Although, this measure is regarded as a brief screening measure to be used on populations who have not be in treatment or even thought about treatment, the CAGE is useful for identifying those individuals who may be dependent on alcohol (Raistrick et al., 2007).

Harm reduction strategies

There is much public and scientific debate as to the role of government in tackling excessive alcohol consumption and in developing and implementing harm reduction strategies. It is essential that any alcohol related public health policy considers the mounting evidence of alcohol related harm to individuals and society and that alcohol harm reduction policies are evidenced based. Alcohol is regarded as an ordinary commodity in commercial trading terms. Babor et al. (2010) suggest that this hinders and often obstructs the way that local and national policies are implemented, which can result in ineffective control policies. They cite examples of tax reduction and increased availability.

The main focus of the UK government since the late 1990s has been on harm reduction rather than the causes and motivation of drinking behaviour. This can result in interventions that appear to focus on responding to problems, rather than avoiding those problems in the first place.

Reactive interventions

This focus has inherent problems and interventions tend to only deal with the consequences of excessive alcohol consumption. For example, one city centre in the UK has had numerous city centre problems as a result of excessive alcohol consumption (road traffic accidents involving intoxicated individuals, alcohol related violence, glass injuries). The resultant intervention was to close the city centre roads, extra police were deployed and field hospitals were set up as the constraints on A&E departments and ambulance services were overwhelmed; this was all at the expense of tax payers.

In the UK, premises that sell or supply alcohol must comply with the Licensing Act, 2003. The potential to apply for 24-hour drinking licences became operational in 2005. In 2010 the licensing authority amended this act by announcing five new conditions of the licensing Act applicable to all licensed premises in England and Wales. These are: A ban on irresponsible promotions; a ban on dispensing alcohol directly into customers' mouths; mandatory provision of free tap water; age verification policy and the availability of smaller measures.

Regulation and licensing

The Licensing Act 2003 proposed changes to British drinking culture. One of these changes was the potential to apply for 24-hour drinking licensing which became operational in 2005. The key aim was to reduce harm, such as alcohol related violence and injury and reduce crime. The main argument put forward was that if opening hours were to be extended it would dramatically reduce the concentrated drinking periods where individuals drank as much as they could before 'last orders' and closing time. For the government this was 'pivotal' in combating alcohol crime and anti-social behaviour (Mistral et al., 2007). Plaudits cited Mediterranean society where individuals sat in café bars drinking coffee until the early hours. However, findings such as those from Stockwell and Chikritzhs (2009) who evaluated the impacts of trading hours on alcohol consumption found that 'extended late night trading hours lead to increased consumption and related harms'. Alongside the implementation of the 2003 Act, the Government at the time 'proposed tougher enforcement against licensees, shopkeepers and disorderly drinkers, better management of venues and voluntary agreements with the industry' (Eldridge and Roberts, 2008). Hadfield et al. (2009) reports qualitative findings from participants who were 'sceptical of centrally driven enforcement campaigns' – however, they also noted that the general public felt as 'if something was being done'. Hadfield also found that while there was considerable negotiation with licensees there was still a clear government message that local agencies should work together to reduce alcohol- related problems. In 2008 the Department for Media, Culture and Sport published an evaluation of the licensing Act which emphasised the positive aspects of the Act. Many more were quick to point out that far from reducing alcohol related harm the Act has led to increases in alcohol consumption and alcohol related harm. Eldridge and Roberts point out the flaws in the thinking behind its implementation and cites one example to outline this: 'rather than encouraging 'family friendly' venues, the Act has unwittingly permitted an expansion in the number of lapdancing or 'gentlemen's clubs'.

Since the implementation of the 2003 licensing Act there appears to be conflicting responses and messages from the government in relation to policy and regulations surrounding the selling and consumption of alcohol. Hadfield et al. (2009) reports participants stating that they 'saw aspects of youth culture and wider societal attitudes to alcohol as providing positive endorsement for hedonistic, sometimes aggressive comportment' (i.e., these are the expected outcomes of drinking for many young people). The consequences for such hedonistic behaviour are well documented (Shepherd, 2007). Hadfield further suggests that much time and effort is dedicated to police time in controlling city centres which limits resources and little can be done in terms of managing increasing problems with drunkenness. Thus, reactive interventions become the norm.

Community harm reduction interventions

In 2004 the Alcohol Education Research Council funded the UK Community Alcohol Prevention Programme (UKCAPP). The objective was to develop and evaluate three projects in the large cities of Glasgow, Cardiff and Birmingham which aimed to reduce alcohol related harm. The broad aims for the development of appropriate interventions for all three projects were to: increase awareness of excessive alcohol consumption and the resultant consequences; to engage with licensing premises to promote best practice in terms of harm reduction; to look at ways of improving the general environment and finally, to improve transport links. The interventions should develop and foster links between community partnerships in order to tackle local issues relating to excessive alcohol consumption. All three interventions demonstrated some success, but Mistral et al. (2007) suggest that the lack of rigorous analysis makes the findings weak.

Jones et al. (2010) reviewed effective approaches to reducing harm in drinking environments. The review included studies from Europe (including four from the UK), USA, Canada, New Zealand and Australia. Overall they report the methodological quality of the included studies as being weak. However, Jones highlights three studies which were well designed and showed evidence of effectiveness. All three of these studies evaluated multi-component programmes such as: community mobilisation, stricter enforcement of licensing laws, bar staff training and policy relating to the premises. Effective projects encouraged multi-agency partnerships between all stakeholders (such as the police, licensees, local authorities and health services). Outcomes from effective projects suggested a reduction in road traffic accidents, personal assaults and underage sales. Bar staff training interventions had very little impact overall. Specific training on risk management had some effect on reducing aggression. Brief interventions targeted specifically at drinkers to reduce alcohol consumption or promote sensible drinking had little effect. Jones found that campaigns to enforce alcohol sales laws through police and other approaches were not effective in reducing harm.

Pricing

Despite the recognition of the problems and associated harm and consequences that excessive alcohol consumption can lead to there is a much debate as to the effectiveness of interventions to do this. The majority of individuals who consume moderate levels of alcohol have no problems or issues and accept it as 'legal recreational drug' (Plant and Plant, 2006); as a result they feel that the implementation of policies such aspricing control has a negative effect on them. Thus there are 2 distinct sides of the argument; liberal attitudes to alcohol versus the well documented negative consequences of excessive alcohol consumption).

Purshouse et al. (2010) evaluated the evidence on the impact of alcohol pricing and promotion policies on alcohol consumption and its related consequences; they considered the impact of age, gender and consumption levels (Their findings clearly indicate the need for policy-makers to consider the 'heterogeneity and complexity' of populations when developing price regulation policy and assessing its impact.

Labelling

A study in Australia investigating the impact of labelling on young people's consumption levels found that out of a sample of 44 participants in focus groups, the majority were aware of the existence of standard drink labels. These standard drink labels outlined the total units in the drink and the recommended guidelines for unit consumption. It was reported by the participants that the majority of people took notice of the drinks labels with sole purpose of making decisions about deliberately choosing the strongest drink to consume (Jones and Gregory, 2009). The authors found that when drinks were labelled it resulted in reported increase of drinking levels.

Regulation of marketing

The alcohol industry spends many times more annually on advertising and marketing than is spent on sensible drinking campaigns. Hastings and Sheron (2011) believe that the UK's voluntary advertising code of contact has:

> resulted in such preposterous contradictions as a proscription on marketers associating alcohol with sporting prowess or youth culture while allowing them to sponsor premiership football and music festivals.
>
> (p. 720)

Hastings and Angus (2009) are clear that alcohol marketing is central to both the development and maintenance of the heavy drinking cultural norms in the UK and that this is especially influential on the young. New outlets for pro-alcohol messages, such as social media and viral transmissions are further evidence for the failure of a voluntary code of practice in alcohol marketing and that regulation is necessary for harm reduction.

Gordon et al. (2010) found that both awareness of and involvement with alcohol marketing at age 13 was predictive of both uptake of drinking and increased frequency of drinking at age 15, even when other variables such as parental drinking status were controlled for. Participants were aware of alcohol related advertising across 5 different media, including sports sponsorship. The authors suggest that these findings add weight to existing evidence that young people are directly affected by alcohol advertising and that regulatory policy should change in light of this.

Harm reduction interventions in health care and other settings

Since the start of the millennium a number of research projects have explored the feasibility of screening to identify hazardous and harmful drinking as a pre-cursor to delivering brief motivational interventions. Accident and Emergency departments have long had high rates of alcohol related admissions, with reported attendances of up to 70% at a given period (John et al., 2002). Evidence to support the implementation of screening and delivery of brief interventions has been mixed. John et al. (2002) found that A&E staff recognised the 'window of opportunity' for screening using a brief measure such as the FAST and at the time nurses expressed interest in being trained to deliver brief interventions. In 2009 Alwyn and John were commissioned by the Welsh Assembly Government to explore the current views of staff regarding the delivery of screening and brief interventions and clearly there has been a change in staff attitudes in recent years. The majority of key staff reported that it was not appropriate to deliver interventions in A&E departments, rather it would be better to implement interventions in call back clinics, such as trauma or maxillofacial units. Screening was thought to be a good idea as long as it did not impact on staff time.

Harm reduction through education

Educational initiatives for reducing alcohol related harm fall into three main groupings: media marketing approaches; school based initiatives; and Higher Education based campaigns.

The broad aims of educational harm reduction initiatives are to prevent and/or reduce alcohol related risky behaviour through increasing knowledge and risk awareness; and developing appropriate and sensible attitudes to drinking alcohol. There is a substantive literature base of a wide variety of such initiatives in each of the three broad groupings. Reviews of evidence of effectiveness have, however, tended to produce limited positive outcomes (e.g. Foxcroft et al., 2003, in school based settings; John and Alwyn, 2010, in Higher Education settings; and Gordon et al., 2006, with broad media campaigns). Babor et al. (2010) observe that:

> given the extent of initiatives in this area and the diversity of interventions that have been implemented, there are relatively few that point to long-term impact on drinking behaviour or alcohol related problems.

(p. 199)

Educational interventions in the school setting

Harm reduction programmes aimed at adolescents usually have additional objectives over the ones outlined above, such as delaying the onset of alcohol use; changing adolescent beliefs and attitudes to alcohol use including perceived peer drinking behaviour; and enhancing protective factors such as social skills and levels of self-esteem. Indicators of 'success' in adolescent harm reduction programmes have been defined by researchers such as Foxcroft et al. (2003) as delayed alcohol initiation behaviours, including: first alcohol use; first alcohol use without permission; and first drunkenness.

The UK and national strategies (for example, Safe, sensible and social, 2007) highlight the need for government strategy to give special focus to young drinkers under 18, specific objectives include reductions in the numbers of under 18s drinking alcohol and in the amounts they consume.

There is a plethora of alcohol misuse prevention programmes designed for young people, but a succession of systematic reviews of such programmes conducted over a 12-year period (e.g. Velleman, 2009; Mistral, 2009; Foxcroft et al., 2002, 2003, 2006) conclude that the evidence of impact on future drinking behaviour is mixed and the lack of methodological rigour in many studies with promising outcomes means that no particular approach can be recommended. In fact, the static nature of consumption frequency statistics and the increase in units consumed in this age group since the new millennium suggest that the educational messages being supplied are missing their targets significantly.

The fact that such messages are often contradictory to what young people see in the culture around them, specifically the centrality of alcohol consumption and drinking behaviour, may go some way to explain why these school based messages fall on deaf ears.

Room (2005) observes that there is an artificiality to the process of school based alcohol education, with an adult controlled (school) forum where educational interventions take place and a young person controlled leisure forum in which experimentation with alcohol takes place. He suggests that a different approach entirely may now be appropriate and proposes that it might be more useful to focus on improving the quality of what teenagers know about drinking and intoxification, rather than ineffective attempts at changing their behaviour.

Despite the repeated reviews stating that alcohol education has little effect, there are some chinks of light in the darkness. There appears to be some evidence that educational messages are more effective when tailored for specific subgroups and specific situations and that behaviour change (rather than simply increased knowledge) is more likely to result from interventions that are interactive (HEA, 1997; Anderson et al., 1994) and involve young people at the design stage (Ranzetta et al., 2003). Although family processes and family social influence have been identified as an important influence on teenage alcohol use, prevention programmes have not usually included parents or guardians as an integral part of the prevention process (Elmguist, 1995; Foxcroft et al., 1997).

Strengthening families approaches

Recent systematic reviews (e.g. Velleman, 2009; Foxcroft et al., 2002, 2003) suggest that interventions that engage the whole family are most likely to produce positive effects over the longer term. These tend to address multiple substances and focus on improving family support systems, communication and parental skills and control. Specific examples with evidence for effectiveness include the STARS (Start Taking Alcohol Risks Seriously) school and family programme (Werch et al., 2003) where at 12 months follow up, individuals in the intervention group were significantly lower in intention to drink in the next six months than those in the control group.

The Iowa project strengthening families programme (SFP) is cited by many reviewers as an effective intervention designed to prevent teenage substance misuse and which appears to be attaining lower drug use and improving family relationships (Molgaard and Spoth, 2001; Spoth et al., 2005, 2008). However, this is an intensive intervention both in terms of time and resources, mostly used with families deemed to be 'at risk' by welfare and other agencies. It may not be appropriate as a general educational-type intervention for 'mainstream' families, as research in this area demonstrates that parents tend to be reluctant to engage in school based alcohol programmes (e.g. Alwyn and John, 2005). Velleman (2009) points out that family take up of such programmes can be as low as 25%. A further consideration is the cultural transferability of these programmes (the majority of studies have been conducted in the USA). One study has been reported where the SFP was adapted for UK families (Coombes et al., 2006, 2009), with promising results

Young people focused approaches

Other harm reduction interventions have been identified as having some effect (Velleman, 2009). These interventions tend to take place in school settings but they are not simply educational messages; they focus on factors such as social skills, drink refusal training and dealing with peer pressure. Most school-based programmes are universal in nature in that they target whole populations, regardless of individual risk level. They are also the most popular and most frequently evaluated harm reduction interventions that are targeted at adolescents (Jones et al., 2009). Examples of promising approaches here include Project Northland (Perry et al., 1996), which focused on enhancing substance refusal skills and demonstrated a significant effect two years post-intervention. Botvin et al. (2001, 2003) also reported encouraging findings at two year follow up from a programme designed to enhance life skills, including building confidence and self-esteem. This programme provided annual 'booster sessions' after the intervention was completed. The authors suggest that this intervention is also appropriate for younger, primary aged children.

Considerations

Systematic reviews tend to focus on specific research designs, favouring RCTs over methodologies that may be more challenging in terms of rigorous evaluation. It remains a possibility that those interventions that are difficult to evaluate could have something to offer.

Sheron et al. (2008) point out that young people suffer disproportionately from high alcohol-related mortality. They believe that a much more holistic approach to tackling young people's alcohol consumption is needed with education, treatment and enforcement agencies working in partnership. The All Wales School Liaison Programme (AWSLP) has made some attempt to undertake such an approach, with a broader focus that encompasses anti-social behaviour and other substance misuse as well as alcohol. The AWSCLP approach is 'mainly a preventive, generalised and broad-based one that is focussed on formal lessons delivered by uniformed police in the classroom, together with supportive policing activities' (Riddell and Stead, 2011: 5). The evaluation commissioned by the Welsh government suggests positive trends, but no hard behavioural outcome measures have been assessed.

Higher education based initiatives

Excesses in alcohol consumption amongst student populations are well-established, although research on drinking patterns in university and college students has been preponderant in the USA. There has been a general acceptance of this in the past as a normal developmental phase, or 'rite of passage', whereby once students reach the end of their courses, there is a 'growing up effect' at which point their drinking is modified and they take on more adult roles and behaviours. In the UK, governmental targets are driving up the percentage of young people who undertake degree courses and are thus exposed to this high drinking culture. Further, some evidence is suggesting that the growing up effect is disappearing and that students are developing career drinking patterns which will be maintained into their post-university futures. This is an important change when we consider harm reduction; as there has not been a corresponding increase in concern at the levels of consumption and subsequent harms that are the norm amongst our undergraduates. The prevailing cultural belief on the part of society that this is a 'normal part of growing up' is appearing increasingly out of step with the reality of harmful consequences.

In a recent survey of more than four hundred first-year university students in Wales, 88% screened positively as hazardous drinkers on the FAST alcohol screening test (John and Alwyn 2009), with a clear correlation between alcohol consumption, academic performance and attrition. This increasingly high drinking culture is producing extensive side effects in relation to excessive health risks. Cashell-Smith et al. (2007), reported on the extensive alcohol-related sexual risk taking reported by students. Further evidence on the severity of this trend comes from liver experts reporting worrying changes in the age of onset of alcohol related liver disease (Smith et al., 2006).

Harm reduction interventions aimed at undergraduate students

The focus and content of campus programmes and interventions are many and varied; there is a danger of drawing erroneous conclusions regarding effectiveness through an assumption of homogeneity. There are broad universal 'social media'-type campaigns that produce slogans on beer mats in the Students' Union bars interventions with individuals identified through student health services as problem or dependent drinkers and a range in between. The higher education campus context highlights the problems of generalisibility across cultures. Much of the harm reduction research in this sector comes from the USA where most undergraduates are below the legal drinking age and prevention strategies also focus on regulation such as restriction of location of sales outlets and the development of campus alcohol policies (Babor et al., 2010).

There are a number of reasons why the situation is very different in other countries, notably the UK, which cast doubt on the potential of the approaches that are showing some promise in the USA. In the UK undergraduates are legally able to drink alcohol and may have done so for some time. The Students' Union organisation is central to the student experience and the majority of its funding stream comes from alcohol sales, giving it a pivotal role as both part of the problem and the potential solution to excessive campus alcohol consumption. University alcohol policies for the most part relate to staff and not students and universities are loathe to give the impression that they do not want their undergraduates to 'have fun' by making any suggestion of restrictions on drinking (John and Alwyn, 2010).

A number of methodological issues have been highlighted in the literature including identified limitations such as the heterogeneity of outcome measures; the need to validate self-report web-based outcome measures (Saitz et al., 2007); small sample sizes at follow-up (Collins et al., 2002); concerns of failed randomisation (Juarez et al., 2006; McAnally, 2003; Walters et al., 2000); lack of controls; social desirability bias; studies targeted at American or New Zealand student populations; and studies targeted at high risk or designated problem drinkers and either a very limited or absence of follow up. Karam et al. (2007) believe that increasingly, there is a need for more comprehensive studies with systematic methodologies to yield representative results on alcohol use and alcohol-protective factors in college settings.

Promising approaches

The evidence for effectiveness in interventions with students appears to mirror those with adult populations in that the approach and mode of delivery are significant. Larimer and Cronce found that those interventions that used motivational approaches, skills based interventions and gave personalised feedback of consumption related risk were the most promising (2007). The authors caution that much of this research suffered from significant limitations

The mode of delivery of interventions is important. Research evidence continues to provide support for Brief Motivational Interventions (BMI) in terms of student drinking, especially if they are multi-component, with Personal Normative Feedback (PNF), feedback from Blood Alcohol Concentration levels (BAC), skills training and protective behavioural strategies incorporated. Decisional balance exercises either alone or with other BMI components also have mixed support (Carey et al., 2006) and MI with no personalised feedback does not appear to be effective (McNally and Palfai, 2003). In contrast with normative feedback, evidence of mailed or computerised motivational feedback in the absence of a face-to-face intervention continues to be supported (Chiauzzi et al., 2005).

Web-based interventions are increasingly common in research trials with student populations. They are anonymous and can reach large numbers relatively easily. The evidence on outcome is inconsistent and student engagement relatively poor. Further controlled trials are needed to fully investigate their efficacy and to understand if different elements are required in order to engage low and high-risk drinkers, as well as cross-cultural generalisiblity

Interventions are less successful in reducing problems when targeted at heavy drinkers or other high-risk groups. Such students are likely to have heavy drinking peers and be embedded in more alcohol-involved social networks. Therefore, there is an increasing need for tailored interventions that address deep structure such as core beliefs, values and norms (Carey et al., 2007)

Social normative interventions

The social normative approach has developed exponentially over the past few years and merits a separate commentary. What is now generally understood by 'social norms theory' was developed by Perkins and Berkowitz in 1986, after their investigation into student drinking behaviour appeared to demonstrate a 'pluralistic ignorance effect'; thus, students overestimate both the alcohol use and approval of drinking of others. This effect has been consistently demonstrated on American college campuses (John and Alwyn, 2010). This has led many researchers to conclude that changing these misperceptions of norms will lead to a reduction in the alcohol consumption of individual students. The main formats for these social normative interventions fall into two groups:

1. *Social marketing approaches*, which rely on mass communication methods to change individual misperceptions. Surveys are conducted to establish the actual levels of alcohol consumption in the target population and these 'corrected drinking norms' are then broadcast universally, in an

attempt to redress the mis-perceptions. This may be costly and impersonal and such interventions can be very difficult to evaluate due to lack of control of extraneous variables. Researchers have also reported difficulties if the average consumption for a particular population is elevated, as this cannot then be usefully employed as a harm reduction strategy.

2. *Individual feedback approaches*, which can include a range of information including actual behavioural norms, individual misperceptions, personal drinking pattern feedback and associated risks. Delivery can be via a number of modes, including e-mail, web-based, paper-and-pen and face-to-face. The target population can also range from identified problem drinkers to a universal campus or institution-wide one. Difficulties are again evident if the mean consumption of the target population is high.

The NIAAA (National Institute on Alcohol Abuse and Alcoholism), in a 2007 review of American college and university alcohol interventions, suggests that while social normative approaches are popular, the research evidence is mixed, with inconsistencies in methodology causing problems for the rigorous evaluation of effectiveness. In a review in 2010, John and Alwyn conclude that the evidence of effectiveness is surprisingly scant, considering the immense popularity of social normative interventions with researchers, politicians and elements of the drinks industry. A review by Weschler et al. (2003) found that this approach actually increased consumption in two studies.

Media/marketing campaigns

The purpose of mass media campaigns is to inform and educate the public with the aim of influencing drink related behaviour. Messages are generally universal in nature, but may have a specific target topic or population, such as pregnant women or young people. The additional objective of mass media messages is to counter the alcohol industry produced pro-drinking advertisements. Specific techniques to refute industry messages are often known as 'counter-advertising, such as warning labelling. Social marketing is a more recent variation on mass media campaigning, where the techniques of commercial advertising are used to pursue specific social goals. The alcohol drinks industry has involved itself in public health campaigns in a number of ways, including financial support and harm reduction messages. According to Smith et al. (2006), such industry sponsored campaigns are ineffective; and are perceived as ambiguousby the general public. The potential outcome here is that seemingly pro-health messages from alcohol producers can result in both increased sales and an elevated reputation for responsibility and social concern.

Wakefield et al. (2010) review a range of social marketing projects and conclude that there is little evidence of effectiveness in terms of behaviour change, despite the often high profile nature and dissemination of such campaigns. For example, a recent social marketing campaign to reduce student drinking in a UK city received an award, but fails to report data relating to actual reduction in consumption of alcohol. Babor et al. (2010: 202) conclude that 'Despite their good intentions, PSAs [public service announcements] are an ineffective antidote to the high quality pro-drinking messages that appear much more frequently as paid advertisements in the mass media.'

Conclusion

Harm reduction in the context of alcohol consumption generates unique considerations because of alcohol's status as a legal drug that is freely available. That alcohol can cause considerable harm at both individual and societal levels is beyond dispute. We have reviewed a wide range of harm reduction strategies including licensing laws; labelling and pricing; voluntary marketing; and the strategies that focus on individual behaviour such as education, brief interventions and screening. The common denominator of all of these would appear to be an overall lack of consistent effectiveness to make a difference.

There are many contradictions apparent in alcohol related harm reduction. It is clear that the success of public health and school based educational initiatives are constrained by the wider social context in which they occur. Their effectiveness is reduced by the overriding cultural norms and attitudes to drinking.

The conflict between the freedom of the drinks industry to market a legal product and attempts to deliver messages relating to sensible consumption patterns on the part of the population, is one that appears to exercise successive governments. The evidence suggests, however, that the laissez faire approach of increasing availability with the assumption that this will somehow decrease the urgency and therefore levels of consumption, is totally flawed. The increasing trends in drunken children and young adults presenting with premature liver disease clearly demonstrate that reducing alcohol related harm is a public health priority that cannot be left to voluntary participation by the drinks industry. The government must legislate in terms of availability by increasing pricing and reducing sales outlets; and in terms of changing prevailing cultural norms through the regulation of advertising and marketing.

References

Alwyn, T. and John, B (2005) *From Lollipops to Alcopops: Developing Sensible Attitudes to Alcohol in Children and Parents*, Report to the Alcohol Education Research Council, London: Alcohol Education Research Council.

Alwyn, T. and John, B. (2009) *An Assessment of Alcohol Related Attendances and Staff Attitudes to Screening and Treatment for Drinking Problems at Emergency Departments in Wales*, Report to the Wales Assembly Government, Cardiff: Wales Assembly Governent.

Anderson, K. (1995) *Young People and Alcohol, Drugs and Tobacco*, WHO regional publications, European series no. 66. Copenhagen: WHO.

Anderson, P., Babor, T.F. and Edwards, G., et al. (eds) (1994) *Alcohol and the Public Good*, Oxford: Open University Press.

Babor, T., de la Fuente, J.R., Saunders, J. and Grant, M. (1989) *AUDIT – the Alcohol-use Disorders Identification Test: Guidelines for Use in Primary Health Care*, Geneva: World Health Organization, Division of Mental Health.

Babor, T., Caetano, R., Casswell, S., Edwards, G., Giesbrecht, N. (and 10 others) (2010) *Alcohol: No Ordinary Commodity*, 2nd edn, New York: Oxford University Press.

Beich, A., Thorsen, T. and Rollnick, S. (2003) Screening in brief intervention trials targeting excessive drinkers in general practice: systematic review and meta-analysis, *BMJ*, 327 (7414), 536–40.

Botvin, G., Griffin, K. W., Diaz, T. and Ifill-Williams, M. (2001) Preventing binge drinking during early adolescence: one- and two-year follow-up of a school-based preventive intervention, *Psychology of Addictive Behaviors*, 15 (4), 360–5.

Botvin, G., Griffin, K., Paul, E. and Macauley, A. P. (2003) Preventing tobacco and alcohol use among elementary school students through life skills training, *Journal of Child & Adolescent Substance Abuse*, 12 (4), 1–17.

Carey, K.B., Carey, M.P., Maisto, S.A. and Henson, J.M. (2006) Brief motivational interventions for heavy college drinkers: a randomized controlled trial, *Journal of Consulting and Clinical Psychology*, 74 (5), 943–54.

Carey, K.B., Scott-Sheldon, L.J.A., Carey, M.P. and DeMartini, K.S. (2007) Individual-level interventions to reduce college drinking: a meta-analytic review, *Addictive Behaviours*, 32 (11), 2469–94.

Chashell-Smith, M.L., Connor, J.L. and Kypri, K. (2007) Harmful effects of alcohol on sexual behaviour in a New Zealand university community, *Drug and Alcohol Review*, 26 (6), 645–51.

Chiauzzi, E., Green, T.C., Lord, S., Thum, C. and Goldstein, M. (2005) My student body: a high risk drinking prevention web site for college students, *Journal of American College Health*, 53, 263–74.

Chief Medical Officer for England (2001) *Annual Report 2001/2*, www.doh.gov.za/docs/reports/annual/2001–02/contents.html, London: Department of Health, accessed 4 June.

Collins, S.E., Carey, K.B. and Sliwinski, M.J. (2002) Mailed personalized normative feedback as a brief intervention for at-risk college drinkers, *Journal Studies on Alcohol*, 63 (5), 559–67.

Coombes, L., Allen, D., Marsh, M. and Foxcroft, D. (2006) *Implementation of the Strengthening Families Programme (SPF) 10–14 in Barnsley: The Perspectives of Facilitators and Families*, Research Report no. 26, Oxford: School of Health and Social Care, Oxford Brookes University.

Coombes, L., Allen, D., Marsh, M. and Foxcroft, D. (2009) The Strengthening Families Programme (SFP) 10–14 and substance misuse in Barnsley: the perspectives of facilitators and families, *Child Abuse Review*, 18, 41–59.

Crawford, M.J., Patton, R., Touquet, R., Drummond, C., Byford, S., Barbara, B., Reece, B., Brown, A. and Henry, J.A. (2004) Screening and referral for brief intervention of alcohol-misusing patients in an emergency department: a pragmatic randomised controlled trial, *Lancet*, 364 (9442), 1334–9.

Department of Health, Home Office, Department for Education and Skills, Department for Culture, Media and Sport (2007) *Safe. Sensible. Social: The Next Steps in the National Alcohol Strategy*, London: UK Government.

Elmguist, D. L. (1995) A systematic review of parent-oriented programs to prevent children's use of alcohol and other drugs, *Journal of Drug Education*, 25 (3), 251–79.

Eurocare European Alcohol Policy Alliance (2011) *Eurocare's Response to 'The Reforms of the CAP towards 2020': Impact Assessment*, Brussels: Eurocare European Alcohol Policy Alliance.

Foxcroft, D.R. (2006) *Alcohol Misuse Prevention for Young People: A Rapid Review of Recent Evidence*, World Health Organization Technical Report, Geneva: WHO, October.

Foxcroft, D.R. and Tsertsvadze, A. (2011) Universal school-based prevention programs for alcohol misuse in young people, *Cochrane Database of Systematic Reviews 2011*, 5.

Foxcroft, D.R., Lister-Sharp, D. and Lowe, G. (1997) Alcohol misuse prevention for young people: a systematic review reveals methodological concerns and lack of reliable evidence of effectiveness, *Addiction*, 92, 531–7.

Foxcroft, D., Ireland D., Lowe, G. Breen, R. (2002) Primary prevention for alcohol misuse in young people, *Cochrane Database of Systematic Reviews*, 3.

Foxcroft, D.R., Ireland, D., Lister-Sharp, D.J., Lowe, G. and Breen, R. (2003) Longer-term primary prevention for alcohol misuse in young people: a systematic review, *Addiction*, 98, 397–411.

Gordon, R., MacKintosh, A.M. and Moodie, C. (2010) The impact of alcohol marketing on youth drinking behaviour: a two-stage cohort study, *Alcohol and Alcoholism*, 45 (5), 470–80.

Gordon, R., McDermott, L., Stead, M. and Angus, K. (2006) The effectiveness of social marketing interventions for health improvement: what's the evidence?, *Public Health*, 120 (12), 1133–9.

Health and Social Care Information Centre (2010) *Statistics on Alcohol: England, 2010*, London: NHS National Statistics.

Health Education Authority (1997) *Health Promotion Effectiveness Review*, London: Health Education Authority.

Hadfield, P., Lister, S. and Traynor, P. (2009) 'This town's a different town today': policing and regulating the night-time economy, *Criminology and Criminal Justice*, 9 (4), 465–85.

Hastings, G. and Angus, K. (2009) *Under the Influence: The Damaging Effect of Alcohol Marketing on Young People*, London: British Medical Association, BMA Board of Science.

Hastings, G. and Sheron, N. (2011) Alcohol marketing to children, *BMJ*, 342, d1767.

Hibell, B., Guttormsson, U., Ahlström, S., Balakireva, O., Bjarnason, T., Kokkevi, A. and Kraus L. (2009) *The 2007 ESPAD Report: Substance Use among Students in 35 European Countries*, Stockholm: ESPAD.

HM Government (2007) *Safe. Sensible. Social: The Next Steps in the National Alcohol Strategy*, London: Department of Health.

Hodgson, R., Alwyn, T., John, B., Thom, B. and Smith, A. (2002) The FAST alcohol screening test, *Alcohol & Alcoholism*, 37 (1), 61–6.

John, B. and Alwyn, T. (2009) *Mapping Student Alcohol Consumption & Drinking Pattern: Perceptions and Beliefs of Students at Higher Education Institutions in Wales*, Report to the Wales Assembly Government, Cardiff: Wales Assembly Government.

John, B. and Alwyn, T. (2010) *Alcohol Related Social Norm Perceptions in University Students: Effective Interventions for Change*, peer reviewed report for Alcohol Education Research Council, www.aerc.org.uk/documents/pdfs/finalReports/AERC_FinalReport_0061.pdf, accessed May/June 2011.

John, B., Alwyn, T., Hodgson, R. J., Smith, A.J. and Waller, S. (2002) The feasibility of alcohol interventions in accident and emergency departments, *Drugs and Alcohol Today*, 2 (2), 8–16.

Jones, L., James, M., Jefferson, T., Lushey, C., Morleo, M., Stokes, E., Sumnall, H., Witty, K. and Bellis, M.A. (2007) *A Review of the Effectiveness and Cost-Effectiveness of Interventions Delivered in Primary and Secondary Schools to Prevent and/or Reduce Alcohol Use by Young People under 18 Years Old*, NICE: PHIAC 14.3a, Alcohol and Schools: Review of Effectiveness and Cost-effectiveness, Liverpool: National Collaborating Centre for Drug Prevention.

Jones, L., Hughes, K., Atkinson, A.M. and Bellis, M.A. (2010) Reducing harm in drinking environments: a systematic review of effective approaches, *Health and Place*, 17 (2), 508–18.

Jones, S.C. and Gregory, P. (2009) The impact of more visible standard drink labelling on youth alcohol consumption: helping young people drink (ir)responsibly?, *Drug and Alcohol Review*, 28 (3), 230–4.

Juarez, P., Walters, S.T., Daugherty, M. and Radi, C. (2006) A randomized trial of motivational interviewing and feedback with heavy drinking college students, *Journal of Drug Education*, 36 (3), 233–46.

Karam, E., Kypri, K. and Salamoun, M. (2007) Alcohol use among college students: an international perspective, *Current Opinion in Psychiatry*, 20, 213–21.

Larimer, M.E. and Cronce, J.M. (2007) Identification, prevention and treatment revisited: individual focused college drinking prevention strategies 1999–2006, *Addictive Behaviours*, 32, 239–46.

McNally, A.M. and Palfai, T.P. (2003), Brief group alcohol interventions with college students: examining motivational components, *Journal of Drug Education*, 33 (2), 159–76.

Mistral, W. (2009) *A Review of the Effectiveness of National Policies and Initiatives to Reduce Alcohol-related Harm among Young People*, Bath: University of Bath and Avon and Wiltshire Mental Health Trust, Mental Health R&D Unit.

Mistral W, Velleman R, Mastache C et al. (2007) UKCAPP: an evaluation of 3 UK community Alcohol Prevention Programmes, Bath: University of Bath and Avon and Wiltshire Mental Health Partnership NHS Trust.

Molgaard, V. and Spoth, R. (2001) The strengthening families program for young adolescents: Overview and outcomes, *Residential Treatment for Children & Youth. Special Issue: Innovative Mental Health Interventions for Children: Programmes That Work*, 18, 15–29.

NIAAA (2007) *What Colleges Need to Know: An Update on College Drinking Research*, NIH Publication number 07–5010, 1–12, London: NHS.

NICE (2011) *Alcohol Use Disorders: Diagnosis, Assessment and Management of Harmful Drinking and Alcohol Dependence*, Clinical Guideline 115, National College for Mental Health London: NHS

Perkins, H.W. and Berkowitz, A.D. (1986) Perceiving the community norms of alcohol use among students: some research implications for campus alcohol education programming, *International Journal of the Addictions*, 21, 961–76.

Plant, M. and Plant, M. (2006) *Binge Britain: Alcohol and the Nation's Response*, Oxford: Oxford University Press.

Perry, C.L., Williams, C.L., Veblen–Mortenson, S., Toomey, T.L., Komro, K.A., Anstine, P.S., McGovern, P.G., Finnegan, J.R., Forster, J.L., Wagenaar, A.C. and Wolfson, M. (1996) Project Northland: outcomes of a community-wide alcohol use prevention program during early adolescence, *American Journal of Public Health*, 86, 956–65.

Purshouse, R.C., Meier, P.S., Brennan, A., Taylor, K.B. and Rafia, R. (2010) Estimated effect of alcohol pricing policies on health and health economic outcomes in England: an epidemiological model, *Lancet*, 375 (9723), 1355–64.

Raistrick, D., Heather, N. and Godfrey, C. (2007) *Review of the Effectiveness of Treatment for Alcohol Problems*, London: National Treatment Agency.

Ranzetta, L., Fitzpatrick, J. and Seljmani, F. (2003) *Megapoles: Young People and Alcohol*, London: Greater London Authority.

Riddell, S., Stead, J., Lloyd, G., Baird, A. and Laugharne, J. (2011) *Evaluation of the All Wales School Liaison Core Programme*, Cardiff: Welsh Assembly Government.

Roberts, M. and Eldridge A. (2007) *Expecting 'Great Things'? The Impact of the Licensing Act 2003 on Democratic Involvement, Dispersal and Drinking Cultures*, University of Westminster, www.ias.org.uk/resources/ukreports/cci/cci-0707.pdf, accessed 16 May 2011.

Room, R. (2005) What to expect from a 'social aspects' organisation and what to expect from school-based alcohol education, *Addiction*, 100 (8) 1072–3.

Royal College of Psychiatrists (2011) *Our Invisible Addicts*, First Report of the Older People's Substance Misuse Working Group of the Royal College of Psychiatrists, CRI 165, London: Royal College of Psychiatrists.

Saitz, R., Palfai, T. P., Freedner, N., Winter, M.R., McDonald, A. Lu, J., Ozonoff, Al., Rosenbloom, D.L. and Dejong. W. (2007) Screening and brief intervention online for college students: the ihealth study, *Alcohol and Alcoholism*, 42 (1), 28–36.

Shepherd, J. (2007) Preventing alcohol related violence: a public health approach, *Criminal Behaviour and Mental Health*, 17 (4), 250–64.

Sheron, N., Olsen, N. and Gilmore, I. (2008) An evidence-based alcohol policy. *GUT*, 57 (10), 1341–4.

Sheron, N., Hawkey, C. and Gilmore, I. (2011) Projections of alcohol deaths: a *wake*-up call, *Lancet*, 277 (9774), 1297–9.

SIPS (2008) (Screening and Intervention Programme for Sensible drinking), sources from www.sips.iop.kcl.ac.uk/, accessed May 2011.

Smith, S., Touquet, R., Wright, S. and Das Gupta, N. (1996) Detection of alcohol misusing patients in accident and emergency departments: the Paddington alcohol test (PAT), *Emergency Medical Journal*, 13, 308–12.

Smith, S., White, J. and Nelson, C., Davies, M., Lavers, J. and Sheron, N. (2006) Severe alcohol-induced liver disease and the alcohol dependence syndrome, *Alcohol Alcoholism*, 41, 274–7.

Spoth, R., Randall, G.K., Shin, C. and Redmond, C. (2005) Randomized study of combined universal family and school preventive interventions: patterns of long–term effects on initiation, regular use and weekly drunkenness, *Psychology of Addictive Behaviours*, 19 (4), 372–8.

Spoth, R., Randall, G., Trudeau, L., Shin, C. and Redmond, C. (2008) Substance use outcomes $5^{1}/_{2}$ years past baseline for partnership-based, family-school preventive interventions, *Drug and Alcohol Dependence*, 96, 57–68.

STARS (2009) *STARS (Start Taking Alcohol Risks Seriously)*, U.S. Department of Health and Human Services, Substance Abuse and Mental Health Services Administration Centre for Substance Abuse Prevention, Washington, DC: US Department of Health and Human Services.

Stockwell, T. and Chikritzhs, T. (2009) Do relaxed trading hours for bars and clubs mean more relaxed drinking? A review of international research on the impacts of changes to permitted hours of drinking, *Crime Prevention and Community Safety*, 11, 153–70.

Velleman, R. (2009) *Alcohol Prevention Programmes: A Review of the Literature for the Joseph Rowntree Foundation*, London: Joseph Rowntree Foundation.

Wakefield, M. A., Loken, B. and Hornik, R. C. (2010) Use of mass media campaigns to change health behaviour, *Lancet*, 376 (9748), 1261–71.

Walters, S. T., Bennett, M. E. and Miller, J. E. (2000) Reducing alcohol use in college students: a controlled trial of two brief interventions, *Journal of Drug Education*, 30 (3), 361–72.

Wechsler, H., Nelson, T. F., Lee, J. E. Seibring, M., Lewis, C. and Keeling, R. P. (2003) Perception and reality: a national evaluation of social norms marketing interventions to reduce college students' heavy alcohol use, *Journal of Studies on Alcohol*, 64 (4), 484–94.

Werch, C.E., Owen, D.M., Carlson, J.M. DiClemente, C.C., Edgemon, P. and Moore, M. (2003) One-year follow-up results of the STARS for Families alcohol prevention program, *Health Education Research*, 18 (1), 74–87.

WHO (2009) *Handbook for Action to Reduce Alcohol Related Harm*, Geneva: World Health Organization for Europe

WHO (2008) *Health Related Behaviours in School Age Children*, Geneva: World Health Organization for Europe.

Williams, S., Brown, A., Patton, R., Crawford, M.J. and Touquet, R. (2005) The half-life of the 'teachable moment' for alcohol misuing patients in the emergency department, *Drug and Alcohol Dependence*, 77 (2), 205–8.

Wittchten, H.U. (1994) Reliability and validity studies of the WHO – Composite International Diagnostic Interview (CIDI): a critical review, *Journal of Psychiatric Research*, 28, 57–84.

Chapter 16

TOBACCO HARM REDUCTION

Jonathan Foulds and Steven Branstetter

Introduction

Despite widespread awareness in developed countries that tobacco smoking is extremely harmful to health, a large proportion (typically 20-40%) of the adult population of most developed countries continues to smoke (Mackay et al., 2002). While surveys suggest that the majority of smokers in most developed countries would rather quit (Mackay et al., 2002; WHO, 1997), only a small proportion of them (<5%) succeed in quitting each year, and most smokers do not even plan to quit within the next six months. As a result, the rate of decline of smoking prevalence remains very slow in most developed countries, and smoking continues as the single biggest cause of premature death (Mackay et al., 2002). The concept of trying to reduce the harm to health caused by tobacco is not a new one. The approach taken by the tobacco industry has largely consisted of a series of failed attempts to develop and market less harmful tobacco products (product modification), combined with far greater attempts to minimize the perception that their products are harmful at all (Glantz et al., 1996). Until relatively recently, two of the main approaches taken by health advocates have consisted of: (1) *cessation*: trying to encourage cessation among existing smokers; and (2) *prevention*: trying to prevent uptake by current non-smokers. Some progress has been made in encouraging cessation (Raw et al., 1998; Parrott et al., 1998; Fiore et al., 2008), and attempts at prevention have had limited success (Reid, 1996; Backinger et al., 2003; Farrelly et al., 2005; Bauer et al., 2000). The net effect has been a steady but slow decline in smoking prevalence in many western countries. However, there is some evidence that this progress is slowing down, and that this may be partly due to remaining smokers being classed as more dependent and/or less motivated to quit (Fagerstrom et al., 1996). This has led to renewed consideration of 'harm reduction' strategies by health advocates. Because most smokers either cannot or will not quit smoking completely in the near future, consideration has been given to strategies designed to produce harm reduction rather than harm minimization. Because the term 'harm reduction' refers to the intended (but sometimes doubtful) aim, rather than the process, the phrase 'nicotine maintenance' may be preferable as it more accurately describes the process typically involved in most harm reduction strategies.

For the purposes of this chapter, 'tobacco harm reduction' and 'nicotine maintenance' can be regarded as synonymous, and are defined as, 'an intervention (policy, advice treatment, etc.) designed to reduce the harm to health from tobacco without requiring or aiming for complete abstinence from all tobacco constituents (including nicotine) within 6 months'.

One major review of this topic was carried out by the US Institute of Medicine in 2001 (IOM, 2001). It was pointed out that conclusive evidence is lacking for most tobacco harm reduction strategies. Even in cases where there is good evidence that the strategy reduces harm for those individuals directly involved, there could still be a net harm to public health if the people who pursue the harm reduction strategy would otherwise have quit tobacco/nicotine completely, or if a much larger

Harm Reduction in Substance Use and High-Risk Behaviour: International Policy and Practice, First Edition.
Edited by Richard Pates and Diane Riley.
© 2012 Blackwell Publishing Ltd. Published 2012 by Blackwell Publishing Ltd.

number of people take up the less harmful tobacco/nicotine strategy than would otherwise have used tobacco. Because many of the health effects of tobacco take decades to occur, it is prohibitively time-consuming and expensive to prove conclusively that a given strategy has long-term harm reduction effects, or to prove that these effects are not outweighed by unintended societal effects (e.g., widespread tobacco use increasing total harm). We are therefore forced to estimate the likely effects of supposed harm reduction strategies, based on the best available evidence.

Nicotine maintenance strategies

Tobacco harm reduction is not a single strategy but rather is an 'umbrella' label that is frequently used to refer to a number of different strategies. The most widely discussed strategies are listed below and each will be described in some detail. For each of these strategies, the key question is whether or not there is sufficient evidence that the strategy is likely to lead to a net reduction in harm to health from tobacco.

1. switching to a potentially less harmful smoked tobacco product;
2. switching to a less harmful smokeless tobacco product;
3. reducing the number of cigarettes smoked;
4. facilitating temporary periods of abstinence via short-term nicotine replacement;
5. facilitating long-term tobacco abstinence with long-term maintenance pharmaceutical products.

Switching to potentially less harmful smoked products

It has been clear for some time that the tobacco industry cannot be relied upon to provide accurate information about the relative harmfulness of its products, and that far greater regulation and disclosure is required (Glantz et al., 1996; Sweanor, 1999). It is also clear that the tobacco industry has been somewhat successful in convincing not only the public but also a significant proportion of health professionals that it has developed products that are significantly less harmful than previous products (Glantz et al., 1996). The inaccuracy of this claim has only been widely recognized relatively recently, along with increasing awareness that it is the nicotine delivery characteristic of a tobacco product that determines how it is used, and therefore how harmful it is likely to be (Glantz et al., 1996; US Dept of Health and Human Services, 1988; Royal College of Physicians, 2007).

Most recently there has been a debate regarding the optimal direction of future tobacco regulation policy. Among the various policies being suggested are two quite separate options:

1. Require the industry to gradually reduce the permissible nicotine delivery of its products down to the point where they can no longer deliver reinforcing doses of nicotine. The primary aim here is to gradually put an end to nicotine addiction from tobacco (Henningfield et al., 1998).
2. Require the industry to gradually reduce the permissible delivery of harmful constituents from its products (without substantially altering nicotine delivery), down to the point where they can no longer deliver detectable quantities of harmful substances (i.e., ultimately requiring a non-combustion delivery device). The primary aim here is to put an end to the most serious health consequences of nicotine addiction (Russell, 1991; Foulds and Ghodse, 1995; Bates et al., 1999).

Each of these strategies has pros and cons. Over time, option 1 will reduce the number of people addicted to tobacco. However smokers may be able to find ways around the legislation. For example, in parts of the United States with higher taxes on manufactured than roll-your-own cigarettes, new cigarette making machines have been developed, allowing customers to buy cheap loose tobacco at an outlet (e.g. a gas station) and then walk to the next counter and have an on-site cigarette machine turn it into a carton of ready-rolled cigarettes. Smuggling of contraband (high nicotine/tar cigarettes) may be a problem for both strategies. However, it may be particularly difficult to prevent legal ultra-low nicotine delivery cigarettes (option 1) from being replaced by contraband, high nicotine delivery cigarettes (which would also avoid taxes in the smuggling process) as they would appear identical to the eye. Option 2 requires the gradual phasing out of smoked tobacco, perhaps making enforcement easier at the local and individual level.

More recently, a combined approach (combining options 1 and 2) to regulating tobacco has been proposed (Henningfield et al., 2005). Regardless of which policy is adopted, it would need to be backed up by a more powerful regulatory authority than has been the case previously (Royal College of Physicians, 2007). Until such an authority exists (with the powers recently given to the United States Food and Drug Administration being the first real test case), and can enable health professionals to provide accurate information on the relative risks of tobacco products, there is no reliable basis for promoting one type of cigarette as being less harmful than another. It is now widely recognized that cigarettes formerly marketed as 'Light', 'Ultralight' or 'Mild' are no less harmful than regular cigarettes. The primary method of reducing the machine-measured tar and nicotine yields has been by adding small ventilation holes in the filter, thus diluting the smoke. However, it is now clear that smokers 'compensate' for the reduced nicotine delivery by simply increasing their average puff volume, therefore absorbing a similar amount of toxins from each type of cigarette (Benowitz, 2001; O'Connor et al., 2006).

More recently the tobacco industry has attempted to develop new types of cigarettes that are claimed to produce smoke that is lower in some specific toxins (Carballo et al., 2006). As with light cigarettes, it is doubtful whether any of these modified products are really any less harmful when smoked by consumers. Given that tobacco smoke contains over 4,000 chemicals (including dozens of carcinogens), it appears unlikely that the health risks from inhaling smoke will be reduced significantly by reducing the levels of a few of those toxins (IOM, 2001). The development of novel cigarette-like products that heat rather than burn the tobacco offers more promise as the resulting aerosol is qualitatively different from smoke. However, to date none of these products have achieved significant market shares.

For now, therefore, there appears to be little likelihood of meaningful harm reduction being achieved via smokers switching to modified cigarettes. Such a strategy appears more likely to repeat the 'Lights and Milds fiasco' which probably led to many smokers continuing to smoke in the false belief these cigarettes are less harmful.

There is, however, relatively good evidence that smokeless tobacco is less harmful than smoked tobacco (Royal College of Physicians, 2007; Foulds et al., 2003; Rodu and Godshall, 2006). Where existing products can be demonstrated to be less harmful, then there is no rationale for banning the less harmful product while allowing the more harmful one to flourish. The example of Sweden (which has high use of smokeless tobacco, low smoking prevalence and a very low proportion of tobacco attributable deaths) suggests that permitting truly less harmful products to be marketed may facilitate a net reduction in harm (Foulds et al., 2006; Bates et al., 2003). This topic is discussed in more detail in the next section.

Switching to smokeless tobacco

As recently as the beginning of the twentieth century, forms of smokeless tobacco (tobacco products that are chewed, sucked or sniffed) were the dominant form of tobacco use. The earliest of these products, a dry snuff which was typically used nasally, is now very uncommon even in countries where it is still freely available (including Germany, India, the USA and some parts of Africa). In some countries however, including India and Sweden, other smokeless tobacco products continue to compete with cigarettes as the most widely used product (Foulds et al., 2003; Reddy et al., 2006). The use of smokeless tobacco in its various forms is in fact common throughout the world, with chewing tobacco and oral snuff (tobacco that is sucked rather than chewed) being used in North America, snus (a moist snuff designed to be placed in the mouth) being widely used in Sweden and more recently introduced in other countries, and paan and gutka (both oral tobacco products) in south-east Asia.

All of these commonly used varieties deliver pharmacologically active doses of nicotine by direct absorption through the lining of the mouth. These different products vary as much as 130-fold in their content and delivery of tobacco toxins (McNeill et al., 2006) some have very high concentrations of tobacco-specific nitrosamines (TSNAs) and are a significant cause of oral cancer (Idris et al., 1998) whereas others, including the snus used in Sweden, have relatively low concentrations of TSNAs and appear to either not to cause cancer, or to present a much lower level of risk (Royal College of Physicians, 2007; Roosaar et al., 2006; Rosenquist et al., 2005; Zatterstrom et al., 2004). Given the harmful effects of nicotine on the foetus, however, all of these products are potentially harmful in pregnancy (Royal College of Physicians, 2007; England et al., 2003). It has been proposed that the variety used in Sweden (snus) is around 90% less harmful to health than smoking (Levy et al., 2004) and has had a net beneficial effect on the health of men in Sweden by acting to reduce the number of daily smokers (Foulds et al., 2003).

Awareness that smokeless tobacco can compete with cigarettes for market share, and that some forms of smokeless tobacco may be markedly less harmful to health than smoked tobacco, has led to a renewed interest within the public health community in the role of smokeless tobacco in reducing smoking-caused mortality and morbidity. This issue has caught the attention of some of the major cigarette manufacturers, who have begun to test market new smokeless tobacco products around the world.

The 2007 Royal College of Physicians report (2007) reviewed the evidence on the health risks of smokeless tobacco. It concluded that, despite the fact that there are many forms of smokeless tobacco which differ substantially in risk profiles, as the known risks are lower than those from smoking and as there is little or no excess risk for COPD or lung cancer, 'in relation to cigarette smoking, the hazard profile of lower risk smokeless tobacco products is very favourable'. Given that smokeless tobacco is much less harmful than smoking, the issue of how smokeless may influence smoking rates is very relevant to judging its overall health impact. If people who start using smokeless are at higher risk of starting smoking or have a lower probability of quitting smoking (all other things being equal), this would add significantly to the health impact of smokeless tobacco use. Conversely, if smokeless tobacco use reduces risk of smoking or helps smokers to quit, that should also be considered in weighing its harmfulness, both for the individual and for public health.

Unfortunately, there is very little available information on patterns of use of smokeless tobacco and effects on smoking prevalence outside of Sweden. Rodu and Godshall (2006) have reviewed the evidence from national surveys in the United States. They reported that the 1986 US Adult Use of Tobacco Survey found that 7% (1.7 million) of male ex-smokers had used smokeless tobacco to help them quit smoking cigarettes, as compared with 1.7% of male ex-smokers (405,000) who had used organized smoking cessation programmes to help them quit smoking. The 1991 U.S. National Health Interview Survey revealed that a third of adult smokeless tobacco users were former cigarette smokers (around 1.8 million). The 1998 NHI Survey revealed that 5.8% of daily snuff users reported quitting smoking cigarettes within the past year, that daily snuffers were three times more likely to report being former smokers than were never snuff users, and that daily snuff users were four times more likely to have quit smoking in the past year than never snuff users.

The question of whether smokeless use acts as a gateway to smoking in the United States has been the subject of heated debate. Kozlowski et al. (2003) have reported that a maximum of 23% of US young smokeless users followed the gateway to smoking, based on the finding that 35% of 23–34 year-old smokeless users had never smoked, and 42% smoked before they used smokeless. They found that those who used cigarettes before moist snuff were 2.1 times more likely to have quit smoking (95% CI 1.21, 6.39) than cigarette-only users. They concluded that the large majority of US smokeless users are non-gateway users, that causal gateway effects should be of minor concern for policy, and that smokeless tobacco may be more likely to prevent smoking than cause it. However, Haddock et al. (2001) in a study of recruits to the US Army, and Tomar (2003) in a longitudinal study of almost 4,000 US male adolescents, both found that young men who started using smokeless tobacco were more likely to subsequently smoke. Collectively, these and other studies in the USA do not provide a clear overall message on the likely impact of smokeless tobacco on smoking behavior.

Recent studies in Sweden, however, appear to be consistent in finding that Swedes who start using snus are less likely to become smokers and Swedish smokers who start using snus are more likely to quit smoking (Gilljham and Galanti, 2003; Ramstrom and Foulds, 2006; Furberg et al., 2005; Rodu et al., 2005; Stegmayr et al., 2005). The data from one of these studies is shown in figure 16.1.

This study (Ramstrom and Foulds, 2006) found that the odds of initiating daily smoking were significantly lower for men who had started using snus than for those who had not (OR = 0.28; 95% CI: 0.22–0.36). Among male primary smokers, 28% started secondary daily snus use and 73% did not. 88% of those secondary snus users had ceased daily smoking completely by the time of the survey as compared with 56% of those primary daily smokers who never became daily snus

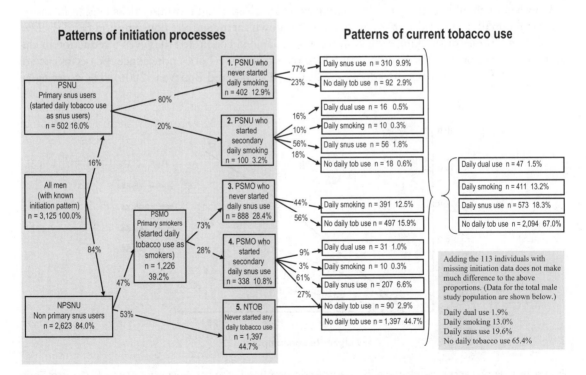

Figure 16.1 Pathways of male tobacco use in Sweden. (Source: Ramström and Foulds, 2006.)

users, (OR = 5.7; 95% CI: 4.9–8.1). Among men who made attempts to quit smoking, snus was the most commonly used cessation aid, being used by 24% on their latest quit attempt.

One potential reason for more switching from smoking to smokeless in Sweden than the United States is that in Sweden the public health authorities have updated their information on health risks according to recent scientific evidence (Ahlbom et al., 1997) whereas in the United States the public have been informed that smokeless tobacco is just as harmful as smoking cigarettes (Carmona, 2003; Kozlowski and Edwards, 2005). In an environment in which smokers are informed and believe that smokeless tobacco is just as harmful to health as smoking, one would not expect many to switch for health reasons. The epidemiology of tobacco use in Sweden suggests that if the public are offered a substantially less harmful smokeless tobacco product along with access to accurate information on relative risks, a substantial proportion can switch to the less harmful product.

Smoking reduction (as opposed to cessation)

The idea of reducing cigarette consumption is largely based on the evidence from large epidemiological studies showing a clear dose response relationship between the number of cigarettes smoked by an individual and that individual's risk of having a smoking-related disease. The most striking dose response relationship is typically found for lung cancer (Law et al., 1997), as shown in figure 16.2.

Thun et al. (1997) examined mortality from chronic obstructive pulmonary disease (COPD) in the second Cancer Prevention Study (CPS-II) and found that the relative risks increased from 5.9 in women smoking 1–9 cigarettes per day, to 25.2 for women smoking 40 or more cigarettes per day (relative to never-smoking women). Similarly, the Nurses Health Study (Stampfer et al., 2000) found adjusted relative risks of coronary heart disease of 3.1 for women smoking up to 14 cigarettes per day and 5.5 for those smoking 15 or more per day.

However, it should be noted that reductions in some disease and mortality risks tend to be disappointingly small or non-existent when smokers cut down their cigarette consumption per day. Two recent large studies of smoking reduction from Scandanavia concluded that even a reduction in cigarette consumption of at least 50% maintained over many years does not reduce the occurrence of smoking related diseases (Godtfredsen et al., 2002; Tverdal and Bjartveit, 2006). The Norwegian

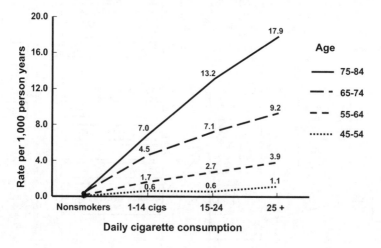

Figure 16.2 Lung cancer risk by age and cigarette consumption in Cancer Prevention Study, II. (Source: Thun et al., 1997.)

study followed up over 50,000 smokers for 3–23 years, including a group of over 475 heavy smokers at baseline who reduced their cigarette consumption by over half for the duration of the study. The main comparison groups in the study were as follows:

- *Never smokers*: People who at both examinations stated that they did not smoke cigarettes daily, and at the first examination said that they had never done so previously (n = 19,000).
- *Ex-smokers*: People who at both examinations stated that they did not smoke cigarettes daily, and at the first examination said that they had done so previously (7,000).
- *Quitters*: People who at the first examination stated that they smoked cigarettes daily, but had quit smoking at the time of the last examination (9,700).
- *Moderate smokers*: People who at the first examination stated that they smoked 1–14 cigarettes per day, and at the last examination said that they smoked cigarettes daily (12,400).
- *Reducers*: People who at the first examination stated a consumption of ≥15 cigarettes per day, and at the last examination reported a consumption of at least 50% less cigarettes per day (475).
- *Heavy smokers*: People who at the first examination stated a consumption of ≥15 cigarettes per day, and at the last examinations did not fall into the categories of reducers or quitters (6,500)

When these 'reducers' were compared to continuing smokers, they had no reduction in mortality, nor any significant reductions in smoking-caused diseases of any diagnostic category. The adjusted all-cause death rate for the different smoking categories is shown in figure 16.3.

The authors concluded that, 'it may give people false expectations to advise that reduction in consumption is associated with reduction in harm'. This is likely because smokers who cut down cigarettes per day 'compensate' by inhaling more from each cigarette in order to obtain their preferred dose of nicotine (Benowitz, 2001; Hatsukami et al., 2006). It has also been established that the duration of smoking (i.e. number of years of smoking) is a much larger determinant of some disease risks (e.g. lung cancer) than the number of cigarettes smoked per day (Knoke et al., 2004). Thus many epidemiological studies use the term 'pack years' (packs of cigarettes per day multiplied by the number of years of smoking) as a crude measure of smoking 'dose' and this measure is often significantly related to disease risk.

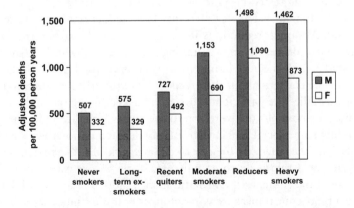

Figure 16.3 Death rates for heavy smokers, smokers who reduced cigarette consumption by > 50% and other categories of smokers and ex-smokers. (Source: Ttverdal and Bjartveit, 2006.)

Hughes (2000) identified five key questions we need to address before advocating Smoking Reduction as a treatment goal. These are:

1. Can smokers successfully reduce their smoking (and what proportion can do this)?
2. Can smokers maintain reduced smoking in the medium to long term (and what proportion can do this)?
3. How much 'compensation' will occur (i.e. compensatory increases in smoke inhalation per cigarette as the number of cigarettes per day is reduced)?
4. Will reduced smoking significantly decrease the health risk of smoking?
5. Will advocacy of smoking reduction promote or undermine cessation?

This section provides a comment on Hughes' review (Sweanor, 1999). Can smokers successfully reduce their smoking in the long term?: Professor Hughes cited data from the California Tobacco Survey (1990–1) (Pierce et al., 1999) and the COMMIT trial which found that 30–43% reductions in reported cigarettes per day were maintained for 2–3 years in non-abstinent smokers (Royal College of Physicians, 2007). This suggests that where there is a supportive environment, smokers can reduce their reported cigarette consumption in the medium term. It has been suggested that many smokers do this 'spontaneously' in the course of their smoking career. However, it should be noted that the circumstances of these two studies were not representative of the situation in most countries of the world or even cities in the USA for that matter (e.g., California was implementing some of the most radical restrictions on smoking in public places at the time, and the COMMIT trial involved a comprehensive community anti-smoking intervention). It is therefore not clear that the smokers in these studies were 'spontaneously' cutting down, as opposed to being forced to restrict by workplace and other smoking bans, or were exaggerating the extent of their reduction due to social pressure in these contexts. It is therefore questionable whether as many people would be as successful at 'spontaneous' smoking reduction in more typical contexts. Close inspection of the results of Hughes et al's analyses of the COMMIT data reveal that 23% of smokers of at least 10 cigarettes per day in 1988 reported a reduction of at least 25% in cigarette consumption by 1990 and 10% maintained this reduction in 1992. Only 3% of the total sample maintained a 50% or greater reduction in cigarettes per day at both 2 and 4 year follow-ups. This study did not involve biochemical measures and so could not examine the extent of compensatory smoking.

How much compensation occurs?: Hughes found that in six experimental trials of smoking reduction in smokers not interested in quitting (Hughes et al., 1999; Glasgow et al., 1985; 1983; Fagerstrom et al., 1997; Rennard et al., 1990), quite large reductions in cigarettes perday (–15% to –63%) were achieved. Although reductions in measured expired carbon-monoxide tended to be smaller (suggesting some compensation was taking place), these were still substantial (–19% to –44%). The three studies with medium-term follow-ups found little loss of effects over 6–30 months.

However, there is some concern about the precision of expired carbon-monoxide as a measure of smoke intake. In such studies the participants are being asked by the researchers to try to cut down their smoking as much as possible and to return to the clinic periodically for support and measurement. There is therefore some social pressure to comply (leading to possible exaggeration of compliance), and particularly to cut down on the day of a clinic visit in order to demonstrate compliance. As carbon-monoxide has a relatively short half life, it may be sensitive to relatively short-term reductions on the day of the clinic visit. One naturalistic study of relapsers which reported on compensation and used a biochemical measure with a longer half life (thiocynate) was the MRFIT trial. This study reported no reduction in thiocyanate despite a self-reported reduction in cigarettes per day of 26% (Hughes et al., 1981). Thiocyanate is not itself without problems, and future studies should use cotinine as a measure of long-term reduction in smoke exposure (in participants not using NRT).

The most impressive reductions in cigarette consumption and expired carbon-monoxide have been obtained in studies of smokers cutting down and substituting with nicotine replacement (Bolliger et al., 2000). While it is perfectly understandable that NRT would help with reduction, and particularly reduce the amount of compensatory smoking, there are doubts about whether this could be sustained in the long term in a non-research context in which smokers have to pay the full cost for the NRT.

There is good evidence that smoking-related morbidity and mortality are highly dose related to the amount of smoking. However, there is also some evidence (e.g., from studies of the effects of passive smoking) of a non-linear relationship between dose and health effects (Law and Hackshaw, 1996). There are also relatively few studies (and certainly no long-term ones) examining the health effects of cutting down. Given that such studies would take many years and be very expensive, and given the evidence from short-term and cross-sectional studies, it seems reasonable to assume that health risk reduction will be proportional to the reduction in toxin intake.

Due to compensatory smoking, the magnitude of the health gain will probably not be accurately estimated by the change in daily cigarette consumption. Those who succeed in reducing their cigarettes per day tend to inhale more smoke from each one than they previously did (in an attempt to get their usual dose of nicotine). In one study by Benowitz and colleagues in the USA (Benowtiz et al., 1986), people who normally smoked an average of 37 cigarettes per day were restricted to only 5 per day for 4 days. It turned out that they inhaled 3 times as much smoke from each cigarette, and so only cut down their smoke exposure by about half, rather than by the 86.5% which would be expected based on the number of cigarettes. Given the possibility that you can get 3 times as much smoke from each cigarette by puffing more intensively, this means that a pack a day smoker would have to cut down to less than 7 per day (i.e., a 65% reduction) to be sure that they had reduced their intake of smoke substantially.

It is also important to bear in mind that while short-term reductions in smoking may reduce some symptoms (e.g., respiratory problems: Rennard et al., 1990) quite quickly, significant reductions in risk for major smoking-related diseases such as COPD and cancer will require that the reduction in smoke intake is maintained for many years.

Does reduced smoking undermine or promote smoking cessation?: Contrary to initial concerns studies of smoking reduction interventions have most often found that participants' motivation to quit smoking actually increased following participation in a reduction programme. For example, Fagerstrom and colleagues found that 93% of participants in their reduction programme reported increased motivation to quit (Rennard et al., 1990). Hughes and Carpenter (2006) reviewed 19 studies of smoking reduction and none reported that reduction undermined future cessation, while 16 reported that reduction was associated with greater future cessation, including the randomized trials of reduction versus non-reduction.

The data from these studies cannot answer the question of whether widespread advocacy of reduction as a goal of treatment, or provision of services to assist with reduction, might prevent individuals who might otherwise have attempted to quit, from doing so.

It is one thing to demonstrate that a significant proportion of smokers can cut down and maintain this in the medium term. It is quite another thing to start to advocate this as a major target for smokers and to use scarce resources (which might otherwise promote cessation) to promote reduction. There is a real risk that if the current clear message that 'The single best thing a smoker can do for their health is to stop smoking' is diluted by adding 'but if you can't stop then try to cut down', then many smokers who would have otherwise tried to quit will go for the easier option.

The idea of setting up 'smoking reduction services' might not be a bad idea in regions which already have sufficient resources to provide good quality smoking cessation services for all smokers who want help to quit; but the reality in most countries is that there are insufficient resources to properly help smokers to quit, without diluting these further by reallocating resources for smokers who want to reduce rather than quit. Given the lack of consistent evidence showing that long-term smoking reduction reduces smoking-related diseases, there is currently insufficient evidence supporting reduced smoking as a treatment goal or endpoint.

Facilitating periods of temporary abstinence with pharmaceutical products

Another approach which is similar to smoking reduction, is that of facilitating periods of temporary abstinence using nicotine replacement. By far the most common scenario here is that an individual will be prohibited from smoking in certain situation (e.g. in the workplace, on public transport, in the hospital) and will use nicotine replacement to reduce their craving and withdrawal symptoms during a period of enforced abstinence. Currently most smokers in these circumstances are forced to take regular cigarette breaks (Borland et al., 1997), and to smoke heavily before and immediately after entering the smoking-restricted situation (Chapman et al., 1997). This compensatory smoking tends to increase over time after implementation of a smoking ban and reduces the potentially large health gains from reduced toxin consumption due to workplace and other smoking bans (Chapman et al., 1999). The net effect of such periods of temporary abstinence may be somewhat similar to the smoking reduction effect and may be enhanced by using NRT. The main difference between 'temporary abstinence' and 'smoking reduction' models is that with temporary abstinence the nicotine replacement is not being presented as a way of permanently cutting down on smoking; rather, it is presented as a means of successfully abstaining for a period of time, with reduced nicotine withdrawal symptoms, where this is perceived as necessary or desirable.

There have been relatively few studies of the use of NRT for this purpose because the products are typically licensed to assist with smoking cessation, This focus on the use of NRT purely to assist an attempt to quit has hindered the potential use of NRT to reduce withdrawal in individuals not trying to quit. Thus many hospitals around the world have complete bans on smoking within its premises (for staff, patients and visitors) but have no organized system of providing NRT for those having to remain within the hospital for long periods of time but who have not made a decision to quit (e.g., inpatients or staff on long shifts). This scenario is repeated in a large number of workplaces. For example, many police forces in the UK have implemented a complete smoking ban in police buildings, including cells. However, they do not have any mechanisms in place to provide NRT to highly nicotine-dependent individuals who are being kept in cells after being charged with criminal offences.

Many addicted smokers are now required to live and work for much of their life in environments in which smoking is prohibited. It seems perfectly reasonable to inform these people that nicotine replacement can and should be used to prevent the mood and performance deficits which result from even relatively short periods of nicotine abstinence (e.g., 8 hours) (Parrott et al., 1996). In situations where the smoker has no choice but to remain in such an environment (e.g., a hospital inpatient, a prisoner, a member of the armed forces) then it is advisable that NRT should be provided routinely and as a treatment for the resultant withdrawal syndrome (Foulds, 2010).

There are a number of important differences between advocating NRT to 'cut down' cigarette consumption and advocating NRT to reduce withdrawal symptoms and craving during a period of temporary abstinence. First, advocating NRT for withdrawal relief does not require a watering down of the clear message on cessation. Second, it avoids the concern in many people's minds about the potential risks of 'simultaneous' smoking and NRT use. Third, the NRT is largely being used in situations in which smoking is not an option (e.g., smoke-free workplaces), and so the smoker does not have the choice of gradually switching to cigarettes. Thus there is no requirement to provide extra resources to assist smokers to reduce, and there is less risk of relapse over time.

Despite these differences, it is likely that the net effect of advocating NRT for temporary tobacco abstinence would be somewhat similar to those which have been claimed for smoking reduction. It is likely that increased provision of NRT in this way would reduce the number of cigarette breaks required in smoke-free workplaces, and reduce the amount of compensatory smoking in these situations. It is also likely that such a policy would: (1) encourage more smokers to try NRT; (2) encourage more smokers to try to quit as they become frustrated with the ongoing costs required to maintain their addiction; and (3) increase awareness among smokers that their craving can be effectively treated with alternatives to tobacco.

Facilitating long-term tobacco abstinence with long-term maintenance pharmaceutical products

Currently virtually all the pharmaceutical products which are licensed to aid smoking cessation are intended to be taken for a relatively short time, usually coinciding with the first 6–12 weeks of the cessation attempt. There is not a large amount of evidence from randomized controlled trials evaluating the effect of longer term availability on abstinence rates. The evidence which does exist is not generally supportive of the need for longer-term maintenance for many smokers. For example, an early trial of nicotine patches found greater relapse after 6 weeks of abstinence in patients allocated nicotine patches compared with patients allocated to placebo patches (Foulds et al., 1993). Another study (Tonnesen et al., 1999) randomized patients to receive 8 or 22 weeks of nicotine patches and found no significant advantage of longer-term patch availability. Overall, therefore, it seems to be the correct strategy to encourage most patients to use an adequate dose of medication during the first 6 weeks of abstinence and then to withdraw from their medication as soon as they feel confident doing so while continuing to abstain from tobacco.

On the other hand, many clinicians comment on the existence of a relatively small proportion of highly addicted smokers who are able to stop smoking with the help of NRT but who consistently relapse within a short time of ceasing medication use. A large proportion of these patients are those who appear to develop clinical levels of depression when attempting to abstain from nicotine/tobacco. It may be that for these individuals there is a rationale for continuing the patient on a maintenance dose of smoking cessation medication (Steinberg et al., 2006; Hall et al., 2004; Tonstadt et al., 2006; Croghan et al., 2007). A recent trial found that use of nicotine patches for up to 6 months yielded better quit rates than 8 weeks of therapy (Schnoll, 2010) and other studies have reported higher quit rates when advising patients to continue to use nicotine replacement therapy 'until you have had fourteen consecutive days without cravings, withdrawal symptoms or near lapses to smoking' (Foulds et al., 2006; Steinberg et al., 2009).The available evidence on long-term use of NRT supports the idea that extremely heavy smokers are more prone to becoming long-term NRT users (Hajek et al., 1988). As more smoking cessation medications become available over the counter from pharmacies or on general sale it will be left more and more to the consumer to decide how long to continue taking the medicine. The available evidence suggests that consumers generally make rationale choices about this (i.e., heavier smokers use medication for longer periods) and if anything, the problems are more to do with under-dosing and use of NRT for too brief a period (e.g. less than 3 weeks) rather than large numbers unnecessarily becoming long-term users (Foulds et al., 2009).

One of the guiding principles of harm reduction should be that it should be possible to provide the public with accurate information with regard to the magnitude of the net reduction in harm which they would be likely to gain by following that strategy. Any strategy which has potential to mislead the public (particularly by implying a larger than likely harm reduction) should be avoided. By this principle, the labelling and marketing of cigarettes according to their FTC measured tar, nicotine and CO yields should be avoided as it falsely implies to the consumer that they would be likely halve their health risk by switching from 10 mg tar yielding cigarettes to 5 mg tar yielding cigarettes (Henningford et al., 1994).

It would also appear to be somewhat difficult to inform a smoker how much they had reduced their risk of disease by cutting down from 25 cigarettes per day to 15 cigarettes per day. However, we could with some confidence inform a smoker that if they chew an adequate dose of nicotine gum during their 10-hour smoke-free work-shift/flight/hospital stay then this would substantially (i.e. at least 50%) reduce the severity of nicotine-withdrawal-related bad mood, poor concentration and tobacco craving. There is little reliable evidence on which to base advice on long-term use of smoking cessation medications, although individual patients and/or clinicians should be able to choose this option if it were indicated on an individual basis.

Iit should be understood that if either of the two main 'tobacco modification' policies discussed above were to be implemented, then this may require a far larger proportion of the smoking population to seek alternative sources of nicotine than is currently the case. In such a scenario it might be anticipated that a larger number (and possibly proportion) of ex-smokers may seek and/or require long-term maintenance on an alternative (or smoke-free) nicotine delivery device. It may be that the success of such policies would be dependent on the easy availability of inexpensive, 'palatable' nicotine replacement medications which would in effect replace tobacco as a source of nicotine. It is therefore important that current policy does not discourage the development or marketing of such products in a way which may jeopardize future restrictions on tobacco products.

Conclusions

1. Switching to supposedly less harmful smoked products is unlikely to result in either individual or societal health gains.
2. Switching to a low-nitrosamine smokeless tobacco product (e.g., snus) will substantially lower health risks as compared with smoking, and may help some smokers quit smoking who would otherwise fail to do so.
3. Some smokers not planning to quit are able to significantly reduce their cigarette consumption, and this appears to increase the likelihood of a quit attempt. However, studies of smokers who have maintained reduced cigarette consumption have not found the anticipated health improvements. This may be due to compensatory increases in the volume of smoke inhaled per cigarette.
4. Dependent smokers should also be encouraged to use NRT to treat nicotine withdrawal symptoms during periods of temporary abstinence (such as hospitalization, smoke-free workplaces, etc.).
5. Current evidence does not support the routine use of long-term maintenance on nicotine replacement therapy but this may be appropriate for some smokers who feel at continued risk of relapse during short-term pharmacotherapy. Product labelling should be adjusted so as not to strongly discourage continued NRT use (Foulds, 2008).
6. Clinicians should continue to focus on encouraging smokers to try to quit smoking completely, and assisting them by providing safe and effective treatments (such as approved medications and counseling).

Note

This chapter is a modified and updated version of a paper previously published in Spanish: Foulds, J. (2007), Estrategias de reduccion del dano en el tabaquismo. In C.J. Ruiz and K. Fagerstrom (eds), *Tratado Tabaquismo*.

References

Ahlbom, A., Olsson, U.A. and Pershagen, G. (1997) Health hazards of moist snuff, *National Board of Health and Welfare*, 11: 1–30, Sweden.

Backinger, C.L., Fagan, P., Matthews, E. and Grana, R. (2003) Adolescent and young adult tobacco prevention and cessation: current status and future directions, *Tob Control*, 12 (supple. 4), 46–53.

Bates, C., Fagerstrom, K., Jarvis, M.J., Kunze, M., McNeill, A. and Ramstrom, L. (2003) European Union policy on smokeless tobacco: a statement in favour of evidence based regulation for public health, *Tob Control*, 12 (4), 360–7.

Bates, C., McNeill, A., Jarvis, M., Gray, N. (1999) The future of tobacco product regulation and labelling in Europe: implications for the forthcoming European Union directive, *Tob Control*, 8 (2), 225–35.

Bauer, U.E., Johnson, T.M., Hopkins, R.S. and Brooks, R.G. (2000) Changes in youth cigarette use and intentions following implementation of a tobacco control program: finding from the Florida Youth Tobacco Survey, 1998–2000, *JAMA*, 284, 723–8.

Benowitz, N.L. (2001) Compensatory smoking of low-yield cigarettes. In National Cancer Institute (ed.), *Risks Associated with Smoking Cigarettes with Low Machine-measured Yields of Tar and Nicotine*, Smoking and Tobacco Control Monograph 13, Bethesda: NCI.

Benowitz, N.L., Jacob, P., Kozlowski, L. and Yu, L. (1986) Influence of smoking fewer cigarettes on exposure to tar, nicotine and carbon monoxide, *N E J Med*, 315, 1310–13.

Bolliger, C.T., Zellweger, J.P., Danielsson, T., Biljon, X.V., Robidou, A., Westin, A., Perruchoud, A.P. and Sawe, U. (2000) Smoking reduction with oral nicotine inhalers: double blind, randomised clinical trial of efficacy and safety, *BMJ*, 321, 329–33.

Borland, R., Cappiello, M. and Owen, N. (1997) Leaving work to smoke, *Addiction*, 92, 1361–8.

Caraballo, R.S., Pederson, L.L., Gupta, N. (2006) New tobacco products: do smokers like them?, *Tob Control*, 15 (1), 39–44.

Carmona, R. (2003) Can tobacco cure smoking? A review of harm reduction: testimony before the US House Subcommittee on Commerce, Trade, and Consumer Protection, Washington, DC, 3 June.

Chapman, S., Haddad, S. and Sindhusake, D. (1997) Do work-place smoking bans cause smokers to smoke 'harder'? Results from a naturalistic observational study, *Addiction*, 92, 607–10.

Chapman, S., Borland, R., Scollo, M., Brownson, R.C., Dominello, A. and Woodward, S. (1999) The impact of smoke-free workplaces on declining cigarette consumption in Australia and the United States, *Am J Public Health*, 89, 1018–23.

Croghan, I.T., Hurt, R.D., Dakhil, S.R., Croghan, G.A., Sloan, J.A., Novotny, P.J., Rowland, K.M., Bernath, A., Loots, M.L., Le-Lindqwister, N.A., Tschetter, L.K., Garneau, S.C., Flynn, K.A., Ebbert, L.P., Wender, D.B. and Loprinzi, C.L. (2007) Randomized comparison of a nicotine inhaler and bupropion for smoking cessation and relapse prevention, *Mayo Clin Proc*, 82 (2), 186–95.

England, L.J., Levine, R.J., Mills, J.L., Klebanoff, M.A., Yu, K.F. and Cnattingius, S. (2003) Adverse pregnancy outcomes in snuff users, *Am J Obstet Gynecol*, 189 (4), 939–43.

Fagerstrom, K.O., Kunze, M., Schoberberger, R., Breslau, N., Hughes, J.R., Hurt, R.D., Puska, P., Ramstrom, L. and Zatonski, W. (1996) Nicotine dependence versus smoking prevalence:comparisons among countries and categories of smokers, *Tobacco Control*, 5, 52–6.

Fagerstrom, K.O., Tejding, R., Ake, W. and Lunnell, E. (1997) Aiding the reduction of smoking with nicotine replacement medications: hope for the recalcitrant smoker?, *Tob Control*, 6, 311–16.

Farrelly, M.C., Davis, K.C., Haviland, M.L., Messeri, P. and Healton, C.G. (2005) Evidence of a dose-response relationship between 'truth' antismoking ads and youth smoking prevalence, *Am J Public Health*, 95 (3), 425–31.

Fiore, M.C., Jaen, C.R., Baker, T.B. et al. (2008) *Treating Tobacco Use and Dependence: 2008 Update – Clinical Practice Guideline*, Rockville: US Department of Health and Human Services, Public Health Service, May.

Foulds, J. (2008) Improving NRT labeling and correcting public misperceptions, *Addiction*, 103, 1379–80.

Foulds, J. (2010) Use of nicotine replacement therapy to treat nicotine withdrawal syndrome and aid temporary abstinence, *International Journal of Clinical Practice*, 64 (3), 292–4.

Foulds, J. and Ghodse, A.H. (1995) The role of nicotine in tobacco smoking: implications for tobacco control policy, *J Royal Society of Health*, 115, 225–30.

Foulds, J., Ramstrom, L., Burke, M. and Fagerstrom, K. (2003) The effect of smokeless tobacco (snus) on public health in Sweden, *Tob Control*, 12, 349–59.

Foulds, J., Steinberg, M.B., Williams, J.M. and Ziedonis, D.M. (2006) Pharmacotherapy for tobacco dependence: past, present and future, *Drug and Alcohol Review*, 25, 57–69.

Foulds, J., Stapleton, J., Hayward, M., Russell, M.A.H., Feyerabend, C., Fleming, T. and Costello, J. (1993) Transdermal nicotine patches with low-intensity support to aid smoking cessation in outpatients in a general hospital: a placebo-controlled trial, *Arch Fam Med*, 2, 417–23.

Foulds, J., Hughes, J., Hyland, A., Le Houezec, J., McNeill, A., Melvin, C., Okuyemi, K., Shiffman, S., Wassum, K., Williams, L. and Zeller, M. (2009) *Barriers to Use of FDA-Approved Smoking Cessation medications: Implications for Policy Action*, Society for Research on Nicotine and Tobacco, March, www.attud.org, accessed 22 February 2012.

Furberg, H., Bulik, C. and Lerman, C., et al. (2005) Is Swedish snus associated with smoking initiation or smoking cessation?, *Tob Control*, 14, 422–424.

Gilljham, H. and Galanti, M.R. (2003) Role of snus (oral moist snuff) in smoking cessation and smoking reduction in Sweden, *Addiction*, 98, 1183–9.

Glantz, S.A., Slade, J., Bero, L.A., Hanauer, P. and Barnes, D. (1996) *The Cigarette Papers*, Berkeley: University of California Press.

Glasgow, R.E., Kleges, R.C. and Vasey, M.W. (1983) Controlled smoking for chronic smokers:an extension and replication, *Addictive Behaviours*, 8, 143–50.

Glasgow, R.E., Klesges, R.C., Klesges, L.M., Vasey, M.W. and Gunnarson, D.F. (1986) Long-term effects of a controlled smoking program: a 2 and a half year follow-up, *Behav Ther*, 16, 303–37.

Godtfredsen, N.S., Holst, C., Prescott, E., Vestbo, J. and Osler, M. (2002) Smoking reduction, smoking cessation, and mortality: a 16-year follow-up of 19,732 men and women from the Copenhagen Centre for Prospective Population Studies, *Am J Epidemiol*, 156 (11), 994–1001.

Gray, N., Henningfield, J.E., Benowitz, N.L., Connolly, G.N., Dresler, C., Fagerstrom, K., Jarvis, M.J. and Boyle, P. (2005) Toward a comprehensive long term nicotine policy, *Tob Control*, 14 (3), 161–5.

Haddock, C.K., Weg, M.V., Debon, M., Klesges, R., et al. (2001) Evidence that smokeless tobacco use is a gateway for smoking initiation in young adult males, *Prev Med*, 32 (3), 262–7.

Hajek, P., Jackson, P. and Belcher, M. (1988) Long term use of nicotine chewing gum. Occurrence, determinants, and effect on weight gain, *JAMA*, 260 (11), 1593–6.

Hall, S.M., Humfleet, G.L., Reus, V.I., Munoz, R.F. and Cullen, J. (2004) Extended nortriptyline and psychological treatment for cigarette smoking, *Am J Psychiatry*, 161 (11), 2100–7.

Hatsukami, D.K., Le, C.T., Zhang, Y., Joseph, A.M., Mooney, M.E., Carmella, S.G. and Hecht, S.S. (2006) Toxicant exposure in cigarette reducers versus light smokers, *Cancer Epidemiol Biomarkers Prev*, 15 (12), 2355–8.

Henningfield, J.E., Kozlowski, L.T., Benowitz, N.L. (1994) A proposal to develop a meaningful label for cigarettes, *JAMA*, 272, 312–14.

Henningfield, J.E., Benowitz, N.L., Slade, J., Houston, T.P., Davis, R.M. and Deitchman, S.D. for the Council on Scientific Affairs AMA (1998) Reducing the addictiveness of cigarettes, *Tobacco Control*, 7, 281–93.

Hughes, G.H., Hymowitz, N., Ockene, J.K., Simon, N. and Vogt, T.M. (1981) The multiple risk factor intervention trial (MRFIT), *Prev Med*, 10, 476.

Hughes, J.R. (2000) Reduced smoking:an introduction and review of the evidence, *Addiction*, 95 (supple. 1), S3–7.

Hughes, J.R. and Carpenter, M.J. (2006) Does smoking reduction increase future cessation and decrease disease risk? A qualitative review, *Nicotine Tob Res*, 8 (6), 739–49.

Hughes, J.R., Cummings, K.M., Hyland, A. (1999) Ability of smokers to reduce their smoking and its association with future smoking cessation, *Addiction*, 94, 109–14.

Idris, A.M., Ibrahim, S.O., Vasstrand, E.N., Johannessen, A.C., Lillehaug, J.R., Magnusson, B., Wallstrom, M., Hirsch J.-M. and Nilsen, R. (1998) The Swedish snus and the Sudanese toombak: are they different?, *Oral Oncology*, 34, 558–66.

IOM (Institute of Medicine) (2001) *Clearing the Smoke: Assessing the Science Base for Tobacco Harm Reduction*, ed. K. Stratton, P. Shetty, R. Wallaceand S. Bondurant, Washington, DC: National Academy Press.

Knoke, J.D., Shanks, T.G., Vaughn, J.W., Thun, M.J. and Burns, D.M. (2004) Lung cancer mortality is related to age in addition to duration and intensity of cigarette smoking: an analysis of CPS-I data, *Cancer Epidemiol Biomarkers Prev*, 13 (6), 949–57.

Kozlowski, L.T. and Edwards, B.Q. (2005) 'Not safe' is not enough: smokers have a right to know more than there is no safe tobacco product, *Tob Control*, 14 (supple 2), ii3–7.

Kozlowski, L.T., O'Connor, R.J., Edwards, B.Q. and Flaherty, B.P. (2003) Most smokeless tobacco use is not a casual gateway to cigarettes: using order of product use to evaluate causation in a national US sample, *Addiction*, 98, 1077–85.

Law, M. and Hackshaw, A.K. (1996) Environmental tobacco smoke, *Brit Med Bull*, 52, 22–34.

Law, M., Morris, J.K., Watt, H.C. and Wald, N.J. (1997) The dose-response relationship between cigarette consumption, biochemical markers and risk of lung cancer, *Br J Cancer*, 75 (11), 1690–3.

Levy, D.T., Mumford, E.A., Cummings, K.M., et al. (2004) The relative risks of a low-nitrosamine smokeless tobacco product compared with smoking cigarettes: estimates of a panel of experts, *Cancer Epidemiol Biomarkers Prev*, 13, 2035–42.

Mackay, J. and Eriksen, M. (2002) *The Tobacco Atlas*, Geneva: World Health organization.

McNeill, A., Bedi, R., Islam, S., Alkhatib, M.N. and West, R. (2006) Levels of toxins in oral tobacco products in the UK, *Tob Control*, 15 (1), 64–7.

O'Connor, R.J., Cummings, K.M., Giovino, G.A., McNeill, A. and Kozlowski, L.T. (2006) How did UK cigarette makers reduce tar to 10 mg or less?, *BMJ*, 332 (7536), 302.

Parrott, A.C., Garnham, N.J., Wesnes, K. and Pincock, C. (1996) Cigarette smoking and abstinence: comparative effects upon task performance and mood state over 24 hours, *Human Psychopharmacology*, 11, 391–400.

Parrott, S., Godfrey, C., Raw, M., West, R., and McNeill, A. (1998) Guidance for commissioners on the cost effectiveness of smoking cessation interventions, *Thorax*, 53 (S5, pt 2) S1–38.

Pierce, J.P., Gilpin, E.A., Emery, S.L., White, M.M., Rosbrook, B., Berry, C.C. and Farkas, A.J. (1999) Has the California tobacco control program reduced smoking?, *JAMA*, 281, 37.

Ramström, L.M. and Foulds, J. (2006) The role of snus (smokeless tobacco) in initiation and cessation of tobacco smoking in Sweden, *Tob Control*, 15 (3), 210–14.

Raw, M., McNeill, A. and West, R. (1998) Smoking cessation guidelines for health professionals: a guide to effective smoking cessation interventions for the health care system, *Thorax*, 53 (S5, pt 1) S1–19.

Reddy, K.S., Perry, C.L., Stigler, M.H. and Arora, M. (2006) Differences in tobacco use among young people in urban India by sex, socioeconomic status, age, and school grade: assessment of baseline survey data, *Lancet*, 18367 (9510), 589–94.

Reid, D. (1996) Tobacco control: an overview, *Brit Med Bull*, 52, 108–120.

Rennard, S.I., Daughton, D., Fujita, J., Oehlerking, M.B., Dobson, J. R, Stahl, M.G., Robbins, R.A. and Thompson, A.B. (1990) Short-term smoking reduction is associated with reduction in measures of lower respiratory tract inflammation in heavy smokers, *Euro Resp J*, 3, 752–9.

Rodu, B., Godshall, W.T. (2006) Tobacco harm reduction: an alternative cessation strategy for inveterate smokers, *Harm Reduct J*, 21 (3), 37.

Rodu, B., Nasic, S. and Cole, P. (2005) Tobacco use among Swedish schoolchildren, *Tob Control*, 14, 405–8.

Roosaar, A., Johansson, A.L., Sandborgh-Englund, G., Nyren, O. and Axell, T.A. (2006) Long-term follow-up study on the natural course of snus-induced lesions among Swedish snus users, *Int J Cancer*, 119 (2), 392–7.

Rosenquist, K., Wennerberg, J., Schildt, E.B., Bladstrom, A., Hansson, B. and Andersson, G. (2005) Use of moist snuff, smoking and alcohol consumption in the aetiology of oral and oropharyngeal cell carcinoma: a population-based case-control study in southern Sweden, *Acta Oto-Laryngologica*, 125, 991–8.

Royal College of Physicians (2007) *Harm Reduction in Nicotine Addiction, Helping People Who Can't Quit: A Report of the Tobacco Advisory Group of the Royal College of Physicians*, London: Royal College of Physicians, October.

Russell, M.A.H. (1991) The future of nicotine replacement, *B J Addiction*, 86, 653–8.

Schnoll, R.A. (2010) Effectiveness of extended duration transdermal nicotine therapy: a randomized trial, *Ann Intern Med*, 152 (3), 144–51.

Stampfer, M.J., Hu, F.B., Manson, J.E., Rimm, E.B. and Willett, W.C. (2000) Primary prevention of coronary heart disease in women through diet and lifestyle, *New England Journal of Medicine*, 342 (1), 16–22.

Stegmayr, B., Eliasson, M. and Rodu, B. (2005) The decline of smoking in northern Sweden, *Scand J Public Health*, 33, 321–14.

Steinberg, M.B., Foulds, J., Richardson, D.L., Burke, M.V. and Shah, P. (2006) Pharmacotherapy and smoking cessation at a tobacco dependence clinic, *Prev Med*, 42 (2), 114–19.

Steinberg, M.B., Greenhaus, S., Schmelzer, A.C., Bover, M., Foulds, J., Hoover, D.R. and Carson, J.L. (2009) Randomized trial of triple combination extended duration pharmacotherapy versus standard duration nicotine patch alone for smokers with medical illness, *Annals of Internal Medicine*, 150 (7), 447–54.

Sweanor, D. (1999) Tobacco and nicotine regulation: time to redress the balance. In C. Tudor-Smith (ed.), *Tackling Tobacco*, Cardiff: Health Promotion Wales.

Thun, M.J., Myers, D.G., Day-Lally, C., Namboodiri, M.M., Calle, E.E., Flanders, W.D., Adams, S.L., Heath, C.W. (1997) Age and exposure-response relationships between cigarette smoking and premature death in Cancer Prevention Study II. In D. R. Shopland, D. M. Burns, L. Garfinkeland J.M. Samet (eds), *Changes in Cigarette-related Disease Risks and Their Implications for Prevention and Control*, Smoking and Tobacco Control Monograph no. 8, Bethesda: DHSS, National Cancer Institute, NIH Publication number 97–4213.

Tomar, S. (2003) Is use of smokeless tobacco a risk factor for cigarette smoking? The U.S. experience, *Nicotine Tob Res*, 5 (4), 561–9.

Tonnesen, P., Paoletti, P., Gustavsson, G., Russell, M.A.H., Saracci, R., Gulsvik, A., Rijcken, B. and Sawe, U. (1999) Higher dosage nicotine patches increase one-year smoking cessation rates: results from the European CEASE trial, *Eur Resp J*, 13, 238–46.

Tonstad, S., Tonnesen, P., Hajek, P., Williams, K.E., Billing, C.B. and Reeves, K.R. (2006) Varenicline Phase 3 Study Group. Effect of maintenance therapy with varenicline on smoking cessation: a randomized controlled trial, *JAMA*, 296 (1), 64–71.

Tverdal, A. and Bjartveit, K. (2006) Health consequences of reduced daily cigarette consumption, *Tob Control*, 15 (6), 472–80.

US Department of Health and Human Services (1988) *The Health Consequences of Smoking: Nicotine Addiction*, Washington, DC: US Government Printing Office.

World Health Organization (WHO) (1997) *Tobacco or Health: A Global Status Report*, Geneva. Switzerland.

Zatterstrom, U.K., Svennson, M., Sand, L., Nordgren, H. and Hirsch, J.M. (2004) Oral cancer after using Swedish snus (smokeless tobacco) for 70 years: a case report, *Oral Dis*, 10 (1), 50–3.

Chapter 17

DRUGS AND HARM REDUCTION: CANNABIS AND THE CANNABINOIDS

Stefan Brugger, Laurence J. Reed, James Stone and David J. Nutt

Introduction

Human use of psychoactive preparations of the plant species *Cannabis sativa* and *Cannabis indica* has a long history. The practice is believed to have originated between five and six thousand years ago in the steppes of Central Asia or China, although evidence for the cultivation of hemp is even older (Merlin, 2003). Today, cannabis is the most widely used illicit drug in the world (UNODC, 2010). Prevalence rates are particularly high among young people: an estimated 30% of Europeans aged 15 to 24 have tried the drug and over a quarter have used it in the last month (EMCDDA, 2010). While such widespread use is indicative of an inherent perception that cannabis use is safe, there has been growing concern that there are longer term harms associated with cannabis.

First and foremost, cannabis smoking shows clear relationship with cardiovascular complications and accidents associated with cannabis intoxication. These are uncontroversial 'indirect' harms associated with cannabis and should prompt straightforward harm reduction strategies. This chapter however focuses on the potential harms associated with exposure to cannabinoids per se and how these may be mitigated or treated. Specifically, there are the concerns that long-term cannabis use may lead to cognitive impairment, addiction and dependence, and chronic psychiatric complications such as psychosis and schizophrenia. The potential associations between cannabinoid exposure and psychiatric complications are particularly pertinent, given that the cannabinoids are a potentially very useful source of novel pharmaceutical development. For example, cannabis itself is actively under investigation and development as valuable treatments for a variety of common chronic pain conditions including cancer-related and neuropathic pain (Martín-Sánchez et al., 2009; Aggarwal et al., 2009). Similarly, drug development targeting the cannabinoid systems is actively being pursued with the aim of producing analgesic agents with superior efficacy and side effect profiles for this potentially enormous market (Pisanti et al., 2009; Anand et al., 2009).

Thus, the number of people who will potentially be exposed to cannabis and the cannabinoids – whether licitly or illicitly – will represent a significant proportion of the population at all ages. Hence there is a pressing need to examine the evidence of harm related to cannabis and cannabinoid use, and to examine to what extent a better understanding of the neurobiology of the cannabinoid system may ameliorate these harms. This chapter first examines the neurobiology of the cannabinoids and the cannabinoid systems before examining in-depth the evidence for the harms of chronic cannabis and cannabinoid use with respect to dependence, cognitive impairment, and psychosis and schizophrenia. In conclusion, we summarise the strength of the current evidence, the areas for further research, and the prospects for development of patterns of cannabis and cannabinoid use that maximises benefit while minimising harm.

Harm Reduction in Substance Use and High-Risk Behaviour: International Policy and Practice, First Edition.
Edited by Richard Pates and Diane Riley.
© 2012 Blackwell Publishing Ltd. Published 2012 by Blackwell Publishing Ltd.

Uncontroversial 'indirect' harms of cannabis and the cannabinoids

In recreational use, cannabis is frequently smoked, often with tobacco. Cannabis smoking has been associated with a greater risk of respiratory symptoms compared with non-smokers, even after accounting for the effects of tobacco smoking (Moore et al., 2005). The evidence linking cannabis smoking to impaired lung function and development of COPD is inconsistent, although it has been suggested that this inconsistency may be due to geographical variation in the availability of cannabis preparations and methods of smoking (Reid et al., 2010). A recent systematic review found little evidence for an association between cannabis and lung cancer after adjusting for tobacco smoking, although there was evidence of increased tar exposure and lung histopathological changes in cannabis smokers compared with non-smokers and tobacco-only smoking controls (Mehra et al., 2006).

One possible harm reduction strategy with respect to lung diseases would be to encourage the use of vaporisers to administer cannabis. Among heavy users, use of vaporisers rather than smoking has been associated with fewer respiratory symptoms and also potentially with improved lung function (Earleywine and Barnwell, 2007; Van Dam and Earleywine, 2010). Alternatively, it seems plausible that cannabis smoked without tobacco may be less harmful than when smoked with tobacco – simply because it burns at a lower temperature. Use of water pipes ('bongs') would further reduce the temperature of the inhaled smoke. It is also worth noting that use of a vaporiser or other tobacco-free method of administration would eliminate the various well-documented harms of concomitant tobacco smoking, including the risk of subsequent development of nicotine dependence. This is especially important in light of recent studies showing that in some cultures cannabis smoking in adolescence is associated with regular tobacco use and nicotine dependence in adulthood, which raise the possibility that cannabis acts as a 'reverse-gateway drug' for tobacco (Patton et al., 2005; Timberlake et al., 2007).

Ingestion is also a popular method of cannabis administration and one which also has potential harm-reduction implications. Cannabinoids are highly lipophilic and can easily be extracted into oil or butter for use in cooking, thereby avoiding all harms associated with smoking. However, effective titration of dose becomes more difficult. When smoked, onset of the psychoactive effect of Δ^9–THC occurs within just a few minutes, allowing the user to alter their rate of intake according to their level of intoxication, whereas the effects of orally administered cannabis take considerably longer to manifest themselves. Thus freed from the negative feedback supplied by rapid-onset intoxication, a user's ingestion of cannabinoids may reach substantially higher levels than intended, leading to undesired aversive effects (Moreira and Wotjak, 2010).

Short-term and effects and pharmacology

Cannabis contains approximately 500 psychoactive compounds, including no fewer than 70 different cannabinoids (Elsohly and Slade, 2005). While different preparations of cannabis – hashish, herbal, skunk (sinsemilla) – contain varying proportions of each compound, the main psychoactive ingredient is Delta-9-Tetrahydrocannabinol (Δ^9–THC), whose properties are mediated by its partial agonism at cannabinoid 1 (CB1) receptors (Pertwee, 2006).

The most frequently cited effect of cannabis among recreational users is one of 'relaxation' (Green et al., 2003), although acute anxiety reactions have been reported, especially in previously naive subjects (Crippa et al., 2009). Other common negative effects include paranoia, drowsiness, depression, dizziness and feelings of hunger (Gonzalez, 2007). Experimental administration of Δ^9–THC to healthy subjects under controlled conditions reproduces these effects and has allowed detailed measurement of significant increases in 'positive' psychotic symptoms and a range of neuro-psychological deficits in memory, verbal reasoning and decision-making (D'Souza et al., 2004; Morrison et al., 2009; Gonzalez, 2007). Other reported psychiatric consequences of cannabis consumption include anxiety states such as depersonalisation (Medford et al., 2003) and even koro, a culture-specific syndrome characterised by the belief that one's external genitalia are shrinking, or retracting into the body and the fear that they will disappear altogether (Chowdhury and Bera, 1994).

Synthetically produced Δ^9–THC, (dronabinol) and nabilone, a synthetic analogue of THC, are used medically as antiemetics for refractory chemotherapy-associated nausea and vomiting (Pertwee, 2009), while Sativex, an oromucosal spray containing approximately equal quantities of Δ^9–THC and cannabidiol (CBD) is used to treat spasticity in multiple sclerosis (Lakhan and Rowland, 2009). Cannabis itself is actively under investigation and development as source of valuable treatments for a variety of common chronic pain conditions including cancer-related and neuropathic pain (Martín-Sánchez et al., 2009; Aggarwal et al., 2009). Similarly, drug development targeting the cannabinoid systems is actively being pursued with the aim of producing analgesic agents with superior efficacy and side effect profiles for this potentially enormous market (Pisanti et al., 2009; Anand et al., 2009).

The central nervous system cannabinoid CB1 receptor is remarkably abundant, being expressed on a variety of neuronal and non-neuronal cell types, and particularly concentrated in the frontal neocortical areas, substantia nigra, putamen and pallidum. Retrograde endocannabinoid signalling via presynaptic CB1 receptors modulates the balance of excitatory and inhibitory activity in the reward circuitry of the basal forebrain. Activation of CB1 receptors has been shown to be involved in the regulation of reinforcement to addictive substances (Lupica and Riegel, 2005; Maldonado et al., 2006), as well as the regulation of feeding behaviour (Di Marzo and Matias, 2005; Williams and Kirkham, 2002), which explains the 'munchies' frequently described by cannabis users. Indeed, both cannabis and dronabinol appear to be effective appetite stimulants capable of treating anorexia-induced weight loss in patients with HIV and AIDS (Haney et al., 2007).

A relatively novel positron emission tomography (PET) tracer, MK-9470, gives a quantitative measure of CB1 distribution in the human brain (Burns et al., 2007), and has been shown to demonstrate an inverse relationship with novelty seeking traits within cortical and subcortical regions including the amygdala (Van Laere et al., 2009). This tracer may be useful in examining the role of CB1 receptors in resolving some of the relationships observed between cannabis use and psychiatric disorder to which this chapter is devoted.

Neuroimaging the acute effects of cannabis and the cannabinoids

Some drugs of abuse are believed to exert their reinforcing effects by increasing synaptic dopamine levels in the ventral striatum (Wise, 2004). In animal models, THC administration is known to be reinforcing in certain situations (Panagis et al., 2008) and has been shown to increase striatal dopamine levels (Fadda et al., 2006), although perhaps by an 'atypical' mechanism (Lupica et al., 2004).

The evidence for an effect of THC on dopaminergic neurotransmission in humans is decidedly weaker. The effect on brain dopamine levels of THC administration has been assessed using positron emission tomography (PET) and single photon emission computed tomography (SPECT) dopamine D2 receptor tracers. One group has reported a small but significant (3–4%) reduction in striatal binding of the PET tracer [^{11}C]raclopride (indicative of 136% increased dopamine release) following inhalation of 8 mg vaporised THC (Bossong et al., 2008). However this result was not replicated in a subsequent [^{11}C]raclopride study, which found no significant changes in striatal binding following oral administration of 10 mg THC, despite increases in psychosis-like symptoms (Stokes et al., 2009). A further study employing the SPECT tracer [123I]IBZM and 2.5 mg intravenous THC likewise failed to demonstrate any effect on dopamine receptor binding, suggesting that THC administration in humans does not cause a significant dopamine release in striatum (Barkus et al., 2010). It is also interesting to note that THC-induced effects are not significantly attenuated by haloperidol, which suggests that they are not mediated via increased activation of striatal D2 receptors (D'Souza et al., 2008a).

Stokes and colleagues did find significant cannabis-induced reduction in [^{11}C]raclopride binding in extrastriatal regions, specifically the frontal and temporal cortex. Despite concerns as to the validity of assaying changes in cortical dopamine levels using [^{11}C]raclopride (Egerton et al., 2009), the authors concluded that this finding was indeed best accounted for by a THC-induced increase in dopamine concentration (Stokes et al., 2010). COMT genotype was also found to correlate with changes in [^{11}C]raclopride binding in cortical regions. This finding is especially interesting in light of research linking dopaminergic dysfunction in frontal regions to cognitive and negative symptoms in schizophrenia (Howes and Kapur, 2009; Goldman-Rakic et al., 2004; Abi-Dargham and Moore, 2003), and the finding of a lower prevalence of neuropsychological defects in patients presenting with a first episode of psychosis who also have a history of cannabis use (Yücel et al., 2010).

Long-term effects of cannabis and the cannabinoids

Evidence for non-acute effects of chronic cannabis consumption comes largely from cross-sectional retrospective studies. A meta-analysis of neuropsychological data by Grant and colleagues revealed small but significant negative effects of prolonged cannabis use on measures of learning and memory (Grant et al., 2003). Subsequent studies suggested that that while these effects resolved with abstinence, persistent deficits in decision-making and inhibitory control remain, although it is possible that these are antecedent to cannabis use (Gonzalez, 2007).

A recent systematic review of 41 neuroimaging studies found poor evidence for any relationship between chronic cannabis use and brain structure, although there was some evidence for lower cerebral blood flow, particularly in the prefrontal region (Martín-Santos et al., 2010). In contrast, four proton magnetic resonance spectroscopy studies have reported interesting findings in relation to cannabis. Hermann and colleagues found a significant reduction in N-acetylaspartate concentration – a surrogate marker of neuronal integrity (Moffett et al., 2007) – in the dorsolateral prefrontal cortex (DLPFC) associated with cannabis use in recreational users (Hermann et al., 2007), while a study of users of multiple drugs reported a significant negative association between NAA levels and cannabis use in Brodmann area 45, also located in the frontal cortex (Cowan et al., 2009), and a recent study of adolescent chronic cannabis users found a reduction in NAA levels in the anterior cingulate cortex (ACC) (Prescot et al., 2011). Reduced NAA levels have also been reported in the basal ganglia in chronic cannabis users (Chang et al., 2006). It is worth noting that reductions in frontal NAA levels are also a consistent finding in patients with chronic and first-episode schizophrenia (Brugger et al., 2011).

Association between cannabis use and development of psychotic illness

A number of lines of evidence are suggestive of an association between cannabis use and psychosis. Higher than average levels of cannabis use have been noted amongst people reporting experience of psychotic symptoms in general population surveys (Johns et al., 2004) and in patients presenting with and receiving treatment for psychotic illness (Barnett et al., 2007; Green et al., 2005; Koskinen et al., 2010). In patients with schizophrenia, these levels have increased dramatically over time, at a rate far outstripping that seen in the general population or indeed in patients with other psychiatric illnesses (Boydell et al., 2006). Longitudinal studies have consistently reported findings of association between cannabis use and psychotic symptoms (Moore et al., 2007).

Several causal explanations for these associations have been proposed (Degenhardt et al., 2003). One hypothesis is that use of cannabis, particularly if prolonged or heavy, causes psychotic illness/ schizophrenia: (1) in vulnerable individuals already likely to develop the disease; and (2) in a significant proportion of users who were otherwise at low risk. Alternatively, cannabis may be precipitate psychotic illness but only in those at high risk of developing it anyway. Finally, it is possible that psychotic illness increases susceptibility to cannabis dependence (the so-called reverse causation hypothesis (Ferdinand et al., 2005)), or that heavy cannabis use/dependence and psychotic illness share certain genetic or environmental risk factors. If the association between cannabis use and psychotic illness is indeed one of causation, we would expect to observe the characteristic temporal order of that relation: cannabis use should precede later psychosis. We might also hope to discern a dose-response effect, whereby the prevalence of psychosis increases with greater frequency and intensity of antecedent cannabis use (Hill, 1965).

Is this the case? A number of longitudinal cohort studies (and systematic reviews thereof) have attempted to answer this question (Minozzi et al., 2010), the most recent and thorough of which identified 11 papers reporting data from 7 such studies (Moore et al., 2007). Meta-analyses of this data showed that people reporting use of cannabis (ever) were at increased risk of developing psychotic symptoms relative to non-users (adjusted odds ratio 1.41). This risk was higher still in the most frequent users (adjusted odds ratio 2.09) (Moore et al., 2007). A differential effect of age of first use was found in one study: first use of cannabis before the age of 16 was more strongly associated with psychotic symptoms (Arseneault et al., 2002).

The effect of cannabis use on risk of developing a psychotic *disorder*, rather than psychotic symptoms, was evaluated in three studies cited by Moore and colleagues, although the severity threshold for meriting the description of disorder differed in each. While pooled analyses of data from these studies confirmed the presence of a significant association, it is worth examining each individually.

The 1969 Swedish Conscripts Cohort study of 50,087 male subjects (Andréasson et al., 1987; Zammit et al., 2002) found that cannabis use (ever) reported at conscription (aged 18–20) was associated with later development of schizophrenia, even after adjustment for a number of confounding factors (odds ratio: 1.5). The relationship was dose-dependent (odds ratio for heaviest users: 3.1). Conscripts diagnosed with psychosis at baseline were excluded.

The Dunedin multidisciplinary health and development birth cohort (1972–3) study of 1,037 individuals found that cannabis use recorded at age 15 or 18 was associated with later development of a schizophreniform disorder (Arseneault et al., 2002). However, this association was no longer significant after controlling for the presence of childhood psychotic symptoms, recorded at age 11. Additionally, the study did not account for the possibility that later-developing psychotic symptoms (i.e. between ages 11 and 15) influenced subsequent cannabis use.

Finally, the Netherlands Mental Health Survey and Incidence Study (NEMESIS) of 4,045 psychosis-free individuals (aged 18–64) sampled from the Dutch general population (van Os et al., 2002) found a significant association between cannabis use and later development of psychotic symptoms clinically assessed as 'needing care'.

The evidence from longitudinal studies is therefore compatible with the hypothesis that cannabis use is a significant factor in the aetiology of psychotic disorder, whether narrowly or widely construed. The fact that both the Swedish Conscript and NEMESIS studies specifically excluded individuals exhibiting psychotic symptoms at baseline significantly reduces the plausibility of the hypothesis that 'reverse causation' – increased cannabis consumption consequent to the development of psychotic symptoms – is solely to account for this association. However, this evidence does not rule out the possibility that the association is at least partly mediated indirectly by some common underlying causal factor.

Modelling studies of the association between cannabis use and psychosis

The hypothesis that cannabis is responsible for the development of schizophrenia in significant numbers of individuals who would not otherwise develop the illness can be examined using the techniques of epidemiological modelling. In such studies, the hypothesis is assumed to be the case and changes in incidence and prevalence of schizophrenia consequent to increasing levels of cannabis use are predicted. The predictions of the model can then be compared with real-world epidemiological data, in light of which the reasonableness of the assumptions can be evaluated.

A study modelling the effect of increased cannabis use in Australia since the 1980s predicted a substantial increase in the incidence (and later, prevalence) of schizophrenia. However, no evidence for an increased incidence or prevalence of schizophrenia was found (Degenhardt et al., 2003). The authors concluded that there was no support for the hypothesis that cannabis use had caused schizophrenia in individuals who would otherwise not have developed the disease. However, a reduction in the age of onset of psychosis over time was noted, and this was compatible with an alternative hypothesis: that cannabis use had accelerated the onset of schizophrenia in individuals who were highly likely to have become psychotic anyway. A similar UK-based study contrasted predicted increases of 29% and 12% in incidence and prevalence by 2010 (Hickman et al., 2007) with evidence from the UK General Practice Research Database of stable or slightly declining rates of schizophrenia (Frisher et al., 2009).

Effect of cannabis use on outcomes in psychotic disorder

The suggestion that a major effect of cannabis use is to accelerate the onset of psychosis in susceptible individuals is strongly supported by evidence from a recent meta-analysis of studies examining differences in age of onset for substance-using and non-substance using patients. The findings were striking: average age of onset was 2.7 years earlier in samples of cannabis users relative to samples of non-drug users; furthermore, the proportion of cannabis users in 'mixed' patient samples (i.e. samples containing users of different substances) was significantly and independently predictive of the variation between these samples in average reduction in age of onset relative to non-user groups (Large et al., 2011). There is also evidence for an interaction between cannabis use and the COMT Val158Met polymorphism in determining age of onset of psychosis (Estrada et al., 2011; Pelayo-Terán et al., 2010). Given the association between early onset of psychosis and poor clinical outcomes (Rabinowitz et al., 2006; Lauronen et al., 2007), measures aimed reducing cannabis use by people at high risk of psychosis constitute an important harm-reduction strategy even if many of these individuals will ultimately develop a psychotic illness later in life.

In individuals already diagnosed with a psychotic disorder, a number of follow-up studies have found associations between continued cannabis use and poorer outcomes independent of effects of the former upon age of onset. These outcomes include severity of positive symptoms, thought disorder and hostility, a more continuous course of illness (i.e. fewer remissions) and more frequent hospitalisations (Grech et al., 2005; Caspari, 1999). Patients with psychosis appear to be more sensitive to the acute symptom-worsening effects of cannabis, as well as effects on cognitive functions such as attention, memory and executive functioning than healthy individuals (D'Souza et al., 2005). A study of subjects at ultra-high risk (UHR) of psychosis and those with a recent onset of schizophrenia examined the effects of cannabis in the prodromal phase, finding greater levels of anxiety, depression and psychotic symptoms, both immediately following use and in the long term, compared with cannabis users from the general population (Peters et al., 2009). Conversely, abstinence from cannabis use after a first episode of psychosis has been associated with long-term functional improvements (González-Pinto et al., 2009).

Why, then, do patients with psychosis continue to use cannabis with a greater prevalence than the general population? Self-medication is a possible explanation – perhaps to reduce negative and affective symptoms (Compton et al., 2004; Spencer et al., 2002). A recent 'experience sampling' study which tracked the cannabis use, mood and psychotic symptoms of a group of patients and controls on a near-hourly basis, suggests an answer. Use of cannabis had a greater positive effect on mood in the patient group compared to the controls, as well as a greater tendency to induce psychotic symptoms. However, the timescales on which these two effects operated differed: decreases in negative affect correlated with recent cannabis use; whereas increases in psychotic symptoms correlated only with previous cannabis use. This difference in timing may explain the continued use of cannabis by patients with psychosis despite the profoundly negative consequences (Henquet et al., 2010).

Cannabis dependence syndrome

Δ^9–THC and other CB1 agonists are reinforcing in animal models of reward including intravenous and intracranial self-administration, conditioned place preference and drug discrimination. With chronic use, tolerance develops and, following the administration of a CB1 antagonist (rimonabant), withdrawal phenomena are seen (Panlilio et al., 2010; González et al., 2005). Tolerance also develops in humans, while abstinence symptoms include anger, irritability, anxiety, sleep difficulty, appetite problems and depression, lasting up to 14 days (D'Souza et al., 2008b; Ramaekers et al., 2009). These may appear mild in comparison with the dramatic withdrawal syndromes associated with benzodiazepines and alcohol (Budney et al., 2004); this comparative mildness may be due to the relatively lengthy half-life of Δ^9–THC in the blood (Karschner et al., 2009).

Nevertheless, cannabis dependence is a highly prevalent phenomenon. In Europe, an estimated 1% of European adults use cannabis on a daily or almost-daily basis (EMCDDA, 2010). Survey data from the US suggest that 10% of people who ever use cannabis will meet the criteria for dependence by the age of 54 (Wagner and Anthony, 2002), with recent evidence suggesting that this risk is more than twice as high in male users than in female users (Wagner and Anthony, 2007) (although note higher risks to users of either gender of developing cocaine or alcohol dependence). Concomitant tobacco smoking also appears to be a risk factor for the transition to dependence or 'problematic use' (Agrawal and Lynskey, 2009; Ream et al., 2008). Problems associated with cannabis use form a major part of the workload of drug treatment services across Europe and constitute the primary reason for referral in 21% of cases, second only to heroin (EMCDDA, 2010).

Treatment options for cannabis dependence are remarkably limited. Several different types of psychotherapy have been developed specifically for cannabis-dependence, including cognitive behavioural (CBT), motivational and group therapy approaches; all have been found to be effective in reducing levels of cannabis intake and symptoms of dependence. However, few patients achieve prolonged periods of abstinence (Denis et al., 2006).

A number of medications have been investigated as potential pharmacotherapies for cannabis dependence. Administration of oral Δ^9–THC at doses producing no discernible intoxication (10 mg, 3–5 times/day) in outpatient and laboratory studies has been shown to reduce craving, anxiety, mood disturbance, anorexia and sleeping problems associated with withdrawal (Haney et al., 2003c; Budney et al., 2007), with higher doses (30 mg 3 times/day) completely eliminating withdrawal symptoms (Budney et al., 2007). Oral Δ^9–THC has also been shown to be well-tolerated in adolescent cannabis users, a particularly important group from a harm-reduction perspective (Gray et al., 2008). A reduction in withdrawal symptoms and improved treatment retention were noted in the first randomised placebo-controlled trial of oral Δ^9–THC in treatment-seeking patients (dose: up to 20 mg twice daily), although no improvement in abstinence rates after 6–8 weeks of treatment were seen (Levin et al., 2011). The effectiveness of higher doses in treatment-seeking patients has yet to be established.

An alternative approach would be to *block* the rewarding effects of cannabis, perhaps most obviously via blocking the cannabinoid CB1 receptor. Administration of the CB1 antagonist rimonabant has been shown to attenuate the effects of cannabis in humans (Huestis et al., 2001) and could thus provide a degree of insurance against relapse in dependent patients undergoing withdrawal. While trials of rimonabant as an anti-obesity agent were terminated due to concerns about its propensity to induce serious neuropsychiatric side effects (Topol et al., 2010), the potential benefits are likely to be considerably greater in cannabis dependence. Use of CB1 antagonists in the treatment of cannabis dependence should therefore be explored in more detail.

The opioid antagonist naltrexone, known to reduce the rewarding effects of THC in animals, has also been investigated as a potentially useful pharmacological agent in the treatment of cannabis dependence. However, the results have not been encouraging: in heavy users, naltrexone pre-treatment *enhanced* the subjective and reinforcing effects of smoked cannabis and orally administered Δ^9–THC and had a negative impact on performance in a number of cognitive tasks assessing attention, learning and memory (Cooper and Haney, 2010; Haney et al., 2003a). Although another study produced different results – namely that naltrexone reduced the effects of low dose (20 mg) oral Δ^9–THC in cannabis smokers (Haney, 2006) – the abuse potential in at least a subset of users would appear to preclude the use of this medication in a clinical setting.

Other investigations have focused on direct palliation of some of the unpleasant symptoms of cannabis withdrawal. Lofexidine, an α2-adrenoceptor agonist, was found to improve sleep and reduce 'relapse' in a sample of non-treatment seeking temporarily abstinent patients but exacerbated anorexia and weight loss, while the combination of lofexidine and orally administeredΔ^9–THC appeared to produce synergistic improvements in sleep, craving and measures of 'relapse' (Haney et al., 2008). The antidepressant nefazodone has shown some potential in reducing the anxiety associated with cannabis withdrawal in non-treatment seeking patients (Haney et al., 2003b), although this effect was not replicated randomised placebo-controlled trial. Additionally, nefazodone failed to show any superiority over placebo in reducing other withdrawal symptoms or in increasing abstinence rates (Carpenter et al., 2009). The same trial also failed to find any significant benefit of the smoking-cessation drug bupropion.

A number of other drugs have also been investigated. These include the highly sedating and appetite-stimulating antidepressant mirtazapine, which (perhaps not surprisingly) has been shown to significantly improve symptoms of sleep disturbance and anorexia in non-treatment seeking users undergoing a period of temporary abstinence, while having no effect on other symptoms of withdrawal (Haney et al., 2010). Likewise, the sedative/hypnotic zolpidem reduced sleep disruption in abstinent cannabis users (Vandrey et al., 2011). Drugs that do not appear to have a significant positive impact upon symptoms of withdrawal or on abstinence levels include the GABA-B receptor agonist baclofen (Haney et al., 2010) and divalproex sodium (valproate) (Levin et al., 2004; Haney et al., 2003c), while the results of a randomised placebo controlled trial of the anxiolytic agent buspirone are strongly equivocal (McRae-Clark et al., 2009). While the existence of an open label trial of the potentially toxic mood stabiliser lithium carbonate may appear to suggest a degree of desperation in the search for effective pharmacotherapies for cannabis dependency, the results do suggest the possibility that this medication may actually be of some clinical usefulness (Winstock et al., 2009). Another emerging alternative approach to treatment is to target the cognitive dysfunction associated with chronic cannabis use with both neuropsychological interventions and pharmacological cognitive enhancers such as anti-cholinesterase inhibitors (Sofuoglu et al., 2010) or modafinil (Sugarman et al., 2011).

A positive role for cannabidiol?

Cannabidiol is the second most abundant cannabinoid found in Cannabis sativa. Unlike Δ^9–THC, it has no psychotomimetic effects but appears to oppose the actions of cannabinoid CB1 and CB2 receptor agonists; however the mechanism of action is unknown and probably does not involve a direct interaction with the receptor (Mechoulam et al., 2007). In healthy subjects, cannabidiol and Δ^9–THC appears to have opposing effects: Δ^9–THC is anxiogenic, whereas cannabidiol appears to be anxiolytic and also to attenuate the psychotomimetic effects of Δ^9–THC. Furthermore, the two cannabinoids were shown to have the opposite effects on regional brain activation (as indexed by fMRI-measured BOLD responses) in verbal recall and response inhibition tasks, during visual and auditory processing and in a task designed to elicit an emotional response (viewing fearful faces) (Bhattacharyya et al., 2010; Fusar-Poli et al., 2009).

Cannabidiol may also exert an antipsychotic effect in the context of recreational cannabis use. Different preparations of cannabis (skunk/sinsemilla, hashish etc.) vary in the relative concentrations of cannabidiol and Δ^9–THC they contain. Morgan and Curran analysed hair samples of a group of cannabis smokers and non-smokers to determine exposure to Δ^9–THC and/or cannabidiol, and found significantly higher levels of positive schizophrenia-like symptoms in the 'Δ^9–THC only' group compared to both the 'no cannabinoids' group and the 'Δ^9–THC and cannabidiol' group. Levels of Δ^9–THC did not differ significantly between the two cannabis-exposed groups, suggesting a genuine antipsychotic effect of cannabidiol (Morgan and Curran, 2008).

In a further study, measures of cannabis users' memory, affective state and schizophrenia-like symptoms were assessed under two conditions: following acute intoxication with a cannabis preparation of their own choosing; and in a drug-free state. These measures were then compared in two subsets of individuals: those smoking cannabis with the highest cannabidiol content; and those smoking cannabis with the lowest cannabidiol content (no significant difference in Δ^9–THC levels were found). In this acute setting, high levels of cannabidiol did not protect against psychotomimetic symptoms but did significantly reduce subjects' anxiety levels and appeared to completely protect against the memory-impairing effects seen in smokers of low-cannabidiol preparations (Morgan et al., 2010b). Furthermore, high-cannabidiol preparations were shown to reduce subjects' attentional bias to cannabis-related cues following intoxication, whereas low-cannabidiol preparations did not. Attentional bias, a measure of the incentive salience of a stimulus, is believed to index a subject's 'appetite', in this case for further consumption of cannabis (Morgan et al., 2010a).

Subjects smoking low-cannabidiol preparations also reported higher levels of subjective 'liking' for drug related stimuli.

Cannabidiol may also be protective against the increased risk of development of clinical levels of psychosis, a phenomenon associated with cannabis use. A case control study found that cannabis-smoking patients presenting with a first episode of psychosis were more likely to users of high-potency, low-cannabidiol cannabis (sinsemilla) than matched cannabis-using and otherwise healthy community controls (Di Forti et al., 2009). Cannabidiol may also have neuroprotective properties. Inverse correlations have been reported between cannabidiol content of a subject's preferred cannabis preparation and the degree of NAA reduction in the putamen/globus pallidum (Hermann et al., 2007) and the degree of grey matter volume loss in the right hippocampus (Demirakca et al., 2011).

Cannabidiol may also be useful medically in the treatment of established psychosis. Preliminary trial data comparing cannabidiol and amilsulpride found that while both treatments showed similar efficacy, cannabidiol was associated with significantly fewer side-effects (Leweke et al., 2009), while an open label trial also suggested that cannabidiol may be useful as an add-on therapy for psychosis associated with Parkinson's disease (Zuardi et al., 2009). Given the serious and disabling side effects of most types of antipsychotic medication (Muench and Hamer, 2010), as well as their limited efficacy in a significant subset of patients (Asenjo Lobos et al., 2010), this finding may prove very significant. Taken together, while these results suggest that cannabidiol may have a potential role in the treatment of both cannabis dependence and psychosis, they do suggest that we should be very worried about the trend for diminishing levels of cannabidiol in 'street' cannabis. Policies to reverse or attenuate this trend and alert users to the potential additional dangers associated with low-cannabidiol preparations might constitute an effective harm-reduction strategy.

Summary and conclusions

Despite the fact that cannabis and the cannabinoids have been used in human society for many thousands of years, we still have great difficulty getting to grips with the harms associated with its use. The obvious harms – those of respiratory disease, increased accidents, are uncontroversial, but non-specific and indirect. The most pressing concern is the extent to which cannabis and the cannabinoids contribute to psychiatric disorder – cognitive impairment, cannabis dependence, and psychosis and schizophrenia. Here a basic consensus is emerging from the literature: a dependence syndrome exists – but it is relatively mild; there is an association with cognitive impairment, but it is relatively mild (and less than that associated with alcohol misuse); there is an association with schizophrenia – to the extent that it clearly exacerbates the condition, although evidence for a strong role in causation of the disorder is still relatively weak. While further large cohort studies will refine our understanding of the association between cannabis use and psychiatric risks, it is unlikely that that they will be able to determine whether cannabis use is truly causative. This lack of clear understanding of the risks of cannabis use is unsatisfactory given the fact that cannabinoid use is increasing in our society and a large number of people will be exposed to cannabis and the cannabinoids. Furthermore, drug development based upon the cannabinoid system show great promise in the treatment of a variety of chronic conditions, in particular chronic pain, cancer treatment and treatment of appetite disorders. Will these be associated with psychiatric complications? We remain deplorably ignorant of the basic neuropharmacology of the cannabinoid system, and there is a pressing need for experimental medicine studies of this system. In particular, cannabidiol appears to show particular promise; however a range of compounds directed at the CB1 and CB2 systems may be very useful. Only when we have a better understanding of the neuropharmacology of this system will we gain a firmer grasp on the harms associated with cannabis and the cannabinoids.

References

Abi-Dargham, A. and Moore, H. (2003) Prefrontal DA transmission at D1 receptors and the pathology of schizophrenia, *Neuroscientist*, 9, 404–16.

Aggarwal, S.K., Carter, G.T., Sullivan, M.D., Zumbrunnen, C., Morrill, R. and Mayer, J. D. (2009) Medicinal use of cannabis in the United States: historical perspectives, current trends, and future directions, *Journal of Opioid Management*, 5, 153–68.

Agrawal, A. and Lynskey, M.T. (2009) Tobacco and cannabis co-occurrence: does route of administration matter?, *Drug and Alcohol Dependence*, 99, 240–7.

Anand, P., Whiteside, G., Fowler, C.J. and Hohmann, A.G. (2009) Targeting CB2 receptors and the endocannabinoid system for the treatment of pain, *Brain Research Reviews*, 60, 255–66.

Andréasson, S., Engström, A., Allebeck, P. and Rydberg, U. (1987) Cannabis and schizophrenia A Longitudinal Study of Swedish Conscripts, *Lancet*, 330, 1483–6.

Arseneault, L., Cannon, M., Poulton, R., Murray, R., Caspi, A. and Moffitt, T.E. (2002) Cannabis use in adolescence and risk for adult psychosis: longitudinal prospective study, *British Medical Journal*, 325, 1212–13.

Asenjo Lobos, C., Komossa, K., Rummel-Kluge, C., Hunger, H., Schmid, F., Schwarz, S. and Leucht, S. (2010) Clozapine versus other atypical antipsychotics for schizophrenia, *Cochrane Database of Systematic Reviews (Online)*, 11, CD006633. DOI: 10.1002/14651858.

Barkus, E., Morrison, P.D., Vuletic, D., Dickson, J., Ell, P.J., Pilowsky, L.S., Brenneisen, R., Holt, D.W., Powell, J., Kapur, S. and Murray, R.M. (2010) Does intravenous Δ9-tetrahydrocannabinol increase dopamine release? A SPET study, *Journal of Psychopharmacology*, DOI: 10.1177/0269881110382465.

Barnett, J.H., Werners, U., Secher, S.M., Hill, K.E., Brazil, R., Masson, K., Pernet, D.E., Kirkbride, J.B., Murray, G.K., Bullmore, E.T. and Jones, P.B. (2007) Substance use in a population-based clinic sample of people with first-episode psychosis, *British Journal of Psychiatry*, 190, 515–20.

Bhattacharyya, S., Morrison, P.D., Fusar-Poli, P., Martin-Santos, R., Borgwardt, S., Winton-Brown, T., Nosarti, C., O'Carroll, C.M., Seal, M., Allen, P., Mehta, M.A., Stone, J.M., Tunstall, N., Giampietro, V., Kapur, S., Murray, R.M., Zuardi, A.W., Crippa, J.A., Atakan, Z. and McGuire, P.K. (2010) Opposite effects of [Delta]-9-Tetrahydrocannabinol and cannabidiol on human brain function and psychopathology, *Neuropsychopharmacology*, 35, 764–74.

Bossong, M.G., van Berckel, B.N.M., Boellaard, R., Zuurman, L., Schuit, R.C., Windhorst, A.D., van Gerven, J.M.A., Ramsey, N.F., Lammertsma, A.A. and Kahn, R.S. (2008) [Delta]9-Tetrahydrocannabinol induces dopamine release in the human striatum, *Neuropsychopharmacology*, 34, 759–66.

Boydell, J., van Os, J., Caspi, A., Kennedy, N., Giouroukou, E., Fearon, P., Farrell, M. and Murray, R.M. (2006) Trends in cannabis use prior to first presentation with schizophrenia in South-East London between 1965 and 1999, *Psychological Medicine*, 36, 1441–6.

Brugger, S., Davis, J.M., Leucht, S. and Stone, J.M. (2011) Proton magnetic resonance spectroscopy and illness stage in schizophrenia: a systematic review and meta-analysis, *Biological Psychiatry*, 69, 495–503.

Budney, A.J., Hughes, J.R., Moore, B.A. and Vandrey, R. (2004) Review of the validity and significance of cannabis withdrawal syndrome, *American Journal of Psychiatry*, 161, 1967–77.

Budney, A.J., Vandrey, R.G., Hughes, J.R., Moore, B.A. and Bahrenburg, B. (2007) Oral Delta-9-Tetrahydrocannabinol suppresses cannabis withdrawal symptoms, *Drug and Alcohol Dependence*, 86, 22–9.

Burns, H.D., van Laere, K., Sanabria-Bohórquez, S., Hamill, T.G., Bormans, G., Eng, W.-S., Gibson, R., Ryan, C., Connolly, B., Patel, S., Krause, S., Vanko, A., van Hecken, A., Dupont, P., de Lepeleire, I., Rothenberg, P., Stoch, S.A., Cote, J., Hagmann, W.K., Jewell, J. P., Lin, L.S., Liu, P., Goulet, M.T., Gottesdiener, K., Wagner, J. A., de Hoon, J., Mortelmans, L., Fong, T.M. and Hargreaves, R.J. (2007) [18F]MK-9470: a positron emission tomography (PET) tracer for in vivo human PET brain imaging of the cannabinoid-1 receptor, *Proceedings of the National Academy of Sciences*, 104, 9800–5.

Carpenter, K.M., McDowell, D., Brooks, D.J., Cheng, W.Y. and Levin, F.R. (2009) A preliminary trial: double-blind comparison of nefazodone, bupropion-SR, and placebo in the treatment of cannabis dependence, *American Journal on Addictions/American Academy of Psychiatrists in Alcoholism and Addictions*, 18, 53–64.

Caspari, D. (1999) Cannabis and schizophrenia: results of a follow-up study, *European Archives of Psychiatry and Clinical Neuroscience*, 249, 45–9.

Chang, L., Cloak, C., Yakupov, R. and Ernst, T. (2006) Combined and independent effects of chronic marijuana use and HIV on brain metabolites, *Journal of Neuroimmune Pharmacology*, 1, 65–76.

Chowdhury, A.N. and Bera, N.K. (1994) Koro following cannabis smoking: two case reports, *Addiction*, 89, 1017–20.

Compton, M.T., Furman, A.C. and Kaslow, N.J. (2004) Lower negative symptom scores among cannabis-dependent patients with schizophrenia-spectrum disorders: preliminary evidence from an African American first-episode sample, *Schizophrenia Research*, 71, 61–4.

Cooper, Z. and Haney, M. (2010) Opioid antagonism enhances marijuana's effects in heavy marijuana smokers, *Psychopharmacology*, 211, 141–8.

Cowan, R.L., Joer, S.J.M. and Dietrich, M.S. (2009) N-acetylaspartate (NAA) correlates inversely with cannabis use in a frontal language processing region of neocortex in MDMA (Ecstasy) polydrug users: A 3 T magnetic resonance spectroscopy study, *Pharmacology Biochemistry and Behavior*, 92, 105–10.

Crippa, J.A., Zuardi, A.W., Martín-Santos, R., Bhattacharyya, S., Atakan, Z., McGuire, P. and Fusar-Poli, P. (2009) Cannabis and anxiety: a critical review of the evidence, *Human Psychopharmacology: Clinical and Experimental*, 24, 515–23.

D'Souza, D.C., Abi-Saab, W.M., Madonick, S., Forselius-Bielen, K., Doersch, A., Braley, G., Gueorguieva, R., Cooper, T.B. and Krystal, J.H. (2005) Delta-9-tetrahydrocannabinol effects in schizophrenia: Implications for cognition, psychosis, and addiction, *Biological Psychiatry*, 57, 594–608.

D'Souza, D.C., Perry, E., MacDougall, L., Ammerman, Y., Cooper, T., Wu, Y.-T., Braley, G., Gueorguieva, R. and Krystal, J.H. (2004) The psychotomimetic effects of intravenous Delta-9-Tetrahydrocannabinol in healthy individuals: implications for psychosis, *Neuropsychopharmacology*, 29, 1558–72.

D'Souza, D.C., Ranganathan, M., Braley, G., Gueorguieva, R., Zimolo, Z., Cooper, T., Perry, E. and Krystal, J. (2008a) Blunted psychotomimetic and amnestic effects of [Delta]-9-Tetrahydrocannabinol in frequent users of cannabis, *Neuropsychopharmacology*, 33, 2505–16.

D'Souza, D., Braley, G., Blaise, R., Vendetti, M., Oliver, S., Pittman, B., Ranganathan, M., Bhakta, S., Zimolo, Z., Cooper, T. and Perry, E. (2008b) Effects of haloperidol on the behavioral, subjective, cognitive, motor, and neuroendocrine effects of Δ-9-tetrahydrocannabinol in humans, *Psychopharmacology*, 198, 587–603.

Degenhardt, L., Hall, W. and Lynskey, M. (2003) Testing hypotheses about the relationship between cannabis use and psychosis, *Drug and Alcohol Dependence*, 71, 37–48.

Demirakca, T., Sartorius, A., Ende, G., Meyer, N., Welzel, H., Skopp, G., Mann, K. and Hermann, D. (2011) Diminished gray matter in the hippocampus of cannabis users: Possible protective effects of cannabidiol, *Drug and Alcohol Dependence*, 114 (2–3), 242–5.

Denis, C., Lavie, E., Fatséas, M. and Auriacombe, M. (2006) Psychotherapeutic interventions for cannabis abuse and/or dependence in outpatient settings, *Cochrane Database of Systematic Reviews (Online)*, 3, CD005336– DOI: 10.1002/14651848.

Di Forti, M., Morgan, C., Dazzan, P., Pariante, C., Mondelli, V., Marques, T.R., Handley, R., Luzi, S., Russo, M., Paparelli, A., Butt, A., Stilo, S.A., Wiffen, B., Powell, J. and Murray, R. M. (2009) High-potency cannabis and the risk of psychosis, *British Journal of Psychiatry*, 195, 488–91.

Di Marzo, V. and Matias, I. (2005) Endocannabinoid control of food intake and energy balance, *Nat Neurosci*, 8, 585–9.

Earleywine, M. and Barnwell, S.S. (2007) Decreased respiratory symptoms in cannabis users who vaporize, *Harm Reduction Journal*, 4, 11.

Egerton, A., Mehta, M.A., Montgomery, A.J., Lappin, J.M., Howes, O.D., Reeves, S.J., Cunningham, V.J. and Grasby, P.M. (2009) The dopaminergic basis of human behaviors: a review of molecular imaging studies, *Neuroscience & Biobehavioral Reviews*, 33, 1109–32.

Elsohly, M.A. and Slade, D. (2005) Chemical constituents of marijuana: the complex mixture of natural cannabinoids, *Life Sciences*, 78, 539–48.

EMCDDA (2010) *Annual Report (2010): The State of the Drugs Problem in Europe*, European Monitoring Centre for Drugs and Drug Addiction.

Estrada, G., Fatjó-Vilas, M., Muñoz, M.J., Pulido, G., Miñano, M.J., Toledo, E., Illa, J.M., Martín, M., Miralles, M.L., Miret, S., Campanera, S., Bernabeu, C., Navarro, M.E. and Fañanás, L. (2011) Cannabis use and age at onset of psychosis: further evidence of interaction with COMT Val158Met polymorphism, *Acta Psychiatrica Scandinavica*.

Fadda, P., Scherma, M., Spano, M.S., Salis, P., Melis, V., Fattore, L. and Fratta, W. (2006) Cannabinoid self-administration increases dopamine release in the nucleus accumbens, *Neuroreport*, 17, 1629–32.

Ferdinand, R.F., Sondeijker, F., van der Ende, J., Selten, J.-P., Huizink, A. and Verhulst, F.C. (2005) Cannabis use predicts future psychotic symptoms, and vice versa, *Addiction*, 100, 612–18.

Frisher, M., Crome, I., Martino, O. and Croft, P. (2009) Assessing the impact of cannabis use on trends in diagnosed schizophrenia in the United Kingdom from 1996 to 2005, *Schizophrenia Research*, 113, 123–8.

Fusar-Poli, P., Crippa, J.A., Bhattacharyya, S., Borgwardt, S.J., Allen, P., Martin-Santos, R., Seal, M., Surguladze, S.A., O'Carrol, C., Atakan, Z., Zuardi, A.W. and McGuire, P.K. (2009) Distinct Effects of {Delta}9-Tetrahydrocannabinol and Cannabidiol on Neural Activation During Emotional Processing, *Arch Gen Psychiatry*, 66, 95–105.

Goldman-Rakic, P.S., Castner, S.A., Svensson, T.H., Siever, L.J. and Williams, G.V. (2004) Targeting the dopamine D_1 receptor in schizophrenia: insights for cognitive dysfunction, *Psychopharmacology*, 174, 3–16.

Gonzalez, R. (2007) Acute and Non-acute effects of cannabis on brain functioning and neuropsychological performance, *Neuropsychology Review*, 17, 347–61.

González, S., Cebeira, M. and Fernández-Ruiz, J. (2005) Cannabinoid tolerance and dependence: A review of studies in laboratory animals, *Pharmacology Biochemistry and Behavior*, 81, 300–18.

González-Pinto, A., Alberich, S., Barbeito, S., Gutierrez, M., Vega, P., Ibáñez, B., Haidar, M. K., Vieta, E. and Arango, C. (2009) Cannabis and first-episode psychosis: different long-term outcomes depending on continued or discontinued use, *Schizophrenia Bulletin*, 37 (3), 631–9.

Grant, I., Gonzalez, R., Carey, C.L., Natarajan, L. and Wolfson, T. (2003) Non-acute (residual) neurocognitive effects of cannabis use: a meta-analytic study, *Journal of the International Neuropsychological Society*, 9, 679–89.

Gray, K.M., Hart, C.L., Christie, D.K. and Upadhyaya, H.P. (2008) Tolerability and effects of oral [Delta]9-tetrahydrocannabinol in older adolescents with marijuana use disorders, *Pharmacology Biochemistry and Behavior*, 91, 67–70.

Grech, A., van Os, J., Jones, P.B., Lewis, S.W. and Murray, R.M. (2005) Cannabis use and outcome of recent onset psychosis, *European Psychiatry*, 20, 349–53.

Green, B., Young, R. and Kavanagh, D. (2005) Cannabis use and misuse prevalence among people with psychosis, *British Journal of Psychiatry*, 187, 306–13.

Green, B., Kavanagh, D. and Young, R. (2003) Being stoned: a review of self-reported cannabis effects, *Drug and Alcohol Review*, 22, 453–60.

Haney, M. (2006) Opioid antagonism of cannabinoid effects: differences between marijuana smokers and non-marijuana smokers, *Neuropsychopharmacology*, 32, 1391–1403.

Haney, M., Bisaga, A. and Foltin, R. (2003a) Interaction between naltrexone and oral THC in heavy marijuana smokers, *Psychopharmacology*, 166, 77–85.

Haney, M., Hart, C., Ward, A. and Foltin, R. (2003b) Nefazodone decreases anxiety during marijuana withdrawal in humans, *Psychopharmacology*, 165, 157–65.

Haney, M., Hart, C.L., Vosburg, S.K., Nasser, J., Bennett, A., Zubaran, C. and Foltin, R.W. (2003c) Marijuana withdrawal in humans: effects of oral THC or Divalproex, *Neuropsychopharmacology*, 29, 158–70.

Haney, M., Gunderson, E.W., Rabkin, J., Hart, C.L., Vosburg, S.K., Comer, S.D. and Foltin, R.W. (2007) Dronabinol and marijuana in HIV-positive marijuana smokers, *Journal of Acquired Immune Deficiency Syndromes*, 45, 545–54.

Haney, M., Hart, C., Vosburg, S., Comer, S., Reed, S. and Foltin, R. (2008) Effects of THC and lofexidine in a human laboratory model of marijuana withdrawal and relapse, *Psychopharmacology*, 197, 157–68.

Haney, M., Hart, C., Vosburg, S., Comer, S., Reed, S., Cooper, Z. and Foltin, R. (2010) Effects of baclofen and mirtazapine on a laboratory model of marijuana withdrawal and relapse, *Psychopharmacology*, 211, 233–44.

Henquet, C., van Os, J., Kuepper, R., Delespaul, P., Smits, M., Campo, J.A. and Myin-Germeys, I. (2010) Psychosis reactivity to cannabis use in daily life: an experience sampling study, *British Journal of Psychiatry*, 196, 447–53.

Hermann, D., Sartorius, A., Welzel, H., Walter, S., Skopp, G., Ende, G. and Mann, K. (2007) Dorsolateral prefrontal cortex N-Acetylaspartate/Total Creatine (NAA/tCr) loss in male recreational cannabis users, *Biological Psychiatry*, 61, 1281–9.

Hickman, M., Vickerman, P., Macleod, J., Kirkbride, J. and Jones, P.B. (2007) Cannabis and schizophrenia: model projections of the impact of the rise in cannabis use on historical and future trends in schizophrenia in England and Wales, *Addiction*, 102, 597–606.

Hill, A.B. (1965) The environment and disease: association or causation?, *Proceedings of the Royal Society of Medicine*, 58, 295–300.

Howes, O.D. and Kapur, S. (2009) The dopamine hypothesis of schizophrenia: version III – the final common pathway, *Schizophrenia Bulletin*, 35, 549–62.

Huestis, M.A., Gorelick, D.A., Heishman, S.J., Preston, K.L., Nelson, R.A., Moolchan, E.T. and Frank, R.A. (2001) Blockade of effects of smoked marijuana by the CB1-selective cannabinoid receptor antagonist SR141716, *Arch Gen Psychiatry*, 58, 322–8.

Johns, L.C., Cannon, M., Singleton, N., Murray, R.M., Farrell, M., Brugha, T., Bebbington, P., Jenkins, R. and Meltzer, H. (2004) Prevalence and correlates of self-reported psychotic symptoms in the British population, *British Journal of Psychiatry*, 185, 298–305.

Karschner, E.L., Schwilke, E.W., Lowe, R.H., Darwin, W.D., Pope, H.G., Herning, R., Cadet, J.L. and Huestis, M.A. (2009) Do Δ9-tetrahydrocannabinol concentrations indicate recent use in chronic cannabis users?, *Addiction*, 104, 2041–8.

Koskinen, J., Löhönen, J., Koponen, H., Isohanni, M. and Miettunen, J. (2010) Rate of cannabis use disorders in clinical samples of patients with schizophrenia: a meta-analysis, *Schizophrenia Bulletin*, 36, 1115–30.

Lakhan, S. and Rowland, M. (2009) Whole plant cannabis extracts in the treatment of spasticity in multiple sclerosis: a systematic review, *BMC Neurology*, 9, 59.

Large, M., Sharma, S., Compton, M.T., Slade, T. and Nielssen, O. (2011) Cannabis use and earlier onset of psychosis: a systematic meta-analysis, *Arch Gen Psychiatry*, archgenpsychiatry, 5.

Lauronen, E., Miettunen, J., Veijola, J., Karhu, M., Jones, P.B. and Isohanni, M. (2007) Outcome and its predictors in schizophrenia within the Northern Finland 1966 Birth Cohort, *European Psychiatry*, 22, 129–36.

Levin, F.R., Mariani, J.J., Brooks, D.J., Pavlicova, M., Cheng, W. and Nunes, E.V. (2011) Dronabinol for the treatment of cannabis dependence: a randomized, double-blind, placebo-controlled trial, *Drug and Alcohol Dependence*, 16 (1–3), 142–50.

Levin, F.R., McDowell, D., Evans, S.M., Nunes, E., Akerele, E., Donovan, S. and Vosburg, S.K. (2004) Pharmacotherapy for marijuana dependence: a double-blind, placebo-controlled pilot study of divalproex sodium, *American Journal on Addictions/American Academy of Psychiatrists in Alcoholism and Addictions*, 13, 21–32.

Leweke, F.M., Koethe, D., Pahlisch, F., Schreiber, D., Gerth, C.W., Nolden, B.M., Klosterkötter, J., Hellmich, M. and Piomelli, D. (2009) S39-02 antipsychotic effects of cannabidiol, *European Psychiatry*, 24, S207.

Lupica, C.R. and Riegel, A.C. (2005) Endocannabinoid release from midbrain dopamine neurons: a potential substrate for cannabinoid receptor antagonist treatment of addiction, *Neuropharmacology*, 48, 1105–16.

Lupica, C.R., Riegel, A.C. and Hoffman, A.F. (2004) Marijuana and cannabinoid regulation of brain reward circuits, *British Journal of Pharmacology*, 143, 227–34.

Maldonado, R., VAlverde, O. and Berrendero, F. (2006) Involvement of the endocannabinoid system in drug addiction, *Trends in Neurosciences*, 29, 225–32.

Martín-Sánchez, E., Furukawa, T.A., Taylor, J. and Martin, J.L.R. (2009) Systematic review and meta-analysis of cannabis treatment for chronic pain, *Pain Medicine*, 10, 1353–68.

Martín-Santos, R., Fagundo, A.B., Crippa, J.A., Atakan, Z., Bhattacharyya, S., Allen, P., Fusar-Poli, P., Borgwardt, S., Seal, M., Busatto, G.F. and McGuire, P. (2010) Neuroimaging in cannabis use: a systematic review of the literature, *Psychological Medicine*, 40, 383–98.

McRae-Clark, A.L., Carter, R.E., Killeen, T.K., Carpenter, M.J., Wahlquist, A.E., Simpson, S.A. and Brady, K.T. (2009) A placebo-controlled trial of buspirone for the treatment of marijuana dependence, *Drug and Alcohol Dependence*, 105, 132–8.

Mechoulam, R., Peters, M., Murillo-Rodriguez, E. and Hanuš, L.O. (2007) Cannabidiol: recent advances, *Chemistry & Biodiversity*, 4, 1678–92.

Medford, N., Baker, D., Hunter, E., Sierra, M., Lawrence, E., Phillips, M.L. and David, A.S. (2003) Chronic depersonalization following illicit drug use: a controlled analysis of 40 cases, *Addiction*, 98, 1731–6.

Mehra, R., Moore, B.A., Crothers, K., Tetrault, J. and Fiellin, D.A. (2006) The association between marijuana smoking and lung cancer: a systematic review, *Arch Intern Med*, 166, 1359–67.

Merlin, M. (2003) Archaeological evidence for the tradition of psychoactive plant use in the old world, *Economic Botany*, 57, 295–323.

Minozzi, S., Davoli, M., Bargagli, A.M., Amato, L., Vecchi, S. and Perucci, C.A. (2010) An overview of systematic reviews on cannabis and psychosis: discussing apparently conflicting results, *Drug and Alcohol Review*, 29, 304–17.

Moffett, J.R., Ross, B., Arun, P., Madhavarao, C.N. and Namboodiri, A.M.A. (2007) N-Acetylaspartate in the CNS: from neurodiagnostics to neurobiology, *Progress in Neurobiology*, 81, 89–131.

Moore, B.A., Augustson, E.M., Moser, R.P. and Budney, A.J. (2005) Respiratory effects of marijuana and tobacco use in a U.S. sample, *Journal of General Internal Medicine*, 20, 33–7.

Moore, T.H.M., Zammit, S., Lingford-Hughes, A., Barnes, T.R.E., Jones, P.B., Burke, M. and Lewis, G. (2007) Cannabis use and risk of psychotic or affective mental health outcomes: a systematic review, *Lancet*, 370, 319–28.

Moreira, F.A. and Wotjak, C.T. (2010) Cannabinoids and anxiety, *Current Topics in Behavioral Neurosciences*, 2, 429–50.

Morgan, C.J.A. and Curran, H.V. (2008) Effects of cannabidiol on schizophrenia-like symptoms in people who use cannabis, *British Journal of Psychiatry*, 192, 306–7.

Morgan, C.J.A., Freeman, T.P., Schafer, G.L. and Curran, H.V. (2010a) Cannabidiol attenuates the appetitive effects of [Delta]9-Tetrahydrocannabinol in humans smoking their chosen cannabis, *Neuropsychopharmacology*, 35, 1879–85.

Morgan, C.J.A., Schafer, G., Freeman, T.P. and Curran, H.V. (2010b) Impact of cannabidiol on the acute memory and psychotomimetic effects of smoked cannabis: naturalistic study, *British Journal of Psychiatry*, 197, 285–90.

Morrison, P.D., Zois, V., McKeown, D.A., Lee, T.D., Holt, D.W., Powell, J.F., Kapur, S. and Murray, R.M. (2009) The acute effects of synthetic intravenous 9-tetrahydrocannabinol on psychosis, mood and cognitive functioning, *Psychological Medicine*, 39, 1607–16.

Muench, J. and Hamer, A.M. (2010) Adverse effects of antipsychotic medications, *American Family Physician*, 81, 617–22.

Panagis, G., Vlachou, S. and Nomikos, G.G. (2008) Behavioral pharmacology of cannabinoids with a focus on preclinical models for studying reinforcing and dependence-producing properties, *Current Drug Abuse Reviews*, 1, 350–74.

Panlilio, L.V., Justinova, Z. and Goldberg, S.R. (2010) Animal models of cannabinoid reward, *British Journal of Pharmacology*, 160, 499–510.

Patton, G.C., Coffey, C., Carlin, J.B., Sawyer, S.M. and Lynskey, M. (2005) Reverse gateways? Frequent cannabis use as a predictor of tobacco initiation and nicotine dependence, *Addiction*, 100, 1518–25.

Pelayo-Terán, J.M., Pérez-Iglesias, R., Mata, I., Carrasco-Marín, E., Vázquez-Barquero, J.L. and Crespo-Facorro, B. (2010) Catechol-O-Methyltransferase (COMT) Val158Met variations and cannabis use in first-episode non-affective psychosis: clinical-onset implications, *Psychiatry Research*, 179, 291–6.

Pertwee, R.G. (2006) Cannabinoid pharmacology: the first 66 years, *British Journal of Pharmacology*, 147, S163–S171.

Pertwee, R.G. (2009) Emerging strategies for exploiting cannabinoid receptor agonists as medicines, *British Journal of Pharmacology*, 156, 397–411.

Peters, B.D., De Koning, P., Dingemans, P., Becker, H., Linszen, D.H. and De Haan, L. (2009) Subjective effects of cannabis before the first psychotic episode, *Australian and New Zealand Journal of Psychiatry*, 43, 1155–62.

Pisanti, S., Malfitano, A.M., Grimaldi, C., Santoro, A., Gazzerro, P., Laezza, C. and Bifulco, M. (2009) Use of cannabinoid receptor agonists in cancer therapy as palliative and curative agents, *Best Practice & Research Clinical Endocrinology & Metabolism*, 23, 117–31.

Prescot, A.P., Locatelli, A.E., Renshaw, P.F. and Yurgelun-Todd, D.A. (2011) Neurochemical alterations in adolescent chronic marijuana smokers: a proton MRS study, *NeuroImage*, 57 (1), 69–75.

Rabinowitz, J., Levine, S.Z. and Häfner, H. (2006) A population based elaboration of the role of age of onset on the course of schizophrenia, *Schizophrenia Research*, 88, 96–101.

Ramaekers, J., Kauert, G., Theunissen, E., Toennes, S. and Moeller, M. (2009) Neurocognitive performance during acute THC intoxication in heavy and occasional cannabis users, *Journal of Psychopharmacology*, 23, 266–77.

Ream, G.L., Benoit, E., Johnson, B.D. and Dunlap, E. (2008) Smoking tobacco along with marijuana increases symptoms of cannabis dependence, *Drug and Alcohol Dependence*, 95, 199–208.

Reid, P.T., MacLeod, J. and Robertson, J.R. (2010) Cannabis and the lung, *Journal of the Royal College of Physicians of Edinburgh*, 40, 328–3.

Sofuoglu, M., Sugarman, D.E. and Carroll, K.M. (2010) Cognitive function as an emerging treatment target for marijuana addiction, *Experimental and Clinical Psychopharmacology*, 18, 109–19.

Spencer, C., Castle, D. and Michie, P.T. (2002) Motivations that maintain substance use among individuals with psychotic disorders, *Schizophrenia Bulletin*, 28, 233–47.

Stokes, P.R.A., Mehta, M.A., Curran, H.V., Breen, G. and Grasby, P.M. (2009) Can recreational doses of THC produce significant dopamine release in the human striatum?, *NeuroImage*, 48, 186–90.

Stokes, P.R.A., Egerton, A., Watson, B., Reid, A., Breen, G., Lingford-Hughes, A., Nutt, D.J. and Mehta, M.A. (2010) Significant decreases in frontal and temporal [11C]-raclopride binding after THC challenge, *NeuroImage*, 52, 1521–7.

Sugarman, D.E., Poling, J. and Sofuoglu, M. (2011) The safety of modafinil in combination with oral [increment]9-tetrahydrocannabinol in humans, *Pharmacology Biochemistry and Behavior*, 98, 94–100.

Timberlake, D.S., Haberstick, B.C., Hopfer, C.J., Bricker, J., Sakai, J.T., Lessem, J.M. and Hewitt, J.K. (2007) Progression from marijuana use to daily smoking and nicotine dependence in a national sample of U.S. adolescents, *Drug and Alcohol Dependence*, 88, 272–81.

Topol, E.J., Bousser, M.-G., Fox, K.A.A., Creager, M.A., Despres, J.-P., Easton, J.D., Hamm, C.W., Montalescot, G., Steg, P.G., Pearson, T.A., Cohen, E., Gaudin, C., Job, B., Murphy, J. H. and Bhatt, D.L. (2010) Rimonabant for prevention of cardiovascular events (CRESCENDO): a randomised, multicentre, placebo-controlled trial, *Lancet*, 376, 517–23.

UNODC (2010) *World Drug Report 2010*, United Nations Office of Drugs and Crime (UNODC) United Nations Publications, www.unodc.org/unodc/en/data-and-analysis/WDR-2010.html, accessed 6 February 2011.

van Dam, N.T. and Earleywine, M. (2010) Pulmonary function in cannabis users: support for a clinical trial of the vaporizer, *International Journal of Drug Policy*, 21, 511–13.

van Laere, K., Goffin, K., Bormans, G., Casteels, C., Mortelmans, L., de Hoon, J., Grachev, I., Vandenbulcke, M. and Pieters, G. (2009) Relationship of type 1 cannabinoid receptor availability in the human brain to novelty-seeking temperament, *Arch Gen Psychiatry*, 66, 196–204.

van Os, J., Bak, M., Hanssen, M., Bijl, R. V., De Graaf, R. and Verdoux, H. (2002) Cannabis Use and Psychosis: A Longitudinal Population-based Study, *American Journal of Epidemiology*, 156, 319–27.

Vandrey, R., Smith, M.T., McCann, U.D., Budney, A.J. and Curran, E.M. (2011) Sleep disturbance and the effects of extended-release zolpidem during cannabis withdrawal, *Drug and Alcohol Dependence*, 117 (1), 38–44.

Wagner, F.A. and Anthony, J.C. (2002) From first drug use to drug dependence; developmental periods of risk for dependence upon marijuana, cocaine, and alcohol, *Neuropsychopharmacology: Official Publication of the American College of Neuropsychopharmacology*, 26, 479–88.

Wagner, F.A. and Anthony, J.C. (2007) Male–female differences in the risk of progression from first use to dependence upon cannabis, cocaine, and alcohol, *Drug and Alcohol Dependence*, 86, 191–8.

Williams, C.M. and Kirkham, T.C. (2002) Observational analysis of feeding induced by [Delta]9-THC and anandamide, *Physiology & Behavior*, 76, 241–50.

Winstock, A., Lea, T. and Copeland, J. (2009) Lithium carbonate in the management of cannabis withdrawal in humans: an open-label study, *Journal of Psychopharmacology*, 23, 84–93.

Wise, R.A. (2004) Dopamine, learning and motivation, *Nat Rev Neurosci*, 5, 483–94.

Yücel, M., Bora, E., Lubman, D.I., Solowij, N., Brewer, W.J., Cotton, S.M., Conus, P., Takagi, M.J., Fornito, A., Wood, S.J., McGorry, P.D. and Pantelis, C. (2010) The impact of cannabis use on cognitive functioning in patients with schizophrenia: a meta-analysis of existing findings and new data in a first-episode sample, *Schizophrenia Bulletin*, 25 July (Epub ahead of print), PMID:20660494.

Zammit, S., Allebeck, P., Andreasson, S., Lundberg, I. and Lewis, G. (2002) Self reported cannabis use as a risk factor for schizophrenia in Swedish conscripts of 1969: historical cohort study, *British Medical Journal*, 325, 1199.

Zuardi, A., Crippa, J., Hallak, J., Pinto, J., Chagas, M., Rodrigues, G., Dursun, S. and Tumas, V. (2009) Cannabidiol for the treatment of psychosis in Parkinson's disease, *Journal of Psychopharmacology*, 23, 979–83.

Chapter 18

THE RESURRECTION OF PSYCHEDELIC RESEARCH

Amanda Fielding

Psychoactive plants have been used by humans since the dawn of civilisation. They have been called in many cultures the *flesh of the gods*, and have been worshiped as deities or as a means of directly communicating with the divine. Psychoactive substances have thus played a key role in the formation of our cultural history, in shamanic practice, aboriginal healing ceremonies, rites of passage, divination and in mysteries of death and rebirth. These traditions still exist in a few undisturbed indigenous cultures around the world. Psychoactive substances are also still used in the more esoteric branches of mainstream religions, such as the Sufis in the Islamic tradition and the Brahmins and Sadhus within Hinduism. Christianity has always had an uneasy relationship with altered states of consciousness, although the writings of great mystics, such as Saint Teresa of Avila, bear a remarkable similarity to the expressions of a psychedelic experience.

The association of psychedelic substances with sacred rites has a history stretching back thousands of years. In Central and South America, the pre-Columbian cultures such as the Olmecs, Maya and Aztecs used mind-altering plants in their rituals. Of these sacred plants the most well-known are the cactus named *peyote* (*Anhalonium Lewinii*), the sacred mushroom named *teonanacatl* (*Psilocybe mexicana*) and *ololiuqui*, or morning glory seeds (*Rivea corymbosa*). In the South American jungle, the brew *ayahuasca* is still used as a religious sacrament. The Amazon basin is also known for a variety of psychedelic snuffs. Preparations using the bark of the shrub *iboga* (*Tabernanthe iboga*) have long been used by African tribes. In low doses it is used as a mild stimulant during the hunt or on long canoe trips; in higher doses it is used as a ritual sacrament. Natural psychedelic substances have had a prodigious impact on both the spiritual and cultural life of pre-industrial societies including our own.

The classical world, from which our modern western culture emerged, was imbued with the deep influence of psychedelic insights through the esoteric ceremonies at Eleusis, which continued for well over two thousand years, influencing such seminal thinkers as Socrates, Plato, Aristotle and Marcus Aurelius, among innumerable others. The mysteries involved the transformational experience of death and rebirth, brought about by imbibing the *kykeon*, a psychedelic brew thought to be based on ergot, a fungus that grows on rye which is the essential ingredient of LSD.

It seems likely that the use of psychoactive substances was an integral part of Homo sapiens' cultural evolution, and aided the development of human consciousness. It has been suggested that psilocybin was the original 'tree of knowledge' of mystical and biblical fame. The addition of psilocybin to the hominid diet may have enhanced eyesight, sexual enjoyment, language abilities and lateral thinking, thereby giving the mushroom-eaters an edge in the game of survival. These early experiences with psychoactive plants led to the development of shamanistic societies which based their divinations on altered states of consciousness, in which knowledge from the psychic depths wells up in oracular fashion. Shamanism in turn led to the alchemical and yogic traditions, and to spiritual and religious practices in general.

Harm Reduction in Substance Use and High-Risk Behaviour: International Policy and Practice, First Edition.
Edited by Richard Pates and Diane Riley.
© 2012 Blackwell Publishing Ltd. Published 2012 by Blackwell Publishing Ltd.

The growing power of the Christian church after Constantine's Edict of Milan of 313 AD led to the persecution of those who engaged in mystical experiences, eventually paving the way for the Papal Inquisition, which finds its modern manifestation in the current *war on drugs*, an unwinnable struggle that sadly causes far more harm and suffering than it manages to prevent. However, there has recently been growing enthusiasm for a reconsideration of how we should best regulate the worldwide use of psychoactive substances, with the aim of minimising the harms associated with their use, based on the latest scientific evidence. This move is encouraging as, particularly in respect to the psychedelics, there is a need for a regulatory system which will maximise the safeguards against harmful use, while permitting their use for scientific, medical, therapeutic and spiritual purposes.

A recent history of psychedelic use in the west

Mescaline was isolated and identified by German chemist Arthur Heffter in 1897. It was the first psychedelic substance that was explored in a systematic fashion under laboratory conditions.

The most famous, or indeed infamous of all psychedelics, LSD-25 was first synthesised on 16 November 1938 by the chemist Albert Hofmann at the Sandoz Laboratories in Basel, Switzerland as part of a larger research programme searching for medically useful ergot alkaloid derivatives. After the initial synthesis, it was given to be tested on animals and, since no effects were found, it was discarded. Five years later, Dr Hofmann had a premonition that he should re-synthesise LSD-25 and, following the synthesis in 16 April 1943, in some unexplained, serendipitous way he experienced a hallucination which reminded him of the mystical episodes of his childhood. This led him to take what he presumed would be a tiny dose (250 µg) of the substance three days later. Thus the first intentional ingestion of LSD occurred on April 19, 1943 (Hofmann, 2010). However, to his amazement, because of the unique power of the substance – 3,000 times more powerful than mescaline – his experiment turned out to be a major ordeal. Thus at the very birth of the LSD movement, both the inspiring beauty and the threatening horror were experienced by its creator.

After Dr Hofmann's discovery, the first clinical paper on LSD by Profesor Walter A. Stoll was published in 1947. This newly synthesised psychoactive substance, that could yield such monumental changes in consciousness with such miniscule doses (measured in micrograms), caused a commotion in the world of science, leading, by the end of the 1960s, to the publication of several thousand scientific articles, many books, six international conferences, and the use of LSD as a aid to psychotherapy in the treatment of over 40,000 patients (Hintzen and Passie, 2010). LSD was originally perceived as being useful clinically as a *psychotomimetic*, that is, as capable of producing a model of psychosis, and it was hoped that, by ingesting small doses of this substance, psychiatrists would gain unparalleled insights into the nature of previously mysterious disorders such as schizophrenia, which would lead to new approaches to treatment. This model soon expanded to include the use of LSD as a novel aid in psychotherapy for such conditions as depression and addiction.

Albert Hofmann presumed that, like mescaline, LSD's non-medicinal use would be confined to artistic and literary circles, to such exceptional thinkers as Aldous Huxley and Ernst Jünger: 'I had not expected that LSD, with its unfathomably uncanny profound effects, so unlike the character of a recreational drug, would ever find worldwide use as an inebriant.' However, his discovery led to LSD becoming a widely used recreational drug used by millions in the 1960s and 1970s, fanned on by the cry of 'turn on, tune in, drop out'. The creator of this iconic phrase, Dr Timothy Leary, explains the importance of LSD and psychedelics 'like every great religion of the past we seek to find the divinity within and to express this revelation in a life of glorification and the worship of God. These ancient goals we define in the metaphor of the present – turn on, tune in, drop out'.

By the end of the 1960s, fuelled by the fear of the 'corrosive effects' on the values of the western middle classes and the profound psychological effects, the authorities panicked, and LSD was declared a Schedule One drug, and on 6 October, 1966 LSD became illegal in the U.S. and the rest of the world were soon to follow. The sad fact is that because of the excesses of a minority of users in the 1960s and the historic taboo associated with altered states of consciousness, governments overreacted by prohibiting not only the recreational use, but also the scientific research into how these substances work and how they might be used to the benefit of humankind. Tragically, the baby was thrown out with the bath water, and both psychotherapy and neuroscience lost an invaluable tool.

The resurrection of psychedelic research

The long history of the use of psychedelic plants in sacred ceremonies throughout the world contrasts sharply with the extremely short history of scientific investigation into the effects of psychoactive compounds, which with illegality became completely taboo.

At its current pace the twenty-first century will undoubtedly be remembered as the century of Neuroscience. Humanity's ability to alter its own brain function is likely shape history just as powerfully as did the development of metallurgy in the Bronze Age and mechanisation in the Industrial Age. Now our growing ability to alter brain functioning can be used to treat mental dysfunction and also enhance some mental processes.

Finally, after decades of prohibition, there are the first glimmers of interest from the fields of neuroscience and psychiatry of the potential uses of psychedelics as a valuable tool in the exploration of consciousness and as an aid in the treatment of mental dysfunction. Since research using psychedelics was prohibited (mainly by taboo), the art of brain imaging has blossomed, along with huge advances in neuroscience. Serotonin, a chemical structure similar to LSD, was discovered shortly after LSD, and more recently many other neurochemicals, such as anandamide and the endorphins came to light, all of which allow us to better understand the complex interactions which underlie the workings of the brain.

The Beckley Foundation

A better understanding of what consciousness is, how it works, and what are the changing factors that underlie its full range of states, is centrally important not only to the individual but also to society as a whole. It was to delve into these questions that in 1998 I set up the Beckley Foundation. My aim was to investigate the neurophysiology underlying conscious states, and how physiological changes in the brain – that occur with age, meditation or due to the ingestion of psychoactive substances – are reflected in changes in our consciousness and cognitive functioning, and how these changes may be beneficial or detrimental to health and well-being. At an early age I was aware of the incredible potential of the psychedelics and developed a passion to learn about how these psychoactive compounds affected the brain. I set up the Beckley Foundation to help start the process of exploration which the established scientific community was ignoring because of societal taboo.

To begin this exploration I sought collaborations with leading scientist from around the world and set about initiating, directing and supporting a programme of research at leading institutions.

I was particularly interested in opening the doors of research into LSD, as that was in my opinion the Cinderella of psychoactive substances, neglected and vilified because of adverse publicity in the 1960s, instead of being recognised as a totally non-addictive tool of psychic transformation.

Lifting the veil on conscious experience

Psychedelics are an amazing tool for modern neuroscience, they change consciousness in a reliable and effective way, allowing us to correlate profound changes in experience with neurophysiological changes; in this way we can discover much more about a fuller range of conscious experiences. Surely there are few things more important in life than a better understanding of how we might enhance our consciousness. The combination of using a psychedelic substance to alter consciousness and modern brain imaging technology enables us to tackle this deep problem in a new and truly inspiring way.

Due to their lack of recreational use in the 1960s, psilocybin and MDMA (ecstasy) carried less historical baggage than LSD and therefore was easier to obtain permissions for research. In the mid-1990s Heffter headed by Franz Vollenweider began research using MDMA and psilocybin with human participants. In 2006 Roland Griffiths and his team at Johns Hopkins completed a beautifully designed and widely publicised project investigating the potential relationship between psilocybin and mystical experiences.

It had always been my aim to open up research into the physiology underlying the actions of LSD and this desire was finally realised in spring of 2007 after two years of seeking approvals, when the Beckley Foundation working with a neuroscientist at University of Berkeley, California, received the final approvals for the first study in recent times using LSD with human participants. This initial study was to investigate the safety factors of taking LSD in an experimental setting and to examine the changes in connectivity between different regions of the brain, in particular exploring the reputed association between LSD and enhanced creativity. These initial studies opened the door sufficiently to allow future work into these potentially valuable compounds to begin to grow.

After many years of working at opening up psychedelic research in the UK. The Beckley Foundation along with Prof. David Nutt and Robin Cahart Harris at Imperial College London, were able to carry out the first neuroscientific study using MRI and psilocybin. The study focuses on how psilocybin alters cerebral blood flow, and if it may aid in the emotional recall of distant memories, which would throw light on why psilocybin may be beneficial in psychotherapy. This study is also producing unexpected data about how psilocybin affects cerebral blood flow, and how this may affect depression.

The Beckley Foundation is particularly interested in how the use of psychedelics may increase the experience of the mystical, both in high level meditators and non-meditators. These states have the potential to be harnessed for the purpose of alleviating suffering, as well as occasioning mystical experiences at will by the ingestion of psilocybin. Collaborating with Prof Roland Griffiths and Matt Johnson at Johns Hopkins we are running a pilot study into how psilocybin facilitated mystical experience may be used as an aid to psychotherapy to treat resistant forms of addiction.

There are other research projects that are utilising the valuable transformational properties of psilocybin in psychotherapy to treat disorders such as obsessive-compulsive disorder and are also investigating how the spiritual experiences facilitated by psilocybin can be used as a healing factor in patients who are psychologically distressed by their diagnosis of cancer. At UCLA, Dr Charles

Grob is examining the use of psilocybin in a controlled setting to reduce the psychospiritual anxiety, depression, and physical pain of terminal cancer patients. Dr Stephen Ross at New York University is investigating how psilocybin can be used to reduce psychosocial distress associated with the diagnosis of cancer.

Following the approvals we gained at Berkeley, Dr Peter Gasser, in Switzerland obtained approvals for a study to explore the use of LSD for anxiety relating to life-threatening illness. This study was sponsored by the Multidisciplinary Association for Psychedelic Studies (MAPS) with the Beckley Foundation as a supporting sponsor. Patients who received LSD found that the experience aided them emotionally in coming to terms with their illness; importantly none of them experienced panic reactions or other untoward events.

Dr Michael Mithoefer and his wife Ann have, since the new millennium, been investigating MDMA-assisted psychotherapy in subjects suffering from treatment-resistant post-traumatic stress disorder (PTSD) and have found that MDMA is highly successful the treatment of PTSD without any evidence of causing harm to the patients.

This brief review illustrates that these pioneering studies are awakening the scientific world to the use of psychoactive compounds to assist in the treatment of a wide range of maladies.

Minimising harms associated with psychedelics

Psychedelics are very powerful substances and as Albert Hofmann discovered in his first intentional trip on LSD, have the power to shake the very foundations of the identity. Like any powerful substance they have the potential to cause great harm, but if used responsibly either for clinical or private use there are many potential benefits. If we need proof of this fact we need only to look through humankind's history to see countless examples of the safe ceremonial and spiritual use of psychedelics by generations of shamans, healers and entire cultures.

A crucial factor in using psychedelics safely is the set and setting they are used in. Set and setting describes one's mindset and the setting in which the user has the experience. The set can be seen as the mental state of the person when they take a psychedelic, such as their thoughts, mood or expectations. While the setting refers to the physical or social environment the person is in when they take a psychedelic. The social support network surrounding an individual has been shown to be particularly important in the outcome of the psychedelic experience.

I also believe in the importance of taking extra vitamin C and glucose during the psychedelic experience. The vitamin C ensures that the body does not run out of adrenaline, while the extra glucose maintains a normal sugar levels in the brain to help maintain concentration. This helps to avoid the dangers of prolonged hypoeglycaemia. Providing these steps are taken there is no reason that a psychedelic experience cannot be used to successfully treat a broad spectrum of psychological and physical disorders and as a tool to expand our consiousness without causing any harm. Stanislav Grof describes the situation succinctly:

> The question whether LSD is a phenomenal medicine or a devil's drug makes as little sense as a similar question asked about the positive or negative potential of a knife. Naturally, we will get a very different report from a surgeon who bases his or her judgment on successful operations and from the police chief who investigates murders committed with knives in back alleys of New York City. Similarly, the image of LSD will vary whether we focus on the results of responsible clinical or spiritual use, or naive and careless mass self-experimentation of the younger generation, or deliberately destructive experiments of the military circles or secret police.

The effects of psychedelics

Many people I have met over the years who have done exceptional things, such as looking after the poor in Africa, starting a school for 500 untouchables in India, discovering how to duplicate DNA, have told me that in their opinion they would never have done such things without the insights they acquired through a psychedelic experience. Whether Francis Crick discovered DNA on LSD is debatable, but what isn't in doubt is his great interest in the substance. In a draft lecture written in 1967, he talks of LSD and asks 'if a chemical were produced which was non-addictive and made people more intelligent', would we object to it? We as a society need to find out more about these compounds which can affect our consciousness so fundamentally. Our species is currently in the midst of a spiritual crisis, in the last two thousand years we have evolved at such a rapid pace in terms of what we can accomplish, but this has not been measured with an equal spiritual or moral growth, this is where the careful use of psychedelics may offer an individual a path to greater insight. The prudent responsible use of these substances may also help treat deep-seated psychological issues which are ever more common in our society, from stress or trauma to addiction and facing death. They also offer the possibility of finding out more about consciousness itself, the holy grail of neuroscience, and the core experience which defines us all, which still we know so little about.

The future of psychedelics

It is vital that we increase our knowledge about these mysterious and powerful compounds that affect our very consciousness. That we learn how to use them beneficially and we reform the way in which we regulate their use to reflect their enormous potential to mankind. I believe that the future of research using LSD, Psilocybin and other psychedelics for clinical/therapeutic applications, neuroscientific, and non-medical investigations has never looked better, and is of immense potential benefit to humanity. In the Garden of Eden, Adam and Eve choose to eat the forbidden fruit from the tree of knowledge of good and evil. Now humankind again has the chance to learn from these great gifts of nature.

In order for humankind to evolve we need to understand better what underlies the fuller range of conscious states and, through that knowledge, learn how to make better use of those states for the deepening of our self-awareness. It will also be possible to use this knowledge to treat the ever-increasing incidence of psychological scars and other ailments that are a product of modern society. It is a tragedy of our times that these substances are prohibited by antiquated laws; it is my hope that ground-breaking research will throw new light on the value of psychoactive substances as tools to assist humans to evolve and become a happier, healthier and a more fulfilled species. With any luck this could help our troubled species to become a better custodian of the wonderful planet we inhabit.

References

Hintzen, A. and Passie, T. (2010) *The Pharmacology of LSD*, Oxford: Beckley.
Hofmann, A. (2010) *Hofmann's Elixir, LSD and the New Eleusis*, ed. A. Fielding, Oxford: Beckley.

Chapter 19

HARM REDUCTION AND SEX WORKERS: A NEW ZEALAND RESPONSE: TAKING THE HARM OUT OF THE LAW

Catherine Healy, Calum Bennachie and Raewyn Marshall

Introduction

Harm Reduction, as a concept, developed in New Zealand within the context of HIV prevention in the mid-1980s and throughout the 1990s (Patterson, 1996: 41). The emergence of the needle exchange programme (NEP) and related political debates enabled the use of expressions such as 'reducing and minimising the risk of disease' (Luke, 2007: 366) which were forerunners to the harm reduction discourse. The rhetoric of 'reducing risk' was useful to secure funding from the government for peer managed needle exchange programmes. By the late 1980s independent needle exchange organisations were operating in the main cities throughout New Zealand. In addition, a number of pharmacies nationwide had opted in to the NEP and were also providing needle exchange services.

Sex workers were one of the targeted populations that the government and AIDS activists identified as requiring specialised programmes in respect to HIV prevention. It took the formation of the New Zealand Prostitutes Collective (NZPC) for effective programmes to be put in place. Although founded slightly before needle exchanges, NZPC was not funded until afterwards (Davis and Lichtenstein, 1996: 6). Until that time, the voices of sex workers had been muted – only heard through court hearings related to prostitution cases. These cases included soliciting, brothel keeping, living on the earnings and procuring for the purposes of prostitution.

Background

In 1987, sex workers were motivated to form their own organisation – the New Zealand Prostitutes Collective (NZPC) – by concerns related to the potential threat of HIV on their lives and issues pertaining to the illegality of sex work and how these compromised sex workers' occupational safety and health. There were a number of negative public perceptions, often portrayed in hostile media reports, depicting sex workers as being 'a reservoir of disease, out of control of their lives and irresponsible' (Healy et al., 2010: 46), often drug addled and posing a risk in terms of the transmission of HIV to the general public. There were few articles expressing genuine concern for the sex workers themselves.

Sex workers didn't have an organised voice until

Harm Reduction in Substance Use and High-Risk Behaviour: International Policy and Practice, First Edition.
Edited by Richard Pates and Diane Riley.
© 2012 Blackwell Publishing Ltd. Published 2012 by Blackwell Publishing Ltd.

a group of nine Wellington women working in massage parlours met to discuss forming an organisation to represent sex workers in New Zealand. Soon after, they connected with other sex workers, including those working on the streets and as escorts. Women, transgendered people and male sex workers were all part of the mix.

(Healy et al., 2010: 46)

In 1988 a representative of NZPC was appointed to the National Council of AIDS by the Minister of Health. This was the first appointment of a recognised sex worker to an official body which was charged with advising government. It signalled that a new approach was emerging from government to engage with sex workers. Later that same year, the Minister of Health negotiated a contract modelled on the principles of the Ottawa Charter which enabled NZPC to provide community based HIV prevention services to sex workers throughout the country (Chetwynd, 1996: 136–47). Based on the Ottawa Charter, NZPC devised its own programmes specific to the diverse needs of sex workers. These programmes included the operation of community drop-in centres with peer-operated needle exchanges and outreach services to sex work venues.

As these programmes unfolded, it became apparent that the police and their enforcement of the laws surrounding sex workers created problems for NZPC and its HIV prevention agenda and this triggered the initial call for the decriminalisation of prostitution from NZPC, with the backing of several prominent politicians (NZPC, 1989: 12–13). While it was not illegal to be a sex worker, the activities associated with sex work such as soliciting, procuring, brothel keeping and living on the earnings were against the law. The majority of sex workers under the guise of 'masseuse' or escort, worked from massage parlours and escort agencies, as well as a small number of street-based sex workers. Many sex workers were subject to police scrutiny and sometimes arrested and convicted in court for soliciting (Healy et al., 2010: 45–6).

Most sex workers worked underground in massage parlours, where the police had the legal right to enter at any time and check a register of names. Sex workers with drug convictions, including those related to the possession of a small amount of marijuana as well as other drugs, were forbidden from working in this indoor branch of the sex industry. This approach gave the police arbitrary powers over the lives of many sex workers and in particular those who used drugs. There was a concern that the heavy scrutiny by the police and their recording of the names of sex workers compromised their health and safety:

In many ways, the registration hinders women if they have had a prior drug conviction, regardless of how long ago this may have occurred and their current health status, making it illegal for them to work in any massage parlour. This then forces women into working at other less safe venues and locations, with less access to harm reduction and safer sex information, support and products.

(Drugs Health Development Project, 2001: 2)

During the period prior to law reform it appeared to NZPC that sometimes the police colluded with the licensed massage parlour proprietors to maintain a large degree of control over these sex workers, including frequently searching their bags for drugs. Sex workers who were known to use drugs would have to tolerate appalling workplace conditions and exploitative practices, knowing they were vulnerable to being expelled from this major branch of the sex industry without any means of redress. Sex workers would feel vulnerable carrying condoms in light of these determined police searches and the illegality of sex work in massage parlours.

It was usual for condoms, which were subsidised by Ministry of Health for the distribution by NZPC to sex workers, to be seized by the police and presented as evidence to achieve prostitution-related convictions (Abel et al., 2010: 76). Furthermore, the Public Health Association (PHA) noted: 'Health promotion resources funded by Regional Health Authorities and produced by the NZPC were also presented to the Court to contribute to the pattern of evidence' (PHA, 2001: 5).

There were other areas of tension which related to sex workers being registered on a police database (Abel, 2010: 91; PUMP, 2001: 11). The Prostitution Law Review Committee (PLRC) reported that sex workers who wished to move to other occupations ran the risk of being prevented from doing so if their connection to sex work was discovered through standard security and reference checks (PLRC, 2008: 70).

Sex workers were placed at risk as they were inhibited from reporting violence to the police. Abel (2010: 27) reports that Pyett and Warr (1997; 1999) were concerned that sex workers were unwilling to contact the police when they were victims of violence 'Due to perceptions of disconnection from the justice system because of their illegal status.' There were similar feelings in New Zealand sex workers (Jordan, 2010: 40), with two-thirds of sex workers surveyed in Christchurch prior to law reform stated they did not believe the majority of police cared enough about their safety (Plumridge and Abel, 2000). There was a fear that they would be prosecuted for their involvement in sex work. Furthermore, they were reluctant to disclose their involvement in sex work to health professionals (Plumridge and Abel, 2000) and as a result missed opportunities for more appropriate healthcare.

Public health experts also noted that while decriminalisation would not on its own remove the stigma associated with sex work, it would reduce some of the significant abuses associated with it (PHA, 2001: 5). Sex workers themselves are always very clear as to the causes of the harms involved in sex work. They identify the illegal nature of sex work as causing harm, along with the perception that they are criminals. There is stigma associated with this perception which causes harm.

The fall-out from convictions related to prostitution had far-reaching consequences. Sex workers who were working in licensed massage parlours instantly lost their jobs and were prohibited from working in this indoor branch of the sex industry for ten years. This often meant that sex work options were severely reduced. For sex workers who were used to working in these managed environments, it meant relocating to unfamiliar branches of the sex industry, such as street-based sex work or working as escorts providing outcalls to clients in places of the client's choice.

NZPC recollects that street based sex workers were obvious targets for police and were sometimes harassed by the street patrols that would search their bags for drugs and condoms. Sometimes they were arrested while going about their daily business unrelated to sex work on suspicion of soliciting for sex in a public place. They were removed in police vans to be detained, photographed and finger printed at police stations. This resulted in court appearances and these sex workers were usually convicted and fined. Curfews would also be imposed as additional punishment, which would severely erode a sex workers' ability to earn a living.

This pattern of enforcement created a revolving door scenario, where the sex workers would then have to return to a new site on the street to try to avoid future detection by the police.

This dislocation from working in familiar territory undermined the safety of these sex workers. Mutually supportive peer groups comprised of street-based sex workers watching out for each other's safety would be fragmented; outreach teams from the NZPC and other service providers would have to re-establish contact; known safe places which could be relied on in a time of crisis would be out of reach; income would be affected with the disruption, creating financial stress.

In addition there could be further repercussions. Names of sex workers who had been convicted would be published in daily newspapers. The information could be used by the authorities against them, including questioning such things as their suitability as parents. Landlords of sex workers could be pressured by the police to evict them from their accommodation or face the consequences of being prosecuted for illegally living on the earnings of prostitution. All these circumstances caused real harm to sex workers.

NZPC advocated for a more supportive social environment where sex workers would have a full spectrum of rights and protections. The criminalisation of sex workers was identified as being a major impediment to their safety, health and well-being and the cause of significant harm (Jordan, 2010: 40; Abel, 2010: 41–6).

Reorienting the law: a harm reduction strategy

NZPC campaigned vigorously to change the law. It built a profile in the media and spoke out against the harm caused to sex workers by the enforcement of the anti-prostitution laws. It proposed that the laws be decriminalised and gathered community support for this end. A range of non-government and government funded bodies – including those with an interest in public health, human rights, people who use drugs and women's organisations – and recognised that sex workers' safety health and well-being would be better served by significant changes to the law. An organisation which provided needle exchange programmes for a wide range of people and professions, including sex industry workers (DHDP, 2001: 5) identified concerns related to the dissemination of harm reduction information, education and products in a criminalised environment.

Eventually a bill was put before Parliament proposing the decriminalisation of prostitution. Tim Barnett, the Labour MP who sponsored the bill, debated the decriminalisation of prostitution as a harm reduction model for sex workers (Barnett et al., 2010: 62, 65).

The overall intention of the Bill was to shift the focus away from the criminal law – which was there to prosecute sex workers, inflated the risks of prostitution and rewarded the strong while punishing the weak – to one where there was an expectation that sex workers would be protected from harm (Barnett, 2003). Public Health authorities endorsed the decriminalisation of prostitution and submitted that

> Our submission is not concerned with questions relating to the desirability or morality of sex work. Our concern is whether legislation changes would reduce the harm that results from social and legal marginalisation and enhance the health status of all those involved with the sex industry; sex workers, their clients and their partners, friends, families and communities.
>
> (PHA, 2001: 4)

The Prostitution Reform Act (PRA) passed in 2003 and is considered as a harm reduction model for sex workers.

NZPC believes that it is not the nature of sex work that causes harm, but rather it is the laws and policies applied to sex workers in a criminalised environment that cause real harm. The PRA provides a legal environment in which sex workers are able to exercise their rights and therefore reduce harm.

The aims of the PRA are to decriminalise prostitution and create a framework that safeguards the human rights of sex workers and protects them from exploitation while promoting their welfare, occupational health and safety and to be conducive to public health. It also prohibits the use of persons under the age of 18 in prostitution.

There are many features related to the PRA which sex workers say contribute to their overall safety and well-being. This legal approach allows them to operate from a wide range of venues, including large and small managed brothels. Since decriminalisation, there has been an increase in sex workers who are choosing to cut out the third-party management tier (Abel et al., 2007:

97–100). NZPC understands this is because they believe their occupational safety and health is best served by determining and managing their own sex work conditions. These sex workers work for themselves, or with other sex workers as equals, from small owner operated brothels (SOOBS). Street based sex work is also permitted, although controversy still continues in some cities and neighbourhoods regarding the location of sex workers and brothels.

These workplace options ensure most sex workers can work within the law with expectations of having rights and protections, wherever they work. There are no laws prohibiting sex workers with drug or other convictions from working in any branch of the sex industry. However, people with convictions for some drug offences, violent crime or money laundering are prohibited from operating brothels but can appeal against this decision on the basis that these are historical crimes.

Government agencies, some of which had had no previous involvement with the sex industry had to adjust to this decriminalised environment and engage with sex workers and brothel operators in a new way.

The Department of Labour (DoL) developed Occupational Safety and Health (OSH) guidelines specifically for the sex industry. To do so, they consulted with sex workers and sex worker organisations including NZPC and Scarlet Alliance, Australia (OSH, 2004: 7). These guidelines carry information related to 'any issue, task or condition in a workplace that may impact on the health and well-being of the people who are working there' (OSH, 2004: 17). The guidelines reinforce the PRA, acknowledging the rights of sex workers to go unharmed.

The Guidelines explain: 'Operators, sex workers and clients have roles and responsibilities under the laws dealing with prostitution, occupational safety and health and public health' (OSH, 2004: 21). In this decriminalised environment, sex workers are also covered by Employment Relations and Accident Compensation law. There is information informing sex workers about regulatory agencies and unions which can assist them in complaints. Advice is provided relating to sexual health and education for sex workers, their clients and management. Sex workers are advised to undertake sexual health assessment based on their specific needs and do not have to work under a regime of imposed mandatory testing. There is practical information related to avoiding condom breakage or slippage and pregnancy as well as information related to disinfecting equipment used for sex work.

The Guidelines advise:

> When as part of their regular work, employees are to operate equipment such as that used in B&D [bondage and discipline] fantasies, it is imperative for the safety of both employees and clients that the employer provides comprehensive training on safe use of the equipment for the employee.
>
> (OSH, 2004: 36)

Other information refers to the cleanliness of workplace amenities, body fluid spills, heating and lighting. There are concerns raised about psychosocial factors, including the vulnerability of sex workers who use drugs and the potential for clients to exploit them. Security and safety from violence is explained, with suggestions for the training of brothel operators and sex workers on how to identify potentially dangerous situations, how to protect sex workers and to develop strategies to eliminate risks (OSH, 2004: 51–60). The DoL also facilitates in labour disputes which occur between sex workers and brothel operators. Sex workers are able to utilise mediation services to resolve their differences including contracts or unfair employment practices.

The legal recognition of sex work as work has opened up the possibility of using other legislation to protect sex workers from harm, such as the Health and Safety and Employment Act 1992. Inspectors can visit brothels to check on the physical conditions such as heating or the way in which hazards are managed in the workplace, including the prevention of violence and security issues.

There is also potential to address bullying and workplace stress. For sex workers who encounter sexual harassment by brothel operators in the workplace, their complaints can be upheld by the Human Rights Act 1993. Sex workers have taken advantage of this, but unfortunately, the Human Rights Act does not extend to protection on the basis of employment as a sex worker and discrimination continues to occur.

Disputes related to money can be resolved through the Disputes Tribunal, accessible through the local district court. Clients and brothel operators have appeared before this tribunal and have had to recompense sex workers for unpaid monies owing.

The Ministry of Health (MoH) designed, in consultation with NZPC, health promotion signs to be displayed in brothels encapsulating the section in the PRA which states that clients must take all reasonable steps to use a condom and other safer sex barriers for penetrative sex or face a fine. The effect of this law has been to support sex workers in dealing with clients who are resistant to using condoms and other safer sex practices that prevent transmission of HIV and STIs. While sex workers and operators are also covered by these laws they have only been enforced against clients. Sex workers are positive in respect to this part of the PRA but NZPC has concerns that it could be used to the detriment of sex workers and result in more harm. Sex workers may feel they are not able to report a mishap if they do have unsafe sex and they may be vulnerable to entrapment through inappropriate checks by authorities, or even subjected to malicious complaints from others. Medical Officers of Health are able to inspect brothels to ensure signs are displayed and do so on a complaints driven basis. A typical scenario is driven by a sex worker's concern about pressure from brothel managers to relax their standards in relation to some safer sex practices.

The police have experienced a significant change in their relationship with sex workers. Previously as enforcers of the anti-prostitution laws, the police had enormous powers over sex workers. Often these powers, when unleashed would result in harm to sex workers. Sex workers now have an expectation that the police are there to uphold their right to protection from those who would cause them harm.

In this decriminalised setting, police have been able to build positive relationships which are focused on solving crimes committed against sex workers. The PLRC found that

> Christchurch Police consider the PRA has made co-operation and the good relations between street-based workers and frontline officers, possible. Street-based workers offer Police useful information about activity on the streets, while Police provide information about potential offenders who may pose a risk to street workers.
>
> (PLRC, 2008: 121)

Furthermore, the PRA can militate against police corruption which some sex workers have complained of prior to the law change. A street based sex worker in this decriminalised environment was able to successfully provide evidence to a court which resulted in a corrupt police officer being convicted of a charge of misusing his authority to get sex from a prostitute (TVNZ, 2009).

Just as violence in society continues to exist, violence against sex workers remains. However, the PRA has changed attitudes of sex workers to the police (Abel, 2010: 235). As a result of this, the PRA

> had helped to increase the reporting of violence to the Police, particularly by street workers. There were also indications that incidents of violence against sex workers were being taken more seriously and that in some cases the Police response assisted in resolving situations.
>
> (Mossman and Mayhew, 2007: 10)

Decriminalisation in New Zealand has also meant that sex work safety issues can be discussed openly with people who are starting sex work. Brothel operators can share information with prospective sex workers and face up to their responsibilities as employers. The need for brothels to disguise the nature of their business when hiring sex workers no longer exists in the decriminalised sector. The PRA enables brothel operators to explain to people who apply to work in a brothel, issues of safety in the workplace relevant to sex workers. People are therefore in a position to make informed choices and are not misled through duplicitous procurement into sex work.

Harm reduction for sex workers is best met within a decriminalised environment. As Abel (2010: 325) indicates:

> decriminalisation does minimise the harm associated with the sex industry. Sex workers in New Zealand now have greater control over their working environment and are able to utilise the law to more readily negotiate condom use. The realisation of their human rights has enabled sex workers in New Zealand to claim legitimacy in an occupation often conceptualised as unlawful, immoral and unethical. In so doing, the PRA has facilitated the evolution of 'prostitution' into 'sex work' in New Zealand.

The harm of stigma and discrimination

There are strong arguments for addressing stigma around and discrimination against, sex workers and sex work, as the effects are far reaching. In the Australian Capital Territory (ACT) in Australia there has been legislative reform to prohibit discrimination against sex workers.

> Discrimination affects sex workers in a myriad of ways in their professional and personal lives; in judgments made by family and friends, the provision of goods and services, planning laws and decisions, the response of some police to sex worker complaints and in the differential application of sexual assault laws. Many sex workers are reluctant to tell their family and friends how they are employed. Fear of discrimination can also limit sex worker participation in community activities. For some women, there is an additional fear that revealing their occupation may jeopardise custody of their children. Fear of discrimination is a key impediment to sex worker complaint-making to the police and to human rights and other regulatory bodies.
>
> (Scarlet Alliance, 2007)

Sex workers need access to services that are non-discriminatory and acknowledge sex work as work. These services need to be wide ranging and cover all aspects that impact negatively on the lives of sex workers. These should include, but not be limited to, services which relate to justice systems, the provision of housing, general and specific health services, as well as commercial services (such as banks) and access to education.

The provision of non-discriminatory services can assist sex workers to overcome the harmful effects of stigma, even in the most hostile of legal environments. Much of this stigma is societal stigma, though it is often reinforced by prurient media representations and anti sex work campaigners who use language which 'reflects not merely a dislike of sex work, but a hatred of sex workers' (Bennachie and Marie, 2010: 24). It is therefore also important to ensure that anti-discrimination legislation includes sex workers to safeguard them from this harm by seeking to reduce stigmatisation against them.

It is important for countries who are considering changing the law on sex work to avoid legislation that causes harm to sex workers and undermines harm reduction efforts.

Sweden passed a law that criminalised the client of sex workers in 1999. As a result of this law, sex workers reported that they were subjected to a system of police harassment (Kulick, 2005: 209); street based clients are so nervous there is no time for sex workers to negotiate with them to assess their suitability before getting into the client's car; good clients are no longer inclined to contact the police as 'whistleblowers' if they suspect sex workers are in coercive situations as they did before the law was implemented; and sex workers are forced to work alone and cannot work together, making them more vulnerable to dangerous situations (Jacobsson, 2009). In the evaluation completed by the Swedish Government, sex workers stated the law stigmatised them (Skarhed, 2010: 129). The author stated that as the purpose of the Act was to combat prostitution, the stigmatisation reported by sex workers may be seen as a good thing (Skarhed, 2010: 130).

Levels of stigma can affect how people make decisions related to safer sex practices (Bruce et al., 2008; Preston et al., 2007). In combating the harm of HIV, it is important that sex workers are supported in their choices to work safely. HIPS (Helping Individual Prostitutes Survive) utilises a harm reduction model through programmes that 'strive to address the impact that HIV/AIDS, sexually transmitted infections, discrimination, poverty, violence and drug use have on the lives of individuals engaging in sex work' (HIPS, 2010). Programmes such as these and peer based, sex worker led initiatives, such as NZPC, which respect the choices of sex workers are critical to harm reduction efforts.

Harm reduction for sex workers in hostile legal environments

Internationally, sex workers are exposed to diverse treatment under law. But even in hostile legal environments, harm reduction strategies are being utilised. Sex worker peer advocacy groups and support initiatives now exist in many countries. These organisations are able to identify circumstances which are causing harm to sex workers and to develop responses to combat this harm, including lobbying for legislative change.

In Liverpool, UK, Merseyside police have, since 1996, treated violence against sex workers as a hate crime. Thus, when sex workers in Liverpool report violence against them, it is afforded an enhanced response, with greater police resources being given (Campbell and Stoops, 2010: 9).

There are other harms which can impact heavily on the safety health and well-being of sex workers. Aboriginal sex workers in Canada stress the importance of violence reduction and sex work-positive strategies, along with outreach programmes that are culturally specific to avoid the harms of discrimination and social isolation (Van der Meulen et al., 2010: 35).

In Hong Kong, organisations concerned with sex workers and peer support spoke out in the media and were able to build public sympathy and awareness around human rights violations which impact on sex workers. Sex workers felt ignored by the police and that their complaints against violence were not being taken seriously. This public support created an opportunity for the organisations to lobby and influence police policy in order that they better protect sex workers (JJJ Association and Zi Teng, 2010: 13–14). Sex worker groups meet regularly with a task force established within the police to help sex workers.

Many sex worker groups urge that it is important to demarcate between the harms of trafficking and sex work. Anti-trafficking campaigns should not harm sex workers. In their view, it is important not to conflate sex work with trafficking.

For example, since 1997, Durbar Mahila Samanwaya Committee (DMSC), a sex worker organisation in Kolkata, India, has taken a strong stance against trafficking of underage girls and women who have been forced, coerced or duped into sex work as it is 'DMSC's experience that Immoral

Trafficking (prevention) Act (IT(P)A), as enforced by the police, is insufficient to combat this trafficking with any great success' (DMSC, undated).

DMSC has established Self Regulatory Boards (SRBs) throughout sex work venues in Kolkata and other places they operate which

> serve as a double check to prevent entry of minor girls and unwilling adult women into sex work, control the exploitative practices in the sector, regulate the rules and practices of the trade and institute social welfare measures for sex workers and their children.
>
> (DMSC, undated)

These boards have links with the departments of Social Welfare, Labour and Health within West Bengal state and seek to make recruitment of young people and people who have been coerced non-viable for sex work venues. This has led to a unique anti-trafficking mechanism designed to reduce harm to young people or people who have been coerced, duped or forced into sex work.

> DMSC feels that the central focus should be on the trafficked girl/woman and efforts should be to rescue, repatriate and/or rehabilitate her. DMSC activists, being sexworkers and residing in sex work sites, are uniquely positioned to do this successfully. In areas where SRBs are functioning, trafficking of girls/women for sex work has become unviable for traffickers and other site controllers.
>
> (DMSC, undated)

Conclusion

Harm reduction does not mean that sex workers want to be 'rescued' and taught how to sew. Sex work is work and in view of this, it should be recognised that sex workers need equal protection under law. It is important to challenge the harms caused by bad law and stigma and, where possible, to resource peer-led initiatives which provide supportive services that are of relevance to sex workers. The over-arching approach to harm reduction and sex workers should be to champion their human rights.

References

Abel, G., (2010) Decriminalisation: a harm minimisation and human rights approach to regulating sex work, thesis submitted for the degree of Doctor of Philosophy of the University of Otago, Dunedin.

Abel, G., Fitzgerald, L. and Brunton, C. (2007) *The Impact of the Prostitution Reform Act on the Health and Safety Practices of Sex Workers*, Commissioned by Prostitution Law Review Committee, Christchurch, New Zealand: Department of Public Health and General Practice, University of Otago, 97–100.

Abel, G., Healy, C., Bennachie, C. and Reed, A. (2010) The Prostitution Reform Act. In G. Abel, L. Fitzgeraldand C. Healy (eds), *Taking the Crime Out of Sex Work: New Zealand Sex Workers Fight for Decriminalisation*, Bristol: Policy Press.

Agustin, L.,(2010) *Swedish Report Based on Wrong Danish Numbers for Street Prostitution*, www.lauraagustin.com/swedish–report–based–on–wrong–Danish–numbers–for–street–prostitution, accessed 1 March 2011.

APCOM (2010) *Image of APNSW T-shirt*, www.msmasia.org/tl_files/2010%20news/10-10_News/tshirtsw_apnsw.jpg, accessed 1 March 2011.

Barnett, T. (2003) *Speech on the Prostitution Reform Bill: Second Reading*, Hansard, www.parliament.nz/en-NZ/PB/Debates/Debates/a/9/a/47HansD_20030219_00001132-Prostitution-Reform-Bill-Second-Reading.htm, accessed 1 March 2011.

Barnett, T., Healy, C., Bennachie, C. and Reed, A. (2010) Lobbying for decriminalisation. In G. Abel, L. Fitzgerald, and C. Healy (eds), *Taking the Crime Out of Sex Work: New Zealand Sex Workers Fight for Decriminalisation*, Bristol: Policy Press.

Bennachie, C. and Marie, J., (2010) Their words are killing us: the impact of violent language of anti-sex work groups, *Research for Sex Work*, 12, 24–5.

Bruce, D., Ramirez-Valles, J. and Campbell, R., (2008) Stigmatization, substance use and sexual risk behaviour among Latino gay and bisexual men and transgender persons, *Journal of Drug Issues*, 22, 235–60.

Campbell, R. and Stoops, S., (2010) Taking sex workers seriously: treating violence as hate crime in Liverpool, *Research for Sex Work*, 12, 9–10.

Chetwynd, J., (1996) The Prostitutes Collective: a uniquely New Zealand institution. In P. Davis (ed.), *Intimate Details and Vital Statistics*, Auckland: Auckland University Press.

Davis, P. and Lichtenstein, B. (1996) Introduction: AIDS, sexuality and the social order, in New Zealand. In P. Davis (ed.), *Intimate Details and Vital Statistics*, Auckland: Auckland University Press.

Drugs Health Development Project (2001) Submission to the Justice and Electoral Select Committee on the Prostitution Reform Bill 2000.

Durbar Mahila Samanwaya Committee (undated) *Anti Trafficking*, www.durbar.org/html/anti_trafficking.asp, accessed 1 March 2011.

Healy, C., Bennachie, C. and Reed, A. (2010) History of the Prostitutes Collective. In G. Abel, L. Fitzgeraldand C. Healy (eds), *Taking the Crime Out of Sex Work: New Zealand Sex Workers Fight for Decriminalisation*, Bristol: Policy Press.

Herek, G. (2004) Beyond 'homophobia': thinking about sexual prejudice and stigma in the twenty-first century, *Sexuality, Research and Social Policy*, 1 (2), 6–24.

Helping Individual Prostitutes Survive (2010) *About Us*, http://hips.org/about/, accessed 1 March 2011.

Jacobsson, P. (2009) *We Want to Save You! (And If You Don't Appreciate It, You Will Be Punished!)*, Stockholm: Hungarian Civil Liberties Union, www.youtube.com/watch?v=7D7nOh57-I8, accessed 1 March 2011.

JJJ Association and Zi Teng (2010) Fighting for our rights: how sex workers in Hong Kong are negotiating for more respect and protection, *Research for Sex Work*, 12, 13–14.

Jordan, J. (2010) Of whalers, diggers and 'soiled doves': a history of the sex industry in New Zealand. In G. Abel, L. Fitzgeraldand C. Healy (eds), *Taking the Crime Out of Sex Work: New Zealand Sex Workers Fight for Decriminalisation*, Bristol: Policy Press.

Kulick, D. (2005) Four hundred thousand Swedish perverts, *GLQ: A Journal of Lesbian and Gay Studies*, 11 (2), 205–35.

Larsson, A. (2010) *Sexköp: Frågan om förbud delar Europa*, www.bra.se/extra/pod/?action=pod_show&id=1084&module_instance=12&apropa=true, accessed 1 March 2011.

Luke, S.M. (2007) Needle exchange networks: the emergence of 'peer-professionals', a thesis submitted in fulfilment of the requirements for the Degree of Doctor of Philosophy in Sociology at the University of Canterbury.

Mossman, E. and Mayhew, P. (2007) *Key Informant Interviews: Review of the Prostitution Reform Act 2003*, Wellington: Victoria University of Wellington.

NZPC (1989) Submission to the Justice and Electoral Select Committee on the Crimes Bill 1989, Wellington.

Occupational Safety and Health (2004) *A Guide to Occupational Health and Safety in the New Zealand Sex Industry*, Wellington: Occupational Safety and Health Service, Department of Labour, www.osh.dol.govt.nz/order/catalogue/pdf/sexindustry.pdf, accessed 1 March 2011.

Patterson, R. (1996) Softly, softly: New Zealand law responds to AIDS. In P. Davis (ed.), *Intimate Details and Vital Statistics*, Auckland: Auckland University Press.

Plumridge, E. and Abel, G. (2000) Services and information utilised by female sex workers for sexual and physical safety, *New Zealand Medical Journal*, 113 (1117), 370–2.

Press, The (2010) *Sentence for Under-age Sex Acts*, www.stuff.co.nz/the-press/news/christchurch/4444175/Sentence-for-under-age-sex-acts, accessed 1 March 2011.

Preston, D.B., D'Augelli, A.R., Kassab, C.D. and Starks, M.T. (2007) The relationship of stigma to the sexual health of rural men who have sex with men, *AIDS Education and Prevention*, 19 (3), 218–30.

Prostitution Law Review Committee (2008) *Report of the Prostitution Law Review Committee on the Operation of the Prostitution Reform Act 2003*, Wellington: Ministry of Justice.

Public Health, Association (2001) Submission to the Justice and Electoral Select Committee on the Prostitution Reform Bill 2000.

PUMP, (Pride and Unity for Male Prostitutes) (2001) Submission to the Justice and Electoral Select Committee on the Prostitution Reform Bill 2000.

Pyett, P. and Warr, D. (1997) Vulnerability on the streets: female sex workers and HIV risks, *AIDS Care*, 9, 439–547.

Pyett, P. and Warr, D. (1999) Women at risk in sex work: strategies for survival, *Journal of Sociology*, 35 (2), 183–97.

Scarlet Alliance (2007) *Comment On: Sex Workers' Rights and Regulation in the ACT*, www.scarletalliance.org.au/library/actcoss_07, accessed 10 March 2011.

Skarhed, A. (2010) *Förbud mot köp av sexuell tjänst en utvärdering 1999–2008*, Stockholm: Justitiedepartementet.

TVNZ (2009) *Verdict in Sex Extortion Case*, http://tvnz.co.nz/national-news/verdict-in-sex-extortion-case-3152086, accessed 1 March 2011.

Van der Meulen, E., Yee, J. and Durasin, E.M., (2010) Violence against indigenous sex workers: Combating the effects of criminalisation and colonisation in Canada, *Research for Sex Work*, 12, 35–7.

Chapter 20

HARM MINIMISATION: GAMBLING

Sally Gainsbury and Alex Blaszczynski

Gambling is a recreational activity that, when restricted to affordable limits, is experienced as an enjoyable socially acceptable leisure pursuit. For the majority of individuals, participation in gambling is comparable to purchasing and participating in a range of other recreational activities, such as a night out at the cinema or theatre, skiing, shopping or eating out at restaurants. However, for a minority of community members, gambling behaviour can become episodically or chronically excessive resulting in significant negative consequences with associated gambling-related harms affecting personal, familial, marital, social, employment and legal functioning. The major effect of excessive gambling is to undermine the financial security, interpersonal trust, stability and marital relationship of a family unit. In contrast to alcohol and illicit substance abuse, there are no observable external signs identifying the presence of excessive gambling, leaving parents, spouses and children unaware of the extent of the problem until a crisis leads to its disclosure. Recognising the potential for harm, governments and gambling operators have a responsibility to implement public health oriented harm-minimisation measures designed to minimise excessive gambling behaviour and its negative outcomes across all strata of the general population.

In contrast to the consumption of substances where physiological levels (and thresholds for harm) are quantified by the presence of alcohol or illicit drugs in the blood, there are no equivalent measures available for gambling. In gambling there is no specific or stable level of participation that can be expressed in terms of time and monetary expenditure that is reliably associated with harm: excessive gambling is relative to each individual's personal financial circumstances and disposable discretionary income and time. Accordingly, setting harm-minimisation standards of 'safe' gambling expenditure, comparable for example to medical recommendations for safe levels of consumption of four standard drinks or less per day for males, is not possible. Rather, individuals must be educated to recognise and set their own limits and to gamble responsibly.

The concept of harm-minimisation was initially applied in response to ancillary harms resulting from unhealthy procedures associated with illicit drug use, specifically hepatitis C and HIV viral infections. Extending the principle and strategies of harm minimisation to the field of gambling is fraught with potential problems unless important fundamental differences are taken into consideration when formulating policies and procedures. Defined strategies with specific targets must be formulated, evaluated and monitored following implementation. This chapter aims to outline the key elements of harm minimisation for gambling in an effort to guide regulators, policy-makers, industry operators and community groups, in designing and implementing successful public health initiatives. Various harm-minimisation strategies and the empirical evidence for their effectiveness across international jurisdictions are outlined.

Harm Reduction in Substance Use and High-Risk Behaviour: International Policy and Practice, First Edition.
Edited by Richard Pates and Diane Riley.
© 2012 Blackwell Publishing Ltd. Published 2012 by Blackwell Publishing Ltd.

Gambling in society

Gambling refers to the act of wagering an item of value, typically money, on the outcome of any event that is determined by chance. Gambling has a long and colourful history with waxing and waning waves of popular support. In the last four decades, gambling has become widely accepted as a popular recreational or entertainment activity. This normalisation of gambling has occurred as a result of several socio-political and economic influences and technological changes. These have led to increased liberalisation of legislation and attitudes, increased density and distribution of venues and gaming machines providing greater accessibility to, and availability of, gambling, and the market penetration of PC-based internet and mobile device communication facilities. Popular land-based forms of gambling include casino games (e.g., roulette, craps, blackjack), poker, electronic gaming machines (EGMs; slots, pokies, fruit machines, video lottery terminals), bingo, keno, lotteries, scratch lotteries, sports betting, horse and dog race wagering. These are supplemented by bets on games of skill (e.g., backgammon, mah-jong, poker card games), sporting, political or social events (e.g., betting on local and international sports events, who will win *American Idol*, when the next election will be held), and dice games, coin tossing and raffles. Gambling can take place in a specified gambling venues (e.g., casino, racetrack, betting shop, EGM clubs, bingo halls) or made available through licensed outlets (e.g., lottery terminals in news outlets). Alternatively, bets can be placed with bookies, friends or relatives, over the phone and increasingly through the internet or other interactive channels such as mobile phones and televisions.

Gambling is a multi-billion dollar worldwide industry, with legalised annual global gambling revenue estimated to increase substantially reaching US$155 billion by 2012. Approximately 65–90% of adults worldwide report gambling at some level on some form each year, with the majority doing so recreationally and in the absence of any significant negative consequences. Current epidemiological research estimates that between 1% and 5% of adults in the general population meet criteria for problem or pathological gambling. Problem gambling is characterised by the presence of excessive money and/or time spent gambling such that adverse consequences including significant distress or life disruption for the gambler, others, or for the community emerge.

Pathological gambling is classified as a psychiatric disorder and categorised as a disorder of impulse control. It's essential features include persistent and recurrent excessive gambling behaviour that disrupts personal, family or vocational interests and is diagnosed according to an individual satisfying five out of a set of ten criteria listed in the Diagnostic and Statistical Manual of Mental Health Disorders (DSM-IV: APA, 2000). Criteria include constant preoccupation with gambling, gambling increasing amounts of money (tolerance), unsuccessful attempts to control gambling (impaired control), feeling restless and irritable when attempting to cease (withdrawal), 'chasing losses', lying and committing illegal acts, and jeopardising other significant life areas including relationships, employment, or education. These criteria are derived from the substance dependence disorders with DSM-V proposing to reclassify pathological gambling as a non-substance related behavioural addiction in its addiction category.

Both problem and pathological gambling are associated with lost productivity (inability to concentrate at work due to anxiety and depression, gambling during work hours), termination of employment due to poor productivity, performance or embezzlement, marital breakdown, family separation and child neglect, crime and bankruptcy, poor physical health. At the emotional level, attendant stresses and concerns over finances and disclosure of debt and/or crimes contribute to the emergence of substance abuse, depression, anxiety and suicide. These all represent a significant health and social burden through the provision of treatment services and legal costs. The Australian Productivity Commission (2010) estimated that the cost of problem gambling to the community was US$4.1 billion leading to their conclusion that policy measures with even modest effectiveness in reducing harm will often be worthwhile. Problem gambling is often used as a generic term to cover both problem and pathological gamblers and this convention will be used in this chapter.

Although potentially all forms of gambling may create harm, certain forms appear to be more closely related to problem gambling, and as such, represent more appropriate targets for harm-minimisation strategies. These include forms of gambling that offer high event frequencies (i.e., rapid and continuous betting) and/or the frequent placement of large single bets. Contributing to excessive gambling are superimposed elements of skill or perceived skill, size and frequency of prizes/payouts, perceived probability of winning, and easy access to additional of funds (credit betting and ATMs) (Reith, 2006). In this context, electronic gaming machines (EGMs) in their various configurations represent one of the most preferred forms of gambling and consequently, the primary form associated with problem gambling and its rapid development. As a consequence, EGMs have been referred to as the 'crack cocaine of gambling' (Dowling et al., 2005).

Research has estimated that problem gamblers account for approximately 23–40% of EGM expenditure (Productivity Commission, 2010; Williams and Wood, 2004), indicating that the small proportion of 1% to 5% of such players are accounting for a disproportionately large percentage of expenditure. A significant minority of internet gambling also met criteria for problem gambling with rates ranging from 14% to 43% amongst various samples (Wood and Williams, 2007), figures that are much higher than the proportion of problem gamblers found in the general population and comparable to, if not exceeding, land-based gamblers.

There are no known specific causes of problem gambling, rather, problem gambling behaviour seems to develop through the interaction of a multiplicity of social, psychological and biological factors. These include genetic/biological predispositions, early gambling experiences, influences of family and friends, irrational thoughts and beliefs, co-morbid conditions including substance abuse, depression and anxiety and personality traits including impulsivity and risk-aversion. Although there is no exact pathway or single motivation leading to problem gambling, some sectors of the population are more vulnerable than others; individuals in lower socio-economic classes (poor, unemployed, welfare dependent, homeless and poorly educated) have higher rates of problem gambling than the general population (Shaffer and Korn, 2002; Volberg, 1994). Within these groups, males, single and/or under 35 years of age are also more likely to be at risk of developing gambling problems (Reith, 2006). Whatever factors contribute to this socio-demographic profile of problem gamblers, it is clear that those less able to afford to gamble have the highest exposure to gambling opportunities and therefore over-represented among treatment-seeking problem gamblers.

Recognition of gambling-related harms

In a mature market social adaptation processes, that is, that community members learn to adapt to the presence of gambling in their environment (LaPlante and Shaffer, 2007), will lead to a reduction in the incidence of problem gambling. Setting this aside, competing commercial forces, increased liberalisation of legislation and the introduction of new forms of gambling opportunities will ensure that a proportion of gamblers will continue to exhibit problem gambling behaviours. From a public health perspective, problem gambling represents (and is predicted to remain) a substantial health and social burden on the community.

The expression of community concern is demonstrated in the increasing number of media stories describing gambling-related harm and the exertion of political pressure for appropriate responses from governments and industry operators. Questions of duty of care and failure to comply with the responsible provision of gambling has led to the emergence of a number of lawsuits including class action cases seeking compensations for losses and hardship have been launched against regulators and operators. These claims are based on the argument that gamblers were not offered adequate information or warnings on which to base informed choices and the failure to instigate adequate procedures for protection against harm, for example, detection of self-exclusion breaches or credit checks.

Following the publication of the National Research Council (1999) and Productivity Commission (1999) reports in Australia, evidence of the existence and impact of problem gambling became irrefutable resulting in the condition gaining prominence as a topic of public health concern. With mounting community pressure, industry operators introduced voluntary codes of conduct complemented by government imposed mandatory requirements in the form of responsible gambling statutory regulatory Acts. These Acts and voluntary codes of conduct were designed specifically to achieve three goals: (1) a reduction in the incidence rate (new cases over a defined timeframe); (2) a reduction in the prevalence (number of existing cases) of problem gambling; and (3) to minimise harm associated with any and all levels of gambling.

The use of harm-minimisation to guide efforts to reduce the incidence of problem gambling finds its origin in efforts initially developed to decrease harms associated with the use of illicit drugs, and later extrapolated to alcohol consumption and safe sex programmes. Although abstinence might be the ideal target objective for at-risk individuals, the majority of those at risk do not or experience intense difficulties in ceasing their consumption. Therefore, alternative solutions based on the premise of continued use/consumption are required not only for heavy users/abusers but also communities in general.

The concept originated from attempts in the 1980s to restrict the spread of various blood-borne diseases including hepatitis and human immunodeficiency virus (HIV) associated with the intravenous injection of illegal drugs, such as heroin. Harm minimisation (commonly used interchangeably with harm reduction) was distinguished from the reduction of drug use, and understood as a set of strategies that decrease the prevalence of behaviours related to the spread of incurable viruses, although they might not reduce drug use in itself. In this context, harm minimisation measures included needle exchange programmes, the provision of bleach kits and the development of methadone maintenance programmes. Subsequent harm minimisation programmes include community-based drive home services after drinking alcohol to reduce alcohol-related car accidents and the distribution of free condoms to reduce the spread of sexually transmitted infections.

Although there is no singular accepted definition of harm minimisation, it is important to distinguish its core elements before an effective framework for gambling can be applied. In global terms, *harm-minimisation strategies aim to minimise the risks associated with gambling and facilitate responsible gambling, without overtly disturbing those who gamble in a non-problematic manner.* This corresponds with the three commonly mentioned aspects of harm-minimisation reported by Stockwell (2001): (1) accepting that while the targeted activity will continue in society, its harmful impacts can be reduced without necessarily requiring a decrease in its use; (2) empowering users to minimise the risk of harm; and (3) developing empirical evidence of the net reduction of harm. Harm-minimisation strategies attempt to reduce harms by utilising public health and social regulatory approaches that have a wide-reaching scope in targeting all segments of society including sub-populations considered to be vulnerable or 'at-risk'.

In many respects it is important to appreciate a point of departure for gambling from the original inherent aims and objectives of harm minimisation as found in substance use. The underlying premise for substance use harm minimisation holds that interventions are not to be specifically directed toward a reduction in consumption but rather the minimisation of ancillary or secondary harms flowing from participation. For example, safe injecting rooms or the provision of clean needles is directed toward minimising infections consequent to needle sharing. In alcohol consumption, the intent is to minimise motor vehicle related and industrial injuries through random blood testing. In these cases, the intent is to modify patterns of behaviours in order to prevent or reduce ancillary harm consequent to unhealthy practices or irresponsible acts. In contrast, with gambling, all harm minimisation initiatives are by necessity directed toward modifying actual gambling behaviours. This is because all harms associated with gambling have their origin in the act of gambling beyond one's affordable limits. For example, a majority of problem gamblers commit crimes to maintain their habitual behaviours. To reduce the commission of gambling-related criminal acts, the target strategy must involve an overall reduction in actual gambling expenditure such that the pressure to obtain money from alternative sources is eliminated.

It is important to note that the intrinsic harms related to the gambling are directly related to levels of consumption. As losses accumulate, it is the presence of financial tensions that form the origin of subsequent harms. In some ways it can be argued that this is similar to other public health topics such as alcohol consumption, which does not cause domestic violence or crime directly but contribute to their occurrence. In the case of gambling, as there is a 'house edge' favouring the operator, there will be a negative monetary return rate to the player in the long term. Therefore, the average gambler will consequently have diminished amounts of time and money available for other needs. However, potential indirect negative consequences stemming from excessive gambling, particularly when such gambling exceeds levels of affordability, include marital and employment problems, domestic violence and child neglect as well as crime and bankruptcy. Thus, in contrast to substance use, harm-minimisation approaches in gambling have their primary focus on decreasing gambling involvement. An alternative and perhaps controversial perspective is to redefine *harm minimisation* as a concept in gambling to one of *harm prevention* since the objective is to prevent the development of, and current harms associated with, excessive gambling behaviours.

Research indicates that, similar to alcohol use, there is a functional relationship between participation and monetary expenditure expressed as a percentage of gross income (Currie et al., 2006; Shaffer, 2005). A risk curve analysis of harm among gamblers in the general population found that gambling at any level appears to carry some risk of harm (Currie et al., 2006). Evidence also suggests that problem gambling is not a chronic condition but dynamically shifts across low, medium, problem, and pathological levels over time with high rates of spontaneous remission from problem gambling (Abbott, 2007; Hodgins and el-Guebaly, 2000; Slutske et al., 2003). Therefore, these findings suggest that harm minimisation initiatives targeting the full spectrum of participation are appropriate if the incidence and ultimately the prevalence, of problem gambling and gambling related harm is to be achieved.

In considering the most appropriate definition of harm-minimisation, Blaszczynski et al. (2001: 25) argued that the aims of harm minimisation are:

- to prevent vulnerable individuals from developing gambling problems;
- to reduce the current prevalence of problem gamblers within the community;
- to reduce the negative social and health consequences associated with problem gamblers for individuals, their families and their communities;
- to maintain a reasonable level of enjoyment from gambling by recreational gamblers;
- to ensure that the livelihood of those associated with the gaming industry is not unnecessarily compromised.

They further contend that the basic assumptions inherent in the harm-minimisation approach are that:

- Gambling is a recreational activity that is common among individuals and within the community.
- Many individuals are able to engage in gambling without negative consequences to their lifestyle or to the community.
- A proportion of participants, family members and others suffer significant harm as a consequence of excessive gambling.
- Complete prohibition is not a realistic option.
- Harm reduction involves individuals at risk reducing gambling to a safe level of the behaviour.
- Harm reduction implies that safe levels of participation are possible.

Harm minimisation and responsible gambling

In gambling, harm minimisation is subsumed within the framework of *responsible gambling*. Within this framework, responsible gambling strategies are designed to ensure the provision of safe gambling products and environments, prevention of exploitation, unacceptable inducements and misleading claims, and the provision of sufficient, relevant and timely information on which gamblers can make informed choices relating to their level of participation. In this context, dilution and confusion regarding the actual definition and theoretical basis of harm minimisation strategies continues to persist. Several researchers (Cantinotti and Ladouceur, 2008; Lenton and Single, 1998; MacCoun, 1998; Marlatt, 1996; Stockwell, 2006) make a clear distinction between demand reduction, supply reduction, and harm minimisation. Demand reduction is aimed at motivating users to lower their participation in an activity, such as encouraging the reduction of consumption through media campaigns, increasing costs of consumption through price increases, or increasing levels of inconvenience by providing fewer options or outlets.

Demand reduction strategies for gambling include preventive and warning messages, modification of gambling features and venues such as providing clocks and activity summaries, removing ATMs from gambling venues, reducing incentives to play and restricting marketing and advertisements.

Conversely, supply reduction focuses on reducing the physical availability of a substance or activity with constraints put in place by policy-makers and providers. Examples of this strategy include fewer retail outlets from which to purchase alcohol and tobacco and restricted trading hours. Supply reduction strategies for gambling include reducing the density and distribution of venues and electronic gaming machines, modifying games by slowing game speed, reducing trading hours, prohibiting certain games (e.g., internet gambling).

In most jurisdictions policy decision-makers accept that gambling is a legitimate recreational activity. Therefore, the accepted premise is that it is not reasonable to prevent the majority of individuals who gamble within affordable limits from participating in gambling activities. This is similar to the stance taken towards other legalised, but potentially harmful products including tobacco, alcohol and increasingly other public health targets including junk food in light of the increasing rates of obesity and associated health consequences. A balance is required between various strategies to ensure that gambling-related harms are minimised, without overtly disrupting recreational gamblers or gambling-related businesses.

In the absence of government intervention, there are mixed incentives for gambling operators to introduce and promote the effectiveness of voluntary measures to reduce gambling problems. This is

Figure 20.1 Strategies to reduce gambling-related harms. (Note: this figure is partially based on Cantinotti and Ladouceur, 2008.)

particularly the case for strategies that aim to reduce levels of participation by a minority whose expenditure represents a disproportionate percentage of total revenue; accordingly, operators are confronted with an inherent conflict of interest in that effective responsible gambling or harm minimisation strategies will by their very objectives, compromise revenue. It has also been argued that governments face a similar conflict of interest due to the substantial tax generated by gambling. Therefore, the implementation of strategies to reduce gambling problems must consider both the benefits and costs of gambling to individuals, families and society and only be implemented when they are shown to be necessary and effective in significantly reducing gambling-related harms (figure 20.1).

Targets for reducing gambling-related harms

Each form of gambling must be considered individually in terms of the most appropriate harm minimisation strategy; however, some forms of gambling are more commonly targeted than others, largely based on their perceived capability to cause or be associated with gambling-related harms. These include games with high event frequency (i.e., that are fast and allow for continual betting) and/or that involve an element of skill or perceived skill. Size of payouts, perceived overestimates of the probability of winning, and the possibility of using credit to play are factors also associated with higher levels of problematic play (Reith, 2006).

Gambling forms with these characteristic features include electronic gaming machines, internet gambling and sports betting (LaPlante et al., 2008; Productivity Commission, 2010; Wardle et al., 2007; Wood and Williams, 2009). An international review (Reith, 2006) noted that most research has found gambling problems are created by numerous complex associations between individuals, the environment and exposure to gambling opportunities. A dilemma for policy decision-makers is that the characteristics of gambling that lead some players into serious harm can be much the same characteristics that make them fun for recreational gamblers (fast games, attractive jackpots, free games, variable payouts and the capacity to win cash prizes, including jackpots). These features are specifically developed and refined to attract gamblers; however vulnerable gamblers are also highly attracted to these features. Therefore, the difficulties confronting gambling regulators and industry operators are the appropriate implementation of effective initiatives that balance the needs of individuals (recreational versus problem gamblers) and society.

Empirical evaluation

To achieve their principal aim, harm-minimisation strategies should be based on empirical evidence demonstrating their effectiveness in achieving their intended objectives for targeted individuals. Historically, such measures have been extrapolated from other fields, principally alcohol and tobacco consumption, without consideration of how these should be modified and applied appropriately for gambling. There is currently limited empirical evidence to guide and inform policy decision and calls for particular measures are often based on face-validity in the absence of data. Furthermore, even empirical studies that aim to test harm-minimisation strategies have failed to adequately take into consideration conceptual theories proposing the mechanism or process by which changes in behaviour occur. As a result, costly interventions are implemented that do not serve their intended purpose, for example, placing clocks on gaming machines or removing ATMs from gaming floors. In addition, scant attention is paid to prospects of unintended effects or compensatory changes in the behaviour of gamblers. For example, in an evaluation of a proposed strategy of slowing reel spins on EGMs, which was expected to reduce supply and subsequently reduce gambling-related problems, it was found that this modification negatively affected the enjoyment of all participants, recreational and problem gamblers alike. Furthermore, the study's authors concluded that problem gamblers who play slowly and spend more time playing would experience an increase in the negative consequences of gambling due to longer sessions of play (Blaszczynski et al., 2001). This emphasises again the critical importance of empirical evaluation for verifying the efficacy of proposed harm minimisation measures and strategies to reduce gambling-related harms. Some proposed harm-minimisation strategies may place large burdens and potential loss of profits for the industry without commensurate benefits being demonstrated. Effective policies should be informed by research determining the success of proposed strategies.

Demand reduction strategies

Warning messages

Messages warning consumers of the potential harmful outcomes associated with use of a particular product have been used for decades on tobacco and alcohol products and have subsequently been implemented for gambling products. Warning messages for gambling products can inform individuals of potential risks of gambling, encourage responsible gambling within personal limits and provide accurate information about probabilities of winning and how outcomes are determined. The key objective of warning messages and signs are to reduce harm by changing, or preventing the development of problematic behaviour. Most international jurisdictions mandate the use of warning signs in gambling venues, particular EGM venues and casinos. The content of these messages differs between jurisdictions; however, little empirical research has been conducted to establish the most effective message content and placement of signage.

To be effective warning messages must be prominently placed, attract attention, and convey an easily comprehensible message. For example, dynamic signs that appear on EGM screens are more likely to be noticed than static signs on EGMs and rotating message content may reduce habituation to signs and reduction of effectiveness. Monaghan and Blaszczynski (2010a) suggest that there is limited evidence that simply warning individuals of the risks associated with gambling or providing player information is sufficient to modify problematic behaviour; however, it may be a necessary step to raise awareness of potential harms. Empirical studies of warning signs for EGMs (Monaghan and Blaszczynski, 2010b) demonstrate that signs that encourage players to reflect on, appraise, evaluate and self-regulate their actions are effective in promoting appropriate thoughts and behavioural changes than signs informing players of the odds of winning or designed to correct irrational thoughts. These may subsequently reduce the incidence of gambling-related harms by reducing the extent to which individuals gamble beyond their means.

Modification to games

Modifications can be made to various forms of gambling. These may include the addition of features that allow players to track their gambling in terms of time and money spent, particularly for EGMs and internet gambling. Similarly, gambling machines should offer displays of cash rather than credits or tokens to increase the salience of the money being wagered. As discussed previously, identifying and modifying features of EGMs that make them appealing and engaging would likely reduce gambling, and subsequent negative consequences, but this is also likely to disrupt non-problem gamblers. Proposed modifications include modifying the size of the screen and reducing audio and visual features, particularly when EGMs are not being played to avoid prompting gamblers to initiate gaming sessions.

Research has demonstrated that the occurrence of *near wins* and *losses disguised as wins* influence player behaviour. *Near wins* refer to outcomes that make it seem as though a win was narrowly missed, for example, displaying two out of three matching symbols on an instant scratch ticket or four out of five matching symbols on the reels of an EGM. These outcomes may be configured to occur with a greater frequency by gambling operators to encourage gamblers to continue to play in the hopes of reaching a jackpot, behaviour based on irrational thoughts and misunderstanding of randomness and mutual exclusiveness of chance events. *Losses disguised as wins* occur when an outcome is displayed as a win, even though the gambler lost money from the wager (Dixon and Harrigan, 2010); for example, an EGM indicating that a player has won, when in fact their win was smaller than the amount wagered. Players have been shown to respond physiologically to these actual losses as though they had won (Dixon and Harrigan, 2010), thus encouraging continued gambling. Some jurisdictions prohibit EGMs from displaying near misses more commonly than would be expected and regulations that reduce the occurrence of both of these phenomena may discourage continued gambling.

Venue modifications

Aside from modifications made directly to the form of gambling, such as EGMs, gambling venues can be modified in an effort to minimise gambling-related harms by reducing demand for continued gambling. For example, prominently displaying clocks and allowing natural light into gambling venues have been implemented to assist gamblers in setting appropriate time limits. The proposed removal of ATMs nearby gambling services areas aims to make gamblers who run out of money travel further to access cash, providing them with a break in play and opportunity to consider whether they should continue gambling. Some jurisdictions have mandatory restrictions on venues offering inducements to gamble; for example, venue operators being prohibited from offering free or discounted liquor, or free credits, as inducements for people while gambling.

Restrictions must balance the broad appeal of inducements for recreational players and the inducements that may lead to problem gambling or exacerbate existing problems. For example, the banning of free alcohol and refusing to serve intoxicated customers is argued to act as an attempt to decrease excessive gambling amongst gamblers who are inebriated. But a survey of 1,000 EGM players in Australia found that not being able to drink alcohol at all while playing EGMs decreased the enjoyment, money spent, session length and play frequency for a significant proportion of players across different risk levels for problem gambling.

Pre-commitment

Pre-commitment strategies provide individuals the opportunity to constrain their behaviour when in gambling venues. These strategies reduce demand for gambling based on the individual limits that a gambler wishes to set for themselves as opposed to mandatory limits on gambling behaviour set by regulators. Several industries offer pre-commitment options to consumers, for example in the form of pre-paid mobile phones, gift and debit cards and capped internet plans, although such strategies are not commonly seen in other public health fields. In gambling, pre-commitment typically takes the form of a *smart card* or computer chip device with limits preset by the individual player in terms of limits on time and monetary expenditure by day, week and month. The rationale behind this strategy is that when an individual is emotionally aroused during a gambling session they find it more difficult to set appropriate limits and make rationale, informed choices. Therefore, by making these choices before they enter the gambling venue when in a *cold* emotional state, an individual can more effectively set limits.

Despite the potential success of pre-commitment strategies, particularly for continuous forms of gambling, several obstacles limit the universal effectiveness of these measures. Limits are still determined by the individual meaning that problem gamblers retain the option of continuing to set excessively high limits or establish a buffer that enables them to choose to continue gambling subject to outcomes of a session. The infrastructure to determine what appropriate financial limits should be established for individual players and to monitor compliance, are costly and not currently available. Rigorous evaluation is suggested for the implementation of a pre-commitment system relative to the jurisdiction and form of gambling in question and consideration given to both voluntary and mandated practices.

Marketing restrictions

Advertising is typically seen as a legitimate commercial strategy for promoting a business's products. As with the promotion of other 'unhealthy' products including tobacco, alcohol and junk food, there are significant concerns that it can increase the availability of and 'normalisation' of gambling, inappropriately attract children, reinforce consumer misconceptions and exacerbate problem gambling. Hence, many international jurisdictions have implemented marketing restrictions on gambling. Restrictions on marketing include the placement and content of advertisements. For example, similar to laws that prohibit tobacco products from being displayed behind the counter of stores that are visited by minors, regulations in some jurisdictions prohibit advertising the presence of EGMs in venues with restaurant and entertainment areas that can be accessed by children. Similarly, gambling advertisements are commonly prohibited from being shown during television slots frequently watched by children. Despite some mandated restrictions on advertising, there are several potential policy gaps that require further attention to reduce demand for gambling and subsequent problems. One example is the involvement of gambling companies, particularly, internet gambling sites, in sponsorship of sporting teams and events. This has been argued to have a strong impact on impressionable children and to increase the association between gambling and a healthy activity such as major sporting events (Monaghan et al., 2009). Marketing regulations must also be continually updated to appropriately regulate new forms of gambling and technology, for example internet gambling and the use of cell phones to recruit players with offers of free credit. Overall, restrictions on advertising aim to reduce the demand for gambling by vulnerable populations such as youth and problem gamblers and ensure that all messages are accurate representations of gambling products and services.

Supply reduction strategies

Evidence suggests a link between gambling accessibility and harm although this relationship is complex and non-linear (Productivity Commission, 2010). For example, studies from Australia, New Zealand and the USA indicate that increasing densities of EGMs are associated with increased prevalence rates of problem gambling with geographical proximity to venues associated with problem gambling (Ministry of Health, 2008; Rush et al., 2007; Storer et al., 2009; Welte et al., 2004). Similarly, Lund (2009) found that, following a temporal ban of EGMs in Norway between 2007 and 2008, gambling participation and calls to help-line services declined. However, there is conflicting evidence regarding the causal relationship between gambling accessibility and gambling problems and it has been argued that in mature markets, individuals habituate and adapt to exposure to gambling (LaPlante and Shaffer, 2007; Sévigny et al., 2008). Further, with the rising popularity of internet gambling, access and availability is increasingly difficult to regulate. Nevertheless, efforts should be made to limit supply in conjunction with effective demand reduction and harm minimisation strategies.

Modifications to games

Proposed modification of EGM physical features include modifying reel spin speed, the removal of the stop button, double-up and free features, and the insertion of pauses and/or messages on the EGM screen during play. These modifications all reduce the number of games that can be played per minute. Some of these modification, for example, slowing game speed, limiting denominations of notes accepted by bill acceptors, and imposing a cap on total credits that can be inserted at any one time can be classified as supply reduction because they result in a direct decrease in the capacity to maintain previous levels of gambling (Cantinotti and Ladouceur, 2008). Such modifications are analogous to policies that require limit the alcohol content of drinks.

The exact factors that make EGMs more problematic have not been determined resulting in the challenge of addressing the risky variables while preserving the leisure aspects of play. Modifications can be made to slow down and disrupt the continuous nature of some forms of gambling, including internet gambling, casino games, and in-play sports wagering. If problem gambling is related to these features, such supply reduction strategies should have an impact on the incidence of problem gambling behaviour; however, as noted, they may also decrease the pleasurable aspects of gambling for recreational gamblers and subsequent gaming revenue and taxes.

Features that interrupt play (requiring more low-denomination notes to be inserted during a session) or impose forced breaks in play (messages interrupting a game) offer opportunities for gamblers to re-appraise their behaviour and decisions to continue gambling thereby discouraging further play. Since, however, EGM players, particularly problem gamblers, often report experiencing dissociation during sessions, this strategy may not be effective. A potential negative consequence may be that rather than limiting themselves to one large note (e.g., $50), individuals may insert multiple smaller bills and experience temptation to bet 'just a little more' resulting in spending more than they intended. Smart cards or other pre-commitment measures can also be used as a supply reduction strategy as they constitute a form of electronic agreement that the gambler makes with the gambling establishment to contain expenditure to pre-set limits. When a gambler exceeds their pre-specified amount of money, various features can be activated including an automated shutdown and inability to continue to gamble. Again these are limited in the extent to which all EGMs require smart cards and other gambling opportunities available.

Venue modifications

In most international jurisdictions, gambling opportunities are limited to those over 18 or 21 years of age, similar to legal drinking ages. The motivation behind restricting access is to protect minors, who are not yet able to discern potentially harmful effects or are more likely to engage in risky behaviours due to developmental immaturity. In Nova Scotia, Canada, the service hours of EGMs were restricted after midnight in response to data suggesting that problem gamblers were playing on EGMs between midnight and the establishments' closing time (Corporate Research Associates, 2006). This measure reduces the availability of gambling after a particular time; however, casinos in Nova Scotia remain open after midnight allowing for the possibility that problem gamblers will move to such a venue to continue gambling. Evaluation of this modification found that it had some impact on higher risk gamblers in terms of reduction in expenditure, although some did shift to other venues and net revenues decreased by between 5% and 9% (Corporate Research Associates, 2006). Similar modifications were made to gambling venues in the Canadian province of Newfoundland and Labrador including a 25% reduction in the number of EGMs, venues restricted to opening between noon and midnight, slowing play by 30% and removing the stop-button feature – further slowing play. After a period of decline, revenue appears to be returning to previous levels. Analogous restrictions are in place in Australia, with each state mandating a period of shutdown from between 8 and 4 hours for most gaming venues. Studies evaluating mandated shutdowns in Australia found that these measures have only a small impact on problem gamblers, although they do not appear to adversely affect recreational gamblers or result in decreased gambling profits (Productivity Commission, 2010).

Similar to laws limiting the number and locations of liquor outlets, gambling venues are restricted in numbers, locations and the number of and forms of gambling they are allowed to supply. These restrictions are largely based on the perceived risks associated with each form of gambling. Casino games and EGMs are heavily restricted by regulators in terms of the number of venues and games that can be offered in an effort to moderate the accessibility drivers of problem gambling. Restrictions have also been placed on the location of gambling venues and the provision of gambling products, such as lottery tickets, in airports and near schools or shopping centres. Again, there is limited evidence to support the effectiveness of these restrictions on the availability of gambling on rates of problem gambling in the community. Following a detailed national review, the Australian Productivity Commission (2010) concluded that EGM caps in place were largely ineffective in addressing gambling related harms. Nevertheless, they noted that existing limits should not be relaxed and further reducing the number of gambling venues in a particular area could be seen as a useful transition to a model of accessibility centred on destination gambling rather than community-wide gambling, a view consistent with other international jurisdictions.

Recent judicial determinations that poker card games represent games of skill and not chance have implications for this form of gambling to be provided in unrestricted venues. The potential risk is that poker games will fall outside gaming regulatory requirements and therefore outside the domain of responsible gambling and harm minimisation.

Self-exclusion

Self-exclusion strategies are voluntary agreements entered into by an individual and a gambling operator whereby the individual agrees that they will not enter particular gambling venues and authorise venue staff to deny them access to or remove them from, premises if detected. The agreement places the responsibility on the self-excluded individual with the aim to reduce the availability of gambling opportunities in an effort to help problem gamblers cease or limit their gambling behaviour. As these agreements are initiated by the player, they can be considered a form of demand reduction; however, as they are considered to be a measure taken by gambling operators to limit access to gambling opportunities for problem gamblers and are binding, they are classified as a supply reduction strategy. Similar agreements are in place in some jurisdictions, including Australia and the UK, with respect to venues that serve alcohol.

Despite the implementation of self-exclusion strategies in numerous international jurisdictions and across a wide range of gambling forms, relatively little research has evaluated the efficacy of these strategies. There is some evidence that self-exclusion programmes result in decreases in expenditure, frequency and duration, reduction in problem severity and negative consequences, and a reduction in related psychological distress for a small minority of those who elect to use this facility. Given that only 1% or so of problem gamblers use self-exclusion, efforts are required to increase utilisation rates, increase the effectiveness of detection and enforcement of breaches, and to increase the extent to which self-exclusion agreements are applied to different gambling venues and across jurisdictions. With increased technological capabilities to assist in offering, promoting and enforcing self-exclusion, such programmes may become more successful in reducing gambling-related harms. They remain an important element of any harm reduction strategy.

Harm-minimisation strategies

Effective strategies should consider the elements of each form of gambling that would be predicted to change gambling behaviour for individuals at risk of experiencing harm. A range of potentially effective harm-minimisation strategies have been recommended and implemented across international jurisdictions.

Legalisation and legal control of gambling

Given the increasing popularity and acceptance of gambling as a form of entertainment, governments internationally are taking steps to legalise and regulate gambling opportunities in an effort to provide a safer playing environment and capitalise on revenue and taxes. Offering legalised gambling also reduces the appeal of illegal gambling, which acts to reduce criminal activity and potential dangers for gamblers including fraud, without necessarily requiring gamblers to modify the extent of their gambling. A cost-benefit analysis is required to determine the optimal conditions for this measure to prove successful (Cantinotti and Ladouceur, 2008).

Services for gamblers

Treatment services should be made available to gamblers in an effort to reduce existing behaviours and harms. Similarly, introducing and promoting alternative entertainment options for those visiting gambling venues or for those taking a break from gambling would result in a possible reduction in the likelihood that individuals would gamble excessively. Preliminary research from the USA, Canada, New Zealand and Australia also suggests that prohibiting cigarette smoking in gambling venues may be a demand reduction strategy as individuals have to take a break to smoke and may gamble less.

On-site crisis interventions for distressed gamblers are also a harm minimisation measure as they provide immediate support for gamblers who may be considering suicide. In such situations the focus is not on modifying or decreasing gambling behaviour, but protecting the individual, although behavioural change may be the target of subsequent interventions. Crisis intervention services may also be provided through telephone helplines and internet-based therapies including live chat options.

Assistance for families of problem gamblers

Harm minimisation strategies also consider the impacts of problem gambling on the families of gamblers. Children and partners of problem gamblers are at risk of experiencing violence, financial distress and neglect and such programmes have as their aim, the prevention or reduction of harm to significant others. Examples of these programmes include emergency accommodation for families of problem gamblers, measures taken to provide appropriate childcare for gamblers at gambling venues to reduce risk of neglect from being left in cars, although this latter approach could be argued to expose children to gambling and the development of favourable attitudes towards gambling – modelling by parents and the normalisation of gambling behaviour. Educational awareness campaigns of the harm caused to families may be viewed as a demand reduction strategy if it results in individuals gambling less.

Conclusions

Harm minimisation strategies are commonly used in other public health fields, but must be carefully considered before being extrapolated and applied to gambling scenarios. Various forms of gambling present unique challenges and risks to players and interventions successful in other fields may not always be effective for gambling. Reducing gambling-related harms often requires the reduction of gambling itself and consequentially should be classified as demand or supply reduction strategies. Although used in a variety of different contexts and definitions, for the purposes of this chapter, harm minimisation refers to a particular set of measures in the gambling field that reduce the potential hazards associated with excessive gambling, without necessarily reducing the use of gambling products. This fits with the original definition of harm minimisation, which recognises that abstinence or reduced use is not necessary or practical for all individuals and individuals who engage in an activity without experiencing problems should not be overtly disrupted or have their entertainment reduced.

In 2001, Blaszczynski et al. stated that there is an imperative need for systematic research to be conducted on all facets of harm minimisation. Empirical research and evaluation of proposed harm minimisation strategies should guide and inform policy and enable key stakeholders to protect community members from the harmful effects of excessive gambling without introducing additional unforeseen consequences for either problem or recreational gamblers.

It is important that the inherent conflict of interest faced by operators with regard to demand and supply reduction measures be addressed. Whether measures derive from industry self-regulation or formal government regulation, the incentive for venues to implement these effectively would be heightened by regulators taking steps to monitor compliance, introducing mechanisms for handling complaints and penalties for serious breaches. To achieve a reduction in gambling-related harms it is important to consider the costs and benefits of many elements of gambling and apply various strategies that use techniques designed to reduce demand and supply ultimately leading to a reduction in excessive gambling and consequent harms.

References

Abbott, M. (2007) Prospective problem gambling research: contribution and potential, *International Gambling Studies*, 7, 123–44.

American Psychiatric Association (2000) *Diagnostic and Statistical Manual of Mental Health Disorders*, 4th edn, text revision, Washington, DC: American Psychiatric Association.

Blaszczynski, A., Sharpe, L. and Walker, M. (2001) *Final Report: The Assessment of the Impact of the Reconfiguration on Electronic Gaming Machines as Harm Minimisation Strategies for Problem Gambling*, Sydney: University of Sydney Gambling Research Unit, University of Sydney.

Cantinotti, M. and Ladouceur, R. (2008) Harm reduction and electronic gambling machines: does this pair make a happy couple of is divorce foreseen?, *Journal of Gambling Studies*, 24, 39–54.

Corporate Research, Associates. (2006) *Video Lottery Program Changes: Impact Analysis*, www.nsgc.ca/pdf/VLTimpactanalysisreport.pdf, accessed 21 June 2007.

Currie, S., Hodgins D., Wang, J., el-Guebaly, N., Wynne, H. and Chen, S. and (2006) Risk of harm among gamblers in the general population as a function of level of participation in gambling activities, *Addiction*, 101, 570–80.

Dixon, M. and Harrigan, K. (2010) Losses disguised as wins in modern video slot machines, presentation given at Discovery 2010 Conference, Toronto, Canada, April.

Dowling, N., Smith, D. and Thomas, T. (2005) Electronic gaming machines: are they the 'crack-cocaine' of gambling, *Addiction*, 100, 33–45.

Hodgins, D.C. and el-Guebaly, N. (2000) Natural and treatment assisted recovery from gambling problems: comparison of resolved and active gamblers, *Addiction*, 95, 777–89.

LaPlante, D. and Shaffer, H. (2007) Understanding the influence of gambling opportunities: expanding exposure models to include adaptation, *American Journal of Orthopsychiatry*, 77 (4), 616–23.

LaPlante, D., Schumann, A., LaBrie, R.A. and Shaffer, H.J. (2008) Population trends in internet sports gambling, *Computers in Human Behavior*, 24, 2399–414.

Lenton, S. and Single, S. (1998) The definition of harm reduction, *Drug and Alcohol Review*, 17, 213–20.

Lund, I. (2009) Gambling behaviour and the prevalence of gambling problems in adult EGM gamblers when EGMs are banned: a natural experiment, *Journal of Gambling Studies*, 25, 215–25.

MacCoun, R.J. (1998) Toward a psychology of harm reduction, *American Psychologist*, 53, 1199–1208.

Marlatt, A.G. (1996) Harm reduction: come as you are, *Addictive Behaviors*, 21, 779–88.

Ministry of Health (New Zealand) (2008) *Raising the Odds? Gambling Behaviour and Neighbourhood Access to Gambling Venues in New Zealand*, Wellington: Ministry of Health.

Monaghan, S. and Blaszczynski, A. (2010a) Electronic gaming machine warning messages: informative versus self-evaluation, *Journal of Psychology: Interdisciplinary & Applied*, 144 (1) 83–96.

Monaghan, S. and Blaszczynski, A. (2010b) Impact of mode of display and message content of responsible gambling signs for electronic gaming machines on regular gamblers, *Journal of Gambling Studies*, 26 (1), 67–88.

Monaghan, S., Derevensky, J. and Sklar, A. (2009) Impact of gambling advertisements on children and adolescents: policy recommendations to minimize harm, *Journal of Gambling Issues*, 22, 252–74, www.camh.net/egambling/issue22/06monaghan-derevensky.html, accessed 1 May 2009.

National Research Council (1999) *Pathological Gambling: A Critical Review*, Washington, DC: National Academy Press.

Productivity Commission (1999) *Australia's Gambling Industries: Final Report*, Canberra: Commonwealth of Australia.

Productivity Commission (2010) *Gambling*. Report no. 50, Canberra: Productivity Commission.

Reith, G. (2006) *Research on the Social Impacts of Gambling: Final Report*, Edinburgh: Scottish Executive Social Research.

Rush, B., Veldhuizen, S. and Adlaf, E. (2007) Mapping the prevalence of problem gambling and its association with treatment accessibility and proximity to gambling venues, *Journal of Gambling Issues*, 20, www.camh.net/egambling/issue20/05rush.htm, accessed 21 April 2009.

Sévigny, S., Ladouceur, R., Jacques, C. and Cantinotti, M. (2008) Links between casino proximity and gambling participation, expenditure and pathology, *Psychology of Addictive Behaviours*, 22, 295–301.

Shaffer, H. (2005) From disabling to enabling the public interest: natural transitions from gambling exposure to adaptation and self-regulation – commentary, *Addiction*, 100, 1227–30.

Shaffer, H. and Korn, D. (2002) Gambling and related mental disorders: a public health analysis, *Annual Review of Public Health*, 23, 171–212.

Slutske, W., Jackson, K. and Sher, K. (2003) The natural history of problem gambling from age 18 to 29, *Journal of Abnormal Psychology*, 112, 263–74.

Stockwell, T. (2001) Harm reduction, drinking patterns and the NHMRC drinking guidelines, *Drugs and Alcohol Review*, 20, 121–9.

Stockwell, T. (2006) Alcohol supply, demand, and harm reduction: what is the strongest cocktail?, *International Journal of Drug Policy*, 17, 269–77.

Storer, J., Abbott, M. and Stubbs, J. (2009) Access or adaptation? A meta-analysis of surveys of problem gambling prevalence in Australia and New Zealand with respect to concentration of electronic gaming machines, *International Gambling Studies*, 9 (3), 225–44.

Volberg, R. (1994) The prevalence and demographics of pathological gamblers: Implications for public health, *American Journal of Public Health*, 84 (2), 237–41.

Wardle, H., Sproston, K., Orford, J., Erens, B., Griffiths, M.D., Constantine, R. and Pigott, S. (2007) *The British Gambling Prevalence Survey 2007*, London: Stationery Office.

Welte, J.W., Wieczorek, W.F., Barnes, G.M., Tidwell, M.C. and Hoffman, J.H. (2004) The relationship of ecological and geographic factors to gambling behaviour, *Journal of Gambling Studies*, 20, 405–23.

Williams, R.J. and Wood, R.T. (2004) The proportion of gaming revenue derived from problem gamblers: examining the issues in a Canadian context, *Analyses of Social Issues and Public Policy*, 4, 33–45.

Wood, R.T. and Williams, R.J. (2007) Problem gambling on the internet: Implications for internet gambling policy in North America, *New Media & Society*, 9, (3), 520–42.

Wood, R. and Williams, R. (2009) *internet Gambling: Prevalence, Patterns, Problems, and Policy Options*, Final Report prepared for the Ontario Problem Gambling Research Centre, Guelph, Ontario, Canada.

Chapter 21

YOUNG PEOPLE AND HARM REDUCTION IN THE UK: A COMMUNITY PERSPECTIVE

Mags Maher

Separate needs of young people

For too long young people have not been recognised as a separate group by drug services and while there have been attempts made to work with young people between the ages of 18 to 21 years, very few services have taken on the challenge of working with young people under the age of 18. This has been influenced by two factors: (1) the close partnerships required in working with social services taking account of child protection issues, (2) the National Drugs Treatment Agency (NTS) do not collect separate data for young people's services.

Drug users under the age of 18 are a challenge and specialist services should be established to accommodate this. Young people often do not recognise the existence of a problem, which is compounded by the belief that they are invincible and the 'it won't happen to me syndrome'. There is little awareness of the risks involved when using drugs and because of their immaturity an inability to think through situations removes recognition of consequences.

Additionally, some young people who have come from disaffected or disadvantaged backgrounds are unable to manage their emotions and may walk around in a heightened state of anxiety. This may be translated into anger and/or agitation and thus their drug use may be destructive as are some of life choices.

In the UK that the majority of young people will have come into contact with or will know someone who is using drugs and/or alcohol by the time they are 13 years old. By the time they are 15 or 16 years old they will know more than the professionals about recent and current trends in drug use which raises the question of why we keep old style 'prevention education' rather than use harm reduction messages (see also chapter 3 by Julian Cohen).

Since the 1990s the UK has not recognised the problems associated with being a young person in the twenty-first century such as being expected to grow up quickly and deal with adult themes, being exposed to information and concepts way beyond their years through the media, internet and so forth, struggling to find an identity and deal with the mixed messages that are constantly being given by adults. All of these factors should be taken into consideration when providing a service for under 18s who use drugs.

The borough of Luton

Luton is about 25 miles (40 kilometres) outside of London, a new town which was developed in the 1960s as an overspill for London. Luton remains a replica of London, on a smaller scale. In the 1960s it was attractive, being a 30-minute commute into the City of London by train. Like London

Harm Reduction in Substance Use and High-Risk Behaviour: International Policy and Practice, First Edition.
Edited by Richard Pates and Diane Riley.
© 2012 Blackwell Publishing Ltd. Published 2012 by Blackwell Publishing Ltd.

it has a very diverse population and although it has experienced some strained relationships in the past, Luton has embraced diversity and this is reflected in the town.

Luton itself has a very diverse population, our project works with young people from Asia, Bangladesh, Pakistan, Afghanistan, Poland, Czech Republic, Serbia, Jamaica, the Caribbean Islands and Britain. Those young people who are born in Britain generally use the drugs belonging to the stimulant family or from the party scene. What is interesting is that all the other nationalities still choose heroin as their drug of choice with those from Eastern Europe having the highest number of injectors. This group of young people have learnt bad injecting techniques and present with a variety of injecting problems. Language is often a barrier and the staff provide information via DVD and/or written information which has been translated. The diversity of the young people in Luton is attributed partly to its airport which is located five minutes from the town centre and many children and young people are trafficked into the country through this route. If they do not present to social services they are soon placed within the sex industry by organised gangs.

Luton remains a poor town with many people claiming benefits from the social welfare system. A number of services have been set up in the borough specifically for young people. An example of services provided is the Teenage Pregnancy Team (Luton Community Services NHS) which in 2007/2008 reported the area to have the highest rate of teenage pregnancy in the UK. The team worked hard to reduce this as well as the high rate of sexually transmitted infections amongst its young population and the rate of teenage pregnancies fell 2008–10.

The town has a number of problems with a high rate of domestic abuse, a high level of drinking amongst young people in the town, with many arriving at A&E (Accident & Emergency) on a Friday and Saturday night, and a large number of drug dealers in the area. Many young women are enticed into the sex industry and injection drug use, the taboo nature of which drives the problem underground.

Luton has a large university, is host to one of the world's largest annual carnivals and has a large shopping centre and library. Luton's drug services work in partnership with many agencies including Education in schools and colleges, Luton Social Services, Council Housing, Criminal Justice (e.g. Probation and Youth Offending Service), Child & Adolescent Mental Health services and drug services such as Addaction, Luton CAN (Community Drugs Project), Alcohol Services and Luton Drug & Alcohol Specialist Service which works with Dual Diagnosis.

The Luton underground (drug service for young people in Luton)

The Luton Underground is a community based service operating with a harm reduction philosophy for young people living in Luton aged 25 and under. The service was set up initially around 2003 to meet the needs of young people who were unable to access a specific young people's service. It was considered that young people have different needs and require a different approach to the delivery of care and treatment. Prior to this young people had to attend the adult service for treatment.

We provide a needs-led, holistic and evidenced-based service to young people who reside in Luton with a primary drug misuse need/s. The service is particularly keen to promote its work to those hard-to-reach young people who may resort to criminal activities or leading a risky lifestyle in order to finance their addiction.

The services provided include:

• assessment and key-working for drug treatment;
• substitute opioid prescribing;

- symptomatic prescribing for other non-prescribed drug misuse;
- physical health checks;
- mental health assessment and interventions including those with severe and enduring mental illness;
- drug intervention programme for youth offenders;
- chlamydia screening;
- pregnancy testing;
- condom card scheme;
- structured counselling and psychotherapy;
- care coordination;
- blood borne virus testing;
- overdose prevention and advice;
- immunisation and vaccination;
- safeguarding of children initiatives.

The Luton underground's harm reduction philosophy

The Harm Reduction philosophy is embedded in practice and we support the achievement of positive emotional outcomes (recovery) within a harm reduction framework. We operate an open door Policy and have a low threshold service which removes barriers. Typical examples of this include allowing dogs into the service and letting the young people who access the service to be in control of the interaction and disclosure of information. In essence we operate a one stop shop which includes all primary care and we engage in outreach as we believe in the importance of meeting young people in their own environment. This supports engagement and builds on the therapeutic alliance, so it is not uncommon for key workers to meet young people in nail parlours, burger joints, youth clubs, at home and so forth. The young people have been supported to voice what they want and need from both the service and the staff and have shaped this service by participating in service user involvement forums. Also they have helped in a local needs assessment and they are encouraged to make complaints with regard to anything with which they are not happy such as. staff comments, attitudes, and interactions. We see this as a feedback process which allows us as a staff team to reflect on our practice, prejudices and communication skills. The young people are also involved in meeting and greeting new comers to the service and participate in delivery of drug awareness sessions at schools and colleges.

Those that we work in partnership with include: Social Services, Youth Offending Service (YOS), Education, Community Mental Health Teams (CMHTs), Child and Adolescent Mental Health Services (CAMHS), GPs, pharmacists, Teaching Primary Care Trust (TPCT), SNAP (Social Needs Art Project: voluntary sector organisation providing therapy through art, drama and photography) and housing. We have developed joint working protocols and our communication is enhanced through regular liaison, attendance at their team meetings, attendance at care plan reviews and lead professionals meetings. We work collaboratively to provide intensive support packages to secure the achievement of positive emotional outcomes and independence and our Commissioner who heads up LDAP (Luton Drug & Alcohol Partnership) recently ran a series of Partnership days which focused on improving the client journey.

The workforce comprises of a multidisciplinary team consisting of a range of practitioners including nurses, doctors, administrators, drug and alcohol workers, counsellor and an 'emotional well-being' drug worker. All the staff are expected to be compliant with corporate mandatory training such as, Infection Control and Safeguarding of Vulnerable Adults and Children. These are monitored centrally in collaboration with the Training Department of NHS Luton and all staff are subject to an annual appraisal process that are monitored centrally in collaboration with NHS Luton Human Resource Department. All the staff are also subject to mandatory checks such as Criminal Record Bureau checks and all related disclosure requirements.

The promotion of self-care

The Luton Underground also supports self-care through a range of initiatives including the availability of treatment information. For example harm reduction leaflets and advice such as *safer injecting techniques; overdose awareness and prevention* distributed freely and easily accessible throughout the service including the drop in. The nurse consultation room has leaflets and information on blood-borne virus infection on hepatitis A, B and C, HIV as well as sexual health information on chlamydia and safer sex practices. Key work rooms and the activities room have information on drug and alcohol treatment and related health risks. Information on medication such as methadone and subutex is readily available on request in different languages and can be downloaded. Information on other agencies with other interventions is also available and a forum within the young person team which promotes inclusiveness and service user empowerment is promoted and updated regularly through the Service User Board in the Drop In.

Educating our stakeholders

The work with young people who are using drugs is highly emotional and very complex with many cases being deemed as high risk and requiring safeguarding procedures. Because of this the Luton Underground actively participates in the delivery of training across the borough which includes running a workshop titled 'Colluding With Silence' – Training includes identifying the risk indicators of children and young people being groomed and sexually exploited, drugs awareness, and working with young problem drug users and is given to professionals and students of social work and nursing, with a view to educating the next generation of professionals entering this field.

Our failure to meet the needs of young people who use drugs

We currently live in a society where drug users are both demonised and criminalised for the failures of society and the failure of the caring professions to honour their responsibilities in offering effective and appropriate treatment. Few professionals speak up about what is in effect is right and wrong with our treatment of other human beings. Children and young people grow up with damage and *'children are blamed, given anti-social behaviour orders, locked up, paying the price for adult incompetencies'* (Batmanghelidjh, 2006).

A lost generation

The 1980s brought a number of changes, such as new drug trends among the young, including the introduction of party drugs and stimulants. Britain was dealing with a 'lost generation' of young people, the innovation and creativity of new music, fashion, art and direction was probably at one of the lowest points in British history. Young people using drugs prior to this time had been influenced by beatniks, mods and rockers, the hippie scene followed by the punk scene, the new romantics and so on. These music scenes brought all young people together under one banner speaking to their generation and making them feel a part of something bigger than themselves with a common interest and understanding.

By the early 1980s under conservative rule in the UK the young hit a brick wall and came to a standstill with no direction to go in or sense of belonging. Drug users were portrayed as 'dirty low lifes' sleeping on street corners looking totally emaciated and hopeless with syringes hanging out of their arms and a clear message, strongly suggesting that if in this state they would run the risk of contracting HIV. The young in this country were in need and looking for a new direction, a new era – a decade they could claim for themselves and a generation to belong to.

It was at this directionless time for many that MDMA took centre stage and became popular in Britain as the 'love drug' and influenced a whole generation of young people. Young people started to create again, and new music started to be filter onto the scene. Young people were able to go into clubs and raves, dancing till dawn and leaving with many new friends; for most young people the 'typical opiate user' became a thing of the past.

The introduction of MDMA brought about experimentation with various other drugs including alcohol, LSD and powder cocaine. Cannabis was mostly available as resin or hash. By the late 1980s the Conservative government fuelled by media and hype started to come down very heavily on raves, making them illegal and bit by bit the 'party scene' became a thing of the past leaving many young people reminiscing about 'the good old days'. Their 'love drug' went underground as the media continued to exaggerate reports and headlines about this 'mysterious drug', linking it to illegal raves and young people who were wreckless and out of control. The results of which were that the quality of MDMA was reduced, and initially cost increased. Consequently young people in their endeavours to recapture what was being quickly lost on the dance scene started to experiment with a cocktail of various other drugs including GBH and ketamine which together with alcohol created the 'dance trance' culture in clubs or run down squats and warehouses. Powdered cocaine increased in popularity and started to become a regular feature on the club scene. Throughout this period heroin was used by some young people as the drug to help with the 'come down or crash' from stimulants but both alcohol and cannabis were more frequently being used to help with this.

Politics and young people's services

The New Labour government launched the ten-year drug strategy *Tackling Drugs to Build a Better Britain* in 1998 and numerous policy measures have been introduced since the 1990s to overcome the negative effects of problem drug use on community safety and public health. Drug policy and practice has primarily focused on tackling the use of illegal drugs amongst individual drug users by increasing the range of treatment programmes, imposing tougher legal sanctions on both the drug users and their suppliers and establishing widespread public information campaigns. There has been little or no focus on children, young people and families even though they have been high on the National Agenda for the years 2005–10.

The Department of Health (DoH) published a White Paper, *Choosing Health: Making Healthy Choices Easier* in 2004 which set out key principles for supporting individuals to make healthier and more informed choices in relation to their health. This paper specifically recognised that young people needed opportunities to learn about their world in ways that would provide positive things to do as an alternative to experimenting with drugs. Reference was also made to the need for adequate information provision and clearer messages for young people about drugs. More recently, policy and practice has changed considerably and has focused on aims that specifically reduce drug use amongst young people and improve care for children affected by drug-using parents. Specific examples include the Advisory Council on the Misuse of Drugs (ACMD) inquiry into the needs of children of problem drug using parents (Hidden Harm, ACMD, 2003). In a more recent report on the use of drugs by young people, the ACMD recommended that the government should continue investing in reducing the number of children and young people living in relative poverty as a key way in which to reduce young people's involvement in drugs.

In 2008 the *Every Child Matters: Change for Children* introduced a programme that included a specific policy focus on children, young people and drugs. Choosing not to take illegal drugs is one of the five aims within the Every Child Matters outcomes 'Be healthy'. As part of this agenda, the former Department for Education and Skills, the Home Office and the Department of Health agreed on a joint approach to the development of targeted and specialist services to prevent drug related harm to children and young people. The approach comprises three main objectives: fostering closer links locally, regionally and nationally between the existing drug strategy and Every Child Matters programme; ensuring that the needs of vulnerable children and young people are met; and building service and workforce capacity.

Just before the *Every Child Matters* programme was rolled out the Department for Children, Schools and Families (DCSF) published *The Children's Plan10* in December 2007. This plan aims to build on the work of the Every Child Matters programme and recognises the need to do more to tackle drug misuse by parents, improve the quality and coverage of specialist drug treatment for young people who experience the most serious harm from drugs and strengthen the role of both schools and children's services in drug prevention. *The Children's Plan* recognises and acknowledges that the voluntary and community sector plays a central role in the delivery of specialist drug services and makes reference to the need for the DCSF to fully support the drug sector by working effectively in partnership with schools and local authorities.

The government has also published cross-departmental targetsfor the period 2008–11. Several targets underpin the delivery of the 2008 drug strategy including reducing the proportion of young people frequently using illicit drugs, alcohol or volatile substances and reducing the harm caused by alcohol and drugs. This target is measured by the number of drug users entering into and remaining in effective treatment, the rate of drug related offending and the percentage of the public who perceive drug use or dealing to be a problem in their local area. One national indicator relates specifically to substance misuse and young people and is defined by the percentage of young people reporting either frequent misuse of drugs/volatile substances or alcohol, or both. Relevant central government departments will be assessed against these targets, as well as being reflected in local government performance indicators. It is hoped these will refocus central and local targets aimed at reducing drug taking. Voluntary and community sector (VCS) support to meet these targets should be recognised by local partnership arrangements.

While government policy and approach towards drug treatment and drug use has changed since the 1990s, the drug culture has continued to change amongst young people and there is now a situation where cocaine has crept into the pub culture and is regularly used with copious amounts of alcohol. A new generation of young people use a combination of crystal and tablet MDMA, ketamine, cocaine powder, cannabis/skunk, alcohol and sometimes heroin. The quality of these drugs is generally very poor with reports of as little as 5% purity of cocaine being detected. The 'legal high' mephedrone or M-cat was increasing in popularity amongst young people until its ban in the UK.

Mephedrone's popularity was said to be as a result of high purity, low cost, knowing the source and not having to buy from dealers.

While the government have been introducing stringent measures to reduce and control the use of drugs, young people have continued to create cocktails of substances that will allow them to experience the pleasure enhancement they are seeking. While policy has concentrated more on 'encouraging' young people to stop using drugs it has not taken account of the fact that very disturbed children take a very long time to show visibly improved outcomes. The problem in presenting outcomes in the way that is currently being demanded is that clinicians are trying to exclude those children and young people from their services who are likely not to provide 'positive outcomes since lack of positive outcomes will mean reduced funding. Stakeholders engaged in partnership work with drug services do not have a clear grasp or understanding of harm reduction and demand that drug services 'make the young person stop taking drugs' and strongly advocate for abstinence with the threat of ceasing the continued provision of positive support for the young person. In truth *'Our social care structures are doing a bad job . . . being forced to mimic business values'* (Batman-ghelidjh 2006) at the expense of the country's most disaffected young who use a combination of substances, very often without the appropriate harm reduction advice, learning instead through experimentation which leaves them vulnerable to exploitation.

What we are working with today and moving forward

Risk reduction needs to focus on the behaviour or other factors that place the young person at risk, for not just disease, but abuse, exploitation, bullying, crime, homelessness, unwanted pregnancy and health complications such as emphysema and TB. Harm reduction must introduce and involve a range of approaches to prevent and reduce drug-related harm which is caused by the above factors and behaviours including *prevention*, *early intervention*, *specialist treatment*, *supply control*, *safer drug use* and *abstinence*. Drug services have a responsibility to educate their partner stakeholders that harm reduction is concerned with recognising that the containment and reduction of drug related harms is a more feasible option than efforts to eliminate drug use entirely.

A broader perspective on harm reduction within service delivery

For the Luton Underground it became evident very early on that harm reduction in relation to working with young people was going to have to take on a much broader perspective, because identifying the risky behaviours related to drug use also had to embrace all the risk factors affecting that young person's life. Not only had drug use and drug culture changed dramatically among young people but also their lives: they were trying to manage adult lives and themes, issues that they were neither emotionally nor mentally competent or equipped to do. A harm reduction philosophy was embedded in day-to-day practice and placed no expectation on the young people other than to support the expectations they had of themselves and focusing on achieving positive emotional outcomes. An open door policy was implemented which aimed at a rapport and a therapeutic alliance with the young people. They were also allowed to voice their opinions and changes could be implemented in line with their views. The recruitment of staff has had to ensure that charismatic and committed staff are employed allowing young people freedom of expression as well as treating them as individuals, respecting their views, learning from their expertise and feedback and advocating on their behalf when facing injustice and marginalisation.

An example of the work of Luton underground

A young person was placed on a reparation order as part of the panel agreement for common assault and they were ordered to do 30 hours reparation. This same young person was using skunk, cocaine, alcohol and intermittently ecstasy pills. First contact with this young person was difficult as they presented as very withdrawn with clear evidence of a lack of self-confidence and self-esteem. This young person could not socially adapt to the conditions of reparation; and they were taken back to court for tougher sentencing. Further work with this young person showed that they were paranoid when working with others and found it hard to trust anyone. During one of the sessions it came to light that her grandmother, who had raised her, assaulted her regularly with her walking stick. It became evident that reparation would not support this young person to make positive life changes that would enable her to relinquish her past and build the confidence and self-esteem she needed for the future.

Looking at this case and others that we have worked with it became clear that this system is not taking into account the wider issues that the young person may be finding hard to deal with. As highlighted by Goldson and Muncie (2007) there is a blurring between children in need and children in trouble, with the system clearly criminalising more children in need then in trouble. Those children 'who are most heavily exposed to correctional interventions, surveillance and punishment within the youth justice system, are routinely drawn from some of the most disadvantaged families, neighbourhoods and communities' (Goldson and Muncie, 2007: 60)

This case study is typical of a number of young people who approach our service for advice and support with their drug use, the majority eventually make disclosures of sexual abuse, domestic abuse, self-harming, suicidal ideation, mental health difficulties and involvement in the sex industry. Frequently abortion is considered as a form of contraception and young people as young as 22 are suffering with emphysema and their general health is very poor. Sexual favours in exchange for a packet of cigarettes or a roof over their heads for the night is also common practice. Sexually transmitted infection rates among young people reflected that 8 out of 10 young people being tested for chlamydia at our service receive positive results.

Embracing the principles of harm reduction when working with young people

When working with young people the central idea of harm reduction is one that recognises that some young people always have and always will engage in behaviours which carry risk, such as casual sex, prostitution and drug use. Approaches to young people using drugs has to embrace the core principles of harm reduction starting with and accepting the fact that that the use of drugs is a common and enduring feature of human experience. Acknowledgement must be made that drug use provides them with benefits that must be taken into account if responses to drug use are to be effective.

Harm reduction responses to drug use must incorporate the notion of a hierarchy of goals, young people's most compelling needs must be supported and addressed through the provision of accessible and user friendly services. Stakeholders and Drug Services must both work from the premise that the young person's decision to use drugs is accepted as fact.

Practitioners cannot afford to focus merely on abstinence. The harm reduction approach recognises that short-term abstinence oriented treatments have low success rates, and anecdotal evidence has shown us that this is especially so in the case of young people.

Finally drug services that are working with young people must seek to maximise the range of intervention options that are available, and engage in a process of identifying, measuring, and assessing the relative importance of drug-related harms and balancing costs and benefits in trying to reduce them. The Luton Underground runs numerous workshops including: graffiti, photography, animal care, who do I want to be? (principles and values), human rights, harm reduction and drugs education, sexuality support group, government funded kids support group, condom card scheme, chlamydia screening, smoking cessation, and drop in. Our interventions include: outreach, crisis intervention, problem solving, brief interventions, befriending, peer support, CBT, structured intervention, prescribing, harm reduction packs, party packs, survival pack (for young women selling sex) and practical support with food, travel expenses, and bills.

A new perspective for young people's services

Harm reduction services would benefit from considering the implementation of Maslow's hierarchy of needs from top down as a treatment pathway for young people as this would allow harm reduction philosophy to be translated into practice on a day-to-day basis. If young people are supported to attain some self-actualisation in relation to their risky behaviours then there is a platform to raise their basic awareness around issues related to morality, creativity, problem solving, lack of prejudice and the acceptance of facts. Once this awareness of self has been achieved then the young person can start to build on their self-esteem, confidence, achievement and respect of both themselves and others. At this stage a young person will have started to demonstrate positive emotional outcomes and an increase in maturity which with the right support will increase their ability to embrace love and belonging and address issues related to friendships, family and sexual intimacy. Then work can be done around safety which would include security of the body, of employment, of resources, the family, health and accommodation. Safe and secure housing is also an important factor for these young people. Once these four steps have been achieved then work can be done on the physiological factors (basic needs) such as food, water, sleep, gas, electric and homeostasis. This is a long journey for any service to support and the outcomes will be slow to achieve, but harm reduction is a thread that can run through this whole process and so support young people to achieve their aspirations.

Note

The Speaking Out project has published a briefing paper on the government's Comprehensive Spending Review which includes further information about public service agreements. The briefing is available to download from the Speaking Out pages at www.childrenengland.org.uk or www.ncvys.org.uk.

References

Advisory Council on the Misuse of Drugs (2003) *Hidden Harm: Responding to the Needs of Children of Problem Drug Users*, London: Home Office.
Advisory Council on the Misuse of Drugs (2006) *Pathways to Problems: Hazardous Use of Tobacco, Alcohol and Other Drugs by Young People in the UK and Its Implications for Policy*, http://publications.everychild-matters.gov.uk/eOrderingDownload/DCSF-00331-2008.pdf.

Bateman, T. and Pitts, J. (2005) *The RHP Companion to Youth Justice*, Dorset: Russel House Publishing.

Batmanghelidjh, C. (2006) *Shattered Lives*, 1st edn, London and Philadelphia: Jessica Kingsley.

Burnett, R. and Appleton, C. (2004) *Joined-up Youth Justice: Tackling Youth Crime in Partnership*, Lyme Regis: Russell House Publishing.

Burney, E. (2005) *Making People Behave: Anti-social Behaviour and Policy*, Cullompton: Willan Publishing.

Choosing Health: Making Healthy Choices (2004) www.dh.gov.uk/en/Publicationsandstatistics/Publications/ PublicationsPolicyAndGuidance/DH_4094550, accessed 6 July.

DCSF (2007) *The Children's Plan*, www.dcsf.gov.uk/publications/childrensplan/, accessed 6 July.

Goldson, B. and Muncie, J. (2007) Youth justice with integrity beyond Allen's 'New Approach'. In Z. Davies and W. McMahon (eds), *Debating Youth Justice: From Punitive to Problem Solving?* London: London Centre from Crime and Justice Studies.

HM, Government (2005) *Every Child Matters: Change for Children – Young People and Drugs*, www.everychildmatters.gov.uk/_files/9660D91BB1755A6E288998AAE145297F.pdf.

Home Office (1989) No More Excuses, www.nationalarchives.gov.uk/ERORecords/HO/421/2/cpd/jou/nmes. htm, accessed 6 July 2010.

Pitts, J. (1989) Cited in E. Burney (2005) *Making People Behave: Anti-social Behaviour and Policy*, Devon: Willan Publishing.

Pitts, J. (2003) *The New Politics of Youth Crime: Discipline or Solidarity*, 2nd edn. London: Macmillan, Russell House.

Smith, R. (2007) *Youth Justice: Ideas, Policy and Practice*, 2nd edn, Devon: Willan Publishing.

Tackling Drugs to Build a Better Britain, www.archive.official-documents.co.uk/document/cm39/3945/3945 .htm, accessed 6 July.

Chapter 22

MAKING TOOLS FOR HARM REDUCTION: THE STORY OF EXCHANGE SUPPLIES

Jon Derricott

This chapter describes and explains the history and continuing development of Exchange Supplies, a unique UK based social enterprise that designs, produces, and supplies a wide range of practical resources aimed at reducing the harm caused by drug use: 'tools for harm reduction'. We produce printed resources, videos, and injecting equipment that has all been specifically designed for drug users. We also organise the National Drug Treatment Conference, and the National Conference on Injecting Drug Use and maintain several websites, including www.exchangesupplies.org which has over 5,000 pages of information, all of it available free of charge.

Exchange Supplies is based on a small industrial estate in the quiet south-west English town of Dorchester. The company has grown up since the 1990s, and currently employs around 20 people, most based in Dorchester where new product development, customer support, and the day-to-day processing, pick, pack and despatch of products and publications is based in 4 industrial units.

In this chapter, I'll look first at the historical development of the company as a social enterprise and, for non-UK readers, provide a context to the history with a description of the arcane UK legal situation regarding the supply of items used for the preparation and administration of drugs (usually referred to as 'paraphernalia'), as that is central to the story. I will also describe in detail some products including citric acid, water for injections (WFI), aluminium foil, and nevershare syringes. The chapter concludes with a look at some particularly notable recent developments and some tentative thoughts about what the future may hold.

The beginning

Exchange Supplies came about because as activists in harm reduction, it became clear that if we didn't take the initiative and develop our first product – citric acid sachets – no one else would. We', are Andrew Preston and myself, who in 2000 were both working as freelance drug trainers and writers. Prior to that Andrew had worked for ten years as a community drug worker with the local drug treatment agency in Dorchester, and I had previously similarly worked as a community drug worker and then gained valuable experience as training and development manager at HIT in Liverpool.

At that time, we were becoming increasingly concerned by the problems caused by limited access by injecting drug users (IDUs) to citric acid, the most commonly used acidifier for UK street heroin. IDUs were frequently turning to more dangerous alternatives such as lemon juice and vinegar,

Harm Reduction in Substance Use and High-Risk Behaviour: International Policy and Practice, First Edition.
Edited by Richard Pates and Diane Riley.
© 2012 Blackwell Publishing Ltd. Published 2012 by Blackwell Publishing Ltd.

which carried an additional risk of the development of fungal infections. As freelancers, we found ourselves in a position to be able to explore solutions to this problem.

Perhaps naively, we had spent some years trying to interest some of the existing suppliers of injecting equipment in our ideas. The enormous drawback with this approach was that many of our suggestions, though unquestionably worthwhile, were technically illegal at the time under an obscure and little used section of the Misuse of Drugs Act 1971 (MDA) – see 'Our products and the law' below. Those individuals that did show some initial interest, were unable to pursue the project further when they explained to their managers the (in reality very distant) possibility of prosecution for supply of drug paraphernalia. It gradually became clearer to us that no one else was going to do this, and that if we wanted to see it happen, then we would have to drive it.

How exchange supplies developed

The nascent idea of Exchange Supplies as a business began in 1992, when Andrew started self-publishing drug information publications for drug users including the methadone handbook and safer injecting handbook. Gradually building a substantial catalogue of work aimed at both drug users and health professionals gave him an understanding of the rudiments of running a successful growing business, that proved essential when executing the launch and development of the citric acid sachets, and the other products that followed.

We formed Exchange Supplies as a limited company because we didn't want to have to put anyone in the position of being a trustee or member of a management committee with responsibility for our actions, as we felt they would be obliged to counsel caution in areas on (or sometimes slightly over) the edge of legality. We also wanted to maximise our independence so that we could innovate in areas that we felt were priorities for reducing drug related harm, rather than always being forced to follow funding streams that are often heavily influenced by changing political agendas.

We have both needed to acquire a lot of new knowledge and skills in the process of building Exchange Supplies to its current position. In a deliberate process of developing the skills and knowledge that are fundamental to the success of all businesses, Andrew has developed a particular aptitude for, and understanding of business through continual attendance at training events and seminars. The growth of the company would simply not have happened without his drive and enthusiasm.

Key elements of the business success include the development of an annual, coherent business plan, a focus on customer service, and an efficient warehousing and despatch facility. The careful management of a growing workforce and recruiting a staff team with a mix of backgrounds including harm reduction, drug use, and more traditional business skills has also been crucial in ensuring our success.

The business model we've used has essentially been one of developing products and services for which there is a need, and then investing profits made from their sale into new products. As we have grown, we have been able to accelerate the rate of new product development.

It hasn't all been about business skills: another skill set we have developed in recent years has been that of film-making. Having recognised the huge potential of film to deliver complex messages, I underwent a rapid learning curve to become a competent one-man documentary film unit, in order that we can make accessible films quickly and cheaply. This means that rather than having to always hire in an expensive crew to make our commissioned work, we can film it ourselves, and invest in better equipment to drive further improvements in the quality of our work.

Exchange supplies: a social enterprise

Defining ourselves as a social enterprise developed as we analysed the things that made us different from other suppliers. A full discussion of what social enterprises are, and what they are not is beyond the scope of this chapter, but essentially the key differentiator of social enterprises is that they have clear social and/or health objectives, and surpluses are invested in the furtherance of those objectives. These are two criteria that we have always kept at the forefront of what we do.

Our mission, is to reduce drug related harm and improve and prolong the lives of drug users by:

- developing and supplying effective equipment and resources;
- publishing quality information;
- influencing policy and practice;
- offering the highest standards of service and customer satisfaction; giving value for money; and
- providing employment, training and career opportunities for drug users.

This means that we invest all we can in product development, conferences and educational events, drug user involvement and free availability of information online. This includes a huge range of harm reduction and drug information films on our YouTube channel.

Social enterprises have a distinct and valuable role to play in helping create a strong, sustainable and socially inclusive economy. Successful social enterprises can play an important role in helping to:

- drive up innovation, productivity and competitiveness;
- contribute to socially inclusive wealth creation;
- enable individuals and communities to work towards regenerating their local neighborhoods;
- show new ways to deliver public services; and
- help to develop an inclusive society and active citizenship.

All this is made more possible because, unlike 'normal' businesses, social enterprises are not driven by the need to maximise profit for shareholders and owners.

An important element of our social mission has been our commitment to offering employment and training opportunities to current and former drug users. The varied nature of our work means that we are able to offer a range of jobs, from occasional employment for people working towards entering the employment marketplace, to regular part-time work that fits with the UK's benefits system, through to full-time complex work at the heart of our operation.

Another key element of our social mission, and success, has been our website exchangesupplies.org. When we first began developing the sachets, the web was the perfect medium for communicating what was a rapidly changing picture. As the company has grown we've remained committed to freely providing as much harm reduction information as possible on our website. Over the years, augmented by the conference archives, this has developed into one of the largest harm reduction resources on the internet. Building this resource has contributed to the development of a huge amount of goodwill and customer loyalty from the field, which has been a key element in our success.

Our products and the law

Since the inception of needle and syringe programmes (NSPs) paraphernalia supply has been a complex and problematic legal issue in the UK. The two main legal issues have centered on

- the Misuse of Drugs Act 1971, which has a subsection 'section 9a' that made it an offence for a person to supply any article – except a syringe or needle – in cases where, 'the supplier believes it may be used by the recipient to administer an unlawful drug or prepare an unlawful drug for administration';
- the Medicines Act 1968, under the Medicines Act, water for injections was deemed a 'prescription only medicine' (POM). This meant that it could not legally be supplied by NSPs.

Section 9a was drafted to enable prosecution of drug dealers selling complete drug kits and the implements with which to take them. Needles and syringes were specifically exempted in the mid-1980s to allow NSPs to operate lawfully. It was really only of academic interest to the UK drug field, it was, and is rarely used by the police for its intended purpose. Probably because in several attempted prosecutions for sale of cannabis and cocaine consumption implements, defendants have successfully used the 'it's an ornament' defence.

Citric acid

People who inject brown street heroin need to use an acid to allow the heroin to be able to dissolve into an injectable solution. The acid of choice for most UK IDUs is citric acid – a fairly weak and benign acid when compared to many others and most often used in cooking. Easy access to citric acid started to become a problem for UK injectors in the late 1990s following a letter to the *Pharmaceutical Journal* questioning the legality of supplying it to IDUs. Many nervous pharmacists simply stopped supplying it, which in turn meant that there were suddenly many IDUs throughout the UK looking for easily available alternatives.

There are many possible alternative weak acids that can be used for injection preparation, the most commonly available being lemon juice and vinegar. The problem with the use of lemon juice and vinegar, is that their use can lead to fungal infections (particularly Candida albicans, commonly known as 'thrush') being introduced into the circulatory system (Shankland and Richardson, 1989), causing eyesight problems through retinal damage and in some cases, severe problems with heart valves.

Citric acid supply was central to the establishment and development of Exchange Supplies. This was because in spring 2001, we were alone in being willing to manufacture single use sachets of citric acid made specifically for IDUs. At this time, the supply of citric acid to IDUs remained illegal, so it was crucial for the success of this initiative that a way was found to enable drug treatment services to be able to supply it in their local areas without fear of being prosecuted for doing so. We were in a good position to facilitate this because while working for the drug treatment service in Dorchester, Andrew had negotiated the UK's first local agreement with a police service (Dorset), that they would not prosecute agencies supplying citric acid in breach of the law. Other areas were successfully able to negotiate their own local agreements using this model and as a result, over the next two years, citric acid supply became widespread throughout UK drug agencies.

Research on the effects of widespread citric supply has been limited, but encouraging (Garden et al., 2003; Beynon et al., 2007). In Scotland, it was found that IDUs valued the provision of single-use citric acid sachets and were more likely to attend at NSPs as a result of it being provided. On Merseyside, it was found that the number of attendances by long-term users of NSP increased, but the number of syringes given out to new attenders decreased, which may have been a result of staff concerns about the number of citric sachets (and thus syringes) given out to new clients. These two studies were conducted in 2003 and 2005, since then, citric provision has become firmly established (and expected by clients) throughout the UK.

The first area to provide widespread supply of citric acid to drug users was Glasgow. The pharmacist who managed the scheme, Kay Roberts, was also a member of the Advisory Committee on the Misuse of Drugs (ACMD), which is responsible for advising UK governments about drugs and drug policy. Kay put the issue on the agenda of the ACMD technical committee and in late 2001 the ACMD recommended a change in the law to allow the supply of citric acid to IDUs.

The commercial success of citric supply enabled us to begin to develop properly as a social enterprise, and initiate the supply of other items of paraphernalia (the next item being sterile spoons) and these were subsequently supplied throughout the UK in a similar manner to citric acid. In November 2002 the Home Office issued a consultation document requesting responses to the proposal to amend section 9A and in August 2003, the supply of citric, swabs, spoons and filters was made legal. Water for injections (WFI) was also included, but warrants its own separate story below.

Water for injections

WFI has a place of its own in the history, because although post August 2003 it was now deemed legal to supply under the MDA, it remained illegal under the Medicines Act 1968, because like all injectable preparations it was a prescription only medicine (POM).

In an attempt to get around the legislation and allow drug treatment services to be able to supply injectors with a better source of water to use for the preparation of injections than the tap, or even less safe alternatives, we introduced 1.4 ml plastic ampoules of *sterile* water (WFI, whilst also sterile, has an even more rigorous manufacturing process). This was an attempt to allow drug services to safely supply single-use ampoules of sterile water, particularly to high risk groups such as the homeless who can sometimes find it difficult to find clean water sources.

This initiative met with enough success between September 2003 and June 2004 to prompt a complaint from an established company in the field, to the Medicines and Healthcare Regulatory Authority (MHRA). The MHRA felt obliged to require us to stop selling the ampoules and an order that we quarantine all remaining stock on the grounds that it was 'presented as a medicine', and therefore needed a medicines licence.

This meant that the remaining stock of these ampoules subsequently had to be destroyed. This prompted a letter writing campaign to the MHRA, complaining about the absurdity of the position, and urging for the reclassification of WFI. Following a widespread consultation process, supply of WFI to UK drug users without a prescription, by drug workers finally became legal in June 2005 (SI, 2005, no. 1507: The Medicines for Human Use (Prescribing) (Miscellaneous Amendments) Order).

Unfortunately, although this made the supply of water completely legal in terms of both the Medicines Act and the MDA, the only 2 ml licensed water for injections available in the UK was (and at the time of writing remains) in a glass ampoule, which is not ideal.

Aluminium foil

It would be desirable to see section 9a of the MDA repealed, rather than continually tinkered with. This is because the law as it is achieves little and the process of changing the law to allow the supply of specific items is ponderous, uncertain and serves to stifle innovation. A case study that demonstrates this is the issue of aluminium foil.

The promotion of smoking heroin on aluminium foil as a safer alternative to injecting has been practised unofficially on a small scale in the UK for a long time. Some projects had previously been giving out foil simply torn from a household roll. Promotion of foil was a part of a massive culture shift in the Netherlands from being a overwhelmingly injecting culture in the 1980s, to the situation that exists today where 9 out of 10 users of cocaine and heroin smoke rather than inject their drug (Grund and Blanken, 1993; KOOLS, 2011). Interestingly, the Netherlands has never had laws outlawing drug paraphernalia provision, enabling them to act quickly to support it when a trend towards heroin smoking rather than injecting was observed by researchers.

We began manufacturing and supplying foil in April 2007, presenting it in packs of ready-cut foil that can easily be given out in NSPs and discretely carried by drug users. This intervention is supported by advice and instruction to users on pipe making and how to minimise loss of drugs in smoke. As foil provision remains illegal in the UK at the time of writing, we are also providing advice and instruction to treatment services on how to go about getting agreements with their local police and Crown Prosecution Services not to prosecute them for breaching the law. This latter strategy is very similar to that which we did with citric earlier in the decade. Curiously, although successful overall as an initiative, some areas have had much more difficulty in gaining local agreements about foil than was previously the case with citric acid. This is despite the fact that smoking drugs, whilst not without its own risks, is widely acknowledged to be a much less harmful route of drug administration than injecting for the vast majority of people. The legal position around foil at the time of writing (January 2011) is that having been reviewed by the ACMD in 2010, a recommendation was made to exempt it from section 9a of the MDA. The decision about whether to implement this recommendation now rests with the Home Secretary.

The nevershare syringe

The nevershare syringe with plungers in a range of colours to prevent accidental sharing is perhaps the best single example of our ability to turn important information gained from research, into practical tools to reduce drug related harm.

In 2004 the Effective Interventions Unit of the Scottish Executive Drug Misuse Research Programme, published the findings of their video ethnography research project (Effective Interventions Unit, 2004), which examined the injecting practices of injecting drug users in Scotland. One of the stark findings from the project was that *accidental* sharing of syringes was very common, and that this was mainly driven by the difficulty of identifying individual syringes, as they all looked the same. As the conclusion of the report says:

> Apart from the one IDU who was seen to inject with another's needle/syringe, the participants in the other 48 injection episodes believed that their pre-used needles had been used only by themselves. However, some participants admitted that they have may have used another person's needle/syringe by mistake. This could happen in two ways. Firstly, cohabiting IDUs often stored their used needle/syringes next to each other's and then had difficulty in distinguishing one from another. Secondly, needle/syringes could be confused where two or more people were injecting together, put their needle/syringes down next to each other's and then could not tell which was theirs. By far the most common type of needle/syringe used by IDUs in the study was the fixed 1ml insulin needle/syringe. This was used in 85% (88/103) of all injections. On only eleven occasions were these needle/syringes observed as marked in some way that could differentiate them from those belonging to other IDUs.

We thought that these findings were very important, likely to be universally relevant and therefore, should be as widely publicised as possible. Our initial response to the research was to commission a documentary training film based around it. In the course of making the film with Professor Avril Taylor, the idea was raised of producing syringes that could easily be differentiated from each other, to avoid the problem of 'mix-ups'.

Our first response to make a syringe marker, was to produce different coloured 'caps', which fitted on the end of the syringe plunger, allowing each user to easily identify their own syringe. Although potentially effective it had two substantial drawbacks: first, it added to the cost of the syringe (the syringe IDs had to be purchased in addition to the syringe), and, second, it required the injecting drug user to apply the marker so wasn't always in place when it was needed.

It became clear that a new syringe, with difference built into the product was needed. We then set out on the long and difficult process of producing such a syringe. This meant identifying a suitable contract manufacturer to manufacture a product for us, and then working with them through the licensing issues to manufacture syringes with plungers in 5 different colours and sorting out all the logistical and financial issues involved in purchasing, storing and nationally distributing millions of syringes.

At the end of the process, we became the producers of the first syringe in the world that had been specifically produced with injecting drug users in mind. All the other syringes distributed across the world were designed with the healthcare market in mind rather than IDUs. An example of why this is not always ideal, is that the most widely used syringe across by IDUs across the world, the 1ml insulin syringe has its' scale graduated in insulin units. At best this is simply an oddity for IDUs, but at worst it can cause confusion about dose if a person moves from using a 1 ml insulin syringe graduated in insulin units to using a 2 ml separate syringe barrel that is graduated in millilitres. For this reason, alongside its primary aim of being easily identifiable, we thought it a simple but important step to make the scale on the nevershare syringe graduated in millilitres.

The introduction of the nevershare syringe has been a steadily building success story, with most IDUs immediately understanding the benefits. Resistance to the concept where it has occurred, has most often come from professionals, some of whom feel that a syringe designed with an inherent acceptance that re-use is a reality, undermines a basic message not to re-use equipment. Unfortunately though, NSPs do not (and almost certainly never will) provide anywhere near enough syringes for a new one to be used for every injection, and unless or until that is the case, reuse of syringes is inevitable.

There are estimated to be approximately 130,000 people in the UK who currently inject illicit drugs, injecting on average three times a day. This means that there are somewhere around 142,000,000 injections per year in the UK. According to a European Monitoring Centre for Drugs and Drug Addiction report, published in 2010 (EMCDDA, 2010), there were no reliable data for syringe distribution in the UK in the years 2003-8, although an ACMD estimate of 23,000,000 for 2005 (probably derived from the National Needle Exchange Survey conducted in that year) is mentioned in a footnote. If true, this would represent an average of considerably less than one syringe per injector per day, and is a very long way short of one syringe per injection.

Some IDUs do use a new sterile syringe each time they inject, but the large number who can't are forced to re-use injecting equipment. Prevention of deliberate and accidental re-use of someone else's equipment is a priority for harm reduction services. We chose to brand the new syringe as the 'nevershare', because preventing sharing (currently at around 20% according to the latest report from the Health Protection Agency, 2010) is a more immediate public health priority than preventing re-use.

In February 2009, the National Institute for Clinical Excellence (NICE, 2009) published guidance for needle and syringe programmes that recommended that agencies should 'encourage people who inject drugs to mark their syringes and other injecting equipment or to use easily identifiable equipment to prevent mix- ups'.

Harm reduction works: a national campaign

In 2008 as part of an action plan to reduce drug-related harm (NTA, 2007), the English Department of Health (DH) and the National Treatment Agency (NTA) announced plans to produce a campaign targeted at those most at risk of drug-related death (DRD). Our unique combination of knowledge of harm reduction issues coupled with experience of drug user involvement, and track record of development of successful social marketing campaigns meant Exchange Supplies won the contract to design and produce the campaign.

The materials we produced can be viewed in electronic form at www.harmreductionworks.org.uk/, hard copies were made available, free of charge, to drug agencies and individuals in England and via exchangesupplies.org.

A wide range of campaign materials were commissioned, using a range of media (print, web based and video) aimed at drug users, their family and carers, drug treatment staff and commissioners of services, to improve their knowledge of relevant issues and improve their response to them.

The campaign focuses on eight specific areas:

- HIV, hepatitis B and C;
- overdose prevention and dealing with overdose;
- safer injecting practice;
- injection of crack cocaine;
- femoral injecting.

The process of producing such a wide range of resources over the relatively short time of 18 months was challenging. Following widespread consultation, it was decided that many key messages of the campaign would be best delivered via video resources. These have been distributed via DVD, and in an effort to maximise their impact, are also publicly available on YouTube.

Only one of the video resources 'Keep walking', is not available on youtube. This is because it begins with the IDUs talking about the positive aspects of femoral injecting (there can be a human tendency to just listen to the positives when contemplating an activity) and also because it also contains a few very graphic scenes. The film is aimed at current femoral injectors, encouraging them to consider the likely physical impact of long-term femoral injecting by following a group of long-tem femoral IDUs through ultrasound imaging of their femoral veins.

Using video enabled us to create short, filmed demonstrations of skills such as syringe cleaning and hand washing that are much more easily followed than printed instructions and do not require literacy as a prerequisite. We also made a full-length documentary training film that looked at the prevention of blood-borne virus epidemics through the eyes of expert commentators.

Alongside this we also commissioned higher budget short films on avoiding and dealing with overdose (one, 'Mr Mange goes over' using animation and black humour), CGI animation and pop video techniques to help to stimulate and maintain the viewer's interest. The films can be viewed on the Harm Reduction Works YouTube channel, which can be accessed via the campaign website.

The future

Our mission remains unchanged, we want to continue to work to do all we can to reduce drug related harm, and improve and prolong the lives of drug users. Although we have now ticked many of the boxes on our 'BBV prevention priority list', there is still much to do. Our main challenge over the coming years will be to continue to fund and develop these new ideas. The current climate is one of increasing pressure to reduce prices, from competitors who don't have our research and development overheads. Introducing new products and services also becomes more difficult in a market that will almost certainly have less scope for expansion and uptake of new harm reduction innovations because of changing political agendas and cuts in public spending. However, we have demonstrated that it is possible for harm reductionists to use business methodology to rapidly develop, and scale up, innovation and that a partnership between a social enterprise, drug users, and health professionals can achieve things that previously seemed impossible.

References

Beynon, C.M., McVeigh, J., Chandler, M., Wareing, M. and Bellis, M. (2007) The impact of citrate introduction at UK syringe exchange programmes: a retrospective cohort study in Cheshire and Merseyside, UK, *Harm Reduction Journal*, 4, 21.

Department of Health (2005) Statutory Instrument 2005 no. 1507, *The Medicines for Human Use (Prescribing) (Miscellaneous Amendments) Order 2005*, London: HMSO.

Effective Interventions Unit (2004) *Examining the Injecting Practices of Injecting Drug Users in Scotland*, Edinburgh: Scottish Government, www.scotland.gov.uk/Publications/2004/02/18871/32890, accessed 15 January 1011.

EMCDDA (2010) *Annual Report on the State of the Drugs Problem in Europe*, Lisbon: EMCDDA.

EMCDDA (2011) *Table HSR-5: Syringes Provided through Needle and Syringe Programmes (NSPs), 2003, 2005, 2007 and 2008*, www.emcdda.europa.eu/stats10/hsrtab5, accessed 15 January 2011.

Garden, J., Roberts, K., Taylor, A. and Robinson, D. (2003) *Evaluation of the Provision of Single Use Citric Acid Sachets to Injecting Drug Users*, Edinburgh: Scottish Centre for Infection and Environmental Health.

Grund, J.P. and Blanken, P. (1993) *From Chasing the Dragon to Chinezen: The Diffusion of Heroin Smoking in The Netherlands*, Rotterdam: Erasmus University.

Health Protection Agency (2010) *Shooting Up: Infections among Injecting Drug Users in the United Kingdom, 2009, an Update*, London: Health Protection Agency.

Kools, J.P. (2011) *The Dutch Experience in Promoting Transition away from Injecting Drug Use 1991–2010*, www.exchangesupplies.org/article_moving_from_fix_to_foil_dutch_experience_by_John-Peter_Kools.php, accessed 15 January 2011.

National Institute for Clinical Excellence (2009) *Public Health Guidance 18: Needle and Syringe Programmes – Providing People Who Inject Drugs with Injecting Equipment*, London: NICE.

National Treatment Agency (2007) *Reducing Drug Related Harm: An Action Plan*, London: National Treatment Agency, Department of Health.

Shankland, G.S. and Richardson, M.D. (1989) Possible role of preserved lemon juice in the epidemiology of candida endophtalmitis in heroin addicts, *European Journal of Clinical Microbiology and Infectious Diseases*, 8 (1), 87–9.

Section IV
Regions

Chapter 23

HARM REDUCTION IN CENTRAL AND EASTERN EUROPE

Tomas Zabransky, Jean Paul Grund, Alisher Latypov, David Otiashvili, Raminta Stuikyte, Otilia Scutelniciuc and Pavlo Smyrnov

Central European countries

History

In the Central European ex-communist countries, harm reduction approaches have a fairly substantial history, particularly in the western part of former Czechoslovakia – nowadays the Czech Republic. The first programmes began in the Department for Treatment of Addictive Disorders at the General Teaching Hospital in Prague, where the staff provided clean needles to 'treatment resistant cases of addicted injectors' in the early 1980s (Zábranský, 2002). The same department was one of the several Czech medical facilities that experimented with provision of medical opioids[1] to patients dependent on a home-made opiate called 'braun'[2] who repeatedly relapsed after traditional, abstinence oriented treatments, in the 1970s and 1980s; according to the medical doctors involved, the results were generally positive. Remarkably, these pioneering harm reduction activities were not driven by a threat of HIV and other blood borne infections, but rather by individual health and social welfare concerns (first author's personal communication). The first official substitution treatment programme started in Prague in 1991, when the head physician of the NGO drop-in illegally imported several kilos of methadone hydrochloride from Switzerland, declared it to customs and after several hours of arrest was released and granted (exceptional) permission by the Ministry of Health to provide substitution to severely addicted opioid users in Prague. This permission, however, was not repeated in 1994, and most of the (rather veteran) patients returned to street heroin and 'braun' use, with all its dire consequences. Needle exchange programmes have faced no difficulties since their official launch in Czech drop-in centres (1991) and street based programmes (1994), and they have developed into what is seen as services with sufficient coverage today.

In 1988, in response to the only epidemic of HIV in drug users in the region that affected as many as 30% of injectors of 'kompot '[3] (by that time the majority of Polish problem drug users (Danziger, 1994), the first documented Polish needle exchange programme was started. MONAR, a faith-based rehabilitation programmes network, launched a needle exchange on a bus which drove through the major open drug scenes of the country. At the end of 1989, after the communist dictatorship was peacefully dismantled, Poland implemented several needle exchange programmes as

---

[1] Most commonly used pharmaceuticals were Diolan® (containing ethylmorphine), and Temgesic® (containing buprenorphine).

[2] Derived from the German word for the brown colour of the solution, containing mostly hydrocodone and hydrocodeine that was produced from codeine-containing pharmaceuticals.

[3] Home-made acetylated opium solution.

Harm Reduction in Substance Use and High-Risk Behaviour: International Policy and Practice, First Edition.
Edited by Richard Pates and Diane Riley.
© 2012 Blackwell Publishing Ltd. Published 2012 by Blackwell Publishing Ltd.

part of outpatient addiction treatment clinics These programmes faced substantial resistance from conservative parts of society, and – especially in the early 1990s – were seen as rather marginal (see, e.g., Chopin, 1992).

Hungary began experimenting with opiate substitution in 1989[4] and started its first NSP in 1992 (Csorba et al., 2003). In Slovakia (the eastern part of former Czechoslovakia), the first needle exchange programmes did not appear until the mid-1990s, and opioid substitution treatment was piloted only in the late 1990s (Slabý et al., 2004).

After the fall of the communist regime, the primarily biologically oriented psychiatric ('narcologic', 'alcohologic-toxicologic', etc.) medical systems were poorly equipped and lacked the human and other resources to react appropriately to the quickly changing situation with regard to drug availability and patterns of use. The heritage of the Soviet-styled medical system, which focused mainly on repression and coercion, was another burden. The specialised non-governmental organisations (NGOs) took over some of the initiatives in the drugs field in Central Europe and helped to tackle the drug related problems in the region.

In Poland, MONAR, that was created in 1978, became a formal association in 1980 and gradually established itself as the major provider of rehabilitation, prevention and, finally, and somewhat reluctantly, of harm reduction, pushing forward the state-based players in the field. Under the leadership of the UNDP in Poland chaired by Kasia Malinowska-Sempruch a set of 'cascade training programmes' was created in the mid-1990s and reached hundreds of key professionals in the field in both governmental and non-governmental sectors, and established harm reduction as a key element of drug policy in the country.

In the Czech Republic, the first two NGOs – previously prohibited in the communist regime – appeared in 1991 and were soon followed by many others. These programmes were ambitious in that they did not limit themselves to primary prevention or policy advocacy: instead, they established themselves as providers of many novel services for problem drug users and for drug dependent clients (Kalina, 2007). The 'Christmas Memorandum' that was sent to the Czech Government in the dawn of the newly established Czech Republic by representatives of major NGOs then active in the drug field (Höschl et al., 1992) urged the Czech government to define its drug policy formally and to establish a National Drug Commission. In a swift response, the first inter-ministerial body of its kind at a high governmental level in the new democracy was established in January 1993. This demonstration of the importance of NGOs for the Czech drug policy ushered in a period of constant involvement of the NGO sector in the drug field. This is currently reflected in the most developed network of NGOs in drug services (including harm reduction) of all post-communist countries.

Unlike Poland and the Czech Republic, the role of NGOs in harm reduction in other CEE countries has been rather limited. The first two NGO-based harm reduction programmes were established in Slovakia only in 1997 (Slabý et al., 2004); the very first OST programme was established in 1999 in the capital city Bratislava, and the second one was established in 2005 in Banska Bystrica, with no further development of the network since then.

In Hungary, the first needle exchange was conducted in 1993 from the 'drug bus' which was supported by the municipal government of Budapest, but it took five more years before needle exchange programmes 'went out of the capital' (see Csorba et al., 2003: ch. 4). Opiate substitution treatment began in 1989 in Hungary with the use of codeine and dihydrocodone, methadone was introduced in 1992 (all in one clinic in Budapest), and there has been gradual development of the network outside the capital city since 1995.

---

[4] Albeit one British expat was receiving his methadone in Budapest since 1992 (Chopin, 1992).

Of the four Central European member states of EU, the Czech Republic was the first to explicitly mention harm reduction measures in the National Drug Strategy as its key element; the third Czech National Drug Strategy (for the period 2001–4) placed primary prevention, treatment and resocialisation, law enforcement and harm reduction as the complementary and mutually irreplaceable 'four pillars of Czech drug policy' and all the subsequent Czech Drug Strategies (2005–9; 2010–18) did so as well.

Hungary lists harm reduction strategies in its framework document to the National Drug Strategy 2001–8 as one of the 'details of the objectives' (Government of the Republic of Hungary, 2000); remarkably, the Hungarian 2001–8 National Drug Strategy is one of the few National Drug Strategies evaluated externally. The importance of harm reduction for successful anti-drug policy was further strengthened in the subsequent National Drug Strategy (Government of the Republic of Hungary, 2009). This, however, is under constant attack by the new Hungarian government and its further implementation is uncertain at the time of writing this chapter (see, e.g., HCLU, 2011).

Poland was explicit in placing harm reduction as one of five areas of the general aim of the National Programme for Counteracting Drug Addiction 2006–10 (Government of the Republic of Poland, 2006), and again in the subsequent Programme for 2011–16 (Government of the Republic of Poland, 2011) that sets the goal, inter alia, to 'further develop harm reduction programmes' explicitly.

While the Slovak Republic connects itself rhetorically with the EU Drug Strategy and Drug Action Plans, where harm reduction is made explicit as the essential element of drug policy (European Community, 2005; 2008), none of its strategic drug policy documents does so. Harm reduction is implicit in the national drug policy papers of Slovakia, as well as of several regional and municipal drug strategies. Slovakia mentions in its Anti-Drug Strategy (Government of the Slovak Republic, 2009) the commitment 'to provide adequate care and assistance to these groups and instruments that prevent the spread of drug abuse-related diseases, HIV and hepatitis in particular' (p. 8) and 'through targeted prevention, to prevent high-risk behaviour of drug users' (p. 17), merely repeating the weak language of the 2009 CND Political Declaration (Fifty-second Session of the Commission on Narcotic Drugs, 2009), and fails to follow the more concrete language of the two crucial EU documents that were approved by the Slovak Government and other EU member states in 2005 and 2008.

Patterns of drug use in the region and specific responses

Czech Republic

The Czech Republic (pop: 10.5 million) is the only European country where the main drug traditionally injected is not opiate(s), but methamphetamine;[5] this has been the case since the late 1970s. Out of the estimated 37,000 problem drug users, approximately 35,300 (app. 0.5% of the population aged 15–64) are estimated to be current injectors, and two-thirds of them inject primarily methamphetamine (Mravčík et al., 2010).

Like other countries in the region except Poland, the HIV rate in the general population and drug users is very low, with around 0.1% in IDUs (accounting for some 7% of all known cases) and far below 0.01% in the general population. The viral hepatitis C is concentrated almost exclusively in

---

[5] Called 'pervitin' in the Czech Republic; 'Pervitin' was the brand name of methamphetamine produced by Germany during World War II.

the drug injecting population with an estimated prevalence around 23% (Mravčík et al., 2010), which puts it to the lowest strata in the EU.

Low-threshold programmes have been developed all over the country with good coverage responding to the regional differences in the extent of the drug problem. Overall, in 2009 there were 95 HR programmes that distributed 4.9 million sterile needles/syringe sets to approximately 30,000 problem drug users in the Czech Republic. This would provide coverage for around 80% of the target population.

After a period of 'wild substitution' (see above) the OST programmes were standardised by Guidelines from the Ministry of Health in 1998. In 2009, methadone, buprenorphine and buprenorphine/naloxone were used for OST that covered approximately 4,800 patients in no less than 34 medical facilities (Mravcik et al., 2011), accounting for some 25% of the estimated problem opiate users.

The major role of methamphetamine in the problem drug scene made professionals in the field seek specific interventions that would reflect the specific needs of pervitin users. Of those that seem successful the most noteworthy is the distribution of gelatine capsules for oral use of methamphetamine; this protects the veins – and the gastric mucosa – of the users while reportedly making the effect comparable with that of injecting the drug (Mravcik et al., 2011).

Hungary

In Hungary (pop: 10 million), the only available estimates of the number of problem drug users relate to the two-years period of 2007–8, when the estimated number of drug injectors in the country is reported as 6,146 for the given two years, the estimates of heroin of users 3,130 and the number of amphetamine users 27,223 persons (National Focal Point Hungary, 2011). However, there are few details about the methodology of calculation of these numbers and they are thus difficult to interpret.

According to a sentinel study in 676 injecting drug users who were using specialised services in 2009, the seroprevalence of HIV was 0.7%, and viral hepatitis C antibodies were found in 24.4% of the sampled institutionalised population of drug injectors (Bozsonyi et al., 2010). Twenty-one existing low-threshold programmes distributed 392,336 syringes to 2,399 clients in 2009, with a substantial increase from 2005 (105,390 syringes for 959 clients). Ten treatment units provided OST to a total of 992 clients using methadone or buprenorphine/naloxone composite in 2009 (National Focal Point Hungary, 2011).

Poland

With a general population of 38.2 million people, the number of problem drug users was estimated to be as high as 100–125,000 in 2005, of whom 25–27,000 were opioid injectors (Malczewski et al., 2010). The 2008 survey in 13 needle exchange programmes found 78% of the clients had used opioids in 30 days prior to the survey (with 50% reporting heroin use) and 61% had used amphetamines in the same period (Malczewski et al., 2009).

Contrary to other three Central European countries, injecting drug use has played a major role in the dynamics of HIV infection in Poland, accounting for 45% of 12,874 cases diagnosed in 1985–2009. The incidence of new diagnoses has steadily decreased in IDUs since 2003 with 45 newly identified HIV + IDUs in 2008 and 49 cases in 2009. The HIV prevalence in IDUs is comparatively high – estimated at 10.3% for 2009 – but decreasing in the sentinel studies from two major cities (from 18% in 2005). This steady decrease in both diagnosed incidence and seroprevalence is usually attributed to: (1) compartmentalisation of a small group of drug users; (2) reduction in the injecting of 'kompot' that was pushed out by heroin and non-medical use of pharmaceutical opioids; (3) successful implementation of needle and syringes exchange programmes (NSP) and, to a somehow lesser extent; (4) generally improved living conditions (Alcabes and Zielinski, 2004). However, the seroprevalence of viral hepatitis C remains high, at around 50% of Polish injectors (results of the study conducted by Epidemiology Department of the National Institute of Public Health cited in Malczewski, et al., 2010).

Despite the long tradition of officially recognised needle exchange programmes, the number of NSPs in the country (13) is remarkably low, as is the number of distributed needles and syringes (318,763) and people using NSPs (3,130), given the estimated number of IDUs and the relatively high prevalence of blood-borne diseases in IDUs. Since the new millennium, we have seen a substantial decrease in the number of distributed needles (from 1,277,570 in 2002), the number of programmes (from 21 in 2002) and the number of cities where NSP were available (from 23 in 2002 to 13 cities in 2009). Little is known about the reasons for such decreases in coverage of NSP in Poland (Malczewski et al., 2010), but factors include a gradual shift in the paradigm of the influential MONAR association to more strictly abstinence-oriented services, decreases in funding, the absence of open local drug scenes which would make the operation of NSPs easier, and the failure of programmes to adjust services to changing drug scenes.

Altogether, 17 substitution programmes operated in Poland in 2009, providing services to approximately 1,900 clients, which represent 7% of opioid injectors in the country (Malczewski et al., 2010). OST is unavailable in most of the country, with the major reason given being the unwillingness of the major public funder – National Health Fund – to support substitution programmes that use mostly methadone and, increasingly, buprenorphine as a substitution drug.

Slovakia

The general population of Slovakia is 5.4 million people; the latest (2008) available estimate of problem drug use calculated the point estimate at 10,600 problem drug users. However, given the wide 95% confidence interval of the calculation (8,200–33,500) and the unrealistically sudden drop in the mid-point estimate from a rather stable three-years row of approximately 18,000 PDUs in 2005–7 (Reitox National Focal Point in Slovakia, 2009), the authors of the calculation note the possible reporting bias – the geographical coverage of the estimation decreased substantially after a sudden fall in the number of low threshold facilities in the country between 2007 and 2008 (see below). Regardless of the accuracy of the problem drug use estimate, the Slovak Republic experienced a major shift in problem drug use in the early 2000s, when the number of opiate users was surpassed by the increased number of methamphetamine injectors using predominantly home-made pervitin, as in the neighbouring Czech Republic (see treatment data and qualitative information quoted by the Slovak Reitox Focal Point, 2010).

The level of HIV infection remains very low in both the general population and among drug users in Slovakia, with 342 diagnosed HIV positives in 1985–2009; however, the seroprevalence in IDUs tested in 2008 was substantially higher (2%) than in previous years. The seroprevalence of viral hepatitis C in the only treatment facility that conducts the testing routinely remains above the regional average, at 52% (data from the Centre for Treatment of Drug Dependencies in Bratislava quoted in Reitox National Focal Point in Slovakia, 2009).

In 2008, altogether 223,721 syringes and/or needles were provided by Slovak harm reduction programmes to 3,184 clients, and additional 30,637 syringes were distributed by the Centre for Treatment of Drug Dependencies to its patients. The drop in the numbers of distributed needles and clients served when compared with 2007 (420,627 needles and syringes to 3,658 injecting clients and patients) relates to a drastic reduction in the geographic coverage of harm reduction services following a sudden change in funding criteria by the Slovak government in 2008. Subsequently, out of 7 organisations and 14 programmes, 2 organisations and 5 programmes ceased their operations resulting in, for example, services being provided to only 68 clients in Eastern Slovakia in 2008 compared with 578 in 2007. The number of clients and injecting equipment distributed in Bratislava, where 2 major organisations and the majority of programmes operate, increased in the given period, suggesting that the need for such services probably increased in other regions (that are now left with no services) as well.

Methadone substitution treatment is provided in only 2 programmes in Slovakia, serving approximately 500 patients. Since 2007 this number of OST patients has been complemented by patients receiving buprenorphine/naloxone pharmaceutical composite preparation in psychiatric outpatient facilities; according to the Reitox National Focal Point in Slovakia (2009), the number of the latter is increasing.

Harm reduction in prisons

Prisons in Central Europe have been reluctant to introduce harm reduction services; among the reasons quoted in personal communications with prison officers is the unwillingness to publicly recognise the magnitude of the drug problem and the safety concerns of the staff regarding 'dangerous' freely distributed needles. NSPs are not allowed to operate in any of the Central European prisons. In the prisons of Poland and of Czech Republic, opiate substitution treatment is available for patients who were identified by their doctors *before* they started their sentence; this is driven by the guidance that treatment available in the community must be available in the prison setting as well if indicated *lege artis*, as defined by the EU and UN bodies (see. e.g., Council of Europe, 1998; WHO, 2005).

Key challenges and current developments

While the funding which is mostly provided by domestic donors and national governments or other public funds is generally regarded as desirable by both private and public international donors, developments in Central Europe show the shortcomings of this arrangement, when all major service providers are dependent on the 'procurement of services' by the respective national governments. Single source funding is risky by definition, but when the funding is politically driven, the risk multiplies. In these times of economic crises, that first hit the EU in 2008, cuts in funding in the social and health areas are politically convenient. This is especially so in the field of addictions, where, according to the erroneous but widespread belief: 'those in need of help are responsible for the poor health and social state they find themselves in'.

This is clearly demonstrated by the situation in Poland and Slovakia in particular, and to a lesser but still palpable extent in the other two countries of Central Europe, where in last three years the coverage and extent of harm reduction services has been either substantially reduced or is stagnating. This happens in situations where economic decline and social welfare cuts increase the risk factors associated with harmful drug (and alcohol) use, and when new patterns of use of both old and new drugs require novel interventions, and more of what has proven to work in protecting public health and public security. Thus, the international (and supranational, i.e. EU) funders of drug services, particularly those concerned about controversy, may want to rebuild their developmental strategies for transitional and newly developed countries.

Baltic countries

History

As in other newly independent countries that emerged after the disintegration of Soviet Union, the history of harm reduction in the Baltics dates back to the end of 1990s. All three Baltic States started low threshold needle exchange programmes for IDUs in 1996–7, but other developments show important differences in these countries. Different stakeholders from the HIV or drug treatment sectors steered these innovations. In Estonia and Latvia harm reduction began mainly through HIV responses since following independence most drug dependency treatment facilities became dysfunctional (I Can Live, 2009). In Estonia, the very first harm reduction programme was initiated and opened by a non-governmental HIV prevention group in Tallinn in 1997.

In Latvia, a governmental HIV prevention agency, the AIDS Prevention Centre, now part of the Public Health Agency, set up the first needle exchange programme in 1997; in 2002–4 it grew into a low threshold programme network in 11 cities co-funded through municipal, governmental and international support (CEEHRN, 2004; Government of the Republic of Latvia, 2010). In Lithuania, the leading (then called) narcologists[6] initiated one programme in Klaipeda in 1996 and another one in Vilnius Narcology Centres (now restructured into Centres for Addictive Disorders), which simultaneously introduced and developed pharmacological treatment with methadone (UNAIDS and ODCCP, 2001).

Opiate substitution treatment (OST) was first introduced in Lithuania in 1995 in response to the appeal of mothers of people who use drugs and drug treatment professionals (I Can Live, 2009; CEEHRN, 2004). By 2001, Lithuania had become a centre of excellence for the post-Soviet countries, where people from similar post-Soviet narcology systems could observe OST policies and practices implemented along with other integrated drug dependence programmes. It was also the first country of the former Soviet Union to introduce pharmacological therapy in primary mental healthcare and to form a drug user organisation of OST clients (CEEHRN, 2003). Latvia and Estonia introduced OST in 1996 and 1999 respectively. The start was modest and development was slow: until 2008, Latvia had OST available only in one city with less than 100 clients and, until the start of the Global Fund project in 2003, Estonia had less than a total of 20 clients in 3 sites (Sile and Pugule, 2008; CEEHRN, 2004).

While the initial start-up of programmes in Baltic countries in 1995–2001 was extensively supported by the Open Society Institute, the further recognition of harm reduction at the national level was related to the following two factors:

1. the outbreak of HIV infection among IDUs that peaked in 2000–2003 (i.e. in the time of preparations of and feedback to the 2001 UNGASS on HIV/AIDS) brought a national and international pressure to prioritise evidence based responses among IDUs in national HIV programmes that was felt by the Baltic countries;
2. the accession process to the European Union and the 2004 membership required adherence of national policies to those in the EU where harm reduction was and continues to be embraced by the EU drug strategies as recommended by a specific EU Council Recommendation as of 2003.

In 2002–6, Estonia and Latvia started to scale up pilot needle exchange programmes supported with substantial external funds from the Global Fund and Nordic Task Force (Government of the Republic of Estonia, 2010; Government of the Republic of Latvia, 2010). In parallel, fierce opposition to harm reduction peaked in 2003–5 in the region, coordinated by European Cities against Drugs

---

[6] In the Soviet system, medical doctors specialised in treatment of alcohol and other drug addictions.

(ECAD) who found strong support among politicians, particularly in Lithuania. The threat and gradual withdrawal of the Open Society Institute's support caused a quick consolidation of main harm reduction advocates into an 'I Can Live Coalition', which was founded in 2004 (I Can Live, 2009). The last major phase in harm reduction development was in 2006–11, when a joint UNODC and Baltic governments project was implemented aiming to improve national legislation and strategies, supporting innovative low threshold services (notably in Latvia and Lithuania), and improving the quality of opioid substitution therapy.

Currently, all countries have harm reduction as an integral part of their national strategies; recognition and funding level varies from explicit mentioning and funding of harm reduction in Estonia's national HIV and drug strategies to continuous political discussions around 'methadone' and 'harm reduction' in Lithuania (Rotberga, 2011; Government of the Republic of Estonia, 2010; I Can Live, 2011).

Specifics of drug use in the region and specific responses

Estonia

Since 2002, following a noticeable decrease in heroin availability, the main injection drug has been fentanyl (marketed as 'China White', 'White Persian' or 'Afghan'), along with amphetamine (Talu et al., 2009); heroin availability has been very low since 2008 (National Institute for Health Development, 2009).

Estonia has one of the highest rates of problem drug use and the highest HIV prevalence and incidence in the EU. A 2004 survey estimated the number of IDUs as high as 13,800 and the injecting drug use prevalence at 2.4% among people aged 15–24 and 1.4% for the age cohort 15–64 (Uusküla et al., 2007). Injecting drug use disproportionally affected the Russian-speaking population of Estonia in the north-east region of the country including Kohtla-Järve and in the capital city Tallinn, where HIV prevalence among IDUs was 48–59% and HCV ranged between 76 and 90% in 2007 (Government of the Republic of Estonia, 2010). These rates are high even among young injectors who have been injecting for less than three years (between 34 and 50% HIV prevalence) (Uusküla et al., 2008).

Harm reduction is one of the three priorities of the national HIV programme and it is explicitly mentioned in the national drug strategy. Funding for harm reduction including needle exchange and some OST with methadone primarily comes from the national HIV budget, and some municipalities (such as the capital city of Tallinn) contribute regularly to these programmes. The first national funding started in 2001 (National Institute for Health Development, 2009; Government of the Republic of Estonia, 2010). Current coverage with syringe exchange services is generally perceived to be good. In 2009, 36 needle exchange programmes distributed 2.3 million syringes or 167 syringes per estimated IDU. Geographically, they are concentrated in the most affected areas and are mainly run by NGOs with government and municipal funding. According to the 2007 study, 64% of IDUs in Tallinn and 75% in Kohtla-Järve visited syringe exchange during the month prior to the survey; 48% of IDUs in the capital and 65% in Kohtla-Järve indicate syringe exchange programmes as their main source for syringes and needles. A range of services in low threshold programmes focused only on HIV prevention until recently, when STI services were added and more emphasis has been placed on integration of TB and HBV prevention. However, more needs to be done to ensure universal access to nine interventions included in the UN comprehensive package for the prevention, treatment and care of HIV among IDUs, as well as to overdose prevention and other drug services (Government of the Republic of Estonia, 2010).

Comparatively, OST is less developed than NSP. Since the end of the Global Fund-supported programme in 2007, coverage has not increased and in 2009 was between 4 and 6% of IDUs, with 660 patients in treatment with either methadone or buprenorphine. Polydrug use is sometimes referred to as a reason for the low scale of OST in the country. No substitution therapy for amphetamine injectors is provided and there are no safer injection rooms (Government of the Republic of Estonia, 2010; National Institute for Health Development, 2009; WHO and UNODC, 2008).

Latvia

Harm reduction services report that the Latvian drug scene is hidden and dispersed with heroin and amphetamines being the main injecting drugs (Rotberga et al., 2010). According to 2009 Health Economy Centre estimations, problem drug users make up 1% of the adult population. Among them, 23% had HIV and 74% had HCV, according to recent reports (Government of the Republic of Latvia, 2010; Karnīte et al., 2010).

In 2010, the Latvian network of 'Low Threshold Centres' had 18 programmes operating in 16 municipalities. They provided needle exchange, condoms, information and counselling, as well as some HIV testing, with funding from national and local governments. Unlike in Estonia, few NGOs are engaged in harm reduction in Latvia, and most services are run by municipal agencies – some with very limited numbers of clients. In the last few years, international support has been provided to 'Low Threshold Centres' network to increase coverage of needle exchange programmes, with a wider introduction of outreach elements involving peer educators and using peer driven interventions. Latvian governmental agencies estimated that in 2009 needle exchange networks reached 27% of IDUs. At the same time, a relatively low number of sterile syringes were distributed: less than 20 syringes per year for each estimated IDU in 2010 (Upmace, 2010; UNODC and WHO/Europe, 2011).

Less than 2% of IDUs are provided with OST; by the end of 2010, there were 271 OST clients receiving methadone and 49 clients receiving buprenorphine (21.9% of these clients were HIV positive). Over the last few years, methadone services have expanded geographically from 1 city in 2007 to 3 cities in 2009 and to 10 municipalities at the end of 2010. More attention has recently been given to improving the quality of services and some effects of the integration of services have been seen: 5 patients receive methadone in the National TB clinic, and methadone is covered by a general state insurance scheme. In spite of those recent positive developments, external experts note that negative attitudes towards methadone among medical professionals, rigid prescription regulations and absence of OST in correctional facilities remain as the key challenges to further OST scale up (UNODC and WHO/Europe, 2011).

Latvia health budgets have been badly affected by the economic crisis: funding and the number of services have been reduced, limitations on access to HIV, hepatitis B and C treatments have increased, and even HIV testing has been reduced. Criticisms by national and international experts has concentrated on the fact that funding cuts were not used for increasing efficiency and prioritisation of funds to the most HIV-affected groups such as IDUs, men who have sex with men and prisoners. National HIV programme evaluators characterised the effects of financial cuts on prison health budgets as 'catastrophic', as illustrated by a 45% decrease in prison health personnel (UNODC and WHO/Europe, 2011).

Lithuania

Among estimated 5,400 IDUs, heroin and locally produced amphetamines are the main drugs of choice (Drug Control Department, 2010; Rotberga et al., 2010). The country reports the lowest prevalence of both injecting drug use and HIV in the Baltics. The prevalence of HIV among IDUs is 8% in the capital city of Vilnius, but HCV rates are similar to those found in other Baltic capitals (82% among Vilnius-based IDUs) (Rüütel et al., 2010; Karnīte et al., 2010).

Although Lithuanian started programmes with much enthusiasm, this country now has the least established political commitment to harm reduction among the three Baltic countries. There are no targets for needle exchange and OST in national programmes, no government funding for needle exchange, and the UNODC indicates the political environment in Lithuania as 'not favourable for harm reduction' (Rotberga, 2011). The recent national drug programme does not prioritise services for people with drug dependency (Seimas of the Republic of Lithuania, 2010). At the end of 2010, there were 12 needle exchange sites that distributed only around 30 needles per IDU annually. The main funding for programmes comes from municipalities which provided 38–50% of funding for needle exchange programmes in 2007–9. The National Drug Control Department provided funding for these programmes in 2007–8, but the budget was abolished in the face of economic crisis and the political hostility towards harm reduction (Rotberga et al., 2010).

On a positive note, Lithuanian opioid substitution therapy has remained as the best developed in the Baltic States. In 2011, more than 700 IDUs (estimated 13.1% of all IDUs) were enrolled in OST with methadone in 21 sites and, as needed, could continue therapy in the police custody centres but not in prisons (Rotberga, 2011). Methadone is covered through state insurance and all programmes provide psychosocial support. Buprenorphine (with or without naltrexone) is used in private clinics (55 clients in 2009). A strong base of methodological support, clinical guidance and medical post-graduate training has been created by the Vilnius Centre for Addictive Disorder, Vilnius University, the Lithuanian Psychiatry Association and other institutions (Drug Control Department of the Republic of Lithuania, 2010).

HR in prisons

The Baltic States have the highest prison populations per capita in the European Union and average rates in the context of Eastern Europe and Central Asia (Walmsley, 2009). Drug dependence problems are acknowledged directly or indirectly in all three countries by prison authorities indicating high levels of problem drug use: approximately 26% of incarcerated people using drugs in Estonia (Kivimets, 2011), 15% of prisoners being injecting drug users in Lithuania (Drug Control Department of the Republic of Lithuania, 2010). This recognition followed high HIV incidence and prevalence rates in prisons being reported since 2000, including a major HIV outbreak in one Lithuanian prison in 2002 (Juodkaite et al., 2008). Currently between 4.2 and 14% of the prison population are HIV positive, and existing studies indicate continued drug injection, high HCV rates, unsafe sexual practices, and sharing needles in prisons (Lohmus and Trummal, 2009; Stover, 2008; Government of the Republic of Latvia, 2010; Prison Department of the Republic of Lithuania, 2011).

Disinfectants for cleaning needles, drug education, abstinence-based drug treatment, and HIV testing are available in Baltic prisons. However, despite high prevalence and incidence rates of HIV and HCV, and high rates of injecting drug use, none of the three countries have introduced needle exchange in prisons (Government of the Republic of Estonia, 2010; Government of the Republic of Latvia, 2010; ECDC, 2010). Methadone programmes inside prisons have been introduced only by Estonia, which initially limited it to 2–3 patients per year, mainly for detox, but by 2011 had made substitution therapy available in all prisons and reported 48 patients on treatment as of March 2011 (Kivimets, 2011). A necessary step towards this development was an introduction of methadone in the police detention stations, so that OST clients would not interrupt treatment upon arrest. OST is also made available in police detention in Lithuania (Rotberga, 2011). Latvia plans to pilot OST in prisons by 2013 (Government of the Republic of Latvia, 2010).

NGO involvement in provision of services for prisoners is very limited in Latvia and Lithuania. In Estonia, the NGO Convictus Eesti provides HIV support, education and counselling in most prisons and their services are funded by the Ministry of Justice (Stover, 2008; Rotberga, 2011). The main challenges to introducing needle exchange and opioid substitution therapy in the Baltic prisons are related not to legislative barriers but to the lack of political will and leadership, negative attitudes of prison authorities and staff towards harm reduction, and to limited support for opioid substitution therapy in general. Furthermore, prison health is managed by the Ministry of Justice authorities instead of the Ministry of Health (Government of the Republic of Latvia, 2010; Rotberga, 2011; Juodkaite et al., 2008; Stover, 2008; Semenaite et al., 2008).

Key challenges and current developments

Since the 1990s, harm reduction in the Baltics has made needle exchange, opioid substitution therapy and some other services available and more accessible to people who inject drugs in community settings. Most of these changes were introduced not because of committed response to problem drug use or protection of rights of people who use drugs, but because of the devastating HIV epidemic (Stuikyte et al., 2009). Dedicated national government officials, NGO advocates and international supporters helped to stabilise the HIV crisis among IDUs in the Baltics, following the peak in 2000–2, but did not prevent extremely high HCV rates.

The three countries are at different levels of harm reduction development, with Estonia leading in establishing low threshold programmes and political commitment, and Lithuania in providing OST services. To have a substantial public health impact, harm reduction services in all three countries need to be substantially scaled up, ensuring the integration of health, social and legal services for IDUs.

So far, few positive developments have occurred in prisons despite the fact that drug use and blood-borne infections rates are substantially higher there than in the community setting. No needle exchange programmes are available in prisons in any of the three countries, and only Estonia has started to scale up the availability of OST in the prison settings. Given the size of prison populations and high proportion of IDUs among prisoners, the countries should consider ways to reduce rates of incarceration of IDUs: reconsider their drug legislation and practices, actively apply alternatives to incarceration and scale up community health and social services.

Membership in the European Union has facilitated the development of harm reduction programmes along with better drug policy. This membership and economic advancements also mean a national responsibility to sustain and expand programmes and allocate necessary funding for both NGO and governmental sectors. National and municipality funds have become the main sources of harm reduction services, but this funding is fragile and less predictable than previous international support. Recently, Latvia and Lithuania have been seriously affected by the economic crisis and health funding, including for IDUs, has been cut by 12–25% (Rotberga, 2011). Given the lack of political support for harm reduction in the country and a one-time window opened for Lithuania by the Global Fund in 2011, Lithuanian NGOs will seek support for advocacy and scaling up harm reduction (I Can Live, 2011).

As a review of Estonia's transition from the Global Fund support to national funding stated, 'it may be true that the government *can* afford to allocate new funds to sustain and expand HIV/AIDS services . . . but it may not always *want* or *choose* to' (OSI, 2008). Continued advocacy by NGOs with involvement of people who use drugs, experts and other stakeholders will be needed for the Baltic societies and governments to both *want* and *choose* to respect rights of people who use drugs and reduce drug related harms for individuals and societies at large.

Moldova

History

The implementation of harm reduction activities in the Republic of Moldova can be divided into three phases. In phase I (1997–9), projects were piloted in community settings (2 sites) and in prison (1 site). In phase II (2000–2), national scaling up of harm reduction was initiated, and by the end of 2002, 7 NSPs were operating (Scutelniciuc et al., 2009). The first two phases were financially and technically supported by UNAIDS Moldova and the Soros Foundation Moldova. Since 2003, the implementation of harm reduction activities has been rapidly scaled up in phase III, with new funding (see below) being available.

Based on the lessons learnt from the first phase, a governmental decision set the regulatory framework for harm reduction activities for 1999–2000 (Government of the Republic of Moldova, 1998). Since 2001, harm reduction activities have been guided by the national HIV programmes, which have a separate strategy on harm reduction for groups at higher risk of HIV (Government of the Republic of Moldova, 2001; 2005). The Global Fund grants (rounds 1 and 6) have been and still are the main funding sources for harm reduction activities, and thus the implementation is fully dependent on external funding (Scutelniciuc et al., 2009; National Coordination Council, 2010). The first methadone substitution treatment programme was established in the community setting in 2004 and in prisons in 2005. In 2007, the restrictive enrolment criterion was removed,[7] improving the access to OST (Scutelniciuc et al., 2009).

Specifics of drug use and specific responses

There are an estimated 25,000 people who inject drugs, living on the right bank of the Dniester River[8] (1% of the adults aged 15–64) (Bivol, 2011). Even in this relatively small country, injecting drug use and its consequences have substantial geographical/regional disparities (Scutelniciuc et al., 2009). In 2009, the main injected drug in the last month was home-made acetylated extract of opium[9] (92.2% in Balti,[10] 69.2% in Chisinau[11] and 87.6% in Tiraspol[12]). Methamphetamines were used mostly in Chisinau, the capital city (15.3% of respondents). Other types of injecting drugs registered lower values. Safer injecting practices have been mostly adopted: more than 85.0% of injectors used sterile syringes at last injection (86.0% in Tiraspol, 97.7% in Balti and 98.8% in Chisinau) and more than 75.0% (77.6% in Tiraspol, 92.4% in Balti and 98.8% in Chisinau) had

---

[7] Being registered officially as drug user (Hoover and Jurgens, 2009).

[8] As a result of the political conflict on the Dniester River (1991–1992), the territory of the Republic of Moldova is *de facto* divided into the territory on the right bank and the territory on the left bank of the Dniester River (so-called 'Transnistria'). The territory on the right bank of the Dniester River is controlled by the Chisinau authorities, while that on the left bank is controlled by the self-proclaimed, internationally unrecognised 'authorities' from Tiraspol – the biggest city of this region.

[9] 'Shirka'.

[10] The biggest city in the northern part of the country (right bank of Dniester River).

[11] The capital city, located in the central part of the country (right bank of Dniester River).

[12] The biggest city of the Transnistria region (left bank of Dniester River).

consistently used sterile syringes during the last month. The indirect sharing of injecting equipment[13] remains still very high in all studied areas (65.6% in Chisinau, 61.9% in Balti, 81.8% in Tiraspol). The rates of reported safe sexual behaviour are lower, with 45.1% in Chisinau, 50.3% in Balti, and 66.1% respondents in Tiraspol having reported more than once sexual partner in the last 12 months and only half (51.8% in Chisinau, 52.2% in Balti and 49.5% in Tiraspol) reporting a consistent use of condoms in last month with casual partners (National Centre of Health Management, 2010). In Eastern Europe, the Republic of Moldova is among countries with the highest HIV prevalence in people who inject drugs. In 2009,[14] the prevalence of HIV in the sampled IDU population was 16.4% in Chisinau, 39.0% in Balti and 12.2% in Tiraspol (National Coordination Council, 2010). In the sampled populations, 20.8% in Tiraspol, 77.9% in Chisinau and 70.2% in Balti were infected with hepatitis C, whereas 7.7% in Tiraspol, 10.3% in Chisinau and 14.2% in Balti were infected with hepatitis B (National Centre of Health Management, 2010). The weighted average HIV prevalence at the national level is estimated as high as 17.4% on the right bank of Dniester River (Bivol, 2011).

In locations studied, harm reduction coverage of the target IDU population [15] is still low (7.4% in Chisinau, 29.2% in Balti, 16.7% in Tiraspol) (National Coordination Council, 2010). Altogether, at the end of 2010, harm reduction services were implemented in 20 territorial-administrative units (urban area with surrounding rural area) using stationary/mobile NSPs and outreach workers. Geographical/regional disparities were taken into account when locating the harm reduction services and their catchment areas. On the left bank, because of the local public authorities' resistance, the harm reduction services are available only in Tiraspol city, its surrounding localities, supported by the same source as those on the right bank. During 2010, 1,563,854 syringes were distributed in communities of the whole internationally recognised Moldovan territory (Soros Foundation Moldova, Harm Reduction Programme, 2011).

Methadone substitution treatment is available only in the two biggest cities (Chisinau and Balti) and exclusively on the right bank of the Dniester River.[16] The obstacles to the access to this treatment were identified as follows: geographical access, no permission for take-home doses, and the limited working hours of the methadone-dispensing office. The evaluation conducted in 2007–8 found that: (1) the overall methadone substitution treatment coverage in the country (both community and prison settings) and the impact of methadone substitution treatment on the HIV epidemic remained very low; and (2) methadone substitution treatment in healthcare facilities still lacked a full multidisciplinary approach (Subata, 2008). At the end of 2010, there were 303 patients enrolled in methadone substitution treatment in community settings (621 ever enrolled) (Soros Foundation Moldova, Harm Reduction Programme, 2011).

Harm reduction services are maintained by international sources, except for expenditures on maintenance of premises and salaries for staff of methadone substitution treatment programmes (National Coordination Council, 2010).

---

[13] The respondents who reported at least one of the following practices during the last month: drawing up a drug solution from a common jar, injecting drugs using a preloaded syringe, or front-/back-loading.

[14] Survey conducted in 2009 among IDUs in three main cities: municipality of Balti, municipality of Chisinau and Tiraspol, RDS sampling method.

[15] With all three main interventions: receiving HIV testing, receiving free condom and free needle/syringe, all of them at least once in the previous 12 months.

[16] Left bank authorities are resistant to the implementation of methadone substitution treatment.

Harm reduction in prisons

The Republic of Moldova can be viewed as an example of best practices in the field of harm reduction service provision in the penitentiary setting (Hoover and Jurgens, 2009). Programmes for inmates are conducted for the most part by the medical services of the institutions, with inmate volunteers involved in outreach. In 2010, the harm reduction information component[17] was implemented in all 17 penitentiary institutions, while needle exchange was implemented in 9 of them, operating on a 24/7 basis. At the end of 2010, substitution treatment was available in 6 prisons. During 2010, 80,408 syringes were distributed in prisons on the right-bank, and at the end of the year there were 60 inmates on methadone substitution treatment (259 ever enrolled in penitentiary setting) (Soros Foundation Moldova, Harm Reduction Programme, 2011).

By 1 July 2011, the number of detainees in right-bank prisons reached 6,245 (4,067 convicts and 2,178 under penal investigation) (Department of Penitentiary Institutions of the Republic of Moldova, 2011). A survey conducted in 2010 in these facilities found 3.0% of last year prevalence of reported injecting drug use and 8.9% of lifetime prevalence of reported injecting drug use (which is considered to be underreported). Among inmates, prevalence rate of HIV was 3.4%, 15.5% for HCV, and 16.3% for HBV (National Centre of Health Management, 2010). In October 2010, three prisons on the Left Bank started needle exchange programmes.

Key challenges and current development

Currently, harm reduction services offer a minimal set of services: distribution of syringes and condoms, information, education, and referral to other services (Scutelniciuc et al., 2009). Because syringes can be bought in pharmacies without prescription and are cheap enough (about 0.1$), the pharmacies are the main source of syringes (96.2% for IDUs in Chisinau, 63.1% in Balti and 71.1% in Tiraspol) (National Centre of Health Management, 2010), but they do not provide harm reduction information or treatment referrals. An evaluation of prevention activities conducted in 2010 showed that existing HIV prevention services are not attractive, unable to reach those most hidden and at risk, and are not designed to address emerging risk sub-groups, such as sexual partners of people who inject drugs, female injectors and young injectors (Bivol et al., 2010). Scaling-up of methadone substitution treatment and removal of existing obstacles to accessing services are needed in if they are to have any impact on the HIV epidemic in the country. Taking into account the alarming situation on the left bank of the Dniester River, scaling up is urgently needed there (National Coordination Council, 2010).

The current grant offered by the Global Fund will end in 2012. After that date, there are no other secured funds to support harm reduction services and so it is crucial that these start to receive public funding.

Ukraine

Ukraine has one of the largest and fastest growing HIV epidemics in Europe. Data from routine epidemiological surveillance show that the epidemic is still concentrated in the ID population (Kruglov et al., 2009). The number of IDUs in the Ukraine is estimated to be between 230,000 and 360,000 (Berleva et al., 2010).

---

[17] Distribution of information materials and carrying out sessions on HIV prevention.

History

The first Ukrainian harm reduction project started in Odessa (in the 'Palermo' area of the city) in 1996 under the umbrella of the Ukrainian AIDS Centre; later, this was transformed into the NGO 'Faith, Hope, Love'. This initiative was facilitated and funded by UNAIDS as a follow-up reaction to the epidemic outbreak in Belarus (known as the 'Svetlogorsk case') and the first cases of HIV in Mykolaiv, Odessa and Crimea region. The decision to pilot this project was made at the city level and all framework documents of the project were approved by Odessa city council. This pilot was followed by three other projects in 1997 in Poltava (project 'Anti-SPID'), Mykolaiv (project 'Blagodiynist'), and in Odessa; all these were supported by UNAIDS (mostly training for project staff), and by International Harm Reduction Development (IHRD) of the Open Society Institute (financial resources for salaries and procurement of commodities). In 1998, a substantially wider initiative was supported by IHRD in Donetsk ('Society for supporting HIV-positive people'), Vinnitsa ('Stalist'), Zhitomir, Sumy ('Krok na zustrich'), Simferopol ('Nadezhda i spasenie'), and Kharkov ('Chervona strichka'). In addition to harm reduction among IDUs, HIV prevention programmes among commercial sex workers (CSW) were initiated in 1998. This was the period of gradual expansion of harm reduction projects to new regions and organisations. All these projects were also supported by small grants from other foreign donors in addition to funding from UNAIDS and OSI Foundations. In 2000–5, harm reduction projects were supported inter alia by USAID-funded projects through the International HIV/AIDS Alliance. Due to restrictions on USAID funds, the procurement of syringes and needles was funded by IHRD.

At the end of the 1990s, new regions in western and central Ukraine were launching their harm reduction initiatives (including Kyiv-based organisations 'Eney' and 'Krok za krokom'). All projects in new regions were approved by local governments after advocacy efforts, meeting with local journalists, communities and government officials.

In 2003, Ukraine received a Global Fund Round 1 grant supporting harm reduction activities as part of its broader HIV prevention efforts. By that time, Ukraine had more than 20 civil society organisations with good access to IDUs, experience in providing harm reduction services and enough technical capacity for further scale-up of the programmes. The year 2004 became a turning point for scaling up the harm reduction services in Ukraine and by the year 2011 more than 80 NGOs in all 25 oblasts were reaching 170,000 IDUs annually, or about 60% of total IDU population in Ukraine (International HIV/AIDS Alliance in Ukraine, 2011).

Overall, local governments positively responded to harm reduction initiatives. At the same time at national level, harm reduction was not acknowledged until February 2009, when it was listed as one of the services in the National HIV/AIDS programme for 2009–13. Finally in 2010, 14 years after the first pilot project, harm reduction was included in the HIV/AIDS Law of Ukraine as a guaranteed service for IDUs, thus, officially legalised at the national level.

Specifics of drug use and specific responses

The drug scene in Ukraine can be characterised as a 'do it yourself' approach. Most drugs are homemade by drug users or drug dealers from ingredients either locally grown or obtained from the pharmacy. The most popular drugs are the opiates 'shirka' (acetylated opium) and 'electroshirka' (desomorphine, known in Russia as 'krokodil'), and amphetamine-type stimulants such as 'vint' (methamphetamine). Most of these drugs are prepared in the solution form and are used intravenously. Opium extract is more popular among the older IDU population, and amphetamine/

methamphetamine solutions are more popular among younger IDUs (Booth et al., 2009; Booth et al., 2008). In the age group under 25 years of age, the proportion of those who use stimulant drugs increased from 22% in 2006 to 57% in 2009, while the use of opiates decreased from 87% to 64% in the same period. The proportion of female IDUs who use stimulants is larger than those who use opiates (Pohorila et al., 2010). Young and female drug users are substantially harder to reach with harm reduction programmes than are older male users. Older male IDUs with a long history of drug use predominate in the use of harm reduction services (Datsenko et al., 2009; International HIV/ AIDS Alliance in Ukraine, 2009). The need to reach young and female drug users and those who use stimulants has led to the development of new outreach and retention strategies. Since 2007, Ukraine has been successfully implementing peer-driven interventions among IDUs that facilitate recruitment of young and female IDUs as well as those who use stimulants. In addition, new pro-grammes have been developed that are sensitive to gender, age and specific patterns of drug use and help to actively engage these groups (Burrows et al., 2009).

Community based harm reduction projects have become a good basis for developing health ser-vices for IDUs and are now offered as a package of interventions to all project clients at the NGO outreach points. These interventions also include HIV, STI and HCV counselling and rapid testing with referral to a medical facility in the case of a positive result for diagnosis and treatment.

HR in prison

To date, there are no harm reduction activities in the penitentiary system of Ukraine.

Key challenges and current development

The successful scale-up of harm reduction became possible in Ukraine only because of a combina-tion of the sound capacity of civil society organisations and timely financial support from external donors. Civil society and community-based organisations are still the only implementers of harm reduction services. International donors, mainly the Global Fund and USAID, remain the only fund-ing sources for the harm reduction programmes. To date, the Ukrainian government has demon-strated neither political will nor commitment to HIV prevention among most-at-risk groups. The government also does not provide funding for these programmes. Unfortunately, despite silent acceptance, the medical personnel, law enforcement bodies and government officials cannot be con-sidered key supporters of the harm reduction approach. Regardless of the recent 'legalisation' of harm reduction, widespread stigmatisation and criminalisation of drug users is still a sad reality in Ukraine. Syringe exchange and substitution therapy are not allowed in Ukrainian prisons, which are one of the most risky environment for the spread of HIV among IDUs. In January 2011, syringe exchange points came under another attack from law enforcement and drug control authorities in many regions of the country. Since its initiation, substitution therapy has continuously been subject to police intrusions and abuses directed towards patients and doctors. Although harm reduction programmes have been implemented for many years in Ukraine, much more advocacy and educa-tional efforts are needed in order to have harm reduction widely and firmly accepted as a public health approach.

References

Alcabes, P. and Zielinski, A. (2004) Lessons learned about communicable disease control: HIV/AIDS in Poland, 1994–2004. Paper presented at the Leczenie substytucyjne i rehabilitacja narkomanii, Katowice.

Berleva, G.O., Dumchev, K.V., Kobyshcha, Y.V., Paniotto, V.I., Petrenko, T.V., Saliuk, T.O. et al. (2010) *Estimation of the Size of Populations Most-at-risk for HIV Infection in Ukraine in 2009*, Analytical report based on sociological study results, Kyiv: AIDS Alliance.

Bivol, S. (2011) Results of the modes of transmission exercise in the Republic of Moldova, Chisinau.

Bivol, S., Vladicescu, N., Lazarescu, L., Dumitrasco, A. and Osadcii, O. (2010) Evaluation of HIV prevention programmes in the Republic of Moldova 2010, Chisinau: unpublished.

Booth, R.E., Lehman, W.E., Dvoryak, S., Brewster, J.T. and Sinitsyna, L. (2009) Interventions with injection drug users in Ukraine, *Addiction*, 104 (11), 1864–73.

Booth, R.E., Lehman, W.E., Kwiatkowski, C.F., Brewster, J.T., Sinitsyna, L. and Dvoryak, S. (2008) Stimulant injectors in Ukraine: the next wave of the epidemic?, *AIDS Behav*, 12 (4), 652–61.

Bozsonyi, K., Csesztregi, T., Dudás, M., Horváth, G.C., Keller, É., Koós, T. et al. (2010). *2010 National Report to the EMCDDA by the Reitox National Focal Point: 'Hungary' – New Developments, Trends and In-depth Information on Selected Issues*, 1st edn, Budapest: National Focal Point HU.

Burrows, D., Thumath, M., Beletsky, L., Manukyan, A., Hardacre, P., Birgin, R. et al. (2009) From beyond boutique to epidemic control: evaluation report of HIV prevention activities by International HIV/AIDS Alliance Ukraine, unpublished report, AIDS Projects Management Group.

CEEHRN (2003) *HIV/AIDS Prevention Amongst Injecting Drug Users in Lithuania: Best Practices*, Vilnius: October.

CEEHRN (2004) *Harm Reduction Mapping*, Databases of needle exchange and opioid substitution sites in the countries of Central-Eastern Europe & Central Asia 2002–3.

Chopin, K. (1992) Too many advisers, not enough aid, *British Medical Journal*, 304 (6839), 1429.

Council of Europe (1998) *Recommendation No. R (98) 7 of The Committee of Ministers to Member States Concerning the Ethical and Organisational Aspects of Health Care in Prison*, https://wcd.coe.int/wcd/com.instranet.InstraServlet?command=com.instranet.CmdBlobGet&InstranetImage=530914&SecMode=1&DocId=463258&Usage=2, accessed 12 September 2011.

Csorba, J., Dénes, B., Miletics, M. and Nyizsnyánszki, A. (2003) *Harm Reduction Programs in Hungary*, 1st edn, trans. D. Bánki, Budapest: HCLU.

Danziger, R. (1994) Discrimination against people with HIV and AIDS in Poland, *British Medical Journal*, 308 (6937), 1145–7.

Datsenko, A., Smyrnov, P. and Broadhead, R.S. (2009) Overcoming stagnation in harm reduction projects in Ukraine: the introduction of peer-driven intervention for IDUs. Fifth European Conference on Clinical and Social Research on AIDS and Drugs, Vilnius, 28–30 April.

Department of Penitentiary Institutions of the Republic of Moldova (16 August 2011) *Information on the Number of Detainees in the Penitentiaries of the Republic of Moldova by 1st of July 2011*, Chisinau.

Drug Control Department under the Government of the Republic of Lithuania (2010) *2010 National Report (2009 data) to the EMCDDA by the Reitox National Focal Point Lithuania: New Development, Trends and In-depth Information on Selected Issues*, ed. E. Jasaitis, E, invited coauthor E. Subata.

ECDC (2010) *Implementing the Dublin Declaration on Partnership to Fight HIV/AIDS in Europe and Central Asia: 2010 Progress Report*, Stockholm: ECDC.

European Community (2005) *EU Drugs Strategy (2005–12)*, 2009, from www.emcdda.europa.eu/html.cfm/index6790EN.html, accessed 12 September 2011.

European Community (2008) *EU Action Plan on Drugs 2009–2012*, http://ec.europa.eu/justice_home/fsj/drugs/docs/com_2008_567_en.pdf, accessed 12 September 2011.

Fifty-second Session of the Commission on Narcotic Drugs (2009) *Political Declaration and Plan of Action on International Cooperation towards an Integrated and Balanced Strategy to Counter the World Drug Problem*, New York: United Nations.

Government of the Republic of Estonia (2010) *UNGASS Country Progress Report – Latvia: Reporting period: January 2008–December 2009*, submission date: 31 March.

Government of the Republic of Hungary (2000) *National Strategy to Combat the Drug Problem: Conceptual Framework of the Hungarian Government's Anti-drug Strategy*, Budapest: Government of the Republic of Hungary.

Government of the Republic of Hungary (2009) *National Strategy for Tackling the Drugs Problem 2010–2018*, Budapest: Government of the Republic of Hungary.

Government of the Republic of Latvia (2010) *UNGASS Country Progress Report – Latvia: Reporting Period: January 2008–December 2009*, submission date 31 March.

Government of the Republic of Moldova (1998) *Governmental Decision on the Implementation of Urgent HIV Prevention Activities among Injecting Drug Users*, Chisinau: Monitorul Oficial.

Government of the Republic of Moldova (2001) *National Programme on Prevention and Control of HIV/AIDS and STIs for 2001–2005*, Chisinau: Monitorul Oficial.

Government of the Republic of Moldova (2005) *National Programme on Prevention and Control of HIV/AIDS and STIs for 2006–2010*, Chisinau: Monitorul Oficial.

Government of the Republic of Poland (2006) *National Programme for Counteracting Drug Addiction 2006–2010*.

Government of the Republic of Poland (2011) *National Programme for Counteracting Drug Addiction 2011–2016*.

Government of the Slovak Republic (2009) *National Anti-Drug Strategy for the Period 2009–2012*.

HCLU (2011) *Sign the Petition to Save Evidence-based Drug Policy in Hungary!*, http://drogriporter.hu/en/drugstrat, accessed 12 September.

Hoover, J. and Jurgens, R. (2009) *Harm Reduction in Prison: The Moldova Model*, New York: Open Society Institute.

Höschl, C., Kalina, K., Bém, P., Těmínová, M. and Presl, J. (1992) *Memorandum on the Drug Policy Addressing the Members of the Czech Government* [*Memorandum o drogové politice pro členy vlády ČR*], Prague.

I Can Live (2009) *Advocating for the Promotion and Development of Harm Reduction Programmes in Lithuania*, ed. E. Matuizaite, E. Subata and V. Ambrazeviciene,Vilnius.

I Can Live (2011) *Information Bulletin* [*Informacinis biuletenis*] [in Lithuanian], no. 13.

International HIV/AIDS Alliance in Ukraine (2009) Programmatic reports on HIV prevention programs among IDUs.

International HIV/AIDS Alliance in Ukraine (2011) Programmatic reports on HIV prevention programs among IDUs.

Juodkaite, D., Uscila, R. and Stover, H. (2008) *Lithuanian Legislation and Policy Analysis on HIV/AIDS Prevention and Care among Injecting Drug Users in Prisons Settings*, Report to the UNODC regional project, HIV/AIDS prevention and care among injecting drug users and in prison settings in Estonia, Latvia and Lithuania, Vienna: UNODC.

Kalina, K. (2007) Developing the system of drug services in the Czech Republic, *Journal of Drug Issues*, 37 (1), 181.

Karnīte, A., Uuskula, A., Raag, M., Rüütel, K., Talu, A., Abel-Ollo, K., Caplinskas, S., Caplinskiene, I., Upmace, I. and Ferdats, A. (2010) Prevalence of hepatitis C infection and related factors among injecting drug users in Estonia, Latvia and Lithuania. Eighteenth International AIDS Conference 2010, *Abstract Book*, abstract no. WEPE0559.

Kivimets, K. (2011) Continuity of methadone maintenance therapy in prison system in Estonia. Ministry of Justice of the Republic of Estonia. *Proceedings of the UNODC Baltic Final Conference in Riga*, 24–5 March, www.unodc.org/documents/balticstates//EventsPresentations/FinalConf_24-25Mar11/Kivimets_25_-March.pdf, accessed 12 September 2011.

Kruglov, Y.V., Maksimenok, O.V., Gural, A.L., Martsynovska, V.A., Nguen, I.V. and Kyslyh, O.M. (2009) *HIV Infection in Ukraine: Information Bulletin 31*, Kiev: Institute of Epidemiology and Infectious Diseases named after L.V. Gromashevsky at AMS Ukraine, Ukrainian AIDS Prevention and Control Center, Ministry of Health of Ukraine.

Law on HIV/AIDS (2009) 2009-11-17, Article 5, par. K (2009).

Lõhmus, L. and Trummal, A. (2009) *HIV and Drug Use Related Knowledge, Attitudes and Behaviour among Prisoners in 2008*, Tallin: National Institute for Health Development.

Malczewski, A., Struzik, M. and Jaśkiewicz, A. (2009) Pierwsze ogólnopolskie badanie klientów oraz programów niskoprogrowych w 2008 roku. Projekt francusko-polski (maszynopis) (unpublished manuscript), Warsaw: Centrum Informacji o Narkotykach i Narkomanii – Krajowe Biuro ds. Przeciwdziałania Narkomanii.

Malczewski, A., Bukowska, B., Jabłoński, P., Struzik, M., Kidawa, M., Strzelecka, A. et al. (2010) *Poland: New Development, Trends and In-depth Information on Selected Issues*, 1st edn, Warsaw: National Bureau for Drug Prevention.

Mravcik, V., Nechanska, B. and St'astna, L. (2011). Ambulantní péče o uživatele a závislé na návykových látkách v ČR ve zdravotnické statistice od roku 1963 [Outpatient care for substance users and addicts in the Czech Republic in Health Statistics since 1963], *Epidemiol Mikrobiol Imunol*, 60 (2), 64–73.

Mravčík, V., Pešek, R., Horáková, M., Nečas, V., Škařupová, K., Št'astná, L. et al. (2010) *Výroční zpráva o stavu ve věcech drog v České republice v roce 2009* [*The Czech Republic: Drug Situation 2009*], vol. 8, Praha: Úřad vlády ČR [Office of the Czech Government].

Mravcik, V., Skarupova, K., Orlikova, B., Zabransky, T., Karachaliou, K. and Schulte, B. (2011). Use of gelatine capsules for application of methamphetamine: A new harm reduction approach, *International Journal on Drug Policy*, 22 (2), 172–3.

National Centre of Health Management (2010) *Integrated Bio-behavioural Survey in High Risk Groups*, Chisinau: National Centre of Health Management.

National Coordination Council (2010a) Application to the 10th round of funding to Global Fund, Chisinau: National Coordination Council.

National Coordination Council (2010b) *Republic of Moldova Progress Report*, Chisinau: National Coordination Council.

National Focal Point Hungary (2011) *Problem Drug Use: Facts and Figures*, http://drogfokuszpont.hu/?lang=eng&menu=119&pid=162, accessed 12 September 2011.

National Institute for Health Development (2009) *Report about the Drug Situation in Estonia in 2009 (Based on Data from 2008)*, ed. A. Talu, K. Abel-Ollo, K. Vals, A. Ahven and H. Tarn, Talinn: NIHD, Estonian Monitoring Centre for Drugs.

Open Society Institute (2008) *Sustaining and Expanding ART Access in a Post-Global Fund Context: Lessons from Estonia – Access to Essential Medicines Initiative of the OSI*, New York: Open Society Institute, Public Health Program, www.soros.org/initiatives/health/focus/access/articles_publications/publications/estonia_20080825/estonia_20080901.pdf, accessed 12 September 2011.

Pohorila, N., Taran, Y., Kolodiy, I., Diyeva, T. (2010) *Behavior Monitoring and HIV-infection Prevalence among Injection Drug Users (Analytical Report Based on Results of Linked Survey)*, Kiev: AIDS Alliance in Ukraine.

Prison Department of the Republic of Lithuania (2011) *Main Statistical Data for the 2010 Activities of Prison Department and Its Subordinate Establishments and State Enterprises* [*Kalėjimų Departamento ir jam pavaldžių įstaigų bei valstybės įmonių 2010 metų veiklos pagrindiniai statistiniai duomenys*] [in Lithuanian], www.kalejimudepartamentas.lt/getfile.aspx?dokid=8C800328-3801-43DB-ACFC-BC16FF2FE333, accessed 12 September 2011.

Programmatic Reports (2011) *Programmatic Reports of HIV Prevention Programs among IDUs (2011)*, Kiev: International HIV/AIDS Alliance in Ukraine.

Reitox National Focal Point in Slovakia (2009) *2009 National Report (2008 data) to the EMCDDA by the Reitox National Focal Point: New Development, Trends and In-depth Information on Selected Issues*, Bratislava: Reitox National Focal Point in Slovakia.

Rotberga, S. (2011) Results of project 'HIV/AIDS prevention and care among injecting drug users and in prison settings'. *Proceedings of the UNODC Baltic Final Conference in Riga in 24–25 March, 2011*, www.unodc.org/documents/balticstates//EventsPresentations/FinalConf_24-25Mar11/Rotberga_24_March_v2.pdf, accessed 12 September 2011.

Rotberga, S., Skilina, I. and Kelpsaite, J. (2010) *Inventory of Harm Reduction Agencies in Latvia and Lithuania*, UNODC Project Office for the Baltic States, 25 October 2010, www.unodc.org/documents/balticstates//EventsPresentations/NSP_25-26Oct10/SRotberga_25102010.pdf, accessed 12 September 2011.

Rüütel, K., Raag, M., Caplinskiene, I., Karnite, A., Talu, A., Abel-Ollo, K., Ferdats, A., Caplinskas, S. et al. (2010) HIV-prevalence and risk behaviors among injecting drug users in Riga, Tallinn and Vilnius. Eighteenth International AIDS Conference 2010, *Abstract Book*, abstract no. CDC0293.

Scutelniciuc, O., Condrat, I., Plamadeala, D., Cocirta, A., Slobozian, V., Susanu, A. et al. (2009) *2008 Drug Situation in the Republic of Moldova: Annual Report*, Chisinau: Reclama.

Seimas of the Republic of Lithuania (2010) *Decree Regarding Approval of National Drug Control and Drug Use Prevention Program for 2010–2016 [Nutarimas dėl Nacionalinės narkotikų kontrolės ir narkomanijos prevencijos 2010–2016 metų programos patvirtinimo]* [in Lithuanian], no. XI-1078, Valstybės žinios, 2010-11-11, no. 132–6720.

Semenaite, B., Januleviciene, R., Kezys, G. et al. (2008) *Rapid Assessment and Response on Drug use in Marijampolė Correction House, Lithuania*, Report for UNODC & Prison Department at the Ministry of Justice of the Republic of Lithuania.

Sile, L. and Pugule, I. (2008) *Evaluation of Pharmacological Treatment of Persons Dependent on Opioids in Latvia [Farmakologiskas opioidu atkaribas arstešanas novertešana Latvija]* [in Latvian], Drug Monitoring Center within the Public Health Agency of Latvia in collaboration with UNODC, Riga.

Slabý, B., Okrúhlica, Ľ., Luha, J., Guláš, J., Tomková, E., SlovÍková, M., et al. (2004) *Drug Situation and Drug Control in the Slovak Republic [Stav drogových závislostí a kontrola drog v Slovenskej republike]*, 1st edn, Bratislava: Urad vlády Slovenskej republiky.

Soros Foundation Moldova, Harm Reduction Programme (2011) *Report on the Implementation of Harm Reduction Programme in 2010*, Chisinau: Soros Foundation Moldova.

Stover, H. (2008) *Evaluation of National Responses to HIV/AIDS in Prison Settings in Estonia*, Vienna: UNODC, http://unosek.org/documents/balticstates/Library/PrisonSettings/Report_Evaluation_Prisons_2008_Estonia.pdf, accessed 12 September 2011].

Stuikyte, R., Otiashvili, D., Merkinaite, S., Sarang, A. and Tolopilo, A. (2009) *The Impact of Drug Policy on Health and Human Rights in Eastern Europe: 10 years after the UN General Assembly Special Session on Drugs*, Vilnius: Eurasian Harm Reduction Network (EHRN).

Subata, E. (2007) *Evaluation of Methadone Maintenance Therapy in the Republic of Moldova*, Vilnius: Government of Moldova, http://aids.md/aids/files/658/report-methadone-maintenance-therapy-moldova-2007-en.pdf, accessed 12 September 2011.

Subata, E. (2008) *Evaluation of the Opioid Substitution Therapy in the Republic of Moldova*, Vlinius.

Talu, A., Rajaleid, K., Abel-Ollo, K., Rüütel, K., Rahu, M., Rhodes, T., Platt, L., Bobrova, N. and Uusküla, A. (2009) HIV infection and risk behaviour of primary fentanyl and amphetamine injectors in Tallinn, Estonia: implications for intervention, *International Journal of Drug Policy*, 21 (1), 56–63.

UNAIDS and ODCCP (2001) *Drug Abuse and HIV/AIDS: Lessons Learnt – Case Studies Booklet: Central and Eastern Europe and the Central Asian States*, Geneva: UNAIDS, http://data.unaids.org/publications/IRC-pub02/jc673-drugabuse_en.pdf, accessed 12 September 2011.

UNODC and WHO/Europe (2011) *Mid-term Evaluation of the Latvian National HIV Programme: 2009–2013*. Report by Ulrich Laukamm-Josten, Pierpaolo de Colombani, Kees de Joncheere, Roger Drew, Irina Eramova, Signe Rotberga, Heino Stöver and Anna Zakowicz, Copenhagen: World Health Organization.

Upmace, I. (2010) HIV prevention program in Latvia: overview and perspectives. *Proceedings of the Conference Harm Reduction in the Baltic States: The Way Forward*, 25–6 October, Riga, www.unodc.org/documents/balticstates//EventsPresentations/NSP_25-26Oct10/Upmace_25102010.pdf, accessed 12 September 2011.

Uusküla, A., Rajaleid, K., Talu, A., Abel, K., Rüütel, K. and Hay, G. (2007) Estimating injection drug use prevalence using state wide administrative data sources: Estonia, 2004, *Addiction Research and Theory*, 15 (4), 411–24, ISSN 1606-6359.

Uusküla, A., Kals, M., Rajaleid, K., Abel, K., Talu, A., Rüütel, K., Platt, L., Rhodes, T., DeHovitz, J. and Des Jarlais, D. (2008) High-prevalence and high-estimated incidence of HIV infection among new injecting drug users in Estonia: need for large scale prevention programs, *Journal of Public Health*, 30 (2), 119–25.

Walmsley, R. (2009) *World Prison Population List*, 8th edn, London: International Centre for Prison Studies, King's College London.

WHO (2005) *Status Paper on Prisons, Drugs and Harm Reduction*, vol. 1, Copenhagen: World Health Organization.

WHO and UNODC (2008) *Evaluation of Fighting HIV/AIDS in Estonia*, by Roger Drew, Martin Donoghoe, Agris Koppel, Ulrich Laukamm-Josten, Claudio Politi, Signe Rotberga, Anya Sarang and Heino Stöver, Copenhagen: World Health Organization.

Zábranský, T. (2002) Problem drug use and treatment responses. In EMCDDA (ed.), *2002 Report on the Drugs Situation in Candidate Central and Eastern European Countries*, Lisbon: EMCDDA, 15–28.

Chapter 24

HARM REDUCTION IN WESTERN EUROPE

Richard Pates

Introduction

This is a complicated subject to address for two reasons. First, prior to 1989 there was a natural division between the countries of the EU (plus Norway and Switzerland) and the countries of Eastern Europe (behind the so called Iron Curtain) but some of the countries of Eastern Europe are now members of the EU so this division is not so clear. Harm reduction in the countries formally known as Eastern Europe is the subject of different chapter in this book (see chapter 23) so this chapter will be concerned with some of the countries west of the former Iron Curtain in the south plus the countries of Scandinavia and the Mediterranean islands which are either independent (Malta) or an archipelago of islands which are part of another European country. The second complication is because much of the early work in harm reduction took place in parts of northern Europe, especially in the UK and the Netherlands (see chapter 2 for the history of harm reduction). It is not appropriate to repeat this in a chapter of limited length. This chapter will briefly review where basic harm reduction measures are in place across the area and then discuss some of the innovative ideas coming from this region and some of the major barriers to harm reduction in some countries.

Beginnings

Although as has been discussed in chapter 2 there were attempts at harm reduction many years ago, the introduction of what is now considered harm reduction probably began in the early 1980s as a response to the threatened HIV epidemic, although some workers in the Netherlands had given out clean syringes in previous years in an attempt to stem the spread of hepatitis in drug injectors. HIV suddenly posed a huge threat to public health when the implications of the disease were recognised and this produced responses at government levels. For example, the committee that advised the UK government on drug policy (Advisory Council on the Misuse of Drugs, ACMD) produced a report which stated that the threat of HIV was more serious than drug misuse and suggested a hierarchy of reduction of harm by moving from injection to oral use, reducing the quantities of drugs consumed and finally to abstinence (ACMD, 1988). There were also leaflets produced for every household in the UK, some of which were frankly obscure and coy, such as leaflets delivered to every household in the UK the message of which was 'don't die of ignorance' and leaflets with picture of falling tombstones and icebergs which had little face validity for the intended recipients. There was however a recognition of the need to improve services for injecting drug users and this produced an injection of funding enabling services to be established all over the country for treatment. That this came from a conservative government not known for compassion or a belief in community was all

Harm Reduction in Substance Use and High-Risk Behaviour: International Policy and Practice, First Edition.
Edited by Richard Pates and Diane Riley.
© 2012 Blackwell Publishing Ltd. Published 2012 by Blackwell Publishing Ltd.

the more remarkable but probably reflected the fear of HIV spreading from drug users and the gay community to the more establishment communities.

In the UK this response to HIV led to the creation of community drug teams and the availability of widespread methadone prescription for opiate dependents (the main problematic drug of the 1980s) and the introduction of needle exchanges. Both of these were not without problems, because of local opposition, sometimes from within the medical profession by people who did not believe in giving out drugs to drug addicts (would you give whisky to an alcoholic they used to ask) or would you prescribe doses ineffective for treatment, in an arbitrary fashion. To some, needle exchanges were a sign of condoning injecting drug use. However, both of these interventions were an important step in public health but in some cases as may be seen in this book, necessary but not sufficient to deal with the problem entirely.

The practice of substitute prescribing had always had a place in the treatment of opiate problems in the UK and was confirmed as good practice by the Rolleston Committee (1926). However, there were no firm rules about prescribing and dispensing of methadone, which in under-prescribing for some users had the consequence of the need to top up on street drugs for which the services would then punish the user by withdrawing the prescription. The system of 'loose' dispensing (e.g. dispensing two weeks supply as a take-home dose at one time) also led to methadone leaking onto a black market.

So if these two interventions were seen to be important methods of reducing harm from injecting drug use should they have been adopted across all communities? From a growing base of drug problems from the early 1980 onwards most Western European countries had significant drug problems but chose to deal with them in different ways or to ignore them. The Netherlands responded quickly and used innovative methods to reach injecting drug users such as the use of the famous methadone buses which provided a daily low threshold service to many parts of Amsterdam.

How common are harm reduction measures throughout Europe?

A recent monograph on harm reduction in Europe was published by the EMCDDA (Rhodes and Hedrich, 2010) and this provides a comprehensive evidence based review of current harm reduction efforts in Europe. As Cook, Bridge and Stimson (2010) found when looking at the diffusion of harm reduction in Europe that all the countries of Western Europe with the exception of Iceland had needle and syringe exchange programmes, all the countries with the exception of Iceland had opioid substitution therapy available but other harm reduction measures were less common. For example only Germany, Luxembourg, Netherlands, Norway, Spain and Switzerland had drug consumption rooms, only Germany, Luxembourg, Portugal, Spain and Switzerland had needle and syringe exchange available in prisons and some western European countries (Cyprus, Greece and Iceland) still did not have opioid substitution therapy available in prisons.

Among their conclusions (Cook et al., 2010) about the role of harm reduction is that 'Europe has had a significant impact on the diffusion of harm reduction globally' and that 'The European Union has played a crucial role in promoting and supporting harm reduction at the United Nations.'

A recent film made by the Hungarian Civil Liberties Union (2011) called *The State of Harm Reduction in Europe*, filmed at the inaugural meeting of the European Harm Reduction network, showed interviews with a number of professionals from a dozen countries in Europe. They discussed the success of harm reduction in reducing the spread of blood-borne viruses and overdose deaths plus the effects of politics in various countries which overall indicated the wide spread of harm reduction in Europe in 2011.

Decriminalisation of drugs in Portugal

In 2001 drugs were decriminalised in Portugal. In effect possession and use were still illegal but became technical violations of the law and were removed from the criminal realm although trafficking remained a criminal offence (Greenwald, 2009). Although other states in the European Union have developed de facto decriminalisation (e.g. by not prosecuting the use of some drugs such as cannabis which are perceived to have less serious consequences for use) no other country has actually changed legislation to decriminalise all drugs. Greenwald reports that the law has become increasingly popular in Portugal since 1991 with very few political factions except some on the far right wanting a repeal of the law. Dealing drugs to minors or those with a mental illness remains a criminal offence although minors found in possession are subject to the same process as adults.

There were concerns that drug use would escalate and that Portugal would become a haven for drug tourists but so far this has not happened. Of those cited for drug offenses 95% were found to be Portuguese and virtually none came from other EU countries. Although Portugal's rates of drug use have not decreased they have stabilised and become among the lowest in Europe, drug related pathologies such as sexually transmitted infections and drug related deaths have fallen considerably. Newly diagnosed cases of HIV and AIDS among drug users have fallen year by year since 2001 (Greenwald, 2009).

This has been attributed to the greater opportunity for access to health services and a lack of fear of prosecution. Those who are cited for drug use or possession go before a 'Dissuasion Commission' of three members appointed by the Justice Ministry the Health Ministry and the government's coordinator of drug policy. Non-addicted users may be fined as a last resort although in practice these fine are usually suspended.. Those who are deemed to be addicted will have sanctions suspended on condition that they accept the treatment offered.

A dual track approach in Finland

Finland is an interesting example of the use of harm reduction policies in a slightly different way. Another chapter in this book (Monaghan, chapter 6) describes harm reduction from the law enforcement perspective, as a way of involving police in the processes of harm reduction. Tammi (2007) describes how in Finland there has been a marriage of harm reduction policies with a strict prohibitionist policy and he describes how typically harm reduction is seen as an arm of public health policy where the main outcome is to reduce the health risks related to drug use. An extension of this is reflected in a concern for human rights and social equality. What Tammi concluded was that in Finland harm reduction had its roots in criminal policy and rather than being contradictory to prohibitionist policy, harm reduction has become part of it (see table 24.1).

In a previous paper Tammi (2005) described how the policy was formulated when a response was needed to an increase in drug use and drug related harm in Finland in the late 1990s. A committee was established in 1997 known as the Drug Policy Committee which had to reconcile the views of the police authorities who were advocating strict controls leading to a 'drug free' society and the views of social welfare, health and criminal policy alliance which pursued a policy of harm reduction. Harm reduction was proposed as a partial solution to the growing drug problem against fears that it would destroy the strict prohibitionist policies and thus harm reduction became to be seen as the source of the crisis. There were fears that harm reduction would be seen to dilute the prohibition policy and lessen the deterrent effect of the law. This committee produced Finland's first national drug strategy. Finland had a tradition from the 1960s and 1970s of humane and rational criminal

Table 24.1 Harm reduction vs. punitive prohibition

Harm reduction	><	Punitive prohibition
Individualism	><	Collectivism
Individual is free also to act to his/her own disadvantage		Public good is always primary vis-à-vis to the individual
Inclusion	><	Exclusion
Drug user is a normal member of a community		Drug user is a deviant special case
Pragmatism	><	Dogmatism
Drug policy should be based on knowledge and situation-specific considerations		Drug policy should be based on value goals that justify the means despite costs
Emancipation	><	Paternalism
Control of drug users should be alleviated		Drug users should be punished for and/or cured of drug use

Source: Tammi, 2007.

policy aimed at minimising social harm and the protection of the population minorities who were the targets of control. The strategy produced was a compromise of stricter criminal control on drug users but a further elaboration of harm reduction policy (Tammi, 2005).

The harm reduction initiatives were the establishing of health counselling centres with needle exchange facilities and extending the provision of substitute prescribing which has had the effect of creating specialist services based on medical expertise and 'an increasing involvement of the medical profession in addressing drug problems' (Tammi, 2007). Alongside this there has been an intensification of the criminal justice control of drug use. Thus the adoption of harm reduction has not seen an adoption of more liberal policies or an undermining of traditional prohibitionist policies. Tammi suggests that a combination of harm reduction and prohibitionist policies has resulted in a dual track policy. He states that at first the relationship between the two tracks was fragile but soon became 'established and institutionalised'. Although this approach has now settled down it has resulted in a diminution of the former socio-psychological approaches to treatment to the more medicalised and desocialised version of prohibition (see table 24.2).

As Tammi (2007) suggests there is a similarity in what is being asked in prohibition and harm reduction policies. Quoting Levine (2003) he says that harm reduction is not asking drug users to give up drugs but to make the process safer for themselves and others and the prohibitionists message to governments would be that governments are not being asked to legalise drugs but to allow some programmes like needle and syringe exchange and substitution programmes to reduce the harmful aspects of prohibition.

Finland appears to have taken a different approach to its Scandinavian neighbours; Sweden has a long history of taking a very punitive view of drugs in policy terms and very slow to adopt harm reduction measures. There is a cherished view of a drug-free society and a view of harm reduction threatening the Swedish ideals of that. Denmark had a more liberal approach and had adopted more harm reduction measures but with more penal control (Tammi, 2007). Iceland as a contrast has no needle and syringe exchange and no substitution programmes. Norway has these harm reduction programmes plus the availability of a drug consumption room. Tammi suggest that this mixture of harm reduction and increased involvement of the criminal justice system is also happening in France (who were very late in adopting harm reduction measures) and even Britain where the Labour government moved responsibility largely from health to the criminal justice system with a focus on reducing drug related crime.

Table 24.2 Progression of the two-track drug policy in Finland

Year	Track 1: Criminal control	Track 2: Harm reduction
1995	Police Act (402/95) permits wiretapping, telecommunications and technical surveillance	3–5 people in substitution treatment
1996		
1997	Drug Strategy 1997 reinforces restrictive drug police line, including total ban on experimentation and use of drugs. Number of companies that subjected their staff to drug testing: 103	Drug Strategy 1997 supports harm reduction measures. Substitution treatment programmes (STP) launched. Needle exchange programme (NEP) starts in Helsinki
1998		
1999		Consensus statement by Medical Society Duodecim and Academy of Finland takes a stand for substitution treatment and needle exchange
2000	Drug strategy of the police emphasises street-level policing of drug use and dealing. Number of companies that subjected their staff to drug testing: 464	NEPs in 12 cities (4,800 clients, 564,500 injection sets exchanged). STP's extended (Decree 607/2000) 200 people in STPs
2001	Amendment of the Penal Code defines drug use as a category of crime in itself, a "drug-use offence". Police Act (21/01; later 525/05) permits new unconventional detection methods, such as undercover activities and pseudo purchase (e.g. of drugs)	
2002	3.103 people fined for drug use by the police	NEPs in 22 cities (9.300 clients, 1.1 million injection sets exchanged). STPs extended (Decree 289/2002)
2003	4.151 people fined for drug use by the police (an increase of 33.8%)	Decree on the amendment to the Communicate Disease Act (1383/2003) puts the cities and municipalities under obligation to arrange needle-exchanges when needed
2004	4.420 people fined for drug use by hte police (an increase of 6.5%). The Act on the Protection of Privacy in Working life (759/2004) incorporates provisions related to drug testing, e.g. on the employers' right to process in certain situations information on job applicants' and employees' drug use	600–700 people in STPs
2005		NEPs in 30 cities (11.800 clients, 1.9 million injection sets exchanged). 900–1000 people in STPs

Source: Tammi, 2007.

Switzerland

Switzerland has a reputation as a conservative country and yet have produced some of the more innovative and liberal policies on harm reduction in Europe. Switzerland is not a member of the European Union and lies land locked in the centre of Western Europe, with a high standard of living from successful business, especially banking. It has a political system that relies much on referenda and thus participation of the citizens of the country. Introducing new policies requires consensual agreement and this has included changes in federal laws on drugs.

In 1993 and 1994 two popular initiatives were presented on the drug question (Büechi and Minder, 2001), one initiative called 'Youth without Drugs' which was a call for a strict, abstinence oriented drug policy. The other called 'For a Reasonable Drug Policy' which proposed the opposite calling for decriminalisation of drug use, the cultivations of plants used to produce drugs and legal possession and purchase of drugs for personal use. The federal government thought both initiatives were too extreme and recommended rejection of them which the Swiss voters did the first by a majority of 70% and the second by a majority of 74%. In 1996 an expert commission (the Schild Commission) was asked by the Swiss government to examine the law on narcotics and psychotropic substances, which resulted in recommendations of decriminalisation of drug use and the medical prescription of heroin as a new therapy (subject to scientific evaluation).

An outdoor area of tolerance was established in a park in Zurich where drug users and drug use was tolerated and later were allowed in other Swiss cities such as Bern and Basle. These were subsequently closed in 1995/6 because they had become unmanageable. The Zurich 'Platzspitz' (needle park) had attracted drug users from outside the city and even the country and drug related harms increased. Switzerland now has comprehensive harm reduction measures in place including needle and syringe exchange, drug substitution treatment (heroin as well as methadone and buprenorphine), outreach services, needle and syringe exchange in prisons and supervised injection sites (Public Health Agency of Canada, 2003).

The heroin prescribing project

The heroin prescribing project is run through special clinics established in the mid 1990s and was closely monitored and researched. Most of the heroin prescribed is for self-injection and the rest in the form of fast or slow release tablets for oral consumption. The main objectives of the heroin assisted therapy were:

- to reach heroin dependent people who are unable to profit from other forms of treatment;
- to improve the health and social status of the participants;
- to reduce the risk taking of participants (including HIV infection);
- to compare the results to those of other treatment approaches especially methadone maintenance).

During the research phase 800 patients received heroin, patients were more than 20 years old, had been dependent on heroin for more than 2 years, had not been helped by other treatment approaches, had evident health and social problems and were prepared to comply with the programme (Büechi and Minder, 2001). The programme was run in 16 treatment centres, the research was supervised by a safety assurance group and the research monitored through WHO by an international expert group. The results showed the following (Büechi and Minder, 2001):

- general improvements to physical and mental health;

- social stabilisation: homelessness decreased from 12% to 1%, permanent employment increased from 14% to 32% and unemployment reduced from 44% to 20%;
- after 22 months 19% of the participants switched from the heroin assisted treatment to another form of treatment for example methadone maintenance or abstinence oriented therapy;
- the use of illicit heroin and cocaine reduced rapidly, benzodiazepine use decreased less rapidly and the use of cannabis and alcohol reduced minimally;
- there was less delinquency;
- there was a reduction of contact with the drug scene.

Heroin prescription is now part of the treatment options available in Switzerland. One of the reasons reported for the success of the project is that because the clients had to attend the treatment centre three times per day and that taking heroin in a supervised way removes the glamour of heroin use and turns it into a dull routine medical procedure, and the image of heroin use has shifted from one of rebellion to an illness (Laurance, 2006).

Supervised injecting rooms

Another aspect of innovative policy in Switzerland was the establishment of safe injecting rooms (or facilities). The first one in Switzerland was established in Bern in 1986 as a response to a rapid increase in HIV infection among injecting drug users (Haemmig and van Beek, 2005). This remains the prime objective of after injecting rooms – to reduce morbidity and mortality among injecting drug users. Although supervised drug injecting facilities had been tried before in a number of countries, this was the first attempt to initiate a professional interface between the injecting drug users and health professionals in an institutionalised way.

There are now about 30 such facilities in Switzerland and are allowed under Swiss law because they do not distribute illicit drugs or allow drugs to be sold or traded. Typically they are either mobile or fixed facilities operating in areas with open drug scenes, located within a larger centre which includes a cafeteria, counselling room and primary care clinic, open 7 hours per day and 7 days per week, entry is controlled and restricted and although the police will refer drug users to the service and do not arrest those around the centre, they will assist with dangerous situations and enforce laws concerned with drug trafficking (Public Health Agency of Canada, 2003).

Supervised injecting rooms are supervised by health professionals, and can provide clean injecting equipment, condoms, provide information and guidance on safer injecting as well as other health matters and can offer referral into treatment when required. They are in effect an easily accessible, low threshold outreach service and are established in areas of known open drug use which have been subject to public health and public order concerns. They can also provide information about changes in drug use patterns such as potency of new batches of drugs etc.. to help reduce risks of overdose.

Success of safer injecting rooms is difficult to measure but a report on the Bern facility concluded that it had been instrumental in reducing overdose deaths although as Haemigg and van Beek point out the fatal overdoses only declined in Switzerland in 1993 after after injecting rooms were introduced. They also noted that there had been no reported fatal overdoses in these facilities anywhere in the world and that one other advantage of the avoidance of overdose is that of hypoxia (when the brain is deprived of oxygen during overdose) which causes damage to the brain and other organs which may be cumulative after several non-fatal overdoses.

Reuters (2010) in an article on Swiss drug policy quoted a former Swiss president, Ruth Dreifuss, as saying that they had changed perspective and introduced the notion of public health and extend a friendly hand to drug users by authorising research into syringe exchange programmes, safer injection rooms (and heroin prescribing) etc.. Dr Ambrose Uchterhagen chair of the Research Institute for Public Health and Addiction at Zurich University quoted in the same Reuters report said that now some 70% of the opiate or cocaine users were in treatment, the number of injectors with HIV has been reduced by 50% over 10 years, overdose mortality has been reduced by 50%.

Switzerland seems to be a good example of sensible public health policy of harm reduction which has been evaluated and taken forward. One cannot translate policies from one culture to another but notice should be taken of the Swiss experience.

United Kingdom

Harm reduction has been part of UK drug policy for many years, at least in terms of substitute prescribing. As discussed in the history chapter in this book (chapter 2) the Rolleston Committee in 1926 recommended that opiate-dependent patients were prescribed substitute medication under certain conditions which included *'when every effort possible in the circumstances has been made, are made unsuccessfully, to bring the patient to a condition of which he is independent of the drug it may become justifiable in certain cases to order regularly the minimum dose which has been found necessary either in order to avoid serious withdrawal symptoms, or to keep the patient in a condition in which he can lead a useful life'*. Although these words were written in 1926, many decades later they still hold true and it is possible that the United Kingdom is the only county in the world who has adopted this policy over time. This was of course against the background of a very small number of opiate users in the country and was manageable by doctors with small populations of opiate dependent individuals. The law allowed any drug except opium to be prescribed, but this essentially meant opiate based products before the development of synthetic opioids such as methadone and pethedine.

This situation remained consistent until the 1980s with the advent of the HIV epidemic. This was despite various changes in the law and the introduction of the Misuse of Drugs Act 1971 which was partly as a result of mis-prescribing by a few errant doctors in the London area. This policy of substitute prescribing was maintained albeit in different venues such as Drug Dependency Units from the 1970s onwards. The 1980s saw the arrival of HIV in the UK and the effect was very localised. This depended partly on luck as to whether the virus arrived in the injecting drug user population early; second, whether there were sufficient treatment services available and, third, the attitudes of policing in terms of confiscation of injecting equipment etc.. There was therefore, the example of Glasgow and Edinburgh in Scotland where there was a prevalence of less than 4% amongst drug users in Glasgow but in Edinburgh, a city only 40 miles away, the prevalence rose to over 85% (Robertson et al., 1986), by 1986 and this was related to the aforementioned conditions.

The arrival of the HIV threat produced a response from the UK government of a large expansion of funding for drug treatment services which led to the development of more community based services and changes in the law allowed for the provision of clean needles and syringes from needle exchanges. The Advisory Council on the Misuse of Drugs (ACMD) in a report in 1988 stated *'we have no hesitation in concluding that the spread of HIV is a greater danger to individual and public health and drug misuse'*. Therefore the scene was set for a rapid expansion in drug treatment services and the introduction of harm reduction policies for which the United Kingdom was rightly recognised in a leading role along with Australia and the Netherlands. In 1996 Stimson wrote an editorial in the influential journal Addiction suggesting that Britain had avoided a major epidemic of HIV infection amongst drug injectors because it had rapidly adopted harm reduction measures.

This is certainly true in that the rate of HIV infection amongst drug users has not been particularly high anywhere in Britain other than Edinburgh and even in Edinburgh after the introduction of harm reduction measures the HIV prevalence dropped substantially. This cannot be said of hepatitis C which has become a major health problem amongst drug injectors in Britain, because as Crofts and colleagues (2000) showed that the transmission of hepatitis C is possible even where needles and syringes have not been shared but in an environment where injecting takes place. This is likely to occur because other injecting paraphernalia such as filters, tourniquets and spoons can be shared (see chapter 22 of this volume where Derricott discusses the development of the supply of these materials through illegal exchanges). The law also had to be changed to allow for the supply of these materials.

One of the unintended consequences of the harm reduction movement and especially the prescription of substitute medication (mainly methadone) is the neglect of the logical end point of treatment and getting people drug free or no longer dependent on methadone. This has resulted in a large population of methadone dependent individuals who have been on methadone for many years or decades but who are still dependent on the drug and the services that supply it. This has become a focus for the so-called recovery movement of people who seek to help drug users become drug free. This is discussed fully in chapter 12 of this book by Neil Hunt; this is an example where the best intentions of harm reduction may have created a large problem of a big population of methadone dependent individuals.

The other aspect of harm reduction that needs to be addressed in the United Kingdom (as elsewhere) is the whole process of injecting. There is now an excellent network of needle and syringe exchanges as standalone services, as part of treatment services and from pharmacies. It is a self-evident truth that a person would be very unlikely to start injecting without having observed others injecting or having been injected by others or having been taught to inject by others. Therefore if people can be persuaded to make the transition from injecting, then this is a major harm reduction initiative. One of the reasons why people inject is because it delivers the drug quickly and economically to the body (and thus the brain). Therefore to try to suggest alternatives is difficult because although smoking will deliver the drug very quickly to the body, the waste of drug compared to injecting may be considered to be a price too high to pay. However, for many people there may be strong reasons to stop injecting which may include health and the difficulty of finding veins or pressure from others.

One of the initiatives that have been promoted in the UK by Neil Hunt and his colleagues (2009) has been a project called 'Breaking the Cycle'. This is based on a number of papers which have examined initiation into injecting and ways of trying to help people to stop injecting or to stop initiating neophytes into injecting. Accepting that current injectors play a role in others' decisions to inject, that most people who inject disapprove of initiating others and that injectors do not always realise that they may unintentionally increase the chances of someone trying to inject Hunt and colleagues devised a programme which tackled the issue of initiation into injecting using a variety of methods. They found this could be carried out by workers in needle exchanges, treatment centres and prisons and also by using injectors themselves as peer teachers. Using motivational interviewing techniques and by explaining the process of social learning as the process by which many people learn about injecting they ask people to examine the whole process of injecting and the passage of information about injecting. The project has been translated to several other parts of the world successfully but local injecting culture needs to be considered. Research by Hunt and colleagues (1998) showed that this intervention was not only feasible as a brief intervention but also was effective in reducing initiation and injecting in front of others.

The United Kingdom has been an important player in the development of harm reduction but work still needs to be done as the above initiative shows. Needle exchange is still not policy in prisons and we have yet to see the effectiveness of the recovery movement on helping people become drug free. It also had a history of substitute prescribing for amphetamines which was often innovative but has now been discouraged because of the paucity of good research evidence (see chapter 13 on stimulants for a fuller discussion of this).

An initiative was announced in October 2011 allowing general practitioners (family doctors) across the United Kingdom to prescribe naloxone emergency injecting kits. These kits were developed in Scotland were available from January 2012. The kits consist of:

- a yellow plastic box (due to change to a white opaque box soon);
- a pre-filled syringe;
- 2 × 23 gauge 1 1/4 inch muscle needles;
- patient information leaflet.

They have been produced by a pharmaceutical company which manufactures naloxone and who approached the UK Medicines and Health Care Regulatory Agency (MHRA) the body which must license the product for prescribing. The drug which works by rapidly reversing opioid overdose can be administered legally by anyone and not only saves lives by reversing a potentially fatal overdose but can help avoid the brain and other organ damage caused by the hypoxic effects of overdose. It also buys valuable time while waiting for emergency services such as the ambulance. This could make a major difference to the rate of overdose deaths in the United Kingdom.

France

France was late adopting harm reduction measures and it was not until 2004 that harm reduction was incorporated into the country's public health regulations, and in from 2008 it became one of the 5 'axes' of the government drug strategy. There are now 120 low-threshold agencies funded by public health insurance which provide a main thrust for services (EMCDDA, 2010). Sales of syringes from pharmacies were allowed in 1987 and by 2006 130 needle and syringe exchanges were in existence and there were 225 syringe dispensing machines. There were also 40 drop-in counselling services and methadone buses to supplement the distribution of substitute medication. Most of France is covered by harm reduction services.

One of the innovative projects in France has been the distribution of crack smoking kits (Espoir Goutte d'Or, 2004). There was recognition of the damage caused by crack smoking in terms of lesions, cuts and burns due to the use of hot and often broken crack pipes. This allows the transmission of infections especially hepatitis C. The kits, known as 'kit base' include the following:

- a glass measure to be used as a pipe;
- 4 plastic tips to reduce the sharing of the glass measure, reduce the burns caused by the heat, to lengthen the pipe to allow a better visibility during consumption and the cooling of the smoke;
- 8 sheets of aluminium foil and rubber bands to make filters to replace the filters made of electric wire the making of which often causes injury;
- 4 alcohol impregnated pads to clean the hands as well as the paraphernalia;
- 3 samples of cream to alleviate irritation of the skin, hydrate and facilitate healing of the tissues;
- a condom and lubricant gel;

- a user's manual giving instructions to the users concerning the use of the kit plus prevention messages.

When the project was evaluated it was found that contact with crack smokers doubled in half a year from 4,617 in 2003 to 8,624 in 2004. Contact with crack users was considered problematic by drug services. In terms of outcomes the majority of people questioned (71%) reported being more attentive to the risks, and 23% no longer shared their smoking equipment. The percentage of people who reported lesions to the lips from burns dropped from 47% to 18%, and the sharing of the pipe or the tip reduced from 41% to 25%.

This is a really innovative project with a difficult to reach group and demonstrates again not only the effectiveness of the 'kit base' but also the rationale for providing something as an incentive to facilitate contact.

The Netherlands

The Netherlands has been in the forefront of harm reduction since the late 1960s. In 1974 Erik Fromberg established a centre known as the HUK which was a drug consumption room, supported by local government (Blok, 2008). At the HUK addicts could cash their unemployment benefits, get a meal and a shower and buy drugs from the house dealer and use a needle exchange and get medical help where necessary. The Dutch therefore pioneered needle exchange even before the HIV epidemic in an attempt to control the spread of hepatitis among injecting drug users and introduced the methadone buses in Amsterdam in 1979 (Blok, 2008) in an attempt to provide low threshold, easy access substitute prescribing for opiate dependent injectors. They also made a clear distinction between 'hard' drugs (opiates and cocaine etc.) and 'softer' drugs such as cannabis. Cannabis was sold legally in small quantities in coffee shops.

Responsibility for the treatment of drug dependent individuals is delegated to regional and local authorities and is mainly delivered by non-governmental organisations on a regional level, by private organisations including physicians, hospitals and private clinics. It is also provided in regional public hospitals.

Possibilities for drug treatment interventions in the Netherlands are diverse. Outpatient substitution treatment is dominant for opiate dependence. Psychosocial interventions are again more frequently provided to complement substitution treatment in order to attain longer-term effectiveness and to reduce relapses and to promote social reintegration (EMCDDA, 2010).

Methadone has been the most commonly prescribed substitution substance but Heroin-assisted treatment (HAT) was also introduced in 1998 and high-dosage buprenorphine treatment was introduced in 1999. HAT is only provided in specialised treatment centres and is used for controlled groups of treatment-resistant opiate users. Methadone, is available in outpatient settings and in mobile treatment venues.

In 2007 (when the latest treatment data was available) there were a total of 12,715 clients in opioid subtitution treatment, 12 000 on methadone maintenance treatment and 715 clients receiving diamorphine prescriptions.

Needle exchanges are available in all Dutch cities and much of it is carried out by outreach workers and to a lesser extent by pharmacists. There are low threshold services offering shelter and drop-in services for street problem chronic drug users, and 'living room' facilities for prostitutes. Outreach programmes also work towards reducing drug related public nuisance often working between treatment workers, civil authorities and the police and outreach work is often brief educational interventions undertaken by peers.

The Netherlands has come under pressure from various other countries especially the United States who have often viewed the Netherlands as being soft on drugs and yet they have shown that harm reduction works and that users remain in contact with the services. One of the more recent changes has been efforts to make the coffee shops less of an attraction for drug tourists and keep them for Dutch citizens and also to reduce the numbers of them licensed in various cities – again a pragmatic response to a perceived problem.

Conclusion

This chapter has discussed harm reduction in Western Europe but has not examined every country in depth but rather looked at areas of particular interest or noteworthy interventions. The variety of interventions across Europe has been wide with some countries still being resistant to a range of harm reduction interventions. Parts of Western Europe such as the United Kingdom and the Netherlands have had many years experience in some forms of harm reduction and have helped introduce these ideas to the rest of the world.

References

ACMD (1988) *AIDS and Drug Misuse*, part 1, London: Home Office.

Blok, G. (2008) Pampering 'needle freaks' or caring for chronic addicts? Early debates on harm reduction in Amsterdam, 1972–82, *Social History of Alcohol and Drugs*, 22 (2), 243–61.

Bechi, M. and Minder, U. (2001) *Swiss Drug Policy, Harm Reduction and Heroin-Supported Therapy*, Vancouver: Fraser Institute.

Cook, C. Bridge, J. and Stimson G. (2010) The diffusion of harm reduction in Europe and beyond. In T. Rhodes and D. Hedrich (eds), *Harm Reduction: Evidence, Impacts and Challenges*, Luxembourg: EMCDDA, Publications Office of the European Union.

Crofts, N., Caruana, S., Bowden, S. and Kerger, K. (2000) Minimising harm from hepatitis C virus needs better strategies, *British Medical Journal*, 321 (7 October), 889.

EMCDDA (2010) *Country Overviews*, European Monitoring Centre for Drugs and Drug Addiction, www.emcdda.europa.eu/publications/country-overviews, accessed 21 October 2011.

Espoir Goutte d'Or (2004) *Rapport d'évaluation du 'Kit-Base': Le 'Kit-Base' un nouvel outil pour la reduction des risqué*, Paris: Espoir Goutte d'Or et STEP.

Greenwald, G. (2009) *Drug Decriminalization in Portugal: Lessons for Creating Fair and Successful Drug Policies*, Washington, DC: Cato Institute.

Haemmig, R. and van Beek, I. (2005) Supervised Injecting Rooms. In R. Pates, A. McBride and A. Arnold (eds), *Injecting Illicit Drugs*, Oxford: Wiley-Blackwell.

Hungarian Civil Liberties Union (2011) *The State of Harm Reduction in Europe*, http://drogriporter.hu/en/eurohm_marseille, accessed 8 November.

Hunt, N., Stillwell, G., Taylor, C. and Griffiths, P. (1998) Evaluation of a brief Intervention to prevent initiation into injecting, *Drugs: Education, Prevention and Policy*, 5 (2), 185–93.

Hunt, N., Derricott, J., Preston, A. and Stillwell, G. (2009) *Break the Cycle: Preventing Initiation into Injecting*, 2nd edn, Dorchester: Exchange Supplies.

Laurance, J. (2006) Heroin the solution?, *Independent*, Friday 2 June.

Levine, D.G. (2003) Global drug prohibition: its uses and crises, *International Journal of Drug Policy*, 14, 145–53.

Public Health Agency of Canada (2003) *Harm Reduction and Injection Drug Use: an international Comparative Study of Contextual Factors Influencing the Development and Implementation of Relevant Policies and Programs*, Ottawa: Public Health Agency of Canada.

Reuters (2010) *Reuters Examines How Harm Reduction Policies in Switzerland Could Serve as a Model for Reducing Spread of HIV/AIDS among IDUs*, www.reuters.com/article/2010/10/25/us-swiss-drugs-idUS-TRE69O3VI20101025, accessed 21/09/2011

Rhodes, T. and Hedrich, D. (2010) *Harm Reduction: Evidence, Impacts and Challenges*, Luxembourg: EMCDDA, Publications Office of the European Union.

Robertson, J.R., Bucknall, A.B.V., Welsby, P.D., Roberts, J.J.K., Inglis, J.M., Peutherer, J.F. and Brettle, R.P. (1986) An epidemic of AIDS related virus (HTLVIII/LAV) infection among intravenous drug abusers in a Scottish general practice, *British Medical Journal*, 292, 527–30.

Rolleston Report (1926) *Report of the Departmental Committee on Morphine and Heroin Addiction*, London: HMSO.

Scottish Drugs Forum (2011) *UK GPs to be given go-ahead on prescribing Scottish Take Home Naloxone Kits*, www.sdf.org.uk/sdf/5111.html, accessed 21 October.

Stimson, G. (1996) Has the United Kingdom averted a major epidemic of HIV-1 infections among drug injectors?, *Addiction*, 91 (8), 1085–8.

Tammi, T. (2005) Discipline or contain? The struggle over the concept of harm reduction in the 1997 Drug Policy Committee in Finland, *International Journal of Drug Policy*, 16 (6), 382–92.

Tammi, T. (2007) *Medicalising Prohibition. Harm reduction in Finnish and International Drug Policy*, Research Report 161, Helsinki: STAKES.

Chapter 25

HARM REDUCTION IN RUSSIA, SOUTH WEST AND CENTRAL ASIA

Tomas Zabransky, Alisher Latypov, Ivan Varentsov, David Otiashvili and Jean Paul Grund

Russia

History of HR in Russia

The very first harm reduction projects for drug users in Russia were launched in Saint Petersburg, Yaroslavl and Moscow in 1996 in response to a significant rise in drug use and related HIV epidemics in the drug injecting population. In this period, syringe exchange programmes – both street-based and in drop-in centres – were implemented by teams of outreach workers operating under the umbrella of newly allowed non-profit non-governmental organisations (NGOs) in these cities. At the beginning of 2000s, there were more than 70 harm reduction (HR) programmes aimed at HIV prevention among injecting drug users (IDUs) in the Russian Federation (Non-Profit Partnership 'ESVERO', 2011).

Initially, the attitude of state authorities to harm reduction programmes was neutral or even (cautiously) positive. This was particularly apparent in those regions and cities where the administration supported such activities not only rhetorically, but also contributing financially to the implementation of harm reduction programmes. For example, in Altay region the first HR programme, which started working in 1999, was based at the Altay regional AIDS centre (government medical facility for HIV-positive people) and in Biysk in 2000 such programme was totally funded from the municipal budget (Altay regional AIDS Centre, 2009). Altogether, around 40% of projects' budgets were co-funded by local authorities in Russia during that period. In some regions, harm reduction projects were even included in regional and city programmes targeting HIV and drug prevention.

For a certain period of time, HR programmes were officially supported by the federal government: in 1999 and 2002, Gennadiy Onishchenko, the Chief Sanitary Inspector of the Russian Federation, issued two decrees of the Ministry of Health in which the necessity of country-wide introduction of harm reduction activities aiming to reduce the spread of HIV was stated explicitly (Onishchenko, 2002). However, even though the official position towards HR was rather positive compared to what we face in Russia now, opioid substitution therapy (OST) was never accepted by the authorities to be a HR measure and methadone has been in Schedule One of controlled narcotic substances since 1998 (Government of the Russian Federation, 1998). The overall attitude of the government bodies and the official position of the Ministry of Health towards harm reduction programmes gradually changed after the new Minister of Health took her position at the end of 2007. In 2008, she still confirmed that all drug projects and programmes including those providing harm reduction services, which had been initiated by non-profit organisations under the Global Fund to fight AIDS, Tuberculosis and Malaria (Global Fund) funding, would continue their work if they did not contradict

Harm Reduction in Substance Use and High-Risk Behaviour: International Policy and Practice, First Edition. Edited by Richard Pates and Diane Riley.
© 2012 Blackwell Publishing Ltd. Published 2012 by Blackwell Publishing Ltd.

existing Russian laws (Golikova, 2008). However, by 2009 her position had significantly changed: during the Meeting of the State Security Council on 8th September 2009 the Minister of Health stated that harm reduction programmes had produced only negative results in Russia and did not bother to provide any evidence in support of her statement (Golikova, 2009). In February 2011 at the meeting with UN High Commissioner for Human Rights Navanethem Pillay, Minister Tatyana Golikova confirmed that despite the globally positive outcomes of OST and its extensive use in the majority of developed countries, Russia was to stay the only country with very high levels of HIV among drug users where substitution therapy is not used. 'Till now we have no evidence from the world community of the OST effectiveness' she stated at the meeting (Medportal.ru, 2011)

To date there are only some 33 HR projects in Russia; these are able to continue their work through funding from the Global Fund Round Five grant that is implemented by the Non-profit partnership to support social prevention programmes in public health 'ESVERO'. In April 2010 its total coverage was estimated at 102 800 drug users, distributing 13 million sterile syringes and/or injection sets annually (Petunin, 2010). At the time of completing this chapter, all HR programmes were expected to be closed with the completion of the Global Fund Round Five grant in September 2011.

Specifics of drug use in the country

The estimated number of people who regularly use illegal drugs in Russia is around 5 million (Yegorov, 2010), out of whom about 1.6 million are estimated to use illicit opiates (UNODC, 2009: 5). As of the end of 2009, over 555,000 people were officially registered as drug users, among whom 70% were recorded in the narcological registry as injecting drug users (Kirzhanova and Sidoryuk, 2010). According to a recent pooled estimate, around 37% of injecting drug users are infected with HIV; in some regions, HIV prevalence among drug injectors was found to be at the level of 75%. As of 31 December 2009, Russian authorities had diagnosed a cumulative total of 567,558 HIV infections (Federal Scientific-Methodological Centre for the Prevention and Control of AIDS in the Russian Federation, 2010). According to official statistics, about 80% of HIV infections diagnosed between 1987 and 2008 were due to shared use of unsterile drug injecting equipment (Federal Scientific-Methodological Centre for the Prevention and Control of AIDS in the Russian Federation, 2009). In some cities, up to 90% of people who use injecting drugs are infected with hepatitis C (Public Mechanism for Monitoring the Drug Policy Reform in the Russian Federation, 2011).

According to the results of an online survey conducted in 2011 by the Andrey Rylkov Foundation among 29 respondents (harm reduction service providers and drug users) from 22 cities, almost all respondents stated that the most important recent trend in the drug scene was associated with a drastic decrease in the availability and quality of heroin and a simultaneous increase in its price. In their view, that development alone could explain the related transition of drug users to the consumption of readily available, cheaper and more dangerous homemade substances based on codeine-containing pharmaceuticals. Among these substances, the one used most widely was referred to as 'krokodil', reportedly containing desomorphine, mixed by some users with other opiates and chemical substances. The use of tropicamid[1] in combination with desomorphine, heroin and sometimes on its own was also noted by several participants.

With Russian authorities focusing primarily on supply reduction measures at the expense of demand reduction and harm reduction services, the emergence of 'krokodil' in the wake of dramatic decrease in heroin availability on the illicit drug markets in many Russian cities has also been linked with a sharp increase in fatal overdoses among drug users (Ataiants et al., 2011).

---

[1] Pharmaceutical eye drops with antimuscarinic effects (used to obtain mydriasis in inflammatory illnesses of eye).

HR in prison settings

Russia has the second largest prison population in the world, ranging from 850,000 to over one million people in prison in a year.[2] Repressive laws, including laws on drug-related crimes, lead to prison overcrowding and extremely poor public health and sanitary conditions (Bobrik et al., 2005). According to a study conducted in Russian penitentiary institutions, between 28 and 65% of drug users have had prison experience, with drug use in prison being common and HIV and TB prevention programmes unavailable (Sarang et al., 2006). Lack of medical treatment for prisoners has been declared as ill-treatment on many occasions by the European Court of Human Rights (ECHR).[3] Harm reduction programmes have no access to prison settings in Russia and harm reduction approaches are prohibited there (Public Mechanism for Monitoring the Drug Policy Reform in the Russian Federation, 2011).

Current developments, outlook and immediate needs

Starting in 2004, harm reduction programmes in Russia have been financed almost exclusively by the Global Fund Round Three, Four and Five HIV grants. Speaking in May 2008 at the Second International Conference on HIV/AIDS in Eastern Europe and Central Asia, the Minister of Health Tatyana Golikova, the Chief Sanitary Inspector Gennady Onishchenko and the presidential aide Igor Shuvalov confirmed that Russia will support all projects implemented in Russia within the Global Fund programmes including HR ones (AIDS Infoshare, 2008). However, the Russian government failed to keep its promises – within the budget of the federal target programme 'Preventing and combating social diseases in 2007–2011' no funds were allocated for HIV prevention among vulnerable groups in 2010 (Goliusov, 2010). Currently, at the heart of the Russian 'priority strategy' to tackle the HIV epidemic is the promotion of a healthy lifestyle among the general population and the development of 'responsible attitudes' to one's own health (Skvortsova, 2009).

The last Global Fund-funded harm reduction programmes will have to terminate their work as the Round Five HIV grant comes to its conclusion by the end of this year (2011). In this regard, the worst-case scenario is that there may not remain a single harm reduction programme in the Russian Federation after 2011. These harm reduction programmes will cease to exist, as will, probably, the majority of non-governmental organisations that have been engaged in their implementation. On August 11, 2011, the Ministry of Health and Social Development of the Russian Federation announced a tender for the provision of secondary and tertiary HIV prevention services to the most at risk populations including IDUs within the national project 'Health' in 2011 (Ministry of Health of the RF, 2011). At first sight, it may seem that the Ministry of Health wants to initiate state-funded harm reduction projects in Russia because, according to tender, these prevention services should be based on the work of outreach teams. In fact, however, all that these outreach workers would be able to do is to provide IDUs with information and refer them to state medical facilities. As stated in the tender, they will not be allowed to distribute even condoms among their clients, let alone syringes and needles; and all these activities are expected to be implemented within just 39 days.

According to a report that was presented at the 54th session of the Commission on Narcotic Drugs (Public Mechanism for Monitoring the Drug Policy Reform in the Russian Federation,

---

[2] By the end of 2008 the total number of prisoners was estimated to be around 891,700 people – see Walmsley (2010).
[3] See, e.g., the following cases of the ECHR: *Alexanyan vs Russia* of 05/06/2009; *Salmanov vs Russia* of 31/10/2008; *Dorokhov vs Russia* of 14/05/2008; *Khudobin vs Russia* of 26/01/2007; *Popov vs Russia* of 11/12/2006; *Romanov vs Russia* of 20/01/2006; *Kalashnikov vs Russia* of 15/10/2002.

2011), in order to fulfil the drug demand reduction provisions of the 2009 Political Declaration and to curb the expansion of the HIV epidemic among IDUs, the following steps must be urgently undertaken by the Russian government:

- Remove legal barriers and initiate the widespread provision of opioid substitution therapy with the use of methadone and buprenorphine, in accordance with guidance from the World Health Organization (2009). Immediate access to substitution therapy should also be provided in tuberculosis hospitals and AIDS-centres as well in facilities serving pregnant women dependent on opioids.
- Remove legal barriers and provide financial and technical support to harm reduction programmes, including needle and syringe programmes, in accordance with the targets recommended by WHO, UNAIDS and UNODC.

Additionally, any legal barriers that restrict 'free exchange of objective health-related information on drug dependency treatment and harm reduction' should be removed (Public Mechanism for Monitoring the Drug Policy Reform in the Russian Federation, 2011).

South West Asia: Southern Caucasus

History

In the three Southern Caucasus countries harm reduction services were introduced in late 1990-early 2000 and were supported by the Open Society Institute and its country offices. First institutionalised NSPs were launched in Tbilisi and Batumi (Georgia) in 2001, involving both non-governmental organisations and state agencies. Namely, NGO Sasoeba (Tbilisi) and the Public Health Department of the Ministry of Health (MoH) of the Autonomous Republic of Ajaria (Batumi) pioneered needle and syringe programmes with financial support from the Open Society-Georgia foundation (Usharidze, 2011).

Opioid substitution therapy was introduced in Azerbaijan in 2004, in Georgia one year later, and in Armenia only in 2009. Again, OSI played a major role financially in supporting OST in Armenia, while the Azerbaijan programme is funded by the state and the Georgia programmes by the Global Fund on AIDS, Tuberculosis and Malaria (GFATM) and the Ministry of Health agencies. This treatment modality remains extremely limited in both Armenia and Azerbaijan, while it has been dramatically scaled up in Georgia in the last four years and is now available to over 1200 patients with opioid dependence (Javakhishvili et al., 2011).

In Georgia, harm reduction is a relatively well-developed strategy. This has happened as a result of the attention of a number of international donors,[4] concern about the threat of HIV/AIDS spreading in the post-Soviet region since the 1990s, and – compared with other countries in the region – involvement of a relatively large number of NGOs. However, neither the Georgian government nor other public bodies have ever supported organisations providing harm reduction services except for OST.[5]

---

[4] Global Fund, UN agencies, the European Union and its Member States, the Open Society Institute and other private donors.

[5] Which is rather seen as 'standard medical treatment, i.e. classic demand reduction strategy that might embrace some elements of harm reduction in its low threshold modifications' (see, e.g., Zabransky, 2004).

The technical and financial support of the international donors has been reflected in the increasing number of NGOs active in the field of harm reduction. The Georgian Harm Reduction Network (GHRN) was established in 2006 and by the end of 2010, 18 NGOs active in the field were members of the network. In the last few years, Georgian harm reduction organisations have increased the scope of their activities; in addition to needle exchange and distribution projects, they routinely provide voluntary counselling and testing for their clients, enter the public debates on drug policy development, and conduct awareness-raising activities to secure the sustainability and further development of harm reduction interventions and programmes.

Similarly, harm reduction programmes receive little or no support from governments in Armenia and Azerbaijan. It was through active support from OSI that the Harm Reduction Network was established in Azerbaijan in 2009, uniting some 24 non-governmental organisations from different regions of the country.

After declaring independence in early 1990s, the Southern Caucasus countries encountered a number of difficulties related to the transition period – uncontrolled state borders and territories, civil wars, high level of crime, corruption, crisis of values followed by social pessimism, protracted social, economic and political crises, and unemployment. A dramatic increase in drug use and in problem drug use in particular co-occurred in all three countries in this period. In 1993, all the three new republics adopted all three UN drug control conventions (Nasriyan et al., 2004). In the following years, all countries followed a similar path of establishing intergovernmental Commissions or Committees to tackle the substance use problem and strengthen the fight against illicit drug circulation. New laws on Narcotic Drugs and Psychotropic Substances were adopted in 1999 in Azerbaijan and in 2002 in Armenia and Georgia. Importantly, the Georgian law legitimated opiate substitution treatment and created a legal background for its introduction three years later (Nasriyan et al., 2004).

Presently, the governments of the three states are facing the same challenge – an urgent need to develop a multidisciplinary, modern approach to the drug use and illicit drug trade, based on balanced and sound legislation that prioritises fundamental human rights. In Armenia and Azerbaijan, non-medical uses of controlled substances, as well as possession of small amounts without intention to sell constitute an administrative offence (UNODC and Canadian HIV/AIDS Legal Network, 2010; Government of the Republic of Armenia, 2009). In sharp contrast, Georgia has one of the strictest drug control legislations in the region; drug use *per se* may lead to criminal liability with imprisonment for up to one year (in cases of consumption of illicit substances for a second or more times within one calendar year) (Otiashvili et al., 2008).

Harm reduction is mentioned in policy documents in all three countries, albeit at different levels:

- The Armenian National Programme on Combating Drug Addiction and Illicit Trafficking provides support for harm reduction interventions and measures to eliminate stigma and discrimination against persons with drug addiction (Government of the Republic of Armenia, 2009).
- The New Georgian Law on HIV/AIDS adopted in 2009 explicitly supports the harm reduction approach and emphasise the need for relevant interventions, including in prison settings (Parliament of Georgia, 2009).
- In Azerbaijan, harm reduction projects were among the key activities for HIV prevention included in the *National Programmatic Strategy on HIV/AIDS (2009–2013)* (UNODC and Canadian HIV/AIDS Legal Network, 2010).

Specifics of drug use in the region, and specific responses

Georgia

It is estimated that there were approximately 40,000 regular injecting drug users in Georgia in 2009 (Sirbiladze, 2010). Thus, problem drug use prevalence (in the case of Georgia defined as regular injecting use) is estimated to be 1.5% for the age group of 15–64, approximately 2.5 times higher than the average prevalence in Europe (European Monitoring Centre for Drugs and Drug Addiction, 2007). Injecting drug users comprised 58.4% of registered cumulative HIV cases in Georgia (Government of Georgia, 2010) and hepatitis C infection has been diagnosed in 50–60% of drug injectors (Otiashvili, et al., 2008; Shapatava et al., 2006; Tkeshelashvili-Kessler et al., 2005). Levels of HIV-risk-injecting behaviour and unprotected sex are seemingly quite high throughout Georgia. Recent studies showed that sharing injecting equipment varied from 52% to 73% of injecting drug users (Otiashvili et al., 2006; Tkeshelashvili-Kessler, et al., 2005).

Home-made opiates and heroin were the main drugs of injection in Georgia in the late 1990s–early 2000s (Gamkrelidze et al., 2004). In 2004, a sudden change in use of illicit opioids occurred, resulting in a significant increase of buprenorphine (namely, the pharmaceutical drug Subutex® that has been smuggled from EU countries) injectors. In 2005, 39% (235 of 603) of all drug users in Georgia admitted for inpatient treatment were buprenorphine injectors (Javakhishvili et al., 2006). Buprenorphine at that time was not a registered medication in Georgia and was available only on the black market. In recent years the country has witnessed a significant increase in injecting use of home-made meth/amphetamine type stimulants (Otiashvili et al., 2010).

In 2009, harm reduction programmes served a total of about 4000 clients, providing information and education, distributing sterile injecting paraphernalia, condoms, and naloxone, and offering voluntary counselling and testing for HIV, HCV and HBV (Kirtadze, 2010). Based on the Sirbiladze (2010) estimation, coverage of prevention programmes for the main risk group – IDUs – remained extremely low, not exceeding 10% of injectors. It is of no surprise that the country failed to effectively halt the HIV epidemic; in the general population we still see a low prevalence of less than 0.1%, but the annual incidence of newly registered cases in the last decade steadily increased by approximately 25% per year (Government of Georgia, 2010).

Opioid substitution therapy was introduced in 2005, fully funded by a grant of the Global Fund to Fight AIDS, Tuberculosis and Malaria (GFATM). Alongside some 70–80 patients detoxified at the cost of the state budget each year, the GFATM-subsided OST is the only drug dependence treatment that is provided free to patients (Chikovani et al., 2010). Acknowledging the importance and positive impact of this treatment modality, the Georgian government started to co-fund OST in 2008. In the state supported programmes, the cost of methadone is covered by the state and patients pay for the services of the staff; the cost of such treatment is 150 GEL per month. This has resulted in a rapid expansion and increased availability of the treatment; as of January 2010, there were 14 programmes operating throughout 8 regions of the country (and one OST programme was established in a penitentiary institution – strict regimen prison no. 8), providing treatment to 1200 patients. About 800 patients receive treatment in state co-funded programmes and 400 receive it in GFATM-funded programmes (Javakhishvili et al., 2011).

Armenia

There are strikingly contradictory estimates of the prevalence of problem drug use in Armenia reaching from 2,000 to 11,000 injectors (Government of the Republic of Armenia, 2009). With one of the world's lowest reported rates of HIV in the country, the main modes of HIV transmission in

Armenia are through injecting drug use (41%) and heterosexual intercourse (50.2%) (Government of Armenia, 2010). According to the *Behavioral and Biological HIV Surveillances* conducted in October–November 2007, HIV prevalence among IDUs was 6.78%. With the support of GFATM, Armenia has achieved universal access to ARV treatment. Opiate substitution treatment remains at a pilot stage and was being provided to 128 patients as of July 2011 (Beglaryan, 2011).

Azerbaijan

The prevalence of HIV in the general population is low in Azerbaijan and does not exceed 0.1%. Annual incidence has been steadily increasing in recent years with shared used of unsterile injecting equipment driving the epidemic (62.6% of registered cases) (Government of Azerbaijan, 2010). HIV prevalence among IDUs in Azerbaijan is the highest among three countries and varies by regions from 1.3% to 33%, with the average national estimate around 10.3%. With about 300,000 injecting drug users in the country it is estimated that only 1.75% of IDUs received HIV prevention services in 2007-2008 (Mathers et al., 2008). In 2009, the coverage of ARV treatment was 78.9% of those in need. Agonist treatment for opioid injectors is provided to some 120 patients a year (UNODC and Canadian HIV/AIDS Legal Network, 2010).

Harm reduction in prisons

The numbers of prisoners in Southern Caucasus countries are reported as follows: 5,100 (165 per 100 thousand of population) in Armenia, 19,559 (228/100,000) in Azerbaijan and 23,995 in Georgia (the 6th highest world prison rate, 547/100,000) (International Centre for Prison Studies, 2011). Data on the situation related to drug use and associated problems in penitentiary institutions are extremely scarce in all countries of the region, and the same is true for information on prison-based interventions. Different sources suggest that significant numbers of prisoners serve prison terms for drug related offences; 7000 prisoners were treated for drug dependence in Azerbaijan between 1989 and 2007 (UNODC and Canadian HIV/AIDS Legal Network, 2010) and about 30% of prisoners were incarcerated in Georgia for drug related crimes (Otiashvili, et al., 2008).

The prevalence of HIV in prisons is much higher than in the general population in all three countries: 2.3% in Azerbaijan (UNODC and Canadian HIV/AIDS Legal Network, 2010), 1.6% in Armenia (Dolan et al., 2007), and 1.76% in Georgia (Otiashvili, et al., 2008). In all three countries, the response to the problem of elevated HIV risks in prisons is inadequate and is limited mostly to provision of information, and HIV counselling and testing. Armenia operates the only prison-based needle and syringe programme in the region (Government of the Republic of Armenia, 2009), while Georgia is the only country offering OST to some 50 persons in one penitentiary institution in Tbilisi.

Current developments and key challenges

National drug policy in all three countries is largely focused on supply reduction, a priority that is reflected in national policy documents and funding (UNODC and Canadian HIV/AIDS Legal Network, 2010; Stuikyte et al., 2009). While countries are now paying some attention to drug demand and giving harm reduction a larger role in national policy, drug policy in the region remains unbalanced and probably constitutes the main barrier to introducing and/or expanding effective interventions to reduce harms associated with drug use.

Of the three countries, Georgia obviously represents the most outstanding case of an unbalanced approach with its draconian drug legislation and troubling legal practices. Georgia's drug policies and legislation are some of the harshest in Eurasian region. Current drug policy – on the level of rhetoric – has endorsed a balanced approach but in reality preference has been given to law enforcement interventions. This has a direct impact on both the rights and health of drug users: currently there are more drug users in prisons than in treatment facilities (Javakhishvili et al., 2011; Otiashvili et al., 2010). The national drug policy of Georgia includes strict criminal drug legislation, forced drug testing of very high numbers of Georgians and the deprivation of human rights of drug users. It remains one of a few countries where the mere non-medical use of controlled drugs constitutes a criminal offence, even in the absence of being found in possession of any narcotics; in other words, rapid urine tests with all their limitations in specificity are routinely considered sufficient evidence for both administrative and criminal sanctions by the Georgian courts. As a result of existing misbalanced policy, resources are driven away from public health and social programmes. Coverage of prevention and treatment services is extremely low and does not exceed 5–10% of those in need. The legal environment creates barriers for drug users who want to access existing limited services and to seek assistance, which in turn increases the risk of transmission of HIV/AIDS and other blood borne viruses.

None of the countries of the region have adequately responded to the increase in problem drug use. None of the three national drug treatment and HIV prevention systems can meet more than 10% of the demand for harm reduction and drug treatment services (UNODC and Canadian HIV/AIDS Legal Network, 2010; Stuikyte et al., 2009). Most of the new policies and services – including needle exchange, user outreach, counselling on safer injecting behaviour, condom distribution, integration of drug treatment services, and opioid substitution therapy – were initiated through the support from international donors and were introduced not because of any committed response of the governments to drug use and problem drug use, but because of the region's devastating HIV epidemic. This casts grave doubts on the future of harm reduction programmes after major international donors withdraw from the country (for example, the Global Fund).

If there is to be a significant improvement in responding to the drug problem in the foreseeable future, the South-Caucasian governments must acknowledge the need to introduce new policies based on respect for human rights and public health principles. Such considerations would necessarily include the reallocation of financial resources – most of which are now spent on repressive, ineffective interventions such as forced drug testing – to evidence-based and cost-effective public health strategies.

Central Asia

History

In Central Asia, Kyrgyzstan is often considered by many as a regional 'pioneer' of harm reduction, marking the way forward for other countries. Needle and syringe programmes (NSP) were first introduced in Kyrgyzstan in 1999, and by 2000 NSPs were established in selected prisons. Two years later, Kyrgyz government officials authorised the launch of methadone maintenance therapy programme through funding from Soros Foundation Kyrgyzstan and UNDP, with Kyrgyzstan becoming the first country of the Commonwealth of Independent States to offer this therapy to people with opiate dependence (Wolfe, 2005).

While Kazakhstan, Tajikistan and Uzbekistan also had some of their first non-governmental and externally funded NSPs operational in the late 1990s – early 2000s, there has been major resistance to opioid substitution therapy (OST). In these countries, OST has either been started only very recently, has already been discontinued, or has remained at a 'perpetual pilot' phase (Latypov, 2010) – in other words, rhetorically welcome, but in reality blocked for many years by administrative obstructions purportedly created at different levels of state administration.

Currently, harm reduction appears institutionalised to a certain but different extent in the national healthcare systems and policies of four of the five Central Asian countries. These countries have also introduced their respective guidelines for harm reduction service provision, although endorsement of harm reduction can be seen most explicitly in the context of national responses to HIV/AIDS, while other state policies may remain repressive, effectively serving as barriers to access to harm reduction services (Ministry of Health of the Republic of Tajikistan, 2010; Schonning and Stuikyte, 2009; Latypov, 2007). With all countries of the region retaining their old Soviet policies of registration and control of 'deviant' populations and pursuing administrative and penal approaches to drug use, commercial sex work, and in the case of Uzbekistan and Turkmenistan, continuing to criminalise sex between consenting males, both non-governmental and governmental harm reduction service providers often opt to refer to their facilities as 'trust points' and/or 'friendly rooms' in order to send a clear message to their clients that they are 'trustworthy' and are not going to pass on their personal information to state authorities (International Lesbian, Gay, Bisexual, Trans and Intersex Association, 2010; Latypov, 2008).

Turkmenistan has not been part of the on-going institutionalisation of harm reduction in Central Asia. According to the official data (i.e., governmentally produced statistics), the HIV/AIDS problem does not exist in the country at all. On one occasion the government of Turkmenistan suggests that only five cases of HIV/AIDS were diagnosed in the country by 2003 and reported a cumulative total of only two cases to WHO and UNAIDS (Medecins Sans Frontieres, 2010; Rechel and McKee, 2005). According to the most recent International Crisis Group's (ICG) report, whenever the issue of HIV is raised with the Turkmen government officials, many of them 'just smile awkwardly and lower their eyes' (ICG, 2011). However, both anecdotal reports and historical evidence from Turkmenistan suggest that opiate use may be rampant and shared use of needles and syringes widespread (Latypov, 2011b; Rechel and McKee, 2005; Institute for War and Peace Reporting, 2004).

Injecting drug use in the region and specific responses

While various estimates of injecting drug use have been proposed by individual republics, the most recent data reported by the national governments and used for programmatic purposes indicates that Kazakhstan has an estimated number of 124,400 IDUs and an adult national prevalence rate of about 1% (Government of Kazakhstan, 2010). Kyrgyzstan, according to the UNODC, has 0.8% of the total adult population aged between 15 and 64 or about 26,000 people dependent on opiates, among whom about 25,000 are IDUs (The Government of Kyrgyzstan, 2010; UNODC, 2007a). In Tajikistan, national and international partners propose that the number of IDUs is 25,000, with a possible range of 20,000–30,000 (AIDS Project Management Group [APMG], 2009). Finally, according to the latest UNODC estimate reported in 2006, the prevalence of opioid use in Uzbekistan is estimated at 0.8% of the adult population, which makes a total of around 130,000 opioid users. The prevalence of IDU is estimated to be about 0.5%, or 80,000 IDUs in the country (UNODC, 2006). Overall, the estimated regional IDU prevalence rate in Central Asia (0.64% among 15–64 year olds) substantially exceeds the global average prevalence rate (0.37%) (Reference Group to the United Nations on HIV and Injecting Drug Use, 2010).

Throughout these four republics, heroin is the primary drug of choice for injecting drug users. In 2009, 91.8% of IDUs recruited in the Kazakh national sentinel surveillance study (n = 4,860) reported intravenous heroin use. Similarly, the majority of opiate injectors in Kyrgyzstan consume heroin and the proportion of injecting heroin users has grown over the past few years from 92% in 2006 to almost 98% in 2009 (Soliev, 2010). In another recent study among female IDUs (n = 73) conducted in Southern Kyrgyzstan (Osh and Jalal-Abad cities) in December 2007–January 2008,

98% of respondents indicated that heroin was their main drug of choice (Dzhalbieva et al., 2009). In Tajikistan, in the most recent sentinel surveillance study conducted among IDUs (n = 1,657) in 2009, 98.4% were heroin injectors (Tumanov et al., 2010). In another study conducted by APMG among IDUs (n = 1,690), the majority were heroin injectors as well, and 90% reportedly never administered heroin through a non-injection route (APMG, 2009). Data reported by the Uzbek authorities in 2007 suggest that in a sample of 3,743 IDUs, 91% were heroin users (Inogamov, 2007). This is hardly surprising given that Afghan heroin is widely and readily available throughout the region, with a retail price for one dose in southern Tajikistan comparable to the price of a bottle of beer (Latypov, 2011a).

Since the start of the millennium, Central Asian republics have faced some of the fastest growing HIV epidemics in the world, and have recently been described as a 'hotspot' of the global HIV epidemic (UNICEF, 2010; Thorne et al., 2010). Injected opiate use with unsterile equipment served as a major driving force of this epidemic (Reference Group to the United Nations on HIV and Injecting Drug Use, 2010). Sentinel surveillance studies conducted in the above four republics around the mid-2000s point to a regional HIV prevalence of about 11.8% among IDUs (Reference Group to the United Nations on HIV and Injecting Drug Use, 2010). According to the latest findings from these annual studies, in a sample of 4,680 active IDUs recruited at 22 sites across the country in 2009, the prevalence of HIV among IDUs in Kazakhstan was 2.9%, HCV prevalence was 60.3% and syphilis was 10.9%. Among males, HIV prevalence was 2.8% and among females HIV prevalence was 3.6% (Soliev, 2010) which would probably suggest an increased role of sexual transmission for female drug users. In Kyrgyzstan, in a sample of 900 IDUs recruited at 5 sites in 2009, HIV prevalence was 14.3%, HCV was 54.2%, and syphilis was 12.1%. HIV prevalence was nearly twice as high as it was reported to be in 2006 (7.4%). In Uzbekistan, according to the 2009 sentinel surveillance study among IDUs (n = 4,098), the overall national HIV prevalence was 11% in the surveyed IDUs (Government of Uzbekistan, 2010; 2011). Tajikistan has the highest HIV prevalence among IDUs of all four Central Asian republics that provide data on the HIV situation. According to the sentinel surveillance study conducted in 2009 among 1,657 IDUs at 8 sites, the prevalence of HIV among IDUs in Tajikistan was 17.3%, HCV prevalence was 32.6% and syphilis was 9.6% (Tumanov et al., 2010).

Below is a brief overview of country-specific responses to injecting drug use, as they were reported in a range of recent reports and studies.

Kazakhstan

According to the Kazakh Republican AIDS Centre, the rates of coverage of IDUs (recruited in sentinel surveillance studies) with any HIV prevention activities (no definition of coverage provided) has been growing steadily from 29% in 2006 to 44% in 2007, 50% in 2008 and 60% in 2009 (Tukeev, 2010). As for coverage with specific HIV prevention activities, data for the year 2009 show that 20,510,779 sterile needles-syringes were distributed in Kazakhstan to 58,521 injecting drug users through the existing network of trust points. This implies a coverage rate of 47%, with an average of 350 syringes per IDU reached in 2009 (Soliev, 2010). Furthermore, 7,099,650 condoms and 160,553 information, education and communication (IEC) materials were distributed among these IDUs in 2009. In the same year, 43,010 IDUs received voluntary HIV counselling and testing through 'trust points' in 2009 (Government of Kazakhstan, 2010). By the end of 2009, there were 168 trust points operational in the country including 24 mobile trust points, which served as key platforms for needle and syringe exchange programmes (Government of Kazakhstan, 2010).

Access to opioid substitution therapy (OST) remains extremely limited in the country, with about 50 IDUs receiving it in 2010. In that year, OST was available in two sites across the country (Pavlodar and Temirtau cities). While the Government was planning a substantial expansion of OST in 2011, plans were put on hold for some time after opponents of OST unfolded a well-orchestrated campaign against substitution therapy claiming that OST allegedly comes 'under the dressing' of the fight against the spread of HIV/AIDS, disguised as a 'humanitarian aid' of international organisations (Latypov, 2011b).

In 2008, the Kazakh government introduced more severe anti-drug provisions in its Criminal Code, making some drug offences punishable with up to 20 years of imprisonment or with a life sentence. Drug use *per se* is not criminalised, but Kazakhstan's narcotic drug schedules are among the strictest in Central Asia, and the possession of any amount of heroin between 0.01 grams (sic) to 1.0 gram is considered as a 'large quantity' leading to criminal liability. Possession of any amount of heroin up to 0.01 grams is an administrative offence (Government of Kazakhstan, 2011; UNODC and Canadian HIV/AIDS Legal Network, 2010). This makes drug users very easy targets for the Kazakh police, especially when they are close to drug dealing points, although drug dealers themselves are rarely detained because of widespread corruption among the law enforcement agencies. Police officers reportedly often plant drugs on injecting drug users and extort bribes from drug users and their relatives. Harassments, physical violence and unauthorised arrests of drug users by the police are common (Human Rights Watch [HRW], 2003).

Kyrgyzstan

According to the Government of Kyrgyzstan, 38.4% of the IDU population were reached with a package of HIV prevention activities (which usually included information, education and communication (IEC), HIV testing, condoms and sterile needles-syringes) in 2009 (Government of Kyrgyzstan, 2010). Other authors also suggest that 2,508,717 needles-syringes were distributed to 16,388 IDUs in Kyrgyzstan in 2009 (Soliev, 2010). This implies a coverage rate of 65.5% of the estimated IDU population (n = 25,000), and an average of 153 needles-syringes per IDU reached in 2009. Furthermore, a total of 2,231,360 condoms were distributed among IDUs in Kyrgyzstan in 2009 (Soliev, 2010). Kyrgyz government also reports that nearly 40% of the IDU population had an HIV test in 2009 and know their test results (Government of Kyrgyzstan, 2010). However, an earlier study conducted in December 2007–January 2008 in a smaller sample of female IDUs (n = 73) found that only 6% of participants had their HIV tests in the previous 12 months before the interview (although 23% in this sample were HIV positive and knew their status at the time of interview) (Dzhalbieva et al., 2009).

According to the latest data from Kyrgyzstan, there were 43 NSPs operational in the cities of Bishkek, Jalal-Abad and Osh and in Chui, Jalal-Abad and Osh oblasts in 2009. Kyrgyzstan is also a home to the Central Asian Training and Information Centre on Harm Reduction (Schonning and Stuikyte, 2009; Government of Kyrgyzstan, 2011). Reportedly, NGOs also enjoy good working relationship with the management of the Ministry of Interior and senior police officers support harm reduction services for drug users (Usenko and Mukambetov, 2006). Until 2006, there were only two OST sites in the country (Bishkek and Osh cities), with only 145 clients enrolled in the OST programme. By the end of December 2008, the OST programme in Kyrgyzstan has been substantially scaled up and reached 729 clients at 12 sites, including one site in prison. At that time, an evaluation of OST by the WHO concluded that for participants of the OST programme in Kyrgyzstan, 'all health indicators, social performance, drug use, risk behavior and crime' had improved since their enrolment (Moller et al., 2009). By the end of 2009, the number of sites had increased to 17, with three sites at penitentiary institutions; these sites were reaching about 1,100 clients (Latypov et al., 2010). Furthermore, Kyrgyz public health authorities' data suggest that as of January 1, 2010, there were 20 OST sites across the country, reaching as many as 1,195 clients, including 95 women (7.9%) (Government of Kyrgyzstan, 2011).

Tajikistan

As of late 2010, there was a total of 47 NSPs operational in Tajikistan, while a total of 2,774,697 needles-syringes were distributed among IDUs in Tajikistan in 2009 (Soliev, 2010; Government of Tajikistan, 2010). Data from the capital city Dushanbe also suggest that drug users may often prefer to purchase their syringes from local pharmacies, where they can be bought very cheaply and without any restrictions (Ibragimov et al., 2011). Furthermore, according to the GFATM, 18% of the estimated number of IDUs (5,482/30,000) were reached by HIV prevention services during the first quarter of 2010 (GFATM, 2010).

Opioid substitution therapy became available in Tajikistan only in the middle of 2010, and initially in Dushanbe only (Latypov et al., 2010). By the end of that year, about 50 clients were enrolled in the programme, including some women and people living with HIV (Tajik Drug Control Agency, 2011). When the introduction of OST in the country was authorised by the Tajik government in 2009, the local stakeholders seemed to have reached a consensus on the coverage target of 700 clients by the year 2014 (Latypov, 2010).

As in other Central Asian countries, IDUs in Tajikistan are frequently harassed and physically abused by the police. Interviews with drug users also suggest that corrupt police officers often plant drugs on drug users and extort bribes. Tajik public health officials also recognise and lament the 'police sanctions' against drug users, concluding in their 2007–10 HIV Prevention Strategy that abuse by the police was one of the main reasons for poor utilisation of HIV prevention services by IDUs (Ibragimov et al., 2011; Latypov, 2008; Government of Tajikistan, 2007).

Uzbekistan

According to public health authorities in Uzbekistan, in the 2009 sentinel surveillance study among IDUs (n = 4,098), 81.6% reported the use of sterile injecting equipment during their last injection of drugs; 35.5% received (at least once) information and education materials; 49.4% received sterile needles-syringes; 43% received condoms; 33.7% had their HIV test in the previous 12 months and knew their test results; and 25.8% reported the use of a condom during the last sexual intercourse. Overall, 1,455,325 needles-syringes were distributed to IDUs through the existing network of 235 state-sponsored trust points in Uzbekistan in 2009 (Government of Uzbekistan, 2010; 2011).

In 2009, the Government of Uzbekistan discontinued its OST programme, and the only operational OST site, which was opened in 2006 in the capital city of Tashkent, was closed on the grounds of OST being an 'inappropriate' intervention. Before its closure, 142 clients were receiving OST in Uzbekistan (Kerimi, 2009; Latypov et al., 2010).

Although data on harassment and abuse of drug users by police is limited in Uzbekistan due to difficulties and possible consequences associated with collecting and reporting such data, a study conducted by UNODC suggests that fear of registration or being caught by the police were among the main reasons why 30% of drug users avoided using HIV prevention and harm reduction services in the previous six months before the interview (UNODC, 2006).

Harm reduction in prisons

In 2009, according to the Kazakh Republican AIDS Centre, the average annual number of persons convicted in Kazakhstan was 64,988, or 0.5% of the total population of Kazakhstan, with many of them sentenced for drug-related crimes due to draconian drug laws adopted in the country. As of end of 2009, there were 2,416 PLWH in Kazakh prisons and pre-trial detention facilities, of whom 172 were receiving ART. However, harm reduction services in Kazakh prisons are severely limited (Ganina, 2010; KUIS MIU RK, 2010). A recent study conducted by Aids Foundation East-West indicates that around 14% of inmates in Kazakhstan use injecting drugs while in prison (Reference Group to the United Nations on HIV and Injecting Drug Use, 2010).

According to the statistics of the Kyrgyz government, there were a total of 9,923 inmates incarcerated in Kyrgyz penitentiary institutions by January 1, 2010. The Government of Kyrgyzstan acknowledges that about 35% of all inmates might be using drugs while serving their sentences. Half of these drug users, in their turn, are believed to be IDUs. Kyrgyzstan has NSP and OST programmes as well as other HIV and drug prevention programmes running in its prisons (Almerekova, 2010; Government of Kyrgyzstan, 2011). In the 2009 sentinel surveillance study among inmates, 65% reported the availability of sterile needles-syringes (vs. 68% in 2007) and disinfecting solutions (vs. 60% in 2007); 57% reported the availability of condoms (vs. 48% in 2007); and 46% had their HIV tests (vs. 37% in 2007) (Abbasova, 2010; Karamatova, 2010).

According to the Department of Correctional Affairs of the Ministry of Justice of Tajikistan, the total prison population of Tajikistan decreased from 12,500 inmates in 2005 to 8,000 by the end of 2009. Generally, it is estimated that the total prison population in Tajikistan is about 10,000 inmates. A total of 158 cases of HIV infections were diagnosed among prisoners by December 31, 2009. This translates into about 2% of the total official number of inmates and 8.5% of all diagnosed HIV infections in the country by the end of 2009 (1,853). As of April 2010, 3 PLWH were receiving ART in Tajik penitentiary institutions (Karamatova, 2010; Nurov, 2010). Repeated incarceration was significantly associated with higher rates of HIV infections in Tajikistan, which increased with the number of times a person had been sentenced to a prison term. Thus, the prevalence of HIV was twice as high among those who had been in prison two times and five times higher among those who had been in prison three times compared to those who were serving their first sentence ($p < 0.05$) (Abbasova et al., 2009).

In 2010, nearly every opiate user with a history of conviction interviewed in Dushanbe by NGO SPIN Plus underscored how difficult it was to obtain sterile syringes in penitentiary institutions. The most common way of obtaining a new syringe was to get access to the medical unit under any pretext, sometimes by faking an illness, and then either to purchase syringes from the medical staff, who would sell syringes informally, or to steal them. Often, syringes and needles are used and shared between inmates for several months, until it is no longer possible to sharpen a blunt needle or until the needle breaks. Sometimes, self-made syringes and needles are used. What seems to be clear, however, is that, in the words of one respondent, 'it is far more difficult to find a syringe there than heroin' (Ibragimov et al., 2011).

In Uzbekistan, data on the prison population is extremely limited. However, according to a regional study on HIV/AIDS and drug use conducted by UNODC, 'more than half of the prisoners who had used drugs reported never being treated for their drug dependence' during the whole period of incarceration; and 'a substantial proportion of prisoners who had been tested for HIV never received their test results nor any pre- or post-test counselling' (UNODC, 2007b).

Recent developments and key challenges

- Reliability of data from sentinel surveillance studies in Central Asia is questioned in private conversations by many experts in the field and those involved in conducting these studies, especially in view of possible biases and the dubious quality of self-reported data.

- Registered declines in national HIV prevalence rates among IDUs are often due to methodological changes, when new sites with low prevalence are included in sentinel surveillance studies on an annual basis to achieve stable or decreasing trends in aggregated national prevalence rates.
- No consistent definition of coverage is used throughout the region and at national levels.
- Many harm reduction programmes and services function in urban settings, with coverage in rural areas being very low.
- Quality of harm reduction services is often low, driven by good intentions but lacking in techniques that would better reflect the specifics of the population, and with little or no evaluation efforts.
- Despite increasing reported coverage rates, the HIV epidemic is growing among IDUs and other key risk populations.
- Repressive drug policies and police practices undermine harm reduction and other public health interventions targeted at vulnerable populations.
- Endemic corruption in law enforcement sectors, with the police playing a major role in local drug markets.
- Access to opioid substitution therapy is denied to the overwhelming majority of IDUs.
- Data on fatal drug overdoses is limited and externally funded overdose prevention programmes exist at a negligible scale.
- Kazakhstan is the only country of the region, where a large portion of funding for harm reduction services is provided by the government.
- The special needs of women IDUs are not met.

References

Abbasova, D. (2010) HIV infection epidemiological situation in the institutions of the penitentiary system. Regional conference on HIV Infection Epidemic in Central Asia: Further Development of Epidemiological Surveillance, Almaty, 18–19 May.

Abbasova, D., Bobodjonov, S., and Nurliaminova, Z. (2009) *Results of HIV Infection Sentinel Surveillance among Convicted People, 2008*, Dushanbe.

AIDS Infoshare (2008) Review of the Second AIDS Conference in Eastern Europe and Central Asia [II конференция по вопросам ВИЧ/СПИДа в Восточной Европе и Центральной Азии], *'Steps' AIDSinfoshare* [«Шаги» СПИД Инфосвязь], 8 (3), 6.

Almerekova, B. (2010) Situation related to the spread of socially significant diseases in the penitentiary system of Kyrgyz Republic. Third Central Asian Forum on Infectious Diseases and Drug Use in Prisons, Dushanbe, 21–3 April.

Altay Regional AIDS Center on HIV Prevention and Treatment, Barnaul (2009) *Harm Reduction among Injection Drug Users: The Principles of the Harm Reduction Strategy*, www.antispid.alt.ru/mater/Sn_vreda.doc, accessed 5 August 2011.

APMG. (2009) *Report on Project: 'Support to National AIDS Response to Scale Up HIV Prevention and Care Services in Tajikistan'*, for UNDP, Tajikistan.

Ataiants, J., Latypov, A. and Ocheret, D. (2011) *Drug Overdose: A Review of the Situation and Policy responses in 12 Eastern European and Central Asian Countries* [Передозировка: Обзор ситуации и ответные меры в 12 странах Восточной Европы и Центральной Азии],Vilnius: Eurasian Harm Reduction Network.

Beglaryan, Z. (2011) OST development in Armenia, personal communication with authors.

Bobrik, A., Danishevski, K., Eroshina, K. and McKee, M. (2005) Prison health in Russia: the larger picture, *J Public Health Policy*, 26 (1), 30–59.

Chikovani, I., Chkartishvili, N., Gabunia, T., Tabatadze, M. and Gotsadze, G. (2010) *HIV/AIDS Situation and National Response Analysis: Priorities for the NSPA 2011–2016*, Tbilisi.

Dolan, K., Kite, B., Black, E., Aceijas, C. and Stimson, G. (2007) HIV in prison in low-income and middle-income countries, *Lancet Infect Dis*, 7 (1), 32–41.

Dzhalbieva, I., Ermolaeva I. and Tokombaeva, M. (2009) *The Limitation of Services and Social-Psychological Factors Influencing the Spread of HIV among Female IDUs in the Southern Region of Kyrgyzstan. Report on Research Results*, Bishkek: Public Foundation 'Asteria'.

European Monitoring Centre for Drugs and Drug Addiction (2007) *Statistical Bulletin 2007*.

Federal Scientific-Methodological Center for the Prevention and Control of AIDS in the Russian Federation (2009) *Information Bulletin No. 33 of the Federal Scientific-Methodological Center for the Prevention and Control of AIDS in the Russian Federation* [Информационный бюллетень 33 Федерального научно-методического центра по профилактике и борьбе со СПИДом Российской Федерации], www.hivrussia.ru/files/bul_33.pdf, accessed 15 August 2011.

Federal Scientific-Methodological Center for the Prevention and Control of AIDS in the Russian Federation (2010) *Information Bulletin No. 34 of the Federal Scientific-Methodological Center for the Prevention and Control of AIDS in the Russian Federation* [Информационный бюллетень 34 Федерального научно-методического центра по профилактике и борьбе со СПИДом Российской Федерации], accesssed 15 August 2011.

Gamkrelidze, A., Javakhishvili, J., Kariauli, D., Lejava, G., Stvilia, K., Todadze, K., et al. (2004) *Drug Situation in Georgia: 2003*, Tbilisi: Southern Caucasus Anti-Drug Programme.

Ganina, L. (2010) Analysis of HIV/AIDS epidemiological situation among the convicts for the year 2009, unpublished.

GFATM. (2010) *Tajikistan: Grant Performance Report*, external print version, updated 5 October 2010, www.theglobalfund.org/en/, accessed 10 January 2011.

Golikova, T., (2008) Paper presented at the Second Conference on the HIV/AIDS in Eastern Europea and Central Asia: the extension of availability, prevention, treatment and support for all, Moscow, 3–5 May.

Golikova, T. (2009) Minutes from the Security Council meeting on 8 September, Kremlin, Building 14 G.

Goliusov, A. (2010) The speech of the head of the HIV/AIDS surveillance department of the Federal Service for Surveillance of Consumer Rights Protection and Human Well-Being. Paper presented at Conference on the Problems of Viral Infections in Russia, Moscow, 16 February.

Government of Armenia (2001) On Approving the National Programme on Combating Drug Addiction and Illicit Traffic in Narcotic Drugs in the Republic of Armenia in 2009-2012 and the Programme Implementation Schedule, Yerevan: Government of Armenia.

Government of Armenia (2009) Decision of the Government of the Republic of Armenia, Yerevan.

Government of Armenia (2010) UNGASS Country Progress Report, Reporting period 2008-9 calendar years, Yerevan.

Government of Azerbaijan (2010) *UNGASS Country Progress Report*, Reporting period January 2008–December 2009, Baku.

Government of Georgia (2010) UNGASS Country Progress Report, Reporting period 2008-9 calendar years, Tbilisi.

Government of Kazakhstan (2010) *UNGASS Country Progress Report*, Reporting period January 2008–December 2009, Almaty.

Government of Kazakhstan (2011) Country profile, draft, Central Asian Drug Action Programme.

Government of Kyrgyzstan (2010) *UNGASS Country Progress Report*, Reporting period January 2008–December 2009, Bishkek.

Government of Kyrgyzstan (2011) Country profile, draft, Central Asian Drug Action Programme.

Government of the Russian Federation (1998) *Decree of the Government od the Russian Federation as of 30 June 1998 'On the Approval of the Schedule of Narcotic Drugs, Psychotropic Substances and Precursors That Are Subject to Control in the Russian Federation'* [Постановление Правительства РФ от 30 июня 1998 г. N 681 'Об утверждении перечня наркотических средств, психотропных веществ и их прекурсоров, подлежащих контролю в РФ'], www.nobf.ru/drugs/control/, accessed 5 August 2011.

Government of Tajikistan (2007) *Programme for Countering HIV/AIDS Epidemic in the Republic of Tajikistan for the Period of 2007–2010*, approved by the Resolution of the Government of Tajikistan on March 3, 2007, Ref. No. 86, Dushanbe.

Government of Tajikistan (2010) Programme for countering HIV/AIDS epidemic in the Republic of Tajikistan for the period of 2011–2015, draft.

Government of Uzbekistan (2010) *UNGASS Country Progress Report,* Reporting period January 2008–December 2009.

Government of Uzbekistan (2011) Country profile, draft, Central Asian Drug Action Programme.

HRW (2003) Kazakhstan: fanning the flames: how human rights abuses are fueling *the* AIDS epidemic in Kazakhstan, *Human Rights Watch*, June, 15(4) (D).

Ibragimov, U., Dzhamolov, P., Latypov, A. and Khasanova, E. (2011) *The Needs of Opiate Users in Dushanbe in 2010: A Qualitative Assessment*, Dushanbe: SPIN Plus [in Russian].

ICG (2011) *Central Asia: Decay and Decline*, Asia Report no. 201, International Crisis Group.

Inogamov, Z. (2007) *Results of HIV Infection Sentinel Epidemiological Surveillance among Injecting Drug Users in 14 Sentinel Territories of the Republic of Uzbekistan*, 2007, Tashkent, 19 August.

Institute for War and Peace Reporting (2004) Turkmenistan's rising drugs crisis, *Reporting Central Asia, 295*, 22 June 22.

International Centre for Prison Studies (2011) *World Prison Brief*, accessed 27 July.

International Lesbian, Gay, Bisexual, Trans and Intersex Association (2010) State-sponsored homophobia: a world survey of laws prohibiting same sex activity between consenting adults, *ILGA,* May.

Javakhishvili, J., Kariauli, D., Lejava, G., Stvilia, K., Todadze, K. and Tsintsadze, M. (2006) *Drug Situation in Georgia: 2005*, Tbilisi: Southern Caucasus Anti-Drug Programme.

Javakhishvili, D. J., Sturua, L., Otiashvili, D., Kirtadze, I. and Zabransky, T. (2011) Overview of the drug situation in Georgia, *Addictologie*, 11 (1), 42–51.

Karamatova, Sh. (2010) Epidemiological surveillance of HIV infection among incarcerated people in Central Asian countries: main trends and results. Third Central Asian Forum on Infectious Diseases and Drug Use in Prisons, Dushanbe, 21–3 April [in Russian].

Kerimi, N. (2009) Accessibility of opioid substitution treatment in countries of Central Asia and in Azerbaijan: recent developments and next steps. Fourth Central Asian Partnership Forum on HIV Infection, Almaty, 10–11 November.

Kirtadze, I. (2010) *GHRN Programme Report to the Georgia Health and Social Projects Implementation Centre*, Tbilisi.

Kirzhanova, V. and Sidoryuk, O. (2010) *Data on Prevalence and Incidence of Drug Disorders in the Russian Federation in 1999–2009* [Показатели общей и первичной заболеваемости наркологическими расстройствами в Российской Федерации в 1999–2009 годах], from www.nrca-rf.ru/2_195.html, accessed 5 August 2011.

KUIS MIU RK (2010) Protection of women's health in penal-correctional system. Medical-social problems. Third Central Asian Forum on Infectious Diseases and Drug Use in Prisons, Dushanbe, 21–3 April.

Latypov, A. (2007) Review of Existing Drug Demand Reduction and HIV/AIDS Prevention Policies, Programs and Strategies in Tajikistan: Gaps and Needs for Technical Expertise and Policy Advice, www.untj.org/library/?mode=details&id=355, accessed 28 February 2008.

Latypov, A. (2008). Two decades of HIV/AIDS in Tajikistan: reversing the tide or the coming of age paradigm?, *China and Eurasia Forum Quarterly*, 6 (3), 101–28.

Latypov, A. (2010) Opioid substitution therapy in Tajikistan: another perpetual pilot?, *International Journal of Drug Policy*, 21 (5), 407–10.

Latypov, A. (2011a) Drug use, drug trade and drug control in Central Asia: Four themes, three paradoxes. Conference on the Nature, State and Capacity to Address Illicit Trade in Tajikistan and Its Effects on (In)security in Central Asia, Terrorism, Transnational Crime and Corruption Centre (TraCCC), School of Public Policy, George Mason University, Washington, DC.

Latypov, A. (2011b) The administration of addiction: the politics of medicine and opiate use in Soviet Tajikistan, 1924–1958, Ph.D. diss., University College London.

Latypov, A., Otiashvili, D., Aizberg, O. and Boltaev, A. (2010) *Opioid Substitution Therapy in Central Asia: Towards Diverse and Effective Treatment Options for Drug Dependence*, Vilnius: Eurasian Harm Reduction Network.

Mathers, B. M., Degenhardt, L., Phillips, B., Wiessing, L., Hickman, M., Strathdee, S. A., et al. (2008) Global epidemiology of injecting drug use and HIV among people who inject drugs: a systematic review, *Lancet*, 372 (9651), 1733–45.

Medecins Sans Frontieres (2010) **Turkmenistan's Opaque Health System,** Geneva: MSF.

Medportal. ru. (2011) Golicova told the UN High Commissioner for Human Rights about the uselessness of the OST programs.

Ministry of Health of the Republic of Tajikistan (2010) *Methodological Guidelines for Implementation of Harm Reduction Programmes*, Dushanbe.

Ministry of Health of the Russian Federation (2011) *Open Tender for the Right to Be Contracted by the Government as Provider of Secondary and Tertiary HIV Prevention Services to Groups of Populations Vulnerable to HIV Infection in the Russian Federation in the Framework of the Priority National Programme 'Health' in 2011* [Открытый конкурс - ИНН 7707515977 КПП 770701001 (Минздравсоцразвития России): На право заключения государственных контрактов на оказание услуг по реализации мероприятий вторичной и третичной профилактики ВИЧ-инфекции среди ключевых групп населения, уязвимых к ВИЧ-инфекции, в субъектах Российской Федерации в рамках реализации Приоритетного национального проекта «Здоровье» в 2011 году], http://zakupki.gov.ru/pgz/public/action/orders/info/common_info/show?notificationId=1364729, accessed 15 August.

Moller, L., Karymbaeva, S., Subata, E. and Kiaer, T. (2009) *Evaluation of Patients in Opioid Substitution Therapy in the Kyrgyz Republic*, Copenhagen: World Health Organization Regional Office for Europe.

Nasriyan, N., Javakhishvili, J. and Nalbova, A. (2004) *Drug Situation in Southern Caucasus, 2004: Annual Report*.

Non-Profit Partnership 'ESVERO' (2011) *History of RHRN,* from http://eng.esvero.ru/vssv_story.shtml, accessed 20 July 2011.

Nurov, R. (2010) Priority directions for activities in the field of protection of health and social adaptation of convicted people in the Republic of Tajikistan. Third Central Asian Forum on Infectious Diseases and Drug Use in Prisons, Dushanbe, 21–3 April.

Onishchenko, G. (2002) *The Decree No. 28 as of 9 October 2002 'On Activization of Measures to Counter the Spread of HIV in the Russian Federation'* [Постановление №28 от 9 октября 2002 года «Об активизации мероприятий, направленных на противодействие распространению ВИЧ-инфекции в Российской Федерации»].

Otiashvili, D., Gambashidze, N., Kapanadze, E., Lomidze, G. and Usharidze, D. (2006) Effectiveness of needle/syringe exchange program in Tbilisi, *Georgian Med News*, 140, 62–5.

Otiashvili, D., Sarosi, P. and Somogyi, G. (2008) *Drug Control in Georgia: Drug Testing and the Reduction of Drug Use?*, Briefing paper 15, Witley: Beckley Foundation Drug Policy Programme, May.

Otiashvili, D., Kirtadze, I. and Zabransky, T. (2010) How effective street drug testing is? Paper presented at the NIDA International Forum, Scottsdale.

Otiashvili, D., Zabransky, T., Kirtadze, I., Piralishvili, G., Chavchanidze, M. and Miovsky, M. (2010) Why do the clients of Georgian needle exchange programmes inject buprenorphine?, *Eur Addict Res*, 16 (1), 1–8.

Parliament of Georgia (2009). Law of Georgia on HIV/AIDS, 30/11/2009 #2042-IIs, Tbilisi.

Petunin, E. (2010) Complex approach to the implementation of the HIV prevention programs among IDUs. Presentation at the HIV/AIDS Partnership Forum. Moscow, 15 April.

Public Mechanism for Monitoring the Drug Policy Reform in the Russian Federation. (2011) *Report on the Course of Implementation by the Russian Federation of the Political Declaration and Plan of Action on International Cooperation towards an Integrated and Balanced Strategy to Counter the World Drug Problem*, Vienna: CND.

Rechel, B. and McKee, M. (2005) *Human Rights and Health in Turkmenistan*, London: European Centre on Health and Societies in Transition, London School of Hygiene and Tropical Medicine.

Reference Group to the United Nations on HIV and Injecting Drug, Use. (2010). **Consensus statement of the Reference Group to the United Nations on HIV and Injecting Drug Use 2010**. Retrieved March 1, 2011, from www.idurefgroup.com

Sarang, A., Rhodes, T., Platt, L., Kirzhanova, V., Shelkovnikova, O., Volnov, V., et al. (2006) Drug injecting and syringe use in the HIV risk environment of Russian penitentiary institutions: qualitative study, *Addiction*, 101 (12), 1787–96.

Schonning, S. and Stuikyte, R. (2009) *Needs Assessment Report for the Central Asian Training and Information Center on Harm Reduction*, Commissioned by Central Asia AIDS Control Project.

Shapatava, E., Nelson, K. E., Tsertsvadze, T. and del Rio, C. (2006). Risk behaviors and HIV, hepatitis B, and hepatitis C seroprevalence among injection drug users in Georgia. *Drug Alcohol Depend*, 82 (supple. 1), S35–8.

Sirbiladze, T. (2010) *Estimating the Prevalence of Injection Drug Use in Georgia: Consensus Report*, Tbilisi: Bemoni Public Union.

Skvortsova, V. (2009) The response letter of the Ministry of Health signed by Deputy Minister – regarding the open letter 'Forgotten epidemic'.

Soliev, A. (2010) Analysis on epidemiological situation and responses based on second generation sentinel surveillance system among injecting drug users, Tajikistan, Kazakhstan, Kyrgyzstan, 2006–9. Regional Conference on 'HIV Infection Epidemic in Central Asia: Further Development of Epidemiological Surveillance, Almaty, 18–19 May.

Stuikyte, R., Otiashvili, D., Merkinaite, S., Sarang, A. and Tolopilo, A. (2009) *The Impact of Drug Policy on Health and Human Rights in Eastern Europe: 10 Years after the UN General Assembly Special Session on Drugs*, Vilnius: Eurasian Harm Reduction Network.

Tajik Drug Control Agency (2011) *Review of the Drug Situation in the Republic of Tajikistan for 2010*, Dushanbe: Drug Control Agency under the President of the Republic of Tajikistan.

Tkeshelashvili-Kessler, A., del Rio, C., Nelson, K., and Tsertsvadze, T., (2005) The emerging HIV/AIDS epidemic in Georgia, *Int J STD AIDS*, 16 (1), 61–7.

Thorne, C., Ferencic, N., Malyuta, R., Mimica, J. and Niemiec, T. (2010) Central Asia: hotspot in the worldwide HIV epidemic, *Lancet Infectious Diseases*, 10, 479–88.

Tukeev, M. (2010) *HIV Infection Epidemiological Situation in the Republic of Kazakhstan*, Almaty, 9 October 9.

Tumanov, T., Asadulovev, K. and Chariev, N. (2010) *Analysis of Epidemiological Situation and Response Measures Based on the Data from Second Generation System Sentinel Surveillance among Injecting Drug Users in the Republic of Tajikistan in 2009*, Dushanbe.

UNICEF (2010) *Blame and Banishment: The Underground HIV Epidemic Affecting Children in Eastern Europe and Central Asia*, New York: United Nations Children's Fund.

UNODC (2006) *Problem Drug Use in Uzbekistan: National Assessment on Drug Abuse 2006*, Tashkent: UNODC Regional Office for Central Asia.

UNODC (2007a) *Illicit Drug Trafficking in Central Asia*, Tashkent: UNODC Regional Office for Central Asia.

UNODC (2007b) *Regional Study on Drug Use and HIV/AIDS. Regional Summary: Kyrgyzstan, Tajikistan and Uzbekistan*, Tashkent: UNODC Regional Office for Central Asia.

UNODC (2009) *2009 World Drug Report*, vol. 1, Vienna: United Nations Office for Drugs and Crime.

UNODC and Canadian HIV/AIDS Legal Network (2010) *Accessibility of HIV Prevention, Treatment and Care Services for People Who Use Drugs and Incarcerated People in Azerbaijan, Kazakhstan, Kyrgyzstan, Tajikistan, Turkmenistan and Uzbekistan. Legislative and Policy Analysis and Recommendations for Reform*, United Nations Office on Drugs and Crime Regional Office for Central Asia, Canadian HIV/AIDS Legal Network.

Usenko, D. and Mukambetov, A. (2006) *Report on Rapid Assessment in Bishkek and Chui Region*, CARHAP.

Usharidze, D. (2011) History of harm reduction in Georgia, personal communication with authors.

Walmsley, R. (2010) *World Prison Population List*, 8th edn, London: King's College London, School of Law.

WHO, UNODC and UNAIDS (2009) Technical Guide for Countries to Set Targets for Universal Access to HIV Prevention, *Treatment and Care for Injecting Drug Users*, Geneva: World Health Organization.

Wolfe, D. (2005) *Pointing the Way: Harm Reduction in Kyrgyz Republic*, Bishkek: Harm Reduction Association of Kyrgyzstan Partners' Network.

World Health Organization (2009) *Guidelines for the Psychosocially Assisted Pharmacological Treatment of Opioid Dependence*, Geneva: World Health Organization.

Yegorov, I. (2010, 4 February) Mindless needles: interview with the head of the Federal Drug Control Service [Иглы без разума], *Rossiiskaya Gazeta*,www.rg.ru/2010/02/04/igly.html, accessed 5 August 2011.

Zabransky, T. (2004) *Drogová Epidemiologie [Drug Epidemiology]*, 1st edn, Olomouc: Nakladatelstvi Univerzity Palackého [Palackýs University Press].

Chapter 26

HARM REDUCTION IN SOUTH, SOUTH EAST AND EAST ASIA

Jimmy Dorabjee

Introduction

The Asian region is home to more than half of the total Global population. The two most populous countries in the world, China and India, the upcoming economic tigers of the region, lie in Asia. The two largest illicit opium producing regions of the world, the Golden Triangle and Golden Crescent, are located in South and South East Asia, ensuring the abundant and widespread availability of opium and its alkaloids, morphine and heroin. In addition, India, which until the 1990s was the world's largest producer of licit opium for medicinal purposes, also contributes a proportion to the domestic market for illicit opiates. Until the mid-1970s, cannabis and opium were the two most common drugs that were traditionally used across Asia, predominantly through oral ingestion. Since the 1990s, South East Asia has witnessed an explosive increase in the use of amphetamine-type stimulants (ATS) especially among the younger population and the use of ATS continues to grow unabated.

This chapter describes the development of harm reduction in South, South East and East Asia. For the purpose of this chapter, Asia refers to 26 countries stretching from Afghanistan in the west to China in the east. Except for a handful of small scale NGO run programmes in a few countries in the 1990s, harm reduction emerged late in the Asian region as a response to the threat of wide-spread HIV infection among people who inject drugs (PWID) and from them to their sexual partners and the general community. Further, harm reduction became reluctantly acceptable to Asian governments only after a series of explosive HIV epidemics among PWID had already been well established and continued to spread to new populations in several countries. Despite a growing acceptance of the effectiveness of harm reduction as a public health approach to HIV prevention and control, the coverage of harm reduction programmes is unable to match the explosive spread of HIV and hepatitis C infection in PWID.

HIV infection in PWID was first detected in Bangkok, Thailand. In 1988, the prevalence of HIV infection rose from < 1% to ~ 40% among injectors in Bangkok (Kitayaporn, 1998). In 1989, 146 inmates of a drug detoxification centre in Ruili County, Yunnan Province, People's Republic of China tested positive for HIV (Ma *et al.*, 1990) and later that year, the first case of HIV in PWID was documented in Manipur State, North East India. Since then, HIV epidemics among the PWID have been documented in almost all the countries in the region.

With an estimated 5.5 million people who inject drugs in the Asian region (Mathers et al., 2010) and poor access to even the most basic of harm reduction tools such as sterile syringes and opioid substitution therapy, the sharing of contaminated injecting equipment has played a driving role in the initiation, acceleration and perpetuation of HIV epidemics in many Asian countries. Thailand,

Harm Reduction in Substance Use and High-Risk Behaviour: International Policy and Practice, First Edition.
Edited by Richard Pates and Diane Riley.
© 2012 Blackwell Publishing Ltd. Published 2012 by Blackwell Publishing Ltd.

Malaysia, Myanmar, Nepal, Cambodia, China, Vietnam and Indonesia continue to document high prevalence of HIV among PWID.

Historical perspective

Since time immemorial the use of mind altering substances was common and countries in the Asian region including Cambodia, Vietnam, Thailand, Laos, China, Nepal, Bangladesh and Pakistan have been traditional consumers of cannabis and opium, with cultural norms restricting the use of cannabis and opium to the adult male population' (Charles et al., 2005; UNODC, 2007; WHO, 2001). In India and Nepal cannabis use has been linked to Hindu religious festivals like Shiv Ratri and Krishna Ashtami – the birth of Lord Krishna and participation in bhajan (religious chanting) sessions. Indeed, occasions like Holi, 'the festival of colours', are not complete without the sharing of a traditional offering of *bhang* – a drink made with crushed cannabis leaves. Opium is also offered at the harvest festival in a ceremony called 'akha teej', intended to strengthen family marital clan bonds and put aside old feuds (WHO, 2001). In rural Myanmar, opium was an integral part of the culture, used in religious festivals and for medicinal purposes (UNAIDS/UNODCCP, 2000).

While the use of opium and cannabis was culturally accepted, traditional forms of opioids began to give way to the aggressive marketing of heroin from the Golden Triangle and Golden Crescent regions. The high purity of heroin manufactured in the South East Asian region, coupled with the reduced availability of opium, resulted in a switch from oral use of opium to heroin injecting, a more efficient and cost-effective mode of drug use. The cruder, less refined products from the Golden Crescent region were more suited to inhalation and by the mid 1980s, cheap and abundant supplies of dark brown heroin, known locally as smack or brown sugar, flooded South Asian markets.

Impact of drug control laws and polices

The legal and political environment determines national responses to drug trafficking and use within their borders. The introduction of stricter drug control laws and policies in Asian countries resulted in a significant decline in the use of culturally sanctioned traditional drugs and the introduction of harder drugs and the injecting of drugs.

In 1976, Joseph Westermeyer's prophetic paper titled 'Pro heroin effects of anti opium laws' alerted us to the unintended negative consequences of law enforcement initiatives that followed the introduction of strict anti opium laws in Hong Kong, Laos and Thailand. Westermeyer commented that all three countries followed a pattern that began with government passing and enforcing laws banning the production, sale and use of opium under pressure from North American, European and international interests. He noted that within a decade, most of the former opium users in Hong Kong and Thailand switched to the use of heroin and all new recruits began with heroin rather than opium. The pattern was striking as not only did it occur in three different locations but also at three different decades, beginning in Hong Kong during the late 1940s and 1950s, in Thailand during the 1960s and in Laos during the 1970s suggesting a causal relationship between the new narcotic laws and heroin use (Westermeyer, 1976).

Since then, many Asian countries including Pakistan, Thailand (McCoy, 1991), India (Charles et al., 2005), Nepal, China and Indonesia have enacted tougher anti-narcotics laws under intense pressure from the West and the UN conventions, resulting in the lower availability of traditional drugs such as opium. The enforcement of the harsh narcotics and drug laws and stricter control measures over the relatively harmless traditional drugs that were used orally set the stage for the emergence of widespread heroin injecting, followed years later by the large scale use of amphetamine type-stimulants.

For example, India introduced the Narcotic Drugs & Psychotropic Substances (NDPS) Act in 1985. Within a few years, local opium dens and cannabis outlets disappeared and reports of the widespread smoking of heroin in major metropolitan cities began to appear, with some heroin injecting. A few years later when law enforcement activities reduced the availability of heroin, the injecting of licit buprenorphine and other pharmaceutical drugs such as diazepam, chlorphener-amine maleate, promethazine, pethidine and dextropropoxyphene began across the country (Kumar and Daniels, 1994; Dorabjee and Samson, 1998; Bharadwaj, 1995; Biswas et al., 1994; Kumar et al., 2000) While heroin continued to be freely available in the North Eastern States of India bordering Myanmar, drug users in metropolitan cities of Delhi, Chennai and Kolkata started to inject pharmaceuticals such as buprenorphine, often cocktailing with antihistamines and benzodiazepines which were easily available over the counter in chemists (Dorabjee and Samson, 1998) Bangladesh and Nepal have witnessed similar patterns of heroin use followed by epidemics of buprenorphine injecting that began in South Asia and continues till today.

The evidence suggests that the new legislation exacerbated the problems arising from such structural changes and far from reaching its goal of eradicating drug use, enforcement of the Indian NDPS Act (1985) appears to have inadvertently facilitated a shift to harder drugs and riskier modes of consumption (Charles et al., 2005; Dorabjee and Samson, 2000) In Thailand, the tough enforcement policies against opium in the 1970s led to the substitution of opium with injected heroin (McCoy, 1991; Westermeyer, 1976).

The history of opium use in China has been documented since the seventeenth century. It was estimated that more than 100 million people smoked opium in China in the early twentieth century and about 15 to 20 million were considered addicted to opium. With the foundation of the People's Republic of China in 1949, the Government under Mao's leadership implemented programmes that effectively reduced opium trade and use for three decades. In the late 1970s China introduced its 'open door' policy and with increased trade of licit goods, the trade in illicit goods, including narcotics, re-emerged. With its borders in close proximity to the Golden Triangle and Golden Crescent, China became a major transhipment route for heroin trafficked to western countries, reporting some of the world's largest seizures of heroin, 10.8 metric tonnes seized in 2004 (UNODC, 2006). The trafficking of large amounts of heroin through China facilitated easy availability of the drug to local markets leading to China becoming a major consumer of heroin, with use concentrated in the provinces that shared borders with the countries of the Golden Triangle.

Although opium is still used, the injecting of heroin has become widespread in China and heroin remains the most popular drug of choice today. Apart from heroin, drugs such as amphetamine-type stimulants (ATS), diazepam, bingdu (methamphetamine) or maguo (a derivative of methamphetamine), ecstasy and ketamine are popular. Drug users in China are required by law to be registered with the authorities and the number of registered drug users in China increased from 70,000 in 1990 to 1.3 million in 2009. However, registered drug users comprise only a fraction of the actual number which is estimated to be between 6 to 7 million, the majority of whom inject heroin.

Traditional responses to drug use

With deterrence and punishment the focus of drug policy and abstinence the predominant philosophy of drug dependence treatment in South East Asia, the region has seen a proliferation of compulsory drug treatment centres managed by the police, army or other uniformed services. South Asia has followed a balanced approach of prevention, treatment and care with an abundance of detoxification and rehabilitation centres funded by international organisations and governments in a variety of hospital settings, psychiatric wards and NGO-run rehabilitation centres.

Governments in South East Asia have responded to illicit drugs by the criminalisation of drug use and have adopted particularly harsh policies in response to drug use and trafficking (WHO/WPRO, 2009). Dependent drug users are considered to be criminals and are subjected to disproportionately severe punishments meted out including detention in compulsory centres for extended periods of time. Even where policy changes have mandated that drug users be viewed as patients in need of medical treatment, periodic law enforcement crackdowns on drug use and users have continued, highlighting the disconnect between public health and drug control policies, and undermining access to harm reduction services.

International and Regional Drug Control Frameworks as well as individual countries' national drug laws effect harsh penalties for possession and use of illicit drugs (table 26.1). Several countries in the region including China, Indonesia, Lao PDR, Malaysia, Singapore, Thailand and Vietnam still retain the death penalty for drug offences (HAARP, 2009).

A major barrier to the introduction of evidence informed approaches and harm reduction has been the positions taken by influential regional bodies such as the Association of South East Asian Nations (ASEAN) declaring the aspiratory goal 'A drug free Asia by 2015', and the UNODC's slogans such as 'A drug free world – we can do it' that have spurred Asian countries to bear down heavily on drug use and conduct a 'war on drugs' approach which has translated into a 'war on drug users' across the region.

The most infamous example of the 'war on drugs' occurred in January 2003, when the Thai government of Prime Minister Thaksin Shinawatra announced an aggressive 'War on drugs' aimed at stopping all illicit drug supply and trafficking in Thailand, treating all known drug users and involving communities in monitoring and preventing drug use. Blacklists containing 329,000 names of people supposedly involved in the drug trade were compiled by the police, village heads and the Office of the Narcotics Control Board. By the end of April 2003, some 2,637 people had been killed,

Table 26.1 Drug control frameworks

International drug control frameworks	Regional drug control frameworks
The Single Convention on Narcotic Drugs (1961): all practicable measures for the prevention of abuse of drugs and for the early identification, treatment, education, aftercare, rehabilitation and social reintegration of the persons involved	*ASEAN and China Cooperative Operations in Response to Dangerous Drugs (ACCORD)*: in Pursuit of a Drug-Free ASEAN and China 2015, a plan of action to address both the demand and the supply of drugs
The Convention on Psychotropic Substances (1971): controls over a number of synthetic drugs according to their abuse potential	*ASEAN Senior Officials on Drug Matters (ASOD)*: a plan of action for drug control
The Convention against Illicit Traffic in Narcotic Drugs and Psychotropic Substances (1988): appropriate measures which includes interventions to counteract the social and health consequences of drug dependence	*Memorandum of Understanding (MOU) on Drug Control*: China, Lao PDR, Myanmar, Thailand, Vietnam and Cambodia – a drug control framework that encompasses the Greater Mekong Region China, Indonesia, Malaysia and Philippines (2004)

Source: Kumar, S. and Dorabjee, J. (2012) Compulsory centres for people who use drugs in Southeast Asia: looking for alternatives, draft report.

of whom 68 were shot by the police claiming it was in 'self-defense' (Siam Voices, 2011). More than 250,000 drug users were treated in healthcare settings or military type camps. It is ironical that the International Harm Reduction Associations 14th International Conference on the Reduction of Drug Related Harm was held in early April of 2003 in Chiang Mai, Northern Thailand, while this campaign was at its peak.

Compulsory drug treatment centres for people who use illicit drugs currently exist in 11 countries across Asia (table 26.2). Cambodia, China, Indonesia, the Lao People's Democratic Republic, Malaysia, Thailand and Vietnam operate compulsory drug treatment centres and re-education through labour centres for drug users (WHO/WPRO, 2009) that are akin to prison settings.

In Vietnam, around 50,000 drug users were residents in compulsory rehabilitation centres (known as 06 centres) nationwide in 2007, about 25% of total number of drug users in the country, with about 30,000 of these in Ho Chi Minh City. The terms of commitment in the 06 centres have increased to 5 years in Ho Chi Minh City and generally 2 years elsewhere. China and Vietnam continues to treat drug use as a 'social evil' and responses such as crackdowns, mass arrest, forced detoxification and incarceration of drug users are common. Enforcement strategies include arrest quotas for beat police, use of paid informants and bounties for turning in dealers and users, besides the further expansion of compulsory detoxification centres and re-education through labour camps (Hammett et al., 2007).

In China the Standing Office of the National People's Congress enacted the 'Regulations on Prohibition against Narcotics' that specified three levels of management of drug use. In the first, drug users are sent to detoxification centres managed by the Ministry of Public Health for a period of 7–30 days (Qian et al., 2006). In case of relapse following detoxification at these centres, they are sent to compulsory detoxification centres administered by the Public Security Bureau, where they

Table 26.2 Compulsory drug treatment in the region

Country	Nature of 'compulsory treatment' provided	Number detained (12 months)	Number detained at any one time
Brunei Darussalam	1 mandatory drug rehabilitation facility	Not known	Not known
Cambodia	14 compulsory camps	1505–1719	Not known
China	700 compulsory detoxification centres, 300 re-education through labour camps	300,000	Not known
Iran (Islamic Republic of)	Temporary compulsory rehabilitation centres reported but number unknown	Not known	Not known
Lao Peoples Democratic Republic	7 compulsory drug rehabilitation centres involving drug detoxification	Not known	833
Malaysia	28 compulsory drug treatment centres	Not known	6,848
Myanmar	26 major and 40 minor compulsory treatment centres	1,492	Not known
Thailand	90 compulsory treatment sites	40,680	Not known
Turkmenistan	1 compulsory detention site	6,546	Not known
Vietnam	109 centres with entry via committal by family, the community or arrest for drug possession	Not known	>60,000

Source: WHO, UNAIDS, UNICEF, 2010.

spend at least 6 months participating in a combination of detoxification treatment, physical exercise, and manual labour. Those who relapse after compulsory detoxification are mandated to undergo 2 to 3 years of re-education through labour centres administered by the Justice Bureau. Drug users are not allowed to leave the compulsory detoxification centres and labour camps. The Regulations on Prohibition against Narcotics states that the main reason for the detoxification centres is to reduce demand for drugs and their use, drug related crimes and to prevent the transmission of HIV. Yet, there is no evidence that those who receive frequent detoxification change their HIV related injecting and sexual risk behaviours. There were reported to be 746 compulsory drug rehabilitation facilities and 168 Rehabilitation through Labour Centres with a population of 200,000 and 120,000 respectively in 1999. In June 2006 alone, 269,000 drug users were interned in rehabilitation centres and 71,000 of them were sent to re-education through labor camps. With 1000 sites across China at the end of 2006, over 600,000 drug users had been admitted to these centres, most of whom (95%) were heroin users (Li et al., 2010).

Malaysia has traditionally imposed strict punitive measures with the widespread arrest and incarceration of drug users and the death penalty for trafficking offences. The 1952 Dangerous Drugs Act has regularly been amended to impose harsher penalties for illicit drug use. A zero-tolerance approach is practised, with the laws authorising police to detain those suspected of drug use for up to two weeks, force them to undergo urine testing, and to send those testing positive for illicit substances to compulsory treatment camps. Repeat offenders who are found in possession of any amount of illicit drugs face mandatory flogging and imprisonment. The possession of 15 grams of heroin or 200 grams of marijuana is punishable by death, and around 230 people have been hanged under this statute since 1975. In January 2005, authorities announced that possession of a syringe would be punishable with incarceration (WHO and Malaysian MOH, 2011).

The government run rehabilitation centres admit heroin dependents for 2 years of detention in a drug-free residential rehabilitation centre followed by 2 years of supervised parole. Relapse after discharge from these centres is very common. The failure of the custodial approach to stem drug use and HIV transmission led to the introduction in 1996 of some medical treatments which were limited to medically supervised detoxification and drug counselling.

The Malaysian government drug control agency estimated approximately 350,000 people who use drugs in 2004, and in 2008, the UN Reference Group estimated between 170,000 and 240,000 injectors (United Nations, 2008). Malaysia's 31 prisons currently hold 36,040 people, and in 2007 about 40% of the prison population were incarcerated on drug related charges (HIV and AIDS data hub for Asia Pacific, 2010). There are at least 16 other detention centres, including drug treatment centres, illegal immigrants' depots and juvenile institutions in Malaysia.

The arbitrary detention of people who use or are suspected of drug use, the mistreatment of detainees and the continued growth in numbers of compulsory drug treatment centres has drawn global attention to the existence of these centres in South East Asia. The lack of evidence supporting these approaches, the practice of repressive policies, violation of the right to health and human rights abuses in these centres has drawn criticism from human rights groups, civil society and the UN.

Below is the story of Jaa from Malaysia which was heard by delegates to the International Conference on the Reduction of Drug Related Harm in Bangkok, Thailand in 2009. It illustrates a common experience of inmates who have been through South East Asian rehabilitation centres.

> Jaa narrated the horrors of mandatory rehabilitation in one of Malaysia's 28 drug rehabilitation centres. As a drug user, Jaa spent most of his adult life in and out of prisons and mandatory rehabilitation. 'I have been into them 16 times' he cried 'and I cannot begin to describe the 30 years experience and torture I

faced in prisons and rehabilitation centres.' But he did describe them, with tears and encouraging claps from the audience. He talked of being caned and hit with baseball bats. 'I had ping pong balls on my head' he said referring to the swellings caused by the beatings. 'And when I was in pain and going through cold turkey, I was made to perform oral sex by the guards' Jaa concluded that the situation was changing for the better in Malaysia but the strict policy of incarcerating drug users, and the command and control approach to rehabilitation did not serve to encourage or develop him in anyway whatsoever. All it did was to break him down.

The beginnings of harm reduction

The beginnings of harm reduction in the context of drug use is difficult to clearly define, as harm reduction is now equated with HIV prevention for PWID and not as drug treatment. This is mainly the outcome of many years of concerted advocacy efforts promoting needle syringe exchange and methadone or buprenorphine substitution, long after the HIV epidemic had swept through PWID in many Asian countries. In South Asian countries, harm reduction services, particularly opioid substitution therapy, are only provided to drug injectors as an HIV prevention strategy. It is still debated whether non injectors should be eligible to receive methadone or buprenorphine substitution.

The earliest methadone programme began in Hong Kong long before HIV infection entered the consciousness. The Hong Kong Methadone Treatment Programme is operated by the Department of Health of the Government of the Hong Kong Special Administrative Region. The methadone programme started in 1972 as a pilot serving primarily as a crime prevention initiative. In 1976, it was formally launched and currently there are 20 clinics across the region. Today, the programme is well accepted and broadly recognised and has continued to provide services at easily accessible centres suited to the schedules of working PWID. One of the outcomes of the methadone programme in Hong Kong is that it maintained low HIV prevalence among MMT participants through the years, averaging 0.3 to 0.4% during 2004–8 (UNODC and UNAIDS, 2009).

Hong Kong's methadone clinics have provided an important link between marginalised people and health and social services. Apart from medical assessments by doctors, services provided at the clinics include counselling by doctors, social workers and peer counsellors, referral services including the referral of HIV positive methadone users to the Department of Health HIV clinic and tetanus vaccination.

Nepal is bordered by countries with extensive HIV epidemics among PWID, including Myanmar and North East India. The Lifesaving and Life giving Society (LALS), a community based NGO established in 1991, began outreach services with needle syringe exchange to PWID in Kathmandu, Nepal. The outreach teams included ex-drug users, nurses and social workers. LALS is widely recognised as the first known harm reduction programme in Asia. A year later in 1992, Sharan an NGO in Delhi with community health clinics and drug treatment programmes for marginalised communities, began a small scale pilot buprenorphine substitution programme for heroin users from the slum colonies in Delhi, India. The pilot was evaluated by the Indian Council for Medical Research in 1996 who reported the programme had established the efficacy of buprenorphine treatment, was acceptable to heroin users, appeared to induce a low level of physical dependence and significantly diminished the self-administration of heroin. In 1999, Sharan initiated partnerships with 6 NGOs in the cities of Chennai, Imphal, Kolkata and Mumbai to provide a range of harm reduction initiatives including OST, NSP, wound and abscess management and treatment for STI among 1,500 PWID and their sexual partners. When the project ended in 2002, over 20,000 drug users had received harm reduction services and set the stage for government acceptance and endorsement for harm reduction.

Like many of its neighbours in the region, Bangladesh had witnessed a rapid shift from oral use to injecting of drugs, along with a surge in risk related behaviours among the drug users. Bangladesh is surrounded by countries with significant HIV epidemics among PWID. In 1998, CARE Bangladesh began a needle exchange programme in Dhaka City that was later expanded to other major cities. The high coverage of the needle exchange programme in Bangladesh has successfully maintained low HIV prevalence among the estimated 20,000 to 40,000 PWID.

In Kuala Lumpur, Malaysia the IKHLAS Centre began providing drop in health facilities for drug users on the streets of Chow Kit, also giving out needles and syringes in 1994. In Mae Chan district of Northern Thailand bordering Myanmar, a community based needle exchange for the Akha tribals from three villages began in 1992. As a result of opium eradication and easy availability of cheap heroin, the Akha had switched from traditional opium use to the easily available high-quality Burmese heroin. The village committee in each village undertook the responsibility for distributing clean needles and syringes and disposing of old ones.

All these were small-scale harm reduction programmes that proved valuable in demonstrating that harm reduction was not only a western concept and could be done in Asia, but they were too few and small in scale to have any measurable impact.

The early history of the development of harm reduction in Asia would be incomplete without mention of some important initiatives that played a catalytic role and set the stage for what followed. In 1994 Dr Nick Crofts from the Macfarlane Burnet Centre for Medical Research, Melbourne, and Dr Alex Wodak from St Vincent's Hospital, Sydney, in collaboration with Aaron Peak and Sujata Rana from the Lifesaving and Lifegiving Society, organised the first workshop on harm reduction in Asia in Kathmandu, Nepal. The workshop was attended by many Asians who went on to become leaders in the Asian harm reduction movement.

In 1995, an article published in the journal *AIDS* by Nick Crofts and colleagues described the few harm reduction programmes in Asia and concluded that the 'prevention of HIV infection among PWID is possible and occurring in Asia on a small scale and that the urgent challenge is to increase the scale of what is now a demonstratedly effective response to meet the scale of the epidemic (Crofts et al., 1995)'.

In 1996, the Indian State of Manipur in North East India, struggling to cope with high levels of drug injecting and extremely high HIV prevalence rates, became the first in Asia to adopt Harm Reduction as the official State Policy to address HIV amongst PWID. With 80% of PWID infected with HIV, Manipur had the dubious distinction of being called the AIDS capital of Asia.

In 1996, at a satellite workshop held just after the International Conference on the Reduction of Drug related Harm in Hobart, Australia, representatives of the few Asian harm reduction programmes met to share their experiences for development of a manual on harm reduction in Asia. Authored by Nick Crofts, Genevieve Costigan and Gary Reid from the Centre for Harm Reduction, Burnet Institute, Melbourne, the Manual for Reducing Drug Related Harm in Asia was published in 1999 and became a seminal publication that was one of the main resources available to Asian audiences.

The participants at the satellite workshop in 1996 decided to form the Asian Harm Reduction Network to nurture and support harm reduction in the Asian region. The network soon became instrumental in advocating and promoting harm reduction and linking the few isolated programmes in the region and a forum for disseminating information on good practices in Asia through newsletters and a website, exposing harm reduction to a much wider audience. Initially based at the Macfarlane Burnet Institute for Medical Research in Melbourne, Australia, the Secreteriat moved to an office at the Centre for Disease Control, Region 10, Chiang Mai, Thailand in 1997. At the same time, UNAIDS and WHO began to endorse and promote harm reduction principles and methodology to prevent and control the rapid diffusion of HIV epidemics among PWID across the region.

Another significant development in the regions response to drug use and HIV came from the UN. Co-chaired by UNAIDS and UNODC, the United Nations Regional Task Force on Drug Use and HIV/AIDS Vulnerability in Asia and the Pacific was established in 1997 to support the United Nations System identify priorities and propose strategies, guidelines and options for collaborative activities on HIV vulnerability and drug use in the Asia Pacific region (United Nations, 2006). The Task Force went through two distinct phases, starting with a period of confrontation between the public security and public health authorities. However, drug control and HIV prevention activities implemented on the ground catalysed an environment more conducive to the second phase, one of advocacy and dialogue.

Holding regular meetings, the Task Force was a forum for collaboration between a wide range of stakeholders. Regional meetings held in China, Indonesia, Myanmar and Thailand between 1999 and 2001 were an important forum for moving the agenda at the country level. The Task Force generated better communication, especially on sensitive issues such as HIV risk in prisons, between different agencies in countries with assistance from international experts. The regional meetings allowed the host countries as well as the participants and observers to share information and discuss plans to implement HIV prevention programmes for drug users and their families. In 2005, the Task Force was reconstituted and renamed the United Nations Regional Task Force on Injecting Drug Use and HIV/AIDS for Asia and the Pacific and continued to lobby for policy change to enable harm reduction in the region.

Technical assistance, capacity building and training programmes were organised by UN organisations, academic and medical research organisations, funders and INGOs targeted at government, law enforcement and public health authorities. These workshops introduced evidence of the effectiveness, health benefits and cost-effectiveness of harm reduction, and created the enabling environment that resulted in changes to laws and policies legitimising harm reduction. The substantial funding made available for HIV prevention among PWID by development agencies, notably the Australian AusAID, United Kingdom's DfID and the United States USAID, significantly contributed to the piloting, initiation and establishment of harm reduction in countries across the region.

By the early 2000s, many Asian countries began to embrace harm reduction principles and initiate HIV prevention programmes for people who inject drugs, followed by the expansion and scale up of programmes. At the end of 2010, out of 25 Asian countries reporting the injecting of drugs, 16 countries had endorsed harm reduction in their national policies and introduced needle and syringe programmes, while 12 countries had begun opioid substitution therapy, mainly with methadone and buprenorphine (IHRA, 2010).

The new era: harm reduction in the context of HIV

The acceptance, development and expansion of harm reduction programmes in countries that have traditionally employed deterrence and punishment as the primary response to the use of drugs is a remarkable achievement and a triumph for public health. What is striking is that in a few countries harm reduction has been driven by law enforcement agencies responsible for the administration of drug control. For example, while the Ministry of Health in Myanmar procrastinated for years, the Central Committee for Drug Abuse Control (CCDAC) recognised the serious consequences of not responding to the high HIV prevalence among Burmese PWID on the country's future and supported the initiation of needle syringe programmes and other harm reduction initiatives in Myanmar.

In spite of the continued growth and use of compulsory drug treatment centres, China has made some bold changes in laws and policies to facilitate the implementation and scale up of harm reduction. In response to the emergence and escalation of HIV among PWID as well as the high relapse rates from abstinence based treatment, China introduced NSP and methadone maintenance in 2004 (Zou 2002) and has since dramatically scaled up the number of methadone maintenance treatment (MMT) clinics and NSP outlets across the country. With its immense political and economic influence over other South East Asian countries, China presents a shining example of pragmatic public health by adopting harm reduction policies and scaling up interventions to manage the impact of HIV among drug users (Wu et al., 2007).

The vigorous scaling up of the methadone programme in China is numerically stunning: from 34 MMT clinics at the end of 2004 (Zuo, 2002) to 500 MMT clinics by early 2008, and more than 680 clinics covering 27 provinces and serving some 242 000 heroin users by the end of 2009. The number of new HIV cases prevented due to the MMT programme during 2008 and 2009 is estimated at 3,377 and 3,900 respectively (UNGASS, 2010). Other benefits attributed to the national MMT programme include a reduction in consumption of heroin by an estimated 16.5 tons and 22.4 tons, respectively, and a reduction in the value of the drugs trade by an estimated 6.077 billion RMB and 8.3 billion RMB, respectively (UNGASS, 2010).

As a consequence, MMT is considered a crime reduction strategy that is strongly supported by the Public Security Bureau in China, and MMT has been incorporated into the AIDS Regulations as a treatment for heroin dependence (Wu et al., 2007). Recognising the role of law enforcement as a barrier to HIV prevention among drug users, a Training Module for Law Enforcement on Harm Reduction was developed and introduced by the AusAID funded Asia Regional HIV/AIDS Project in 2005–6, and is now an integral component of the training curriculum for police officers at the Yunnan and Guangxi Police Academies (Asia Regional HIV/AIDS Project, 2005).

In Vietnam as in China, policy is now guided by pragmatism and evidence to support harm reduction for HIV prevention among drug users, despite the retention of otherwise severe policies towards drug users (Hammett et al., 2007). Under the legal framework of the Law on HIV, the national pilot MMT programme began in Hai Phong and Ho Chi Minh City (HCMC) in May 2008 and in Ha Noi in 2009 (Ministry of Health, Viet Nam, 2010) Currently methadone clinics are functioning in 11 centres and will be scaled-up to 245 MMT clinics by 2015 covering about 80,000 heroin users (IRIN, 2011). But these changes did not materialise overnight; they were the result of a combination of efforts over many years by different parties to showcase, sensitise and convince politicians, public health, and law enforcement agencies of the benefits of alternative approaches through workshops, study tours to other countries, conference attendance and initiation of pilot projects.

In Malaysia, drug control through strict legal sanctions and severe punishments was the predominant response to drug use. Recognising that this approach failed to control HIV among people who inject drugs, the Malaysian government accepted harm reduction and started needle and syringe programmes and opioid substitution therapy as a means to reduce HIV transmission among PWID. Buprenorphine has been available in private clinics since 2002 and methadone was first introduced in 2005 in government-sponsored healthcare settings. The pilot methadone maintenance therapy programme in 2005 was under the Ministry of Health and government and hospitals began methadone services as part of the programme. The success of the programme led to an expansion in the coverage in 2007 to 5,000 drug users. By June 2010, there were 211 free methadone service delivery outlets with 13,471 registered clients, while an additional 20,000 individuals were accessing fee-based substitution treatment through private practitioners. Over 18,000 PWID have accessed sterile injecting equipment through the 240 service delivery sites. Needle and syringe programmes in Malaysia have mainly been the responsibility of civil society groups and this continues to be the case.

While the examples above have been showcased due to the immense impact the changes in government policy have had on the lives of millions of drug users, other initiatives owned by civil society and people who use drugs have also arisen.

Of particular noteworthiness is the **Asian Consortium on Drugs, HIV, AIDS and Poverty** (ACDHAP) whose Response Beyond Borders (RBB) consultations have brought grassroots workers, people who use drugs, politicians, civil society, UN and parliamentarians together on a platform to seek Asian solutions to Asian problems. The RBB consultations have provided the forum for the development of the Asian Network of People who Use Drugs, and seeded the Asian Parliamentarians for Harm Reduction, a group of Asian Parliamentarians who are supportive of harm reduction.

Another noteworthy development is the Asian Network of People who Use Drugs (ANPUD), the first registered regional network of people who use drugs was established by people who use drugs to unify the voices of their communities to advocate for changes in drug laws and policies that negatively affect their lives and for better access to prevention, treatment and care services across Asia. ANPUD currently has over 250 members in 11 countries throughout the Asian region.

In January 2008, the Response Beyond Borders 'First Consultation on the Prevention of HIV Related to Drug Use' in Goa, India, provided a platform for Asian drug user activists to hold a regional consultation and develop the Goa Declaration, building on the Vancouver Declaration (talkingdrugs, 2011), that gave birth to ANPUD. Between 2008 and 2009 members of ANPUD, now an informal network, set up a Google group forum with the main purpose being to engage with membership to develop the constitution and governance structures.

A small group began to draft a formal constitution that would be necessary to register ANPUD as a non-profit entity. At the same time members met regularly and informally during key events such as the International Harm Reduction Conference in Bangkok in 2009, the Response Beyond Borders Workshops in Phnom Penh and Kathmandu and the International Congress on AIDS in Asia and the Pacific (ICAAP) in Bali.

Since its registration in Hong Kong in February 2010, ANPUD has made its presence strongly felt in the region. Members are involved in a broad range of activities and events in partnership with WHO, UNAIDS and UNODC and are currently conducting a study on the barriers faced by people who inject drugs in accessing hepatitis C diagnosis and treatment in four Asian countries. A hepatitis C regional advocacy strategy to pressurise ministries of health, the Global Fund and UN organisations to provide hepatitis treatment for PWID is being developed.

The formation of ANPUD is underpinned by the principle of 'Meaningful Involvement of People who Use Drugs' (MIPUD), with a strong belief in unity, support, equality, inclusiveness, collaboration and the will to change the current situation faced by people who use drugs in the Asian Region. ANPUD promotes the MIPUD principle in all aspects of the harm reduction response, and believes that people who use drugs must be actively involved and engaged in the design, implementation and evaluation of programmes. ANPUD has vigorously campaigned against the detention of people who use drugs in compulsory treatment centres. ANPUD has been actively involved in the development of the new WHO Regional Strategy titled 'A Strategy to halt and reverse the HIV epidemic among people who inject drugs in Asia and the Pacific, 2010–15 (WHO, 2010)

Recently, ANPUD has established or strengthened National Networks of people who use drugs in India, Nepal, Indonesia and Malaysia. ANPUD continues to advocate for the harmonisation of policies, decriminalisation of drug use and reducing the stigma and discrimination faced by people who use drugs across the region. Further, ANPUD advocates for universal access to a range of diverse, evidence based, locally driven harm reduction approaches in conformity with the *WHO, UNODC, UNAIDS Technical Guidance* (WHO/UNODC/UNAIDS, 2009) in the Asian region with a special focus on access to Hepatitis C diagnosis and treatment.

UN initiatives in support of harm reduction

A number of high-level dialogues and initiatives have been commissioned by UN organisations to examine and address legal and political barriers to the provision and scaling up of harm reduction related to HIV and drug use.

The Economic and Social Commission for Asia and the Pacific (ESCAP) which is the UN body with the authority and mandate to convene intergovernmental meetings adopted the 'Resolution 66/10' which underscores the need 'to ground universal access in human rights and undertake measures to address stigma and discrimination, as well as policy and legal barriers to effective HIV responses, in particular with regard to key affected populations'.

In 2010, SAARCLAW, UNAIDS, IDLO and UNDP initiated a dialogue to promote a legal enabling environment and strengthen the legal response to HIV in South Asia, specifically to:

- promote understanding of rights-based approaches and frameworks to respond to HIV and to support people most at risk of or living with HIV;
- advocate for reform of unjust practices and laws which interfere with effective responses to HIV and contribute to the vulnerability of key affected populations;
- work to eliminate all forms of discrimination and stigmatisation of people living with or affected by HIV.

SAARCLAW is an association of legal communities of the South Asian Association for Regional Cooperation (SAARC) countries comprising judges, lawyers, academicians, law teachers and public officers. SAARCLAW has the status of a Regional Apex Body of SAARC, whose member states are Afghanistan, Bhutan, Bangladesh, India, Maldives, Nepal, Pakistan and Sri Lanka.

In 2010, the Asia Pacific Regional Consultation of the Global Commission on HIV and the Law organised a meeting in Bangkok, Thailand for civil society and people who use drugs to document legal and policy barriers to the HIV response, including the stigmatisation and discrimination of injecting drug users, to advocate and support the reform of discriminatory laws and policies which block effective responses to HIV and contribute to their vulnerability

In November 2011, SAARCLAW, the International Development Law Organization (IDLO), UNAIDS and UNDP have convened a Roundtable Dialogue on 'Legal and Policy Barriers to the HIV Response' in Kathmandu, Nepal to promote an enabling legal environment and strengthen the legal response to HIV in South Asia. The Roundtable intends to bring together legal professionals, advocates, community leaders, government representatives and parliamentarians from South Asian countries to discuss legal and policy barriers to the HIV response, and analyse the impact of the barriers upon the ability of people who use drugs and other key populations to access HIV prevention, treatment, care and support services and recommend strategies to overcome them.

Conclusion

The efforts of the various stakeholders mentioned above have translated into an increasing number of Asian countries embracing the principles of harm reduction. In the past few years, many more countries have initiated or expanded HIV prevention and treatment programmes for people who inject drugs.

The progress is captured by UNAIDS in their 2011 publication entitled *HIV in Asia and the Pacific: Getting to Zero* (UNAIDS, 2011) which reported that the number of needle and syringe programme sites in Asia has increased seven-fold – from 291 in 2006 to 2,200 in 2010 – mainly due to scale-up in Bangladesh, China, Indonesia and Vietnam. However, only Bangladesh and Vietnam reported distributing more than 100 needles and syringes per user per year in 2009 (United Nations, 2011; WHO, 2011; UNODC/UNAIDS, 2011).

Opioid substitution programmes have also increased from 341 sites in 2006, to 1,182 sites in 2010. Bangladesh and Cambodia introduced opioid substitution therapy for the first time in 2010 after a protracted period of procrastination. However, only 5% of the estimated number of people who inject drugs in Asia and the Pacific were reached with substitution programmes in 2010 (UNODC/UNAIDS, 2011).

Despite the increased acceptability and initiation of harm reduction programmes in Asia, coverage with harm reduction remains low in the region. Numerous barriers impede access to harm reduction services by people who use drugs. In many countries, the lack of awareness of services, the distance to services, inappropriate opening hours, fear of arrest, police harassment and fear of being seen by family and friends while attending harm reduction services are just some of the barriers that need to be addressed in order to increase the number and efficacy of services.

Laws and policies in many Asian countries present another significant barrier. For example, the provision of needles and syringes to drug users is illegal and outreach workers are vulnerable to arrest and being charged for the possession of injecting paraphernalia or aiding and abetting the commission of a criminal offence – the use of illicit drugs.

Law enforcement approaches still prevail and a 'war on drugs' approach still dominates in several countries in the region. Law enforcement authorities continue to criminalise the possession of needles and syringes, and mount 'crackdowns' against people who use drugs, even when they are in treatment or visiting drop-in centres for clean needles and syringes or other services. Criminalisation of drug use drives people who inject drugs away from health and HIV services operated by government and nongovernmental agencies. Stigma and discrimination in healthcare settings have the same effect. A few countries have begun to shift away from the compulsory centre approach, including Malaysia, which is transforming its compulsory centres into voluntary 'Cure and Care' clinics.

The disconnection between drug control and HIV prevention policies needs to be resolved and efforts to ensure that policy reform translates into effective service delivery must be made. The legal and policy barriers to HIV prevention and treatment for people who inject drugs must be removed. Collaboration between drug control and law enforcement officials and the health sector needs to be fostered (see also chapter 6 by Monaghan on law enforcement)]. Compulsory centres for people who use drugs need to be replaced with voluntary community based treatment approaches that offer a wide range of options for treatment and care for drug dependence, including expanding services to those in prisons.

In 2010, WHO, UNODC, UNAIDS, the Global Fund and the Asian Network of People who Use Drugs outlined a, three-pronged strategy for controlling HIV among people who inject drugs (WHO, 2010):

1. create a favourable enabling environment for harm reduction, especially by strengthening policy coordination and harmonisation between public health and public security ministries, and by removing policy and punitive legal barriers;
2. provide technical support to governments to scale up community-based harm reduction programmes and to build capacity for developing public health evidence based approaches for users of amphetamine-type stimulants;
3. ensure the availability of good quality strategic information to develop and budget for effective national responses to drug use.

Recognising the negative impact of drug policies on the health and human rights of people who use drugs, the Global Commission on Drug Policy has called for humane and effective drug policies (2011). The report states that drug policies should be evidence- informed and based on human rights and public health principles, and be implemented by involving families, schools, public health specialists and civil society leaders in partnership with law enforcement agencies and other relevant governmental bodies. It recommends that governments: promote policies that effectively reduce consumption and that prevent and reduce harm; invest in evidence-informed prevention, with a special focus on young people; and focus repressive measures on organised crime and drug traffickers in order to reduce the harm associated with the illicit drug use market.

Looking back to the period since the 1990s it is heartening to see that some landmark changes have occurred in Asian countries and that harm reduction continues to grow. It is hoped that ongoing efforts to harness high-level political support will result in the introduction of public health oriented policies to support and strengthen the further development of harm reduction in Asia.

References

Asia Regional HIV/AIDS Project (2005) *Law Enforcement Manual*, Canberra.
Bharadwaj, A. (1995) Self-injecting of drugs gains popularity in Punjab, *Times of India*, 1 July.
Biswas, S. (1994) Hooked to a new high, *India Today*, April.
Charles, M., Bewley-Taylor, D. and Neidpath, A. (2005) *Briefing Paper Ten, October 2005: Drug Policy in India – Compounding the Harm?*, Oxford: Beckley Foundation Drug Policy Programme.
Crofts, N., Costigan, G., Narayanan, P., Gray, J., Dorabjee, J., Langkham, B., Singh, M., Peak, A., Aquino, C. and Deany, P. (1995) Harm reduction in Asia: a successful response to hidden epidemics, *AIDS*, 12 (supple. B), S109–S115.
Dorabjee, J. and Samson, L. (1998) Self and community based opioid substitution among opioid dependent populations in the Indian sub-continent, *International Journal of Drug Policy*, 9, 411–16.
Dorabjee, J. and Samson, L. (2000) A multi-centre rapid assessment of injecting drug use in India, *International Journal of Drug Policy*, 11, 99–112.
Global Commission on Drugs (2011) *War on Drugs: Report of the Global Commission on Drug Policy, 2011*, www.globalcommissionondrugs.org/Report, accessed October.
HAARP (2009) HIV/AIDS Asia Regional Program, *Law and Policy Review*, July, Canberra.
Hammett, T.H., Wu, Z., Duc, T.T., Stephens, D., Sullivan, S., Liu, W., Chen, Y., Ngu, D. and Des Jarlais, D.C. (2007) 'Social evils' and harm reduction: the evolving policy environment for human immunodeficiency virus prevention among injection drug users in China and Viet Nam, *Addiction*, 103, 137–45.
HIV and AIDS Data Hub for Asia–Pacific (2010) Law, policy and HIV in Asia and the Pacific: implications on the vulnerability of men who have sex with men, female sex workers and injecting drug users, www.aidsdatahub.org/en/regional-profile/law-and-policy, accessed 21 September 2011.
IHRA (2010) *The Global State of Harm Reduction*, London: International Harm Reduction Association.

IRIN (2011) *Vietnam: Compulsory Drug Treatment Centres 'Counterproductive'*, Integrated Regional Information Networks, www.irinnews.org/report.aspx?ReportId=92599, accessed 21 September 2011.

Kitayaporn, D., Vanichseni, S., Mastro, T.D., Raktham, S., Vaniyapongs, T., Des Jarlais, D.C., Wasi, C., Young, N.L., Sujarita, S., Heyward, W.L. and Esparza, J. (1998) Infection with HIV-1subtypes B and E in injecting drug users screened for enrolment into a prospective cohort in Bangkok, Thailand, *J Acquir Immune Defic Syndr Hum Retrovirol*, 19, 289–95.

Kumar, M.S. and Daniels, D. (1994) *HIV Risk Reduction Strategies among IDU's in Madras*, New Delhi: CARITAS India.

Kumar, M.S., Mudaliar, S., Thyagarjan, S.P., Kumar, S., Selvanayagam, A. and Daniels, D. (2000) Rapid assessment and response to injecting drug use in Madras, South India, *International Journal of Drug Policy*, 11, 83–98.

Li, J., Ha, T.H., Zhang, C. and Liu, H. (2010) The Chinese government's response to drug use and HIV/AIDS: a review of policies and programs, *Harm Reduction Journal*, 7 (4), DOI: 10.1186/1477-7517-7-4, accessed 21 September 2011.

Ma, Y., Li, Z.Z. and Zhang, K.X. (1990) Identification of HIV infection among drug users in China, *Zhonghua Liu Xing Bing Xue Za Zhi*, 11, 184–5.

Mathers, B., Cook, C. and Degenhardt, L. (2010) Improving the data to strengthen the global response to HIV among people who inect drugs, *International Journal of Drug Policy*, 21 (2), 100–2.

McCoy, A.W. (1991) *The Politics of Heroin: CIA Complicity in the Global Drug Trade*, New York: Lawrence Hill Books.

Ministry of Health, Vietnam (2010) Ministry of Health/UNGASS Country Progress Report Viet Nam. In Ministry of Health, *Socialist Republic of Viet Nam*, Hanoi.

Qian, H., Schumacher, E.J., Chen, T.H., and Ruan, Y. (2006) Injection drug use and HIV/AIDS in China: review of current situation, prevention and policy implications, *Harm Reduction Journal*, 3 (4), DOI: 10.1186/1477-7517-3-4, accessed 21 September 2011.

Siam Voices (2011) Resurrecting Thailand's brutal 'war on drugs', *Siam Voices*, 10 March 2011, http://asian-correspondent.com/49966/the-war-on-drugs-pheu-thais-democratic-deficit/ accessed 20 September.

Talkingdrugs (2011) http://talkingdrugs.org/vancouver-declaration, accessed 21 September.

United Nations (2006) *Background Paper and TOR July 2006*, United Nations Regional Task Force on Drug Use and HIV/AIDS Vulnerability in Asia and the Pacific, New York: United Nations.

United Nations (2008) *Reference Group to the United Nations on HIV and Injecting Drug Use*, New York: United Nations.

United Nations (2011) *Getting to Zero: 2011–2015 Strategy Joint United Nations Programme on HIV/AIDS (UNAIDS)*, New York: United Nations.

UNAIDS (2011) *HIV in Asia and the Pacific: Getting to Zero*, Joint United Nations Programme on HIV/AIDS (UNAIDS)

UNAIDS/UNODCCP, (2000) *Drug Use and HIV Vulnerability: Policy Research Study in Asia*, Task Force on Drug Use and HIV vulnerability, Geneva: UNAIDS/UNODCCP.

UNGASS (2010) *UNGASS Country Progress Report*. In Ministry of Health; of the People's Republic of China, Beijing: Ministry of Health.

UNODC (2006) *World Drug Report*, United Nations Office on Drugs and Crime, Vienna: UNODC.

UNODC (2007) *Legal and Policy Concerns Related to IDU Harm Reduction in SAARC Countries: A Review commissioned by UNODC Regional Office for South Asia*, Lawyers Collective HIV/AIDS Unit, Vienna: UNODC.

UNODC (2011) *World Drug Report 2011*, New York, United Nations Office on Drugs and Crime, Vienna: UNODC.

UNODC and UNAIDS (2009) Methadone treatment in Hong Kong: history, strategy and results, *Experiences from the AIDS Response in China*, 1 (September).

UNODC and UNAIDS (2011) Coordinator's report. Presentation to the Eighth Meeting of the UN Regional Task Force on Injecting Drug Use and HIV/AIDS for Asia and the Pacific, New Delhi, 10–11 February.

Westermeyer, J. (1976) The pro-heroin effects of anti-opium laws, *Arch Gen Psychiatry*, 33, 1135–9

WHO (2001) *Regional Health Forum: WHO South East Asia Region*, 5 (1), Geneva.

WHO (2010) *A Strategy to Halt and Reverse the HIV Epidemic among People Who Inject Drugs in Asia and the Pacific, 2010–2015*, Geneva: WHO.

WHO (2011) *WHO Technical Briefs on Amphetamine-type Stimulants*, Manila, World Health Organization Regional Office for the Western Pacific (WPRO), www.who.int/hiv/pub/idu/ats_brief2.pdf, accessed 18 October.

WHO and Malaysian MOH (2011) *Good Practices in Asia: Scale Up of Harm Reduction in Malaysia*, Geneva and Kuala Lumpur: WHO and Malaysian Ministry of Health.

WHO, UNODC, UNAIDS (2009) *Technical Guidance for Countries to Set Targets for Universal Access to HIV Prevention, Treatment and Care Injecting Drug Users*, Geneva and Vienna: WHO, UNODC, UNAIDS.

WHO, UNAIDS, UNICEF (2010) *Towards Universal Access: Scaling up Priority HIV/AIDS Interventions in the Health Sector*, Progress Report, Geneva: WHO, UNAIDS, UNICEF.

WHO/WPRO (2009) *Assessment of Compulsory Treatment of People Who Use Drugs in Cambodia, China, Malaysia and Viet Nam: An Application of Selected Human Rights Principles*, Geneva: WHO WPRO.

Wu, Z., Sullivan, S.G., Wang, Y., Rotheram-Borus, M.J. and Detels, R. (2007) Evolution of Chinas response to HIV/AIDS, *Lancet*, 369, www.thelancet.com, accessed 21 September 2011.

Zou, K. (2002) The 're-education through labour system in China's legal reform, *Criminal Law Forum*, 12, 459–85.

Chapter 27

HISTORY AND CONTEXT OF HARM REDUCTION IN THE UNITED STATES

Lisa Moore and Allan Clear

Out of necessity, the story of harm reduction in the United States is a story of activism. The United States has been in an ideological, political and material war against drugs and drug users for over a century, with the current offensive running from the Nixon administration to the present (Currie, 1993) The current drug war has served to re-inscribe some of the conditions of pre-civil rights, Jim Crow America: the disenfranchisement of the poor and people of colour, a transfer of wealth and political representation from urban inner-cities to white rural and exurban communities, the re-creation of prison-based slave labor and the concomitant social control of the same urban populations (Abramsky, 2006; Alexander, 2010). The Drug War also demands the cooperation of other nations, regardless of whether or not it serves their interests or sovereignty (United Nations Office on Drugs and Crime, 2010; Levine, 2003).

All of this has been justified by a media-produced terror of crime and of illicit drug users. Political careers are made by toeing the 'tough on crime' line, which implicitly means that one is 'tough' on drugs and drug users (Dyer, 2000). The drug war produced massive political and social inertia supporting the repression and dehumanisation of drug users. This inertia is driven by the tremendous profits garnered by the Prison Industrial Complex and its subsidiary industries.[1] Any efforts to rehumanise drug users and to promote public health constitute a struggle against this inertia, against this hegemony and against the profits made from the oppression of drug users. It requires cross-national collaboration and solidarity. Therefore, it is, by definition, an activist story.

The roots of this story go back earlier than the twentieth century. In the United States, drug policy has always been inextricably linked to politics of the racial or national 'other'. While drug use is ubiquitous, the drug use, and thus the drug users, who are deemed problematic are inevitably those whose race, class, culture or politics are not considered 'American' (Musto, 1987; Morgan, 1981). The first anti-drug user law was created in 1875, ostensibly against opium (Courtwright, 1982). While opium and morphine-based patent medicines were widely used by men, women and children across the country, with the largest group of users being white women in the south, San Francisco, California lawmakers saw fit to ban Chinese opium smoking. They made this decision with the concurrent backdrop of anti-Chinese pogroms and riots, which were rife throughout the western and northwestern United States (Pfaelzer, 2007). This culminated with the Chinese exclusion act of 1882, the Immigration Act of 1924 and finally, the forced incarceration of Japanese Americans during World War II (Takaki, 1993). Similar to the recent crack/powder cocaine sentencing disparity (Coyle, 2002), this is a disparity of legal policies for drugs that are pharmacologically either similar or identical. The difference is not in the drug, but in the drug user.

---

[1] E.g. manufacturing where prison labour is employed well below minimum or union wages, industries that support prisons like food services, phone companies, industries that are supported by the wages of those employed in prisons.

Harm Reduction in Substance Use and High-Risk Behaviour: International Policy and Practice, First Edition.
Edited by Richard Pates and Diane Riley.
© 2012 Blackwell Publishing Ltd. Published 2012 by Blackwell Publishing Ltd.

The drug use of other people of colour has also prompted moral panics and legislation. In the Southwest United States, cannabis smoking was linked to panics about Mexican immigrants. One of the most legendary examples of the moral panic that conflates difference and drugs was the story of the Alabama marshalls who, in 1911, decided to change the size of bullets employed since they believed that smaller bullets would not stop 'negroes on cocaine' (Musto, 1987). In the 1930s, under the first drug czar, Harry Anslinger, and with the Federal Bureau of Investigation's head J. Edgar Hoover, jazz musicians and communists got added to the list of putative drugged subversives (Musto, 1987). And much later, with our most recent drug war, the substances used by the youth, civil rights and anti-war movements became the markers for anti-social evil that are used to justify an increase in policing and in federal power (Epstein, 1990). All of this happened while the pharmaceutical revolution produced more and more mind-altering substances. These legal substances, which are used by populations whose American credentials are unquestioned, are medicalised, not criminalised. Likewise, harm reduction for alcohol and tobacco is much less controversial than it is for illicit substances (Baer and Murch, 1998; Larimer et al., 1998). Medicalisation creates a version of harm reduction, relative to approaches that are solely punitive. Medicalisation offers the space to treat problematic drug use, while under criminimalisation the only solutions are stigmatisation and incarceration. Harm maximisation becomes policy with criminalised drugs.

Interestingly, there is always slippage with this analysis, but the slippage happens when the users (or perceived users) of a drug change. When free-based cocaine was an expensive drug used by the wealthy, the reaction to its use was muted (Reinarman and Levine, 1997b). Cocaine was trendy and, for a time, thought to be non-addictive. In contrast, when crack became a cheap drug of choice, we embarked on a huge moral panic that prompted the sentencing disparity, and endless discourse about how people become immoral monsters from just one hit and how crack exposed babies become adults who are permanently intellectually and morally impaired (Reinarman and Levine, 1997a). Much of the prognostication about the future on crack never happened, except the part about the disintegration of family and community which was, beyond a doubt, caused more by the draconian punishments imposed on the drug users than by the effects of the drug per se (Maurer and Chesney-Lind, 2002).

It is a mistake to ignore or discount this history because it shows the hidden and unspoken ideology that has informed drug policy and harm reduction. Prescription drugs used by white, middle class people are purported to be good, regardless of what harms they cause. The drug use of the poor and of people of colour reflects subversive tendencies and immorality, again regardless of the actual harm (or benefits) seen. Our collective reactions to drug use are married to our racist and xenophobic perceptions of the group who is using. This was true in the 1800s with the Asian exclusion laws (Takaki, 1993). It was true in the 1980s with the sentencing disparity for crack cocaine, where one would have to have 100 times as much powder cocaine as crack to get the same sentence (Coyle, 2002). These policies and politics are deeply linked to the ugly racial politics of this country. So harm reduction, in its desire to overturn laws and ideologies that hurt drug users, cannot be separated from activism that tries to overturn laws and ideologies that repress the poor and people of colour. As long as drug policy is a thinly veiled effort to repress and control the poor and people of colour (Fellner, 2000) harm reduction must be part of the activism to overturn that repression.

Drug policy in the United States also functions to further geopolitical outcomes that may seem far from the outcomes espoused by public health. Like the petrochemical market, another product that engenders addiction and breathtaking profit, the production and consumption of drugs, is of geopolitical import. Whether we go back to the British Opium Wars (Waley, 1958) or to the Vietnam War (where opium and heroin financed the side wars in Cambodia and Laos) (McCoy, 1972) or the current wars in the Golden Crescent, a region cursed with both oil and opium, it is a mistake to pretend that drugs and drug policy aren't a part of broader imperial agendas. With the current status of the United States as the world 'superpower', this agenda impacts the drug policies of practically all nations. In spite of national sovereignty, others become players in our drug war and pawns in our great game (McAllister, 2000). International activism and solidarity need to break these chains. US harm reduction activists need to know that their work changing policy matters both here and abroad, and our colleagues abroad need to know to support US efforts, not just out of altruism but also out of the desire to reduce US interference in their efforts. These truths underscore the impossibility of progressive drug policy in the absence of activism, at least when one examines the US context.

This said, harm reduction has a long history in the United States (Moore, 1995). One might begin that history with the activists who fought the scapegoating of Asian, Latinos and blacks in the early twentieth century or with those who fought the post-1960s backlash against youth culture. This counter-hegemonic struggle continues today with the prison abolition movement and with all efforts that fight the over incarceration of poor drug users of colour; it very much includes the efforts of harm reductionists. These ideological battles function as the backdrop for attempts to create services that actually improve the lives of drug users, especially those who are not willing or ready to become abstinent.

Early harm reduction in the United States: methadone, acupuncture detox and drug testing

There is a pervasive tension between the medical control of drugs and drug users and community control. We reduce harm by allowing medicine to address some of the issues of addiction and drug use. By doing so, the outcomes are infinitely more humane than they would be if left to criminal justice. At the same time, these approaches do not allow for community control and individual empowerment. They convert the drug user from being a 'criminal' to being a 'patient' or 'client', the idea that a user can retain or regain integration into his/her community and have agency as a user and as a person who, ideally, can only be accomplished with community generated and controlled processes. Medicine offers much to 'manage' drug use and to reduce medical harms associated with drug use, but it offers less for people to achieve complete social and interpersonal health.

In the mid-1960s Dole and Nyswander pioneered the development of methadone maintenance as a treatment for opiate addiction. Not since the closing of narcotic maintenance clinics after the passage of the 1914 Harrison Act had addiction been treated as a medical issue. This, in fact, set the stage for the first federally funded harm reduction strategy (Rosenbaum, 1995). The introduction of methadone occurred at a pivotal moment in US history as the counter-culture openly encouraged drug use.

Alternative culture experienced the benefits of drug use and also quickly noticed the negative effects. Peer based drug education expanded during the late 1960s (Do It Now Foundation, 2011) and low threshold, drug-user-friendly medical services in the shape of the free clinic movement placed an emphasis on health over moral judgment. Simultaneous to President Nixon's declaration of the war on drugs in 1971 was an expansion of methadone maintenance spearheaded by Dr Robert Newman, Assistant Commissioner for Addiction Programs in New York City (Newman, 1990). The rapid scale-up of drug treatment to match the need for services was the first of its kind. To date, approximately a quarter of a million people in all fifty states of the nation use methadone (Pollack and d'Aunno, 2008).

While medicine was reluctantly embracing drug users, through methadone detoxification and maintenance, there was also a community resistance to medicalisation (Morales, 1992). This was best exemplified by the acupuncture detox model utilised at Lincoln Hospital in the Bronx and at the Haight Ashbury Free Clinic in San Francisco (Kolenda, 2000). The New York model emerged from a collaboration between the Young Lords and the Black Panther Party (Morales, 1992). Community acupuncture is still used in numerous drug detox and acupuncture settings. This approach can be differentiated from medical approaches because the control lies in the hands of community members, not outsiders; it leads to less, not more, dependency. Acupuncture needle detoxification is something that any community member can enjoy and it serves to reduce the difference between users and non-users by being a community service (Rohleder et al., 2009).

Another community model of harm reduction was developed in San Francisco in the 1970s. The Haight Ashbury Free Clinic, in collaboration with Pharmchem labs, did free drug testing. One could listen to radio station KSAN where they would announce the drug test findings: the drug, neighborhood, purity and adulterants would all be announced. Individuals could anonymously send samples for testing for a fee (Nisker, 2004). This was incredible harm reduction and had it been generalised, it could have decreased drug overdoses, as well as toxicity problems caused by drug adulterants. One of the most intractable harm reduction issues is the lack of control of illicit drug purity and adulterants. The idea that one could have one's drugs tested and that one could shop for drugs based upon actual quality, could theoretically allow the market to improve the safety of drugs. It certainly allowed people to use more safely with an absence of paternalism; science offered information without gatekeeping. Sadly, this testing programme ended in the mid-1970s.

The innovation of drug testing was reinstituted by DanceSafe which has done club based and web based testing of ecstasy, as well as education and counseling in the United States and Canada since the new millennium. Such community based approaches have enormous potential for improving health and increasing the agency of drug users (Henricksen, 2000; Dancesafe, 2011). (See the chapter 14 on Ecstasy and related drugs for further discussion of drug testing as a harm reduction measure.)

Reagan, the drug war and harm reduction

Now here, you see, it takes all the running you can do to keep in the same place. If you want to get somewhere else, you must run at least twice as fast as that!

(The Red Queen, Carroll, 1946)

The 1970s were marked by tension between the anti-drug, anti-1960s moral panic, as evidenced by the drug war and continued efforts to normalise and decriminalise drugs. During the Carter administration, we saw a national effort to decriminalise cannabis. What may be even more notable was the normalisation of drug use. The high school class of 1978 saw more illicit drug use than any other class before or since (Lloyd, 2002). Legislation introduced at the end of the 1970s criminalised purchase and possession of syringes in an attempt to curb injection drug use. Paraphernalia and prescription laws produced the tremendous susceptibility to blood borne infections evidenced in communities of injecting drug users. At the beginning of the HIV epidemic, practically all states had paraphernalia and prescription laws on the books (Lazzarini et al., 1996). Death from AIDS among drug users began escalating in the early 1980s adding another layer of stigma to an already stigmatised population.

Until the election of Ronald Reagan in 1980 it wasn't clear how this tension between the two opposing views of drugs was going to be resolved. The election of Reagan,[2] and the fact that the First Lady, Nancy Reagan, took on drugs as her pet project eroded the gains of harm reductionists in previous years and made it necessary for us to work even harder to create any positive gain (Merritt, 2004). If the Reagan administration created one leg around which drug policy and reaction was organised in the 1980s, the AIDS epidemic created the other. Nancy Reagan's 'Just Say No' campaign found itself countered by the 'Silence = Death' of AIDS activists who decried the malign indifference of government (Crimp, 1988; Gamson, 1989). President Reagan launched the unprecedented expansion of the prison industry until the United States led the world in incarcerating its citizens. Looking abroad for inspiration, we began to look to interventions to stem the spread of HIV. In 1986, Jon Parker and the AIDS Brigade initiated exchanges on the east coast (Boston, New Haven, New York City) and Dave Purchase commenced an exchange programme in Tacoma, Washington (Sorge, 1990; Sherman and Purchase, 2001). The earliest government effort at establishing a needle exchange was initiated by the New York City Health Department, also in 1985. After racial politics stymied the development process, a compromise programme was started in 1988 (Anderson, 1991), at which time activists across the country were successfully organising to start exchange efforts in their communities. In San Francisco, anti-nuclear activists and drug researchers exchanged needles as an act of civil disobedience, with the hopes of triggering the government to start a programme. The government didn't, so what began as civil disobedience became a programme (Moore and Wenger, 1995). AIDS activists in New York, Philadelphia and Chicago also began programmes in advance of government efforts. By the end of the 1980s, non-governmental needle exchanges were operating in practically every major city in the nation. Regular conventions for the nascent movement of underground exchange programmes and the subsequent formation of the North American Syringe Exchange Network acted as catalysts for the rapid spread of mostly extra-legal efforts to start harm reduction services.

Whereas most industrialised nations responded to HIV among drug users with a proactive public health response, the United States continued its policy of restricting help for drug users. The Health Omnibus Program Extension Act of 1988 established support for investment in HIV prevention, testing and education through the Centers for Disease Control and contained a significant clause: 'None of the funds provided under this Act or an amendment made by this Act shall be used to provide individuals with hypodermic needles or syringes so that such individuals may use illegal drugs, unless the Surgeon General of the Public Health Service determines that a demonstration needle exchange programme would be effective in reducing drug abuse and the risk that the public will become infected with the etiologic agent for acquired immune deficiency syndrome' (1988; Vlahov et al., 2001).

Since the government decided to respond to the need for services with a ban, it was the catalytic efforts of an activist movement that helped propel harm reduction services (Downing et al., 2005). Without the direct action of activists, many of whom had personal experience as drug users, the emerging alliance of scientists, government officials, drug treatment specialists and healthcare workers would not have been effective. Members of the AIDS activist group, ACT-UP, initiated new programmes and the movement generated support and was endorsed by researchers from NDRI in New York and the Urban Health Study in San Francisco. From the early 1990s to 2000, the number of exchanges increased to 127, in spite of the federal ban (Des Jarlais et al., 2004).

---

[2] Who was in part elected because of his stern contempt for youth, people of colour or any part of America that did not conform to a 50s white middle-class ideal.

The spread of exchange programmes was supported by the birth and growth of policy and educational groups. The Lindesmith Center, which produced fact-based drug education material merged with the Drug Policy Alliance in 2000 to work on national and local policy issues. Likewise, in 1995, harm reduction activist created the Harm Reduction Coalition, whose mandate was to do education, organising and advocacy with and for active drug users.

New York City once regarded as the global epicentre of injection drug use and HIV experienced a reversal in HIV transmission after the wide-scale implementation of harm reduction services (Des Jarlais et al., 1998). A remarkable partnership between the New York State Department of Health, the American Foundation for AIDS Research, Beth-Israel Medical Center and the underground street-based needle exchange programmes combined to inaugurate a network of programmes that reduced HIV among injectors from a high of 50% in 1992 to 10% in 2002 (Des Jarlais, 2006; Des Jarlais et al., 2005). Similar partnerships emerged in other parts of the country particularly in Northern California, Oregon, Washington State, Chicago and the eastern seaboard. Stimulation of new needle exchange programmes by activists peaked in the mid-1990s to be superseded by the systematic and slower introduction of new programmes by local health departments.

In 1997, when the Democrats were in power in the White House, advocates initiated a campaign to remove the federal ban on the funding of syringe exchange. A wealth of empirical evidence existed which supported the efficacy of syringe exchange in reducing HIV transmission among injection drug users and demonstrated that it did not increase the incidence of drug use (Lurie et al., 1993). There were well over 100 syringe exchange programmes operating in the United States and several federally funded studies existed that further substantiated the positive impact of exchange services on drug user health (Des Jarlais et al., 2004). Advocacy efforts waged by researchers and advocates were successful in influencing then Director of Health and Human Services, Donna Shalala, to certify that the scientific criteria for removing the ban had been met. Despite this certification, President Clinton refused to take the final step and remove the ban (Harris and Goldstein, 1998; Stollberg, 1998).

When the 2006 elections restored congressional control to the Democrats, advocates seized the opportunity to launch a more aggressive campaign to build political support for syringe exchange among elected officials in positions of influence. A ban on the use of funds for sterile syringes that affected the city of Washington, DC, which is governed by the federal government, was overturned in 2006. Advocates read these as signs that they were in a prime position to win support among their elected officials for lifting the ban. All three of the primary democratic presidential candidates in the 2008 election (including President Obama) supported removal of the ban. One year into the presidency of Barack Obama the federal ban on the funding of needle exchange was removed by Congress (Editorial, 2009; Schwartzapfel, 2010).

For a number of years, activists and then local governments have initiated and expanded needle exchange while actively fighting the expressed intentions of the federal government. In many locales, the incidence of HIV has been depressed to levels comparable to European and Australian cities that have enjoyed full government support. This has been accomplished with a largely volunteer workforce. One could easily argue that needle exchange in the United States has been one of the most cost-effective unsupported interventions ever. The failure of government in its responsibilities has given rise to enormous national networks of mutual support, cooperative purchasing of supplies, and mutual aide with wealthier programmes supporting those with fewer resources. The lack of government has led to a lack of governance. This is a strength of harm reduction in the United States but it is also a weakness, because reliance on local volunteers and local politics means that users in one community might be well served while just a few miles away, other users may have nothing. The fragmentation of harm reduction mirrors what is seen in social services generally in the United States. We have a system that necessitates local initiative and can easily foster inequity. As the federal government takes up more responsibility, we expect it to mirror social services even more. We also hope that the unique commitment brought by activists is not lost, as the work becomes increasingly legitimated.

Other drug-user initiated public health

Drug users have organically organised and crafted an alternative approach to user-led community organising which is distinct from user groups in Europe, Canada and Australia. Users spurred a movement through the creation of non-profit organisations and by prioritising user self care. Users addressed health conditions such as endocarditis, abscesses, overdose, cotton fever, hydration, bleaching, hepatitis C, through the development of materials including posters, pamphlets and 'zines which were widely distributed, emulated and subsequently were incorporated into the mainstream healthcare world.

Users and activists self-trained to become wound care experts and treated soft tissue infections on site at harm reduction programmes. Soft tissue infections create tremendous suffering at tremendous cost (Takahashi et al., 2003); harm reductionists produced changes in surgical procedures. They also fought to get wound care clinics sited at needle exchanges rather than at hospitals where staff might be bigoted and where users would be less comfortable. Pioneering user-friendly changes in treatment have made it more likely that people get treatment sooner saving the system money and lessening the chance of wounds causing permanent maiming and disability (Ciccarone et al., 2001).

Since the beginning of the harm reduction movement in the US peer based home delivery of syringes in both urban and rural situations has been a standard offering alongside storefront and street-based syringe exchange. This is referred to as secondary exchange in the literature (Snead et al., 2003). The robust efforts and commitment of active users in secondary exchange has meant that syringe exchange have much more reach in injecting communities than their funding or staffing would both indicate and allow. The initial need for secondary exchange has grown from government neglect but its success reflects indigenous drug user organising and community commitment to disease prevention.

In the late 1990s, staff of the Chicago Recovery Alliance channeled their grief about needless drug overdoses by teaching rescue breathing and distributing naloxone (Bigg, 2011). In 2001 the DOPE Project was started in San Francisco. The health department began a collaboration with this project in 2003 (Enteen et al., 2010). In 2001, the New Mexico Department of Public Health began the first state funded overdose prevention project (Sporer and Kral, 2007). Now, 188 programs have been established in 15 states and Washington DC leading to 10,171 overdose reversals using naloxone (Wheeler et al., 2012). Like everything else, it began with activist syringe exchange staff illegally distributing naloxone to users.

At a pace attendant to the expanding availability of exchange programmes, harm reduction based social services increased in number, innovative programming was developed and implemented. Whereas initial programming was inspired and located at needle exchange programmes, the breadth of programmes providing harm reduction based services has extended into housing organisations, especially AIDS housing, shelters, mental health facilities, and drug treatment programmes among others. When adequately funded, services can include medical care, housing, mental health wound care, HIV/HCV/TB screening, testing and care, case management, support groups and spiritual counseling. As drug users often overuse emergency care, while remaining medically and socially under-served, community-based programmes are invaluable for decreasing morbidity and mortality (French et al., 2000).

It is important to underscore the necessity for such programming in the United States where access to healthcare is usually predicated upon one's ability to pay. The United States continues to be the only rich industrialised country without national health insurance. Furthermore, discrimination continues in medical settings based upon race/ethnicity and class (Williams, 1999). The behaviour of illicit drug use prompts even more discrimination. In 2010 the Harm Reduction Coalition initiated training for medical care personnel to reduce stigma and discrimination (Harm Reduction Coalition, 2010).

Anti-prison activism

Just as pro-incarceration politics and economics have dampened our abilities to do harm reduction, the activism to reduce incarceration has made it easier to support the lives and health of drug users. This activism ranges all over the political spectrum. Decidedly progressive activists like Critical Resistance and Dr Angela Davis, question the legitimacy of incarceration as a way of addressing social and behavioural disorder. They draw comparisons to the chattel slavery of African Americans, and call for abolition of the prison industrial complex (Davis, 2003). In contrast, we are seeing law makers from conservative districts call to decrease incarceration. These calls come from communities which support the premise of incarceration but which seek to reduce costs (Furillo, 2007). The five-fold increase in incarceration since the 1980s has led to enormous financial demands which can only be met in the anti-tax fiscal environment of the United States but the cutting of education, health and infrastructure. So increasingly, conservatives as well as liberals decry the seemingly bottomless pit of incarceration. And finally, we are seeing increasing activism about the more draconian elements of the drug wars. Recently, the Rockefeller laws, which led to the incarceration of tens of thousands of drug users in New York State were overturned (Peters, 2009). The crack/powder cocaine disparity is also being reduced (Eckholm, 2010). As of early 2010, fourteen states and the District of Colombia have legalised the medical use of cannabis in spite of the federal laws banning cannabis for medical or recreational purposes (Eddy, 2010). Harm reduction in the United States cannot proceed without the vigorous opposition to criminalisation and over-incarceration.

International solidarity

The harm reduction movement has remained entrenched in the public health response to HIV transmission due to the seriousness of the immediate threat of HIV to individual and public health and because that is very often the only funding stream for the work. HIV, however, comprises only a minute fraction of the harms users experience in their day-to-day lives and for the majority of users in the United States it is something that can be avoided. Drug related harm falls into two arenas: (1) the actual harm that a drug or a mixing of drugs can cause for an individual and (2) the harm caused by the approach to and application of drug policy. Due to limited resources, harm reduction activists have concentrated almost exclusively on the public health approach to drugs to the detriment of focusing on the main mechanisms of the creation of drug policy which resides with the Office of National Drug Control Policy (ONDCP). Without impacting national drug policy, the ability to improve health and social conditions for drug users is severely hampered – as can be seen by the difficulty of removing the federal ban on the funding of syringe exchange – due to the default position of prioritising law enforcement and drug treatment that adheres to the abstinence approach over the creation of an environment that enables individuals to use drugs in a safer way.

Drug policy is exported globally and reflects US national priorities to the exclusion of the desires of partner countries such as those of the European Union and the drug producing countries (Nadelmann, 1988). Until very recently the international bodies that shape and affect global drug policy, most notably the Commission on Narcotic Drugs (CND) and International Narcotics Control Board, have not been challenged by activists working to shape global drug policy within a human rights and public health framework, but this is now changing. This change also reflects the need to engage domestically with ONDCP. CND, a committee of the United Nations, is dominated by three powers: the United States, Russia and the European Union, and virtually all positions advanced at CND meetings generally reflect the interests of those entities. Japan also plays a major role in maintaining the status quo (Fazey, 2003).

As it does not reflect US interests abroad, the existence of a vibrant harm reduction community and the long-term existence of harm reduction interventions within the United States have not been reflected in its public positioning. In its conclusion of a 10-year review of progress on global policy, CND developed a political declaration that was birthed after a protracted and contentious diplomatic battle over the inclusion of harm reduction as a means of addressing drug demand reduction. Harm reduction did not appear in the final document and despite a consensus based process, 26 countries officially noted their disappointment.

As countries with emerging drug problems seek blueprints to develop their drug strategies they look to the United States and to the United Nations for direction and without having harm reduction as a significant plank in their planning, it will remain imbalanced. And users, their families and their communities are the most adversely affected. US activists have already made their presence felt as reflected in the US statement at the 2009 CND meeting that declared that the United States had accepted the efficacy of syringe exchange as an HIV intervention (Kerlikowske, 2010). Less than a year prior to this statement, ONDCP denied the scientific evidence in support of syringe exchange. Without pressure from the activist community, it is very unlikely that this position would have been publicised.

The US harm reduction movement has now been active since the 1980s. It has grown from a handful of concerned citizens to having a national (albeit still marginal(ised)) voice that has produced concrete change in the lives of drug users. To progress further, activists and policy analysts need to have sustained engagement with the branches of the federal government that develop and implement drug policy as well as continuing to interact with the branches of federal government that produce health policy. Drug users have been central to the development and dialogue that has propelled harm reduction policy and practice within the United States. As interventions and policy become institutionalised, it is imperative that those voices remain heard and their ideas implemented.

References

Abramsky, S. (2006) *Conned: How Millions Went to Prison, Lost The Vote, and Helped Send George Bush to the White House*, New York: New Press.

Alexander, M. (2010) *The New Jim Crow: Mass Incarceration in the Age of Colorblindness*, New York: New Press.

Anderson, W. (1991) The New York Needle Trial: the politics of public health in the age of AIDS, *Am J Public Health*, 81, 1506–17.

Baer, J.S. and Murch, H.B. (1998) Harm reduction, nicotine and smoking. In G.A. Marlatt (ed.), *Harm Reduction: Pragmatic Strategies for Managing High-Risk Behaviors*, New York: Guilford Press.

Bigg, D. (2011) *Chicago Recovery Alliance: Case Study*, http://harmreduction.org/issues/overdose-prevention/tools-best-practices/naloxone-program-case-studies/chicago-recovery-alliance/, accessed 5 March.

Carroll, L. (1946) *Through the Looking Glass*, Kingsport: Grosset and Dunlap.

Ciccarone, D., Bamberger, J., Kral, A. and Edlin, B. (2001) Soft tissue infections among injection drug users: San Francisco 1996–2000, *Morbidity and Mortality Weekly Report*, 50, 381–4.

Comprehensive Alcohol Abuse, Drug Abuse and Mental Health Amendments Act of 1988 (1988) Pub L No 100–690(Title II, Subtitle A) 102 Stat 4193 (Sec 2025 (2). (A)).

Courtwright, D.T. (1982) *Dark Paradise: Opiate Addition in America before 1940*, Cambridge, MA: Harvard University Press.

Coyle, M. (2002) *Race and Class Penalties in Crack Cocaine Sentencing*, Washington, DC: Sentencing Project.

Crimp, D. (1988) AIDS: cultural analysis/cultural activism. In D. Crimp (ed.), *AIDS: Cultural Analysis/Cultural Activism*, Boston: MIT Press.

Currie, E. (1993) *Reckoning: Drugs, the Cities and the American Future*, New York: Hill and Wang.

DANCESAFE (2011) http.//dancesafe.org/, accessed 27 February.

Davis, A.Y. (2003) *Are Prisons Obsolete*, New York City: Seven Stories Press.

Des Jarlais, D.C. (2006) Mathilde Krim, amfAR, and the prevention of HIV infection among injecting drug users: a brief history, *AIDS Patient Care STDS*, 20, 467–71.

Des Jarlais, D.C., McKnight, C. and Milliken, J. (2004) Public funding of US syringe exchange programs, *Journal of Urban Health*, 81, 118–21.

Des Jarlais, D.C., Perlis, T., Arasteh, K., Torian, L.V., Beatrice, S., Milliken, J., Mildvan, D., Yancovitz, S. and Friedman, S.R. (2005) HIV incidence among injection drug users in New York City, 1990 to 2002: use of serologic test algorithm to assess expansion of HIV prevention services, *Am J Public Health*, 95, 1439–44.

Des Jarlais, D.C., Perlis, T., Friedman, S.R., Deren, S., Chapman, T., Sotheran, J.L., Tortu, S., Beardsley, M., Paone, D., Torian, L.V., Beatrice, S.T., Debernardo, E., Monterroso, E. and Marmor, M. (1998) Declining seroprevalence in a very large HIV epidemic: injecting drug users in New York City, 1991 to 1996, *Am J Public Health*, 88, 1801–6.

Do It Now Foundation (2011) *Do It Now Foundation History*, www.doitnow.org/pages/history.html, accessed 27 February.

Downing, M., Riess, T.H., Vernon, K., Mulia, N., Hollinquest, M., McKnight, C., Des Jarlais, D.C. and Edlin, B. (2005) What's community got to do with it? Implementation models of syringe exchange, *Aids Education and Prevention*, 17, 68–78.

Dyer, J. (2000) *The Perpetual Prisoner Machine: How America Profits from Crime*, Boulder: Westview Press.

Eckholm, E. (2010) Congress moves to narrow cocaine sentencing disparities, *New York Times*, 29 July.

Eddy, M. (2010) *Medical Marijuana: Review and Analysis of Federal and State Policies*, Washington, DC: Congressional Research Service.

Editorial (2009) Righting a wrong, much too late, *New York Times*, 26 December.

Enteen, L., Bauer, J., McLean, R., Wheeler, E., Huriaux, E., Kral, A. and Bamberger, J. (2010). Overdose prevention and naloxone prescription for opioid users in San Francisco, *Journal of Urban Health*, 87, 931–41.

Epstein, E.J. (1990) *Agency of Fear: Opiates and Political Power in America*, New York: Putnam.

Fazey, C.S.J. (2003) The Commission on Narcotic Drugs and the United Nations International Drug Control Programme: politics, policies and prospect for change, *International Journal of Drug Policy*, 14, 155–69.

Fellner, J. (2000) *Punishment and Prejudice: Racial Disparities in the War on Drugs*, New York: Human Rights Watch.

French, M.T., McGeary, K.A., Chitwood, D.D. and McCoy, C.B. (2000) Chronic illicit drug use, health services utilization and the cost of medical care, *Social Science & Medicine*, 50, 1703–13.

Furillo, A. (2007) Ruling could spring inmates early: in a rare move, federal judges in Sacramento today will consider setting up a panel that may cap the state's burgeoning prison population, *Sacramento Bee*, 27 June, A3.

Gamson, J. (1989) Silence, death, and the invisible enemy: AIDS activism and social movement 'newness', *Social Problems*, 36, 351–67.

Harm Reduction Coalition (2010) *Understanding Drug-related Stigma: Tools for Better Practice and Social Change*, New York: Harm Reduction Coalition.

Harris, J.F. and Goldstein, A. (1998) Puncturing an AIDS initiative, *Washington Post*, 23 April.

Henricksen, K. (2000) Harm reduction in the rave community, *Focus*, 15, 1–4.

Kerlikowske, R.G. (2010) Opening statement of the Government of the United States of America before the 53rd UN Commission on Narcotic Drugs, Vienna: UN Commisson on Narcotic Drugs, 8 March.

Kolenda, J. (2000) A brief history of acupuncture for detoxification in the United States, *Acupuncture Today*, 1, 1–3.

Larimer, M.E., Marlatt, G.A., Baer, J.S., Quigley, L.A., Blume, A.W. and Hawkins, E.H. (1998) Harm reduction for alcohol problems: expanding access to and acceptibility of prevention and treatment services. In G.A. Marlatt (ed.), *Harm Reduction: Pragmatic Strategies for Managing High-risk Behaviors*, New York: Guilford Press.

Lazzarini, Z., Gostin, L.O., Flaherty, K.M. and Jones, T.S. (1996) Limitations on the sale and possession of syringes; results of a national survey of laws and regulations, 11th International AIDS Conference, Vancouver, 7–12 July.

Levine, H.G. (2003) Global drug prohibition: its uses and crises, *International Journal of Drug Policy*, 14, 145–53.

Lloyd, J. (2002) *Drug Use Trends*, Washington, DC: Office of National Drug Control Policy.

Lurie, P., Reingold, A., Bowser, B., Chen, D., Foley, J., Guydish, J., Kahn, J., Lane, S. and Sorensen, J. (1993) *The Public Health Impact of Needle Exchange Programs in the United States and Abroad*, Atlanta: Centers for Disease Control and Prevention.

Maurer, M. and Chesney-Lind, M. (eds) (2002) *Invisible Punishment: The Collateral Consequences of Mass Imprisonment*, New York: New Press.

McAllister, W.B. (2000) *Drug Diplomacy in the Twentieth Century: An International History*, London: Routledge.

McCoy, A.W. (1972) *The Politics of Heroin: CIA Complicity in the Global Drug Trade*, New York: Harper and Row.

Merritt, J. (2004) *Reagan's Drug War Legacy*, Alternet, 2011, www.alternet.org/drugs/18990/, accessed 26 February.

Moore, L.D. (1995) In harm's way, *Crossroads*, 56, 14–17.

Moore, L.D. and Wenger, L.D. (1995) The social context of needle exchange and user self-organization in San Francisco: possibilities and pitfalls, *Journal of Drug Issues*, 25, 583–98.

Morales, F. (1992) Methadone: genocide of the poor. In K. Hollander (ed.), *Chemical City*, New York: Portable Lower East Side.

Morgan, H.W. (1981) *Drugs in America: A Social History 1800–1980*, Syracuse: Syracuse University Press.

Musto, D. (1987) *The American Disease*, New York: Oxford University Press.

Nadelmann, E.A. (1988) U.S. drug policy: a bad export, *Foreign Policy*, 70, 83–108.

Newman, R.G. (1990) Advocacy for methadone treatment, *Annals of Internal Medicine*, 113, 819–20.

Nisker, W.S. (2004) *The Big Bang, The Buddha and the Baby Boom*, San Francisco: Harper Collins.

Peters, J.W. (2009) Albany reaches deal to repeal '70s drug laws, *New York Times*, 26 March.

Pfaelzer, J. (2007) *Driven Out: The Forgotten War against Chinese Americans*, New York: Random House.

Pollack, H.A. and d'Aunno, T. (2008) Dosage patterns in methadone treatment: results from a National Survey 1988–2005, *Health Services Research*, 43, 2143–63.

Reinarman, C. and Levine, H.G. (1997a) The crack attack. In C. Reinarman and H.G. Levine (eds), *Crack in America: Demon Drugs and Social Justice*, Berkeley: University of California Press.

Reinarman, C. and Levine, H.G. (1997b) Crack in context. In C. Reinarman and H.G. Levine (eds), *Crack in America: Demon Drugs and Social Justice*, Berkeley: University of California Press.

Rohleder, L., van Meter, S., Cooper, M., Gulbransen, M., Goldfedder, J. and Vella, J. (2009) *Acupuncture Is Like Noodles: The Little Red (Cook) Book of Working Class Acupuncture*, Portland, OR: Working Class Acupuncture.

Rosenbaum, M. (1995) The demedicalization of methadone maintenance, *Journal of Psychoactive Drugs*, 27, 145–9.

Schwartzapfel, B. (2010) Swapping politics for science on drug policy, *The Nation*.

Sherman, S.G. and Purchase, D. (2001) Point defiance: a case study of the United States' first public needle exchange in Tacoma, Washington, *Int J Drug Policy*, 12, 45–57.

Snead, J., Downing, M., Lorvick, J., Garcia, B., Thawley, R., Kegeles, S. and Edlin, B. (2003) Secondary syringe exchange among injection drug users, *Journal of Urban Health*, 80, 330–48.

Sorge, R. (1990) A thousand points . . . needle exchange around the country, *Health PAC Bulletin*, 20, 16–22.

Sporer, K.A. and Kral, A.H. (2007) Prescription Naloxone: a novel approach to heroin overdose prevention, *Annals of Emergency Medicine*, 49, 172–7.

Stollberg, S.G. (1998) Clinton decides not to finance needle program, *New York Times*, 21 April.

Takahashi, T., MerrilL, J., Boyko, E. and Bradley, K. (2003) Type and location of injection drug use-related soft tissue infections predict hospitalization, *Journal of Urban Health*, 80, 127–36.

Takaki, R. (1993) *A Different Mirror: A History of Multicultural America*, Boston, MA: Little Brown.

United Nations Office on Drugs and Crime (2010) *World Drug Report*, New York: United Nations.

Vlahov, D., Des Jarlais, D.C., Goosby, E., Hollinger, P.C., Lurie, P.G., Shriver, M.D. and Strathdee, S.A. (2001) Needle exchange programs for the prevention of human immunodeficiency virus infection: epidemiology and policy, *American Journal of Epidemiology*, 154, S70–S77.

Waley, A., (1958) *The Opium War Through Chinese Eyes*, Palo Alto: Stanford University Press.

Wheeler, E., Davidson, P.J., Jones, T.S. and Irwin, K.S. (2012) Community-based opioid overdose prevention programs providing naloxone – United States, 2010, *Morbidity and Mortality Weekly Report*, 61 (6) 101–5.

Williams, D.R., (1999) Race, socioeconomic status, and health: the added effects of racism and discrimination, *Annals of the New York Academy of Sciences*, 896, 173–88.

Chapter 28

HARM REDUCTION IN CANADA: THE MANY FACES OF REGRESSION

Walter Cavalierri and Diane Riley

The authors dedicate this chapter to the memory of Jack Layton, friend and colleague, leader of Canada's New Democratic Party, who died in August of 2011 at age 61. In his eloquent letter to Canadians, released the day after he died, Jack called on us to join together to build on the work he left unfinished, and he left us a guide to how to do it:

'My friends,' he wrote, 'love is better than anger. Hope is better than fear. Optimism is better than despair. So let us be loving, hopeful and optimistic. And we'll change the world.'

Historical background to harm reduction in Canada

Drug policy

The legal framework of the current system of drug control in Canada was laid down in the early part of the twentieth century. In 1908, all medicines, as well as tobacco and alcohol, were on the way to regulation and the Opium Act created drug prohibition, the basis of the current system. An increase in illicit drug use in the 1960s and 1970s was met by greatly increased criminalisation and the associated individual and social costs. Rates of use climbed sharply through the 1960s and early 1970s, despite a large allocation of enforcement resources (Erickson, 1992). The strain on the courts, and the rising numbers of otherwise law-abiding youth being sentenced for drug offences (particularly cannabis possession) created pressures for the liberalisation of Canada's drug laws. The Commission of Inquiry in the Non-Medical Use of Drugs (1972, generally referred to as the Le Dain Commission) was formed in 1969 to address this growing concern about drug use and appropriate responses.

The Le Dain Commission described and analysed the social costs and individual consequences of the criminalisation policy and represents an important step in the development of a policy of harm reduction in Canada. Following much consultation and study, the Le Dain Commission inquiry concluded that drug prohibition results in high costs but relatively little benefit. The majority of the commissioners recommended a gradual withdrawal from criminal sanctions against people who use illicit drugs, along with the development of less coercive and costly alternatives to replace the punitive application of criminal law. The Le Dain Commission served the role of most Royal Commissions: it delayed action on a controversial issue long enough for the public demand for action to subside. Interest in reform of drug policy gradually declined (Single et al., 1991). Attempts to reduce the consequences of criminalisation met with limited success.

Harm Reduction in Substance Use and High-Risk Behaviour: International Policy and Practice, First Edition.
Edited by Richard Pates and Diane Riley.
© 2012 Blackwell Publishing Ltd. Published 2012 by Blackwell Publishing Ltd.

By the mid-1980s there was growing acknowledgment of the serious limitations of law enforcement and education in reducing the demand for drugs. In 1987 the Canadian federal government announced 'Action on Drug Abuse', Canada's Drug Strategy. Canada's Drug Strategy (CDS) gave a means to address substance use with both supply and demand reduction strategies. The new drug strategy brought $210 million in new funding in roughly equal amounts to enforcement, treatment and prevention programming and had the aim of reducing drug-related harm. It defined harm as 'sickness, death, social misery, crime, violence and economic costs to all levels of government'. Canada's Drug Strategy was funded for an initial five-year term ending in April 1992 and was renewed to 1997. The Canadian Centre on Substance Abuse was founded in 1990 as part of this strategy. In its Policy and research Unit, Diane Riley and Eric Single researched and documented alternatives to drug prohibition and promoted the principles and practice of harm reduction and other evidence-based approaches. This unit, often under criticism for its anti-prohibitionist stance, was shut down in 1996 as part of the demise of the drug strategy (Oscapella and Riley, 1997). In Riley's approach, what came to be called pillars were tightly integrated threads, not distinct entities (Riley, 1993; Riley et al., 1999). The term 'Drug Strategy' was reapplied to the remaining efforts in 1998, but it is a strategy without the weight, collaborators, or funding of the forerunners. with drug issues being brought under the general umbrella of 'population health'.

With the introduction of a new drug law in the 1990s, there was an opportunity to address some of the problems of past law and to benefit from what had been learned from the experience of other countries. The new law, the *Controlled Drugs and Substances Act*, however, is soundly prohibitionist; and rather than retreating from the drug war rhetoric of the past it expands the net of prohibition further still. The problems related to criminalising people who use illicit drugs, the social and economic costs of this approach, and its failure to reduce drug availability have still not been addressed. As a result, the costs, both financial and human, of licit drug use remain unnecessarily high while the costs of criminalising illicit drug use continue to rise, steadily, predictably and avoidably. The result: harms increased rather than reduced (Oscapella and Riley, 1997).

In 1994 the Canadian Foundation for Drug Policy (CFDP) was created and during the next several years this small NGO helped to bring about some drug reform, including the legalisation of medical marijuana. In 1999 members of the CFDP wrote a review of drug policy in Canada for the Senate with a view to drug policy reform (Riley, 1998). In 2000 the Senate began an inquiry into the non-medical use of drugs and soon after the House of Commons began its own review of drug policy. The results of both reviews were disappointing, with the most significant being that the Senate called for legalisation of cannabis, but there was little resulting change in policy or practice.

Harm reduction programmes

As in other countries, harm reduction in various forms has been practised for centuries but not explicitly labelled as such. The first form of harm reduction as we define it today was practised in the early 1980s in Toronto, Ontario, in the form of controlled drinking programmes (Riley and O'Hare, 2000). In 1987, as concerns rose in the community about the spread of HIV through injection drug use, bleach programmes were started at Alexandra Park in Toronto; these developed into syringe exchange programmes in 1988 and were taken over by the City of Toronto in 1989 (Riley and McCrimmon, 1988). A grant application submitted by Jack Layton (leader of the New Democratic Party), then Chair of the Toronto Board of Health, and Diane Riley to the Federal government received $11 million in AIDS funding over three years, including funds for syringe exchange and other harm reduction initiatives. This helped to ensure low prevalence of HIV among IDU in that city (Riley, 1993; CPHA, 1994). Syringe exchange programmes were started in Montreal and Vancouver in 1989, and in other urban and rural communities across Canada in the following years (CPHA, 1994). A number of NGOs began to conduct workshops on harm reduction and to carry out advocacy throughout Canada and then internationally. In the late 1980s and early 1990s the number of methadone programmes in Canada increased significantly and became somewhat more liberal in nature.

As in many countries, the real impetus for harm reduction was the rise of HIV infection among injection drug users. In Canada, injection drug use is second only to homosexual/bisexual activity as a means of HIV transmission in men and second only to heterosexual acquisition in women. These individuals are concentrated, for the most part, in the metropolitan areas of larger cities, but there is injection drug use in most urban and rural areas of Canada. In 1997 a health emergency was declared as a result of the rapid increase of HIV infection in injection drug users in Vancouver's Downtown East Side. Prevalence levels had reached more than 20% and incidence rates more than 10%. In 1998, prevalence rates were estimated at between 25 and 35% (Vancouver/Richmond Health Board, HIV Reports; BC Ministry of Health AIDS Surveillance Reports). These rates placed Vancouver in the unenviable position of having the highest levels of HIV infection in injection drug users in the western world. In addition, Vancouver has had the highest levels of overdose deaths in Canada, with more than 3,000 since 1991. The high levels of infection and other drug-related problems have been linked to the poverty and social dislocation of many of the residents of some of its neighbourhoods. This outbreak was one of the main forces behind Vancouver's move toward harm reduction policies and programmes and sent a strong warning message to other cities in Canada, sadly, by no means always heeded (see below).

Traditionally, heroin has been the main drug administered by injection in Canada; Talwin (a depressant) and Ritalin (a stimulant) have also been popular as injectables at various times in different parts of the country, and are still very popular in some provinces. Since the 1990s, cocaine and methamphetamine have been used increasingly by injection drug users, either on their own or in combination with heroin (Riley, 2008). There is also increasing non-medical use of injectable steroids by athletes, dancers and the general male population throughout Canada. Cocaine, in the form of crack, is the most universally used drug in Canada – typically it is smoked, but it is also injected. Prescription opiates have grown in popularity and are readily available through dealers.

Rates of HIV among drug injectors in Canadian cities range from approximately 5% to more than 30%. Some regions of Canada report higher incidence rates, especially among Natives and in correctional institutions (see chapter by Jurgens in this volume) Aboriginal peoples are overrepresented in inner-city injection drug use communities and among clientele using inner-city services such as needle exchange programmes and counseling/referral sites. It is important to note that hepatitis C is a more important issue for most drug users in Canada than is HIV.

Recent developments

The current status of harm reduction in Canada, at both the policy and programme level, is best described as 'in regression'. There are two types of regression; structural regression is the 'natural' process of sanitising that sets in when something radical is institutionalised or professionalised and becomes part of the mainstream, when it 'comes of age'. This is a slow, insidious type of regression. The second type of regression is deliberate and swifter than the first type, and it is often ideologically driven.

Ideologically driven regression has moved Canada's federal drug strategy away from harm reduction. As noted above, the National Drug Strategy of 1987, as well as its revisions in 1992 and 1998, acknowledged the existence of harm reduction. This was a somewhat brave move, even in this essentially prohibitionist and enforcement-oriented strategy, because of Canada's proximity to the United States, with its war on drugs. Good words were far more numerous than good actions, and the majority of funds dispersed under the drug strategies continued to be dedicated to enforcement. According to the Auditor General, in 1991 95% of federal expenditures related to illicit drugs were used for drug law enforcement, with little success to show for it. This percentage has been only slightly modified since then.

The impact of having a 'balanced' drug strategy – even if it was in name only – was ambiguous. On the one hand, federal recognition of harm reduction as a viable public health measure gave licence to supporters in the community as well as in the public service to engage in implementing harm reduction policies and practices, albeit unevenly, across Canada and also gave provinces and municipalities the impetus to incorporate harm reduction into their own drug strategies. Currently, four provinces and two territories explicitly advocate for or include harm reduction as a component of their strategies, as do nine cities and municipalities. One of those cities is Vancouver, whose 'Framework for Action' initiated, in 2001, Canada's infatuation with the concept of 'Four Pillars': harm reduction, prevention, treatment and enforcement.

On the other hand, the federal government's shameless lack of reasonable support for harm reduction and its commitment to enforcement maintained Canada's affection for prohibition and set up harm reduction as a lightening rod for controversy. Harm reduction programmes and services are always forced to prove their worth, even in the face of overwhelming evidence that indeed they *do* work, both on a scientific level and on the level of 'what is right'. Core programme funding continued to be difficult to get, and little if anything was done to address underlying issues which support substance dependency: poverty, trauma, mental illness, stigma, lack of honest information about drugs and drug use, lack of compassion, inequity and disrespect. At the same time, harm reduction was expanding its focus well beyond HIV and HCV prevention, and took it upon itself addressing social justice and the right to health for people using illicit drugs, incorporating the best of health promotion.

In 2008, with the Liberals losing control of governing Canada to neo-conservatives, led by Stephen Harper, the duplicity and hypocrisy of surrounding harm reduction's place in Canada's drug strategy ended. The Liberal's dithering about harm reduction begat the withering that the current government is all too happy to accelerate (Riley and Oscapella, 2006; 2007). Among its earliest actions was the prime minister's announcement of its $64-million-dollar National *Anti-Drug* Strategy.

The National Anti-Drug Strategy was developed through close collaboration between the Canadian government's ministers and senior bureaucrats from the Bush White House, and was stripped of all mention of not just harm reduction in general, but of needle exchange specifically. Harper also put an end to the prior government's plan to decriminalise possession of small quantities of marijuana and removed drug issues from the Ministry of Health, leaving them solely under the jurisdiction of the Ministry of Justice.

The government also promoted a stringent 'law 'n' order' agenda about crime in general, and in particular, youth and drug crime – despite a drop in both the volume and severity of crime consistent over the past few years. The Anti-Drug's Strategy's views are simplistic: drugs are the principal cause of crime, and the best weapons against drugs are incarceration, longer prison sentences, property seizure, and just-say-no-to-drugs education, all of which have spotty records. Under the Anti-Drug Strategy, 70% of the funding is allocated to law enforcement, 4% to prevention; 17% to treatment, and 2% to harm reduction, even though it is not listed in it.

The Conservative's claimed that the Liberals had put Canada on the road to drug legalisation and that they intended to stop this (in truth, legalisation was never the Liberal agenda). Saying that parents and police alike know that the last thing Canada needs is more drugs on our streets, they have declared that get-tough-on-crime-and-criminals policies are needed fix this; prison reform measures are particularly heinous. They have vowed to end house arrests, cut back on probation, and ensure mandatory minimum prison sentences and large fines for 'serious' drug offenders, including marijuana growers and dealers of crystal meth and crack; to prevent the decriminalisation of marijuana; to beef up law enforcement; and to seriously undermine the rights of incarcerated people. All these measures have been passed or are underway.

Despite evidence that this American-style approach has been such a disaster and that even the Americans are retreating from it, a significant proportion of the Canadian electorate is embracing it, largely without informed public debate. Yet this agenda benefits no one save those involved in the illegal trade and black market and the prison-industrial complex. Drugs are more available than ever, stronger and in greater variety, and people continue to be incarcerated, get longer sentences and – even worse – die of highly preventable diseases and conditions. Further, in Canada, the war on drugs has been conflated with its war on terrorism. Canada's supports anti-drug operations in Afghanistan to the tune of many millions, and our troops are heavily involved in this.

Harper's Conservatives blatantly attack harm reduction in their policies (e.g., tough-on-crime bills, continually trying to shut down the safe injection site, Insite), and in their discourses (e.g., distributing pamphlets fraught with inflammatory anti-drug-user and anti-harm-reduction messages).

In the summer of 2007, staff from the Canadian Harm Reduction Network and the Canadian AIDS Society travelled from coast to coast to coast in Canada, researching the state of harm reduction in small-to-medium-sized cities. One result of this project was the report *Learning from Each Other: Enhancing Community-Based Harm Reduction Programs and Practices in Canada* (2008). It was found that, though programmes were sometimes insufficient and spotty, a great deal of inventive and effective work was being done. There was hope, then, that things would get better for people using drugs – even though it was tempered by growing apprehension about the direction of the new federal government.

Three years on, the balance between hope and concern has shifted. There have been no major leaps forward in the provision of services for people who use drugs, and we do the best we can now to maintain what we have and not make waves. In some cases this may mean serving people inadequately or even degrading or undermining harm reduction. Science is vilified, caring is scorned, and mean-spiritedness is becoming institutionalised. When it comes to harm reduction, we are a nation in regression.

A brief overview of harm reduction across Canada[1]

The Territories

The northernmost part of Canada comprises three Territories: Yukon and Northwest Territories and Nunavut. The land area is vast: nearly 4,000,000 square kilometres. The population is small: just over 100,000 people. In the Yukon Territory, the challenges for harm reduction are formidable and include lack of anonymity, sparse populations over large areas, and limited funding. While not

---

[1] This overview is drawn largely from *Learning from Each Other* and an informal survey of members of the Canadian Harm Reduction Network

unlike the situation throughout rural Canada, it is much more so, and people have come up with imaginative solutions tailored to local needs. In Whitehorse (the capital) services have a quality that is much stronger than in other parts of the country: broad community collaboration. Agencies, a service club, volunteers, the local college and community members work together to address the joint issues of drug use and poverty. Programmes are embedded in the community itself, and no one agency takes heat for problems or prejudice. Whitehorse's harm reduction programme is operated by a partnership of three community agencies and Yukon College. The outreach van programme, receives financial backing from the Territorial Government, while some local restaurants provide food and coffee. These collaborations mean that harm reduction is a community initiative in which many have ownership.

The territorial government allows a safer crack kit distribution programme to operate, but does not fund supplies, which are paid for by the local Rotary Club. A spanner in the works is SCAN – the Safer Community and Neighbourhoods programme – which is territory-wide. SCAN programmes have been sprouting up across Canada; they encourage citizens to contact their offices through 'snitch lines' when they suspect that activities such as producing, selling or using illegal drugs, sex work, solvent use or the unlawful sale and consumption of alcohol are taking place in their neighbourhood. Complaints are kept anonymous and result in a boldly coloured lawn or door sign on the residence of the offending person, informing all that it is under surveillance An investigation by the SCAN team of law enforcement personnel eventually takes place. 'Remedies' such as closing down the residence, evicting the occupants and seizing their assets may be applied. Alternative housing and support and treatment for the occupants may be offered; but, in Whitehorse outreach workers state that most people who had been 'marked' simply disappear and cannot be provided with services. Eviction in Whitehorse is cruel and callous. Winter temperatures there often exceed 40 degrees celsius below zero.

The Province of British Columbia is seen by many as the leader in harm reduction in Canada. Though not necessarily an accurate assessment, it *is* the perception, largely because of Insite, Canada's best known safe injection site (this is one of two safe injection sites in Vancouver; the other is at the Dr Peter Centre); VANDU, Canada's largest drug user group; the NAOMI trial (North American Opiate Maintenance Initiative), which successfully addressed recalcitrant opiate addictions with heroin or dilaudid; and the Portland Hotel Society, whose 'Harm Reduction Housing' programme has, since 1993, promoted, developed and maintained supportive, affordable lodging for adult individuals who are considered 'hard to house' and at the highest risk of homelessness. Their principal residents are people with HIV/AIDS, substance misuse problems, forensic issues, mental illness and/or concurrent disorders.

In 2001, Donald MacPherson, Vancouver's Drug Policy Coordinator unveiled Canada's first urban drug strategy, Vancouver's 'Framework for Action', a 'four pillar' approach: harm reduction, prevention, treatment and enforcement. Recently, MacPherson resigned his post and he is not being replaced. Vancouver is a major public battle ground for the federal government's war on harm reduction. Their principal focus is Incite, started in 2003, after many years of planning by local and national activists. Despite its clear success in preventing overdoses and other personal and community harms, the federal government have repeatedly tried to shut it down (see, e.g., Kerr et al., 2005; Wood et al., 2005). The RCMP, too, campaigns against Insite, contributing to public misinformation. Some workers have suggested that Vancouver's preoccupation with Insite is impeding the development of other, much-needed harm reduction services, especially in the suburbs and rural areas. Insite remains open, and other sites for safe injection and inhalation have been proposed in British Columbia and Quebec, but none has moved beyond the speculative stage.

The province is cutting prevention-focused community support for people using drugs, including treatment. They have scrapped many contracts with community social service agencies which work with people suffering from both mental illness and addiction. In many parts of the province, outreach to people who use crack is woefully incomplete: Pyrex pipe stems are not supplied. There is considerable community activism, however, around decriminalisation of marijuana. BC has some of the most innovative harm reduction programmes for women in Canada, including Fir Square and Sheway for pregnant women and mothers.

Victoria, the capital of British Columbia, has an open drug scene second only to Vancouver's. Victoria has been without a fixed-site needle exchange since May 2008 because: residents and businesses object and politicians claim it 'not ready' for a fixed site. Syringes are available in two public health offices, but users tend not to go there. There is some mobile exchange organised by the drug users themselves but mobile services are not allowed in certain sections of the city, including some where drug use is highest. Coquitlam is part of greater Vancouver; in an effort to make it more 'family-friendly', the city will ban exotic dancing and methadone clinics. In another city, Abbotsford, the council has passed an anti-harm reduction bylaw.

The prairies

Recently, the Province of Alberta centralised its health services. Consequences of this move include the loss as of local autonomy and the Non-Prescription Needle Use Initiative, a very effective provincial drug and harm reduction networking scheme. Funds, programmes and staff for programmes practising harm reduction have been cut; coordinated services downgraded; regional needs and differences dismissed; and the province's annual harm reduction conference cancelled. Programmes across the province are no longer able to come together routinely, and many opportunities for training or policy discussion have been curtailed. This has led to greater isolation, fewer mentorship opportunities, diminished opportunities to track trends across the province and less partnership work. A highly successful collaborative model has been replaced with one based on competition among communities for scarce funding. Even so, Edmonton has found a way to continue to support drug user organising and also maintain its innovative overdose-death-prevention programme which provides peers with a supply of naloxone, which they can use to save the lives of people overdosing on opiates. It is the only programme of its kind in Canada.

Within a political atmosphere that is hyper-responsive to public opinion, especially that driven by conservative family and social values it is difficult for policy-makers to support harm reduction publicly, though many seem to favour it privately. The creation of fear is a common theme in Alberta. People pursuing harm reduction activities and applying for funding for programmes report that almost universally report that they avoid words 'harm reduction'.

Saskatchewan's rates of HIV/AIDS are currently the highest in Canada – 20.3 per 100,000 as opposed to the national rate of 9.3, with 75% of those cases found in injection drug users. Its premier wants to halt unlimited needle distribution and mandate a limit of ten needles per visit in all its needle exchange programmes, despite an earlier government-ordered review that found the existing system helps curb disease and reduce healthcare costs. He has, however, offered no new funding for these interventions. In Regina, Saskatchewan's capital city, the return rate of used needles is 94%, one of the highest in the world. Should the premier study what happened in Vancouver in the 1990s, he would see how foolish and ill-informed his idea is: it was tried there; and, before it was altered, Vancouver had attained the highest HIV rate of any major first-world city. Like Vancouver, Saskatchewan's injectable drug of choice is cocaine.

Ontario and Quebec

In Ontario there is ambivalence about harm reduction, but it continues to lead the way in Canada in the implementation of needle distribution and, in some area, crack kits. That leadership is based on a 2006 publication, Ontario Needle Exchange Programs: Best Practice Recommendations. The application of these best practice guidelines is uneven, and some public health personnel still consider needle exchange as 'enabling'. More extensive scorn is directed toward crack kit distribution, including by a number of Medical Officers of Health. Although smaller towns and rural areas continue to be very seriously under-served, there is increased awareness about harm reduction's efficacy in medium-sized cities such as Sudbury, Thunder Bay, Kingston and Kitchener-Waterloo. Methadone is available across the province, though the provincial guidelines for methadone treatment draw strong criticism from clients because of their restrictiveness. There is little access for methadone treatment in locations away from cities and towns, and clinics still have to fight business and residents' associations over locations.

The province recently completed its ten-year mental health and addiction strategy. It was a struggle to ensure that the voice of the drug user was included at a volume even half that of the mental health client, and the strategy is to be accomplished without any new funding.

Even now, though most of those who provide services to people who use or at risk of using illicit drugs are aware of harm reduction, many don't understand what harm reduction really is and neglect even its most basic principle. Worse, many construe it solely as an intervention rather than a way of working, which means that both its health promotion and social justice planks may be ignored. This narrowness is not unique to Ontario.

The city of Ottawa is conservative in its approach to harm reduction; the current police chief continues to lobby for 1-for-1 needle exchange. A few years ago, led by a mayor disinclined to respect evidence, Ottawa closed its highly successful safer crack kit programme. The province's ministry of health subsequently stepped in and saved it by funding a community health centre to take it over. Ottawa does what it must and can do, but there is a sense that homeless people, most of whom do use illicit drugs, are no longer welcome there.

Toronto has long had a vibrant harm reduction community, initiated by a combination of community activists, front-line workers, people with current drug-use experience, academics and even some city politicians. The AIDS Network of Toronto (later the Harm Reduction Network), established in 1987, conducted education and provided syringe exchange, setting up Canada's first needle exchange in a community housing project in 1988. Toronto then led the way in Canada in setting up decentralised needle exchanges under the leadership of Public Health. There are now approximately 30 needle exchange sites across the city, plus a mobile programme. Canada's first drug users' group was established in Toronto in 1991, the FUN Group, and it is still operating. In 1994 the group produced Canada's first video on safer injecting, FIT, and marketed it internationally.

It is encouraging that Toronto has a comprehensive drug strategy and that harm reduction plays a central role in it. However, as in the now defunct federal government drug strategies, no real money has ever been allocated to realising the strategy's potential, and harm reduction is left vulnerable. Toronto has engaged in a five-year effort to sort out whether or not it should set up safe drug-use rooms. Harm reduction has a high profile in the city, but it also has its opponents: neighbourhood and business organisations, police and opportunistic politicians being the most prominent; Toronto's Police Service have maintained a 'War on Drugs' mentality.

Programmes in urban Quebec have been daring and effective, largely because early on they adopted harm reduction as a core principal and made extensive use of indigenous knowledge. Harm reduction was accepted in a full range of institutional and community organisations, including the CACTUS needle exchange, one of Canada's first such programmes. Lately, political support for harm reduction programmes has been slipping and funding more difficult to obtain. Harm reduction has been subjected to baseless criticism from many provincial and municipal politicians and funding has been withdrawn from successful programmes and services.

In the Quebec legislative assembly, the deputy leader of the opposition claimed that a cocaine harm reduction information card produced by a leading Montreal agency was promoting cocaine use. The opposition party has criticised needle exchange and the minister of health will not support the establishment of a safe injection site. The highly praised book, *Drogues: savoir plus, risquer moins*, with over 125,000 copies already in distribution, was pulled off the market: it was too friendly to harm reduction.

In Quebec City, the major harm reduction programme, Point de repères, is fighting for its life, being pushed out of a high-drug-use neighbourhood to facilitate gentrification. For many years, this neighbourhood has been the home base for a large community of illicit drug users; Point de repères is being framed as the reason that these people are coming to the neighbourhood, rather than it being recognised that the agency is in the neighbourhood because the drug users are already there. Quebec City is again enforcing the law that anyone caught with drug paraphernalia (needles, pipes, etc.) will be fined.

Atlantic provinces

In these eastern-most provinces (Nova Scotia; Prince Edward Island; New Brunswick; Newfoundland and Labrador), harm reduction services tend to be more constrained, and even in the cities they stay as conservative as the government, in order to maintain their funding. The focus of needle exchange programmes continues to be mostly on the syringe itself, with access to other safer injecting supplies being limited, as are crack kits, even though the demand for them has increased, often surpassing that for needles as drug-use patterns have changed. The availability of methadone is far more restricted than in Ontario or Quebec. In the past few years, there has been some additional outreach into rural areas, but it is insufficient in coverage and scope of service provision. Satellite harm reduction sites remain scarce, the development of networks of drug users or dealers who can distribute harm reduction equipment has not really taken place, and a culture of clean needle and disposal access is not well supported. Many people see harm reduction as a do-gooders' activity that coddles people who use drugs and helps them to stay hooked, at the taxpayers' expense.

In Nova Scotia, there is no provincial leadership for harm reduction. The needle exchange in the capital, Halifax, in operation since 1992, still exists by grace of discretionary 'grants', not permanent funding, and opportunities for sharing information and ideas, developing provincial or regional strategies or providing basic client support simply don't exist, unless it is through research projects. Programme funding, as elsewhere, is often tied to short-term pilot projects, a dismal practice, with no guarantee of continuity for the programme or the staff; 'Death by pilot' is a common joke. There is also the threat, here as elsewhere, that harm reduction services will be subsumed into a generic mental health and addiction basket, where addiction will play second fiddle to mental health and harm reduction will all but disappear. In this scenario, while it's impossible to fault people for becoming schizophrenic, it's easy to blame (and shame) them for becoming drug-dependent.

The increased presence of police around needle exchanges, as has been the case in Halifax, is ominous. The tensions caused by this and the limitations put on the number of crack pipes available elevate tension and are used to 'justify' municipal sweeps of established street communities. One Chief of Police, in Moncton, New Brunswick, acknowledges the futility of the revolving door approach in which people move in and out of jail and get sicker; recognising the efficacy of nursing and social work interventions; he has become a proponent for harm reduction.

Through all of this, Maritimers remain pragmatic, and there is quiet support for harm reduction. There seem to be more people talking about harm reduction initiatives as a practical approach to addressing the problems arising from illicit drug use – as long as they are not situated in their neighbourhoods. There are also more researchers participating in and fostering community-based research with a focus on harm reduction. This is providing an opportunity to train community researchers and to reach new people with the messages about what 'least harm' might mean. Because of government disdain for harm reduction some workers have become surreptitious and clandestine in providing services necessary for helping people stay alive until they are ready to make changes in their use of substances This noble form of anarchism maintains the stigma endured by people who use drugs. At the same time it makes workers themselves vulnerable and causes burn-out; this is a worker issue throughout Canada.

At-risk groups

There are a number of groups in Canada who would benefit from additional harm reduction services. All of them have elevated rates of HIV. These include, but are not limited to, youth, women, Aboriginal/First Nations people, transgender and transsexual persons, and prisoners. Abstinence-only approaches are widespread, despite their demonstrated shortcomings.

Women, particularly those who work in the sex trade, need special programmes; but few exist. The most effective are those few run by current or former sex-trade workers, most of which are in a constant struggle for funding, especially now that 'family values' are once again in the ascendancy, and the rights of women are being subverted. Many women do not know how to inject drugs properly. This renders them dependent on their partners, who use this as a means of control and to disallow them from making essential life and safety choices; this situation could be rectified through safe drug use sites. Pregnant women and mothers also need programmes which address their needs; there are far too few of these in Canada. Of those programmes that do exist, some of the best programmes are in Vancouver and Toronto; these programmes, too, are at risk.

Transgendered people are the most severely marginalised and least well understood sexual minority; they don't fit in traditional agencies and are often mocked, stigmatised and dismissed because of who they are. They are also at very high risk of drug-related harm, including HIV/AIDS and hepatitis C. There has been little if any change in their status within the communities they interact with, and they receive no recognition from most governments; agencies who work with them struggle for funding.

Prisoners are one of the highest risk groups for injection-related communicable diseases, especially HIV/AIDS and hepatitis C. Yet, healthcare on the inside is far from the equivalent of that on the outside. Corrections Canada closed down a successful safer tattooing programme in its prisons. It steadfastly refuses to consider making new needles available to prison inmates, despite constant pressure from community groups since the 1990s and despite the fact that prison syringe programmes have been successfully implemented elsewhere. It is not that Corrections Canada denies that inmates use drugs and that, as a consequence, some get infected with HIV or HCV while they are incarcerated; in fact, they admit in meetings (but not on paper) that such infection is known to occur in their institutions. It is likely that this situation will only change when legal action is taken (as occurred with methadone availability); a number of NGOs are working on a legal challenge (for more details on prisons in Canada and around the world, see chapter 7, this volume).

Most Aboriginal and First Nations communities continue to embrace and promote an abstinence-based approach to drug use issues, despite all evidence that its treatment and tools do not work for the majority of people who attempt them or on whom they are imposed. Canadian Aboriginals have very high rates of HIV and hepatitis C, suicide and premature death, intense and unbearable poverty, and extreme levels of incarceration: the prison system is the new residential school. Homeless Aboriginal people in Canadian cities may receive the benefit of harm reduction programming. Most live in rural and remote parts of Canada, where the extent of harm reduction, if there is any, is usually in the form of secondary needle exchange and little else. Some Aboriginal leaders recognise that harm reduction could fit into traditional thinking and practices, but most don't; there is much work to be done in this area.

Conclusion

Changes in the practice of social work over the past decades shed light on the structural reduction regression taking place in harm reduction in Canada. Early social work was a magnet for progressive reformers with a strong commitment to social justice, actualised through social action. The ability to show independence of thinking and commitment to justice were the qualities that made the traditional social worker a 'professional'. By the 1950s, social work had virtually deserted idealistic intellectualism and in the process relinquished the utopian vision that guided early practitioners. It moved away from its vision of social justice, to a narrow preoccupation with methods and skills. Increasingly, social work strove to fit the client to the system rather than be concerned with the reduction of inequality and social injustice which had subverted the client's life in the first place. Incrementally and ineluctably, through professionalisation social workers distanced themselves from the people they worked with. Social work became mainstream, increasingly routinised and standardised, with an emphasis on expert-driven, quantitative-research-based practice that stressed standardised, ritualistic, empirically tested forms of treatment – 'best practices' – and where research and theory drove practice across the board, top-down. By and large, social workers have earned a poor reputation with people on the street through losing their connection with the field's radical roots and buying into the new professionalism.

There is evidence that a similar process of regression is taking place in harm reduction, driven by 'experts', once again the people in power, the gatekeepers who have committed themselves to maintaining their status at the expense of the other. Will harm reduction in Canada cease to be user-driven and become distanced and impersonal? The answer at the moment would be 'yes'.

In certain communities, harm reduction has already become part of 'the system'; while not necessarily a bad thing, we must remain watchful. As it moves into mainstream organisations, academia and public policy, harm reduction is given a suit and a haircut, made presentable and told to behave. Acting within a temple of power, as part of the establishment, harm reduction can perpetuate the structure of domination by emphasising the enforcement of social control and order and getting individuals to fit into society, rather than promoting social welfare, responding to societal changes and respecting people's human needs. In this paradigm, the most profoundly disenfranchised users of illicit drugs are further marginalised, stigmatised and neglected in the race to make them meet the providers' expectations of what a client is and how a client must behave in order to get help.

In a publication from the 1990s, Ontario's Centre for Addiction and Mental Health described harm reduction as the best alternative to try 'when efforts to treat, prevent or punish addiction problems have not succeeded'. Second best – to punishment? The director of a street-based youth agency funded to run a harm reduction programme refuses to allow needle exchange to be done by her staff because 'it will give the wrong message'. Another states that she doesn't allow needle exchange on site, because the clients know that she is opposed to their injecting drugs. Harm reduction for whom?

Methadone maintenance programmes (MMT) – at least in Ontario – have become big business, with quasi-franchise operations located around the province. Though this has made MMT more accessible, programmes have not been consistent in offering the supportive services or atmosphere which would make them effective. Many patients are very dissatisfied with the treatment they receive, refer to MMT as a 'cash cow' for doctors who run the clinics, and see methadone itself as 'liquid handcuffs', not just because of restrictive guidelines but also because, as they report, it is difficult to get the prescribers' support when they express the desire to taper off it.

In the area of research, the promotion of and reliance on pilot projects can be harmful to participants, especially when follow-up is not sufficiently thought out. In the above-mentioned NAOMI project, even those whose lives had been turned around by having been prescribed heroin were taken off it at the end of the project and referred to MMT programmes. A criterion for acceptance in NAOMI was evidence of repeated failures with MMT. Clearly both harm reduction research ethics and MMT are areas for future study.

What may keep Canadian harm reduction honest and effective is the inclusion of people with the lived experience of drug use in all phases of policy development and programming, from design through delivery through evaluation and research. This occurs in varying degrees across Canada, and continues to give harm reduction its authenticity and edge.

Harm reduction's regression in Canada is part of a larger context of the federal government's demonisation of drugs and the people who use them. This is a well-funded propaganda campaign, which appeals to fear, prejudice and greed. As a result, we are experiencing a value shift which is deeply upsetting and does not augur well for harm reduction, the well-being of people who use illicit drugs or for any marginalised people. How do we account for the public embrace of current neo-conservative propaganda? Is it simply a case of unenlightened self-interest and a shortage of compassion? Is it a temporary aberration, or is it a radical change in Canadian temperament?

We do know this: those who work with people who use drugs, as both clients and allies, must double and re-double our efforts to ensure that the gains we had made are not forever lost; that harm reduction attains its rightful place among the ways we use to address drug issues, not as a stand-alone 'pillar' but as what *informs* all substance-related programming and work. This means that we give full attention to the consequences of what we do, including the unintended ones. Access to harm reduction services is both a health right and a human right. And rights for oppressed people are an anathema to our current government which – for ideological reasons – ignores not merely rights but also science. The result: 'regression to the mean' . . . in both senses of the term.

References

Alexander, B. (1998) Reframing Canada's 'drug problem', *Policy Options*, 19 (8), 30.
Canadian Harm Reduction Network (2008) *Learning from Each Other: Enhancing Community-based Harm Reduction Programs and Practices in Canada*, www.canadianharmreduction.com/project/index.php, accessed 3 March 2011.
Canadian Public Health Association (1994) Needle exchange in Canada, *Savoir Faire*, Ottawa: CPHA.
Centre for Addiction and Mental Health (CAMH) (2011) www.camh.net/Public_policy/Public_policy_papers/harmreductionbackground.html, accessed 24 February.
Erickson, P. (1992) Recent trends in Canadian drug policy: the decline and resurgence of prohibition, *Daedalus*, 121 (3), 239–67.

Kerr, T., Tyndall, M., Li, K., Montaner, J. and Wood, E. (2005) Safer injection facility use and syringe sharing in injection drug users, *Lancet*, 366, 316–18.

Ontario Ministry of Health (2006) *Ontario Needle Exchange Programs: Best Practice Recommendations*, Toronto: OMH.

Oscapella, E. and Riley, D.M. (1997) Canada's new drug law: some implications for HIV/AIDS prevention in Canada, *International Journal of Drug Policy*, 7 (3), 180–2.

Riley, D.M. (1993) *The Policy and Practice of Harm Reduction*, Ottawa: Canadian Centre on Substance

Riley, D.M. (1998) *Drug policy in Canada: Paper Written as Background Paper for the Senate of Canada Committee on Drug Policy Reform*, Ottawa: Senate of Canada.

Riley, D.M. (2008) Amphetamine use in Canada. In R., Patesand D. M., Riley (eds), *Interventions for Amphetamine Misuse*, Oxford: Blackwell, 101–13.

Riley, D.M. and McCrimmon, M. (1988) *AIDS Prevention for Substance Abuse Treatment Programs: A Canadian Approach*, Toronto: AIDS Network of Toronto.

Riley, D.M. and O'Hare, P. (2000) Harm reduction: history, definition and practice. In J. Inciardi and L. Harrison (eds.), *Harm Reduction and Drug Control*, Newbury Park: Sage, 1–26.

Riley, D.M. and Oscapella, E. (2006) Drug policy in Canada: a decade of dithering. Paper presentedat 17th International Conference on the Reduction of Drug Related Harm, Vancouver, April.

Riley, D.M. and Oscapella, E. (2007) Drug policy in Canada: from dithering to withering. Paper presented at the 18th International Conference on Drug Related Harm, Warsaw, May.

Riley, D., Sawka, E., Conley, P., Hewitt, D., Mitic, W., Poulin, C. Room. R., Single, E. and Topp, J. (1999) Harm reduction: concepts and practices, *Substance Use and Misuse*, 34 (1), 9–24.

Single, E., Erickson, P. and Skirrow, J. (1991) Drugs and public policy in Canada. Rand Conference on American and European Drug Policies, Washington, May.

Vancouver/Richmond Health Board (1992–2009) HIV Reports; BC Ministry of Health AIDS Surveillance Reports.

Wood, E., Kerr, T., Small, W., Li, K., Marsh, D.C., Montaner, J.S. and Tyndall, M.W. (2004) Changes in public order after the opening of a medically supervised safer injecting facility for illicit injection drug users, *Journal of Can. Medical Association*, 171, 731–4.

Wood, E., Tyndall, M.W., Stoltz, J., Small, W., Lloyd-Smith, E., Zhang, R., Julio S.G. Montaner, J.S.G. and Kerret, T. (2005) Factors associated with syringe sharing among users of a medically supervisedsafer injecting facility, *American Journal of Infectious Diseases*, 1, 50–4.

Chapter 29

HARM REDUCTION IN LATIN AMERICA AND THE CARIBBEAN

Diana Rossi

Harm reduction is still a new and not entirely well-understood concept in the Latin American and Caribbean region, where it is associated primarily with injecting drug use (IDU). Since the 1990s when the first tolerated needle exchange programme was established in the City of Salvador in Brazil (Mesquita et al., 2003), the concept is being discussed and broadened to adapt it to local cultural and socio-economic processes.

During the 1990s harm reduction was discussed primarily by healthcare workers dedicated to prevent transmission and treat consequences of the Human Immunodeficiency Virus (HIV) among injecting drug users in the main cities of South America. The harm reduction concept linked to acquired immunodeficiency syndrome (AIDS) among IDU gained attention in Brazil, Argentina, Chile, Paraguay and Uruguay, where programmes were being instituted by national agencies and non-governmental organisations (NGOs). Much of the success in implementing needle and syringe exchange programmes has been due to the work of civil society in Latin America and the Caribbean; this work has been implemented in Argentina, Uruguay, Mexico, and Puerto Rico without large-scale government assistance (Rossi et al., 2009).

During the 1990s, interventions were mainly oriented to distribute preventive information to drug users and their social networks in order to change attitudes towards shared use of paraphernalia to inject drugs. Twenty years after those initial interventions, harm reduction now includes new approaches related to a variety of problems with more emphasis on community intervention. These changes in harm reduction concepts and interventions might be related to:

1. *transformation of drug use patterns*, for example, the increase of non-injecting cocaine use in most of the cities with previous high prevalence of cocaine injection;
2. *the impact of different theoretical paradigms* that influence the understanding of and action towards social problems, particularly the emphasis on individual change as the main goal of preventive interventions.

Transformation of drug use patterns

The successive social and economic crises that affected Latin America and the Caribbean (LAC) during the hegemonic neoliberal period in the 1990s, not only had a profound impact on social integration of the population but also increased vulnerability as a consequence of deepening poverty, cuts in health services, and disillusionment (Friedman et al., 2009). Changes in drug use patterns also occurred influenced by drug traffic and market transformation.

Harm Reduction in Substance Use and High-Risk Behaviour: International Policy and Practice, First Edition.
Edited by Richard Pates and Diane Riley.

Cocaine is the primary drug of choice for injectors in several Latin American countries. Nevertheless, heroin injection has been reported in the northern part of Latin America, in Colombia and in the cities of the Mexico that border the United States of America.

The preference for cocaine is primarily driven by availability as the widespread cultivation, refinement, and transit of this drug is common throughout the region, since the majority of the world's cocaine originates from coca leaf plantations in Colombia, Peru, and Bolivia (Blickman et al., 2006).

Estimates of the number of injecting drug users in LAC vary widely depending on the methodology used and the year in which the estimates were made (Rossi, 2009). The Reference Group to the United Nations on HIV and Injecting Drug Use published an estimate of 580,500 people in Latin America and 24,000 in the Caribbean who inject drugs and live with HIV. The number of IDUs was estimated to be 65,829 in Argentina in 1999; 29,130 in Puerto Rico in 2002; and 800,000 in Brazil in 2003 (Mathers et al., 2008).

Cocaine use trends in Latin America indicate that intranasal and smoking have displaced injection use as preferred routes of administration among drug users. For example, in Argentina, a study with 140 current cocaine injectors that lived in Buenos Aires in 2003, showed changes in the mode of injecting, which became more individual and hidden. Avoiding recognition as an injecting drug user became a primary goal, since the practice is heavily stigmatised and thus associated with negative effects: AIDS and death. Both in single and group injecting practice, the same syringe was used fewer times than in the past. The decrease in the frequency of injecting use, was also related to the poor quality of the cocaine, which no longer had the desired effect. In addition, harm reduction programmes facilitated risk and health management among those users who had been in contact with them (Rossi and Rangugni, 2004).

In the Caribbean crack cocaine use is much more widespread than the intranasal use of powder cocaine, which is limited to the economically elite. The use of coca paste (an intermediate product in manufacturing between coca leaves and purified cocaine) has increased in the cities of Buenos Aires and Montevideo, while crack cocaine is expanding in many Brazilian cities and several Caribbean sites such as Saint Lucia, Jamaica, Trinidad and Bahamas (Day et al., 2010).

According to the Caribbean Drug and Alcohol Research Institute (CDARI), possible explanations for the lack of injection drug use vary from the ease of smoking crack, the lack of heroin in local drug markets and a universally reported needle aversion of the English speaking Afro and Indo-Caribbean people (Day et al., 2010)

To address vulnerability that drug using populations face in South America, a project was financed by the Brazilian Council on Scientific and Technological Development. This project analysed 3604 records from 13 cross-sectional studies that included IDUs, ex-IDUs, and non-injecting drug users (NIDUs). The data were collected between 1998 and 2004 in the cities of Buenos Aires (Argentina); Florianópolis, Gravataí, Itajaí, Porto Alegre, Rio de Janeiro, Salvador, São José do Rio Preto, São Paulo and Sorocaba (Brazil); and Montevideo (Uruguay). While the study showed that there was a high HIV seroprevalence among drug users, especially among IDUs, there was also to some extent a high HIV prevalence among NIDUs. The socio-demographic variables and risk practices denote a population highly vulnerable in terms of HIV transmission, highlighting similar situations of social vulnerability for drug-using population in the three countries (Ralón et al., 2008).

For Latin American and Caribbean drug users, harm reduction measures have included various public health interventions, such as the needle and syringe exchanges, opiate substitution treatment, testing and counselling for HIV, testing and vaccination for hepatitis, prevention and treatment of various sexually transmitted infections (STI) and tuberculosis as well as access to primary healthcare and antiretroviral treatment (ART). Although harm reduction programmes have demonstrated a proven efficacy in reducing HIV transmission among injecting drug users and have been consistently recommended by academics, officials and activists, as well as various United Nations agencies, contextually and culturally appropriate harm reduction coverage is insufficient for Latin America and the Caribbean particularly in a drug using environment that includes NIDU (Rossi, 2009). The absence of knowledge in the application of harm reduction measures is especially evident in the healthcare services that base intervention on the individual change approach.

Impact of different theoretical paradigms on the current concept of harm reduction

The emphasis on individual change as the main goal of preventive interventions was part of the debate among many outreach workers and healthcare professionals receiving HIV infected drug users and their sexual partners in South American healthcare centres. The limits of the emphasis on the risk factors and behavioural change approach were discussed among harm reduction teams working in different Latin American cities (Caiaffa and Bastos, 2006; Galante et al., 2009).

The antecedents for this paradigm change are partially rooted in the of popular education ideas developed by the Brazilian Paulo Freire and of the social psychology approach by Enrique Pichon-Rivière, particularly in Argentina (Freire, 1987; Pichon-Rivière, 1998). These perspectives, embraced by outreach workers, have mingled with harm reduction principles to sustain ideas such as the need for integrating scientific and popular knowledge, and for empowering drug users through engaging them in the design and implementation of preventive projects. Drug users have specific knowledge of drug use practices, its meanings and cultural codes, as well as of the institutional practices of social control.

The Pensamiento Complejo (Complex Thought) theory of Edgar Morin has also influenced the study of drug use, emphasising the complexity of the phenomenon. Morin's theory is based on an integration of knowledge from different disciplines such as nursing, social work, anthropology, psychology, medicine, economy, law, political science, sociology, along with drug users' views (Morin, 1990).

Rose Mayer proposes that the concept of harm reduction formed part of the Collective Health approach in that it focused on building drug users' capacity to take a leading role in their own care (Santos, 2010). In Argentina and Brazil the harm reduction movement and the movement for the reform of mental health laws have taken on a a clinical-political role. Eduardo Passos writes that 'the clinical practice in its relation with the process of production of subjectivity of those defined as mentally ill or drug abusers, necessarily implies that we take risks in an experience both of critique and analysis, a critique-clinical experience of the instituted forms that politically compromises us' (Santos, 2010). The linkages with these approaches have moved the harm reductionists towards the human rights groups working in the region, helping these groups to broaden the views of human rights and giving the people working with the harm reduction approach a well defined framework to discuss the rights of drug users.

At present, the individual-level and behaviour-change orientation that still predominates in many harm reduction programmes is being challenged by the social epidemiology approaches that propose to study risk environments to better understand drug-related harms. 'A "risk environment" framework envisages drug harms as a product of the social situations and environments in which individuals participate. It shifts the responsibility for drug harm, and the focus of harm reducing actions, from individuals alone to include the social and political institutions which have a role in harm production' (Rhodes, 2009).

There is still both a lack of investigation and of interventions that work with this paradigm shift (Strathdee et al., 2010). In a study of 96 metropolitan areas in the USA, Friedman and colleagues found that three measures of legal repressiveness – arrests for possession of cocaine or heroin, police staff per capita, and costs for corrections – were independently associated with HIV prevalence. This suggested that 'legal repressiveness may have little deterrent effect on drug injection and may have a high cost in terms of HIV and perhaps other diseases among injectors and their partners', thus illuminating the social and economic influences on HIV transmission (Friedman et al., 2006). In a recent paper, Friedman and colleagues also demonstrated that arrests do not decrease IDU prevalence (Friedman et al., 2011).

The focus on consequences of criminalisation of drug users is currently part of the main debate among several stakeholders in Latin American governments and the harm reduction concept is expanding to include Pensamiento Complejo minimisation of negative consequences of the USA 'war on drugs'. A recent study has shown how the severity of drug laws has contributed to increase incarceration rates and prison overcrowding in Latin American countries (Metaal and Youngers, 2010).

Drug law reform to achieve harm reduction

Several Latin American governments have been part of a global debate to decriminalise drug use (Cook, 2010). Most of the arguments in favour state that the current drug policy has done nothing to reduce drug supply or demand. It has stigmatised drug users by distancing them from preventive and assistance services and using funds from the judicial system and law enforcement organisations for penalising consumers rather than persecuting dealers. Numerous governments from the region are more open to change than in the 1990s.

The civil society has played a key role in Latin America and the Caribbean to promote and increase health responses in opposition to the criminal response against drug use and in the promotion and implementation of harm reduction policies (Cook, 2010). The Brazilian government invested a fair amount of governmental funds to develop harm reduction services supported by the Ministry of Health with funds from World Bank and other United Nations agencies (Hacker et al., 2005). Also, some multilateral agencies such as the Pan American Health Organization (PAHO) have helped with dissemination and acceptance of harm reduction policy in the region.

This positive trend, however, does not translate into decisive actions, such as the scaling up of harm reduction programmes. Moreover, in the most promising contexts such as Argentina and Brazil, where harm reduction has more background, there has been no progress and it can be argued that there were some setbacks regarding the services provided.

Governmental drug policies in Latin America have mainly focused on prosecuting drug users. However, it is important to note that recently, Argentina, Bolivia, Mexico, Brazil and Ecuador have shown a new approach in deliberations on drug policy, which has a clear impact on broadening the concept of harm reduction to include the negative effects of criminalisation (Rossi et al. 2009; Cook, 2010).

In Argentina, the National Government declared its willingness to change the drug laws that criminalise drug possession for personal use. The current president, Cristina Fernández de Kirchner, has publicly stated that those who are addicted should not be 'condemned as if they were criminals'.[1] On 25 August 2009, the Supreme Court of Argentina voted unanimously in favour of

[1] Clarín (30 July 2008) *Cristina respaldó la despenalización del consumo personal de drogas.* Available at www.clarin.com/diario/2008/07/30/sociedad/s-01725993.htm. In Spanish the president said, 'No me gusta se condene al que tiene una adicción como si fuera un criminal.'

decriminalising personal consumption of illicit drugs, declaring that it was unconstitutional to punish a person for holding or using illegal drugs if it does not endanger others. Although the court order specifically refers to cannabis, it opens the door to judicial reform of the drug laws in Argentina because the arguments are applicable to other illicit drugs as well. The Scientific Advisory Committee on Control of Illicit Traffic in Narcotic Drugs, Psychotropic Substances and Complex Crime of the Chief of Cabinet published a key report on drug users and policies to address this issue. The National Commission on Drug Policy is clearly critical of the prohibitionist-abstentionist model and is responsible to launch the National Drug Plan 2010–15. In addition, the Committee studies possible reforms to the current laws: 'A debate on reform of drug policy is underway in Argentina like never before. Despite the initial confrontational content and contradictory positions within the state, the mechanisms for negotiation are improving and leading to promising results' (Touzé, 2010).

In 2008, Uruguay also gave an important signal of openness regarding drug policy. Uruguay was characterised by having never criminalised drug possession for personal use and expanded that conception in the 51st Session of the Commission on Narcotic Drugs, held in Vienna in March 2008. Uruguay was the spokesman for a claim regarding revised goals at the 1998 United Nations General Assembly Special Session on the World Drug Problem (UNGASS). As part of that claim, Uruguay put forward the resolution 'Integration of an adequate human rights system with the United Nations drug control policy' calling for respect for fundamental human rights and equal access of drug users to social and healthcare services. That statement was co-sponsored by Argentina, Ecuador and Bolivia, as well as by the European Union and Switzerland (Rossi et al. 2009; Cook, 2010). Currently Uruguayan legislators are discussing decriminalisation of cannabis cultivation for personal use.

In Bolivia, the focus has been to establish a legal regime for the coca leaf. In March 2009, Evo Morales sent a formal letter to UN Secretary General calling for the abolition of two sub-articles of the 1961 Single Convention on Narcotic Drugs, which specifically prohibit the chewing of coca leaf (Jelsma, 2011). However, Morales apparently wants to avoid the mis-interpretation by the international community that the Bolivian government condones drug use. The Bolivian law, like the Argentinean, is very repressive towards drug use and trafficking at a small-scale level.

The drug law in Ecuador is also highly repressive and provides a good example of how drug policy may become useless to the local criminal code. Ecuadorian law criminalises the posses-sion for personal use and the traffic and sale of small quantities of drugs. They have minimum sentences of 12 years and maximum of 25 years, while the maximum penalty for homicide is 16 years. That means a user who has drugs for personal use may receive a sentence equivalent to that of a small dealer, and a small dealer can receive a sentence greater than a person who has committed a murder. However, Ecuador has proposed amnesty for small dealers – called 'mules' – and the current President Rafael Correa stressed the need of proportionality of pun-ishment and pardons and of reducing the time of sentencing in the case of the first offense. The reprieve for small traders or drug carriers proposed by the Ecuadorian government was approved by the Constituent Assembly. Under this initiative, between 2008 and 2009 around 1,500 detainees for crimes related to small drug trafficking regained their freedom (Metaal, 2009). The Article 364 of the new constitution, adopted in 2008, states: 'Addictions are a public health problem. The State is responsible to develop coordinated programmes of infor-mation, prevention and control of alcohol consumption, tobacco and narcotic and psycho-tropic substances, in no case will criminalization be permitted nor will persons' constitutional rights be violated.'

In 2008, Mexico faced exponential growth of organised crime, violence and an alarming rise in drug consumption, President Felipe Calderón proposed a bill to the Union Congress as part of his general security strategy. Its aim was to fight small-scale drug dealing, known in Mexico as 'narcomenudeo' by recognising and distinguishing drug users from drug dealers (Cook, 2010). The Law was passed by both Legislative Houses of Congress in April 2009. It also preserves the right of the traditional use of certain drugs by the country's indigenous people. It includes harm reduction as a state policy; which suggests the possibility of increased resources for this intervention strategy. However, according to Hernández Tinajero and Zamudio Angles, although the law represents some significant advances, at least theoretically, it has many negative aspects that could signify a threat to the most basic rights of all Mexicans. First, the law lacks an integrated approach for dealing with demand and supply of drugs as a cultural and health phenomenon as much as it is a market and criminal one. Second, it encourages crime, as it allows undercover police to simulate buying drugs in order to incriminate traffickers. Third, it establishes disproportionate prison sentences for those who enter the illegal drug market due to lack of economic opportunity, the burden of which falls heaviest on the most vulnerable of the community: peasants, poor people, young people and women (Hernández Tinajero and Zamudio Angles, 2009).

In 2006 the Brazilian government approved a new drug law that aimed to adjust the proportionality of punishment, to differentiate between the crimes of possession and trafficking, offering alternatives to incarceration for possession, while keeping the prison sentences for trafficking offences. Experts are now wondering, however, the extent ot which the state can exercise control over police interventions on the streets, which are often illegal, or how much impact the new law can have in the country without reform of the judicial system (Bastos et al., 2007). Critics argue that in fact the law had little effect in distinguishing between consumers and dealers as it does not provide any specific guidance about possession differing amounts of traffic. Critics also argue that the distinction is still based on subjective context criteria such as time or the place of incident. In addition, the law still allows judges to impose penalties of imprisonment if individuals choose not to undergo compulsory treatment. However, in September 2010, the Supreme Court of Brazil ruled that failure to consider non-custodial sentences for individuals found guilty of small-scale drug-dealing offences would violate the Constitution. It is also important to note that in October 2009, the seminar 'Drugs, Harm Reduction and Legislation' was held in the capital, Brasilia. The seminar was conducted by the Commission on Human Rights and Minorities of the Chamber of Deputies. The main objective was to promote discussion on experiences and drug laws – of Brazil and other countries – in order to address and reduce vulnerabilities and harms associated with drug use.

Contrary to the new winds in Latin American countries, Colombia has promoted the re-criminalisation of drug possession for personal use; despite the fact that harm reduction is mentioned as a public policy strategy (Cook, 2010). In 2009, the parliamentary allies of the former president Alvaro Uribe, promoted and achieved an amendment to the Constitution which states that: 'The possession and consumption of narcotic drugs or psychotropic substances is prohibited.' This amendment is contrary to the trend of jurisprudence in the country since 1994, Colombia's Constitutional Court had declared unconstitutional the criminalisation of drug possession for personal use pointing out that adults can have up to 20 grams of cannabis and 1 gram of cocaine. In the Case C-221, the Court ruled that the ban violates the constitutional right of '*free development of personality*'. In July 2009 the Court reconfirmed the 1994 ruling holding that the amounts allowed for personal use were 20 grams of cannabis and 1 gram of cocaine.

In Central America anti-drug policies, strategies and plans are focused on reducing supply and combating drug trafficking. This fact reflects the characteristics of these sub-region countries that have been and are 'bridge' countries for drug trafficking. One clear example of this situation is the implementation of Plan Merida, which the Bush USA administration had articulated with the governments of Mexico, Dominican Republic, Haiti and several Central American countries.[2] The plans currently in place in the region are oriented almost exclusively to the suppression of supply. For instance, the National Anti-Drug Plan El Salvador (2002–8), although proposed as a model of harm reduction, equates drug addiction with drug offenses and money laundering. Furthermore, the national HIV plans in various Central American countries show the poor development of harm reduction in that region. In Nicaragua the national HIV plan 2006–10 included drug users in the list of vulnerable populations for HIV transmission, while Costa Rica, El Salvador, Panama and Belize do not include them yet (Cook, 2010).

Harm reduction debates among civil society organisations

Some countries in the region such as Brazil and Argentina introduced harm reduction policies several years ago; others are in early stages of development, including Colombia and Paraguay. But there are many countries in the region that have not yet adopted harm reduction as public policy: Bolivia, Costa Rica, Cuba, Chile, Peru and Venezuela. In Central America, according to Pascual Ortells, a member of the Foundation Nimehuatzin, 'harm reduction is still pending'. The Caribbean countries have a similar situation (Cook, 2010).

Latin American organisations such as Intercambios Asociación Civil, Asociación de Reducción de Daños de Argentina (ARDA), Associação Brasileira de Redutoras e Redutores de Danos (ABORDA), Rede Brasileira de Redução de Danos (REDUC), Corporación Caleta Sur, Red Chilena de Reducción de Daños, Programa Compañeros, Prever, Instituto de Investigación y Desarrollo Social (IDES) and El Abrojo have pushed forward harm reduction developments in Latin American in meetings, through papers and by interventions. In the Caribbean region, the Caribbean Harm Reduction Coalition, the Caribbean Vulnerable Communities, Rebirth House in Trinidad and Patricia House in Jamaica have led the way in bringing harm reduction interventions to the drug users in the Caribbean (Day et al., 2010).

At the same time, networks of people living with HIV, sex workers and gay movements have also learned and helped to expand harm reduction concept within the AIDS field. Also, organisations working with drug using populations from around the world have interacted and influenced the Latin American and Caribbean groups, such as the International Harm Reduction Association or the International Network of People Who Use Drugs. Groups of organised drug users have increased their interaction with governmental agencies in Argentina, Brazil, Chile, Mexico and Uruguay, although the links among Latin American activists to develop a regional agenda are still weak.

The role played in the region by RAISSS (Network of institutions involved in situations of social suffering) in introducing a broader harm reduction concept is very interesting. RAISSS is a network of organisations from 32 countries, including Brazil, Chile, Haiti, Guatemala, Honduras, El Salvador, Nicaragua, Costa Rica, Panama, Bolivia, Mexico and Colombia with explicit guidance to the community intervention.[3] Community is defined as the 'interaction (in fact a system of interactions) between three subjects: the individual in his subjective dimension, the group (the others, people, informal networks) and the institutions (formal networks) that are

[2] Personal communication, Pascual Ortells, Fundación Nimehuatzin, Nicaragua, by email 02/08/2010.

[3] RAISSS constructed, promoted and implemented the ECO2 model, based in the complexity epistemology of the ethics and the community, technically oriented by Caritas Germany in Latin America and in other regions of the world, www.corpconsentidos.org/docs/20080808133430_red_raisss.pdf.

part of a territory' (Milanese, 2009). In that sense, cure is understood as a way of 'governing, overcoming, accompanying the individual, group and network suffering, without alienating one from the others' (Milanese, 2009). Several organisations of the network work both in prevention and care, assuming and spreading many forms of intervention that are part of the harm reduction approach, although this concept is not always explicit. During the meeting, Drugs, Youth, Violence and Gangs: An Alternative View, held in October 2008, at Ayagualo (El Salvador), RAISSS members signed a statement arguing that

> we have confirmed in the last ten years of sustained work with people living in severe exclusion associ-
> ated with drug use and trafficking, HIV, extreme poverty, living in the streets, sex work, violence and
> other forms of social suffering, that States have not yet succeeded in ensuring the rights and the dignity
> of all people. Therefore . . . we urge the United Nations . . . the presidents gathered at the XVII Summit
> of Heads of State of Iberoamérica, the International Organizations, States and civil society, to integrate
> during the next decade the following priorities in their policies and actions: the guarantee of human
> rights for drug users . . . the implementation of alternative care that integrate prevention, harm reduc-
> tion, treatment and social reintegration, setting aside punitive and stigmatising actions.

These issues were also discussed in a meeting about drug policies held by the network in Brasilia in 2010.

In this context, Intercambios organised the I and II Latin American Conferences on Drug Policy in Buenos Aires in 2009, and in Rio de Janeiro together with the Brazilian civil organisation Psico-tropicus in 2010. During those encounters, Intercambios promoted the dialog among several impor-tant Latin American experts on drug policies. Moreover, the Conferences had important impact on local and international media, thus expanding the concept of harm reduction widely in the Latin-American region.

Conclusion

Harm reduction is at an early stage in the region. The punitive approach has prevailed over the health approach and US policy toward the region has not changed in relation to supply control.

While there are a few countries that have developed harm reduction interventions over several years, many others have not yet discussed the harm reduction perspective. Moreover, in countries where there is a history of harm reduction, the sustainability is fragile and they are very dependent on international funding. Government support – political and financial- is still low in most countries and there is a long road ahead. In all countries of the region, progress depends largely or exclusively on NGOs who work with great effort and, in most cases, with few resources, little support from governments, and confront numerous barriers.

Nevertheless, there is a clear opening in the discussions on the need to change drug laws and incorporate harm reduction in many countries of the region; as yet, this 'opening' has not resulted in the implementation/extension of harm reduction programmes.

At the level of harm reduction assistance, despite the scant development in the region, the role being played by the drug users groups, the organisations working with drug using populations, the network working with social suffering and the networks of people living with HIV is remarkable, particularly in countries where the harm reduction is still pending.

There is increasing non-injecting drug use in the region, with high risk of contracting and/or transmitting HIV and other STI. Several studies show higher prevalence of HIV and STI in nasal and pulmonary cocaine users. It is essential to intensify the research and discuss harm reduction interventions for these problems and to ensure that governments and multilateral agencies incorporate these issues in their agenda.

Note

I particularly thank Graciela Touzé, Paula Goltzman, Pablo Cymerman and Samuel R. Friedman for their suggestions and commentaries to this paper. I also acknowledge support by a Fogarty International Center/ NIH grant through the AIDS International Training and Research Program at Mount Sinai School of Medicine-Argentina Program (Grant # D43 TW001037) and by the Buenos Aires University UBACyT SO44.

References

Bastos, F.I., Caiaffa, W.T., Rossi, D., Vila, M. and Malta, M. (2007) The children of mama coca: Coca, cocaine and the fate of harm reduction in South America, *International Journal of Drug Policy*, 18 (2), 99–106.

Blickman, T., Rangugni, V., Rossi, D., Corda, A., Garibotto, G., Caliocchio, L., Latorre, L. and Scarlatta, L. (2006) *Paco Under Scrutiny: The Cocaine Base Paste Market in the Southern Cone*, Briefing Series Drugs & Conflict, no. 14, Amsterdam: Transnational Institute.

Caiaffa, W.T. and Bastos, F.I. (2006) Harm reduction: milestones dilemmas, prospects, challenges, *Cadernos de Saúde Pública [Reports in Public Health]*, 22 (4), 702.

Cook, C. (2010) *The Global State of Harm Reduction 2010: Key Issues for Broadening the Response*, London: International Harm Reduction Association.

Day, M., Rangugni, V. and Cymerman, P. (2010) *A Review of the State of Harm Reduction in Latin America and the Caribbean Assessing the Current Situation and Response*, Report prepared for the HIV/STI Project of the Pan American Health Organization/World Health Organization.

Freire, P. (1987) *Pedagogia do oprimido*, Rio de Janeiro: Paz e Terra.

Friedman, S.R., Cooper, H.L., Tempalski, B.J., Friedman, R., Flom, P.L. and Des Jarlais, D.C. (2006) Relationships of deterrence and law enforcement to drug-related harms among drug injectors in US metropolitan areas, *AIDS*, 20, 93–9.

Friedman, S.R., Rossi, D. and Braine, N. (2009) Theorizing 'big events' as a potential risk environment for drug use, drug-related harm and HIV epidemic outbreaks, *International Journal of Drug Policy*, 20 (3), 283–91.

Friedman, S.R., Pouget, E.R., Chatterjee, S., Cleland, C., Tempalski, B.J., Brady, J.E. and Cooper, H.L. (2011) Drug arrests and injection drug deterrence, *American Journal of Public Health*, 101 (2), 344–9.

Galante, A., Rossi, D., Goltzman, P. and Pawlowicz, M.P. (2009) Programas de Reducción de Daños en el Escenario Actual. Un cambio de perspectiva, *Escenarios*, 14, 113–21, Universidad Nacional de La Plata.

Hacker, M.A., Malta, M., Enriquez, M. and Bastos, F.I. (2005) Human immunodeficiency virus, AIDS, and drug consumption in South America and the Caribbean: epidemiological evidence and initiatives to curb the epidemic, *Revista Panamericana de Salud Pública*, 18 (4–5), 303–13.

Hernández Tinajero, J. and Zamudio Angles, C. (2009) *Mexico: The Law against Small-scale Drug Dealing – A Doubtful Venture*, Transnational Institute and Washington Office on Latin America, www.tni.org/report/mexico-law-against-small-scale-drug-dealing, accessed 28 February 2011.

Jelsma, M. (2011) *D-Day for Bolivia's Coca Chewing Amendment*, Transnational Institute, www.tni.org/article/d-day-bolivia%E2%80%99s-coca-chewing-amendment, accessed 28 February 2011.

Mathers, B.M., Degenhardt, L., Phillips, B., Wiessing, L., Hickman, M. and Strathdee, S.A. (2008) Global epidemiology of injecting drug use and HIV among people who inject drugs: a systematic review, *Lancet*, 372, 1733–45.

Mesquita, F., Doneda, D., Gandolfi, D., Battistella Nemes, M.I., Andrade, T., Bueno, R., Piconez, E. and Trigueiros, D. (2003) Brazilian response to the human immunodeficiency virus/acquired immunodeficiency syndrome epidemic among injecting drug users, *Clinical Infectious Diseases*, 37 (supple 5), 382–5.

Metaal, P. (2009) *Pardon for Mules in Ecuador: A Sound Proposal*, Transnational Institute and Washington Office on Latin America, www.tni.org/report/pardon-mules-ecuador, accessed 28 February 2011.

Metaal, P. and Youngers, C. (2010) *Systems Overload: Drug Laws and Prisons in Latin America*, Transnational Institute and Washington Office on Latin America, www.druglawreform.info/index.php?option=com_flexicontent&view=category&cid=122&Itemid=46&lang=en, accessed 28 February.

Milanese, E. (2009) *Tratamiento comunitario de las adicciones y de las consecuencias de la exclusión grave*, Manual de trabajo para el operador. Mexico: Plaza y Valdés.

Morin, E. (1990) *Introducción al Pensamiento Complejo*. Barcelona: Gedisa.

Pichon-Rivière, E. (1998) *Diccionario de términos y conceptos de psicología y psicología social*, Buenos Aires: Nueva Visión.

Ralón, G., Bastos, F.I., Latorre, L., Vila, M., Rossi, D., Weissenbacher, M. and Caiaffa, W.T. (2008) Vulnerability associated with HIV transmission among drug users in three countries in South America: Argentina, Brazil, and Uruguay (1998-2004). Seventeenth International AIDS Conference, *Abstract Book*, vol. I, 145–6. Poster, Mexico: MOPE0399.

Rhodes, T. (2009) Risk environments and drug harms: a social science for harm reduction approach, *International Journal of Drug Policy*, 20, 193–201.

Rossi, D. (2009) HIV among People who use drugs in Latin America and the Caribbean. In *Challenges Posed by the HIV Epidemic in Latin America and the Caribbean 2009*, Lima: PAHO, UNICEF and UNAIDS, 29–39.

Rossi, D.and Rangugni, V. (eds) (2004) *Cambios en el uso inyectable de drogas en Buenos Aires (1998–2003)*, coedited for the Intercambios Asociación Civil, Ministerio de Salud y Ambiente de la Nación, Buenos Aires: ONUSIDA y ONUDD.

Rossi, D., Pawlowicz, M.P., Rangugni, V., Zunino Singh, D., Goltzman, P., Cymerman, P., Vila, M. and Touzé, G. (2006) The HIV/AIDS epidemic and changes in injecting drug use in Buenos Aires, Argentina, *Cadernos de Saúde Pública [Reports in Public Health]*, 22 (4), 741–50.

Rossi, D., Harris, S., and Vitarelli-Batista, M. (2009) The impacts of the drug war in Latin America and the Caribbean. In *At What Cost? HIV and Human Rights Consequences of the Global 'War on Drugs'*, New York: Open Society Institute – International Harm Reduction Development Program.

Santos, L.M. (2010) *Outras palavras sobre o cuidado de pessoas que usam Drogas*, Porto Alegre: Conselho Regional de Psicologia do Rio Grande do Sul.

Strathdee, S.A., Hallett, T.B., Bobrova, N., Rhodes, T., Booth, R., Abdool, R., and Hankins, C.A. (2010) HIV and risk environment for injecting drug users: the past, present and future, *Lancet*, 376 (9737), 268–84.

Touzé, G. (2010) *Argentina: ¿Reform on the way?*, series on Legislative Reform of Drug Policies no. 6, Transnational Institute (TNI) and Washington Office on Latin America (WOLA), www.tni.org/briefing/argentina-reform-way, accessed 17 February 2011.

Chapter 30

POLICY AND PRACTICE IN HARM REDUCTION IN AUSTRALASIA

Alex Wodak, John Ryan, Patrick Griffiths, Ingrid van Beek, Monica J. Barratt, Simon Lenton, Kate Dolan, Ana Rodas, Geoffrey Noller and Michael Farrell

This chapter has a different format from the other chapters. The author originally commissioned to write the chapter was unable to deliver it late in the process. We asked a number of distinguished experts from Australia and New Zealand to write a brief piece on their perceptions of the current situation of harm reduction in their countries. What we have now are six contributions and a brief commentary. There is a small overlap between some contributions but this is the nature of these individual contributions and as such they have remained as integrated pieces.

Thirty years of harm reduction in Australia
Alex Wodak

When the Australian people learned in 1984 that a daughter of the then Prime Minister was using heroin, a major national political psychodrama erupted (Reuters, 1984). This ultimately led to a meeting of the Prime Minister and the heads of all the state governments on 2 April 1985 at which harm reduction (referred to in Australia as 'harm minimisation') was accepted as the official national drug policy (Hughes, 2011). Thirty years later, harm minimisation is still Australia's official national drug policy, though now defined as consisting of supply reduction, demand reduction and harm reduction (Ministerial Council on Drug Strategy, 2011). Every few years Australia's response to drugs is reviewed by an independent evaluation (NCADA, 1988; Webster, 1992; Single and Rohl, 1997; Success Works Pty Ltd, 2003; Siggins, 2009). On each occasion, retention of harm reduction has been recommended and accepted. A remarkable feature of Australia's approach to psychoactive drugs since 1985 has been the inclusion of alcohol, tobacco and prescribed drugs along with illicit drugs (Single and Rohl, 1997; NCADA, 1991; Blevins, 1990).

Australian politicians often refer to national responses to illicit drugs as 'the balanced approach'. However, if government expenditure is anything to go by, this approach is hardly balanced. The total expenditure by all Australian governments in response to illicit drugs in 2002–3 was estimated to be $A 3.2 billion of which 75% was allocated to supply control, 10% to prevention, 7% to treatment, 5% to health costs, 2% to other (including research) and 1% to harm reduction (Moore, 2005). Identifying benefits of the not inconsiderable sums allocated to drug law enforcement has proved challenging while the severe unintended negative consequences of supply control have been all too obvious (Costa, 2008). In contrast, the benefits and cost-effectiveness of drug treatment and harm reduction are striking while their unintended negative consequences are minimal (Committee on the Prevention of HIV Infection among Injecting Drug Users in High Risk Countries, 2006).

Harm Reduction in Substance Use and High-Risk Behaviour: International Policy and Practice, First Edition.
Edited by Richard Pates and Diane Riley.
© 2012 Blackwell Publishing Ltd. Published 2012 by Blackwell Publishing Ltd.

Australia was one of the first countries to adopt harm reduction as its official national drug policy. Few countries have been as explicit as Australia when adopting harm reduction. In late 1985, the magnitude of the potential threat of an HIV epidemic among and from people who inject drugs (PWIDs) was recognised officially. Despite the national drug policy of harm reduction, advocacy for the establishment of needle and syringe programmes (NSPs) fell on deaf ears. Consequently, Australia's first NSP had to be established as an act of civil disobedience in November 1986. Soon afterwards, all state governments accepted the need for NSPs and the necessary legislation was passed. By the end of the 1980s, sterile needles and syringes were fairly readily available throughout most of Australia.

Methadone maintenance treatment (MMT) had been available in Australia to a limited extent from 1970. The threat of HIV among PWIDs stimulated the rapid expansion and liberalisation of methadone treatment. The fact that harm reduction was the official national drug policy facilitated the relatively early adoption and vigorous expansion of NSPs and MMT but it still required a major advocacy struggle. In the 1980s and 1990s, Australia was rightly regarded as a world leader in harm reduction.

In 1991, a recommendation to conduct a heroin trial was accepted by a committee of the Australian Capital Territory Legislative Assembly (Bammer and Douglas, 1996). This led to an exhaustive examination of the possible benefits and costs of a heroin trial and the optimal means for conducting such research. At each stage of the process, careful examination showed that the likely benefits were considerable while the risks were small. The penultimate hurdle was a meeting of all nine national health and police/justice ministers on 31 July 1997. The ministers voted 6: 3 in favour of conducting the trial. Nevertheless, a federal cabinet meeting on 19 August overturned this decision and prevented further consideration of a heroin trial on the grounds that such research would 'send a wrong message' (Miller, 2010).

This decision provoked considerable internal criticism as heroin use and problems were increasing rapidly at the time (Mackey, 1998). The Howard government then announced a 'Tough on Drugs' policy which largely amounted to the creation of a perception of intense hostility to harm reduction and support for harsh and punitive measures (Mendes, 2001). The reality was that the same government that was publicly so hostile to harm reduction allocated hundreds of millions of dollars to exporting harm reduction to Asia to prevent epidemic spread of HIV among PWIDs. Vast sums were also allocated to the diversion of drug offenders from the ineffective criminal justice system to more effective drug treatment. After a review of the evidence (Drucker et al., 1998), the Howard government also became the first federal government to allocate funding to the state NSPs (Wodak, 2004).

In the late 1990s, with rapidly increasing numbers of heroin overdose deaths, pressure grew in Sydney, Melbourne and Canberra for the establishment of Medically Supervised Injecting Centres (MSICs). An unofficial MSIC was established in Sydney as an act of civil disobedience, prompting, as intended, the later approval of an official centre which commenced operating in 2001 (Dolan et al., 2000).

By the end of the twentieth century harm reduction had achieved a great deal in Australia. An HIV epidemic among PWIDs had been averted. NSPs from 1991–2000 were estimated to have cost $A 122 million while preventing 25,000 HIV and 21,000 HCV infections and saving $A 2.4–7.7 billion and by 2010, an estimated 4,500 deaths from HIV and 90 deaths from HCV (Health Outcomes International et al.,). A subsequent study estimated that by 2009, 32,050 HIV and 96, 667 HCV infections had been prevented with every dollar spent on NSPs saving $4 in healthcare costs and an astonishing $27 overall (NCHECR, 2009). Several states reduced the punishment for minor cannabis offences with some imposing only civil penalties. All flour was fortified with thiamine to reduce the incidence of a severe form of brain damage (Wernicke-Korsakoff Syndrome) which is prone to occur in people drinking excessive quantities of alcohol (Drew, 1998). Harm reduction approaches were common in the road safety area where alcohol contributes to many car crashes (Loxley et al., 2004).

But harm reduction in Australia this century has now grown stale, complacent and excessively cautious. Heroin trials have now been conducted in six countries with consistently impressive health, social and economic benefits. Although heroin assisted treatment is now provided in five countries, it is still not discussed in Australia. MMT is still only available for about half the heroin users who want this treatment and meet the relevant criteria. The approximately 400 heroin over-dose deaths/year this century are accepted with little apparent concern. The prevalence of hepatitis C remains high with little discussion of prevention. Sniffer dogs and threatening helicopter flights are used widely to detect drugs. Reforms found in many other countries are not even considered including medicinal cannabis, increasing the number of MSICs and introducing civil penalties or just assessment for persons found in possession of quantities of illicit drugs consistent with personal consumption. As the War Against Drugs is increasingly recognised to cause more harms than bene-fits, the time has surely come when harm reduction also has to include reducing the harms of drug policy. Harm reduction still has a long way to go in Australia.

Strategic harm reduction
John Ryan and Patrick Griffiths

The first national meeting of needle and syringe programme (NSP) workers was held in 2002, some fifteen years after the first NSPs were established. Frontline workers were shocked that they shared so many common issues, but existed as islets with little interaction. Hence Anex, a networking harm, reduction non-government organisation became the peak for the Australian NSP and harm reduction workforce, nearly all of which is embedded within mainstream health services including hospital emergency departments and health centres.

Anex does not get funded for its national advocacy work but does receive funding for the *Anex Bulletin*. Developing the *Anex Bulletin* was a recommendation from the first national NSP workers meeting: the Australian front line harm reduction workforce needed connections. Without the *Bulletin*, many workers had no capacity to connect with or be aware of policy or service improvement challenges.

In late 2010 the National Needle and Syringe Programme Strategic Framework was released (DoHA, 2010a), the first of its kind in the world. It has been a long time since Australia has had a harm reduction 'first'. The Framework's journey from concept to finalisation is a good example of how sector ambitions meet the political realities of governance structures. It began with a recom-mendation from the Anex National NSP Policy and Practice Forum which puts harm reduction bureaucrats in the same room as frontline service providers. Anex was tasked to consult nationally and developed an ambitious draft document reflecting the findings of the consultations that was substantially changed once it passed through Government filters. The final Framework recognises many areas for improvement, particularly in metrics and the long overdue need for greater stand-ardisation and substantial improvements in workforce development.

All but a handful of Australia's 3,000-plus NSPs are delivered through the public health system. There are only a few specialist primary health services specifically addressing injecting drug users, and there is no sign of adding to the single safe injecting facility in Sydney. Australia is a highly urbanised nation. Mainstreaming the services, which includes community pharmacies, was the only way in which IDUs living in regional and remote areas could be provided with sterile injecting equipment. The need for investment in staff training comes as national funding for state and territory NSP implementation is no longer 'tied'. Monies are now poured into treasuries without the former conditionality of 'specific purpose payments' which is a major threat to the sector. It makes it even more crucial that return on investment-type evidence is consistently updated in order to lobby for not only maintaining levels of service coverage (Mathers et al., 2010), but also for expansion, which is obviously required if the stubbornly high hepatitis C rates are to be substantially reduced. Untied harm reduction funding is also a threat given that far greater attention is being paid to alcohol than illicit drugs, and mental health is receiving the prioritisation it obviously warrants: but at what cost to harm reduction?

Prison NSP

There are about 30,000 people in Australian correctional facilities (ABS, 2009), an estimated 71% of whom had used illicit drugs in the 12 months before incarceration (AIHW, 2010). Prisons, some of which are privatised, are State and Territory responsibilities (Black et al., 2004; Standard Guidelines for Corrections in Australia, 2004). In the words of the National NSP Strategic Framework, 'injecting drug use in prison and the absence of NSPs in prisons represents a gap, a risk and a limitation in all jurisdictions and requires urgent attention' (DoHA, 2010a). Illicit drug use is widespread throughout prisons, needle sharing is rampant and blood-borne virus transmission rates are alarming (Dolan et al., 2009; Dolan et al., 2010; ANEX, 2010; Miller et al., 2009). Relevant national health strategies agreed to by all jurisdictions call for each government to identify sites to trial an in-prison NSP (DoHA, 2010a; DoHA, 2010c; DoHA, 2010d). As at this point (2011), only the Australian Capital Territory (ACT) Labor Government has publicly explored the possibility of introducing NSP in a prison. The single biggest obstacle has, and remains, opposition from the prison officers' union which threatens industrial action ('needles in, guards out') and exerts pressure throughout the Labor Party to which it is affiliated and thus has substantial voting blocs within parliamentary pre-selection processes.

Political and supporting media strategy has been critical in assisting the ACT government position prison NSP as a responsible public health measure. Anex established a Harm Minimisation in Prisons Committee (HMPC) comprising respected medical leaders (ANEX, 2010). Prominent Australians from across the political spectrum were enlisted as a means of publicly re-positioning prison NSP away from its portrayal as a 'leftist' pro-prisoner rights issue as its opponents often do. Former military leaders have signed up, as has Nobel Laureate Professor Peter Doherty, the eminent and former Australian of the Year Sir Gustav Nossal, a former Governor General and one of our most wealthy and influential business people, Mrs Janet Holmes a' Court.

This was a deliberate strategy aimed at providing government with mainstream support for a public health issue. We advocated for an investigation into potential models and steps to overcome barriers to implementation, the primary obstacle being the union. The Public Health Association was nominated to conduct the investigation in the ACT. Three other jurisdictions have expressed willingness to investigate prison NSP options, but remain extremely reluctant to go public because of union opposition. A primary lesson is that despite numerous peer-reviewed publications endorsing prison NSP, there has been a distinct lack of understanding amongst Australians regarding the precise details of how models have functioned overseas and how trade union opposition has been overcome.

Far from being a leader, Australia is not even a 'follower' when it comes to provision of naloxone to potential overdose witnesses. As a peak body we are frustrated that debate dominated by researchers seems unable to get beyond whether the evidence is of sufficient 'quality' to justify government even piloting naloxone distribution (ANEX, 2010). Pharmacotherapy systems are stretched to breaking point and in the state of Queensland, there is the ridiculous situation in which only female prisoners can access methadone. There is a dearth of quality data and interventions for and with Indigenous Australians who, although only 2.5% of the population, make up a quarter of those in proven hepatitis C incubators, our prisons (Kratzmann et al., 2011).

Harm reduction in Australia: a tale of two decades
Ingrid van Beek

Australia is among 93 countries and territories worldwide that explicitly supports harm reduction (Cook, 2010). Harm reduction is one of the 'three pillars' in its current National Drug Strategy along with demand and supply reduction strategies (Ministerial Council on Drug Strategy, 2011). It has also underpinned Australia's approach to HIV since its first National AIDS Strategy was instituted in 1989.

Australia currently has five among the six indicators of harm reduction policy identified by Cook et al. in 2010, there being only four countries with all six elements at this time. While Australia is among only eight countries globally with a supervised injecting facility (SIF), it is not among the ten countries that provide access to clean needle syringes in prisons.

A study of the effectiveness of Australia's needle syringe programme (NSP) estimated that HIV prevalence among people who inject drugs (PWID) was less than 2% and that there had been a return of up to $7.7 bn in economic and social costs averted for the $150 m invested in NSP from 1988 to 2000 (Health Outcomes International, 2002).

It is widely agreed that key reasons for Australia's success in HIV prevention among PWID included the bipartisan harm reduction approach to what was perceived to be a public health emergency at the time, the involvement of affected communities with government-funded peer organisations being supported from this early stage, and the rapidness with which NSP was implemented in all states and territories.

During this first decade of harm reduction, high quality heroin became increasingly cheap and available throughout Australia, and the annual number of opioid overdose deaths rose to exceed the national road toll in 1999.

This was also the year that the NSW Parliamentary Drug Summit was held, a political response instigated in the weeks immediately before a state election to defuse increasingly shrill calls from the tabloid press to abandon the harm reduction approach altogether. At the Summit, however, compelling evidence for the success of harm reduction was presented and this informed the passage of 172 resolutions including the resolution to support a trial of what became known as the 'Medically Supervised Injecting Centre' (MSIC) in Sydney's Kings Cross, where heroin overdose deaths had been the most concentrated.

The harm reduction field hoped that this Summit heralded a new era of evidence-based drug policy-making, a formal evaluation of the MSIC being undertaken following 18 months of operation to inform its future beyond this trial period, being seen as an example of this.

The opening of the MSIC in 2001 coincided with the emergence of what is now referred to as the 'national heroin shortage'. This shortage persisted in all jurisdictions throughout the next decade until the present time for reasons that remain unclear despite significant research, it may well have been more the result of luck than wisdom.

This national heroin shortage has been accompanied by a plummeting rate of overdose-related deaths (60–70%). There is also evidence that it has led to a contraction in the size of the injecting population (Day et al., 2004) and probably related to this, the overall burden of disease associated with illicit drug use, which has of course been welcomed by all.

While this heroin shortage is considered the main reason for this decrease in opioid overdose mortality at a national level, there is also strong evidence that the MSIC has had a significant impact on overdoses in its immediate vicinity, there having been a 80% decrease in ambulance callouts to overdose-related events in Kings Cross compared to 45% in the neighbouring suburb and 61% elsewhere in the state (Salmon et al., 2010).

Meanwhile the evidence for the continued effectiveness of the NSP also remains strong (National Centre in HIV Epidemiology and Clinical Research, 2009) and yet Australia's continuing progress, particularly in relation to implementing the more contemporary harm reduction strategies appears to have stalled in recent years, the decision to establish a single SIF in Sydney's Kings Cross in 1999 arguably being the last significant step forward in this regard.

When one looks more closely at exactly how NSP was in fact legislated in the various Australian states and territories in the late 1980s, it becomes apparent that the possession of clean injecting equipment (and any other drug paraphernalia) can still be used as circumstantial evidence towards charges of drug self-administration, which remains illegal. Providing such equipment to a drug user can also result in being charged with 'aiding and abetting' (the crime of drug use), or even manslaughter in the event that he/she dies as a result of injecting a drug with that particular needle syringe. This is unless you belong to the only category of persons explicitly exempted in the relevant legislation that is someone authorised to work at a needle syringe programme. This exemption in the NSW legislation was extended to also enable the operation of the MSIC, which has its own Act of Parliament explicitly precluding more than one operating licence to be held at the one time.

This very minimalist and restrictive legislative framework to enable NSP (and later the MSIC in NSW) may have seemed politically expedient at the time to ensure the bipartisan support needed for its immediate implementation. But it is proving not to be sufficiently robust to enable, for example, the distribution of injecting equipment through peer networks of PWID, which is considered vital at this point in time to achieve the very much higher population coverage needed to prevent hepatitis C given its high prevalence among PWID compared to HIV.

The speed with which state governments of all political colours have rejected proposals arising from local communities to establish more SIFs despite the weight of evidence demonstrating the effectiveness of Sydney SIF and others elsewhere in recent years (Hedrich et al., 2010) has only been matched by their resistance to calls to establish NSPs in custodial settings.

Despite the increasingly widespread implementation of peer-administered naloxone programmes throughout the world to reduce opioid overdose-related harm, the response to establish these in Australia has been ambivalent at best to date. Likewise, despite evidence supporting the need to further expand NSP (Kwon et al., 2009) and opioid substitution treatment, government funding for these programmes has plateaued in recent years and they are likely to compete for future resources with other emerging public health issues such as alcohol-related harm, mental health, obesity and diabetes.

While harm reductionists advocate that illicit drug use should be considered a health and social issue instead of a criminal issue, the ongoing criminalisation of drug use throughout Australia directly contradicts this. Even in the politically courageous days of the NSW Parliamentary Drug Summit, the only one of the 172 resolutions passed *not* to be subsequently acted upon was the resolution to repeal the legislation criminalising [drug] self-administration. Despite little evidence that such criminalisation affects the extent of problematic drug use, it constitutes a significant barrier to enabling the broadening of both NSP and SIFs and the adoption of a public health approach to drug use more generally. And yet it continues to receive strong political support.

Meanwhile the fear of a generalised HIV epidemic and an explosive heroin overdose death rate, which may have emboldened politicians of both sides to support compassionate and pragmatic harm reduction approaches has ebbed in recent years, there are signs of an increasing shift towards more values-based belief systems, which tend to see people affected by drug-related issues as being personally responsible for their situations and therefore less deserving of healthcare.

This should make us wonder with the benefit of hindsight, whether we were naive or maybe just too busy at the time to realise how unique and short an opportunity HIV would provide, when still considered a public health emergency, to actually get public policy right. If we had got it right, it would have enabled Australia to deal with other public health issues that emerged later, such as the ongoing transmission of hepatitis C virus among PWID. We might also wonder, whether the efforts to defend the MSIC from concerted and strident attacks over the years by the likes of Drug Free Australia and the UNODC's International Narcotics Control Board, which targeted this single facility in lieu of the entire harm reduction field in Australia, distracted us from doing the groundwork to enable the deeper more fundamental legal reform needed to enable their replication elsewhere.

Perhaps the heroin shortage with its positive impact on heroin-related deaths and other drug-related harms has lulled Australian governments into a sense of security in recent years. But this may well be false since it is presumably only a matter of time before this country sees this or other highly addictive injectable drugs return to its shores, possibly for similarly unclear reasons as those that caused the heroin glut of the late 1990s to cease in 2001.

Assuming that potentially controversial public policy matters are dealt with most sensibly when not in the midst of public health crisis situations, this would seem a good point in time to be proactive about achieving more evidence-based sustainable legal, policy and practice frameworks able to meet future challenges in this regard.

The continuing criminalisation of drug use and possession and distribution of injecting equipment associated with this, the continuing incarceration of drug users in settings with no access to the means of preventing blood-borne infections and the continuing inability to establish additional SIFs should the need arise, remain unfinished business for Australia's harm reduction field.

Internet, digital media and newer synthetic drugs
Monica J. Barratt and Simon Lenton

In Australia, as in other nations, there are two emergent issues which pose particular challenges and opportunities for harm reduction. Recognised as such by Australia's most recent National Drug Strategy (Ministerial Council on Drug Strategy, 2011), these are the increased use of internet and digital technologies and the increasing growth in the number of new synthetic drugs. Australian practitioners have taken advantage of the opportunities presented by high levels of internet use (over 90% of 15–34 year olds, see Australian Bureau of Statistics, 2009) by developing innovative online interventions for treatment of problem drug use (Swan and Tyssen, 2009), and projects that build resilience in young people's lives (Burns et al., 2010; 2009). The challenges of increased internet and digital media use include the sale of new synthetic drugs with unknown legal status, the provision of information on illegal drug manufacture and use, and the existence of a largely unregulated space where alcohol and tobacco are promoted (Ministerial Council on Drug Strategy, 2011).

As a response, Federal legislation is currently proposed in Australia that would mandate Internet Service Providers (ISPs) to block a list of 'refused classification' websites (Bennett Moses, 2010;

Langos, 2010). In addition to sites allowing access to child pornography, this would target media that 'depict, express or otherwise deal with matters of . . . drug misuse or addiction' and/or 'promote, incite or instruct in matters of crime' which may be refused classification, subject to the extent to which they would 'offend reasonable adults', under the *Classification (Publications, Films and Computer Games) Act 1995 (Cth)*. Currently, websites hosted in Australia that are refused classification are issued with a take-down notice, but all other websites remain outside Australia's legal jurisdiction. The proposed legislation seeks to create parity between online and offline content regulation (Bennett Moses, 2010). Worryingly from a harm reduction perspective, independent research has found that the scope of refused classification will be wide enough to encompass online content aimed at promoting safer drug practices through the provision of detailed use instructions (Lumby et al., 2009). As at June 2011, the definition of 'refused classification' is under review (McClelland and O'Connor, 2011).

A significant proportion of Australian drug users access drug-related information through websites (Bleeker et al., 2009; Duff et al., 2007; Gascoigne et al., 2004; Johnston et al., 2006). One example of a website popular among Australians is pillreports.com, a site that enables peers to post reviews of ecstasy pills in their local area including experience reports and reagent testing results. Unlike some European countries, Australia does not have an official illicit tablet monitoring system that provides information to users (see Hales, 2009), meaning that pillreports.com, to some extent, fills this information void although the information is sometimes less-than-reliable. The content and purity of tablets sold as ecstasy is just one example where there is a dearth of relevant and detailed harm reduction information available from more official sources. Government sponsored websites generally offer simple fact sheets, but rarely provide the detailed instructional information that is available peer-to-peer via public online forums where drugs are discussed. In the case of the newer synthetic drugs such as mephedrone and synthetic cannabinoids, internet forums tend to be the first and only sources of available information when new drugs first emerge (e.g., mephedrone in 2007 in Australia, see Camilleri et al., 2010). The ability to remain relatively anonymous, to connect with other like-minded drug users to discuss experiences, and access information that is not otherwise available attracts people to online contexts over and above traditional information channels (Barratt, 2011). At present, the public nature of drug discussion forums used by Australian drug users allows researchers and authorities to monitor emerging drug trends in this country. However, this could change dramatically if, as is proposed, web filtering of drug websites occurs at the Internet Service provider (ISP) level, which would likely simply shift such conversations from public to private networks.

New synthetic drugs have not undergone official review in Australia as they have in the EU (EMCDDA, 2009, 2011; European Monitoring Centre for Drugs and Drug Addiction, 2011; Europol-European Monitoring Centre for Drugs and Drug Addiction (EMCDDA), 2010). Neglible local information is available upon which to base scheduling decisions. Drug possession and supply laws are under state jurisdiction in Australia, which means that there is a wide range of laws across our eight states and territories. Whilst some call for standardising Australian drug laws nationally to avoid such complications, uniform drug laws across the country would curtail the ability of individual states and territories to implement and evaluate drug law reforms (see Room et al., 2010). Synthetic drug manufacturers find ways around these schedules through marketing their products as 'not for human consumption' or by changing the chemical compounds to a variation that is not prohibited under existing schedules. In a recent example, the synthetic cannabinoid *Kronic* was recently scheduled in Western Australia. Within days, the same company began offering a new formulation of Kronic that they claimed was then legal in WA.

There is preliminary evidence that the prohibition of new synthetic drugs may have increased harm to some users, while not achieving any meaningful change in the availability of similar drugs to those who seek them. There is no incentive or requirement for companies to provide information to potential users about the active ingredients or about safer ways to consume the product and users are unlikely to know what the product actually contains. In Australia this issue is of particular relevance because of a shortage of imported MDMA, claimed by law enforcement as due to successful interdiction of precursors in South East Asia (Australian Crime Commission, 2010). Ongoing demand for MDMA-like substances provides a market opportunity for companies selling MDMA alternatives. Similarly, the increase in drug testing policies for Australian mine workers (Holland, 2003) has provided a market for synthetic cannabinoids as a replacement for cannabis which, until recently, have been unable to be detected by workplace drug testing technologies. While MDMA and cannabis have known harms, their newer replacements are even less studied and known. In these cases, well-intended drug policy decisions have led to use of new drugs with unknown potential for harm. How Australia responds to the increasing emergence of new synthetic drugs and the intersection of drug issues with new technologies will be major determinants of the countries success in reducing drug related harm into the future.

Harm reduction in Australian prisons
Kate Dolan and Ana Rodas

Prisons are high-risk settings for HIV infection and transmission, and this has consequences for the spread of HIV in society at large (see also chapter 7 by Jurgens in this book). Controlling the infection rate and spread of HIV in prisons is an important ethical and human rights initiative for the prisoners themselves – and an important public health initiative for society in general. HIV presents enormous challenges for prison authorities worldwide in terms of controlling it (Dolan et al., 2007). Prisoners have characteristics that can increase the risk of HIV transmission (Dolan et al., 1996). Injecting drug users (IDUs) are vastly over-represented, often accounting for more than half of all prison inmates (Dolan et al., 2007), but only 1–3% of the broader community. HIV is usually more prevalent in prison populations than in the surrounding community, and levels of infection reach 50% among prisoners in some countries (Dolan et al., 2007; Jurgens, 2005). Imprisonment is a common and recurring event for most IDUs. Over 60% of IDUs in a 12-city international study reported a history of imprisonment (Ball and Des Jarlais, 1995) and IDUs report an average of five imprisonments (Dolan, 1997; Dolan and Wodak, 1999). One-third of all heroin dependent individuals in the United States pass through a correctional centre each year (Boutwell, 2007). Furthermore, prison populations are dynamic with a vast number of movements of prisoners in and out of the prison setting. The throughput of inmates per year can be several times that of the census population. These two attributes of prison populations – a high proportion of IDUs and a high turnover of inmates – contribute to the spread of HIV among prisoners and the broader community (Dolan et al., 1997). While it is very difficult to document HIV transmission in prison owing to uncertainties regarding precise date of infection, reluctance of reporting risk behaviours and resistance by prison authorities, a growing number of reports has been made (Brewer et al., 1988; CDC, 1986; Horsburgh et al., 1990; Mutter et al., 1994; Taylor et al., 1995).

Prison officers and other prison employees are often overlooked in studies of HIV in prison. Although there have been reports of prison officers becoming infected with HIV (Egger and Heilpern, 1992) and HCV (Rosen, 1997). An investigation found that 9% of prison officers had experienced needlestick injuries (Larney and Dolan, 2008) and syringes confiscated in prison contained the hepatitis C virus (Dolan et al., 2009).

Impressive progress has been made in Australia in response to the use of illicit drugs since the National Campaign against Drug Abuse was launched in 1985. The Strategy includes harm minimisation, evidence-based practice, integration, social justice and coordination (Fitzgerald and Sewards, 2002). Progress has occurred in limiting HIV transmission among IDUs in the community (Wodak and Cooney, 2004), but this will be undermined if efforts to prevent HIV transmission in prison are insufficient. Ultimately, the implementation of HIV prevention strategies *in prison* is essential for HIV control.

The increasing use of illicit drugs in Australia in recent decades and the heavy reliance on law enforcement measures to control drugs have resulted in a steadily growing prison population, an increase in the proportion of inmates with a history of drug use, particularly injecting drug use. In response, prison authorities have established a diverse array of supply, demand and harm reduction strategies. In this chapter we examine Australia's efforts to minimise harm among prisoners.

Supply reduction strategies are designed to disrupt the production and supply of illicit drugs (see table 30.1). The two main specific forms of supply reduction used in Australian prisons were drug detection dogs and urinalysis. All prison systems utilised drug detection dogs and urinalysis. It was apparent these supply reduction strategies were relatively expensive, had not been evaluated and possibly had unintended negative consequences. Supply reduction strategies in Australian prisons need to be evaluated.

Demand reduction strategies aim to reduce the demand for illicit drugs (see table 30.2). Examples include detoxification, methadone treatment, inmate programmes and counselling and drug-free units. While most demand reduction strategies were implemented in every prison system, the level

Table 30.1 Supply reduction measures in Australian prisons: coverage and evaluation

Jurisdiction	Drug detection dogs		Urinalysis programmes	
	Coverage	Evaluation	Coverage	Evaluation
NSW	Y	Y	Y	Y
QLD	Y	N	Y	N
VIC	Y	N	Y	Y
SA	Y	N	Y	N
WA	Y	Y	Y	Y
TAS	Y	N	Y	N
NT	Y	N	Y	N
ACT	Y	Y	Y	Y

Table 30.2 Demand reduction measures in Australian prisons: coverage and evaluation

State	Detoxification		MMT		Inmates programmes/ counselling		TC and drug free	
	Coverage	Evaluation	Coverage	Evaluation	Coverage	Evaluation	Coverage	Evaluation
NSW	Y	N	Y	Y	Y	Y	Y	Y
QLD	Y	Y	Y	Y	Y	N	Y	N
VIC	Y	N	Y	N	Y	Y	N	—
SA	Y	N	Y	Y	Y	N	Y	Y
WA	Y	N	Y	Y	Y	N	Y	N
TAS	Y	N	Y	N	Y	N	N	—
NT	Y	N	Y	N	Y	N	N	—
ACT	Y	Y	Y	Y	Y	Y	N	—

of implementation varied greatly. Some demand reduction strategies were relatively inexpensive. Each type of demand reduction strategy had been evaluated and most evaluations were favourable. There was strong evidence that the availability of demand reduction strategies was insufficient.

The aim of harm reduction strategies is to directly reduce the harms associated with illicit drug use (see table 30.3). The eight harm reduction strategies identified were harm reduction education, peer education, blood-borne viral infection (BBVI) testing, hepatitis B vaccination, condom provision, bleach/detergent provision, naloxone provision and needle and syringe programmes. Only three strategies were implemented in every jurisdiction: BBVI testing, hepatitis B vaccination and naloxone provision, even though these were generally inexpensive. Three strategies had been evaluated: illicit drug peer education, condom provision and bleach provision, all favourably. There was evidence of insufficient implementation of harm reduction strategies.

Extensive evaluation of demand and harm reduction strategies in community settings has suggested similar benefits are likely in correctional environments. Considering the importance of developing a more effective response to drug use in prison, there is an urgent need to improve documentation of all strategies, increase the quantity and quality of evaluation and expand the implementation of those strategies best supported by current evidence, namely demand and harm reduction strategies. In addition, measures to reduce the size of the prison population would have great benefit and achieve considerable savings.

In conclusion, supply reduction strategies were widespread, relatively expensive, had not been evaluated and possibly had unintended negative consequences. Demand reduction strategies had a reasonable level of implementation, were relatively inexpensive and evaluation had been favourable. Harm reduction strategies were least likely to be implemented, were relatively inexpensive and evaluation had been favourable.

Harm reduction in Aotearoa, New Zealand
Geoffrey Noller

In Aotearoa, New Zealand, harm reduction represents the philosophical compass officially guiding responses to a range of public health risks. In practice, however, there exists an ambivalence concerning harm reduction's application, depending on the theatre in which it is deployed. The perceived severity of health risks, moral attributions (e.g. regarding drug use and users) and competing political agendas animate rival views about what remains in some circles a controversial approach to managing harms from risk behaviours.

As with elsewhere in the world, the initial impetus for harm reduction in New Zealand derived from responses to the HIV/AIDS epidemic during the early to mid-1980s. Davis and Lichtenstein (1996) note its early embracing by those at risk of contracting blood-borne viruses (BBVs), for example the gay community and then intravenous drug users (IDUs), and later by policy-makers. This provided the basis of a successful response to the risk of infection from HIV/AIDS, with New Zealand IDU seroprevalence (consistently <1%) amongst the lowest in the world (Aitken, 2002; Ministry of Health, 2009). This is despite a sharp increase in opiate and opioid use in New Zealand among 16- to 64-year-olds between 2004 (0.4%) and 2008 (1.1%), thereby surpassing use in Australia and being significantly attributable to street morphine and diverted methadone (UNODC, 2010). Nonetheless, although ultimately proving effective and being highlighted as such in the minds of policy-makers, as Kemp and Aitken (2004) observe, enthusiasm for harm reduction has fluctuated.

Table 30.3 Harm reduction measures in Australian prisons: coverage and evaluation

	HR education		Peer education		BBV Testing		HBV vaccine		Condoms		Disinfectant	
	Coverage	Evaluation	Coverage	Evaluation	Coverage	Evaluation	Coverage	Evaluation	Coverage	Evaluation	Coverage	Evaluation
NSW	Y	Y[a]	Y	Y	Y	N	Y	N	Y	Y	Y	Y
QLD	N	—	N	—	Y	N	Y	N	N	—	Y	N
VIC[b]	Y	N	Y	N	Y	N	Y	N	Y	N	Y	N
SA	Y	N	Y	N	Y	N	Y	Y?	Y	N	Y	N
WA	Y	Y	Y	N	Y	N	Y	Y	Y	N	N	—
TAS	Y	Y	N	—	Y	N	Y	Y[c]	Y	N	N	—
NT	Y	Y	Y	N	Y	N	Y	N	N	—	Y	—
ACT	Y	Y	Y	Y	Y	Y	Y	Y	Y	Y	Y	Y

[a] Internal evaluation, report not publicly available.
[b] Black et al., 2004.
[c] Prisoners sentenced to six months or longer are offered vaccination.

Sources: Black et al., 2004; AIHW, 2010.

There can be no doubt that the public health risks faced by IDUs, and by association the wider community, have promoted the uptake of harm reduction strategies by consumers and officials alike. In 1986 New Zealand's AIDS Advisory Committee recommended the legalisation of needle and syringe possession, accompanied by the introduction of a suitable means of exchange. Endorsed by the Ministry of Health, this led in 1987 to the introduction of the Health (Needles and Syringes) Regulations, and in 1988 to the implementation of a national Needle Exchange Programme (NEP). As Kemp and Aitken (2004) note, however, an unusual aspect of the NSEP design was the government decision to impose full market costs on needle and syringe 'consumers', a requirement unique among government-sanctioned and implemented programmes at that time.

Injecting equipment was initially distributed principally through pharmacies. In 1989 these provided the bulk of equipment (90%), with consumers accessing the remainder through IDU peer support groups set up as independent trusts (Kemp and Aitken, 2004). By 1996 the proportion of equipment supplied by pharmacies had decreased to 44% as peer groups sought greater involvement, including sourcing equipment directly from wholesalers (Walker and Baker, 1994; Kemp and Aitken, 2004).

That year also saw one IDU peer group attempt trialling free one-for-one (1–4–1; new for used) needle exchange due to access barriers resulting from government-imposed costs. Although a legal decision successfully challenged the Ministry of Health's opposition to the scheme, it was subsequently discontinued for financial reasons. A similar failure occurred at another site in 1999. In 2004, however, the NEP secured government funded unlimited 1–4–1. By 2010 twenty-one exchanges and 171 pharmacies were distributing 2.8 million needles and syringes annually, 80% of these through NEP exchanges (Henderson, 2011).[1]

These figures and the existence of a government-funded NEP imply a strong commitment to harm reduction in New Zealand. Yet other evidence suggests that both officially and structurally, New Zealand continues to struggle philosophically with this approach.

Tensions surrounding harm reduction are apparent in the drafting of New Zealand's National Drug Policy, which claims harm reduction as its guiding principle (Ministerial Committee on Drug Policy, 2007).[2] The first formal policy was promulgated in 1996, initially only for alcohol and tobacco (Ministry of Health, 1996), then two years later for all other drugs (Ministry of Health, 1998). Although beyond the scope of the present text, an examination of policy drafts preceding the 1996 and 1998 documents would suggest a vigorous debate concerning harm reduction's place in New Zealand drug policy.[3] Of this process, commentators have noted that during the drafting of the policy, enforcement and abstinence messages were ultimately privileged over harm reduction (Webb, 1999b), and that no formal analysis of prohibition's negative consequences was undertaken (Abel and Casswell, 1998).

The significance of prohibition is relevant as New Zealand's policy incorporates a purportedly balanced, 'three pillars' approach to drug policy promoted by the United Nations (Costa, 2003): supply control (enforcement), demand reduction (limiting drug use), and problem limitation (treatment). However, the extent to which 'strong law enforcement (to control supply of drugs)' (Ministry of Health, 1998: iii) is compatible with harm reduction is a vital question and one remaining to be resolved in New Zealand drug policy. Certainly other writers consider a fundamental

[1] Personal communication between the author and Charles Henderson, National Manager, Needle Exchange Programme, Aotearoa New Zealand, 8 July, 2011.
[2] New Zealand policy documents refer to harm 'minimisation' rather than 'reduction'. While the latter is more common, some writers acknowledge the use of both terms (e.g. Nadelmann, 1996).
[3] For a detailed analysis see Noller (2008: 98–104).

contradiction between harm reduction and prohibition may exist (Single, 1995), particularly where use reduction becomes a goal (Lenton and Single, 1998).

In this context the difficulties harm reduction faces in New Zealand are most clearly evidenced by the case of cannabis. As is the situation globally, it is the country's most popular illicit drug, with 45% of those aged 16–64 reporting lifetime use and 15% ongoing use (Ministry of Health, 2010) which ranks New Zealanders second only to Canada in the developed world. The same rank (with the US first) applies to New Zealand per capita arrests for cannabis (349 per 100,000; Police National Headquarters, 2007). These statistics are accompanied by an array of enforcement-related harms including: criminal convictions, leading to lost employment and travel opportunities; racial profiling by police whereby Maori (indigenous New Zealanders) are disproportionately arrested, convicted and imprisoned; undermining of respect for the law; and a significant black market.

Significantly, these negative consequences result from a current cannabis policy that, despite the claimed tripartite balanced approach, sees enforcement receiving the overwhelming proportion of resources. A crude analysis of government-related funding for 2005/06 suggests that specifically for cannabis, use reduction measures (police, courts, Justice) deploy 83% of funds, with demand reduction (education) 3% and problem limitation (treatment) 14%.[4]

Criticism of this emphasis on enforcement, with its high costs, limited success and generation of harms, has broadened to drug control in general. A review of the Misuse of Drugs Act specifically noted the negative consequences of enforcement on harm reduction and the need to rethink enforcement objectives and how its performance is measured (Law Commission, 2010:310).

In summary, harm reduction in Aotearoa New Zealand has a chequered history. Its application to reduce the spread of BBVs (HIV/AIDS, hepatitis C) represents arguably the country's most successful public health programme, one for which there is strong official support. However, the philosophical core of harm reduction, with its emphasis on safe practice regarding risk behaviours, sits uneasily alongside the pre-existing architecture of other strategies, notably those of traditional drug control. Its place in the political, moral and social landscape of New Zealand public health is yet to be secured.

Conclusion: harm reduction and the long haul
Michael Farrell

Most of the contributors to this chapter have devoted the best part of their professional lives to the implementation of a broad range of innovative policies and between them have had an extraordinary impact in Australia, in Asia and globally and I thank them for their robust achievements.

The rush and trickle effect seems clear where harm reduction is concerned. A number of the authors report that the policies are become 'jaded, stale, complacent' and that there is a loss of thrust and vigour to contemporary policy. A number of the commentaries indicate that the policies to some extent are a victim of their own success, with a growing complacency around drug use and HIV and a lack of policy and public concern around these issues.

The role that the policy has had in building up a research capacity in Australia that has made it a major contributor to publications and discussion on policy and science globally cannot be

---

[4] Figures are difficult to access, there being no formal complete analysis across the three areas described above. For enforcement see Slack et al. (2008), i.e. NZD$123 million; for treatment data are based on a proportion of service provision (e.g. Adamson et al., 2006), giving a cost of NZD$21.5 million; and for education NZD$4.4 million (personal communication between the author and the Ministry of Health, February 2011).

overstated. The other striking aspect of Australian policy was the way it embraced tobacco, alcohol and other drugs early on and the difference that this comprehensive approach made to a policy focus. In reality one of the most striking aspects of policy has been the reduction in overall cigarette smoking rates and the continued commitment to address getting population levels of tobacco consumption down. The recent initiatives around plain packaging are a world first initiative and have resulted in major scrutiny and pressure on the Australian federal government by the tobacco industry. This focus has also shifted attention away from the problems of injecting.

In many ways the real challenge in Australia is to see how the longer-term strategic goals can be fully underpinned and not subject to day to day political whim. From the drug injecting and HIV perspective what is most striking is the extent to which the rest of the Asia Pacific region suffered a major HIV epidemic. This was bound up with difficulties in implementing approaches to evidence based treatment and the price to be paid in the longer term for such short sighted policies is very significant.

The other challenge has been the shift away from the plant based opiate type products to synthetic stimulants and a range of new synthetic drugs in the Asia Pacific region as well as in Australia. The changing nature of the drug problem has been a challenge for the policy-makers and the drug field, with a rather slow and fumbled response to a changing drug and social climate. All along, the other legal industries of alcohol and gambling have had little change through harm reduction or health improvement.

On balance one is struck by the complexity of the broad field to be covered, the requirement for nimble footed politicians, policy-makers and intervention providers. With an end of term score sheet that would say, started the term very well but seems to have lost his way during the year and could do a lot better and I hope he will pick up and do better next year.

References

ABS (2009) *Prisoners in Australia, 2009*, Canberra: Australian Bureau of Statistics.

Adamson, S.J., Sellman, D., Deering, D., Robertson, P. and de Zwart, K. (2006) Alcohol and drug treatment population profile: a comparison of 1998 and 2004 data in New Zealand, *New Zealand Medical Journal*, 119 (1244), www.nzma.org.nz/journal/119-1244/2284/.

AIHW (2010) *The Health of Australian Prisoners 2009*, Cat. No. PHE 123, Canberra: Australian Institute of Health and Welfare.

Aitken, C. (2002) *New Zealand Needle and Syringe Exchange Programme Review: Final Report*, Wellington: Centre for Harm Reduction.

ANEX (2010a) *Lifesavers: A Position Paper on Access to Naloxone Hydrochloride for Potential Overdose Witnesses*, Melbourne: Anex.

ANEX (2010b) *With Conviction: The Case for Controlled Needle and Syringe Programs in Australian Prisons*, Melbourne: Australia: Association for Prevention and Harm Reduction Programs Australia Inc.

Australian Bureau of Statistics (2009) *Household Use of Information Technology, Australia, 2008–09*, Canberra: Author, www.abs.gov.au/ausstats/abs@.nsf/mf/8146.0.

Australian Crime Commission. (2010) *Illicit Drug Data Report 2008–09*, Canberra: Commonwealth of Australia.

Ball, A. and Des Jarlais, D. (1995) *Multi-centre Study on Drug Injecting and Risk of HIV Infection: A Report Prepared on Behalf of the International Collaborating Group for World Health Organisation Programme on Substance Abuse*, Geneva: WHO.

Bammer, G. and Douglas, R.M. (1996) The ACT heroin trial proposal: an overview, *Med J Aust*, 164690–2, www.mja.com.au/public/issues/jun3/bammer/bammer.html, accessed 15 June 2011.

Barratt, M.J. (2011) 'Refused classification': exploring the unintended consequences of the proposed internet filter for young Australians who use drugs. Paper presented at the Sixth International Conference on Drugs and Young People, Melbourne Convention Centre, Melbourne, 4 May.

Bennett Moses, L. (2010). Creating parallels in the regulation of content: moving from offline to online, *University of New South Wales Law Journal Forum*, 16 (1), 95–108.

Black, E., Dolan, K. and Wodak, A. (2004) *Supply, Demand and Harm Reduction Strategies in Australian Prisons: Implementation, Cost and Evaluation*, ANCD research papers, Canberra: Australian National Council on Drugs.

Bleeker, A., Silins, E., Dillon, P., Simpson, M., Copeland, J. and Hickey, K. (2009). *The Feasibility of Peer-led Interventions to Deliver Health Information to Ecstasy and Related Drug (ERDs) Users*, NDARC Technical Report no. 299, Sydney: National Drug and Alcohol Research Centre, www.med.unsw.edu.au/NDARC-Web.nsf/resources/TR+298-302/$file/TR+299.pdf.

Blevins, F.T.(Chair) for the Ministerial Council on Drug Strategy Sub-committee. (1990) *National Health Policy on Alcohol in Australia and Examples of Strategies for Implementation*, adopted by the Ministerial Council on Drug Strategy 23 March 1989, Canberra: Commonwealth of Australia, www.nationaldrugstrategy.gov.au/internet/drugstrategy/publishing.nsf/Content/4584407086E6AB7ACA2575B4001353FE/$File/ndsp7-8.pdf, accessed15 June 2011.

Boutwell, A.E., Nijhawan, A., Zaller, N. and Rich, J.D. (2007) Arrested on heroin: a national opportunity, *Journal of Opioid Management*, 3, 328–32.

Brewer, T.F., Vlahov, D., Taylor, E., Hall, D., Munoz, A. and Polk, B.F. (1988) Transmission of HIV-1 within a statewide prison system, *AIDS*, 2 (5), 363–7.

Burns, J.M., Ellis, L.A., Mackenzie and Stephens-Reicher, J. (2009). Reach Out! Online mental health promotion for young people, *Counselling, Psychotherapy, and Health*, 5, 171–86.

Burns, J.M., Davenport, T.A., Durkin, L.A., Luscombe, G.M. and Hickie, I.B. (2010) The internet as a setting for mental health service utilisation by young people, *Medical Journal of Australia*, 192 (11 supple.) S22–6.

Camilleri, A., Johnston, M.R., Brennan, M., Davis, S. and Caldicott, D.G. (2010) Chemical analysis of four capsules containing the controlled substance analogues 4-methylmethcathinone, 2-fluoromethamphetamine, alpha-phthalimidopropiophenone and N-ethylcathinone, *Forensic Science International*, 197, 59–66.

CDC (1986) Acquired immunodeficiency syndrome in correctional facilities: a report of the National Institute of Justice and the American Correctional Association, *MMWR: Morbidity and Mortality Weekly Report*, 35 (12), 195–9.

Committee on the Prevention of HIV Infection among Injecting Drug Users in High Risk Countries (2006) *Preventing HIV Infection among Injecting Drug Users in High Risk Countries: An Assessment of the Evidence*, Washington: National Academies Press, www.nap.edu/catalog.php?record_id=11731#orgs, accessed 15 June 2011.

Cook, C. (2010) *IHRA*, London.

Costa, A.M. (2003) Statement by the executive director. Paper presented at the Commission on Narcotic Drugs 46th Session, UNODC (United Nations Office on Drugs and Crime), Vienna, 1–5.

Costa, A.M. (2008) Making drug control 'fit for purpose': building on the UNGASS decade. Report by the Executive Director of the United Nations Office on Drugs and Crime as a contribution to the review of the twentieth special session of the General Assembly, www.unodc.org/documents/commissions/CND-Session51/CND-UNGASS-CRPs/ECN72008CRP17.pdf, accessed 15 June 2011.

Davis, P. and Lichtenstein, B. (1996) In P. Davis (ed.), *AIDS, Sexuality and the Social Order in New Zealand: Intimate Details and Vital Statistics*, Auckland: Auckland University Press.

Day C., Degenhardt, L., Gilmour S. and Hall W. (2004) Effects of a reduction in heroin supply on injecting drug use: analysis of data from needle & syringe programmes, *British Medical Journal*, 329, 428–9.

DoHA (2010a) *National Needle and Syringe Programs Strategic Framework 2010–2014*, Canberra: Australian Government Department of Health and Ageing, www.health.gov.au/internet/main/publishing.nsf/Content/0CF549E9268148FCCA2578000008F55B/$File/frame.pdf.

DoHA (2010b) *Third National Hepatitis C Strategy 2010–2013*, Canberra: Australian Government Department of Health and Ageing.

DoHA (2010c) *Sixth National HIV Strategy 2010–2013*, Canberra: Australian Government Department of Health and Ageing.

DoHA (2010d) *Third National Aboriginal and Torres Strait Islander Blood Borne Viruses and Sexually Transmissible Infections Strategy 2010–2013*, Canberra: Australian Government Department of Health and Ageing.

Dolan, K. (1997) AIDS, drugs and risk behaviour in prison: state of the art, *International Journal of Drug Policy*, 8, 5–17.

Dolan, K., and Wodak, A. (1999) HIV transmission in a prison system in an Australian State, *Medical Journal of Australia*, 171 (1), 14–17.

Dolan, K., Wodak, A., Hall, W., Gaughwin, M. and Rae F. (1996) Risk behaviour of IDUs before, during and after imprisonment in NSW, *Addiction Research*, 4 (2), 151–60.

Dolan, K., Wodak, A. and Hall, W. (1999) HIV risk behaviour and prevention in prison: A bleach programme for inmates in NSW, *Drug and Alcohol Review*, 18 (2), 139–43.

Dolan, K., Kimber, J., Fry, C., Fitzgerald, J., Mcdonald, D., Trautmann, F. (2000) Drug consumption facilities in Europe and the establishment of supervised injecting centres in Australia, *Drug and Alcohol Review*, 19: 337–346http://informahealthcare.com/doi/pdf/10.1080/cdar.19.3.337.346.

Dolan, K., Kite, B., Black, E., Aceijas, C. and Stimson, G.V. (2007) HIV in prison in low-income and middle-income countries, *Lancet Infectious Diseases*, 7 (1), 32–41.

Dolan, K., Larney, S., Jacka, B. and Rawlinson W. (2009) Presence of hepatitis C virus in syringes confiscated in prisons in Australia, *Journal of Gastroenterology and Hepatology*, 24 (10), 1655–7.

Dolan, K., Teutsch, S., Scheuer, N., Levy, M., Rawlinson, W. Kaldor, J., Lloyd, A. and Haber, P. (2010) Incidence and risk for acute hepatitis C infection during imprisonment in Australia, *European Journal of Epidemiology*, 25 (2), 143–8.

Drew, L. (1998). Wernicke's encephalopathy and thiamine fortification of food: time for a new direction?, *MJA*, 168, 534–5. www.mja.com.au/public/issues/jun1/drew/drew.html, accessed 15 June.

Drucker, E., Lurie, P., Wodak, A. and Alcabes, P. (1998) Measuring harm reduction: the effects of needle and syringe exchange programs and methadone maintenance on the ecology of HIV, *AIDS*, 12 (supple. A), S217–S230. www.geo.hunter.cuny.edu/~dgreimer/TEMPALSKI/Drucker.pdf, accessed 15 June 2011.

Duff, C., Johnston, J., Moore, D. and Goren, N. (2007) *Dropping, Connecting, Playing and Partying: Exploring the Social and Cultural Contexts of Ecstasy and Related Drug Use in Victoria*, Melbourne: Premier's Drug Prevention Council, Department of Human Services Victoria, www.health.vic.gov.au/vdapc/archive/erd_full_report_march07.pdf.

Egger, S. and Heilpern. H. (1992) *HIV/AIDS and Australian Prisons*. In J. Norberry, M. Gaughwinand S.A. Gerull (eds), Canberra: Australian Institute of Criminology.

EMCDDA. (2011) *Synthetic Cannabinoids and 'Spice'*, Lisbon: EMCDDA.

European Monitoring Centre for Drugs and Drug Addiction (2011) *Report on the Risk Assessment of Mephedrone in the Framework of the Council Decision on New Psychoactive Substances*, Lisbon: Author.

Europol-European Monitoring Centre for Drugs and Drug Addiction (EMCDDA). (2010) *Joint Report on a New Psychoactive Substance: 4-Methylmethcathinone (Mephedrone)*, London: EMCCDA.

Fitzgerald, J. and Sewards, T. (2002) *Drug Policy: The Australian Approach*, Canberra: Australian National Council on Drugs.

Gascoigne, M., Dillon, P. and Copeland, J. (2004) *Sources of Ecstasy Information: Use and Perceived Credibility*, NDARC Technical Report no. 202, Syndey: National Drug and Alcohol Research Centre, UNSW.

Hales, J. (2009) *A Feasibility Study for an Illicit Tablet Information and Monitoring Service*, Report to the Premier's Drug Prevention Council Victoria, Melbourne: Health Outcomes International, www.health.vic.gov.au/vdapc/archive/itims_jun09.pdf.

Health Outcomes International Pty Ltd, National Centre for HIV Epidemiology and Clinical Research (NCHECR), Drummond, M. (2002) *Return on Investment in Needle & Syringe Programs in Australia*, Final

Report to the Commonwealth Department of Health and Ageing, St Peters: Health Outcomes International, www.health.gov.au/internet/main/publishing.nsf/Content/E1027EFEC83DA846CA257650007AC419/ $File/roisum.pdf, 15 June 2011.

Hedrich D, Kerr T, Dubois-Arber F. (2010) Drug consumption facilities in Europe and beyond. In European Monitoring Centre for Drugs and Drug Addiction, *EMCDDA Monographs – Harm Reduction: Evidence, Impacts and Challenges*, Lisbon: EMCDDA.

Holland, P. (2003) Case-study: drug testing in the Australian mining industry, *Surveillance and Society*, 1, 204–9.

Horsburgh, C.R., Jarvis, J.Q., McArthur, T., Ignacio, T. and Stock, P. (1990). Seroconversion to human immunodeficiency virus in prison inmates, *American Journal of Public Health*, 80 (2), 209–10.

Hughes, C. (2011) *The Australian (Illicit) Drug Policy Timeline: 1985–2011*, Drug Policy Modelling Program, updated 1 February, www.dpmp.unsw.edu.au/dpmpweb.nsf/page/Drug+Policy+Timeline, accessed 15 June.

Johnston, J., Barratt, M.J., Fry, C.L., Kinner, S., Stoové, M. and Degenhardt, L. (2006) A survey of regular ecstasy users' knowledge and practices around determining pill content and purity: Implications for policy and practice, *International Journal of Drug Policy*, 17, 464–72.

Jurgens, R. (2005) *HIV/AIDS and HCV in Prisons: A Select Annotated Bibliography*, Ottawa: Health Canada.

Kemp, R., and Aitken, C. (2004) The development of New Zealand's Needle and Syringe Exchange Programme, *International Journal of Drug Policy*, 15, 202–6.

Kratzmann, M., Mitchell, E., Ware, J., Banach, L., Ward, J. and Ryan J. (2011) *Injecting Drug Use and Associated Harms among Australian Aboriginals*, Canberrra: Australian National Council on Drugs.

Kwon, J.A., Iversen, J., Maher, L., Law, M.G. and Wilson, D.P. (2009) The impact of needle and syringe programs on HIV and HCV transmissions in injecting drug users in Australia: a model-based analysis, *Journal of Acquired Immune Deficiency Syndrome*, 51, 462–9.

Langos, C. (2010) Proposed mandatory filtering for internet service providers (ISPs): a brief insight into how filtering the refused content list may affect Australian ISPs, *Internet Law Bulletin*, 13, 137–9.

Larney, S. and Dolan, K. (2008) An exploratory study of needlestick injuries among Australian prison officers, *International Journal of Prisoner Health*, 3, 164–8.

Law Commission (2010) *Controlling and Regulating Drugs*, Law Commission issues paper 16, Wellington: New Zealand.

Lenton, S. and Single, E. (1998) The definition of harm reduction, *Drug and Alcohol Review*, 17, 213–20.

Loxley, W., Toumbourou, J.W., Stockwell, T., Haines, B., and Scott, K., for the Ministerial Council on Drug Strategy (2004) *The Prevention of Substance Use, Risk and Harm in Australia: A Review of the Evidence*, Report prepared by the National Drug Research Institute and the Centre for Adolescent Health, Canberra: Commonwealth Department of Health and Ageing, www.health.gov.au/internet/main/publishing.nsf/Content/health-pubhlth-publicat-document-mono_prevention-cnt.htm/$FILE/mono_prevention_ch14.pdf, accessed 15 June 2011.

Lumby, C., Green, L. and Hartley, J. (2009) *Untangling the Net: The Scope of Content Caught by Mandatory Internet Filtering*, University of NSW, Edith Cowan University and the CCI ARC Centre of Excellence for Creative Industries and Innovation, www.saferinternetgroup.org/pdfs/lumby.pdf.

Mackey, P. for the Social Policy Group. (1998) *Alternative Treatments for Heroin Addiction*, Current Issues Brief 3 1998–99, Canberra: Commonwealth of Australia, www.aph.gov.au/library/pubs/cib/1998-99/ 99cib03.htm, accesssed15 June 2011.

Mathers, B.M., Degenhardt, L., Ali, H., Wiessing, L., Hickman, M. and Mattick, R.P. (2010) HIV prevention treatment, and care services for people who inject drugs: a systematic review of global, regional, and national coverage, *Lancet*, 375, 1014–28.

McClelland, R., and O'Connor, B. (2011) *Review of National Classification Scheme Starts*, Media release, Retrieved from www.alp.org.au/federal-government/news/review-of-national-classification-scheme-starts/.

Mendes, P. (2001) Social conservatism vs harm minimisation: John Howard on illicit drugs, *Journal of Economic and Social Policy*, 6 (1), Article 2, http://epubs.scu.edu.au/cgi/viewcontent.cgi?

article=1026&context=jesp&sei-redir=1#search="howard+announces+tough+on+drugs", accessed 15 June 2011.

Miller, E.R., Bi, P. and Ryan, P. (2009) Hepatitis C virus infection in South Australian prisoners: sero-prevalence, seroconversion, and risk factors, *International Journal of Infectious Diseases*, 13, 201–8.

Miller, P. (2010) Reporting of the ACT heroin trials, *Journal of Media and Communication Studies*, 2 (1), 001–008, www.academicjournals.org/jmcs/PDF/pdf2010/Jan/Miller.pdf, accessed 15 June 2011.

Ministerial Committee on Drug Policy (2007) *National Drug Policy 2007–2012*, Wellington: Ministry of Health.

Ministerial Council on Drug Strategy (2011) *The National Drug Strategy 2010–2015: A Framework for Action on Alcohol, Tobacco, and Other Drugs*, Canberra: Commonwealth of Australia, www.nada.org.au/downloads/Federal/NationalDrugStrategy2010_2015.pdf, accessed 15 June 2011.

Ministry of Health (1996) *National Drug Policy, Part 1: Tobacco and Alcohol*, Wellington: Ministry of Health.

Ministry of Health (1998) *National Drug Policy, Part I: Tobacco and Alcohol, Part 2: Illicit and Other Drugs – A National Drug Policy for New Zealand*, Wellington: Ministry of Health.

Ministry of Health (2009) *AIDS: New Zealand*, vol. 64: Wellington: Ministry of Health.

Ministry of Health (2010) *Drug Use in New Zealand: Key Results of the 2007/08 New Zealand Alcohol and Drug Use Survey*, Wellington: Ministry of Health.

Moore, T., (2005) *What Is Australia's 'Drug Budget'? The Policy Mix Of Illicit Drug-Related Government Spending in Australia 2005*, Melbourne: Turning Point, www.med.unsw.edu.au/ndarcweb.nsf/resources/Publications_1/$file/DPMP+MONO+1.pdf, accessed 15 June 2011.

Mutter, R. C., Grimes, R. M., and Labarthe, D. (1994) Evidence of intraprison spread of HIV infection, *Archives of Internal Medicine*, 154 (7), 793–5.

Nadelmann, E. (1996) Progressive legalizers, progressive prohibitionists and the reduction of drug-related harm. In N. Heather, A. Wodak, N. Nadelmann, and P. O'Hare (eds), *Psychoactive Drugs and Harm Reduction: From Faith to Science*, London: Whurr Publishers, 34–8.

National Campaign Against Drug Abuse (NCADA) (1988) *Report of the NCADA Task Force on Evaluation: August 1988*, Canberra: Australian Government Publishing Service.

National Campaign Against Drug Abuse (NCADA) (1991) *National Health Policy on Tobacco in Australia and Examples of Strategies for Implementation*, Canberra: Commonwealth of Australia, www.health.gov.au/internet/main/publishing.nsf/Content/9126302FDE02CBD4CA256F1900044D02/$File/ndsp7-9.pdf, accessed 15 June 2011.

National Centre in HIV Epidemiology and Clinical Research (NCHECR) (2009) *Return on Investment 2: Evaluating the Cost-effectiveness of Needle and Syringe Programs in Australia*, Canberra: National Centre in HIV Epidemiology and Clinical Research, UNSW and the Commonwealth Department of Health and Ageing.

NCHECR (2009) *Return on Investment 2: Evaluating the Cost-effectiveness of Needle and Syringe programs in Australia 2009*, Darlinghurst: Australian Government Department of Health and Ageing, www.med.unsw.edu.au/nchecrweb.nsf/resources/Reports/$file/RO-2ReportLQ.pdf, accessed 15 June 2011.

Noller, G. (2008) Cannabis in New Zealand: use, users and policy, unpublished PhD thesis, Dunedin: Otago University.

Police National Headquarters (2007) *New Zealand Crime Statistics 2006/2007: A Summary of Recorded and Resolved Offence Statistics*, Wellington.

Reuters (1984) Wife of Australia's premier tells of the family's ordeal, *New York Times*, 25 September, www.nytimes.com/1984/09/25/world/wife-of-australia-s-premier-tells-of-the-family-s-ordeal.html, accessed 15 June 2011.

Rosen, H.R. (1997) Acquisition of hepatitis C by a conjunctival splash, *American Journal of Infection Control*, 25, 242–7.

Room, R., Fischer, B., Hall, W., Lenton, S. and Reuter, P. (2010) *Cannabis Policy: Moving beyond Stalemate*, Oxford: Oxford University Press.

Salmon, A., van Beek, I., Amin, J., Kaldor, J. and Maher, L. (2010) The impact of a supervised injecting facility on ambulance callouts in Sydney, Australia, *Addiction*, 105 (4), 676–83.

Siggins Miller (2009) *Evaluation and Monitoring of the National Drug Strategy 2004–2009: Final Report*, Canberra: Commonwealth Department of Health and Ageing (CDHA) and the Intergovernmental Committee on Drugs (IGCD). www.health.gov.au/internet/drugstrategy/publishing.nsf/Content/FD973BE3A786C9B0CA257682000E70DC/$File/eval1.pdf, accessed 15 June 2011.

Single, E. (1995) Defining harm reduction, *Drug and Alcohol Review*, 14 (3), 287–90.

Single, E., Rohl, T. (1997) *The National Drug Strategy: Mapping the Future – An Evaluation of the National Drug Strategy 1993–1997*, Prepared for the Ministerial Council on Drug Strategy, Canberra: Commonwealth of Australia. www.health.gov.au/internet/main/publishing.nsf/Content/F8500968AEC6A827CA257567000ED8B1/$File/mapping.pdf, accessed 15 June 2011.

Slack, A., O'Dea, D., Sheerin, I., Norman, D., Wu, J., and Nana, G. (2008) *New Zealand Drug Harm Index*, Report to the New Zealand Police, Wellington: Berl Economics.

Standard Guidelines for Corrections in Australia (revised) (2004) *Standard Guidelines for Corrections in Australia*, revised, Western Australia Department of Justice, Corrective Services NSW, Correctional Services South Australia, Corrective Services ACT, Tasmania Department of Justice, Queensland Department of Corrective Services, Victoria Department of Justice, Northern Territory Department of Justice NT Correctional Services, Canberra.

Success Works Pty Ltd (2003) *Evaluation of the National Drug Strategic Framework 1998–99–2003–04*, Report to the Commonwealth Department of Health and Ageing (CDHA) and the Intergovernmental Committee on Drugs (IGCD), www.nationaldrugstrategy.gov.au/internet/drugstrategy/Publishing.nsf/content/33B3F1FD97B13446CA2575B4001353A3/$File/ndsf_eval.pdf, accessed 15 June 2011.

Swan, A.J., and Tyssen, E.G., (2009) Enhancing treatment access: evaluation of an Australian web-based lcohol and drug counselling initiative, *Drug and Alcohol Review*, 28, 48–53.

Taylor, A., Goldberg, D., Emslie, J., Wrench, J., Gruer, L., and Cameron, S., (1995) Outbreak of HIV infection in a Scottish prison, *British Medical Journal*, 310 (6975), 289–92.

United Nations Office on Drugs and Crime (UNODC) (2010) *2010 World Drug Report*, Vienna: United Nations.

Walker, N., and Baker, M., (1994) *Utilisation of the Needle Exchange Programme in New Zealand (1988–1993)*, Report to the New Zealand Ministry of Health, Wellington. Institute of Environmental Science and Research.

Webb, M.B., (1999b) New Zealand's National Drug Policy, *Drug and Alcohol Review*, 18, 435–44.

Webster, I., (1992) *No Quick Fix: An Evaluation of NCADA 1992*, Canberra: Australian Government Publishing Service.

Wodak, A., (2004) Is the Howard government tough on drugs?, *Social Research Briefs*, 7 (December), Sydney: National Centre in HIV Social Research, http://nchsr.arts.unsw.edu.au/media/File/SRB07.pdf, Retrieved 15 June 2011, accessed 15 June 2011.

Wodak, A., and Cooney, A., (2004) *Effectiveness of Sterile Needle and Syringe Programming in Reducing HIV/AIDS among Injecting Drug Users*, Geneva: World Health Organization.

Chapter 31

HARM REDUCTION IN SUB-SAHARAN AFRICA

Bruce Trathen, Charles D.H. Parry and Neo K. Morojele

Background

Sub-Saharan Africa is currently populated by approximately 800 million people, predicted to almost double by the middle of the twenty-first century (UN, 2010a). It is usually described as consisting of 47 states located south of, or partially within, the Sahara, and including a number of island states which stand in the Indian or Atlantic oceans close to the mainland African continent. Culturally, it is probably the richest region in the World, its diversity reflected in the number of languages spoken (as many as 2,500: UNESCO, 2010) and its pre-colonial demographics (Murdock, 1959). The United Nations (UN) designates it as the world's least developed region; it harbours 33 of the 49 least developed countries (LDCs), as classified by UN measures of low-income, human resource weakness, and economic vulnerability (UN, 2010b). Many of its countries suffer from political instability which is in some cases exacerbated by the trade in illicit substances. According to one recent rating of the 25 countries with the highest risks of instability globally, 9 were in West Africa (Hewitt et al., 2010 from UNODC, 2010).

Sub-Saharan countries are reported as accounting for many of those with the lowest life expectancies (from as low as 37 years in Swaziland) (WHO, 2008) concordant with the region's socio-economic status and its burden of infectious disease. Deaths from AIDS, malaria, diarrhoeal and respiratory disease account for much of the world's child mortality (WHO, 2008); AIDS is the leading cause of death for adults in the region (WHO, 2008), accounting for 92% of AIDS deaths throughout the world (UNAIDS, 2008), many of which are complicated by tuberculosis.

This chapter discusses harm reduction, as 'policies, programmes and practices that aim primarily to reduce the adverse health, social and economic consequences of the use of legal and illegal psychoactive drugs without necessarily reducing drug consumption' (IHRA, 2010b: 2). While recognising the importance of harm reduction measures for minimising problems associated with the use of both legal and illegal drugs, this chapter focuses on measures specifically related to the use of illicit drugs in sub-Saharan Africa. The chapter begins by providing an overview of the prevalence of the use of legal and illicit drugs in sub-Saharan Africa. It then focuses specifically on injecting drug use (IDU), and the main harms associated with heroin and IDU (namely the risks of HIV, hepatitis C infection and risk behaviours). The provision of services for drug users in general, and drug users in prisons are then described. Regional policies and legislation are then reviewed. The chapter then discusses the available evidence regarding harm reduction for drug users in sub-Saharan Africa. In recognition of a relative lack of data, the chapter concludes by providing recommendations on further research that can be done to enhance understanding of service needs of drug users, and highlighting the specific harm reduction activities that can be implemented to assist in minimising the potential for drug use to impact on the HIV epidemic in Sub-Saharan Africa.

Harm Reduction in Substance Use and High-Risk Behaviour: International Policy and Practice, First Edition.
Edited by Richard Pates and Diane Riley.
© 2012 Blackwell Publishing Ltd. Published 2012 by Blackwell Publishing Ltd.

Prevalence of substance use and misuse

The African continent is by far the least documented region of the world in terms of data and information on drug use (UNODC, 2009). For its 2009 World Drug Report, only 38% of African countries responded to the UN annual reports questionnaire (ARQ) in the drug use 'demand' area, even though submission of such reports is mandatory under the provisions of the international drug control treaties. To a large extent this is thought to represent the fact that in many cases member states simply do not have the information. Review of the UN's 2010 World Drug Report, shows that much data has been collated many years in the past, and is of questionable validity (UNODC, 2010). Throughout sub-Saharan Africa, there have been very few studies using validated techniques for estimation of prevalence (such as household surveys or capture-recapture methods) which allow for analysis of trends in illicit drug use in the general population. The only ongoing systematic collection of data on drug use which lends to analysis of trends, is treatment population data compiled on a bi-annual basis in South Africa by the South African Community Epidemiology Network on Drug Use (SACENDU) (Parry et al., 2009b), and in Mauritius by the Patterns and Trends of Alcohol and Other Drug Use (PTAODU) project (NATRESA, 2009). Another useful network, the Southern African Community Epidemiology Network on Drug Use (SENDU), provided trend data for seven countries in the Southern African Development Community (SADC), but came to an end in 2004 (Parry et al., 2003). A number of locally initiated cross-sectional studies in a few countries, most of which involve youth and high school students, represent the only other sources of information apart from anecdotal reports.

In spite of the questionable validity of the data available, the emerging pattern in recent years appears to be one of increasing heroin, cocaine and amphetamine-type-stimulant (ATS) (methamphetamine in particular) use, superimposed on the more traditional and widespread use of tobacco, alcohol and cannabis. Annual prevalence data for Africa as a whole indicate a range of 0.2 to 0.5% of the population using heroin at least once per year (UNODC, 2009). This figure hides the much greater estimated prevalence of opioid use in some countries with estimates as high as 1.95% in Mauritius (largely injecting buprenorphine misuse rather than heroin (IHRA/CUT, 2010)) and 1.3% in Kenya. In Nigeria, a recent study of 402 selected secondary school students in Lagos (mean age 15.9 years) found lifetime prevalence of 3.8% for both heroin and cocaine (Oshodi et al., 2010). In South Africa, a study of a nationally representative sample of high school students in Grades 8–11 (Reddy et al., 2010) revealed lifetime prevalence rates of heroin use of 6.2% (95% CI = 5.2–7.4) and of cocaine use of 6.7% (95% CI = 5.6–7.8). Treatment demand for heroin misuse in South Africa increased seven-fold compared to other substances over an eight-year period from 1998 (Parry et al., 2009b), with 17% of the treatment population consisting of primary heroin users as of late 2009 (Plüddemann et al., 2010). The UNODC (2010) tentatively estimates a total of 1.3 million cocaine users (annual prevalence) throughout the African continent, accounting for an estimated 5% of global use (UNODC, 2010). Lifetime prevalence of cocaine use is estimated at 0.1% in Nigeria and 0.7% in South Africa (Degenhardt et al., 2008), with cocaine treatment demand increasing significantly over the last ten years or so in the latter (Parry et al., 2007).

Asian data reported by the new millennium described the association between trafficking routes and development of substance-specific drug use (Beyrer et al., 2000). In sub-Saharan Africa, heroin and cocaine use, in particular, appears to have increased in response to globalisation of drug trafficking with use of African countries as thoroughfares for the producer countries of South America (cocaine) and Asia (heroin) (IHRA, 2008; Kools, 2008). The value of the drugs trade in Guinea-Bissau (South American cocaine moving to Europe and the USA) has previously been estimated as equivalent to the country's entire national income, with the UNODC estimating that about 27% of the cocaine that entered Europe in 2006 transited African countries (UNODC, 2007). Since 2008 seizures of cocaine in transit to West African countries have reduced dramatically, which may lead in turn to decreased use of the drug in those countries (UNODC, 2010).

Available treatment population data are generally supportive of the hypothesis that trafficking routes lead to demand creation in the areas through which the substance is being trafficked. Eastern and South-Eastern African countries generally describe much greater relative demand for heroin treatment, with Kenya, Mauritius, Seychelles, Tanzania and Mozambique variously reporting between 33% and 87% of treatment populations consisting of primary heroin users (when excluding alcohol and nicotine) (UNODC, 2010). African countries with west-facing coastlines report a relatively greater number of primary cocaine than heroin users in treatment, as compared to countries with east-facing coastlines (UNODC, 2010). South Africa, which has both Indian and Atlantic Ocean coastlines, reports much greater demand for heroin treatment in the eastern coastal region of Kwazulu Natal and the north-eastern province Mpumulanga than in other areas (Plüddemann et al., 2010). For countries which are described in the UNODC's World Drug Report (2010), the pattern is distinct with the ratio of heroin to cocaine treatment greater than one in all countries with eastern coastlines, and less than one in all westerly countries apart from Nigeria. Nigeria is thought to act as a thoroughfare for air transportation of heroin, which may explain this inconsistency (UNODC, 2010).

While alcohol and tobacco probably remain the most commonly used substances throughout sub-Saharan Africa as a whole, the reported use of alcohol varies extremely between different regions. The WHO (2004) reported a number of Eastern African countries as having some of the highest reported lifetime abstinence rates in the world, with the notable exception of Uganda which has the highest recorded per capita consumption in the world at 19.47 litres of pure alcohol. Clausen et al.'s (2009) household survey of 77,165 adults in 20 African countries concluded that lifetime abstinence dominates in African countries, although drinking patterns within countries were diverse. However, adult per capita alcohol consumption (population 15 years and above) throughout the sub-Saharan region has been reported as higher than the global consumption rate (7.4 litres vs. 6.2 litres) and alcohol consumption per adult drinker as 42% higher than the global rate (Roerecke et al., 2008). The data validity is questionable – over 90% of alcohol consumed in Eastern Africa may be unrecorded, with numerous home-brewed and illicit formulations available (WHO, 2004). West and Southern African countries tend to report a more homogenous pattern of alcohol use, with South African treatment admissions being more likely to be alcohol related than any other substance (Plüddemann et al., 2010).

Where estimates of annual prevalence are available cannabis is the substance most frequently used at least once in the last year in all countries, when excluding alcohol and tobacco. Annual prevalence rates approach 20% in some countries with estimated annual prevalence for Africa as a whole in the region of 8% (INCB, 2009). Cumulative lifetime incidence of cannabis use is reported as 8.4% in South Africa and 2.7% in Nigeria (Degenhardt et al., 2008). It is also the primary illicit drug associated with provision of treatment in most sub-Saharan countries, apart from in Kenya, Mauritius and Mozambique, where heroin treatment predominates, in Namibia, where methaqualone (Mandrax, a barbiturate-like substance) is most often the primary drug of use, in Eritrea where inhalant use is more often treated than cannabis use, and in Ethiopia where Khat treatment predominates (UNODC, 2010).

Similar to cannabis use in the region, use of amphetamine-type stimulants (ATS) is usually associated with local production. South Africa routinely dismantles approximately 30 illegal stimulant factories every year (INCB, 2009), which are dependent on internationally supplied precursor chemicals (ephedrine and pseudo-ephedrine). Such precursor chemicals are usually imported for legal purposes, with a proportion of the supply then being diverted for the illicit manufacture of ATS. Increased use of methamphetamine in recent years is reported in South Africa, particularly among adolescents and young adults in Cape Town (Plüddemann et al., 2008a). Other countries where there is evidence from treatment populations for possible widespread amphetamine-type-stimulant use include Namibia, Burkina Faso, Chad and Niger (UNODC, 2009).

The relatively mild stimulant khat (cathinone) is widely used in some East African countries (Fekadu et al., 2007; IHRA, 2008) as well as in South Africa, where an increase in methcathinone production (UNODC, 2009) and use have also been observed.

Inhalant use is evident from treatment data in a large number of countries, and community-based studies, and is usually associated with younger populations, and street children in particular. Inhalant use usually involves the sniffing of benzene, glue and paint thinners.

Use of multiple substances by individual drug users (poly-drug use) appears common in sub-Saharan Africa as elsewhere. Examples include the large majority of a Cape Town, South Africa, population of heroin users, who also use methamphetamine on a regular basis (Plüddemann et al., 2008b), cocaine as a primary drug frequently used with cannabis and/or alcohol in South Africa (Parry et al., 2007) where a heroin/cannabis mixture is also commonly used (Nyaope), and concurrent use of heroin and cocaine reported as common in Nigeria (Adelekan, 2006).

Prevalence of injecting drug use (IDU)

Globally there may be as many as 21.2 million or as few as 11.0 million people who inject drugs, and among them between 0.8 and 6.6 million who are living with HIV (Mathers et al., 2008). Consistent with general data on drug use, sub-Saharan Africa has the greatest paucity of data on IDU worldwide (Mathers et al., 2008). Mathers et al. (2008) estimated that between approximately 0.5 million and 3 million people in the region inject drugs, but these figures are extrapolated from annual prevalence data estimated for only three countries – Kenya (0.16%–1.3%), Mauritius (2.01%–2.13%) and South Africa (0.87%), and South African researchers believe this to represent a gross over-estimate (Parry, 2010, personal communication, June–August). In Mauritius there were estimated to be over 17,000 IDUs in 2006 (Abdool et al., 2006), and 5.1% of adolescents are reported to have injected buprenorphine (IHRA/CUT, 2010). One Tanzanian (Zanzibar) purposively sampled study of 508 self-identified drug users found that 38.9% reported injecting (Dahoma et al., 2006). Reports of injecting drug use occurring (without prevalence estimates) currently exist for a further 28 sub-Saharan countries (IHRA, 2010a).

Injecting drug use appears to be well established in at least Kenya, Mauritius, Nigeria, South Africa, and Tanzania. This is consistent with the prevalence of heroin use in these countries, (as well as the illicit use of the opioid, buprenorphine in Mauritius (IHRA/CUT, 2010) and the greater likelihood of heroin being administered by injection than other substances (Adelekan and Lawal, 2006). In South Africa, treatment data indicate an increased frequency of injecting drug use over the first half of the decade (2000–10), particularly in Johannesburg and Pretoria (Parry et al., 2009b), with a relative stabilisation or even decrease since then in some parts of the country such as Cape Town (Plüddemann et al., 2010). Available treatment data indicate that injecting probably remains largely the preserve of the white population in South Africa (Plüddemann et al., 2010), although an increasing number of anecdotal reports describe injecting among other racial groups (including Indian, coloured (people of mixed ancestry) and black African users) (Trathen, 2010, personal communication). Methamphetamine has in other parts of the world overtaken heroin for some periods as the most commonly injected drug (McAllister and Makkai, 2000) and of note high levels of concurrent use of these substances has been observed in Cape Town, South Africa (Plüdde-mann, 2008b), although injecting does not seem (as yet) to be a frequent route of administration.

HIV, hepatitis C and risk behaviours

UNAIDS reports that sub-Saharan Africa is the region most heavily affected by HIV, accounting for 67% of new HIV infections worldwide. The majority of new HIV infections in the region occur through heterosexual intercourse, but recent epidemiological evidence attributes an increasingly significant role to injecting drug use (UNAIDS, 2009).

Estimates suggest that 221,000 (range 26,000 to 572,000) people who inject drugs are living with HIV in the region (Mathers et al., 2008), although the estimate is believed to be based on incorrect data for South Africa resulting in an inflated figure (Parry, 2010, personal communication). HIV prevalence among people who inject drugs is estimated to be over 40% in Kenya (Mathers et al., 2008) (and previously as high as 88% (Aceijas et al., 2004) and 75% in Mauritius (Sulliman and Ameerberg, 2004). A Tanzanian (Zanzibar) study of 508 self-identified drug users found the prevalence of tested infections to be higher in IDUs as compared with non-IDUs (HIV: 30% vs. 12%; hepatitis C: 22% vs. 15%; syphilis: 17% vs. 10% respectively) (Dahoma et al., 2006). A mainland Tanzania study of 319 heroin users (IDU and non-IDU) found 27% of males and 58% females tested positive for HIV infection with the majority of females engaged in sex work (Timpson et al., 2006). In general, women IDUs in sub-Saharan Africa have higher prevalence rates of HIV than male injectors (IHRA, 2008).

In contrast, Adelekan and Lawal (2006) were unable to demonstrate a significant correlation between IDU and HIV positivity in their review of three studies (n = 1147 street drug users) conducted in Nigeria between 2000 and 2005 with HIV rates similar between non-injecting and injecting drug users. Although limited by small sample sizes and the use of non-probability-based sampling, two studies in South Africa had similar findings. One study in Cape Town, South Africa, in 2004 (Plüddemann et al., 2008b) of 250 heroin users, found a relatively low self-reported HIV prevalence of 5.4% (as compared to a current population prevalence of 11%) (UNODC, 2008), or the provincial prevalence rate of 3.8%, 95% CI = 2.7–5.3 (Shisana et al., 2009). A later South African study (Parry et al., 2009) found that 20% of IDUs who agreed to testing, tested positive for HIV compared to 0% of non-IDUs.

Needle sharing is common in at least some sub-Saharan countries with rates reported as high as 50% in Mauritius (Abdool et al., 2006), but ranging from as low as 11–15% in Nigeria (Dewing et al., 2006). Plüddemann et al. (2008b) found that 86% of the injecting drug users in their Cape Town, South Africa study, had shared a needle at least once in the past. While most IDUs in the region are male (Aceijas et al., 2006; Reid, 2009), women who inject drugs in the region (many of whom are sex workers) are at greatly increased risk of contracting HIV – between two and ten times more likely than men (Reid, 2009). Extremely risky practices such as 'flashblood' (withdrawal of blood back into the syringe before sharing – reported in Tanzania) exacerbate the risk for these women further (McCurdy et al., 2010; Reid, 2009). Dahoma et al.'s (2006) Tanzanian (Zanzibar) study found that 46.1% of 508 subjects reported having shared needles, with IDUs who shared needles having higher HIV (28% v. 15%) and hepatitis C (31% v. 7%) infection rates than those who did not share needles. A mainland Tanzania mixed method study (n = 319) of heroin users found that one-third of IDUs reported sharing (Timpson et al., 2006).

Quite apart from self-administered injections of illicit drugs, medical injections performed with used needles and syringes may explain a proportion of Africa's AIDS epidemic, allowing cyclic transmission within high risk groups treated at sexually transmitted disease clinics (Gisselquist, 2008). In all but one of a cohort of studies of HIV incidence following HIV negative people in Africa between 1984 and 2006, people who received medical injections were more likely to acquire HIV (Gisselquist and Potterat, 2004).

An increasing number of studies also identify the role of non-injecting drug and alcohol use in facilitating sexual transmission of HIV, including among youth misusing amphetamine-type stimulants in South Africa (Plüddemann et al., 2008a; Parry et al., 2009), alcohol misusing non-injecting drug users in Malawi (Bisika et al., 2008), alcohol misusers with HIV in Nigeria (Olisah et al., 2009), alcohol users in Botswana (Pitso, 2004) and 18–24 year olds using alcohol in Uganda (Nazarius and Rogers, 2005). High levels of unprotected sex, multiple partners, increased duration of the sexual act, poor levels of understanding of risk behaviours and infrequent receipt of HIV testing and counselling, are all routinely reported in studies of drug using populations in the region (Abdool et al., 2006; Timpson et al., 2006; Parry et al., 2009). Several studies from the region have found that HIV prevalence rates among people who both use drugs and engage in sex work are higher than in those who only use drugs or only engage in sex work (IHRA, 2008). In 2007, a meta-analysis of 20 African studies concluded that 'Alcohol drinkers were more apt to be HIV positive than non-drinkers' (Fisher et al., 2007: 856), a finding supported by Pithey and Parry's (2009) systematic review. Indeed, Parry et al. (2010) describe the existence of conclusive evidence of a causal link between heavy alcohol use and worsening of HIV disease course, although further research is needed to substantiate causality in terms of HIV acquisition.

The prevalence rate of hepatitis C is estimated at approximately 5.5% in Africa (Sy and Jamal, 2006), and appears to be very low in all populations in South Africa (e.g. Madhava et al., 2002; Prabdial-Sing et al., 2006), while in contrast, a recent survey of Mauritian injecting drug users infected with HIV found that 99.7% were co-infected with hepatitis C (Johnston, 2009 from IHRA/CUT, 2010). In Mombasa, Kenya, HCV prevalence was reported as 70% among people who inject drugs (National AIDS Control Council, 2008). In Zanzibar (Tanzania) rates were reported as 22% for IDUs and 15% for non-injecting drug users, with higher rates among females than males (Dahoma et al., 2006).

Different social behaviours between injectors and non-injecting drug users have been found in different countries in the region – in South Africa, injectors are more likely to inject in private and have a small network of fellow IDUs (Parry et al., 2009), whereas in Tanzania, McCurdy et al. (2005) reported networks of IDUs gathering to inject at existing specific places.

Service provision

Service provision of any type for drug users is extremely limited throughout the sub-Saharan Africa region. Where services do exist, they are usually available only to those who can self-fund or who have medical insurance, which acts to exclude the large majority of the region's population. If services can be accessed, then in most countries treatment is likely to be based on a non-specialist psychiatric model and occur within a general psychiatric ward setting. Such treatment is unlikely to consist of any evidence-based intervention apart from medicated detoxification. International bodies indicate that most countries are far from implementing the comprehensive package of measures recommended by UNODC, UNAIDS and WHO to reverse the HIV epidemic and reduce drug-related harms (WHO, UNODC, UNAIDS, 2009). Harm-reduction specific interventions (opioid substitution therapy (OST) and needle and syringe programmes (NSPs)) are entirely absent at a public-health level apart from in Mauritius, and OST remains unlicensed in any context whatsoever in the large majority of countries, despite the fact that both methadone (a long-acting opioid agonist) and buprenorphine (an opioid partial agonist) are included on the WHO model essential medicines list (WHO, 2010).

Various regional-level efforts are attempting to address the deficits. The sub-Saharan Harm Reduction Network (SAHRN) was established in 2007 to advocate for and support the development of harm reduction services throughout the region (SAHRN, 2010). The TREATNET programme (international network of drug dependence treatment and rehabilitation resource centres) was recently extended to Africa, jointly by UNODC and WHO, to improve the quality of treatment for drug-dependent persons through cooperation, information exchange and the empowerment of selected resource centres. Cape Verde, Côte d'Ivoire, Kenya, Mozambique, Nigeria, Sierra Leone, the United Republic of Tanzania and Zambia are currently participating in TREATNET, and a review of its first phase is due for publication in the fourth volume of the journal *Substance Abuse* (R. Rawson, 2010, personal communication, 11 August).

Equally, recent regional cooperation has led to the creation of a database on African non-governmental organisations (NGOs) active in demand reduction (Wolfe and Malinowska-Sempruch, 2007); a number of such organisations are active in the sub-Saharan region delivering advice and education-based interventions. In Kenya, for example, since November 2006, the AED Capable Partners Programme in Kenya project has provided technical direction to eight Kenyan NGOs to design and implement programmes to reduce the spread of HIV among the local drug using population. Programmes are reported to have been developed utilising conventional outreach models modified for application in Kenya, and various other community-based interventions geared to reduce HIV among drug users (Deveau, 2008). However, according to a 2007 report, among other more traditional Kenyan residential treatment providers there were no or limited onsite HIV services for patients receiving treatment, and among HIV care sites, there was no drug or alcohol screening or referral for addiction treatment (Sullivan et al., 2007). The international narcotics control board's 2009 report (INCB, 2009) also refers to availability of treatment for drug abusers in the Seychelles and Uganda, but the quality and availability of such treatment is not described.

In South Africa a Rapid Assessment Response and Evaluation project funded by the US Centers for Disease Control and Prevention and implemented by the Medical Research Council (MRC) has been underway since late 2005. The first few phases (2005–7) involved undertaking two rapid assessment studies among vulnerable drug using populations, including commercial sex workers (CSWs), men who have sex with men (MSM), and injection (IDUs) and non-injection drug users (NIDUs) who are not CSWs or MSM, as well as with service providers to these populations in Cape Town, Durban and Pretoria. The results of these studies have been published widely (for example, Parry et al., 2008 and Parry et al., 2010). In addition, a WHO manual on conducting outreach to address HIV risk behaviours among IDUs was adapted to be used in South Africa among a broad grouping of drug users, both IDUs and non-IDUs (Medical Research Council, 2007). Since 2007 the project has focused on supporting NGOs (6 between 2007 and 2010: 2 working with MSM, 3 working with drug users in need of treatment and 1 working with street-based sex workers) in these 3 cities to establish targeted condom service outlets (25 in total between 2007 and 2010), to train persons to promote HIV/AIDS prevention through other behaviour change beyond abstinence and/ or being faithful (154 in total), to conduct outreach activities to reach vulnerable drug using populations from the sub-populations referred to above and conduct risk reduction counselling (10,613 drug users reached over 3 years, with many reached on more than one occasion), to establish dedicated service outlets for these sub-populations providing HIV counselling and testing according to national and international standards (25 new outlets have been established to date), and to train individuals counselling and testing according to national and international standards (more than 55 have been trained). Since 2007, 3,872 drug users have received counselling and testing for HIV and received their test results, and of these 1,071 have been referred to other services, such as HIV clinics. A 6-monthly evaluation of the project over the previous 3 years has demonstrated a willingness of the NGOs to expand the skills of their staff and broaden outreach and service delivery activities to address both sexual and drug-related HIV risk in these vulnerable populations, and a strong uptake of VCT and other services. Improved integration of drug treatment, HIV intervention and other services has also occurred through strengthened referral networks and the provision of VCT. A thorough assessment of whether risk reduction goals set by drug users has resulted in concrete behaviour change is now underway, and early indications are that there have been notable increases among drug-using participants in condom use, increased uptake of VCT, decreases in drug use during sex, avoidance of places where risky sex occurs and a reduction in injection related HIV risk behaviours.

Also in South Africa, several projects are underway or have been undertaken that specifically focus on reducing drug-related harm in women associated with contracting HIV or other STIs, or being a victim of substance-related violence. Once such study conducted by the RTI International and the MRC adapted a US-based intervention known as the Women's Coop Study which involved provision of two one-hour intervention sessions which included education on substance abuse, HIV/STIs, and ways of reducing HIV risk, behavioural skills training with male and female condoms, condom negotiation with sex partners and development of risk reduction plans. One-month post-intervention assessments indicated significant reductions in substance use and sex-risk behaviours (Wechsberg et al., 2008).

South Africa probably has the most extensive network of treatment providers within sub-Saharan Africa, but there is limited government support, and publicly funded treatment is restricted to providers operating according to an abstinence-based rationale. The largest coordinated network of programmes falls under the South African National Council on Alcoholism and Drug Dependence (SANCA) with each SANCA site operating as an individual entity (Parry, 2010, personal communication); both residential and community programmes are offered. A relatively large number of abstinence-based specialist private residential facilities are available, but these are inaccessible to the majority. Sublingual buprenorphine, and since early 2010, oral methadone (2 mg/ml), are licensed for use in opioid substitution therapy, but are again inaccessible to the majority, due to absence of public funding, lack of support for these treatments by medical insurance companies, and the limited number of practitioners trained in their prescription. Purchase of needles from pharmacies is not illegal, and is made available by some pharmacists on a client-funded basis. In July 2010, following the announcement at the 18th International AIDS Conference that PEPFAR/USAID sponsored organisations can deliver needle and syringe programmes, a Cape Town NGO, Health4Men, is planning to establish the country's first such programme.

Apart from South Africa, opioid substitution therapy is currently available in only three other sub-Saharan countries – Mauritius, Kenya and Senegal – and in the latter two cases in a very limited fashion for self-funding individuals (Mathers et al., 2010). Tanzania appears likely to be following in the near future, with a recent NIDA announcement (NIDA, 2010) that researched programmes of medication-assisted-therapy are due to commence shortly in Dar-es-Salaam and Zanzibar, with the cooperation of the Tanzanian government.

The single outlier with regard to publicly funded, evidence-based service provision for drug users is Mauritius, where clear evidence of an IDU-mediated HIV/AIDS epidemic exists (Reid, 2009). In 2009 the Mauritian Ministry of Health and the National AIDS secretariat, assisted by UNODC, mobilised $3 million from the Global Fund to Fight AIDS, Tuberculosis and Malaria, to be used in the development of service provision including for those who inject drugs. Mauritius is the only sub-Saharan country with established needle and syringe programmes (IHRA, 2010a). The official programme operates mainly through community-based outreach, reaching 31 sites, while NGOs run 8 fixed sites. Needles, syringes and condoms are delivered to nearly 1 in 3 people who inject drugs in the country (Sulliman, 2009 cited in IHRA, 2010a). OST has been scaled up in Mauritius since over the last several years, but services are still very limited. Over two thousand people are currently believed to be receiving methadone substitution therapy from 14 publicly or NGO-funded sites (Mathers et al., 2010); buprenorphine is not licensed for substitution therapy (IHRA, 2010a), remaining classified in the Mauritian Dangerous Drugs Act 2000 probably due to its role as a frequently illicitly injected opioid in this country. Despite its role-model status in the sub-Saharan region as far as harm reduction is concerned, Mauritius is still seen by some to be lacking in its response; there remains generally poor availability of harm reduction related services compared to the scale of the IDU/HIV epidemic, and a lack of focus on high-risk sub-populations including women, and prisoners (IHRA/CUT, 2010). Hepatitis C is highly prevalent among those infected with HIV (Johnstone, 2009 cited in IHRA/CUT, 2010), and no publicly funded hepatitis C treatment is available (IHRA/CUT, 2010).

Drug use, HIV and treatment in prisons

Throughout the world, the prison population consists of individuals facing greater risk factors for contracting HIV (and HCV and TB) than do the general population. Such characteristics include injecting drug use, poverty, alcohol abuse and living in medically underserved and minority communities (IHRA, 2010a).

Globally, the highest HIV prevalence reported in a national prison population is in South Africa (IHRA, 2010a), where some estimates put the figure as high as 41.4% (Dolan, 2007). South Africa also has the highest incarceration rate in the sub-Saharan region, estimated at 342 per 100,000 population (UNODC, UNAIDS and World Bank, 2007), as compared to a regional average of 84 per 100,000 (IHRA, 2008). Zambia, Burkina Faso, Cameroon, Cote D'Ivoire, Gabon, Malawi and Rwanda are all reported to have prisons with HIV prevalence of greater than 10% among inmates (Dolan, 2007) and HIV prevalence among prisoners who inject drugs in Malawi has been reported as 60–75% (IHRA, 2008). A 2007 UNODC report (UNODC, UNAIDS and World Bank, 2007) indicated that injecting in prisons is likely to be rising in Cape Verde, Cote d'Ivoire, Guinea, Senegal, Nigeria, Kenya, Tanzania, Mauritius. Injecting drug use in prison has also been reported in Ghana (Adjei et al., 2006), but appears absent in Nigeria (Adoga et al., 2009).

International guidelines recommend a range of measures to address enhanced risks in prisons, including HIV/AIDS education, voluntary and confidential HIV testing and counselling, condom provision, prevention of rape, sexual violence and coercion, and HIV care, support and treatment, including antiretroviral therapy (ART) (WHO, UNODC, UNAIDS, 2007). Botswana, Kenya, the Seycelles, Tanzania, Uganda, Zambia, South Africa and Lesotho are reported as providing variable levels of HIV counselling and testing (VCT/HCT), as well as anti-retroviral medication (ARV) to prisoners, whilst condom distribution is reported only in the latter two countries (IHRA, 2008). Prison HIV counselling and testing is also reported in Malawi and Mauritius, in the absence of ARV or condom provision.

WHO, UNODC and UNAIDS recommend that prison authorities in countries experiencing or threatened by an epidemic of HIV infection among prisoners who inject drugs should introduce and scale up needle and syringe programmes urgently (WHO, UNODC, UNAIDS, 2007). Only South Africa and Mauritius offer any form of drug treatment within prisons with over 2,300 prisoners receiving treatment during 2007 in the latter (IHRA, 2008). However neither OST nor NSPs are currently components of these programmes in South Africa, while Mauritius restricts provision of methadone to prisoners (70% of whom are serving sentences due to a drug-related crime (Mauritius Drug Control Master Plan, 2004–9)) who were receiving methadone treatment immediately preceding incarceration. NSPs are not available in Mauritian prisons (IHRA/CUT, 2010).

In Southern Africa, prison diversion programmes which provide treatment as an alternative to incarceration are reported as available in Botswana, Namibia, South Africa and Malawi and compulsory drug treatment occurs for sentenced individuals in Angola, Namibia, South Africa, Swaziland, and Lesotho (IHRA, 2008).

Legislation and policy

Whilst UNODC, WHO and UNAIDS, have expressed clear support for harm reduction, the UNDCP's Legal Affairs Section and the International Narcotics Control Board (INCB) have merely clarified that harm reduction services do not contravene the international drug control conventions (IHRA, 2008). As such, the drug conventions are often used to deny harm reduction services in countries around the world (Wolfe, 2004), due to the perception that introduction of services is optional. With several exceptions, such is the case in sub-Saharan Africa where most countries' drug policies focus exclusively on supply reduction and criminalisation of users (IHRA, 2010a), despite the fact that the relevance of harm reduction has been recognised by the African Union (Special Summit of African Union on HIV/AIDS, Tuberculosis and Malaria, Abuja, Special Summit of African Union on HIV/AIDS, Tuberculosis and Malaria, 2006). The USA's certification process is also believed to have had a major impact on the approach taken at times by some sub-Saharan countries. According to Obot (Obot, 2004), the decertification of Nigeria by the USA administration during the latter half of the 1990s was indirectly associated with an increased emphasis on law enforcement by the Nigerian authorities over all other approaches to the control of drugs.

Contradiction at the international level, is often reflected at the national level, for example in Mauritius, where the HIV/AIDS Act 2006 (which provides a legal framework for NSPs) lacks concordance with the Dangerous Drug Act 2000 (which criminalises all types of drug paraphernalia) (IHRA/CUT, 2010). Such inconsistencies can lead directly to conflict between law enforcement agencies and treatment providers. In Kenya, the 2010–2013 strategic plan for AIDS specifically supports opioid substitution therapy (OST) and needle and syringe programmes (NSPs), although legislation will need to be amended before full implementation (National AIDS Control Council, 2009). Despite this, anecdotal sources report that possession of syringes remains frequently used as a pretext for arrest and extortion by law enforcement agencies, and reservation exists within government as to implementation of opioid substitution treatment.

The drug conventions require countries to formulate a drug master plan, although in Southern Africa, South Africa is the only country to have implemented national legislation requiring this (R Eberlein, 2010, personal communication, July) In Eastern Africa, Djibouti, Ethiopia, Kenya, Madagascar, Mauritius, Seychelles, Tanzania/Zanzibar, and Uganda have all developed plans (R Abdool, 2010, personal communication, June), although some of these may not have been ratified. The Tanzanian National Drug Control Policy (2007) refers to responding to HIV infection among people who use drugs as critical to the response (IHRA, 2008), and Tanzania is currently planning to introduce a pilot OST programme, as detailed in its national strategic plan for substance use and HIV and AIDS for 2007 to 2011 (R. Abdool, 2010, personal communication, June). Mozambique refers to OST in its national drug strategy (IHRA, 2008) and the Mauritian National Multi-sector

HIV/AIDS Strategic Framework (NSF) 2007–11 includes two objectives on reducing HIV transmission among people who inject drugs and prisoners. It sets targets of 80% of people who inject drugs and all prisoners having access to HIV prevention services by 2011 (IHRA, 2008).

The provision of opioid substitution therapy has been legalised in Senegal (IHRA, 2010a) but has only minimal availability in practice. The South African National Drug Master Plan incorporates references to harm reduction (South Africa National Drug Master Plan 2006–11), although harm reduction-specific interventions are not mentioned.

In 2008 the Indian Ocean Commission (representing Mauritius, Madagascar, Reunion, Seychelles and the Comoros) initiated discussions on the introduction of harm reduction policies. Mauritius has the most developed response in the region with government funded OST and NSPs, although there have also been moves to reintroduce the death penalty for drug trafficking, especially for the importation of buprenorphine (IHRA, 2010a). If this occurred, Mauritius would be in the contradictory position of being one of only several countries in sub-Saharan Africa to impose the death penalty for drug-related offences, while also providing the most human rights-friendly treatment in the region for individual drug users. While Nigeria has imposed the death penalty for drug-related offences in the past, the only current sub-Saharan countries to do so are Sudan and the Democratic Republic of Congo (IHRA, 2008).

In West Africa, the heads of state of the Economic Community of West African States (ECOWAS) recently signed the Abuja Declaration (Abuja Declaration, 2009). The document recognises the need to commit to 'provision of treatment and support for those who abuse drugs and those dependent on drugs' (p. 45), and to 'take appropriate steps to make healthcare and social support available, affordable and accessible to those who abuse drugs and those dependent on drugs' (p. 46). The remainder of the declaration focuses almost exclusively on demand reduction related issues, and there is no mention of harm reduction or harm reduction-specific interventions.

Discussion

The International Harm Reduction Association (IHRA) defines 'Harm Reduction' as referring to 'policies, programmes and practices that aim primarily to reduce the adverse health, social and economic consequences of the use of legal and illegal psychoactive drugs without necessarily reducing drug consumption. Harm reduction benefits people who use drugs, their families and the community' (IHRA, 2010b: 2). It further states that 'The harm reduction approach to drugs is based on a strong commitment to public health and human rights' (IHRA, 2010b: 2). International critics of harm reduction argue on a number of grounds encompassing its morality, effectiveness and dangers. Such concerns, as well as others more specific to regional cultural and religious orientation, are reflected in sub-Saharan debate, where resistance to and/or failure of implementation remain endemic at all levels from legislative to service delivery.

Many sub-Saharan countries north of the equator have a majority Muslim population, and for the continent as a whole, the Muslim population is estimated at 40%. Particular challenges associated with HIV risk behaviours and the introduction of harm reduction related measures include gender inequality, stigma, discrimination and misinformation and these may be more pronounced in the Muslim world than elsewhere (Hasnain, 2005). 'The typical response from policy-makers in such countries is to propagate Muslim ideals, mainly abstention from illicit drugs and sexual practices, while sexuality is taboo for discussion' (Hasnain, 2005: 4). However, Hasnain (2005) has also noted that in some countries where HIV/AIDS is a rapidly rising threat, some religious scholars are justifying the provision of condoms and clean needles through Qur'anic and Hadith passages, based on the paramountcy of sanctity of life, and as being permissible as a short-term measure under a state of emergency. The importance of engaging with and educating religious leaders in particular, and collaboration with all stake-holders in general, is considered key (Hasnain, 2005).

Quite apart from the global concerns of Catholicism regarding condom use, non-Catholic sub-Saharan Christian populations may be equally ambivalent regarding the introduction of harm reduction measures on religious or moral grounds. A content analysis study of heroin use disorder specialists in South Africa (dos Santos et al., 2010), recorded views regarding the stigmatisation of heroin use disorders in the traditional white Afrikaner Calvinistic community, which may have contributed to delays in the development of appropriate medical interventions: 'South Africa has not kept up to speed with the rest of the world . . . it was seen as a non-white issue, and because of the Calvinistic culture of this country, it was seen as a moral issue.' Some specialist interviewees in this study were themselves of the opinion that it is immoral to condone and implement needle exchange programmes, and there was widely divergent opinion regarding the use of substitute opioid therapy.

Other examples include that of Zimbabwe, and most likely elsewhere in the region where some Christian communities are described as 'led by ministers or prophets who believe in diagnosis and treatment through prayer, aspire to biblical standards of treatment (the mentally ill achieve instantaneous recovery), and may not allow members of their congregations to visit hospitals or to take medicine' (Mpofu, 2003: 1). The notion of harm reduction is often at odds with the religious teachings that are espoused by members of groups such as these.

In the west, the earlier years of the twentieth century saw the development of a number of abstinence-based policies and movements ('Prohibition' at the legislative level and Alcoholics Anonymous (AA) and later 12-step movements at the service level), which were historically associated with Christian belief. While groups such as AA and 12-step treatment programmes have typically modified their approaches to encompass secularity in the west, this is much less the case in Africa, where religiosity often remains a predominant feature of treatment. Advocacy for an exclusively abstinence-based rationale is often strongest from those who have based their own recoveries on a deep acceptance of the need for abstinence, supported by belief in God. Contemplation of alternatives to abstinence may have the potential to undermine an individual's ongoing recovery, as well as to challenge religious and moral belief systems.

From the wider cultural perspective, indigenous (traditional) healers have been 'serving African communities since time immemorial, understand the belief system of their people, and enjoy a respected place in their society' (dos Santos et al., 2010: 8). Robertson (2006) estimated that 70% of South Africans consult indigenous healers, who include diviners, herbalists, faith healers and traditional birth attendants, while 61% of psychiatric patients had consulted indigenous healers during a 12-month period. Mpofu (2003), in Zimbabwe, describes all classes and racial groups as consulting traditional healers. Omonzejele (2008) describes African perspectives of health and disease as 'usually understood in terms of one's relationship with his ancestors' (p. 120). Mystical beliefs regarding health may not sit easily with western constructs of health and disease, and the latter risk impinging negatively on the successful incorporation of harm reduction interventions, unless they are modified to harmonise with the local context. Many individuals with general health problems already consult both Western-trained and indigenous healers. Quite apart from arguments for engaging with indigenous healers in terms of outreach, capacity and pragmatism (traditional healers are often the first to be consulted by community members), concordance with and effectiveness of treatment would seem likely to be enhanced through holistic policy and thinking.

A holistic approach is consistent with modern appreciation of the social determinants of health which emphasises the interactivity between factors exogenous and endogenous to the individual, as mediated by risk and protective factors of the individual and society (Strathdee et al., 2010). Introduction of interventions of proven effectiveness elsewhere in the world may potentially interact adversely with socially protective factors specific to other regions and cultures, and indeed, simple adoption of mental health practices from the west may sometimes be harmful (Fryers, 1986). Such concerns, together with an ingrained mistrust of western intentions at the political level (Nunn and Wantcheckon, 2010), act to bolster conservatism as to the introduction of new approaches. Corruption (UNODC, 2010), the contradiction of human rights observance for autocratically governed states, poor infrastructure, huge distances to reach services and their general inaccessibility, and the low priority accorded to substance problems given economic status and burden of other diseases, all act further to challenge the introduction of harm reduction services.

Since the 1980s, countries which have led in embracing the harm reduction rationale are those who drew conclusions similar to UK's Advisory Council on the Misuse of Drugs (ACMD, 1988) that the 'threat to individual and public health posed by HIV and AIDS was much greater than the threat posed by drug misuse' (Hunt et al., 2003, p. 2). There can be no reasonable doubt that such is the case throughout sub-Saharan Africa, and it is in attending to the region's burden of infectious disease that the overwhelming arguments for a harm reduction approach arise.

Since HIV infection in Africa occurs mostly by sexual transmission, HIV interventions have not been targeted at people who use drugs (Mathers et al., 2010). This approach ignores the regionally generated evidence for the enhanced risk of sexual transmission of HIV associated with alcohol and stimulant drug use, and denies the potential for injecting drug use to maintain and exacerbate the epidemic. In particular, the core public health message that AIDS is transmissible by needle reuse, has been set aside in many African AIDS prevention programmes which perceive IDU as uncommon (Reid, 2009), and may be stigmatised towards drug users (Parry et al., 2010).

The available data clearly indicates the existence of injecting drug use in the majority of sub-Saharan countries, and is indicative in some areas of increasing incidence. Observation of emerging injecting drug use in other areas of the world reveals the potential for rapid increases in prevalence, as well as associated risk factors for such a development (Renton et al., 2006). Transit of drugs through these areas, decreasing purity, as well as socio-economic hardship, are some of the factors which highlight the vulnerability of sub-Saharan Africa to the development of such an epidemic of injecting drug use. Available treatment data in South Africa have indicated to date that injecting probably remains largely the preserve of the white population (Pluddemann et al., 2010), although this is not the case in other countries in sub-Saharan Africa in which injecting has been recorded. Experience from other world regions shows that injecting first spreads within wealthy groups with subsequent diffusion more generally into the population, before later markedly affecting impoverished communities (IHRA, 2008); of note, an increasing number of South African anecdotal reports describe injecting among less affluent sectors of society (Trathen, 2010, personal communication). HIV infection levels can reach 50–60% one to two years after introduction to a community of IDUs (WHO, 2005), and these figures are consistent with the reported rates for HIV infection among IDUs in the eastern facing states of Mauritius, Tanzania and Kenya. In Kenya, only 38 people who inject drugs are reported as prescribed anti-retroviral therapy (Mathers, 2010) of an estimated 120,000 injectors living with HIV in the country.

Proponents of an exclusively abstinence-based approach to the problem fail to account for the fluctuating levels of motivation for abstinence experienced by dependent drug users, and the resulting difficulties of engaging more than a small proportion of the drug or alcohol using population with such treatment at any one time. In particular, those who advocate residential forms of abstinence-based treatment as a solution have not considered the financial impracticalities of such a response at the public health level. While these modalities of response remain completely valid for motivated individuals with the resources to access them, they cannot provide a solution for the majority of drug users, or impact meaningfully on the HIV epidemic.

The international evidence for the effectiveness of harm reduction programmes in the prevention of HIV infection among injecting drug users is increasingly clear (Vlahov, 2010), and WHO guidance for prevention, treatment and care among people who inject drugs describes an evidence-based comprehensive package of nine interventions (WHO, UNODC, UNAIDS, 2009). These are needle and syringe programmes; opioid substitution therapy and other drug dependence treatment; HIV testing and counselling; antiretroviral therapy; prevention and treatment of sexually transmitted infections; condom programmes for injecting drug users and their sexual partners; targeted information, education and communication (IEC) for IDUs and their sexual partners; vaccination, diagnosis and treatment of viral hepatitis; prevention, diagnosis and treatment of tuberculosis. Together with a community outreach approach, the need for all these interventions, delivered to drug users in Africa in integrated drug/HIV services, has been recognised (Parry et al., 2010). Sub-Saharan governments must develop capacity to provide access and referral to substance misuse and HIV services for vulnerable populations. In particular, provision of subsidies for those NGOs/CBOs that address drug and HIV risks in a comprehensive and integrated manner must be supported, with a move away from the tendency to deliver services in drug and HIV silos. Education regarding HIV drug-related risks must be incorporated into HIV prevention efforts, and into drug services; in particular drug programmes must provide VCT (inclusive of risk reduction counselling) and also screen for substance-related HIV risk behaviour (injection and sexual risk) and HIV programmes for substance-related risk such as poor compliance with anti-retroviral medication and HIV reinfection. VCT must become more localised, mobile and population specific, reaching vulnerable groups. Cross-training must occur for personnel delivering substance abuse and HIV services, with stigma reduction incorporated as a key component. Throughout the region, in view of the predominant sexual mode of transmission of HIV in drug users and their partners, and the increasingly clear role of alcohol in such transmission (Parry, 2010) these interventions should be available to non-IDUs (apart from NSPs) as well as IDUs.

Conclusion

African governments, civil society stakeholders and the general public, even if viewing drug users as low priority for healthcare, must beware the locally generated evidence for enhanced HIV transmission associated with non-injecting drug and alcohol use as well as the evidence from Eastern Europe and Asia for transformation of HIV epidemics concentrated among injecting drug users to generalised heterosexual epidemics (Des Jarlais et al., 2009). The almost complete absence of valid drug use related epidemiological data throughout sub-Saharan Africa acts to prevent informed debate, and leaves the region at risk of an ineffectual reactive response rather than a preventative one, to such an occurrence. Methodologically validated but cost-effective programmes for ongoing monitoring of drug use trends in community as well as treatment populations must be funded at the earliest opportunity. Based on evidence of their effectiveness (Vlahov et al., 2010), needle and syringe programmes, substitute opioid therapy programmes, and other WHO recommended interventions, in conjunction with local rapid assessment and response (RAR) studies, must be implemented if sub-Saharan Africa is to responsibly manage the potential for drug and alcohol use to maintain and exacerbate the HIV epidemic among its general population.

References

Abdool, R., Sulliman, F. and Dhanoo, M. (2006) The injecting drug use and HIV/AIDS nexus in the republic of Mauritius, *African Journal of Drug & Alcohol Studies*, 5 (2), 107–16.

Abuja Declaration (2009) Political Declaration on the Prevention of Drug Abuse, Illicit Drug Trafficking and Organised Crimes in West Africa, *African Journal of Drug & Alcohol Studies*, 8 (1), 43–7.

Aceijas, C., Stimson, G., Hickman, M. and Rhodes, T. (2004) Global overview of injecting drug use and HIV infection among injecting drug users, *AIDS*, 18 (17), 2295–303.

Aceijas, C., Friedman, S., Cooper, H., Wiessing, L., Stimson, G. and Hickman, M. (2006) Estimates of injecting drug users at the national and local level in developing and transitional countries, and gender and age distribution, *Sexually Transmitted Infections*, 82 (S3) iii10–iii17.

Adelekan, M. and Lawal, R. (2006) Drug use and HIV infection in Nigeria: a review of recent findings, *African Journal of Drug and Alcohol Studies*, 5 (2), 140–57.

Adjei, A., Armah, H., Gbagbo, F., Ampofo, W., Isac, K.E., Quaye, I., Hesse, I. and Mensah, G. (2006) Prevalence of human immunodeficiency virus, hepatitis B virus, hepatitis C virus and syphilis among prison inmates and officers at Nsawam and Accra, Ghana, *Journal of Medical Microbiology*, 55, 593–7.

Adoga, M., Banwai, E., Forbi, J., Nimzing, L., Pam, C., Gyar, S., Agabi, Y. and Agwale, S. (2009) Human immunodeficiency virus, hepatitis B virus and hepatitis C virus: sero-prevalence, co-infection and risk factors among prison inmates in Nasarawa State, Nigeria, *Journal of Infection in Developing Countries*, 3 (7), 539–47.

Advisory Council on the Misuse of Drugs (1988) *AIDS and Drug Misuse*, part 1, London: HMSO.

Beyrer, C., Razak, M., Lisam, K., Chen, J. and Lui, X. (2000) Overland heroin trafficking routes and HIV-1 spread in south and south-east Asia, *AIDS*, 14 (1), 75–83.

Bisika, T., Konyani, S., Chamangwana, I. and Khanyizira, G. (2008) An epidemiologic study of drug abuse and HIV and AIDS in Malawi, *African Journal of Drug and Alcohol Studies*, 7 (2), 81–8.

Clausen, T., Rossow, I., Naidoo, N. and Kowal, P. (2009) Diverse alcohol drinking patterns in 20 African countries, *Addiction*, 104 (7), 1147–54.

Dahoma, J., Salim, A., Abdool, R., Othman, A., Makame, H., Ali, A., Abdalla, A., Juma, S., Yahya, B., Shaka, S., Sharif, M., Seha, A., Mussa, M., Shauri, O., Nganga, L. and Kibuka, T. (2006) HIV and substance abuse: the dual epidemics challenging Zanzibar, *African Journal of Drug and Alcohol Studies*, 5 (2), 130–9.

Degenhardt, L., Chiu, W., Sampson, N., Kessler, R., Anthony, J., Angermeyer, M., Bruffaerts, R., Girolamo, G., Gureje, O., Huang, Y., Karam, A., Kostyuchenko, S., Lepine, J., Mora, M., Neumark, Y., Ormel, J., Pinto-Meza, A., Posada-Villa, J., Stein, D., Takeshima, T. and Wells, J. (2008) *PLoS Med*, 5 (7), e141.

Des Jarlais, D., Arasteh, K., Semann, S. and Wood, E. (2009) HIV among injecting drug users: current epidemiology, biologic markers, respondent-driven sampling, and supervised-injection facilities, *Current Opinion in HIV and AIDS*, 4 (4), 308–13.

Deveau, C. (2008) HIV prevention among drug and alcohol users: models of intervention in Kenya, *African Journal of Drug and Alcohol Studies*, 7 (2), 113–26.

Dewing, S., Pluddemann, A., Myers, B. and Parry, C. (2006) Review of injection drug use in six African countries: Egypt, Kenya, Mauritius, Nigeria, South Africa and Tanzania, *Drugs: Education, Prevention and Policy*, 5 (2), 118–29.

Dolan, J. (2007) HIV in prison in low-income and middle-income countries, *Lancet Infectious Diseases*, 7, 32–43.

Dos Santos, M, Rataemane, S., Fourie, D. and Trathen, B. (2010) An approach to heroin use disorder intervention within the South African context: a content analysis study, *Substance Abuse Treatment, Prevention, and Policy*, 5, 13, www.substanceabusepolicy.com/content/5/1/13, accessed 1 August.

Fekadu, A., Alem, A. and Hanlon, C. (2007) Alcohol and drug abuse in Ethiopia: past, present and future, African, *Journal of Drug and Alcohol Studies*, 6 (1), 39–53.

Fisher, J., Bang, H. and Kapiga, S. (2007) The association between HIV infection and alcohol use: a systematic review and meta-analysis of African studies, *Sexually Transmitted Diseases*, 34 (11), 856–63.

Fryers, T. (1986) Screening for developmental disabilities in developing countries: problems and perspectives. In K. Marfo, S. Walker and B. Charles (eds), *Childhood Disability in Developing Countries: Issues in Habilitation and Special Education*, New York: Praeger, 27–40.

Gisselquist, D. (2008) *Points to Consider: Responses to HIV/AIDS in Africa, Asia and the Caribbean*, London: Adonis & Abbey.

Gisselquist, D. and Potterat, J. (2004) Review of evidence from risk factor analyses associating HIV infection in African adults with medical injections and multiple sexual partners, *International Journal of STD and AIDS*, 15 (4), 222–33.

Hasnain, M. (2005) Cultural approach to HIV/AIDS harm reduction in Muslim countries, *Harm Reduction Journal*, 2, 23, www.harmreductionjournal.com/content/2/1/23, accessed 1 August 2010.

Hewitt, J., Wilkenfeld, J. and Gurr, T. (2010) *Peace and Conflict 2010*, Center for International Development and Conflict Management, College Park: University of Maryland.

Hunt, N., Ashton, M., Lenton, S., Mitcheson, L., Nelles, B. and Stimson, G. (2003) *A Review of the Evidence-base for Harm Reduction Approaches to Drug Use*, London: Forward Thinking on Drugs, www.neilhunt.org/publications.htm, accessed 1 August 2010.

IHRA (2008) *The Global State of Harm Reduction 2008*, International Harm Reduction Association, www.ihra.net/contents/551, accessed 1 August 2010.

IHRA (2010a) *The Global State of Harm Reduction 2010*, International Harm Reduction Association, www.ihra.net/contents/245, accessed 1 August.

IHRA (2010b) What Is Harm Reduction?, www.ihra.net/what-is-harm-reduction, accessed 1 August.

IHRA/CUT (2010) *Briefing to the Committee on Economic, Social, Cultural Rights on the Consolidated Second-fourth Reports of Mauritius on the Implementation of the International Covenant on Economic, Social, Cultural Rights*, www2.ohchr.org/english/bodies/cescr/docs/ngos/IHRA_CUT_Mauritius44.pdf, accessed 1 August.

INCB (2009) *International Narcotics Control Board Annual Report 2009*, www.incb.org/pdf/annual-report/2009/en/AR_09_E_Chapter_III_Africa.pdf, accessed 1 August 2010.

Johnstone, L. (2009) *Integrated Behavioural and Biological Surveillance Survey among Injecting Drug Users in Mauritius*, referenced from IHRA/CUT, 2010.

Kools, J.-P. (2008) *Drug Use and HIV risk among Young People in Sub-Saharan Africa*, www.stopaidsnow.org/documents/drug_use_africa_2008_report.pdf, accessed 1 August 2010.

Madhava, V., Burgess, C. and Drucker, E. (2002) Epidemiology of Chronic Hepatitis C Virus Infection in Sub-Saharan Africa, *Lancet Infectious Diseases*, 2 (5), 293–302.

Mathers, B. et al. (2008) For the 2007 Reference Group to the UN on HIV and Injecting Drug Use: global epidemiology of injecting drug use and HIV among people who inject drugs – a systematic review, *Lancet*, 372 (9651), 1733–45.

Mathers, B., Cook, C. and Degenhardt, L. (2010) Improving the data to strengthen the global response to HIV among people who inject drugs, *International Journal of Drug Policy*, 21 (2), 100–2.

Mauritius Dangerous Drugs Act 2000, www.gov.mu/portal/sites/icac/legislations.htm, accessed 1 August 2010.

Mauritius Drug Control Master Plan (2004–9) Referenced from IHRA/CUT (2010).

McAllister, I. and Makkai, T. (2000) The prevalence and characteristics of injecting drug users in Australia, *Drug and Alcohol Review*, 20 (1), 29–36.

McCurdy, S., Williams, M., Kilonzo, G. and Leshabari, M. (2005) Heroin and HIV risk in Dar es Salaam, Tanzania: Youth hangouts, mageto and injecting practices, *AIDS Care*, 17, S65–S76.

McCurdy, S., Ross, M., Williams, M., Kilonzo, G. and Leshabari, M. (2010) Flashblood: blood sharing among female injecting drug users in Tanzania, *Addiction*, 105 (6), 1062–70.

Medical Research Council (2007) *Training Guide for HIV Prevention Outreach to Drug Users*, Cape Town: South African Medical Research Council.

Mpofu, E. (2003) Conduct disorders: presentation, treatment options and cultural efficacy in an African setting, *International Journal of Disability, Community and Rehabilitation* 2003, 2 (1), www.ijdcr.ca/VOL02_01_CAN/articles/mpofu.shtml, accessed 1 August 2010.

Murdock, G. (1959) *Africa, Its Peoples and Their Culture History*, New York: McGraw-Hill.

National AIDS Control Council (2008) UNGASS Country Progress Report, http://data.unaids.org/pub/Report/2008/kenya_2008_country_progress_report_en.pdf, accessed 1 August 2010.

National AIDS Control Council (2009) Kenya National AIDS Strategic Plan 2009/10 to 2012/13, www.nacc.or.ke/2007/images/downloads/knasp_iii_document.pdf, accessed 1 August 2010.

NATRESA (2009) National Agency for the Treatment and Rehabilitation of Substance Abusers, Mauritius, www.gov.mu/portal/site/natresa/menuitem.1cd1e0f1764105a94605b010a0208a0c/, accessed 1 August 2010.

Nazarius, T. and Rogers, K. (2005) Alcohol and its association with sexual abstinence, condom use and risky behaviour among unmarried young people aged 18–24 years in Uganda, *African Journal of Drug & Alcohol Studies*, 4 (1–2), 17–31.

NIDA (2010) http://nidaint.demo2.iqsolutions.com/information/enews_201006.html#what1, accessed 1 August 2010.

Nunn, N. and Wantcheckon, L. (2010) *The Slave Trade and the Origins of Mistrust in Africa*, www.economics.harvard.edu/faculty/nunn/files/Trust_AER_Rev2.pdf, accessed 1 August 2010.

Obot, I. (2004) Assessing Nigeria's drug control policy, 1994–2000, *International Journal of Drug Policy*, 15, 17–26.

Olisah, V., Adekeye, O., Sheikh, T. and Yusuf, A. (2009) Alcohol-related problems and high risk sexual behaviour in patients with HIV/AIDS attending medical clinic in a Nigerian university teaching hospital, *African Journal of Drug & Alcohol Studies*, 8 (1), 17–22.

Omonzejele, P. (2008) African concepts of health, disease, and treatment: an ethical inquiry, *Explore: The Journal of Science and Healing*, 4 (2), 120–6.

Oshodi, O., Aina, O. and Onajole, A. (2010) Substance use among secondary school students in an urban setting in Nigeria: prevalence and associated factors, *African Journal of Psychiatry*, 13, 52–7.

Parry, C., Plüddemann, A. and Strijdom, J. (2003) Developing the Southern African development community epidemiology network on drug use: methods and issues, *Bulletin on Narcotics*, 55 (1–2), www.unodc.org/pdf/bulletin/bulletin_2003_01_01_1_Art8.pdf, accessed 1 August 2010.

Parry, C., Pluddemann, A. and Myers, B. (2007) Cocaine treatment admissions at three sentinel sites in South Africa (1997–2006): findings and implications for policy, practice and research, *Substance Abuse Treatment, Prevention and Policy*, 2 (37), doi: 10.1186/1747-597X-2-37.

Parry, C., Petersen, P., Carney, T., Dewing, S. and Needle, R. (2008) Rapid assessment of drug use and sexual HIV risk patterns among vulnerable drug using populations in Cape Town, Durban and Pretoria, South Africa, *Journal of Social Aspects of HIV/AIDS*, 5, 52–8.

Parry, C., Carney, T., Petersen, P., Dewing, S. and Needle, R. (2009) HIV-risk behaviour among injecting or non-injecting drug users in Cape Town, Pretoria, and Durban, South Africa, *Substance Use and Misuse*, 44 (6), 886–904.

Parry, C., Pluddemann, A. and Bhana, A. (2009b) Monitoring alcohol and drug abuse trends in South Africa via SACENDU (1996–2006): reflections on treatment demand trends over the past 10 years and the project's impact on policy and other domains, *Contemporary Drug Problems*, 36, 685–703.

Parry, C., Rehm, J. and Morojele, N. (2010a) Is there a causal relationship between alcohol and HIV? Implications for policy, practice and future research. Paper presented at the Ninth Biennial International Conference on Alcohol, Drugs and Society in Africa, Abuja, August.

Parry, C., Peterson, P., Carney, T. and Needle, R. (2010b) Opportunities for enhancing and integrating HIV and drug services for drug using vulnerable populations in South Africa, *International Journal of Drug Policy*, 21 (4), 289–95.

Pithey, A. and Parry, C. (2009) Descriptive systematic review of sub-Saharan African studies on the association between alcohol use and HIV infection, *Journal of Social Aspects of HIV/AIDS*, 6 (4), 155–69, www.sahara.org.za, accessed 1 August 2010.

Pitso, J. (2004) Does alcohol use take away condom use? Qualitative evidence from Selibe Phikwe and Mahalapye town districts, Botswana, *African Journal of Drug and Alcohol Studies*, 3 (1–2), 53–73.

Plüddemann, A., Flisher, A.J., Mathews, C., Carney, T. and Lombard, C. (2008a) Adolescent metamphetamine use and sexual risk behaviour in secondary school students in Cape Town, South Africa, *Drug and Alcohol Review*, 27 (6), 687–92.

Plüddemann, A., Parry, C., Flisher, A. and Jordann, E. (2008b) Heroin users in Cape Town, South Africa: injecting practices, HIV-related risk behaviours, and other health consequences, *Journal of Psychoactive Drugs*, 40 (3), 273–9.

Plüddemann, A., Parry, C., Bhana, A., Dada, S. and Fourie, D. (2010) Alcohol and drug abuse trends: July–December 2009 *SACENDU Update*, 27, 1–2.

PrabdiaI-Sing, N., Bowyer, S.S.M. and Puren, A.A.J. (2006) Genotyping hepatitis C virus in South Africa: a comparison of results obtained by partial sequencing of the 51UTR and NS5B regions with a real-time light-cycler genotyping method, *Journal of Clinical Virology*, 36 (supple. 2), S104–5, Abstracts, 12th ISHVLD.

Reddy, S.P., James, S., Sewpaul, R., Koopman, F., Funani, N.I., Sifunda, S., Josie, J., Masuka, P., Kambaran, N.S. and Omardien, R.G. (2010) *Umthente Uhlaba Usamila: The South African Youth Risk Behaviour Survey 2008*, Cape Town: South African Medical Research Council.

Reid, S. (2009) Injection drug use, unsafe medical injections, and HIV in Africa: a systematic review, *Harm Reduction Journal*, 6 (24), 24–34.

Renton, A., Gzirishvilli, D., Gotsadze, G. and Godhino, J. (2006) Epidemics of HIV and sexually transmitted infections in central Asia: trends, drivers and priorities for control, *International Journal of Drug Policy*, 17, 494–503.

Robertson, B. (2006) Does the evidence support corroboration between psychiatry and traditional healers? Findings from three South African studies, *South African Psychiatry Review*, 9, 87–90.

Roerecke, M., Obot, I., Patra, J. and Rehm, J. (2008) Volume of alcohol consumption, patterns of drinking and burden of disease in sub-Saharan Africa, *African Journal of Drug and Alcohol Studies*, 7 (1), 1–16.

SAHRN (2010) www.sahrn.net, accessed 1 August.

Shisana, O., Rehle, T., Simbayi, L.C., Parker, W., Jooste, S., Pillay-van Wyk, V., et al. (2009) *South African National HIV Prevalence, HIV Incidence, Behavior and Communication Survey, 2008: A Turning Tide Among Teenagers?*, Cape Town: Human Sciences Research Council (HSRC) Press.

South Africa National Drug Master Plan (2006–11) www.capegateway.gov.za/ . . . /national_drug_master_plan_(2006–2011)_a.pdf, accessed 1 August 2010.

Special Summit of African Union on HIV/AIDS, Tuberculosis and Malaria (2006) Abuja, 2–6 May, www.africa-union.org/root/au/conferences/past/2006/may/summit/doc/en/SP_PRC_ATM3I_AU_Social_and_Cultural_Factors.pdf, accessed 1 August 2010.

Strathdee, S., Hallett, T., Bobrova, N., Rhodes, T., Booth, R., Abdool, R. and Hankins, C. (2010) HIV and risk environment for injecting drug users: the past, present, and future, *Lancet*, 376, 268–84.

Sulliman, F. and Ameerberg, S. (2004) *Mauritius Epidemiology Network on Drug Use Report: January–June 2004*, Port Louis, Mauritius, NATRESA.

Sullivan, L., Levine, B., Chawarski, M., Schottenfeld, R. and Fiellin, D. (2007) Addiction and HIV in Kenya: a description of treatment services and integration, *African Journal of Drug and Alcohol Studies*, 6 (1), 17–26.

Sy, T. and Jamal, M. (2006) Epidemiology of hepatitis C virus (HCV) Infection, *International Journal of Medical Sciences*, 3 (2), 41–6.

Timpson, S., McCurdy, S., Leshabari, M., Kilonzo, G., Atkinson, J., Msami, A. and Williams, M. (2006) Substance abuse, HIV risk and HIV/AIDS in Tanzania, *African Journal of Drug and Alcohol Studies*, 5 (2), 158–69.

UN (2010a) http://unstats.un.org/unsd/demographic/products/vitstats/, accessed 9 July.

UN (2010b) www.unohrlls.org, accessed 9 July.

UNAIDS (2008) 2008 report on the global AIDS epidemic, www.unaids.org/en/KnowledgeCentre/HIVData/GlobalReport/2008/2008_Global_report.asp, accessed 1 August 2010.

UNAIDS (2009) *Aids Epidemic Update*, Geneva: UNAIDS.

UNESCO (2010) Why and how Africa should invest in African languages and multilingual education: An evidence- and practice-based policy advocacy brief, www.unesco.org/uil/en/UILPDF/nesico/publication/AfricanLanguages_MultilingualEducation_pab.pdf, accessed 1 August.

UNODC(2007) *Cocaine Trafficking in West Africa: The Threat to Stability and Development (with Special Reference to Guinea-Bissau)*, Vienna: UNODC, www.unodc.org/documents/data-and-analysis/west_africa_cocaine_report_2007-12_en.pdf, accessed 1 August 2010.

UNODC (2008) *Epidemiological fact sheet on HIV and AIDS*, Vienna: UNODC.

UNODC (2009) World Drug Report 2009, www.unodc.org/documents/wdr, accessed 1 August 2010.

UNODC (2010) World Drug Report 2010, www.unodc.org/documents/wdr, accessed 1 August.

UNODC, UNAIDS and World Bank (2007) HIV and prisons in sub-Saharan Africa: Opportunities for Action, www.unodc.org/documents/hiv-aids/Africa%20HIV_Prison_Paper_Oct-23-07-en.pdf, accessed 1 August 2010.

Vlahov, D., Robertson, A. and Strathdee, S. (2010) Prevention of HIV in injection drug users in resource-limited settings, *Clinical Infectious Diseases*, 15 (50, supple. 3), S114–21.

Wechsberg, W.M., Luseno, W., Karg, R.S., Young, S., Rodman, N., Myers, B. and Parry, C. (2008) Alcohol, cannabis, and methamphetamine use and other risk behaviours among black and coloured South African women: a small randomised trial in the Western Cape, *International Journal of Drug Policy*, 19, 130–9.

WHO (2004) *Global Status Report on Alcohol 2004*, Geneva: WHO, www.who.int/substance_abuse/publications/global_status_report_2004_overview.pdf, accessed 1 August 2010.

WHO (2005) *Biregional Strategy for Harm Reduction 2005–2009*, www.searo.who.int/LinkFiles/Publications_BiregionalStrategicPlan.pdf, accessed 1 August 2010.

WHO (2008) *Global Burden of Disease 2004: Update (2008)*, Geneva: UNODC, www.who.int/healthinfo/global_burden_disease/GBD_report_2004update_part2.pdf, accessed 1 August 2010.

WHO (2010) *WHO Model Essential Medicines List*, www.who.int/medicines/publications/essentialmedicines/Updated_sixteenth_adult_list_en.pdf, accessed 1 August.

WHO, UNODC, UNAIDS (2007) *Interventions to Address HIV in Prisons: Needle and Syringe Programmes and Decontamination Strategies*, Evidence for action technical paper, GenevaWHO, www.unodc.org/documents/hiv-aids/EVIDENCE%20FOR%20ACTION%202007%20NSP.pdf, accessed 1 August 2010.

WHO, UNODC, UNAIDS (2009) *Technical Guide for Countries to set targets for Universal Access to HIV Prevention, Treatment and Care for Injecting Drug Users*, Geneva: WHO, www.who.int/hiv/pub/idu/idu_target_setting_guide.pdf, accessed 1 August 2010.

Wolfe, D. (2004) Alchemies of inequality: the United Nations, illicit drug policy and the global HIV epidemic. In K. Malinowska-Sempruch and S. Gallagher (eds), *War on Drugs, HIV/AIDS and Human Rights*, New York: International Debate Education Association, 158–89.

Wolfe, D. and Malinowska-Sempruch, K. (2007) *Seeing Double: Mapping Contradictions in HIV Prevention and Illicit Drug Policy Worldwide*. In C. Beyrer and H. Pizer (eds), *Public Health and Human Rights: Evidence-Based Approaches*, Baltimore: Johns Hopkins University Press, 330–61.

Chapter 32

OVERVIEW OF THE HARM REDUCTION SITUATION IN THE MIDDLE EAST AND NORTH AFRICA

Jallal Toufiq

Context

This chapter reviews the current situation of harm reduction policies in the field of drug use in the Middle East and North Africa region (MENA). The MENA comprises 21 countries, from west to east: Morocco, Algeria, Tunisia, Libya, Malta, Egypt, Saudi Arabia, Lebanon, Syria, Israel, Palestine, Jordan, Iraq, Djibouti, Yemen, Oman, Bahrain, United Arab Emirates, Qatar, Kuwait and Iran. The population of the MENA region as it is typically defined is around 400 million people, about 6% of the total world population. The MENA region had a population of 112 million in 1950. The population is approaching a fourfold increase. It will more than double again, to at least 833 million, by 2050. Around two thirds of the population in the MENA region is under 30 years of age, almost the opposite situation of societies in Europe and North America, where more than half of the population is over 40. Even more, the World Bank estimates that some 36% of the total MENA population is less than 15 years of age, versus 21% in the United States and 16% in the European Union.

This young population growth is leading to a real 'youth explosion'. The sole fact that young age, as a demographic variable, is a predictive factor for first drug use and drug misuse gives an idea about the risky situation in the region in terms of incidence of drug use.

In addition, the population growth presents major problems for the economy since it is a concern affecting every aspect of society, from urban services to education. In addition, population pressure is exhausting natural water supplies in many countries, leading to growing dependence on very costly desalination, and forcing permanent dependence on hard-currency-consuming food imports. Demand for water already exceeds the supply in nearly half the countries in the region and annual renewable water supplies per capita have fallen by 50% since 1960. Years of drought and economic turmoil have led to a massive exodus from rural to urban areas creating huge social poverty with the emergence of slums and big cities 'ruralisation', especially in North Africa and Yemen.

Poor education policies and unemployment are critical challenges to regional stability. The MENA region has an average unemployment rate of at least 20% for young males; no real statistics exist for women. The number of young people entering the work force each year will double between now and 2025. This creates a huge pressure on social, educational, political, and economic systems and this effect is compounded by a lack of jobs and job growth, practical work experience and competitiveness.

A young population, unemployment, hyper-urbanisation and a half-century decline in agricultural and traditional trades has led to high levels of stress on society. In addition, many countries of the region have counted on tourism and money transfer from their emigrants working in Europe

Harm Reduction in Substance Use and High-Risk Behaviour: International Policy and Practice, First Edition.
Edited by Richard Pates and Diane Riley.
© 2012 Blackwell Publishing Ltd. Published 2012 by Blackwell Publishing Ltd.

and North America to boost their economy. This has led to great mobility of population and goods, including drugs and 'laundered money'. Moreover, the region is in a very crucial geographic location between Europe, Africa and Asia, at an intersection of three international drug trafficking paths.

The MENA region offers very mixed and sometimes even ambivalent societies: conservative and yet liberal, very rich and outrageously poor, educated and illiterate, so many ingredients adding to a rapid absorption of 'consumption behaviour' globalisation. For example, cell phone service subscription more than tripled in the last few years because of soaring demand among the youth. All this is happening in countries where the poverty is climbing and the socio-economic reforms are too slow.

Besides, most MENA countries are in the majority Muslim, with still quite conservative societies. The use of drugs is forbidden (*haram*) in Islam (Kamarulzaman and Saifuddeen, 2010). Yet, illicit drug use is common in the whole region. In recent decades, there has been a significant increase in the prevalence of drug use in the MENA region and subsequently there has been an increase in injecting drug use and a related HIV/AIDS and hepatitis epidemic. As a result, some of these countries have decided to launch harm reduction (HR) programmes. Most of them, however, are still very shy in responding to the problem, although the preservation and protection of the dignity of human beings and keeping them away from harm and destruction, are the core precept of Islam. The Cairo Declaration on Human Rights in Islam (adopted and Issued at the 19th Islamic Conference of Foreign Ministers, 5 August 1990) states: 'Believing that fundamental rights and universal freedoms in Islam are an integral part of the Islamic religion and that no one as a matter of principle has the right to suspend them in whole or in part or violate or ignore them in as much as they are binding divine commandments'. It also adds the following: Article 2(c) – Obligation to Preserve Life: 'The preservation of human life throughout the term of time willed by God is a duty prescribed by Shari'ah'. Article 17(b) – Right to Medical Services: 'Everyone shall have the right to medical and social care, and to all public amenities provided by society and the State within the limits of their available resources.' And yet, the use of drugs in the MENA region is still perceived by the community as a deviant behaviour or even a crime rather than a complex chronic medical condition needing a bio-psychosocial approach.

History of drug use and current situation in the MENA region

Very little has been done in evaluating the situation regarding drug use and related harms in the region. The pejorative view of drug use has had a negative impact on the management of drug-related harms in the region. Policy-makers are not always willing to assess the situation and are reluctant to put money into related research. Researchers do not have enough resources to conduct epidemiological studies and sometimes they are simply not allowed to do so. Health professionals are so overwhelmed with so many other health priorities that often they just do not want to get involved in drug use management issues. In addition, a huge lack of qualified human resources in the field cripples all the programmes and plans to handle it.

In the United Nations Office on Drugs and Crime 2010 World Report, the MENA region is divided into two regions. The Near and Middle East refers to a sub-region which includes Bahrain, Israel, Jordan, Kuwait, Lebanon, Oman, Qatar, Saudi Arabia, the Syrian Arab Republic, the United Arab Emirates and Yemen. The North Africa region includes Algeria, Egypt, Libyan Arab Jamahiriya, Morocco, Sudan and Tunisia.

The UNODC 2010 WDR states that the estimated number of illicit drug users aged 15–64 years in the year for 2008 in the MENA region was around 25 million (lower figures). For many years, cannabis, khat, tobacco, and to a lesser extent alcohol, were the main drugs of use in the region. Up until the 1980s, heroin and cocaine were not commonly used in the region and apart from tobacco, cannabis is still the main drug used. The main problem drug as reflected in treatment demand is cannabis in North Africa and opiates in the Middle East. Opiate seizures, both opium and heroin, continue to increase in that region. Morphine seizures, in contrast, declined in 2008. The largest seizures continue to be reported from the countries neighbouring Afghanistan, notably the Islamic Republic of Iran and Pakistan. Large increases in cannabis resin seizures in 2008 were reported from the Near and Middle East region.

With regard to drugs of injection, the 2010 WDR shows recent prevalence of heroin use in the region ranges from less than 0.1% in Morocco, up to more than 1% in Yemen, Bahrain and Iran. Heroin trafficking routes go mainly from Afghanistan to Europe through the Middle East and Africa, and also to Europe and North America through North Africa. Cocaine is still not widely used in the region except for North Africa, where it is increasing as the route of traffic from Latin America crosses African sub-Saharan countries to go through North Africa, especially Morocco, to finally reach Europe via Spain, the second largest consumer in Europe. For example, recent prevalence for cocaine use in Morocco is around 0.03%.

Injecting drug use poses a real problem in some countries, especially in Iran, Libya and Bahrain (Shawky *et al.*, 2009). The marginalised and criminalised populations of men who have sex with men and people who inject drugs remain most affected by HIV in this region. The Reference Group to the UN on HIV/AIDS and Injecting Drug Use indicated there are over 300,000 people who inject drugs in the MENA region. Injecting drug use contributes to HIV epidemics in Iran, Bahrain, Libya and several other MENA countries. Iran is particularly concerned with a drug-use-related HIV epidemic. Iran has gone through a significant change in its drug-related HIV epidemic. Iran has always been known as a major global centre of opium production and distribution, and opium smoking has been popular for hundreds of years (INCB, 2005). In the last few decades there has been a fall in opium production and Iran has emerged as a major drug transit country, because of its long border with the world's largest opium producer, Afghanistan. Increased availability and lower prices of heroin have led to a very marked increase in heroin dependency and injecting drug use. In 1969, there were, reportedly, 350,000 opium users, consuming a total of 240 tons of opium a year (McCoy, 1991). By the early 1970s, it was estimated that there were 400,000 drug addicts, mainly opium smokers. In 1975, there were 30,000 heroin users (Moharreri, 1978; McCoy, 1991). Since then, the drug use picture in Iran has totally shifted in nature and type of response. After the 1979 Islamic Revolution, there were some two million drug users (Razzaghi *et al.*, 1999), of which between 200,000 and 300,000 were drug injectors. There was a tremendous increase in drug related deaths and high rates of HIV/AIDS infection among injecting drug users. This has led to a change in policy towards less enforcement and more medical and social approach to drug use and great improvements in drug treatment and an expansion of harm reduction services have emerged.

A Rapid Situation Assessment (RSA) of ten urban sites conducted in 1998/1999 (Razzaghi *et al.*, 1999) reported that injecting drug use in Iran was significantly higher than previously believed. Estimates of the numbers of injecting drug users in Iran ranged from 200,000 to 300,000 (Iranian National Centre for Addiction Studies, 2008). The World Drug Report for 2004 stated that 'Iran could be home to as many as 200,000 injecting drug users' (UNODC, 2004). In July 2001 the Iranian National Committee on AIDS reported that the cumulative total of officially recorded HIV infections was 2,458. Of this total, 1,841 (74.8%) were drug users (Iranian National Centre for Addiction Studies, 2008). The most recent figure for cumulative HIV infections in Iran is 92,000 in 2009 (UNAIDS, 2009, 2010). A RSA of six urban sites in Tehran in 2005/2006 by Razzaghi and colleagues found very high levels of sharing of drug paraphernalia and other unsafe practices among injectors (Razzaghi *et al.*, 2006). The situation is particularly serious inside Iran's prisons, reaching a 63% rate of HIV infection amongst drug users in one institution (reported in UNODC, 2004: 50).

Current policy and practice

Overall, harm reduction in the MENA region is still very limited. Only a few countries are taking the lead in terms of implementing harm reduction policies and programmes. One main concern in many countries is still the lack of accurate data on patterns of drug use, risk behaviours, social influences and infections such as HIV and hepatitis (table 32.1).

The major achievements in harm reduction have been seen in Iran and to a lesser degree in Morocco and Lebanon. The Iranian harm reduction policy is the result of a gradual policy shift over many years (Nassirimanesh *et al.*, 2005). Iran had a supply-reduction policy that criminalised any type of drug use, in any quantity, with no treatment alternatives available. Since the mid-1990s, the law has changed to allow drug users who access treatment to be exempted from the penal punishments they faced in the 1970s and 1980s (Dalvand, 1984; DCHQ, 1997, 2001; Ahmadi, 2000). The first developments under this new policy of expanding treatment were of three types: government supported therapeutic communities, 'Narcotics Anonymous' support groups, and outpatient clinics offering short detoxification programmes. Although these treatment programmes were of variable quality and ranged from abstinence-only programmes to detoxification programmes with high relapse rates, these advances in treatment and rehabilitation of drug users represented a significant step forward.

Table 32.1 Harm reduction initiatives in the MENA region

Country	NSP	OST	Drug consumption rooms	NSP in prisons	OST in prisons	HR policy
Algeria	X	X	x	X	x	X
Bahrain	X	X	x	X	x	x
Egypt	✓	X	x	X	x	x
Iran	✓	✓	x	✓	✓	✓
Iraq	X	X	x	X	x	x
Israel	✓	✓	x	X	x	✓
Jordan	X	X	x	X	x	x
Kuwait	X	X	x	X	x	x
Lebanon	✓	✓	x	X	x	✓
Libya	X	X	x	X	x	x
Morocco	✓	✓	x	X	x	✓
Oman	✓	X	x	X	x	x
Palestine	X	X	x	X	x	x
Qatar	X	X	x	X	x	x
Saudi Arabia	X	X	x	X	x	x
Syria	X	X	x	X	x	x
Tunisia	✓	X	x	X	x	x
United Arab Emirates	x	X	x	X	x	x
Yemen	x	X	x	X	x	X

In the mid-1990s that there was a convergence of drug demand-reduction and HIV prevention approaches. It had become evident that HIV infection was increasing rapidly among injecting drug users, especially in prisons, where a majority of inmates were serving sentences for drug-related crimes and using drugs. Studies in the late 1990s and early 2000 showed that levels of injection drug use with sharing of injecting equipment in correctional settings were extremely high (Ohiri *et al.*, 2006). Iran adopted a pragmatic approach to deal with these problems. In January 2005, an executive order was issued by the Head of the Judiciary on harm reduction, providing a legal framework that would allow for more effective HIV prevention in Iran. According to Ohiri and colleagues, several factors helped catalyse change and bring about Iran's current progressive policies (2006). These were:

1. the important role NGOs and civil society played in advocacy and implementation of successful programmes that reached vulnerable groups;
2. the close cooperation and common understanding between the Ministry of Health, the prison department health authorities, and the judiciary authorities and other stakeholders, on drug treatment and HIV/AIDS, leading to increased government support for implementation of evidence-based harm reduction policies; and,
3. informed advocacy among senior policy-makers paving the way for adoption of harm reduction measures in early 2000. A national harm reduction committee was established with representatives from various ministries, academic centers and NGOs.

Harm reduction programmes are now implemented in both government and non-governmental facilities in Iran. The triangular clinic which integrates services for treatment and prevention of STIs, injecting drug use and HIV/AIDS is used as an example of best practice for the region (WHO, 2004). These clinics are set up in prisons and by NGOs to reach IDU communities in a cost-effective manner.

A unique model for comprehensive harm reduction has been implemented by the Persepolis NGO for several years. Persepolis provides needle exchange, methadone maintenance treatment, general medical care, and referral for voluntary counselling and testing. It runs drop-in centres for IDUs who are based on the street in a continuum-of-care model, and services extend to the provision of food, clothes and other basic needs. At the moment the geographical range of Persepolis is limited; similar services, that can meet the specific needs of a local community, need to be implemented in many communities in order meet the demand not only in Iran but also in other countries in the region.

Implementation of harm reduction in Iran still faces many challenges, the most significant of which are (Nassirimanesh *et al.*, 2005; Ohiri *et al.*, 2006):

1. the imbalance between the predominant international enforcement of supply-reduction and harm reduction interventions;
2. the need to achieve high enough intervention coverage to reverse the trends in HIV prevalence and demonstrate impact to convince critics;
3. disruptions in the supply of methadone and other essential harm reduction materials; and,
4. the lack of human resources, both technical experts and field workers, essential for harm reduction initiatives to reach the necessary minimum threshold for such programmes to be effective.

To scale up and sustain support of its progressive harm reduction policies which can help stem the HIV epidemic in the region, especially if bordering countries adopt and reinforce similar policies, Iran needs to (Nassirimanesh *et al.*, 2005; Ohiri *et al.*, 2006):

1. establish strong monitoring and evaluation systems for existing interventions and programmes, including impact evaluation of the programmes that they are spearheading;
2. support strategies aimed at preventing HIV transmission from IDUs to their spouses and other sexual partners;
3. scale-up existing programmes for street-based IDUs incorporating quality standards for harm reduction services to ensure sustained effectiveness; and,
4. strengthen the capacity of NGOs and other community-based groups to effectively reach the most vulnerable population groups.

Harm reduction programmes are running in many countries in the MENA region. Only three countries do actually have HR policies at the governmental level: Iran, Morocco and Lebanon. Needle and syringe programmes (NSPs) have been introduced to eight countries. Iran, Morocco and, most recently, Lebanon offer both NSPs and opiate substitution therapy. Iran and Morocco have introduced methadone maintenance programmes whereas Lebanon is implementing buprenorphine programmes. Despite all the positive developments and recent improvement in service provision, the majority of MENA drug injectors still do not have access to these key interventions.

Moreover, research is scarce and data availability is poor. There are no structured monitoring systems to assess the real situation in the region and as a result both injecting drug use and HIV are being under-reported in the region. Local and national monitoring systems urgently require strengthening in order to inform targeted responses to drug related HIV epidemics in the region. Some recent advances have been achieved in countries such as Morocco where a national observatory on drugs is being created.

One important development, particularly for civil society, was the creation of the Middle East and North African Harm Reduction Association (MENAHRA). MENHARA has carried out multiple activities with civil society to foster an increase in knowledge and skills in the field. The first Regional Conference on Harm Reduction, which was held in Lebanon in November 2009, was a great opportunity for sharing experiences and raising awareness of key issues with policy-makers and the media. NGOs are really strong in the region and may be called upon in the future to fill the gap seen in the area of harm reduction. Despite a great deal of enthusiasm and willingness on its part, civil society remains quite muzzled as restrictions on the freedom of action of non-governmental organisations in several countries continue to limit the harm reduction response.

Outreach

At least 12 countries have developed community-based drop-in centers. They are designed to provide a means of outreach to drug injectors, including information and education about drug use and the risks of HIV infection, as well as access to clean needles, condoms, and general healthcare.

Needle and syringe exchange programmes (NSPs)

Seven MENA countries have operational NSPs. The first one to implement them was Iran (Mohsenifar, 2009), which had 170 NSPs in 2008 and now has between 428 and 637 sites. Morocco has increased its service provision and several NSPs are now operating, especially in the northern areas of the country; where respondent-driven samplings suggest that between 5% and 15% of heroin users are injecting. Lebanon, reported to have very small-scale service provision in 2008, may now

Table 32.2 Syringe distribution in four countries in the region in 2008

Country	Syringe/year/person	Number of syringes
Lebanon	2.5	2,000
Morocco	6.7	44,696
Oman	<1	2,400
Tunisia	8.7	5,924

have up to six NSPs. Estimates of NSP service coverage are scarce in the region in the absence of monitoring and surveillance systems (table 32.2).

Iran is aiming at universal access; Morocco and Lebanon are rapidly scaling up their services. Research in the region suggests that people who inject drugs commonly share needles and that the need to scale up access to sterile injecting equipment remains urgent.

Opioid substitution therapy (OST)

OST is now officially and legally operational in three MENA countries: Iran, Israel, and Morocco. Recently, Lebanon has adopted a legal framework for OST and many injectors are receiving buprenorphine. Again, research is scarce and no clear data is available on exact numbers of people enrolled in OST programmes. Since the launching of the Methadone Maintenance Treatment Programmes in Morocco, some tens of injectors have been receiving ART through that programme; two residential centres and three drop-in centres are currently providing MMTP in Morocco. Many injectors are getting ART but are not reported as such.

In Iran, the first long-term substitution programme was initiated in 1999 in the southern city of Marvdasht. Managed by a non-governmental organisation (Persepolis), this clinic offered buprenorphine tablets to more than 3,000 clients between 1999 and 2001. In 2000, the first methadone pilot project opened within a government psychiatric hospital serving 140 patients. In 2002, with the support of the United Nations Office on Drugs and Crime's (UNODC's) office in Tehran, a major new outpatient drop-in centre was opened in the capital offering maintenance treatment. Since then, a number of clinics across Iran have offered substitution therapy.

HR in prisons

Very little is done in the MENA region when it comes to promoting harm reduction for drug-using prisoners. Some countries, such as Morocco, are starting to develop new programmes aiming at offering inmates information and education, as well as condoms.

Iran has a history of widespread incarceration of drug offenders (Spencer, 1990). A significant proportion of the prison population is comprised of drug users. Like many other countries, Iran has experienced the surge of HIV, hepatitis or tuberculosis epidemics through drug-related transmission in prisons (Razzaghi, 2001). Subsequently, there has been support from the Iranian prison authorities for the development of treatment and infection prevention services for drug users. Harm reduction services were introduced into Iran's prisons in 2003. Currently, at least forty prisons have developed triangular clinics offering services for drug dependence, HIV and sexually transmitted infections.

Policy developments

Four MENA countries have included harm reduction in their national policies on drugs: Iran, Israel, Lebanon and Morocco. Two more are in the process of doing so, Oman and Bahrain.

Civil society and advocacy for harm reduction

Civil society organisations (CSO) are playing a key role in advocating for harm reduction in the region. The most prominent CSO is the Middle East and North African Harm Reduction Association (MENHARA), which has a regional scope of activities through its three knowledge hubs situated in Iran, Lebanon and Morocco allowing a broad coverage of the region. MENHARA held the first Regional Conference on Harm Reduction in the region in 2009 in Beirut. More than 200 policy-makers, religious leaders and civil society representatives took part in the conference. Up to 2010, through 30 regional workshops and seminars, MENHARA have 560 civil society representatives, media workers, religious leaders and policy-makers. As for NGOs involving current or former drug users, there is not much to mention in the region; one NGO is very active in Morocco (Tangier).

Gaps and opportunities

Implementation of harm reduction in Iran still faces many challenges, the most significant of which are (Nassirimanesh *et al.*, 2005; Ohiri *et al.*, 2006):

1. the imbalance between the predominant international enforcement of supply-reduction and harm reduction interventions;
2. the need to achieve high enough intervention coverage to reverse the trends in HIV prevalence and demonstrate impact to convince critics;
3. disruptions in the supply of methadone and other essential harm reduction materials; and,
4. the lack of human resources, both technical experts and field workers, essential for harm reduction initiatives to reach the necessary minimum threshold for such programmes to be effective.

Many obstacles still hamper the development of harm reduction policies and programmes in the region; the stigma surrounding drug use is the main one. Officials in many countries approach drug use only from the supply reduction angle. Huge amounts of resources are put into combating traffic and money laundering. Prevention, treatment and harm reduction needs are under-estimated and under-funded. Most countries of the region are crippled under the burden of so many other health priorities. An important gap also is the lack of a research tradition in many countries of the region. Very few means are dedicated to research and the link between research and policy-making is almost inexistent. The lack of research in the field of drug use makes it very hard to have a clear idea of the situation and hence to establish evidence-based plans and strategies. The very conservative type of society in the region is also a major obstacle to tackling the problem of drug use as a medical condition. Criminalisation of drug users often curbs the efforts to reach out to them for any kind of intervention, research, treatment, or harm reduction.

The most important gap of all is the lack of qualified human resources in the field of drug use research and treatment. No programme can be effectively and efficiently carried out without highly qualified and well-trained professionals. That is the most insurmountable impediment in the region. Besides, there is no link between academics, NGO workers, health professionals and policy-makers. Thus, data are not shared with policy-makers; scientific knowledge is not transmitted to highly willing field workers; and actions on the ground are not always listed. In short, policies are seldom evidence-based.

Since the new millennium, however, there has been an increasing interest on the part of policy-makers in drug use as a socially expressed phenomenon. More drug-related crimes and felonies are having an impact on the media and the society as a whole. Subsequently, politicians have become more and more aware of the burden and negative impact of such a problem and therefore, are more and more looking for data on this. Also, the very limited governmental resources allocated to the problem in many countries have led policy-makers to encourage NGOs to take over and fill the gap. Clearly, there is a mounting political willingness to handle the problem in the region as community awareness regarding the right of drug users for treatment is also rising.

Recommendations

The following list of recommendations cover the main priorities to be rapidly met in order to improve harm reduction in the region:

1. enhance capacity-building in the field of drug-use related research, addiction medicine, harm reduction, community outreach programmes, and civil society organisation (CSO) skills;
2. fund research and data collection (monitoring and surveillance systems);
3. foster and support CSO activities;
4. create/elaborate legal frameworks to protect the rights of drug users;
5. advocate for harm reduction within the community;
6. raise awareness in policy-makers;
7. allow drug users the right to establish NGOs of their own;
8. link in a consistent way policy-makers, researchers, health professionals and field workers;
9. advocate for evidence-based policies;
10. launch culturally adapted harm reduction programmes;
11. be innovative in dealing with poor resources;
12. evaluate and, if needed, reorient programmes as resources are scarce.

References

Ahmadi, J. and Ghanizadeh, A. (2000) Motivations for use of opiates among addicts seeking treatment in Shiraz, *Psychological Reports*, 87 (3, pt 2) 1158–64.

Cook, C. and Kanaef, N. (2008) *Global State of Harm Reduction 2008: Mapping the Response to Drug-Related HIV and Hepatitis C Epidemics*, London: IHRA.

Dalvand, S., Agahi, C. and Spencer, C. (1984) Drug addicts seeking treatment after the Iranian revolution: a clinic based study, *Drug and Alcohol Dependence*, 14, 87–92.

Drug Control Headquarters (DCHQ) (1997) *The Anti Narcotics Law of the Islamic Republic of Iran (as Amended November 1997)*, Tehran: Drug Control Headquarters.

Drug Control Headquarters (DCHQ) (2001) *The National Drug Control Report: Iran 2000*, Tehran: Drug Control Headquarters.

Global Fund to Fight AIDS, Tuberculosis and Malaria (GFATM) (2009) *Regional Overview: Middle East and North Africa*, Geneva: GFATM.

INCB (International Narcotics Control Board) (2005) *Part Four: Statistical Information on Narcotic Drugs*, www.incb.org/pdf/e/tr/nar/2004/narcotics_part4.pdf, accessed 21 February 2012.

Iranian National Centre for Addiction Studies (2008) *Assessment of Situation and Response to Drug Use and Its Harms in the Middle East and North Africa: Year 2008*, Tehran. Tehran: University of Medical Sciences.

Kamarulzaman, A. and Saifuddeen, S.M. (2010) Islam and harm reduction, *International Journal of Drug Policy*, 21 (2), 115–18.

Mathers, B.M., Degenhardt, L., Phillips, B., Wiessing, L., Hickman, M., Strathdee, S.A., Wodak, A., Panda, S., Tyndall, M., Toufik, A. and Mattick, R.P. (2008) Global epidemiology of injecting drug use and HIV among people who inject drugs: a systematic review, *Lancet*, 372 (9651), 1733–45, for the 2007 Reference Group to the UN on HIV and Injecting Drug Use.

Mathers, B.M., Degenhardt, L., Ali, H., Wiessing, L., Hickman, M., Mattick, R.P., Myers, B., Ambekar, A., Strathdee, S.A. (2010) HIV prevention, treatment and care for people who inject drugs: a systematic review of global, regional and country level coverage, *Lancet*, 375 (9719), 1014–28, for the 2009 Reference Group to the UN on HIV and Injecting Drug Use.

McCoy A. (1991) *The Politics of Heroin: CIA Complicity in the Global Drug Trade*, New York: Lawrence Hill Books.

Moharreri, M.R. (1978) General view of drug abuse in Iran and a one-year report of outpatient treatment of opiate addiction in the city of Shiraz. In R. Peterson (ed.), *The International Challenge of Drug Abuse*, National Institute on Drug Abuse Research Monograph 19, 69–79.

Mohsenifar, S. (2009) Setting up a drug treatment service for female drug users in Iran. Paper presented at Towards Harm Reduction in the MENA Region: A Step Forward, MENAHRA Regional Conference on Harm Reduction, Beirut, Lebanon, November, for INCAS.

Narcotics Control Strategy Report (2001) *Narcotics Control Strategy Report, Iran*, released by the Bureau for International Narcotics and Law Enforcement Affairs, Washington, DC: US Department of State.

Nassirimanesh, B., Trace, M. and Roberts, M., (2005) *The Rise of Harm Reduction in the Islamic Republic of Iran*, Briefing Paper 8, Berkeley: Berkeley Foundation Drug Policy Program.

Ohiri, K., Claeson, M., Razzaghi, E., Nassirimanesh, B., Afshar, P. and Power, R. (2006) *HIV/AIDS Prevention among Injecting Drug Users: Learning from Harm Reduction in Iran*, Washington, DC: Report for World Bank.

Razzaghi, E.M. (2001) Comparison study on socio-economic factors in Iranian injecting users. Presentation at the 12th International Conference on the Reduction of Drug Related Harm, New Delhi, 1–5 April.

Razzaghi, E., Rahimi, A., Hosseni, M., and Chatterjee, A. (1999) *Rapid Situation Assessment (RSA) of Drug Abuse in Iran*, Prevention Department, State Welfare Organization, Ministry of Health, I.R. of Iran and United Nations International Drug Control Program.

Shawky, S., Cherif, S., Kassak, K., Oraby, D., El-Khoury, D. and Kabore, I. (2009) HIV surveillance and epidemic profile in the Middle East and North Africa, *Journal of Acquired Immune Deficiency Syndromes*, 51, 583–95.

Spencer, C. and Agahi, C. (1990–1) Drugs and Iran after the Islamic Revolution: prophesying the next quarter century, *International Journal of Addictions*, 25 (2A) 171–9.

State Welfare Organization (2000) Drug abuse prevention in youth needs a National movement, May 16, Tehran, Iran (unofficial translation).

Toufiq, J. (2010) *Global State of Harm Reduction Information Response*, Morocco: National Center on Drug Abuse Prevention and Research.

UNAIDS (2009, 2010) *AIDS Epidemic Update*, Geneva: UNAIDS.

UNODC (2004) *World Drug Report 2004*, Vienna: United Nations.

World Health Organization (2004) *Best Practice in HIV/AIDS Prevention and Care for Injecting Drug Abusers: The Triangular Clinic in Kermanshah, Islamic Republic of Iran*, Regional Office for the Eastern Mediterranean, Geneva: WHO-EM/STD/052/E.

Section V
Conclusions

Chapter 33

CONCLUSIONS

Richard Pates and Diane Riley

This book has tried to provide a comprehensive view of what is happening in harm reduction across subjects and across continents (as noted in the introduction, key areas such as women, first nations and performance enhancing drugs will be covered in a forthcoming book). Some subjects remain controversial while others have become mainstream in the policy and practice of public health and criminal justice. What is clear is that the situation does not remain static with regard to psychoactive substances. New drugs come onto the market, new ways of taking drugs develop, new risks to health and life emerge, and changes in the political environment affect the policy and the delivery of harm reduction.

The effects of the increasing use of cognitive enhancers have not yet been fully understood and this may have consequences in the future beyond the traditional concerns about drug use, including safety and ethics. Cognitive enhancers are drugs that are taken in the hope of increasing cognitive performance by improved memory, increased concentration, motivation, attention, and even intelligence. They are not illegal as such, but where they are prescription only drugs possession of them may be deemed to be illegal, and there are questions as to whether they work and whether they are safe (Bell, 2006). Some drugs which are amphetamine-type substances such as methylphenidate, Modafinil and Adderall are used in the treatment of narcolepsy and attention deficit hyperactivity disorder (ADHD) in children. Other cognitive enhancers known as 'Nootropics' or smart drugs are claimed to work by altering the brain's supply of neurochemicals and improving the brain's oxygen supply but their efficacy is yet unproven (Wikipedia, 2011). The question as to whether the use of these drugs is fair in environments such as schools and colleges, by giving those taking them an advantage over those not taking them, is similar to the issues raised by the taking of performance enhancing drugs in sport. The other point that needs to be made is that if they work by increasing concentration or attention, they are unlikely to produce a brilliant mind where the raw material is not there (Munkittrick, 2011)!

In the UK and a number of other countries there has been an increase in the sale of so called 'legal highs' in recent years. These are substances that are legal in that they do not come under the provisions of the Misuse of Drugs Act or similar legislation but are nevertheless psychoactive. In 2010 in the UK a drug known as mephedrone (or miaou miaou in street parlance) was being sold on the internet as plant food although it was recognised that this was not its purpose. After a number of reports of deaths the government moved swiftly to ban it despite little scientific evidence that the drug really was implicated in any deaths and little scientific study of the effects and danger of the drug. A recent study (Measham et al., 2011) found that despite the ban the drug was still popular in night clubs and that the ban had had little effect on its use. A further consequence was that another drug, known as Ivory Wave, was marketed which quickly developed the reputation of being 'more dangerous' than mephedrone. It was reputed to produce a rapid psychosis and was 'identified' as the cause of a number of suicides. This drug is still legal, which raises the question of whether the

Harm Reduction in Substance Use and High-Risk Behaviour: International Policy and Practice, First Edition.
Edited by Richard Pates and Diane Riley.
© 2012 Blackwell Publishing Ltd. Published 2012 by Blackwell Publishing Ltd.

government really wishes to play cat and mouse with the producers of new drugs. These drugs, often manufactured in China and sold on the internet, can be reformulated by minor chemical changes to produce something which is not illegal in the country in which the person who purchases it resides.

The rise of manufactured drugs raises the more general question of using drug laws to attempt to reduce drug related harms. Kushlick in chapter 8 of this book examines the role of prohibition and legalisation in drug control. In the UK, the Misuse of Drugs Act (1971) is the legislation concerned with the legality of drugs, but this legislation was drafted in a time when the UK had a very minor drug problem and takes no account of the dangerousness or the real harms associated with different drugs. In 2010, the UK government dismissed the chairperson of the expert committee that advises the government on drug policy (The Advisory Council on the Misuse of Drugs) because he had the temerity to raise the question of the appropriateness of the legislation. New drugs are certainly not covered, nor ever will be by the existing legislation.

Another question raised by the discussion of legal highs is the role of the internet both in the popularising and the marketing of drugs. This is raised by Barratt and Lenton in chapter 30 of this book. The wide availability of all sorts of legal, prescription only, and illegal drugs via the internet is something that was unforeseen when the current legislation in most countries was drafted and introduced.

The development of new drugs will, of course, continue, as it must for both the relief of suffering and the improvement of the quality of life. Heroin was first synthesised just over 100 years ago and marketed by Bayer as, among other things, a treatment for coughs, and was thought to be safe and none addictive. Crack cocaine hit the headlines in many countries in the 1980s (although free basing cocaine had been around for a while) and we had both a substance which could cause a lot of problems and a panic fanned by the authorities and media which hails each 'new' drug as being more dangerous/more addictive than those currently known. The one thing it most surely did was raise the curiosity of drug users to try the 'new' drug. Methamphetamine was the next scare drug; it followed crack, accompanied by the same sort of messages. The popular press in countries such as the UK play a key role in increasing panics around drugs which often makes rational discussion and education about psychoactive substances very difficult indeed. Stories about drugs seem to sell newspapers, magazines and airtime, especially when associated with celebrities.

All of this is set against a background of numerous deaths and health problems from tobacco. As laws have become more restrictive on sales and advertising in the western world, tobacco companies have switched their marketing focus to the developing world. Tobacco companies like alcohol companies make huge profits on their products despite the amount of harm caused and as markets diminish in the developed world they seek to make their profits elsewhere.

Alcohol use is also associated with many more costs to the individual and society than are illicit drugs. In the UK, for example, the escalation of binge drinking by young people is far more worrying than is illicit drug use, as there seems to have been a cultural shift among this group to an acceptance of very heavy drinking and getting drunk as the norm.

Harm reduction has come a long way since the 1980s as the book has demonstrated. Yet in many countries, including those of the developed world, the range and coverage of services is far from adequate. Indeed, in several countries such as Australia and Canada, policies and services have been severely eroded in the past several years, illustrating all too well the fragility of harm reduction. The rights to health and freedom from fear of persecution are basic human rights so it is clear that in many parts of the world there is still a very long way to go. In all cases, there is a pressing need for education of politicians and those involved with criminal justice and law enforcement.

Continuing the theme of a Report Card from the Australia/New Zealand chapter, we can summarise that harm reduction shows much promise but has made disappointing progress in several areas and needs to focus and apply itself more to important matters rather than being distracted by trivia and self-aggrandisement: B.

References

Bell, V. (2006) Know the facts about cognitive enhancers. In R. Hale-Evans (ed.), *Mind Performance Hacks*, Sebastopol: O'Reilly Publishing, 286–90.

Measham, F., Wood, D.M., Dargan, P.I. and Moore, K. (2011) The rise of legal highs: prevalence and patterns in the use of illegal drugs and the first- and second- generation 'legal highs' in South London gay dance clubs, *Journal of Substance Use*, 16 (4), 263–72.

Munkittrick, K. (2011) Cognitive enhancers are not cheating, *Discover Magazine*, 3 March.

Nootropics (2011) *Wikipedia*, accessed 23 September.

INDEX

Harm Reduction in Substance Use and High-Risk Behaviour: International Policy and Practice, First Edition.
Edited by Richard Pates and Diane Riley.
© 2012 Blackwell Publishing Ltd. Published 2012 by Blackwell Publishing Ltd.

British Opium Wars, 371
BrugerForeningen, 129
buprenorphine, 35, 70, 74, 85, 309, 310, 428, 431–3, 435
 to arrestees in police stations in Australia, 64
 availability, 363
 cocktailing with antihistamines and benzodiazepines, 356
 heroin-assisted treatment, 164, 332, 356
 importation of, 435
 as substitution drug, 305, 360
Bush, George H.W., drug policy of, 400–401

C
CACTUS needle exchange, 390
California
 effects of needle exchanges, 143
 wound botulism, among users of black tar heroin, 138
Canada, harm reduction, 382
 drug policy, 382–3
 drug strategy, 383, 385
 harm reduction programmes, 383–4
 historical background, 382–3
 overview of, 386
  atlantic provinces, 390–1
  at-risk groups, 391–2
  Ontario and Quebec, 389–90
  the prairies, 388
  the territories, 386–8
 recent developments, 384–6
Canadian Foundation for Drug Policy (CFDP), 383
cannabidiol (CBD), 231
 positive role for, 237–8
cannabinoids, 230
 aversive effects, 230
 long-term effects of, 232
 neuroimaging, acute effects of, 231–2
 properties, 230
cannabis, 20, 230
 acute effects, neuroimaging, 231–2
 association causing psychotic disorders, 232–4
  effect on outcomes in psychotic illness, 234–5
  modelling studies, 234
 CB1 receptors, role of, 231
 dependence syndrome, 235–7
  administration of Δ^9-THC, 236
  drugs no significant positive impact, 237
  opioid antagonist naltrexone, 236
  use of pharmacological cognitive enhancers, 237
 harm reduction strategy, 230
 for improving psychotic symptoms, 231
 ingredients, 230
 long-term effects of, 232
 negative effects, 230
 preparations of, 230
 as reverse-gateway, 230
 smoking, risk factors, 230
 synthetically produced
  medical importance, 231, 236
Cannabis indica, 229
Cannabis sativa, 229

Caribbean crack cocaine, 396
Caribbean Drug and Alcohol Research Institute (CDARI), 396
cascade training programmes, 302
cautioning policies, 61–4
Central Asia
 harm reduction in prisons, 346–7
 HR, history, 342–3
 injecting drug use in region, 343–4
  Kazakhstan, 344–5
  Kyrgyzstan, 345–6
  Tajikistan, 346
  Uzbekistan, 346
 recent developments and challenges, 347–8
Central Committee for Drug Abuse Control (CCDAC), 362
Central European countries, harm reduction, 301–3
 drug use in the region
  Czech Republic, 303–4
  Hungary, 304
  Poland, 304–5
  Slovakia, 305–6
 key challenges/current developments, 306
 prisons, harm reduction, 306
CGI animation, 296
chewing tobacco, 216. *See also* smokeless tobacco
Chicago Recovery Alliance, 376
Chill Out, 185, 186
China
 decrease in heroin availability, 308
 drug trafficking, 356
 drug users, to be registered with, 356
 IDUs in, 56
 key recommendations from evaluation for, 56
 management of drug use, 358
 opium use, 356, 370
 scaling up of methadone programme, 363
 USAID-funded interventions to address, 55
Chinese opium smoking, 370
chlorpheneramine maleate, heroin uses, 356
chronic hepatitis C virus (HCV) infection, 111
chronic obstructive pulmonary disease (COPD), 218, 230
civil liberties, 113, 323
civil society organisations (CSO), 451, 452
Clinton administration, drug policy on, 375
cocaine, 62, 68, 69, 74, 171, 173, 283, 384, 396, 426, 446
 average blood concentration of, 175
 consumption implements, 292
 crack cocaine, 265, 396, 458
 harm reduction information card, 390
 with heroin
  pharmacology and neurobiology of, 144–5
 lifetime prevalence of, 426
 negroes on cocaine, 371
 as primary drug frequently used with, 428
 production, 108
 seizures of, 427
 vasocontrictive properties, 146
cocaine anonymous (CA), 157